D1073801

Neonatal Medications & Nutrition

A Comprehensive Guide
3rd Edition

KARIN E. ZENK, PHARMD, FASHP

Associate Clinical Professor of Pediatrics,
University of California, Irvine, and in private consulting practice
Formerly, Pharmacist-Specialist in Pediatrics and Neonatology,
University of California, Irvine Medical Center

With

JACK H. SILLS, MD

Medical Director, Neonatal Intensive Care Unit,
University of California, Irvine Medical Center,
Clinical Professor of Pediatrics,
University of California, Irvine

ROBIN M. KOEPPEL, RNC, MS, CPNP, CS

Neonatal Clinical Nurse Specialist/Pediatric Nurse Practitioner,
University of California, Irvine Medical Center

NICU Ink®
BOOK PUBLISHERS
SANTA ROSA, CALIFORNIA

1410 NEOTOMAS AVENUE, SUITE 107
SANTA ROSA, CA 95405-7533

Copyright ©2003 by NICU INK
BOOK PUBLISHERS

Editor-in-Chief: Charles Rait, RN, MSEd, PNC

Managing Editor: Suzanne G. Rait, RN

Editorial Coordinator: Tabitha Parker

Reviewers: Bobby G. Bryant, PharmD
Margaret Conway-Orgel, RNC, NNP
Barbara Noerr, RNC, MSN

Editors: Debbie Fraser Askin, RNC, MN
Beverley J. DeWitt, BA
Carolyn R. Mueller, RN, MSN
Sylvia Stein Wright, BA

Proofreader: Joanne Gosnell, BA

Indexer: Gerry Lynn Messner

Book design and composition by
Marsha Godfrey Graphics

Library of Congress Cataloging-in-Publication Data

Zenk, Karin E.
  Neonatal medications & nutrition : a comprehensive guide / Karin E. Zenk, with Jack H. Sills, Robin M. Koeppel. — 3rd ed.
    p. ; cm.
  Includes bibliographical references and index.
  ISBN 1-887571-10-8
  1. Infants—Diseases—Chemotherapy—Handbooks, manuals, etc. 2. Pediatric pharmacology—Handbooks, manuals, etc. 3. Infants—Nutrition—Handbooks, manuals, etc. 4. Neonatal intensive care—Handbooks, manuals, etc. I. Title: Neonatal medications and nutrition. II. Sills, Jack H., 1952– III. Koeppel, Robin M., 1965– IV. Title.
  [DNLM: 1. Drug Therapy—Infant, Newborn—Handbooks. 2. Infant Nutrition—Handbooks. 3. Intensive Care, Neonatal—Handbooks. 4. Pharmaceutical Preparations—administration & dosage—Handbooks. WS 39 Z54n 2003]
  RJ253.7.C45 Z46 2003
  618.92'01—dc21   2002038660

FOREWORD

This 3rd edition of *Neonatal Medications & Nutrition: A Comprehensive Guide* updates and expands upon the previous two editions. Karin Zenk, PharmD, FASHP, Jack H. Sills, MD, and Robin M. Koeppel, RNC, MS, CPNP, continue to use their wide experience and expertise to provide a truly comprehensive text that succinctly presents crucial information about medications, nutritional products, and immunizations arranged alphabetically by generic name (which we should all use to write our orders). Besides the alphabetic listing, medications are arranged by therapeutic class to assist with drug selection for specific disorders. These extensive sections are complemented again by tables of difficult to find information from a table of reversal agents for respiratory depressants to the Finnegan Withdrawal Score Sheet to compatibilities among infusion drugs. A new section addresses live virus vaccinations and steroid treatment. New listings are included for 28 medications ranging from amiodarone to zidovudine while one surfactant that is no longer available is eliminated. Each entry is referenced to provide the evidence needed to inform therapeutic decisions. It remains the most comprehensive text available for addressing day to day questions concerning medications, nutritional products, and immunizations for the newborn. As you explore this book to locate essential information for neonatal care, it will become an invaluable addition in your library, the pharmacy, and the NICU.

> Robert M. Ward, MD, FAAP, FCP
> Professor of Pediatrics
> Director, Pediatric Pharmacology Program
> University of Utah

DEDICATION

To my husband, Phil,
for his encouragement and support

ACKNOWLEDGMENTS

We very much appreciate the helpful suggestions of the nurses, neonatal physicians (attendings, fellows, house staff), nurse practitioners, clinical nurse specialists, physician assistants, pharmacists, respiratory therapists, dieticians, and others in the University of California Irvine Medical Center neonatal intensive care unit. Their contributions were invaluable in making this a useful text. Our sincerest thanks go to the editorial staff at NICU INK, particularly Suzanne Rait and Tabitha Parker.

TABLE OF CONTENTS

SECTION II—NUTRITION

SECTION III—IMMUNIZATIONS

Table of Contents by Therapeutic Categories and Indications

Drugs used in neonates are listed here by their therapeutic category and by their indication, to assist the prescriber in choosing among the alternatives presented in this book to treat various indications. Please consult the drug monographs for dosages, adverse effects, and other pharmacologic information.

Treatment suggestions list only drugs for which this book contains monographs. The suggestions do not comprise a complete list of the drugs that can or should be used. Drugs are listed in alphabetical order, not in the order in which they should be used or tried. It is essential that other references also be consulted regarding treatment of the listed disorders.

THERAPEUTIC CATEGORIES AND INDICATIONS

THERAPEUTIC CATEGORIES AND INDICATIONS

THERAPEUTIC CATEGORIES AND INDICATIONS

THERAPEUTIC CATEGORIES AND INDICATIONS

THERAPEUTIC CATEGORIES AND INDICATIONS

NOTICE

This book is intended for health care providers caring for infants in the neonatal intensive care unit. It is directed to many disciplines, including nursing, neonatology, family practice, and respiratory therapy, and to neonatal nurse practitioners, physician assistants, dietitians, and pharmacists. Content has been reviewed by nurses, respiratory therapists, physicians, dietitians, and pharmacists to make the book as accurate, practical, and useful as possible.

Although every effort has been made to ensure accuracy, the reader is cautioned to consult the manufacturer's prescribing literature for complete prescribing information on each product. Drug therapy is constantly changing because of ongoing research and clinical experience and is subject to interpretation in the individual practice setting. The authors and editors therefore cannot guarantee the continued currency of the information, nor can they be responsible for errors or omissions, whether caused by negligence or otherwise, or any consequences whatsoever arising from use of this information.

Trade names mentioned do not imply endorsement of any product. Many drugs are not approved for use in neonates, and the reader assumes liability for any problems that may arise from their use.

It is recommended by the editors that this reference not be the only resource used and that all health care workers stay abreast of current literature, ongoing research, and changes in government regulations pertaining to drug administration.

Full knowledge of recommended dose, indications, contraindications, adverse reactions, and nursing implications is imperative prior to administration of any medication. The reader is urged to check the package insert of each drug for any changes in indications, dosage, warnings, and precautions. Verification of action through multiple resources is strongly encouraged.

HOW TO USE THIS BOOK

Neonatal Medications & Nutrition: A Comprehensive Guide, 3rd edition, provides practical, concise information on prescribing medications and nutrition for infants in the neonatal intensive care unit. This reference has been prepared with input from the many disciplines involved in neonatal care. It is intended for neonatal nurses, physicians, nurse practitioners, physician assistants, pharmacists, respiratory therapists, dietitians, and others caring for infants.

SECTION I: Individual medications are presented as monographs. Information on each is presented in the following categories:

Generic name is followed by the **phonetic pronunciation** of the drug name. One or two common **trade** or **brand names** are given in parentheses.

Therapeutic category and subcategory: The drug's classification is provided. Refer to the **USE** section of the monograph for more detailed information.

Synonym: Other names used for the drug may be given.

Information marked with a capsule is particularly important.

Dose: The monograph gives the neonatal dose. Dose adjustment in renal dysfunction is included where appropriate. Please note that some doses are customarily written as mg/kg/dose, whereas others are written as mg/kg/day divided by the number of doses given in a day. For example, for a 1 kg infant:

*250 mg/kg/**dose***   *given three times a day*   *totals 750 mg in a day*

versus

*250 mg/kg/**day***   *divided into three doses*   *equals 83.3 mg per dose*

Please be extremely careful to note whether a dose is "per day" or "per dose."

Administration: Routes by which the drug can be given, instructions for its administration, and precautions regarding administration in neonates are given. For drugs given IV, the rate of infusion and recommended concentration are given. Information regarding proper storage and stability are included where appropriate. For compatibility information, the reader is referred to the appropriate appendix.

Only the dosage forms and strengths that are used for infants are presented; all commercially available dosage forms and sizes are not listed. If a drug is not commercially available as an oral liquid, directions for compounding an oral liquid from the solid dosage form(s) are given.

Cautions/Contraindications: Precautions and specific warnings are discussed.

Use: This section presents indications for which the drug is used in infants.

Mechanism of Action: How the drug exerts its effects in the body is explained.

Adverse Effects: Side effects that may be seen in infants are included; those that apply only to adults are not.

Pharmacokinetics/Pharmacodynamics: Pharmacodynamic data may include onset of action, time to peak action, and duration of action. Pharmacokinetic data may include information on absorption, metabolism, and elimination.

Nursing Implications: Information is given regarding appropriate administration of the drug and monitoring of the infant receiving the medication.

Comments: Additional suggestions for use of the drug, if any, are given here. The therapeutic serum concentration is listed when appropriate. This heading may include a section on **Interactions** containing precautions regarding use with concurrent medications.

References: The sources of the information presented are listed. These can provide a resource for further reading.

SECTION II: Nutrition—Enteral and Parenteral: Provides suggestions for nutritional management of neonates needing intensive care. Includes a table of formulas commonly used in neonates and the rationale for use of each one. Neonatal parenteral nutrition is discussed: when to begin, how to administer safely and effectively, and how to make the transition to enteral nutrition.

SECTION III: Immunizations: Provides information on immunization regulations, schedules, and ordering information. Provides drug monographs on immunizations used in neonates.

SECTION IV: Appendices: The appendices complement and enrich the monographs by presenting additional reference data to increase the safety of drug therapy in the infant. Among them are information on calculations and charts of conversions and equivalents. We hope this book will be a valuable resource in your practice and that you will consult it often.

SPECIAL CONSIDERATIONS IN NEONATAL DRUG THERAPY

Drug efficacy, pharmacokinetics, and adverse effects are dynamic in infants because their growth and organ maturation are dynamic. Health care providers caring for neonates need to be aware of many special considerations to ensure effective drug therapy and avoid therapeutic disasters.

POTENTIAL FOR THERAPEUTIC DISASTERS

Adverse drug effects in neonates, especially preterm infants, are relatively frequent and often unexpected. In one prospective study on adverse drug reactions (ADRs) in 200 neonates, ADRs occurred in 30 percent. Of these ADRs, 15 percent were life-threatening and 25 percent prolonged the hospital stay.[1]

Lack of knowledge regarding developmental pharmacology in neonates has produced therapeutic disasters resulting from toxicity of two types:

- *Toxicity caused by immaturity of metabolism and/or elimination processes*
- *Toxicity due to percutaneous absorption*

TOXICITY DUE TO FUNCTIONAL IMMATURITY

Some drugs have shown themselves to be harmful to neonates, especially low or very low birth weight infants.

- *Sulfonamides* have been implicated as playing a role in the pathogenesis of kernicterus.[2] We now know to avoid sulfonamides in hyperbilirubinemic infants.

- *Chloramphenicol,* given to neonates in doses safe for older infants and children, causes gray baby syndrome, characterized by abdominal distention, vomiting, ashen color, hypothermia, progressive pallid cyanosis, irregular respiration, and circulatory collapse, followed by death in a few hours or days.[3] This syndrome is caused by reduced capacity for glucuronidation of chloramphenicol and decreased glomerular filtration rate, leading to accumulation of the drug and excessive serum concentrations. We now rarely use chloramphenicol, and when we do use it, we monitor serum concentrations and use only neonatal-specific doses.

- *Preservatives* and other ingredients in drug products have caused serious problems in infants. *Benzyl alcohol* in IV solutions used to flush umbilical catheters has caused death in 20 low birth weight neonates.[4] The syndrome included metabolic acidosis, progressive encephalopathy, intracranial hemorrhage, and respiratory depression with gasping. Accumulation of benzyl alcohol's benzoic acid metabolite, which could not be effectively handled by the immature liver of neonates, was the cause. We now avoid use of IV flush solutions containing benzyl alcohol. We also minimize use of drugs containing this preservative—and avoid them whenever medically possible.

An IV formulation of *vitamin E (E-Ferol)* (now withdrawn from the market) was associated with unusual liver and kidney disorders resulting in the death of 38 low birth weight infants. Symptoms were hypotension, thrombocytopenia, renal dysfunction, hepatomegaly, cholestasis, ascites, and metabolic acidosis. Polysorbate 80, used as a carrier in the product, is thought to have been responsible for the adverse effects, rather than the vitamin E.[5]

TOXICITY DUE TO PERCUTANEOUS ABSORPTION

Numerous reports have documented toxicity caused by absorption of drugs and chemicals through the skin of newborns. The skin of infants, especially preterm infants, is much more permeable to drugs than is adult skin.

- *Aniline dye* on freshly marked cloth diapers has resulted in cyanosis caused by methemoglobinemia in newborns.

- *Hexachlorophene (HCP)* skin disinfectant used during bathing to prevent staphylococcal disease has caused neurologic illness associated with cystic lesions in the brain and spinal cord.[6] Because HCP is insoluble in water, a residue remains on the infant's skin after bathing, and cutaneous absorption occurs even through intact skin. We now know to avoid use of HCP for routine daily bathing of newborns, except in term infants to interrupt nursery transmission of *Staphylococcus aureus* when high colonization rates are associated with high rates of staphylococcal infection. It is important to use copious amounts of water during the bath and rinse thoroughly. HCP is not used in preterm infants.[7]

- *Topically applied steroid preparations* may cause serious systemic complications from percutaneous absorption of steroids. Infants are particularly susceptible because their proportion of surface area to weight is relatively high and their skin is thin and very permeable, factors that enhance percutaneous absorption. Occlusion, a condition created by plastic diapers, is one of the most important factors that increases steroid penetration. Suppression of adrenocortical function, iatrogenic Cushing's syndrome, cessation of growth, and infant death due to adrenal failure following abrupt withdrawal from intensive topical steroid application have been reported. Local atrophy of the epidermis may occur. Effects are more pronounced when application is in the diaper area for prolonged periods of time, in infants with extensive skin lesions, and with use of high-potency steroids.[8]

- *Povidone-iodine (Betadine, polyvinylpyrrolidone iodine)* has caused transient iatrogenic hypothyroidism and goiter when used for extensive topical application, such as to an omphalocele. The effect appears to be dose related, is directly related to the degree of prematurity, and is gradually reversible once application is discontinued. Topical administration of povidone-iodine may increase plasma iodine levels. This toxicity is managed by monitoring thyroid function and promptly using replacement therapy if indicated.[9]

- *Isopropyl (rubbing) alcohol* has caused skin burns in preterm infants. Contributing factors are concentration of solution, duration of exposure, hypoperfusion (like that produced by hypoxia, hypothermias, and acidosis), and condition of the skin. Burns have been reported to occur most frequently in extremely low birth weight infants because of the immaturity of their skin.

Burns occurred most often in areas of pressure, where the alcohol pooled underneath the infant; areas exposed to soaked drapes; and areas where ECG electrodes were placed using isopropyl alcohol swabs.[10,11]

To help avoid adverse effects of drugs in neonates, do the following:[12,13]

1. Carefully evaluate and minimize use of topically applied soaps, creams, disinfectants, and drugs.
2. Before using newly marketed drugs in neonates, wait for the publication of articles documenting neonatal dosing, safety, and efficacy.
3. Use preservative-free drugs when possible.
4. Use appropriate neonatal-specific doses.
5. Monitor and document adverse drug reactions.
6. Use clinical pharmacy and unit-dose drug distribution services to optimize drug therapy and reduce medication errors.
7. Remove topical preparations such as iodine from the skin as soon as possible to limit absorption.

EFFECTS OF AGE ON PHARMACOKINETICS AND PHARMACODYNAMICS

Pharmacokinetics and pharmacodynamics differ markedly in infants, children, and adults and are continuously changed by maturational processes.

Absorption

There is relative achlorhydria for the first 10–15 days after birth, with gastric acidity reaching adult values only after two years. Gastric emptying in the neonatal period is irregular, unpredictable, and prolonged, reaching adult values at about six to eight months. Intramuscular absorption is erratic in neonates because of scarce muscle and adipose tissue, particularly in preterm infants. Percutaneous absorption differs from that of adults as well. The skin surface area relative to weight is approximately three times greater in infants than in adults. This, along with increased water content, predisposes infants to enhanced percutaneous absorption relative to adults. Preterm infants have thinner skin, thereby increasing the risk of absorption of many medications.[14]

Volume of Distribution

Developmental changes occur in amount of body water, binding capacity of plasma proteins, and body fat content relative to age. These changes influence the distribution of drugs. The volume of distribution for a number of drugs differs markedly in newborns, infants, and children compared with adults. Water constitutes 78 percent of body weight at birth, but drops to adult levels of approximately 60 percent by 1 year of age.[14]

Protein Binding

Neonates have decreased protein binding compared with adults. Factors that affect drug-protein binding in neonates include low total protein, decreased plasma albumin, decreased plasma globulin, increased unconjugated bilirubin, increased free fatty acids, low blood pH, and decreased α_1-acid glycoprotein. For example, comparative protein binding in the newborn and adult for ampicillin is 10 percent vs 18 percent; diazepam, 84 percent vs 99 percent; lidocaine, 20 percent vs 70 percent; phenytoin, 80 percent vs 90 percent; and theophylline, 36 percent in neonates vs 56 percent in adults.[15]

Several drugs are thought to be able to compete with and displace bilirubin from binding sites on the albumin molecule, thus increasing the risk of an infant's developing kernicterus (bilirubin encephalopathy). Drugs that are administered in low doses, such as digoxin, indomethacin, and furosemide, are not dangerous in this instance because a certain molar amount of the drug is required to occupy a significant fraction of the reserve albumin sites. Cationic drugs and most electroneutral substances, such as aminoglycosides, general anesthetics, and benzodiazepines, are not bound competitively and so will not compete with bilirubin for a binding site. The highest degree of displacement is with x-ray contrast media for cholangiography.[16]

Metabolism

Neonates metabolize drugs at a rate several times lower than that observed in adults. They also may have been exposed *in utero* to agents capable of altering the metabolic activity of liver or kidney excretory functions.[14] The functions of acetylation, glucuronidation, and conjugation with amino acids are all immature at birth, reaching adult levels by six months of age. Alcohol dehydrogenase takes even longer and may not reach adult levels until about five years of age.

Although most drugs are metabolized to less active forms, some may be transformed to active metabolites. For example, the conversion of theophylline to caffeine is important in neonates because the long half-life of caffeine in this population results in significant accumulation. Caffeine serum concentrations average 30 percent of theophylline concentrations in neonates.[17]

Differences in pharmacokinetic values such as volume of distribution and protein binding may cause a lack of efficacy. As a result, the dosages of certain drugs (on a body-weight basis) are larger in infants than those routinely used in adults. These drugs include, for example, gentamicin, digoxin, and pentamidine.

Elimination

Renal function increases with age. Glomerular filtration and tubular secretion reach adult values at about six months of age. The changes in theophylline half-life illustrate the effects of several of these processes dramatically, especially the maturation of kidney and liver function: The half-life of theophylline is about 30 hours in preterm infants, 14 hours in full-term infants less than 6 months of age, 4.6 hours in infants 6–11 months of age, and 3.4 hours in children 1–4 years old.[17] The shorter half-life at 1–4 years is a result of maturation and improvement in liver and renal function resulting in markedly faster metabolism and elimination of the drug. Thus, there is a potential for overdose in infants younger than 1 year of age and a risk for underdose at 1–4 years of age. A better understanding of the factors determining such increases in drug metabolism could lead to better and safer treatment in neonates and infants.[14,18]

GROWTH FACTORS: BODY WEIGHT AND DRUG DOSING

Infants, particularly preterm infants, may have fluctuations in body weight that affect drug dosing. The distribution of most drugs in the body changes with body and organ growth. These developmental changes are important because drug distribution might suddenly change as a result of differential development of one or the other body compartment, resulting in a need for readjustment of drug dosage. Increases or decreases in body weight should alert health care providers to consider adjusting the dose of an infant's medication. The infant's weight on the day that a medication dose was first ordered should be compared weekly with the current weight.

A 10–20 percent change in body weight may indicate that the infant's dose needs to be recalculated. Dose adjustment of drugs with a narrow therapeutic range (such as digoxin, theophylline, and gentamicin) should be considered when there is approximately a 10 percent change in body weight. Changing the dose of other less toxic drugs can be considered with a 20 percent change in body weight. Some drugs, such as multivitamins, do not need to be changed. Clinical judgment should be used to determine whether a dose change is necessary, using as a guide factors such as the infant's serum drug concentration and how well the infant is doing.

It is advisable to use the birth weight of the infant (rather than the actual daily weight) for drug and fluid calculations for the first week of life because the infant is attaining fluid equilibrium at this time and the changes in weight that occur reflect fluid shifts rather than actual weight gain or loss. After the first week, the actual weight can be used.

In seriously ill, very edematous infants, an estimate of the dry weight is made and used to calculate fluids and drugs.

In some cases, the dose is not changed as the infant's weight increases. For example, as phenobarbital is being tapered in preparation for discontinuation, the infant may be allowed to grow out of the dose.

FDA: SCHEDULES OF CONTROLLED SUBSTANCES

There are five controlled substance schedules. Drugs are placed in these schedules as findings are made with respect to each drug (or other substance). The findings required for each schedule are listed here. Schedule I: The drug* has a high potential for abuse. The drug has no currently accepted medical use in treatment in the U.S. There is a lack of accepted safety for use of the drug under medical substance. Schedule II: The drug has a high potential for abuse. The drug has a currently accepted medical use in treatment in the U.S. or a currently accepted medical use with severe restrictions. Abuse of the drug may lead to severe psychological or physical dependence. Schedule III: The drug has the potential for abuse less than the drugs listed in Schedules I and II. The drug has a currently accepted medical use in treatment in the U.S. Abuse of the drug may lead to moderate or low physical dependence or high psychological dependence.

* "drug" refers to "drug or other substance" as stated in the FDA guidelines.

Schedule IV: The drug has a low potential for abuse relative to the drugs or other substances in Schedule III. The drug has a currently accepted medical use in treatment in the U.S. Abuse of the drug may lead to limited physical dependence or psychological dependence relative to the drugs in Schedule III. Schedule V: The drug has a low potential for abuse relative to the drugs in Schedule IV. The drug has a currently accepted medical use in treatment in the U.S. Abuse of the drug may lead to limited physical dependence or psychological dependence relative to the drugs in Schedule IV.

REFERENCES

1. Aranda JV, et al. 1982. Epidemiology of adverse drug reactions in the newborn. *Developmental Pharmacology and Therapy* 5(3–4): 173–184.

2. Silverman WA, et al. 1956. A difference in mortality rate and incidence of kernicterus among premature infants allotted to two prophylactic anti-bacterial regimens. *Pediatrics* 18: 614–625.

3. Weiss CF, Glazko AJ, and Weston JK. 1960. Chloramphenicol in the newborn infant: A physiologic explanation of its toxicity when given in excessive dose. *New England Journal of Medicine* 262: 787–794.

4. Gershanik J, et al. 1982. The gasping syndrome and benzyl alcohol poisoning. *New England Journal of Medicine* 307(22): 1384–1388.

5. Alade SL, Brown RE, and Paquet A Jr. 1986. Polysorbate 80 and E-Ferol toxicity. *Pediatrics* 77(4): 593–597.

6. Shuman RM, Leech RW, and Alvord EC Jr. 1974. Neurotoxicity of hexachlorophene in the human. Part I: A Clinicopathologic study of 248 children. *Pediatrics* 54(6): 689–695.

7. Peter G, and Cashore WJ. 1995. Infections acquired in the nursery: Epidemiology and control. In *Infectious Diseases of the Fetus and Newborn Infant,* 4th ed., Remington JS, and Klein JO, eds. Philadelphia: WB Saunders, 1000–1019.

8. Shohat M, et al. 1986. Adrenocortical suppression by topical application of glucocorticosteroids in infants with seborrheic dermatitis. *Clinical Pediatrics* 25(4): 209–212.

9. Cosman BC, et al. 1988. Hypothyroidism caused by topical povidone-iodine in a newborn with omphalocele. *Journal of Pediatric Surgery* 23(4): 356–358.

10. Schick JB, and Milstein JM. 1981. Burn hazard of isopropyl alcohol in the neonate. *Pediatrics* 68(4): 587–588.

11. Weintraub Z, and Iancu TC. 1982. Isopropyl alcohol burns (letter). *Pediatrics* 69(4): 506.

12. Solomon SL, et al. 1984. Medication errors with inhalant epinephrine mimicking an epidemic of neonatal sepsis. *New England Journal of Medicine* 310(3): 166–170.

13. Zenk KE. 1994. Challenges in providing pharmaceutical care to pediatric patients. *American Journal of Hospital Pharmacy* 51(5): 688–694.

14. Morselli PL. 1989. Clinical pharmacology of the perinatal period and early infancy. *Clinical Pharmacokinetics* 17(supplement 1): S13–S28.

15. Marx CM, Pope JF, and Blumer JL. 1990. Developmental toxicology. In *Clinical Management of Poisoning and Drug Overdose,* 2nd ed., Haddad LM, and Winchester JF, eds. Philadelphia: WB Saunders, 388–435.

16. Brodersen R. 1980. Bilirubin transport in the newborn infant, reviewed with relation to kernicterus. *Journal of Pediatrics* 96(3 part 1): 349–356.

17. Hendeles L, and Weinberger M. 1983. Theophylline: A "state of the art" review. *Pharmacotherapy* 3(1): 2–44.

18. Kearns GL, and Reed MD. 1989. Clinical pharmacokinetics in infants and children: A reappraisal. *Clinical Pharmacokinetics* 17(supplement 1): S29–S67.

SECTION I
DRUG MONOGRAPHS

TABLE OF CONTENTS

A

A

ACETAMINOPHEN (TYLENOL)
(a-seat-a-MIN-oh-fen)

CENTRAL NERVOUS SYSTEM: NON-NARCOTIC ANALGESIC, ANTIPYRETIC

Synonyms: paracetamol, N-acetyl-p-aminophenol APAP

DOSE

Acetaminophen may be dosed per body weight in mg/kg/dose or given as a standardized dose, as shown in Table 1-1.

TABLE 1-1 ◆ ACETAMINOPHEN DOSE SCHEDULE

Age/Weight	Dose	Maximum	Standardized Dosing
Preterm/≤1 kg (2.2 lb)	5–10 mg/kg/dose* given every 8 hours as needed	3 doses/day	Give the exact mg/kg dose calculated. Do not round to a standard dose because small preterm infants have very immature hepatic and renal functions.
Preterm/>1 kg (2.2 lb)	10 mg/kg/dose* given every 8 hours as needed	3 doses/day	Round calculated dose to nearest 10 mg (i.e., give 20 mg, rather than 18 mg, for a 1.8 kg baby).
Term (0–1 month)/ 2.7–5 kg (6–11 lb)	40 mg/dose[†] given every 6–8 hours as needed or 10–15 mg/kg/dose given every 6–8 hours as needed	4 doses/day	Round to 40 and 80 mg increments.
2–3 months/ 2.7–5 kg (6–11 lb)	40 mg/dose[†] given every 4–6 hours as needed or 10–15 mg/kg/dose given every 6–8 hours as needed	5 doses/day	Round to 40 and 80 mg increments.
4–11 months/ 5.5–7.7 kg (12–17 lb)	80 mg given every 4–6 hours	5 doses/day	

Adapted from: Manufacturer's product literature. 1998. *Infants' Tylenol Suspension Drops*. Fort Washington, Pennsylvania: McNeil Consumer Products; and Anderson B, Anderson M, and Hastie B. 1996. Paracetamol prescription habits in a children's hospital. *New Zealand Medical Journal* 109(1031): 376–378.

* Anderson and colleagues state that 30 mg/kg/day achieves effective therapeutic concentrations in neonates, but further studies are needed.[1]

[†] In small-for-gestational-age infants, the 40 mg dose should not exceed 15 mg/kg.

Standardized Dosing: Standardized dosing reduces dosage errors and streamlines dose preparation. Unit-dose oral syringes of acetaminophen can be prepared in advance by the pharmacy in dosages of 10, 20, 30, 40, and 80 mg. (For other oral liquid medications that can be standardized, see Appendix Q: Pharmacist's Suggested Standardized NICU Oral Unit-Dose Syringes for Use with Infants >1 kg.)

Prophylactic Administration with DTP Vaccination: Administer a dose immediately following the DTP vaccination and every 4–6 hours thereafter for 48–72 hours.

Anderson and colleagues state that 30 mg/kg/day achieves effective therapeutic concentrations in neonates, but further studies are needed.[1]

Reduce dose in severe hepatic dysfunction.

ADMINISTRATION

Supplied as: Drops: 100 mg/ml; suppository: 80 mg, 120 mg.

PO: May administer with feedings to reduce GI upset.

- Dilute drops (100 mg/ml) with water before use because they have a high osmolality (16,550 mOsm/kg H_2O). There may possibly be an association between necrotizing enterocolitis and oral administration of hypertonic solutions.[2]

- When giving for pain management prior to a procedure, administer 1–2 hours before the anticipated pain because cerebrospinal fluid (CSF) concentrations lag those of plasma, and site-of-action concentrations equilibrate slowly with those of plasma.[3]

Storage: Store suppositories below 27°C (80°F) or refrigerate.

Choosing the Right Product:

- Liquid acetaminophen is available as an elixir, a liquid, a solution, a suspension, and drops.

- The 100 mg/ml drops are the preferred liquid dosage form because this concentration minimizes dose volume; makes computation and measurement of dose volume easier, reducing the potential for errors; and does not contain alcohol.

- *Acetaminophen and Alcohol:* Many acetaminophen products contain no alcohol, but some may contain as much as 23 percent alcohol. Ethanol-containing medications should be avoided in infants, if possible, because of the potential for undesirable interactions, neuronal dysfunction, and hypoglycemia. Alcohol can also cause neurologic depression, altered liver function, and gastric irritation. Neurologic depression from alcohol in a medication can theoretically cause lethargy and poor feeding, resulting in an unnecessary workup for suspected sepsis.[4]

CAUTIONS/CONTRAINDICATIONS

Contraindicated in infants with acetaminophen hypersensitivity.

Check the alcohol content of the acetaminophen product you are using; avoid giving ethanol-containing products to infants.

Avoid giving acetaminophen for longer than 5 days without physician reassessment. Chronic use can cause hepatotoxicity.

Reduce dose in severe hepatic dysfunction. Pershad and associates report a case fatality from chronic acetaminophen toxicity in an 18-month-old toddler, born 14 weeks premature, who had been receiving less than the standard toxic threshold of acetaminophen pediatric suspension for 4 days prior to presentation. He had been on prolonged parenteral nutrition (PN) as an infant. The authors hypothesize that PN-induced hepatic changes may have diminished the toddler's hepatic reserve, making him more susceptible to acetaminophen toxicity. The authors propose that a different therapeutic acetaminophen dose may be needed for those with underlying risk factors for hepatotoxicity.[5]

Overdose has been associated with acute renal failure.

Advise parents about the potential hepatotoxicity of acetaminophen when it is given to ill children in doses exceeding weight-based recommendations.[6,7] Rivera-Penera and colleagues reported that 39 percent of patients admitted for acetaminophen overdose in their study had severe toxic effects to the liver, and six of them underwent liver transplantation. The researchers reported that a miscalculated dose given multiple times by parents and delay in therapy when the error was discovered and/or toxic symptoms appeared are risk factors for overdose toxicity in children 10 years of age or younger.[7]

Infants with Phenylketonuria: Note that some acetaminophen products (Children's Tylenol chewable tablets, Children's Anacin-3 tablets, Junior Strength Tylenol tablets, and Tempra chewable tablets) contain aspartame (NutraSweet), which is metabolized in the GI tract to phenylalanine. Avoid or use these products with caution in infants with phenylketonuria.

Use

An analgesic that provides temporary relief of mild to moderate pain and discomfort and an antipyretic that provides temporary relief of fever.

Decreases the incidence of fever and pain at the injection site in children receiving a DTP vaccination.

Comparison of Acetaminophen and Aspirin:

- Acetaminophen is usually preferred over aspirin for the treatment of pain or fever in infants because acetaminophen does not affect bleeding time or the ductus arteriosus. Also, it is not associated with Reye's syndrome, as aspirin is.

- Because it is stable in solution, acetaminophen is available in liquid form, whereas aspirin is not stable in solution and therefore is not available as a liquid.

- Aspirin or a nonsteroidal anti-inflammatory agent, rather than acetaminophen, should be used in a clinical disease such as arthritis, where an anti-inflammatory effect is needed.

TABLE 1-2 ◆ COMPARISON OF ACETAMINOPHEN, IBUPROFEN, AND ASPIRIN GIVEN AT NORMAL DOSES

Action or Adverse Effect	Acetaminophen	Ibuprofen	Aspirin*
Duration of action	4 hours	6–8 hours	4 hours
Available as an oral liquid	X	X	
Relieves mild to moderate pain	X	X	X
Anti-inflammatory		X	X
Relieves fever	X	X	X
Inhibits prostaglandin synthesis (closes ductus arteriosus, anti-inflammatory effect)		X	X
GI bleeding, ulceration		X	X
Prolongs bleeding time		X	X
Prolongs prothrombin time			X (at high doses, with fever, or with increased metabolic rate)
Causes thrombocytopenia	X	X	
Inhibits platelet aggregation		X	X
Associated with Reye's syndrome			X

* Aspirin is shown for comparison purposes only. It should not be used in infants for analgesia or antipyresis because of its effects on the ductus arteriosus and on bleeding time and because of its association with Reye's syndrome. Low-dose aspirin is used by some clinicians after cardiac surgery to prevent clotting.

- Table 1-2 compares the actions and adverse effects of acetaminophen, ibuprofen, and aspirin.

MECHANISM OF ACTION

The mechanism of action of acetaminophen is not well understood. It reduces fever through action on the hypothalamic heat-regulating center, which increases the dissipation of body heat.

Acetaminophen's mechanism for reducing pain is unclear. It has poor anti-inflammatory action. Compared with aspirin, it is only a weak inhibitor of prostaglandin synthesis.

ADVERSE EFFECTS

Usually well tolerated when used as directed. Adverse effects rarely occur.

Dermatologic: Rash, hypersensitivity reactions.

Hematologic: Hemolytic anemia, neutropenia, leukopenia, thrombocytopenia.

Hepatic: Jaundice. Causes hepatic necrosis on overdose and with chronic use. In single doses of the appropriate amount, however, there should be no cause for concern about acetaminophen's use in children with chronic liver disease.[8]

Other: Hypoglycemia; rarely, nephrotoxicity.

A

Overdose: May cause severe hepatotoxicity. Prompt treatment with the **antidote acetylcysteine** (Mucomyst) is essential for potentially hepatotoxic serum concentrations. Acetylcysteine is given at a dose of 140 mg/kg PO initially, followed by 70 mg/kg PO every 4 hours for an additional 17 doses.[9] Acetaminophen plasma concentrations are followed. Confer with the poison control center as to whether or not the drug is indicated and for instructions on safe, effective use. Acetylcysteine replenishes the hepatic glutathione stores that are necessary to protect the liver cells against the highly toxic metabolites of acetaminophen. With normal doses, small quantities of acetaminophen are metabolized in the liver by a cytochrome P-450 microsomal enzyme to a toxic intermediate metabolite that is responsible for the acetaminophen-induced liver necrosis. It is then further metabolized to nontoxic form via conjugation with glutathione and ultimately excreted in urine as mercapturic acid.

After an overdose, however, increased hepatic metabolism of acetaminophen by the cytochrome P-450 mixed function oxidase system results in the depletion of liver glutathione stores to critical levels and subsequent accumulation of the toxic intermediate. Infants and young children usually demonstrate less toxicity than adults for equivalent serum concentrations and are less prone to developing hepatotoxicity than adults, perhaps because of lesser metabolism by the P-450 enzyme system and higher turnover rates of glutathione. For information on treatment of acetaminophen overdose, refer to the manufacturer's product literature and toxicology resources. For additional emergency information, contact your regional poison control center or the Rocky Mountain Poison Center (800-525-6115) immediately for treatment recommendations.

Risk factors for dose-dependent hepatotoxicity on overdose include sustained administration of high doses (i.e., ≥90 mg/kg/day) to a sick child (e.g., one with repeated vomiting/diarrhea and poor oral food intake) for more than 1 day,[10] delayed referral and therapy after overdose, concurrent use of "enzyme inducers" (phenobarbital, phenytoin, rifampin), and malnutrition.

PHARMACOKINETICS/PHARMACODYNAMICS

Absorption: Well absorbed from the GI tract after oral administration. Absorption is more erratic and variable with the suppository form.

Peak Effect: Maximum temperature decrease and peak analgesia are at 1–2 hours after peak plasma concentrations because CSF concentrations lag those of plasma.[3] The time to peak plasma concentrations is 10 minutes to 1 hour.

Duration of Action: 4 hours.

Metabolism:

- Acetaminophen is metabolized mostly to the inactive sulfate and glucuronide metabolites. Ability to conjugate glucuronide is immature in the first months of life. Enhanced sulfate conjugation compensates for this deficit, and it provides the main pathway for elimination of acetaminophen in infancy.[11,12] Systemic clearance is lower, and it is necessary to use a lower daily dose, particularly in preterm infants because of their immature hepatic and renal function.

- A small amount of acetaminophen is deacetylated, probably to *p*-amino-phenol, which can cause methemoglobinemia.

- Another small amount of acetaminophen is metabolized to a highly toxic metabolite that is conjugated with hepatic glutathione and inactivated. This toxic metabolite may be responsible for acetaminophen-induced liver necrosis. When acetaminophen is taken at excessive doses or used chronically, glutathione stores can become depleted, leading to insufficient inactivation of the toxic metabolite and then to hepatic necrosis.

Half-life: Newborn: 3.5 hours[12] to 4.9 hours.[11]

Elimination: Excreted in the urine as inactive glucuronate and sulfate conjugates. Systemic clearance is reduced in severe hepatic failure, especially if the failure is caused by acetaminophen poisoning.

Nursing Implications

If treating fever, monitor temperature.

If treating pain, monitor for signs of pain relief. See Table 1-38, page 413.

On discharge, advise parents of the correct dose of acetaminophen for the infant's weight, the correct product to use (caution them not to use adult-strength formulations for infants), use of sponge bathing if fever is unresponsive, and the potential risks of giving too much acetaminophen to a sick, acutely malnourished infant.[10] Parents should be instructed to contact their health care provider immediately if they accidentally give an overdose (for example, if the parents realize in retrospect that they were giving the child the adult-strength rather than the pediatric-strength acetaminophen product).

Comments

Interactions: Large doses or long-term administration of barbiturates, carbamazepine, hydantoins, and rifampin may increase the potential hepatotoxicity of acetaminophen. These drugs can also decrease the therapeutic effects of acetaminophen.

Reference Range: Toxic concentration after overdose: >200 mcg/ml at 4 hours or 50 mcg/ml at 12 hours after overdose. Serum concentration after the usual therapeutic dose: 5–20 mcg/ml 30 minutes to 2 hours after the dose.

References

1. Anderson B, Anderson M, and Hastie B. 1996. Paracetamol prescribing habits in a children's hospital. *New Zealand Medical Journal* 109(1031): 376–378.

2. Ernst JA, et al. 1983. Osmolality of substances used in the intensive care nursery. *Pediatrics* 72(3): 347–352.

3. Anderson BJ, et al. 1998. Paracetamol plasma and cerebrospinal fluid pharmacokinetics in children. *British Journal of Clinical Pharmacology* 46(3): 237–243.

4. American Academy of Pediatrics, Committee on Drugs. 1984. Ethanol in liquid preparations intended for children. *Pediatrics* 73(3): 405–407.

5. Pershad J, Nichols M, and King W. 1999. "The silent killer": Chronic acetaminophen toxicity in a toddler. *Pediatric Emergency Care* 15(1): 43–46.

6. Heubi JE, Barbacci MB, and Zimmerman HJ. 1998. Therapeutic misadventures with acetaminophen: Hepatotoxicity after multiple doses in children. *Journal of Pediatrics* 132(1): 22–27.

7. Rivera-Penera T, et al. 1997. Outcome of acetaminophen overdose in pediatric patients and factors contributing to hepatotoxicity. *Journal of Pediatrics* 130(2): 300–304.

8. al-Obaidy SS, et al. 1996. Metabolism of paracetamol in children with chronic liver disease. *European Journal of Clinical Pharmacology* 50(1-2): 69–76.

9. United States Pharmacopeial Convention/USP DI. 2000. *Drug Information for the Health Care Professional,* 20th ed. Rockville, Maryland: United States Pharmacopeial Convention, 18–20.

10. Kearns GL, Leeder JS, and Wasserman GS. 1998. Acetaminophen overdose with therapeutic intent. *Journal of Pediatrics* 132(1): 5–8.

11. Miller RP, Roberts RJ, and Fischer LJ. 1976. Acetaminophen elimination kinetics in neonates, children and adults. *Clinical Pharmacology and Therapeutics* 19(3): 284–294.

12. Levy G, et al. 1975. Pharmacokinetics of acetaminophen in the human neonate: Formation of acetaminophen glucuronide and sulfate in relation to plasma bilirubin concentration and D-glucaric acid excretion. *Pediatrics* 55(6): 818–825.

ACETYLCYSTEINE

(as-eh-til-SIS-tee-in)

(MUCOMYST)

RESPIRATORY:
MUCOLYTIC

Synonym: N-Acetylcysteine

DOSE

Nebulization:

- 1 ml of a 20 percent solution diluted with normal saline or sterile water for inhalation, to a final volume of 3 ml.
- Give every 6–8 hours.

ADMINISTRATION

Supplied as: 10 percent and 20 percent solution, in 4, 10, and 30 ml vials.

To avoid possible acetylcysteine-induced bronchoconstriction, consider preceding treatment with administration of a bronchodilator, such as albuterol.

Maintain an open airway by mechanical suction as necessary.

Clean nebulizing equipment immediately after use so residues do not occlude fine orifices or corrode metal parts.

Storage: Refrigerate unused portion, mark vial with date and time, then discard 96 hours after opening.[1]

USE

A mucolytic agent used as an adjuvant therapy for abnormal, viscid, or inspissated mucus secretions; facilitates their removal through coughing, postural drainage, or mechanical suctioning.[1]

Used successfully in infants with recurrent or severe atelectasis during mechanical ventilation when other types of therapy (at least 4 days of chest physiotherapy consisting of postural drainage, vibration, percussion, saline lavage, and selective intubation of the atelectatic lung) have failed.[2]

Some investigators do not support the use of acetylcysteine as a mucolytic agent in premature infants with chronic lung disease; they found no improvement in the clinical condition of treated infants and reported that tracheal administration of 0.5 ml of a 5 percent solution led to increased total airway resistance and apnea/bradycardia.[3]

Acetaminophen overdose. Acetylcysteine has been used as an antidote for an overdose of acetaminophen at a dose of 140 mg/kg PO initially, followed by 70 mg/kg PO every 4 hours for an additional 17 doses.[4] Acetaminophen plasma concentrations are followed. Confer with your regional poison control center or the Rocky Mountain Poison Center (800-525-6115) as to whether or not the drug is indicated and for instructions on safe, effective use. (Also see monograph on acetaminophen.)

FIGURE 1-1 ◆ **ACETYLCYSTEINE MECHANISM OF ACTION.**

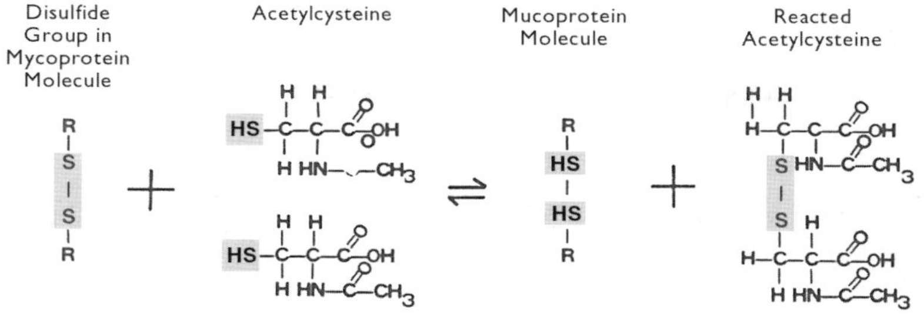

Acetylcysteine reduces the viscosity of mucus by substituting the sulfhydryl for the sulfide bonds in mucoprotein molecules.

From: *Professional Handbook of Clinical Experience.* 1970. Evansville, Indiana: Mead Johnson. Reprinted by permission.

MECHANISM OF ACTION

Acetylcysteine is the N-acetyl derivative of the naturally occurring amino acid cysteine. Its mucolytic effect has been shown to depend on acetylcysteine's free sulfhydryl group, which is thought to open disulfide linkages of mucoproteins, forming a mixed disulfide and a free sulfhydryl group (Figure 1-1).[5] It exerts mucolytic, osmotic, and irritative effects on the mucosa, causing mobilization of secretions. Acetylcysteine does not inhibit ciliary activity.

ADVERSE EFFECTS

Acetylcysteine appears to have a wide margin of safety.[5] The major disadvantages to use of the drug are malodor (acetylcysteine has an unpleasant, rotten-egg odor when administered), nausea, vomiting, and airway irritation, which could result in bronchospasm.

May also cause stomatitis, fever, rhinorrhea, drowsiness, and clamminess.[1]

Acquired sensitization (rash) rarely occurs in respiratory therapists even after frequent and extended exposure.

One group of investigators reported no adverse effects in neonates.[2] Another group reported an increase in total airway resistance and increased frequency of bradycardia and cyanotic spells in some infants.[3]

PHARMACOKINETICS/PHARMACODYNAMICS

Absorption: Following oral inhalation, most of the drug appears to participate in the sulfhydryl-disulfide reactions described under **MECHANISM OF ACTION**; the rest is absorbed from the pulmonary epithelium.

Metabolism: Diacetylated by the liver to cysteine; then metabolized by incorporation into protein chains and conversion to taurine and other metabolic pathways.[1,3] The odor produced during nebulization is caused by the emission of hydrogen sulfide when the drug is degraded.

NURSING IMPLICATIONS

Be prepared to suction the infant after drug administration to control the increased volume of liquefied secretions that may occur.

Consider preceding treatment with a bronchodilator because acetylcysteine may cause airway irritation and (infrequently) bronchospasm.

COMMENTS

Contact with rubber, copper, iron, and cork may inactivate the drug.

EDTA (ethylenediaminetetraacetic acid) is added as a chelating agent to tie up heavy metal ions to preserve the activity of the drug. The slight purple color in opened bottles results from the EDTA's combining with heavy metal ions and does not significantly affect the safety or effectiveness of the drug.[1]

Monitoring: Subjective observations must be used to evaluate the effectiveness of aerosol myocytic agents, making evaluation difficult.[5]

Discontinuation of Treatment: Discontinue use if there is no improvement after 2–4 days, as measured by decreased mucus viscosity with improved ability to remove mucus secretions. Discontinue immediately if bronchospasm occurs, and administer a bronchodilator.[1]

REFERENCES

1. Manufacturer's product literature.
2. Amir J, et al. 1985. Acetylcysteine for severe atelectasis in premature infants (letter). *Clinical Pharmacy* 4(3): 255.
3. Bibi H, et al. 1992. Intratracheal N-acetylcysteine use in infants with chronic lung disease. *Acta Paediatrica* 81(4): 335–339.
4. United States Pharmacopeial Convention/USP DI. 2000. *Drug Information for the Health Care Professional,* 20th ed. Rockville, Maryland: United States Pharmacopeial Convention, 18–20.
5. McEvoy GK. 1994. *AHFS Drug Information.* Bethesda, Maryland: American Society of Hospital Pharmacists, 1762–1764.

ACYCLOVIR (ZOVIRAX)
(ay-SYE-kloe-veer)

**ANTI-INFECTIVE:
ANTIVIRAL**

DOSE

IV:

- *Preterm <33 weeks gestation:* 20 mg/kg/day every 12 hours.
- *Term:* 30 mg/kg/24 hours divided every 8 hours IV for 14 to 21 days.[1]
  - Some experts give 45–60 mg/kg/day every 8 hours for term infants with normal renal function.[1]

PO (**varicella**): 20 mg/kg/dose PO every 6 hours initiated at the first sign of disease and continued for 5 days. The patient should be maintained in a well-hydrated state.

Reduce dose in renal dysfunction. Measure serum creatinine.[2]

ADMINISTRATION

IV—*Rate:* Infuse over 1 hour by syringe pump.

IV—*Concentration:* Less than 7 mg/ml.

IV—*Compatibility:* See Appendix E: Y-Site Compatibility of Common NICU Drugs.

PO: Available as an oral suspension (200 mg/5 ml).

USE

Herpes simplex (HSV-1 and HSV-2) and varicella-zoster (chickenpox) infections. (See also varicella vaccine in SECTION III—Immunizations.)

Inhibits viral DNA synthesis.

Less toxic than vidarabine, easier to administer, and the usual drug of choice.[1,3]

Oral acyclovir therapy initiated within 24 hours of illness for otherwise healthy children with varicella typically results in a 1-day reduction of fever and in approximately a 15–30 percent reduction in the severity of cutaneous and systemic signs and symptoms.[4] The American Academy of Pediatrics has stated that it cannot comment on the use of oral acyclovir in infants 0–12 months because of insufficient data on safety and efficacy in this age group.[1]

ADVERSE EFFECTS

Usually well tolerated.

May cause renal tubular crystallization and transient elevation of BUN and creatinine. Renal dysfunction is especially associated with large doses by rapid IV infusion, but is uncommon and reversible.

Vomiting, vein irritation, tremulousness, and rash may occur.

CNS disturbances (such as agitation, tremors, myoclonus) have been reported.[2]

PHARMACOKINETICS/PHARMACODYNAMICS

Absorption: Oral absorption is only 15–30 percent.

Distribution: Concentration in the CSF is 50 percent of serum level. Neonates have higher serum concentrations of the drug than do older infants receiving the same dose.

Protein Binding: Low (15 percent).

Half-life: Reported as 5 hours with serum creatinine <1 mg/dl and 15.6 hours with creatinine >1 mg/dl.[2]

Elimination: Acyclovir is excreted mostly unchanged in the urine.

NURSING IMPLICATIONS

Monitor renal function closely and strictly monitor I & O.

COMMENTS

Adequate hydration is required to prevent renal tubular crystallization.

Adequate dilution and slow infusion rate are required to prevent vein irritation.

REFERENCES

1. American Academy of Pediatrics, Committee on Infectious Diseases. 1994. *Red Book: Report of the Committee on Infectious Diseases.* Elk Grove Village, Illinois: American Academy of Pediatrics.

2. Englund JA, Fletcher CV, and Balfour HH Jr. 1991. Acyclovir therapy in neonates. *Journal of Pediatrics* 119(1 part 1): 129–135.

3. Whitley R, et al. 1991. A controlled trial comparing vidarabine with acyclovir in neonatal herpes simplex virus infection. *New England Journal of Medicine* 324(7): 444–449.

4. Balfour HH Jr, et al. 1990. Acyclovir treatment of varicella in otherwise healthy children. *Journal of Pediatrics* 116(4): 633–639.

ADENOSINE (ADENOCARD)

(a-DEN-oh-seen)

CARDIOVASCULAR:
ANTIARRHYTHMIC

DOSE

0.1–0.2 mg/kg by rapid IV push over 1–2 seconds.
May also use 0.05 mg/kg/dose followed by 0.1 mg/kg/dose every 2–5 minutes as needed × 3, until supraventricular tachycardia (SVT) is controlled. (Range 0.04–0.25 mg/kg.)[1]

ADMINISTRATION

Supplied as: 3,000 mcg/ml (6 mg/2 ml).

Prepare a 1:10 dilution to improve accuracy of measurement, and double-check dose with another RN: Dilute 1 ml of drug with 9 ml of saline. Concentration will then be 300 mcg/ml.

Rate: Rapid IV push over 1–2 seconds. **Follow by normal saline rapid flush to be sure the drug reaches the circulation. Administer as close to the baby's IV site as possible.**

CAUTIONS/CONTRAINDICATIONS

Do not use in second- or third-degree atrioventricular (AV) block.

Not effective for atrial flutter, atrial fibrillation, or ventricular tachycardia.

USE

Converts SVT, including that associated with Wolff-Parkinson-White syndrome (WPW), to sinus rhythm.[2,3]

Does not have the negative inotropic effects of other antiarrhythmics, has a faster onset of action than digoxin, and appears not to have the serious hemodynamic adverse effects of verapamil.

Can be used repeatedly without risk of accumulation.

MECHANISM OF ACTION

This purine nucleoside that occurs naturally in all human cells slows conduction time through the AV node and interrupts re-entry pathways through the AV node to restore normal sinus rhythm.[2]

ADVERSE EFFECTS

May produce a short-lasting first-, second-, or third-degree heart block (particularly if on carbamazepine concurrently) and other arrhythmias at the time of conversion.

May decrease blood pressure (<1 percent) by vasodilation.

May cause brief dyspnea (12 percent), facial flushing (18 percent), nausea (3 percent).

PHARMACOKINETICS/PHARMACODYNAMICS

Duration of Effect: 20–30 seconds.

Metabolism: Metabolized to inosine and adenosine monophosphate (AMP).[1]

Half-life: <10 seconds.

NURSING IMPLICATIONS

Monitor all vital signs continuously, including systemic blood pressure.

Obtain EKG printout continuously during administration.

Observe for changes in perfusion or respiratory status.[4]

COMMENTS

Interactions: Higher doses of adenosine are required if infant is receiving caffeine or theophylline concurrently. Lower doses may be required if patient is on digoxin or verapamil concurrently. Higher degrees of heart block may occur if patient is on carbamazepine concurrently.

REFERENCES

1. American Heart Association, Emergency Cardiac Care Committee and Subcommittees. 1992. Guidelines for cardiopulmonary resuscitation and emergency cardiac care. Part VI: Pediatric advanced life support. *JAMA* 268(16): 2262–2275. (Comment in *JAMA*, 1992, 268[16]: 2297–2298; and *JAMA*, 1993, 269[20]: 2626.)

2. Case CL, Trippel DL, and Gillette PC. 1989. New antiarrhythmic agents in pediatrics. *Pediatric Clinics of North America* 36(5): 1293–1320.

3. Eubanks AP, and Artman M. 1994. Administration of adenosine to a newborn of 26 weeks' gestation. *Pediatric Cardiology* 15(3): 157–158.

4. Zeigler V. 1991. Adenosine in the pediatric population: Nursing implications. *Pediatric Nursing* 17(6): 600–602.

ALBUMIN
(al-BYOO-min)

BLOOD MODIFIER:
VOLUME EXPANDER

DOSE

5 percent (hypovolemia): 10–20 ml/kg/dose (= 0.5–1 gm/kg/dose). May repeat as needed.[1]

25 percent (hypoalbuminemia): 4 ml/kg (= 1 gm/kg).

Admixture in parenteral nutrition (PN): Up to 1.5 gm/kg per 24-hour volume of PN. Use the 25 percent concentration to minimize fluid volume.[2]

ADMINISTRATION

Rate: Infuse 5 percent solution by syringe pump over 30–60 minutes. The 5 percent concentration may be infused more quickly in emergencies such as hypovolemic shock when rapid volume expansion is needed. Infuse the 25 percent more slowly over 1–2 (preferred) hours.

For neonatal resuscitation, volume expansion with albumin 5 percent may be given over 5–10 minutes.[3] In a study by Lay and colleagues, infusion of albumin 25 percent 1 gm/kg over 10 minutes in infants with RDS resulted in increased blood volume and glomerular filtration rate.[4]

Concentration: May give undiluted. Available as 5 percent (for volume expansion) and as 25 percent (to increase serum albumin without excessive volume). 5 percent = .05 gm/ml; 25 percent = 0.25 gm/ml. (See **CAUTIONS/CONTRAINDICATIONS** for dilution information.)

Filtration: Baxter Hyland recommends a 5-micron filter for albumin 5 percent and 25 percent (range of acceptable filter sizes is 5–15 microns). This manufacturer supplies filters at no charge on request.

Compatibility: See Appendix E: Y-Site Compatibility of Common NICU Drugs.

Other: Refrigerate unused portion of vial; discard after 4 hours. May be administered by coinfusion by Y-site into parenteral nutrition and infused over 24 hours when admixed in TPN.

CAUTIONS/CONTRAINDICATIONS

Warning: **Do not use sterile water to make this dilution because the reduced tonicity of the final solution may cause hemolysis. Hemolysis has been reported in four plasmapheresis patients who received hypotonic albumin solution; one of these patients died.[5]**

USE

A rapid intravascular volume expansion in infants who are hypovolemic. Albumin increases the intravascular colloid pressure by increasing serum albumin level. Albumin has also been used to enhance bilirubin binding in infants with hyperbilirubinemia. The efficacy for volume expansion or bilirubin binding is controversial.

Jefferies and colleagues found that the lungs of neonates with hyaline membrane disease are abnormally permeable to small solutes and that this abnormality persists in infants with subsequent chronic lung disease.[6] Hypoproteinemia is one factor that promotes fluid movement into the lungs. Management includes manipulation of fluid intake, diuretics, and maintenance of a normal serum albumin through optimal nutrition and albumin infusions, when necessary.

Albumin has been used to minimize insulin adsorption to tubing; however, this is not necessary and adds to the cost of treatment (see insulin monograph).

Albumin 5 percent is no longer the fluid of choice for initial volume expansion in neonatal resuscitation. (See Appendix O: Neonatal Cardiopulmonary Resuscitation and Postresuscitation Drug Doses.)

ADVERSE EFFECTS

Hypervolemia and precipitation of CHF.

Rapid infusion over <30 minutes may predispose preterm infants to intracranial hemorrhage.

Risk of infection, because albumin is a blood product.

PHARMACOKINETICS/PHARMACODYNAMICS

The elimination half-life is 15–20 days.

NURSING IMPLICATIONS

Monitor for signs of fluid overload.

Monitor vital signs before, during, and after administration.

Monitor I & O, hemoglobin, hematocrit, urine specific gravity.

COMMENTS

Albumin 5 percent and 25 percent each contain 0.16 mEq Na/ml (in normal saline). If albumin 5 percent with lower sodium concentration is needed, dilute albumin 25 percent to albumin 5 percent using D_5W. (Dilute each 1 ml of albumin 25 percent with 4 ml dextrose D_5W.)

REFERENCES

1. Greene MG. 1991. *The Harriet Lane Handbook,* 12th ed. Chicago: Year Book Medical Publishers.

2. Kanarek KS, Williams PR, and Blair C. 1992. Concurrent administration of albumin with total parenteral nutrition in sick newborn infants. *Journal of Parenteral and Enteral Nutrition* 16(1): 49–53.

3. American Heart Association in collaboration with the International Committee on Resuscitation. 2000. Part 11: Neonatal resuscitation. In Guidelines 2000 for cardiopulmonary resuscitation and emergency cardiovascular care. *Circulation* 102(supplement I): I-343–I-357).

4. Lay KS, et al. 1980. Acute effects of albumin infusion on blood volume and renal function in premature infants with respiratory distress syndrome. *Journal of Pediatrics* 97(4): 619–623.

5. Albumin warning. 1998. *American Journal of Health-System Pharmacy* 55(9): 867.

6. Jefferies AL, Coates G, and O'Brodovich H. 1984. Pulmonary epithelial permeability in hyaline-membrane disease. *New England Journal of Medicine* 311(17): 1075–1080.

ALBUTEROL
(al-BYOO-ter-ole)
(PROVENTIL, VENTOLIN)

RESPIRATORY:
BRONCHODILATOR

A

Synonym: Salbutamol

DOSE

Intermittent Nebulization:

- *Inpatients*—0.083 percent (0.83 mg/ml): 0.6–1.2 ml (0.5–1 mg) every 4 hours (range: every 2–6 hours) diluted to 3 ml with normal saline.
- *Outpatients*—0.5 percent (5 mg/ml): 0.1–0.2 ml (0.5–1 mg) every 4 hours (range: every 2–6 hours) diluted to 3 ml with normal saline.
- *Other dose recommendations:*
  - 2.5 mg in 3 ml saline (total volume = 3 ml).[1,2]
  - 0.05 mg (= 0.06 ml of 0.083 percent solution) regardless of the infant's weight or postnatal age.[3]
  - 0.04 ml/kg of 0.5 percent (= 0.2 mg/kg) in 1.5 ml normal saline every 4 hours. Increase dose to 0.1 ml/kg (= 0.5 mg/kg) or until a significant increase in basal heart rate is seen.[4]
  - 0.01–0.03 ml/kg of 0.5 percent. *Maximum:* 1 ml. Dilute with saline to 3 ml. Up to 4 times daily.[5]

Continuous Nebulization:

- 0.5 percent (5 mg/ml). Monitor severity of bronchoconstriction and heart rate.[3,4]
- May begin with full-strength 0.5 percent solution; as clinical condition improves, taper by diluting to 1:2 and then 1:3 with normal saline. The extra saline may add excessive amounts of fluid to the infant's daily fluid intake, however.

Metered Dose Inhaler (MDI) Using a Spacer:

- 1–2 puffs (= 90 mcg/puff) every 6 hours.

ADMINISTRATION

Choice of Delivery System:

- Intermittent nebulization is the delivery system of choice for most infants.
- For infants with severe bronchoconstriction, where intermittent nebulization is ineffective, consider continuous nebulization.[6]
- Continuous nebulization may significantly increase the fluid intake of the infant—6 ml/hour minimum.
- MDI delivery is used for severely fluid-restricted infants. The MDI method, when used with a spacer, may allow greater amounts of aerosol deposition in the lungs than either intermittent or continuous nebulization.[7]

TABLE 1-3 ◆ ALBUTEROL VOLUME CONVERSIONS: ML TO MG

0.5% (5 mg/ml) Concentrate	0.083% (0.83 mg/ml) Unit-Dose	mg
0.1 ml	0.6 ml	0.5 mg
0.2 ml	1.2 ml	1 mg
0.25 ml	1.5 ml	1.25 mg
0.3 ml	1.8 ml	1.5 mg
0.4 ml	2.4 ml	2 mg
0.5 ml	3 ml (usual adult dose)	2.5 mg

- All three delivery systems can be used for infants on mechanical ventilation.
- Dilute to a final total volume of 3 ml with normal saline or other concurrent medications.

Concentration:

- Table 1-3 gives volume conversions.
- For intermittent nebulization in inpatients: Supplied as 0.083 percent (2.5 mg/3 ml unit-dose = 0.83 mg/ml) solution for inhalation.
- For outpatient use and for continuous nebulization: 0.5 percent (5 mg/ml).

USE

For bronchodilation in reversible airway obstruction.[8]

For infants with significantly impaired respiratory function (such as in RDS) to increase maximal expiratory flow.[7]

To improve lung mechanics in ventilator-dependent infants and those with BPD.[1,9]

MECHANISM OF ACTION

β_2-adrenergic stimulation (bronchial dilation and vasodilation) with minor β_1 effects (increased myocardial contractility and conduction). Stimulates adenyl cyclase, which converts ATP to cyclic AMP. Cyclic AMP mediates cellular responses.

β-agonists (albuterol, isoetharine, isoproterenol, metaproterenol, terbutaline) predominately relax smooth muscle and therefore cause bronchodilation. These drugs may also help enhance mucociliary transport and redistribute pulmonary blood flow. They also inhibit histamine release from mast cells and produce vasodilation. Table 1-4 compares various adrenergic bronchodilators.

ADVERSE EFFECTS

Potential: Tachycardia, tremors, CNS stimulation, hypokalemia, poor growth, hyperglycemia, and perhaps impaired metabolism. Hypertension and cardiac hypertrophy.[10,11]

TABLE 1-4 ◆ COMPARISON OF ADRENERGIC BRONCHODILATORS[16–18]

Drug	Activity*	Relative Aerosol Potency[†]	Dose Form Available	Onset (Minutes)	Inhalation Duration (Hours)
Albuterol	$\beta_1 << \beta_2$	1	Neb & MDI	Within 5	4–6
Metaproterenol	$\beta_1 < \beta_2$	0.37	Neb & MDI	5–30	3–5
Terbutaline	$\beta_1 << \beta_2$	0.43	Inj & MDI	5–30	4–6
Isoproterenol	$\beta_1 = \beta_2$	ND	Neb & MDI	2–5	2–3
Epinephrine	$\alpha, \beta_1,$ and β_2	ND	Neb & MDI	1–5	1–2
Isoetharine	$\beta_1 < \beta_2$	ND	Neb & MDI	Within 5	2–3

ND = No data available

* Activity:
  << = much less than
  α = alpha-adrenergic stimulation (vasoconstriction, pressor effects)
  β_1 = beta 1-adrenergic stimulation (increased myocardial contractility and conduction)
  β_2 = beta 2-adrenergic stimulation (bronchial dilation and vasodilation)

[†] Equivalent number of puffs of albuterol required to produce initial effects equal to 1 puff of the medication tested.

A paradoxical response has been described in term infants, with an increase in airway resistance, possibly resulting from the osmolality or acidity of the product.[12]

Infants with BPD and tracheomalacia may lose central airway tone after bronchodilator therapy, increasing airway obstruction.[13]

In a retrospective study, Abman and colleagues showed a possible relationship between late, sudden, unexpected deaths in hospitalized infants and severe BPD. The infants who died more frequently had left ventricular hypertrophy and received prolonged combination theophylline and β-adrenergic agonist therapy than those who survived.[14]

One study of 19 infants and children indicated that continuous nebulization is safe and well tolerated. There was no significant evidence of cardiotoxicity. Katz and associates reported that heart rates tended to decrease during the study period, possibly as a result of improved respiratory status.[6]

PHARMACOKINETICS/PHARMACODYNAMICS

Onset of Action: Within 5–30 minutes.

Duration of Action: Commonly 3–4 hours.[7,15] Durations of up to 8 hours have been reported.[8]

NURSING IMPLICATIONS

Assess breath sounds before and after administration to determine effectiveness.

Monitor heart rate during and after administration.

Strictly monitor intake and output.

Albuterol nebulization may add significant amounts of fluid intake per day. Monitor for fluid volume overload.

Monitor blood pressure.

COMMENTS

Monitoring: Carefully evaluate effectiveness on an individual basis. Continuous monitoring of heart rate and clinical status is recommended for hospitalized infants, and in selected patients, oxygen saturation monitoring is recommended. Blood gases and pulmonary function testing may also be helpful to assess the need for dose adjustment. Monitor heart rate before, during, and after treatment. Monitor serum potassium. Observe for any other unusual adverse effects. Hold dose and reassess as follows if heart rate exceeds 180 bpm.

- **Dose Titration:**
  - *Reduce the dose* to the next smaller dose and/or increase the interval to the next longer interval when the heart rate exceeds 180 bpm (if baseline heart rate was <150 bpm) or 200 bpm (if baseline heart rate was >150 bpm). A moderate increase in heart rate is expected and may indicate absorption and therapeutic response. Lengthening the interval between doses should be tried when respiratory status has improved. Taper to the lowest effective dose.
  - *Increase the dose* to the next larger dose and/or decrease the interval to the next shorter interval if the infant is still in respiratory distress after a trial of one to three doses. However, do not increase dose if infant is experiencing adverse effects from current dose.

Discontinuation of Treatment: Assess daily the effectiveness of and need for the drug. If there has been no improvement in respiratory status as measured by pulmonary mechanics, change in respiratory support, or clinical status after 24 hours, discontinue the drug. If the heart rate continues above 180–200 bpm despite reduction in dose or lengthening of dosage interval, consider discontinuing the drug or changing to another agent.

REFERENCES

1. Rotschild A, et al. 1989. Increased compliance in response to salbutamol in premature infants with developing bronchopulmonary dysplasia. *Journal of Pediatrics* 115(6): 984–991.

2. Yuksel B, and Greenough A. 1991. Effect of nebulized salbutamol in preterm infants during the first year of life. *European Respiratory Journal* 4(9): 1088–1092.

3. Rush MG, and Hazinski TA. 1992. Current therapy of bronchopulmonary dysplasia. *Clinics in Perinatology* 19(3): 563–590.

4. Blanchard PW, Brown TM, and Coates AL. 1987. Pharmacotherapy in bronchopulmonary dysplasia. *Clinics in Perinatology* 14(4): 881–910.

5. Canny GJ, and Levison H. 1988. Aerosols—therapeutic use and delivery in childhood asthma. *Annals of Allergy* 60(1): 11–19.

6. Katz RW, et al. 1993. Safety of continuous nebulized albuterol for bronchospasm in infants and children. *Pediatrics* 92(5): 666–669.

7. Denjean A, et al. 1992. Dose-related bronchodilator response to aerosolized salbutamol (albuterol) in ventilator-dependent premature infants. *Journal of Pediatrics* 120(6): 974–979.

8. Manufacturer's product literature.

9. Montoyama EK, et al. 1987. Early onset of airway reactivity in premature infants with BPD. *American Review of Respiratory Disease* 136(1): 50–57.

10. Abman SH, and Groothuis JR. 1994. Pathophysiology and treatment of bronchopulmonary dysplasia. Current issues. *Pediatric Clinics of North America* 41(2): 277–315.

11. Zierhut W, and Zimmer HG. 1989. Significance of myocardial alpha- and beta-adrenoceptors in catecholamine-induced cardiac hypertrophy. *Circulation Research* 65(5): 1417–1425.

12. O'Callaghan C, Milner AD, and Swarbrick A. 1986. Paradoxical deterioration in lung function after nebulized salbutamol in wheezy infants. *Lancet* 2(8521-22): 1424–1425.

13. Panitch HB, et al. 1990. Effect of altering smooth muscle tone on maximal expiratory flows in patients with tracheomalacia. *Pediatric Pulmonology* 9(3): 170–176.

14. Abman SH, et al. 1989. Late sudden unexpected deaths in hospitalized infants with BPD. *American Journal of Diseases of Children* 143(7): 815–819.

15. Wilkie RA, and Bryan MH. 1987. Effect of bronchodilators on airway resistance in ventilator-dependent neonates with chronic lung disease. *Journal of Pediatrics* 111(2): 278–282.

16. Ahrens RC, et al. 1987. Use of bronchial provocation with histamine to compare the pharmacodynamics of inhaled albuterol and metaproterenol in patients with asthma. *Journal of Allergy and Clinical Immunology* 79(6): 876–882.

17. Harris JB, et al. 1986. Relative potencies and rates of decline in effect of inhaled albuterol and terbutaline. *Journal of Allergy and Clinical Immunology* 77(1): 147A.

18. McEvoy GK. 1994. *AHFS Drug Information.* Bethesda, Maryland: American Society of Hospital Pharmacists.

ALPROSTADIL

(al-PROS-ta-dil)

(PROSTIN VR PEDIATRIC)

CARDIOVASCULAR:
DUCTUS ARTERIOSUS

Synonyms: PGE_1, prostaglandin E_1

DOSE

Initial: 0.05 mcg/kg/minute by continuous infusion. Titrate to lowest possible rate that maintains response (range 0.01–0.4 mcg/kg/minute). Usual rate is 0.1 mcg/kg/minute.

Maintenance: Once stable improvement is attained, may reduce to half the initial rate.[1]

ADMINISTRATION

Supplied as: 500 mcg/ml 1 ml ampoule for dilution. Refrigerate. Discard after 24 hours.

Administer by neonatal syringe pump by continuous infusion only. Give into a large vein or through the umbilical artery catheter placed at the ductal opening.

See Appendix A for calculation of continuous infusions.

Compatibility: See Appendix E: Y-Site Compatibility of Common NICU Drugs.

CAUTIONS/CONTRAINDICATIONS

Do not use in respiratory distress syndrome.

USE

Maintains patency of the ductus arteriosus (by relaxing its smooth muscle) in neonates with ductal-dependent congenital cyanotic or acyanotic heart disease. It is a temporizing measure until corrective surgery can be performed.

Because of its vasodilating effects, has potential benefit as a pulmonary vasodilator for persistent pulmonary hypertension of the newborn. Almost completely metabolized on one pass through the pulmonary circulation, thus reducing extent of systemic hypotension.[2–4]

ADVERSE EFFECTS

Bone: Cortical hyperostosis is a frequent complication of prolonged use (42 percent at <30 days; 87 percent at 30–60 days; 100 percent at >60 days). PGE_1 stimulates both bone formation and resorption *in vitro* and may promote osteogenesis *in vivo*. Alkaline phosphatase is increased. Reversible bone tenderness or swelling and irritability mimicking osteomyelitis or cellulitis occur in some infants.[5]

Cardiovascular: Cutaneous vasodilation (10 percent, especially with intra-arterial administration) (can sometimes be alleviated by repositioning the catheter); rhythm disturbances (7 percent); hypotension (4 percent); cardiac arrest, edema (1 percent).

CNS: Apnea (12 percent), especially in infants weighing <2 kg; fever (14 percent); seizurelike activity (4 percent); irritability.

Hematologic: Disseminated intravascular coagulation (DIC) (1 percent); inhibition of platelet aggregation.

Other: Hyperthermia, hypoglycemia, diarrhea, gastric outlet obstruction with prolonged use.[6]

PHARMACOKINETICS/PHARMACODYNAMICS

Onset of Action: Maximum PO_2 response at 30 minutes in cyanotic heart disease and much later at 1.5–3 hours (up to 11 hours) in acyanotic heart disease.

Half-life: 5–10 minutes.

Elimination: 80 percent removed by pulmonary vascular bed in one circulatory pass. Excreted as metabolites via the kidney.

NURSING IMPLICATIONS

Monitor for respiratory depression.

Carefully monitor for ductal patency by noting presence and quality of heart murmur, peripheral pulses, capillary refill, improving urine output, and blood gases.

If used for ductal-dependent lesions, a patent IV must be maintained at all times; have a second heparin lock available for immediate use in case of IV infiltration because half-life is so short.

In long-term use, hyperostosis may cause bone tenderness; handle infant gently.

Monitor heart rate and rhythm, blood pressure, respiratory rate, and temperature. Most adverse effects are reversible upon slowing or temporarily discontinuing the infusion. Signs of improvement are improved blood oxygenation with cyanotic heart disease and improved blood pressure, blood pH, and urine output for acyanotic heart disease.

COMMENTS

Equipment to monitor the infant and support respiration should be available when using this drug.

Alprostadil should be stocked in all hospitals that deliver infants because it is a life-saving drug and must be used without delay in certain infants with congenital heart disease.

REFERENCES

1. Manufacturer's product literature. Prostin VR Pediatric. Kalamazoo, Michigan: Upjohn Company.

2. Hammerman C, et al. 1989. Prostaglandin E_1 selectively reduces Group B beta-hemolytic streptococci–induced pulmonary hypertension in newborn piglets. *American Journal of Diseases of Children* 143(3): 343–347.

3. Heymann MA. 1981. Pharmacologic use of prostaglandin E_1 in infants with congenital heart disease. *American Heart Journal* 101(6): 837–843.

4. Freed MD, et al. 1981. Prostaglandin E_1 in infants with ductus arteriosus–dependent congenital heart disease. *Circulation* 64(5): 899–905.

5. Woo K, Emery J, and Peabody J. 1994. Cortical hyperostosis: A complication of prolonged prostaglandin infusion in infants awaiting cardiac transplantation. *Pediatrics* 93(3): 417–420.

6. Peled N, et al. 1992. Gastric-outlet obstruction induced by prostaglandin therapy in neonates. *New England Journal of Medicine* 327(8): 505–510.

ALTEPLASE, RECOMBINANT (ACTIVASE, CATHFLO ACTIVASE, ACTILYSE)
(AL-te-plase)

ANTIDOTE: OCCLUDED CENTRAL CATHETER; BLOOD MODIFIER: THROMBOLYTIC AGENT

Synonym: tissue plasminogen activator (t-PA), recombinant

DOSE

Occluded Central Venous Catheter: 0.25–0.5 mg diluted in NS to volume required to fill line, usually 0.2–0.6 ml. Allow the instilled solution to dwell in the catheter for 2–4 hours; then try to aspirate (Table 1-5).[1]

Choi and colleagues recommend that x-ray evaluation be done to check for proper line placement before alteplase is given because malposition of the catheter is often the reason for occlusion. Their pre-alteplase protocol also includes an attempt to flush the central venous catheter, manipulate the central venous line (CVL) position, and instill hydrochloric acid when blockage is thought to be chemical rather than blood related.[1]

Note: Consult catheter product literature or the catheter manufacturer for catheter volume. For example, the catheter specifications in the package insert for L-CATH Catheter System, Peripherally Inserted Central and Midline Catheters state: "The priming volume for the central polyurethane, 24 Gauge, 1.9 Fr, 30 cm catheter is 0.2 ml." This volume will change if the line has been trimmed prior to insertion. Table 1-5 lists some regimens that have been used in pediatrics. (Also see Appendix F: Restoring Patency to Occluded Central Venous Catheters.)

Lysis of Large-vessel Thrombus (systemic use): Because of the diversity of treatment regimens in the literature, the lack of controlled trials, and the significant incidence of bleeding complications, we provide neither a dose nor a duration recommendation.[2] Doses used in neonates range from 0.1 to 1 mg/kg/hour for a duration of hours to days, as shown in Table 1-6. Duration of therapy is being determined by clinical response or imaging results.

ADMINISTRATION

Supplied as:

- *Injection:*
  - *Activase:* 50 mg (= 29 million units/vial) lyophilized powder with 50 ml diluent (sterile water for injection). Also contains L-arginine, phosphoric acid, and polysorbate 80.
  - *Cathflo Activase:* 2 mg vial as lyophilized powder. Reconstitute with sterile water for injection. Gently swirl until completely dissolved (about 3 minutes). Do not shake.

Occluded Central Venous Catheter:

IV—*Rate:* Instill into lumen of catheter slowly and carefully so as not to inject the drug into the systemic circulation.

TABLE 1-5 ◆ T-PA REGIMENS FOR CLEARING OCCLUDED CENTRAL VENOUS CATHETERS IN INFANTS AND CHILDREN

Reference	Dose and Concentration	Comments
Choi et al. 2001[1]	*Infants ≤2.5 kg:* Instill 0.25 mg diluted in NS to the volume required to fill the line.	A dwell time of 2–4 hours is recommended. After that time, withdraw the drug.
	Infants 2.5–10 kg: Instill 0.5 mg diluted in NS to the volume required to fill the line.	If possible, flush catheter with normal saline. Attempt to aspirate blood. If unsuccessful in obtaining a blood return, repeat once in 24 hours. For a double-lumen line, treat one lumen at a time using the specified dose in each line.
Monagle et al. 2001[15]	*Infants ≤10 kg:* Instill 0.5 mg diluted in 0.9% NaCl to the volume required to fill the line. Use the same amount for a double-lumen central venous line, but treat one lumen at a time.	From a consensus conference on anti-thrombotic therapy in infants and children.
Calhoun et al. 2000[2]	0.5 mg of drug/ml of fluid. *Maximum:* 2 ml/port. Leave t-PA in the catheter for 2 hours; then try to aspirate. May repeat once.	A consensus-of-practice document drafted by a group of neonatologists.
Davis et al. 2000[7]	Instill 0.5 mg/ml initially in the occluded port for 1 hour; then aspirate and flush with 0.9% sodium chloride. If this does not restore patency, increase the dose to 1 mg/ml and then to 2 mg/ml sequentially until the catheter is cleared.	In this study of 58 adult and pediatric patients as young as 1.7 months, 50 catheters (86.2%) were cleared with 0.5 mg/ml, 5 (8.6%) after dose escalation to 1 mg/ml, 1 (1.7%) after escalation to 2 mg/ml, and not cleared in 2 (3.4%). • Aliquots of 0.5 mg/ml, 1 mg/ml, and 2 mg/ml were frozen and stored for ready use and to reduce cost.
Kleta et al. 1998[18]	0.5 mg/0.5 ml was introduced into obstructed central venous catheters for 20–30 minutes.	In patients as young as 3 months, 97% of all obstructed catheters were reopened without side effects. • Aliquots of 0.5 mg/0.5 ml were frozen and stored for ready use and to reduce cost.
Atkinson et al. 1990[13]	1 mg/ml was instilled into the catheter for a dwell time of 4 hours.	Patients were as young as 1.5 years.

IV—*Concentration:* 0.5–1 mg/ml in dextrose or saline.

- For clearing occluded central venous catheters in infants, use of the 0.5 mg/ml concentration may be safer than use of the 1 mg/ml, to avoid a potential systemic dose.

Lysis of Large-vessel Thrombus (systemic use):

IV—*Rate:* Bolus doses have been infused over 10–15 minutes.[3–5] A continuous infusion usually follows the initial bolus (Table 1-6).

IV—*Concentration:* 0.5–1 mg/ml in dextrose or saline.

Storage/Stability: May use up to 8 hours after reconstitution. Discard unused portion because it contains no preservatives.[6]

Cost: Pharmacy preparation of multiple syringes from one 50 mg vial using appropriate sterile technique, then freezing the syringes until needed has been used to offset the high cost of t-PA. Refer to specialized references.[6–9] However, 2 mg vials are now commercially available as Cathflo Activase.

CAUTIONS/CONTRAINDICATIONS

Occluded Central Venous Catheter:

Use caution so as not to flush the t-PA out of the catheter into the systemic circulation. If the infant inadvertently receives a systemic dose of 0.05 mg/kg or more, observe potential bleeding sites (such as catheter insertion sites, cutdown sites), consider checking a fibrinogen level, avoid IM or SC injections, and minimize venipuncture.[10]

t-PA is not effective for occlusions caused by drugs or by calcium and phosphorus precipitates. Use dilute HCl instead.[9] (See Appendix F: Restoring Patency to Occluded Central Venous Catheters and the monograph on hydrochloric acid.)

Clearing occlusions of percutaneous intravenous catheters (PIC lines) used for very low birth weight infants may be difficult because of the very small lumen of these catheters and difficulties in instilling the t-PA. See **NURSING IMPLICATIONS,** below, for a technique that has been used in one unit.

Lysis of Large-vessel Thrombus (systemic use):

Infants with pre-existing intraventricular hemorrhage or cerebral ischemic changes should probably not receive t-PA.[11]

Correct hypertension before initiating t-PA.[11]

If serious bleeding in a critical location occurs (for example, an IVH extension or pulmonary hemorrhage), discontinue t-PA immediately.

Reocclusion is a potential problem after fibrinolytic therapy. The protocol used by Farnoux and colleagues withholds heparin therapy during the t-PA infusion to reduce the risk of bleeding and starts heparin immediately at the completion of t-PA therapy.[3]

Monitoring: Neonates require frequent reassessment of the thrombosis, usually by ultrasound during and after t-PA therapy to assess lysis and long-term outcome.[12] Daily cranial sonography has been recommended.[13] Testing for fibrin/fibrinogen degradation products and/or D-dimers is helpful in determining whether a fibrinolytic effect is present.[11,12] Fibrinogen is followed in most studies with a lower limit of 100 mg/dl, although Weiner and colleagues recommend maintaining the fibrinogen level at >150 mg/dl during the infusion to reduce the risk of bleeding.[11] Levy and colleagues measured the fibrinogen 4 hours after

TABLE 1-6 ◆ **T-PA REGIMENS USED FOR LYSIS OF LARGE-VESSEL THROMBUS IN INFANTS AND CHILDREN**

Reference	Dose and Concentration	Comments
Monagle et al. 2001[15]	0.1–0.6 mg/kg/hour for 6 hours (no initial bolus).	Longer or shorter infusions may be required. Start heparin either during or immediately on completion of thrombolytic therapy.
Weiner et al. 1998[11]	*Initial:* 0.1 mg/kg/hour. Assess fibrinogen blood levels every 4 hours, and adjust the infusion rate to maintain the fibrinogen level at >150 mg/dl. After 6 hours of treatment without response, increase the infusion in 0.1 mg/kg/hour increments at 6-hour intervals. *Maximum:* 0.4 mg/kg/hour.	The two patients with the most severe bleeding complications had received the highest dose: 0.5 mg/kg/hour. Therefore, these investigators now limit the infusion rate to no more than 0.4 mg/kg/hour. Bleeding complications were not seen in patients with fibrinogen >150 mg/dl.
Farnoux et al. 1998[3]	Initial bolus of 0.1 mg/kg over 10 minutes, then 0.3 mg/kg/hour for 3 hours. If that was not successful, up to 4 additional t-PA infusions were given every 12–24 hours.	Fibrinogen assay was done 1 and 4 hours after initiation of each t-PA dose. Heparin was stopped 3 hours before t-PA and restarted at the end of the t-PA infusion.
Fleming et al. 1998[4]	Initially, 0.5 mg/kg infused over a 10-minute period by left subclavian catheter, then 0.2 mg/kg/hour over 3 days.	This regimen was used to treat a staphylococcal endocarditis vegetation in a 0.93 kg infant. Heparin was not used.
Giuffre et al. 1998[5]	*Case 1:* 1 mg/kg IV through the central venous line for 15 minutes, followed by a continuous infusion of 1 mg/kg/hour for 4 hours given 1 time, plus fresh frozen plasma 10 ml/kg. *Case 2:* A dose of 0.5 mg/kg/hour for 6 hours was given through the catheter, plus fresh frozen plasma 10 ml/kg for a total of 3 days.	Treatment was successful in 2 preterm infants with catheter-related intracardiac thrombi. No bleeding complications occurred.

(continued on next page)

starting the drug and adjusted the dose if needed. Fibrinogen was measured every 4 hours until the value stabilized, then daily.[14]

Overdose: Fibrinogen levels help determine the need for cryoprecipitate and/or plasma replacement.[12] In patients having severe hemorrhage, stopping the t-PA infusion and applying direct pressure, when feasible, is usually all that is required to control bleeding. In more severe cases, treatment options include fresh frozen plasma, cryoprecipitate, and the antifibrinolytic drug aminocaproic acid (Amicar).[14,15]

TABLE 1-6 ◆ T-PA REGIMENS USED FOR LYSIS OF LARGE-VESSEL THROMBUS IN INFANTS AND
CHILDREN (CONTINUED)

Reference	Dose and Concentration	Comments
Grieg 1998[19]	0.1 mg/kg/hour for 15 hours.	Successful treatment of a neonatal brachial artery thrombosis, with no adverse effects.
Dillon et al. 1993[20]	Initially, 0.5 mg/kg, then 0.04–0.5 mg/kg/hour.	Two infants responded to only bolus administration. A third responded to bolus plus continuous infusion after 58 hours.
Levy et al. 1991[14]	*Initial:* 0.1 mg/kg/hour. Then increase in a stepwise fashion if no improvement in clot dissolution can be documented, while closely monitoring for bleeding. *Range:* 0.1–0.5 mg/kg/hour.	The authors note that all bleeding in their study was associated with higher doses of 0.46–0.5 mg/kg/hour. Complete clot dissolution occurred in 2 hours to 3 days in most patients. Heparin was discontinued when t-PA was started. Heparin was restarted once the clot dissolved, after which t-PA was discontinued.

USE

Used in neonates to restore patency of central venous catheters occluded by fibrin or clotted blood and for lysis of large-vessel thrombus (systemic use). t-PA has been used in neonates primarily to treat arterial clots, usually caused by an umbilical arterial catheter. t-PA has been used for lysis of catheter-related intracardiac thrombi.[5] Intracoronary t-PA successfully lysed a coronary artery thrombus in an infant with Kawasaki disease.[16]

Advantages of t-PA over Urokinase and Streptokinase:

- t-PA has more action locally at the site of the clot and lower affinity for circulating plasminogen, making for lower systemic effects, than urokinase or streptokinase. t-PA may be more clot-selective than these other drugs.[17]

- t-PA has a short half-life (approximately 5 minutes), allowing fibrinogen levels to return to normal more quickly than with the other drugs, thus reducing the risk of bleeding complications.

- t-PA is a naturally occurring substance and is therefore not antigenic (as is streptokinase).[14] Therefore, a second course of t-PA can be given without the patient's developing resistance to its effects and without risk of anaphylactic reaction.[17]

- t-PA may be successful in treating thromboses resistant to urokinase therapy.[3,14]

MECHANISM OF ACTION

Alteplase is a synthetic tissue plasminogen activator produced by recombinant DNA technology. Alteplase, like other thrombolytics, enhances the conversion of plasminogen to plasmin, which then cleaves fibrin, fibrinogen, factor V, and factor VIII, resulting in clot breakdown.

Neonates have low plasminogen plasma concentrations (50 percent of adult values at birth); thus, neonatal thrombi may not lyse as readily in response to fibrinolytic agents as do adult thrombi, resulting in the need for higher doses of fibrinolytic agents. Because of this, neonates may also need exogenous plasminogen in the form of fresh frozen plasma.[12]

ADVERSE EFFECTS

When Used for Occluded Central Venous Catheter: Bleeding, if excessive amounts of t-PA are inadvertently injected into the systemic circulation. Excessive pressure or force on instillation may force the clot into the systemic circulation. No t-PA–related incidences of hemorrhage, bleeding complications, or coagulation abnormalities (PT, PTT, platelets) were observed in the reports by either Atkinson and colleagues or Davis and coworkers when t-PA was used to treat occluded central lines.[7,13]

When Used for Lysis of Large-vessel Thrombus (systemic use):

Bleeding from puncture sites or internal bleeding (such as intracranial hemorrhage) may occur. Levy and colleagues reported adverse effects of nosebleed, upper GI bleed, and prolonged bleeding from injection sites associated with doses of 0.46–0.5 mg/kg/hour.[14] Weiner and colleagues stated that the two patients in their study with the most severe bleeding complications had received the highest t-PA infusion rate (0.5 mg/kg/hour); bleeding complications were not seen when fibrinogen was maintained at >150 mg/dl.[11] Edstrom and Christensen summarized neonatal case reports in the use of t-PA for thrombolysis in neonates; significant bleeding complications occurred in 13 percent of patients.[10]

Other: Rarely, allergic reactions.

PHARMACOKINETICS/PHARMACODYNAMICS

Onset of Action: Rapid.

Duration of Action: Thrombolysis may continue for approximately 4 hours following administration of alteplase. The prothrombin time may rarely be prolonged for 12–24 hours following cessation of therapy because of the decreased plasma concentration of fibrinogen, decreased plasma factor V and possibly other coagulant effects, and/or the anticoagulant effects of fibrinogen degradation products.[17]

Metabolism: Rapid hepatic metabolism.

Elimination: In the urine as metabolites within 18 hours.

Half-life: Biphasic; distribution phase is about 4 minutes, and elimination phase about 35 minutes.[17]

Nursing Implications

Physicians, nurse practitioners, or nurses with training in management of occluded lines should administer t-PA for occluded central venous catheters. Monitor vital signs continuously.

The following method has been used for neonates in the neonatal intensive care unit at the University of California Irvine Medical Center when a small-lumen PIC line seems too occluded to instill a dose of t-PA:

- Attach a stopcock to the PIC line.
- Attach an empty syringe to one port and the t-PA syringe to the other.
- Turn off the stopcock to the t-PA syringe, and pull up on the empty syringe to create negative pressure.
- Quickly turn off the stopcock to the empty syringe while maintaining the negative pressure. This should draw the t-PA into the lumen of the PIC line.

Comments

Interactions: Increases risk of bleeding in infants concurrently on heparin, indomethacin, or warfarin (Coumadin).

References

1. Choi M, et al. 2001. The use of alteplase to restore patency of central venous lines in pediatric patients: A cohert study. *Journal of Pediatrics* 139(1): 152–156.

2. Calhoun DA, et al. 2000. Consistent approaches to procedures and practices in neonatal hematology. *Clinics in Perinatology* 27(3): 733–753.

3. Farnoux C, et al. 1998. Recombinant tissue-type plasminogen activator therapy of thrombosis in 16 neonates. *Journal of Pediatrics* 133(1): 137–140.

4. Fleming RE, Barenkamp SJ, and Jureidini SB. 1998. Successful treatment of a staphylococcal endocarditis vegetation with tissue plasminogen activator. *Journal of Pediatrics* 132(3 part 1): 535-537.

5. Giuffre B, et al. 1998. Successful use of tissue plasminogen activator (t-PA) in catheter-related intracardiac thrombi of two premature infants. *Acta Paediatrica* 87(6): 695–698.

6. Manufacturer's product literature.

7. Davis SN, et al. 2000. Activity and dosage of alteplase dilution for clearing occlusions of venous-access devices. *American Journal of Health System Pharmacists* 57(11): 1039–1045.

8. Calis KA, Cullinane AM, and Horne MK. 1999. Bioactivity of cryopreserved alteplase solutions. *American Journal of Health System Pharmacists* 56(20): 2056–2057.

9. Phelps KC, and Verzino KC. 2001. Alternatives to urokinase for the management of central venous catheter occlusion. *Hospital Pharmacy* 36(3): 265–274.

10. Edstrom CS, and Christensen RD. 2000. Evaluation and treatment of thrombosis in the neonatal intensive care unit. *Clinics in Perinatology* 27(3): 623–641.

11. Weiner GM, et al. 1998. Successful treatment of neonatal arterial thromboses with recombinant tissue plasminogen activator. *Journal of Pediatrics* 133(1): 133–136.

12. Kastrup EK. 2001. *Drug Facts and Comparisons.* St. Louis: Facts and Comparisons, 190–192.

13. Atkinson JB, et al. 1990. Investigational use of tissue plasminogen activator (t-PA) for occluded central venous catheters. *Journal of Parenteral and Enteral Nutrition* 14(3): 310–311.

14. Levy M, et al. 1991. Tissue plasminogen activator for the treatment of thromboembolism in infants and children. *Journal of Pediatrics* 118(3): 467–472.

15. Monagle P, et al. 2001. Antithrombotic therapy in children. *Chest* 119(1 supplement): S344–S370.

16. Horigome H, Sekijima T, and Miyamoto T. 1997. Successful thrombolysis with intracoronary adminis-
    tration of tissue plasminogen activator in an infant with Kawasaki disease. *Heart* 78(5): 517–518.

17. United States Pharmacopeial Convention/USP DI. 2000. *Drug Information for the Health Care
    Professional,* 20th ed. Rockville, Maryland: United States Pharmacopeial Convention, 2970–2978.

18. Kleta R, Schleef J, and Jurgens H. 1998. Tissue plasminogen activator and obstructed central venous
    catheters (letter). *Medical and Pediatric Oncology* 30(6): 376.

19. Grieg A. 1998. Thrombolysis of a neonatal brachial artery thrombosis with tissue plasminogen activator.
    Journal of Perinatology 18(6 part 1): 460–462.

20. Dillon PW, et al. 1993. Recombinant tissue plasminogen activator for neonatal and pediatric vascular
    thrombolytic therapy. *Journal of Pediatric Surgery* 28(10): 1264–1269. (Discussion in *Journal of Pediatric
    Surgery,* 1993, 28[10]: 1268–1269.)

Aluminum and Magnesium Hydroxides (Maalox)

GASTROINTESTINAL: ANTACID

(a-LOO-mi-num and mag-NEE-zee-um hye-DROX-idez)

Dose

Term Infants <1 Month of Age and Preterm Infants: 0.5–1 ml/kg/dose given every 4–6 hours.

Term Infants >1 Month of Age: 0.5–1 ml/kg/dose given every 1–2 hours.

Maximum: 2–5 ml/dose.

Titrate to maintain gastric pH >3.5.

Use the lowest effective dose, and discontinue as soon as medical condition warrants.

Administration

Supplied as: Suspension. Contains aluminum hydroxide 225 mg and magnesium hydroxide 200 mg per 5 ml.

PO: May give undiluted.

Use

Treatment of hyperacidity.

Treatment of gastric ulcer pain and promotion of healing, prophylaxis of GI bleeding, and treatment of gastroesophageal reflux disease.

Acid suppression, with agents such as histamine H_2-receptor antagonists (ranitidine), preferred to using antacids.

Mechanism of Action

Aluminum and magnesium hydroxides neutralize existing gastric acid. They do not have a direct effect on acid output. Instead, they increase the pH of gastric contents. About 99 percent of gastric acid is neutralized when a gastric pH of 3.3 is achieved.

The acid neutralizing capacity (ANC) of an antacid is the amount (in mEq) of 1 Normal (N) hydrochloric acid that can be titrated to a pH of 3.5 in 15 minutes by a certain dose of antacid. It is a way of comparing the efficacy of various antacid products. Maalox Oral Suspension has an ANC of 13.3.

The combination of aluminum and magnesium salts in Maalox balances the constipating qualities of aluminum and the laxative qualities of magnesium.

Adverse Effects

Aluminum Component: The aluminum in the antacid may cause constipation, phosphate depletion, and bezoar[1] or fecalith formation. Use with caution in patients with decreased bowel motility and related problems. Aluminum may accumulate to toxic levels, particularly in infants with renal failure and/or dehydration. Preterm infants have limited ability to excrete aluminum. Signs of aluminum toxicity include microcytic and/or hypochromic anemia, and osteomalacia. Aluminum-containing antacids may cause hypophosphatemia. Monitor serum levels of phosphorus and aluminum.[2]

Magnesium Component: The magnesium in the antacid may cause hypotonia, apnea, cyanosis, hypermagnesemia, diarrhea, hypokalemia, hypocalcemia, and bezoar formation. Magnesium may accumulate to toxic levels, particularly in infants with renal failure and/or dehydration. Monitor serum levels of magnesium.[3]

PHARMACOKINETICS/PHARMACODYNAMICS

Absorption: Small amounts of aluminum and magnesium are absorbed.

Duration of Action: Duration is determined by gastric emptying time. If gastric emptying is rapid, stomach may empty before much acid is neutralized.

Elimination: Renal and fecal.

NURSING IMPLICATIONS

Consider monitoring gastric pH twice daily until desired pH is achieved.

COMMENTS

Interactions: May reduce absorption of iron, phenytoin, isoniazid, nitrofurantoin, penicillin G, sulfonamides, and digoxin. Antacids may increase the absorption of aspirin.

REFERENCES

1. Kaplan M, et al. 1995. Antacid bezoar in a premature infant. *American Journal of Perinatology* 12(2): 98–99.
2. Tsou VM, et al. 1991. Elevated plasma aluminum levels in normal infants receiving antacids containing aluminum. *Pediatrics* 87(2): 148–151.
3. Brand JM, and Greer FR. 1990. Hypermagnesemia and intestinal perforation following antacid administration in a premature infant. *Pediatrics* 85(1): 121–123.

AMIKACIN (AMIKIN)

(am-i-KAY-sin)

ANTI-INFECTIVE:
ANTIBIOTIC

DOSE

<1.2 kg (0–4 weeks): 7.5 mg/kg/dose given every 18–24 hours[*]
1.2–2 kg:

- 0–7 days of age: 7.5 mg/kg/dose given every 12–18 hours[*]
- >7 days of age: 7.5 mg/kg/dose given every 8–12 hours

>2 kg:

- 0–7 days of age: 10 mg/kg/dose given every 12 hours
- >7 days of age: 10 mg/kg/dose given every 8 hours[1,2]

Reduce dose in renal impairment.

Individualize dose based on serum concentrations.

ADMINISTRATION

IV—*Rate:* Infuse IV over 30 minutes.

IV—*Concentration:* No maximum concentration. Dilute in enough fluid to allow infusion over 30 minutes.

IV—*Compatibility:* See Appendix E: Y-Site Compatibility of Common NICU Drugs.

IM: May give IM if necessary, although the IV route is preferred. No dilution required.

USE

An aminoglycoside antibiotic used to treat multiple resistant Gram-negative bacterial infections, including most Pseudomonas and Serratia.

Use only when sensitivities show that the organism is resistant to gentamicin and sensitive to amikacin.

MECHANISM OF ACTION

Aminoglycosides act on microbial ribosomes to irreversibly inhibit protein synthesis.[3]

ADVERSE EFFECTS

Nephrotoxicity.

Ototoxicity: The risk of ototoxicity with the use of amikacin and other aminoglycosides increases with the degree of exposure to either high peak or high trough serum concentrations. Factors that may increase the risk of ototoxicity include renal impairment, dehydration, excessive dosage, concomitant furosemide administration, and previous use of other ototoxic drugs.

---

[*] See Appendix B: Every-18-Hour Medication Worksheet.

Pharmacokinetics/Pharmacodynamics

Absorption: Very little oral absorption.

Distribution: In uninflamed meninges in 1-day-old infants, CSF values ranged from 0.2 to 2.7 mcg/ml 1–4 hours after a 10 mg/kg dose IV while simultaneous serum concentrations were 15–29 mcg/ml.[4]

Metabolism: Serum half-life is inversely correlated with gestational and chronologic age. Half-life is 7–8 hours in preterm infants 1–3 days old and 4–5 hours in term infants older than 1 week. Hypoxemia prolongs the half-life.[5,6]

Elimination: Excreted unchanged in the urine by glomerular filtration.

Nursing Implications

Monitor blood levels; dose adjustment needed if peak or trough level is out of range.

Monitor renal function.

Comments

Therapeutic Range:

- **Peak:** 20–30 mcg/ml (drawn 30 minutes after a 30-minute infusion).
- **Trough:** <10 mcg/ml (drawn just before the dose). A trough level between 3 and 5 mcg/ml should be above the *in vitro* minimum inhibitory concentration (MIC) values.

References

1. Nelson JD. 1996. *1996–1997 Pocketbook of Pediatric Antimicrobial Therapy,* 12th ed. Baltimore: Lippincott Williams & Wilkins, 16–17.

2. Sáez-Llorens X, and McCracken GH Jr. 1995. Clinical pharmacology of antimicrobial agents. In *Infectious Diseases of the Fetus and Newborn Infant,* 4th ed., Remington JS, and Klein JO, eds. Philadelphia: WB Saunders, 1287–1336.

3. Philips JB, and Cassady G. 1982. Amikacin: Pharmacology, indications and cautions for use, and dose recommendations. *Seminars in Perinatology* 6(2): 166–171.

4. Yow MD. 1977. An overview of pediatric experience with amikacin. *American Journal of Medicine* 62(6): 954–958.

5. Howard JB, et al. 1976. Amikacin in newborn infants: Comparative pharmacology with kanamycin and clinical efficacy in 45 neonates with bacterial diseases. *Antimicrobial Agents and Chemotherapy* 10(2): 205–210.

6. Myers MG, Roberts RJ, and Mirhij NJ. 1977. Effects of gestational age, birth weight and hypoxemia on pharmacokinetics of amikacin in serum in infants. *Antimicrobial Agents and Chemotherapy* 11(6): 1027–1032.

AMINOCAPROIC ACID (AMICAR)
(a-mee-noe-ka-PROE-ik A-sid)

BLOOD MODIFIER:
ANTIFIBRINOLYTIC;
ANTIHEMORRHAGIC.
ANTIDOTE FOR THROMBOLYTICS

Synonym: epsilon-aminocaproic acid

DOSE

Prophylaxis during heparin anticoagulation for extracorporeal membrane oxygenation (ECMO):

Loading Dose: 100 mg/kg IV, infused over 1 hour, *followed by* 20–30 mg/kg/hour by continuous infusion.[1]

Acute Bleeding:

IV: 100 mg/kg (or 3 gm/m^2) loading dose infused over 1 hour, *followed by* a continuous infusion of 33.3 mg/kg/hour (or 1 gm/m^2/hour).[2]

PO: 100 mg/kg (or 3 gm/m^2) loading dose, followed by 33.3 mg/kg/hour (or 1 gm/m^2/hour).[2]

Maximum: 18 gm/m^2/day.

For treatment of acute bleeding syndromes resulting from elevated fibrinolytic activity, treatment is usually continued for about 8 hours or until the bleeding stops.[3]

⌐ Reduce dose in renal impairment.

ADMINISTRATION

Supplied as: 20 ml vial with 250 mg/ml for IV use or 250 mg/ml oral syrup for PO use.

May be given IV or PO. The dose is the same whether given IV or PO.

IV—*Rate:* Infuse slowly, over 1 hour or more.

IV—*Concentration:* 20 mg/ml. Do not give drug undiluted.[3]

IV—*Compatibility:* Compatible with normal saline, D$_5$W, D$_{10}$W, Ringer's solution.

PO: May give with feedings or on an empty stomach.

CAUTIONS/CONTRAINDICATIONS

⌐ Rapid IV administration may cause cardiac arrhythmias, hypotension, and bradycardia.

⌐ Other emergency measures may be needed to enhance hemostasis. Such measures may include transfusion of whole blood, fibrinogen infusions, fresh frozen plasma, or specific clotting factors.[2,3]

⌐ Contraindicated in disseminated intravascular coagulation (DIC) without concomitant heparin because aminocaproic acid may produce potentially fatal thrombus formation in patients with DIC.

Use with caution in patients with cardiac, hepatic, or renal disease.

Monitoring: Monitor for signs of thromboembolic complications.

Use

Used to treat excessive bleeding from increased fibrinolytic activity (hyperfibrinolysis, hyperplasminemia).[2] Hyperfibrinolysis is characterized by a normal platelet count, negative protamine paracoagulation, and reduced euglobulin clot lysis time.

Aminocaproic acid has decreased the incidence of intracranial hemorrhage (ICH) and other hemorrhagic complications of ECMO. In a study of 51 neonates and 5 older children receiving ECMO, those who received aminocaproic acid had significantly less bleeding and required fewer blood transfusions than did patients not receiving the drug. The incidence of ICH in the neonatal patients was reduced, with no infant developing a new or extending a pre-existing ICH.[1]

Used for prophylaxis and treatment of postsurgical hemorrhage, such as reducing postoperative hemorrhage in infants and children with congenital heart disease.[4]

Aminocaproic acid was part of a multimodal intervention required to manage a 14-month-old child with kaposiform hemangioendothelioma, to achieve involution of the lesion and preserve function of the arm.[5]

As an Antidote: Aminocaproic acid may be useful in treating severe hemorrhage caused by thrombolytic agents such as alteplase, streptokinase, or urokinase, although controlled efficacy studies have not been done in humans.[3] (See monograph on urokinase.)

Mechanism of Action

Competitively inhibits the activation of plasminogen, thereby reducing conversion of plasminogen to plasmin (fibrinolysin), an enzyme that degrades fibrin clots as well as fibrinogen, factor V, and factor VIII.[2]

Adverse Effects

Hypotension, bradycardia, and arrhythmia with rapid IV administration.

May elevate serum potassium, particularly in renal dysfunction.

May cause local injection site reactions, pain, and necrosis.[3]

May cause nausea, bloating, diarrhea, nasal stuffiness, and rash, but these are uncommon and reversible.

May cause thrombosis, leukopenia, agranulocytosis, or thrombocytopenia.[3] Fatal aortic thrombosis occurred in one infant on extracorporeal life support who was receiving an infusion of aminocaproic acid in an attempt to decrease the risk of hemorrhagic complications.[6]

May (rarely) cause skeletal muscle weakness with necrosis of muscle fibers with long-term use. Consider the possibility of cardiac muscle damage if this occurs.

Pharmacokinetics/Pharmacodynamics

Absorption: Oral absorption good.

Duration of Action: Approximately 3 hours after a single IV dose.

Elimination: Excreted primarily unmetabolized in the urine.

Half-life: Approximately 2 hours.

Nursing Implications

Monitor blood pressure continuously.

Strictly monitor intake and output.

Observe IV site carefully to avoid extravasation injury.

Comments

Interactions: Aminocaproic acid and thrombolytic agents such as alteplase, streptokinase, and urokinase are mutually antagonistic.

Therapeutic Serum Concentration: 13 mg/dl (= 130 mcg/ml) for inhibition of systemic hyperfibrinolysis.[2]

Aminocaproic acid is not a substitute for fresh whole blood transfusions, fibrinogen infusions, and other emergency measures that may be required in lifethreatening situations.

Parenteral aminocaproic acid contains benzyl alcohol 0.9 percent.

References

1. Wilson JM, et al. 1993. Aminocaproic acid decreases the incidence of intracranial hemorrhage and other hemorrhagic complications of ECMO. *Journal of Pediatric Surgery* 28(4): 536–540; *Discussion* 540–541.

2. United Stated Pharmacopeial Convention/USP DI. 2000 *Drug Information for the Health Care Professional,* 20th ed. Rockville, Maryland: United States Pharmacopeial Convention, 73–76.

3. Medical Economics Data. 2000. *Physicians' Desk Reference,* 54th ed. Montvale, New Jersey: Medical Economics, 1412–1413.

4. Jonas RA. 1995. Advances in surgical care of infants and children with congenital heart disease. *Current Opinion in Pediatrics* 7(5): 572–579.

5. Blei F, Karp N, and Rofsky N. 1998. Successful multimodal therapy for kaposiform hemangioendothelioma complicated by Kasabach-Merritt phenomenon: Case report and review of the literature. *Pediatric Hematology and Oncology* 15(4): 295–305. (Comment in *Pediatric Hematology and Oncology,* 1999, 16[4]: 373–374.)

6. Hocker JR. 1995. Fatal aortic thrombosis in a neonate during infusion of epsilon-aminocaproic acid. *Journal of Pediatric Surgery* 30(10): 1490–1492.

AMINOPHYLLINE
(am-in-OFF-i-lin)

RESPIRATORY:
BRONCHODILATOR;
APNEA/BRADYCARDIA

Synonym: theophylline ethylenediamine

DOSE

Loading: 6 mg/kg/IV.

Rebolus: In neonates, a dose of 1.3 mg aminophylline/kg raises the theophylline serum level approximately 1.4 mcg/ml (volume of distribution in neonates is variable, with a mean of approximately 0.69 liter/kg). To raise the serum theophylline concentration by approximately 2 mcg/ml, give a dose of 1.75 mg aminophylline/kg.

Maintenance: Begin 12 hours after loading dose.

Neonatal Apnea: 2.5 mg aminophylline/kg/dose IV/PO given every 12 hours.

BPD/Bronchospasm:

- *6 weeks–6 months postnatal age:* 12 mg aminophylline/kg/day PO divided every 6–8 hours.
- *6 months–1 year postnatal age:* 15–22 mg aminophylline/kg/day PO divided every 6–8 hours.
- *Continuous IV infusion:*
  - 6 weeks–6 months of age: 0.5 mg/kg/hour.
  - 6 months–1 year of age: 0.6–0.7 mg/kg/hour.
- Hendles and associates have published an equation to estimate theophylline dosage in infants with apnea and bradycardia or asthma 1 year of age or younger to produce serum theophylline concentrations between 5 and 15 mcg/ml:[1,2]

$$\text{Dose of theophylline in mg/kg/hour} = [0.008 \times (\textit{postnatal age in weeks})] + 0.21$$

or:

$$\text{Dose of theophylline in mg/kg/day} = (0.2 \times \textit{postnatal age in weeks}) + 5$$

(To convert the theophylline dose to aminophylline, divide by 0.8, explanation follows.)

- *Example:* What dose of aminophylline drip in mg/kg/hour is needed for a preterm infant 32 weeks gestation, now 5 weeks postnatal age?

$$[0.008 \times (\textit{postnatal age in weeks})] + 0.21 = \text{dose of theophylline in mg/kg/hour}$$

$$[0.008 \times (5)] + 0.21 = 0.04 + 0.21 = 025 \text{ mg theophylline/kg/hour}$$

To convert to aminophylline:

$aminophylline\ mg = theophylline\ mg \div 0.8$

$0.25 \div 0.8 = 0.3\ mg\ aminophylline/kg/hour$

Adjust dose carefully based on serum theophylline concentration, especially when on the higher BPD/bronchospasm doses.

Aminophylline/Theophylline Conversion: Aminophylline is approximately 80 percent theophylline. To convert one to the other, use the following formulas:

$Aminophylline\ mg = theophylline\ mg \div by\ 0.8$

$Theophylline\ mg = aminophylline\ mg \times 0.8$

Aminophylline is commonly given IV, and theophylline is given PO in neonates. (Table 1-7 illustrates conversions among theophylline salts.)

ADMINISTRATION

IV—*Concentration:* Aminophylline may be given undiluted (25 mg/ml) if infused slowly as indicated below. For very small doses measuring <0.1 ml, prepare a 1:10 dilution to improve measurement accuracy.

IV—*Rate:* Infuse over 30 minutes.

IV—*Compatibility:* See Appendix E: Y-Site Compatibility of Common NICU Drugs.

PO: Oral liquid has 21 mg aminophylline (equivalent to 18 mg theophylline) per 5 ml (= 86 percent theophylline).

USE

To reduce the severity and frequency of neonatal apnea and as a bronchodilator in BPD. A marked reduction in the number of apneic episodes is usually seen within a few hours of initiation of therapy. Aminophylline may assist in weaning these infants from the ventilator. Infants who do not respond to aminophylline or caffeine alone may respond to doxapram alone or doxapram plus caffeine or aminophylline.

In treatment of neonatal apnea, caffeine is often preferred to aminophylline because of its efficacy, greater safety, and once-daily dosing, but aminophylline is preferred when bronchodilation is also desired, such as in infants with BPD.[3]

TABLE 1-7 ◆ THEOPHYLLINE CONTENT OF PREPARATIONS

Theophylline Salt	Percent Theophylline	Equivalent Dose (mg)
Theophylline anhydrous	100	1
Theophylline monohydrate	91	1.1
Aminophylline anhydrous	86	1.16
Aminophylline dihydrate	79	1.27

Adapted from: Olin BR. 1994. *Drug Facts and Comparisons.* St. Louis: Facts and Comparisons, 941. Reprinted by permission.

TABLE 1-8 ◆ MAJOR PHARMACOLOGIC EFFECTS OF THE METHYLXANTHINES CAFFEINE AND THEOPHYLLINE

Effect	Estimated Relative Potency[a]	
	Caffeine	Theophylline
CNS		
Stimulation of medullary respiratory centers	++++	+++
Generalized (cortical) enhancement of CNS cellular response to stimulation	+++	+++
Cardiovascular		
Heart: increased rate	– or +	++
Vascular: decreased peripheral vascular resistance	+	+
increased cerebro-vascular resistance	+	+
Smooth Muscle		
Relaxation (i.e., bronchial)	+	+++
Skeletal Muscle		
Stimulation	++	+
Kidney		
Diuretic action	?	++
Gastrointestinal		
Secretion (acid)	++	+
Cellular		
Phosphodiesterase inhibition	+	++
Competitive inhibition of adenosine	++	+++

[a] Comparative potency estimates are based on use of doses in the therapeutic range. Opposite or no effect: –; minimal effect: +; maximal effect: ++++. Very few critically controlled experiments have been conducted comparing the pharmacologic potency of caffeine and theophylline, particularly their CNS effects. No comparative studies have been done in neonates.

From: Roberts RJ. 1984. *Drug Therapy in Infants: Pharmacologic Principles and Clinical Experience.* Philadelphia: WB Saunders, 121. Reprinted by permission.

The major pharmacologic effects of methylxanthines are listed in Table 1-8.

MECHANISM OF ACTION

Theophylline, the active component of aminophylline, relaxes smooth muscle of the bronchi and pulmonary blood vessels, induces a small amount of diuresis, increases gastric acid secretion, and has a mild chronotropic and inotropic effect on the heart.

Some of the mechanisms by which xanthines (theophylline and caffeine) reduce neonatal apnea include increased sensitivity of the CNS medullary respiratory centers to CO_2, stimulation of central inspiratory drive, improvement in skeletal muscle contraction, and improvement in oxygenation via increased cardiac output and decreased hypoxic episodes. (See also monographs for caffeine and theophylline.)

ADVERSE EFFECTS

May cause tachycardia, irritability, transient hyperglycemia, diuresis (may require adjustment of fluids, especially in very low birth weight infants), reduced sleep, GI irritation, and jitteriness.[4]

At serum levels >40 mcg/ml, seizures and cardiac arrhythmias may occur. Chronic toxicity may result in poor weight gain.[4]

Severe tissue injury may occur after IV extravasation.[4]

PHARMACOKINETICS/PHARMACODYNAMICS

Absorption: Well absorbed orally.

Metabolism: In the neonatal liver, theophylline is partially methylated to caffeine. In neonates treated with theophylline, the mean caffeine level is about one-third that of the concurrent theophylline level, although caffeine plasma levels may reach up to 50 percent of theophylline plasma levels. Thus, the overall methylxanthine effect has to account for the sum of the two drugs because both drugs are pharmacologically active.[3,5,6] Both caffeine and theophylline levels could be measured to determine the total xanthine serum concentration, although this is rarely necessary and adds to the cost of therapy.

Clearance Rate: Aminophylline is the ethylenediamine salt of theophylline. The clearance rate of theophylline, the active component of aminophylline, increases with postnatal age as liver function matures. Older infants (>1–2 months) may therefore require higher doses to achieve therapeutic levels and clinical response.

NURSING IMPLICATIONS

Monitor serum levels and for signs of toxicity such as irritability, jitteriness, feeding intolerance, and tachycardia.

If the heart rate increases above 180 bpm or to approximately 20 bpm above normal baseline, withhold the next dose, and check the serum level. The dose may need to be reduced.

Discontinue oral theophylline in infants with suspected necrotizing enterocolitis (NEC) to reduce gastric irritation. Use other means to control apnea.

COMMENTS

Interactions: Cimetidine (but not usually ranitidine or famotidine) and erythromycin reduce the clearance of theophylline, resulting in higher than expected serum theophylline concentrations. Elevated theophylline levels and signs of toxicity have occurred in select patients concurrently receiving theophylline and ranitidine. This is not a general phenomenon, but rather idiosyncratic. Ranitidine does not reduce the clearance of theophylline.[7] Phenobarbital and phenytoin may decrease theophylline levels.

Therapeutic Serum Concentration: 5–15 mcg/ml of theophylline.[3]

When to Draw Serum Levels: In preterm infants being treated for apnea, draw blood for levels after 3 or more days (steady state is reached at approximately 5 days). Serum levels fluctuate only about 2 mcg/ml between dosing intervals; therefore, theophylline level may be drawn at any time during the dosing interval except immediately after the dose.

Therapeutic Range: 5–15 mcg/ml.[3]

REFERENCES

1. Hendles L, et al. 1986. *Applied Pharmacokinetics: Principles of Therapeutic Drug Monitoring,* 2nd ed. Spokane, Washington: Applied Therapeutics, 1105–1108.

2. Hogue SL, and Phelps SJ. 1993. Evaluation of three theophylline dosing equations for use in infants up to one year of age. *Journal of Pediatrics* 123(4): 651–656.

3. Aranda JV, et al. 1991. Treatment of neonatal apnea. In *Neonatal Clinical Pharmacology and Therapeutics,* Rylance G, Harvey D, and Aranda J, eds. Linacre House, Jordan Hill, Oxford: Butterworth-Heinemann, 95–115.

4. Howell J, Clozel M, and Aranda JV. 1981. Adverse effects of caffeine and theophylline in the newborn infant. *Seminars in Perinatology* 5(4): 359–369.

5. Aranda JV, et al. 1976. Pharmacokinetic aspects of theophylline in premature newborns. *New England Journal of Medicine* 295(8): 413–416.

6. Aranda JV, et al. 1979. Metabolism of theophylline to caffeine in human fetal liver. *Science* 206(4424): 1319–1321.

7. Kehoe WA, et al. 1996. Effect of ranitidine on theophylline metabolism in healthy Koreans living in China. *Annals of Pharmacotherapy* 30(2): 133–137.

AMIODARONE (CORDARONE)
(am-ee-OH-da-rone)

**CARDIOVASCULAR:
ANTIARRHYTHMIC**

DOSE

- Use the lowest effective dose to minimize adverse effects.

PO:

- *Loading dose:* 10 mg/kg/day PO as a single daily dose or divided every 12 hours. The loading period is 10–14 days.[1]
- *Maintenance dose:* 5–7.5 mg/kg/day PO given as a single daily dose.[2] Begin 24 hours after the last loading dose.[3] After 1–2 months, may decrease to 2.5 mg/kg/day in some patients, depending on response.[4] Attempt to decrease the dose every 3 months. *Maximum:* 10–15 mg/kg/day.[2]

IV:

The doses and rates of infusion shown here are from the referenced pediatric studies. See **CAUTIONS/CONTRAINDICATIONS** below for advice from the manufacturer of the drug on dose and rate of administration.

- *Loading dose:* 5 mg/kg IV infused over 1 hour.[5–7] Higher doses of 10–15 mg/kg/day may be required.[1, 8] The average loading dose in one study was 6.3 mg/kg.[9]
  - For the management of junctional ectopic tachycardia (JET) after cardiac surgery in infants and children, Raja and colleagues administered a loading dose of 5 mg/kg IV over 1 hour, followed by 5 mg/kg IV infused over 12 hours. The patient was assessed every 12 hours, and the dose of 5 mg/kg IV over 12 hours was repeated as necessary until a satisfactory heart rate and stable hemodynamics were achieved.[6]
- *Maintenance dose:* 5 mg/kg IV given as a single daily dose.[3] Alternatively, the maintenance dose can be begun as a continuous IV infusion.[1,5]

Continuous IV Infusion:

- 5 mcg/kg/minute. Increase gradually, as needed.[5]

Mean effective dose: 9.5 mcg/kg/minute.[5]

Maximum: 15 mcg/kg/minute.[5]

Combination Therapy:

- *Amiodarone with flecainide:*
  - Fenrich and colleagues reported that a combination of flecainide and amiodarone appeared to be safe and effective in controlling refractory tachyarrhythmias in infants and that it may reduce or eliminate the need for early interventional therapy or may allow delay until the child is older. The loading period in Fenrich's study was approximately 9 days when amiodarone (7.5–13.5 mg/kg/day) was used in combination with flecainide (70–110 mg/m^2/day).[10]

- *Amiodarone with propranolol:*
  - Propranolol may enhance the success rate of amiodarone in infants affected by life-threatening and/or drug-resistant supraventricular or ventricular tachyarrhythmias, especially in the treatment of re-entry tachycardias resulting from accessory pathways. Drago and colleagues used the following regimen: an amiodarone loading dose of 10–20 mg/kg/day and a maintenance dose ranging between 3 and 20 mg/kg/day. When amiodarone was ineffective, propranolol was added at a dose of 2–4 mg/kg/day.[11]

ADMINISTRATION

Supplied as: Injection: 50 mg/ml. Tablet: 200 mg.

IV—*Rate:* Infuse over 1 hour.[5,6]

IV—*Concentration:* 1–6 mg/ml.[12] Solutions containing <0.6 mg/ml of amiodarone in D_5W are unstable and should not be used.[13]

- Administer with an inline filter because the drug may precipitate when diluted (immediately on dilution or after standing), increasing the risk of phlebitis. No significant loss of drug was noted as a result of binding to the filter when a 0.22 micron filter was used.[13–15]
- Administer into a central line, if possible. Concentrations 2 mg/ml require a central venous catheter for administration because of the risk of peripheral vein phlebitis.
- Administer using a volumetric infusion pump, not a drop counter, because the product contains polysorbate 80, a surface-active agent that alters drop size. Underdosage may occur if a drop counter is used.
- Administer in a glass or polyolefin container if infusing longer than 2 hours because amiodarone adsorbs to polyvinyl chloride (PVC) containers. PVC tubing and containers may be used for infusions shorter than 2 hours.
- Dilute only in dextrose. Normal saline may induce precipitation.[16]

PO: May give with feedings to reduce GI effects.

- Protect tablets from light. (*Note:* Light protection is not necessary during IV administration.)

Not available as an oral liquid; however, a suspension can be prepared by the pharmacist as follows:

Pharmacist Compounding Directions
Amiodarone Oral Suspension 5 mg/ml[16,17]

Crush three 200 mg tablets. Gradually add 90 ml of methylcellulose 1 percent and 10 ml of simple syrup.

Triturate until uniform consistency. Then add enough purified water USP so that the total volume equals 120 ml (= 600 mg/120 ml or 5 mg/ml). Pour into an amber glass bottle. Protect from light. Shake well before use.

Stability: 7 days.
Storage: Refrigerate.

CAUTIONS/CONTRAINDICATIONS

- Because of the difficulties in dosing this drug and the severity of adverse effects, amiodarone should be administered only by physicians (such as pediatric cardiologists) who are experienced in the treatment of life-threatening arrhythmias, who are thoroughly familiar with the risks and benefits of amiodarone therapy, and who have access to laboratory facilities capable of adequately monitoring the effectiveness and side effects of treatment. Such experienced physicians should direct chronic amiodarone therapy because of the drug's complex pharmacology, poor oral absorption, and potential for long-term adverse effects.[8]

- The parenteral form contains benzyl alcohol and polysorbate (Tween) 80. A benzyl-alcohol-free and polysorbate-free injection (Amio-Aqueous 15 mg/ml, 10 ml) is available from the manufacturer (Academic Pharmaceuticals, Inc. [847-735-1170]) via orphan drug status or compassionate use.

- Change to oral administration as soon as medically warranted to minimize cardiodepressant adverse effects.

- The drug name amiodarone can easily be confused with amrinone, another cardiac drug whose name sounds and looks like amiodarone. To avoid mix-ups, the drug name amrinone has been changed to inamrinone.

- Do not routinely administer amiodarone and procainamide together.[8]

- Concurrent amiodarone may *increase* digoxin serum concentrations to toxic levels; discontinue or reduce dose of digoxin by one-half. Monitor digoxin levels.

- Amiodarone inhibits the metabolism and potentiates the effects of warfarin, causing the prothrombin time to possibly double or triple. Reduce dose of the anticoagulant by one-third to one-half, and closely monitor prothrombin times.

- The manufacturer advises minimizing the potential for the drug to leach out di-(2-ethylhexyl)phthalate (DEHP) from IV tubing during administration to pediatric patents by avoiding administration by continuous IV infusion. Instead, they suggest administration in 1 mg/kg increments over 5–10 minutes per dose as was done by Perry and associates.[9] DEHP in relatively high amounts may alter the development of the male reproductive tract. DEHP is added to IV tubing to make it flexible.

USE

For resistant, life-threatening ventricular arrhythmias unresponsive to conventional therapy with less toxic agents.[2–4,12,18,19]

Also, used to suppress and prevent recurrence of supraventricular arrhythmias unresponsive to conventional therapy,[2,8,9,12,18,19] especially when the arrhythmias are associated with Wolff-Parkinson-White (WPW) syndrome, when surgical treatment is not feasible.[3,7]

Has been used safely and effectively to control junctional ectopic tachycardia (JET) after open-heart surgery in children.[6,20]

Advantages of the drug are that it can be given as a single daily dose and has minimal myocardial depressant effects.[3] Use of amiodarone is more acceptable in infants than in adults because of the lower incidence of adverse effects in infants and the knowledge that, in many neonates, treatment may be needed only for a short time.[21]

MECHANISM OF ACTION

Amiodarone is an iodinated benzofuran with a chemical structure similar to that of thyroxine. Amiodarone is a class III antiarrhythmic agent (prolongs the action potential and effective refractory period of cardiac muscle and Purkinje fibers).[4,22] It also lengthens AV node conduction. Amiodarone inhibits the outward potassium current, prolonging the QT interval.[8] It prolongs refractoriness and slows conduction in accessory pathway tissue in patients with WPW syndrome. The drug has α- and β-blocking effects and is a calcium channel inhibitor. Some of its electrophysiologic effects may be mediated by selective blockade of triiodothyronine (T3) action on cardiac muscle. Amiodarone has a mild, negative inotropic effect, but usually does not depress left ventricular function. It causes coronary and peripheral vasodilation and therefore decreases peripheral vascular resistance (afterload).[22]

ADVERSE EFFECTS

Children seem to be less susceptible to adverse effects than adults, but the incidence is still high.[2] Higher doses and durations of therapy longer than 6 months increase the incidence of adverse effects.[22]

Cardiovascular:

- Hypotension, particularly in the first several hours of IV treatment.[6,9] Treat hypotension initially by slowing the infusion rate; vasopressor drugs and volume expansion may be needed.

- Sinus bradycardia that is atropine resistant but usually responds to dose reduction; some patients may require a pacemaker.[5,6] Second- or third-degree heart block may occur and may be prolonged. Therefore, the patient must be hospitalized during the loading period.[2,9,12]

- Proarrhythmia (drug-induced worsening of arrhythmias),[23] particularly torsade de pointes, may occur rarely.[1,8]
- Electromechanical dissociation occurred after an IV bolus of amiodarone for rapid atrial flutter in a 1-day-old, 36-week gestational age infant.[24]

CNS: Sleep disturbances, behavioral changes, encephalopathy.

Dermatologic: Phlebitis; bluish-gray discoloration of the skin on face, neck, and arms; rash. *Sun sensitivity:* Sunburns may occur even through window glass and thin cotton clothing. Sun sensitivity may last for several months after the drug is discontinued.

Endocrine: Abnormal thyroid function, thyroiditis.[11] New or exacerbated arrhythmias may be a sign of hyperthyroidism.[22] Hypothyroidism developed in a 13-day-old term infant after 27 days of amiodarone.[24]

GI: Hepatic failure, hepatitis,[11] cirrhosis, elevated liver enzyme levels.[8]

Pulmonary:

- *Acute:* Acute pulmonary toxicity (reversible) was reported in a 7-month-old boy with hepatic dysfunction who had received IV amiodarone for 1 week. The cause of this adverse effect may be direct drug toxicity to alveolar macrophages and indirect toxicity from an inflammatory response. Daniels and colleagues advise that a high index of suspicion be maintained and that patients on IV amiodarone be considered for bronchoalveolar lavage if there is worsening pulmonary disease, new or developing infiltrates on chest x-ray, or widening of the alveolar-arterial oxygen gradient. If the characteristic cellular changes of lipid-laden macrophages are present on bronchoalveolar lavage and there is no other cause for this finding, amiodarone should be discontinued.[12,25]
- *Chronic:* Pulmonary interstitial fibrosis (potentially fatal) may occur. Bowers and colleagues reported that after 9 months of amiodarone treatment in an infant who was otherwise asymptomatic, a screening chest radiograph showed a diffuse interstitial infiltrate. The pulmonary fibrosis resolved gradually over 6 months after amiodarone was discontinued. Chronic fibrosis may be a type of hypersensitivity reaction.[26]

Neurologic: Peripheral neuropathy, muscle weakness and wasting.

Ophthalmic: Corneal microdeposits,[11] optic neuritis and/or optic neuropathy.

Monitor: Liver and thyroid function twice a year; regular ophthalmologic exam including funduscopy and slit-lamp procedures; ECG; routine chest x-rays every 3–4 months to screen for pulmonary fibrosis;[26] and assess for peripheral neuritis.

PHARMACOKINETICS/PHARMACODYNAMICS

Absorption: Absorption is slow and variable. About 50 percent (range 22–85 percent) of an oral dose is absorbed.

Onset of Action: Onset of antiarrhythmic action is unpredictable and significantly delayed even when a loading dose is given, as is the development of adverse effects.[2] Antiarrhythmic effects have begun in from 1 hour to 5 days[5] and are generally observed during the first week in pediatric patients.[2]

Both onset and duration of action are shorter in pediatric patients than in adults. The effects (including adverse effects) of amiodarone are prolonged after the drug is discontinued, lasting a few weeks in children and a few months in adults.[2]

Peak Plasma Concentration: 3–7 hours after dose.

Protein Binding: 96 percent.

Metabolism: Metabolized in the liver. The major active metabolite is desethylamiodarone. A dose of 30 mg released approximately 0.9 mg of elemental iodine.[22]

Elimination/Half-life: Elimination is biphasic, with an initial half-life of 2.5–10 days and a terminal half-life of 40–55 days (amiodarone) and 61 days (desethylamiodarone) in adults, possibly shorter in children. Elimination is biliary.

NURSING IMPLICATIONS

Monitor infusion rate carefully to prevent hypotension. Monitor blood pressure. Frequent vital signs should be performed during infusion of this drug to provide early intervention for hypotension.

Observe IV site carefully to prevent IV extravasation injury. Hyaluronidase (Wydase) may be helpful in treating IV extravasations.

Monitor for worsening of pulmonary status.

Caution parents regarding photosensitivity: Use sunscreens and proper clothing.

COMMENTS

Therapeutic Range: 1–2.5 mcg/ml. Therapeutic effect and toxicity are difficult to predict based on plasma concentrations in children. Adverse effects may occur at therapeutic serum concentrations; however, severe toxicity is more common with prolonged amiodarone levels of >2.5 mcg/ml and with the metabolite desethylamiodarone levels of >3 mcg/ml.[4, 22] Consider obtaining amiodarone plasma concentrations if the patient is not responding or has unexpected severe toxicity.

- Bouillon and colleagues individualized the dose of amiodarone in a newborn based on a computer simulation, taking into account the pharmacokinetic parameters of the patient and the individual concentration-effect relationship. The infant's tachycardia was controlled as long as plasma concentrations of amiodarone were above 0.8 micromols/liter.[27]

Interactions: Interactions may occur or continue weeks to months after discontinuation of amiodarone because of its slow elimination.

- Additive cardiac effects may occur with other antiarrhythmics, increasing the risk of tachyarrhythmias. If antiarrhythmic therapy (diltiazem, flecainide, lidocaine, phenytoin, procainamide, quinidine) needs to be added to amiodarone, initiate the additional antiarrhythmic at one-half the usual dose and monitor serum concentrations. Amiodarone inhibits the P-450 enzymes, increasing plasma concentrations of these antiarrhythmic drugs.

- Concurrent amiodarone may *increase*
  - digoxin serum concentrations to toxic levels. Discontinue or reduce dose of digoxin by one-half. Monitor digoxin levels.
  - theophylline plasma concentrations.
- Concurrent β-blockers may cause bradycardia.
- Concurrent cholestyramine may *decrease* amiodarone concentrations.
- Concurrent cimetidine may *increase* amiodarone serum concentrations.
- Amiodarone inhibits the metabolism and potentiates the effects of warfarin, causing the prothrombin time to possibly double or triple. Reduce the dose of the anticoagulant by one-third to one-half, and closely monitor prothrombin times.

REFERENCES

1. Go RM, et al. 1993. Cardiovascular pharmacology. In *Pediatric Pharmacology and Therapeutics,* 2nd ed., Radde IC, and MacLeod SM, eds. St. Louis: Mosby-Year Book, 197–218.

2. Paul T, and Guccione P. 1994. New antiarrhythmic drugs in pediatric use: Amiodarone. *Pediatric Cardiology* 15(3): 132–138.

3. Roberts RJ. 1984. *Drug Therapy in Infants: Pharmacologic Principles and Clinical Experience.* Philadelphia: WB Saunders, 205–208.

4. Gorodischer R, and Koren G. 1992. Cardiac drugs. In *Pediatric Pharmacology: Therapeutic Principles in Practice,* 2nd ed., Yaffe SJ, and Aranda JV, eds. Philadelphia: WB Saunders, 345–354.

5. Figa FH, et al. 1994. Clinical efficacy and safety of intravenous amiodarone in infants and children. *American Journal of Cardiology* 74(6): 573–577.

6. Raja P, et al. 1994. Amiodarone management of junctional ectopic tachycardia after cardiac surgery in children. *British Heart Journal* 72(3): 261–265.

7. Soult JA, et al. 1995. Efficacy and safety of intravenous amiodarone for short-term treatment of paroxysmal supraventricular tachycardia in children. *Pediatric Cardiology* 16(1): 16–19.

8. American Heart Association in collaboration with the International Committee on Resuscitation. 2000. Part 10: Pediatric advanced life support. In Guidelines 2000 for cardiopulmonary resuscitation and emergency cardiovascular care. *Circulation* 102(supplement I): I291–I342.

9. Perry JC, et al. 1996. Pediatric use of intravenous amiodarone: Efficacy and safety in critically ill patients from a multicenter protocol. *Journal of the American College of Cardiology* 27(5): 1246–1250.

10. Fenrich AL Jr, Perry JC, and Friedman RA. 1995. Flecainide and amiodarone: Combined therapy for refractory tachyarrhythmias in infancy. *Journal of the American College of Cardiology* 25(5): 1195–1198.

11. Drago F, et al. 1998. Amiodarone used alone or in combination with propranolol: A very effective therapy for tachyarrhythmias in infants and children. *Pediatric Cardiology* 19(6): 445–449.

12. Medical Economics Data. 2000. *Physicians' Desk Reference,* 54th ed. Montvale, New Jersey: Medical Economics, 3226–3231.

13. Trissel LA. 1998. *Handbook on Injectable Drugs,* 10th ed. Bethesda, Maryland: American Society of Health-System Pharmacists, 78–81.

14. Ward GH, and Yalkowsky SH. 1993. Studies in phlebitis VI: Dilution-induced precipitation of amiodarone HCl. *Journal of Parenteral Science and Technology* 47(July-August): 161–165.

15. Ward GH, and Yalkowsky SH. 1993. Studies in phlebitis IV: Injection rate and amiodarone-induced phlebitis. *Journal of Parenteral Science and Technology* 47(January-February): 40–43.

16. Trissel LA. 1996. *Trissel's Stability of Compounded Formulations.* Washington, D.C.: American Pharmaceutical Association, 13–14.

17. Nahata MC, and Hipple TF. 1992. *Pediatric Drug Formulations,* 2nd ed. Cincinnati, Ohio: Harvey Whitney Books, 10.

18. Etheridge SP, and Judd VE. 1999. Supraventricular tachycardia in infancy: Evaluation, management, and follow-up. *Archives of Pediatrics and Adolescent Medicine* 153(3): 267–271.

19. Pfammatter JP, and Bauersfeld U. 1998. Safety issues in the treatment of paediatric supraventricular tachycardias. *Drug Safety* 18(5): 345–356.

20. Luedtke SA, Kuhn RJ, and McCaffrey FM. 1997. Pharmacologic management of supraventricular tachycardias in children. Part 2: Atrial flutter, atrial fibrillation, and junctional and atrial ectopic tachycardia. *Annals of Pharmacotherapy* 31(11): 1347–1359.

21. Till JA, and Rigby ML. 1991. Treatment of cardiac disorders in the neonate. In *Neonatal Clinical Pharmacology and Therapeutics,* Rylance G, Harvey D, and Aranda JV, eds. Oxford: Butterworth-Heinemann, 126–152.

22. United States Pharmacopeial Convention/USP DI. 2000. *Drug Information for the Health Care Professional,* 20th ed. Rockville, Maryland: United States Pharmacopeial Convention, 89–94.

23. Shuler CO, Case CL, and Gillette PC. 1993. Efficacy and safety of amiodarone in infants. *American Heart Journal* 125(5 part 1): 1430–1432.

24. Gandy J, Wonko N, and Kantoch MJ. 1998. Risks of intravenous amiodarone in neonates. *Canadian Journal of Cardiology* 14(6): 855–858.

25. Daniels CJ, et al. 1997. Acute pulmonary toxicity in an infant from intravenous amiodarone. *American Journal of Cardiology* 80(8): 1113–1116.

26. Bowers PN, et al. 1998. Amiodarone induced pulmonary fibrosis in infancy. *Pacing and Clinical Electrophysiology* 21(8): 1665–1667.

27. Bouillon T, et al. 1996. Amiodarone in a newborn with ventricular tachycardia and an intracardiac tumor: Adjusting the dose according to an individualized dosing regimen. *Pediatric Cardiology* 17(2): 112–114.

AMOXICILLIN (AMOXIL)

(a-mox-i-SILL-in)

ANTI-INFECTIVE: ANTIBIOTIC

DOSE

40 mg/kg/day PO divided every 8 hours.[1] *In severe renal dysfunction* (creatinine clearance <10 ml/minute), give every 12 hours.

UTI Prophylaxis: 20 mg/kg PO as a single daily dose.

Bacterial Endocarditis Prophylaxis: 50 mg/kg PO 1 hour before the procedure, then 25 mg/kg 6 hours after the procedure.[2]

ADMINISTRATION

Supplied as: A suspension: 25 or 50 mg/ml.

PO only.

May be given with feedings. May be mixed with a small volume of formula and given immediately.

Shake suspension well before administering.

Storage: Discard 14 days after reconstitution. Refrigeration is preferable, but not required.

CAUTIONS/CONTRAINDICATIONS

Cross-sensitivity between penicillins occurs; do not use if patient is allergic to penicillin.

USE

A broad-spectrum antibiotic with the same spectrum as ampicillin (see that monograph), except that ampicillin is more effective against Shigella. Preferred over ampicillin for oral therapy because it is better absorbed, causes less diarrhea, and requires fewer daily doses than ampicillin.

For infants with otitis media or urinary tract infections (UTIs) who are to be treated with oral antibiotics. Infants with UTIs should initially receive parenteral antibiotics until bloodstream infection has been ruled out and the susceptibility of the urinary pathogen has been determined.[3]

Spectrum: An analog of ampicillin, with bactericidal activity against many Gram-negative and Gram-positive bacteria. Used to treat susceptible infections of the ear, nose, throat, genitourinary tract, soft tissue, skin, and lower respiratory tract. Its spectrum includes *Haemophilus influenzae, Escherichia coli, Proteus mirabilis, and Neisseria gonorrhoeae.* Gram-positive organisms covered include streptococci (among them, *S. faecalis and S. pneumoniae)* and nonpenicillinase-producing staphylococci.

Prophylaxis of bacterial endocarditis.

For UTI prophylaxis in infants younger than 1–2 months of age because co-trimoxazole and nitrofurantoin, the antibiotics usually recommended,[1] are contraindicated in this age group. Infants younger than 1 month old are at risk for hemolytic anemia from nitrofurantoin. Infants less than 2 months of age are at risk for bilirubin encephalopathy from co-trimoxazole.

MECHANISM OF ACTION

Amoxicillin interferes with bacterial cell-wall synthesis, resulting in bactericidal activity.

ADVERSE EFFECTS

Usually well tolerated.

GI: Uncommonly, diarrhea. Prolonged use of antibiotics may result in fungal or bacterial superinfections.

Hematologic: Rarely, bone-marrow depression, granulocytopenia.

Hepatic: Rarely, hepatitis.

Hypersensitivity Reactions: Rash, fever, bronchospasm, vasculitis, serum sickness, exfoliative dermatitis, Stevens-Johnson syndrome, and anaphylaxis. Amoxicillin (and also ampicillin) cause two different types of rash: One resembles an urticarial hypersensitivity rash seen with other penicillins, and the second is a generalized erythematous, maculopapular rash that is usually nonimmunologic. A higher incidence of the latter rash occurs when these antibiotics are used in patients with viral disease, infectious mononucleosis, cytomegalovirus infections, and lymphatic leukemias, as well as in patients with hyperuricemia who are receiving allopurinol.[4]

PHARMACOKINETICS/PHARMACODYNAMICS

Absorption: Resistant to acid hydrolysis in the stomach. Oral absorption is delayed in neonates compared with children and adults.

Peak Levels: Achieved in neonates within 3–4.5 hours, compared with 1–2 hours in children and adults. Peak serum concentrations and bioavailability are approximately twice those of ampicillin after comparable doses.

Half-life: In term neonates, 3.7 hours; in infants and children, 0.9–1.9 hours.[4,5]

NURSING IMPLICATIONS

Observe infant for rash and signs of anaphylaxis.

Monitor for diarrhea.

REFERENCES

1. Nelson JD. 1996. *1996–1997 Pocket Book of Pediatric Antimicrobial Therapy,* 12th ed. Baltimore: Lippincott Williams & Wilkins, 34, 68.

2. American Academy of Pediatrics, Committee on Infectious Diseases. 1994. *Red Book: Report of the Committee on Infectious Diseases.* Elk Grove Village, Illinois: American Academy of Pediatrics, 529.

3. McCracken GH Jr, and Nelson JD. 1983. *Antimicrobial Therapy for Newborns,* 2nd ed. New York: Grune & Stratton, 13–16.

4. McEvoy GK. 1994. *AHFS Drug Information.* Bethesda, Maryland: American Society of Hospital Pharmacists, 266–267.

5. Ginsburg CM, et al. 1979. Comparative pharmacokinetics of amoxicillin and ampicillin in infants and children. *Pediatrics* 64(5): 627–631.

AMPHOTERICIN B, CONVENTIONAL (FUNGIZONE) AND AMPHOTERICIN B, LIPID BASED (ABELCET, AMPHOTEC, AMBISOME)

ANTI-INFECTIVE: ANTIFUNGAL

(am-foe-TER-i-sin Bee)

DOSE

Amphotericin B, Conventional (Fungizone):

Test: **Choose one:**

- Give 0.25 mg/kg (first day's dose) IV over 6 hours (0.04 mg/kg/hour), monitoring for adverse effects during the first hour.
- Give 0.05 mg/kg IV (*Maximum:* 1 mg) over 1 hour; monitor vital signs for hypotension and arrhythmias. If there are no adverse effects, infuse balance of first day's dose of 0.25 mg/kg over 3–5 hours.

Maintenance: Begin with 0.25 mg/kg/day IV; increase by 0.25 mg/kg/day increments to 1 mg/kg/day.

- In severe disease, 0.3 mg/kg may be given on the first day, then 0.6 mg/kg on day 2 and 1 mg/kg on day 3 as tolerated.
- In life-threatening situations, 0.25 mg/kg increments can be given in successive 4-hour infusions during a 12- to 24-hour period to achieve the maximum total daily dose of 1 mg/kg.[1]
- Once the patient has improved (after 1–2 weeks), the dose may be given every other day (*Maximum:* 1.5 mg/kg/dose/48 hours).[1]
- *Maximum:* The usual maximum is 1 mg/kg/day. For severe, rapidly progressing disease, a short-term maximum dose of 1.5 mg/kg/day can be used.

Duration: Duration of therapy ranges from 2 to 6 weeks, depending on the type and extent of the fungal infection and on the clinical and mycological response. A shorter course of therapy may be successful for catheter-associated infection, provided the catheter is removed.[1] Duration has been expressed in terms of total mg/kg/course:

- *Catheter-associated Candidemia:* 10–15 mg/kg total dose with catheter left in. This may be reduced to 5–10 mg/kg if the catheter is removed, the fungemia is rapidly cleared, and there is no evidence of metastatic infection.[2]
- *Systemic Candidiasis:* as much as 25–30 mg/kg total accumulative dose may be required.[2]

Intrathecal: Initial dose in infants is 0.01 mg, gradually increasing over 5–7 days to 0.1 mg given every other day or every third day.[1,3] Klein and colleagues instilled 0.05 mg every third day for two administrations in an infant with Candida meningitis.[4] For injection, reconstitute with sterile water containing no bacteriostatic agents. Maximum concentration is 0.25 mg/ml; dilute further with CSF fluid and reinfuse.

A

Bladder Irrigation for Candida Cystitis: 50 mcg/ml sterile water for injection. Instill fluid into bladder, clamp catheter for 1–2 hours, then drain bladder. Repeat 3–4 times/day or by continuous irrigation for 2–7 days or until cultures are negative. The bladder capacity of a neonate is approximately 5–10 ml/kg.

Topical: For severe cutaneous Candida not responsive to nystatin, apply liberally to lesions and rub in gently 2–4 times daily for 1–3 weeks, depending on patient response. Available in 3 percent cream, lotion, ointment.

Amphotericin B, Lipid-based (Liposomal)

There is limited experience with lipid-based formulations of amphotericin B in neonates.[5–8] Lackner and associates used liposomal amphotericin B (AmBisome) successfully in two very low birth weight infants with disseminated fungal infections. An initial dose of 1.5 mg/kg/day was infused over 1 hour; the dosage was increased to 5 mg/kg/day within 1 week. Duration of therapy was 26 days in one patient and 14 days in the other. No severe side effects were observed; in one patient, kidney impairment caused by treatment with conventional amphotericin B even improved during therapy with AmBisome.[8] Lipid-based amphotericin B appears to be less nephrotoxic than conventional amphotericin B.

Scarcella and colleagues used liposomal amphotericin B (AmBisome) to treat 40 preterm and 4 term newborn infants with severe fungal infections. Their protocol called for an initial daily dose of 1 mg/kg, then a stepwise increase in 1 mg/kg increments to 5 mg/kg/day. Infusion time was over 30–60 minutes. Doses actually used were 1 mg/kg/day throughout treatment in 6 infants, 3 mg/kg/day in 22 cases, 4 mg/kg/day in 14 cases, and 5 mg/kg/day in 2 cases (osteomyelitis and polyarticular infection in 1 infant and osteoarthritis in the other). The drug was discontinued when all signs and symptoms of infection had resolved and a culture taken 1 week earlier was negative. The cumulative dose ranged from 7 to 139 mg/kg (median, 45 mg/kg). The mean duration of therapy was 22 days (range, 7–49 days). The drug was effective in 73 percent of patients. No fever, chills, phlebitis, or abnormalities in blood pressure or in hepatic, renal, or hematologic indices occurred, except for transient hypokalemia, which responded readily to potassium supplementation.[6]

For a comparison of various lipid-based amphotericin B formulations, see Table 1-9.

ADMINISTRATION

IV—*Rate:* Infuse over 4–6 hours, as tolerated.[3]

IV—*Concentration:* 0.1 mg/ml (maximum for peripheral IV and intrathecal use). For fluid-restricted patients, 0.25 mg/ml in D_5W may be used via a central venous line.[9]

- Stable at room temperature for 24 hours after reconstitution.
- It is not necessary to protect drug from light during infusion.
- *Discomfort:* Pretreatment with acetaminophen or aspirin and diphenhydramine 30 minutes before the infusion, frequently done in older children and adults to reduce the discomfort of infusion, is not usually recommended

TABLE 1-9 ◆ COMPARISON OF LIPID-BASED FORMULATIONS OF AMPHOTERICIN B

Drug	Dose	Concentration	Rate of Infusion	Comments
Abelcet (lipid complex)	5 mg/kg/day as infusion	1–2 mg/ml	2.5 mg/kg/hour	Shake bag or syringe every 2 hours. Do not use an inline filter.
AmBisome (liposomal)	3–5 mg/kg/day as infusion	0.2–2 mg/ml	Infuse over 2 hours. May shorten infusion to 1 hour if tolerated (30-minute infusion has also been used[6]). Increase infusion period if discomfort is present.	May use inline membrane filter of 1 micron or larger mean pore diameter.
Amphotec (cholesteryl)	3–4 mg/kg/day as infusion	0.16–0.83 mg/ml	1 mg/kg/hour	Do not use an inline filter.

in infants. Instead, treat any apparent discomfort during infusion by slowing the rate or temporarily stopping the infusion.

Compatibility: See Appendix E: Y-Site Compatibility of Common NICU Drugs.

Use dextrose, not sodium chloride, flushes before and after amphotericin B administration.

CAUTIONS/CONTRAINDICATIONS

Do not mix in a saline solution.

If BUN rises to >40 mg/dl or serum creatinine rises to >3 mg/dl (or 3 times normal), reduce or discontinue the dose until renal function improves.

Renal insufficiency is **not** a contraindication for amphotericin B.[2]

If patients are salt depleted, renal dysfunction during amphotericin B administration can be decreased by salt loading and assuring adequate hydration.[10,11]

Infants very often need increased potassium supplementation while on amphotericin B.

USE

The most important antifungal for systemic fungal infections and severe superficial mycoses.[2] Its spectrum includes a wide variety of fungal infections, including candidiasis.

MECHANISM OF ACTION

Amphotericin B binds sterols of the fungal cell membrane and produces cell damage and lysis.

ADVERSE EFFECTS

Amphotericin B has a high incidence of adverse effects.[9,12] Toxicity occurs in about half of treated infants.[2]

Cardiovascular: Hypotension, hypertension, arrhythmias.

CNS: Malaise, convulsions (rare).

Dermatologic: Rash.

Electrolytes: Hypokalemia, hypomagnesemia.

GI: Nausea, anorexia, diarrhea (symptoms usually abate as patient develops tolerance to the drug).

Hematologic: Anemia, thrombocytopenia (69 percent),[2] neutropenia, others.

Hepatic: Alteration in liver function tests (50 percent), acute hepatic failure with jaundice and hepatocellular dysfunction.

IV site: Phlebitis, pain affected by concentration and rate of infusion.

Renal: Increased BUN and creatinine, decreased creatinine clearance, diminished ability to concentrate the urine, decreased GFR, and abnormal urine sediment (incidence 80 percent). Renal tubular acidosis, nephrocalcinosis. Renal dysfunction is usually reversible. Alteration in renal function occurred in 54 percent of neonates in one study.[13]

Other: Fever; shaking chills. Tolerance may develop to febrile response.[1,12,14] There is minimal toxicity from bladder irrigation with amphotericin.[1]

PHARMACOKINETICS/PHARMACODYNAMICS

Absorption: Little or no GI absorption.

Distribution: Distributed poorly into CSF (approximately 3 percent of concurrent serum concentration).

Protein Binding: 95 percent. Drug is stored in different organs and re-enters the circulation slowly.

Metabolism: Metabolism is unknown.

Half-life: Half-life in children is 18 hours (range: 12–40 hours). Half-life is markedly increased in neonates.[15]

Elimination: 3 percent of the drug is excreted in the urine, 1–15 percent in the bile. Renal or hepatic failure does not alter blood concentration.[16]

NURSING IMPLICATIONS

Strictly monitor input and output. Monitor renal function because BUN and creatinine frequently increase during drug therapy.

Monitor for electrolyte imbalance, particularly potassium and magnesium.

Monitor for response to therapy, such as improved stability of serum glucose, improved CBCs, and stabilizing condition.

Monitor liver function tests weekly.

The clinical usefulness and validity of measuring amphotericin serum concentrations have not been proven.[16]

Do not mix in a saline solution.

Comments

Interactions: Concurrent aminoglycosides or other nephrotoxic drugs potentiate renal toxicity. Acute pulmonary deterioration has occurred in patients receiving combined granulocyte transfusions and amphotericin.[17] There is synergism between amphotericin and flucytosine.[13] There is a possible antagonism between amphotericin and miconazole or ketoconazole.[18]

References

1. American Academy of Pediatrics, Committee on Infectious Diseases. 1994. *Red Book: Report of the Committee on Infectious Diseases.* Elk Grove Village, Illinois: American Academy of Pediatrics, 562–564.

2. Butler KM, Rench MA, and Baker CJ. 1990. Amphotericin B as a single agent in the treatment of systemic candidiasis in neonates. *Pediatric Infectious Disease Journal* 9(1): 51–56.

3. Miller JM. 1995. Fungal infections. In *Infectious Diseases of the Fetus and Newborn Infant*, 4th ed., Remington JS, and Klein JO, eds. Philadelphia: WB Saunders, 703–744.

4. Klein JD, Yamauchi T, and Horlick SP. 1972. Neonatal candidiasis, meningitis and arthritis: Observations and a review of the literature. *Journal of Pediatrics* 81(1): 31–34.

5. Jarlov JO, Born P, and Bruun B. 1995. *Candida albicans* meningitis in a 27 weeks premature infant treated with liposomal amphotericin-B (AmBisome). *Scandinavian Journal of Infectious Diseases* 27(4): 419–420.

6. Scarcella A, et al. 1998. Liposomal amphotericin B treatment for neonatal fungal infections. *Pediatric Infectious Disease Journal* 17(2): 146–148.

7. Arishi HA, et al. 1998. Liposomal amphotericin B in neonates with invasive candidiasis. *American Journal of Perinatology* 15(11): 643–648.

8. Lackner H, et al. 1992. Liposomal amphotericin B (AmBisome) for treatment of disseminated fungal infections in two infants of very low birth weight. *Pediatrics* 89(6): 1259–1261.

9. Kintzel PE, and Kennedy PE. 1991. Stability of amphotericin B in 5 percent dextrose injection at concentrations used for administration through a central venous line. *American Journal of Hospital Pharmacy* 48(2): 283–285.

10. Gardner ML, Godley PJ, and Wasan SM. 1990. Sodium loading treatment for amphotericin B–induced nephrotoxicity. *DICP: The Annals of Pharmacotherapy* 24(10): 940–946.

11. Heidemann HT, et al. 1983. Amphotericin B nephrotoxicity in humans decreased by salt repletion. *American Journal of Medicine* 75(3): 476–481.

12. Baley JE, Kliegman RM, and Fanaroff AA. 1984. Disseminated fungal infections in very-low-birth-weight infants: Therapeutic toxicity. *Pediatrics* 73(2): 153–157.

13. Cleary JD, Weisdorf D, and Fletcher CV. 1988. Effect of infusion rate on amphotericin B–associated febrile reactions. *DICP: The Annals of Pharmacotherapy* 22(10): 769–772.

14. Chesney PJ, Justman RA, and Bogdanowicz WM. 1978. Candida meningitis in newborn infants: A review and report of combined amphotericin B–flucytosine therapy. *Johns Hopkins Medical Journal* 142(5): 155–160.

15. Benson JM, and Nahata MC. 1989. Pharmacokinetics of amphotericin B in children. *Antimicrobial Agents and Chemotherapy* 33(11): 1989–1993.

16. LeBel MH, LeBel P, and Mills EL. 1992. Antifungal agents for systemic mycotic infections. In *Pediatric Pharmacology: Therapeutic Principles in Practice*, 2nd ed., Yaffe SJ, and Aranda JV, eds. Philadelphia: WB Saunders, 261–275.

17. Wright D, et al. 1981. Lethal pulmonary reactions associated with combined use of amphotericin B and leukocyte transfusions. *New England Journal of Medicine* 304(20): 1185–1189.

18. McEvoy GK. 1994. *AHFS Drug Information.* Bethesda, Maryland: American Society of Hospital Pharmacists, 70–74.

A

AMPICILLIN
(am-pi-SILL-in)

ANTI-INFECTIVE:
ANTIBIOTIC

DOSE

<1.2 kg (0–4 weeks): 100 mg/kg/day divided every 12 hours

1.2–2 kg:

- 0–7 days of age: 100 mg/kg/day divided every 12 hours
- >7 days of age: 100 mg/kg/day divided every 8 hours

>2 kg:

- 0–7 days of age: 100 mg/kg/day divided every 8 hours
- >7 days of age: 100 mg/kg/day divided every 6 hours

Meningitis: Use double the above doses.[1]

This dose has also been used for term newborn infants for possible sepsis:
0–7 days: 100 mg/kg/day divided every 12 hours.

In severe renal dysfunction, prolong dosage interval (i.e., if 25 mg/kg/dose is usually given every 12 hours, give 25 mg/kg/dose every 24 hours).

ADMINISTRATION

Supplied as: Ampicillin suspension is available in 125 mg/5 ml, 250 mg/5 ml, 500 mg/5 ml, and 100 mg/ml drops.

IV—*Rate:* Infuse over at least 3–5 minutes (not faster than 100 mg/minute). May give over 10–30 minutes.

IV—*Concentration:* Reconstitute the 125 mg, 250 mg, or 500 mg vial with 5 ml sterile water or normal saline (not dextrose, because it causes more rapid degradation). *Maximum:* 100 mg/ml.

Note the date and time on the vial, refrigerate, and discard after 8 hours.

IV—*Compatibility:* See Appendix E: Y-Site Compatibility of Common NICU Drugs.

IM: When IV access is limited, may give IM for a few doses if necessary.

PO: Amoxicillin is preferred over oral ampicillin because amoxicillin is better absorbed and causes less diarrhea than ampicillin. Also, amoxicillin can be given with feedings, whereas ampicillin should be given on an empty stomach to optimize absorption.

USE

A broad-spectrum penicillin antibiotic commonly used with gentamicin or cefotaxime to treat suspected or documented neonatal sepsis and/or meningitis. Ampicillin provides coverage for Group B β-hemolytic streptococci, *Listeria monocytogenes*, and enterococci; the gentamicin or cefotaxime provides Gram-negative coverage.

Also effective against many *Haemophilus influenzae* strains, *Proteus mirabilis,* and Salmonella species.

Ampicillin's Gram-negative coverage is not as broad as that of the aminoglycosides or the third-generation cephalosporins.

Ampicillin is not penicillinase resistant.[2]

MECHANISM OF ACTION

Ampicillin is an aminopenicillin that is bactericidal for Gram-positive and some Gram-negative bacteria. Penicillins act by interrupting bacterial cell wall synthesis.

ADVERSE EFFECTS

Usually well tolerated in infants.

Diarrhea is uncommon, especially when the drug is given IV. Ampicillin rarely causes rash or urticaria in neonates.

Mild eosinophilia has been observed in infants.

Oral and/or diaper-area candidiasis may occur.

Alteration of bowel flora may occur after IV administration.

Overgrowth of resistant Gram-negative bacteria and Candida diaper dermatitis and oral thrush occur more commonly after oral administration.[2]

PHARMACOKINETICS/PHARMACODYNAMICS

Absorption: Well absorbed after oral administration; acid stable. Amoxicillin is better absorbed, however, and with fewer adverse GI effects.

Distribution: Concentrations in the CSF vary greatly; levels 2 hours after a 50 mg/kg IV dose exceed the minimum inhibitory concentration (MIC) values of Group B streptococci and Listeria by 50- to 300-fold.[3]

Metabolism: Serum half-life is inversely correlated with birth weight and postnatal age. Half-life in the first week of life is 3–6 hours; thereafter, 2–3.5 hours.

Elimination: Renal. Severe renal impairment markedly prolongs clearance. Also excreted in the bile and undergoes enterohepatic circulation.

NURSING IMPLICATIONS

Do not mix ampicillin and gentamicin in the same tubing; do not mix in same IV bag or bottle, or substantial mutual inactivation may result.

Monitor for development of oral Candida or diaper dermatitis.

COMMENTS

Contains 3.1 mEq sodium/gm of ampicillin sodium.

REFERENCES

1. McEvoy GK. 1994. *AHFS Drug Information.* Bethesda, Maryland: American Society of Hospital Pharmacists, 285–288.

2. Sáez-Llorens X, and McCracken GH Jr. 1995. Clinical pharmacology of antimicrobial agents. In *Infectious Diseases of the Fetus and Newborn Infant,* 4th ed., Remington JS, and Klein JO, eds. Philadelphia: WB Saunders, 1296–1297.

3. Kaplan JM, et al. 1974. Pharmacologic studies in neonates given large dosages of ampicillin. *Journal of Pediatrics* 84(4): 571–577.

AQUAPHOR OINTMENT
(AH-kwah-for OYNT-ment)

**TOPICAL:
EMOLLIENT, PROTECTANT**

Synonym: Aquaphor-Original Ointment

DOSE

Birth Weight <1,500 gm: Apply topically every 6–12 hours for at least the first 14 days of life, then as needed. Use every-6-hour applications for extremely premature, very low birth weight infants.

Birth Weight >1,500 gm: Apply to skin as needed.

ADMINISTRATION

Supplied as: Topical: 16-ounce jar. Pharmacist should repackage 2-ounce jars from the 16-ounce jar for each individual infant.

Topical administration only.

CAUTIONS/CONTRAINDICATIONS

For external use only. Avoid contact with eyes. Do not apply over deep or puncture wounds, infections, or lacerations because its high occlusive ability may lead to maceration and further inflammation.[1]

USE

A topical preparation to help heal severely dry skin.

Pabst and colleagues reported that the use of Aquaphor during the first 2 postnatal weeks improved skin condidion in infants of 26–30 weeks gestation without changing skin bacterial flora. The researchers speculated that improved skin condition may limit transepidermal water loss and decrease portals of entry for pathogens, thereby potentially decreasing fluid and electrolyte imbalances and sepsis in very low birth weight infants.[2] In another study, Aquaphor was shown to decrease transepidermal water loss, decrease severity of dermatitis, and decrease bacterial colonization of axillary skin in preterm infants.[3] A randomized controlled study compared prophylactic application of Aquaphor with local as-needed application. Nosocomial bacterial sepsis (NBS) was more frequent in the study group, in which Aquaphor was applied prophylactically over the entire body (except face and scalp) twice a day through day 14, than in the control group, which received as-needed application only to the site of injury. Although skin condition was better and skin injury less in the prophylactic group, more infants in the prophylactic group had NBS, with the higher incidence resulting exclusively from coagulase-negative staphylococcus infections and occurring only in the smallest infants (501–750 gm). Consider using Aquaphor as needed, rather than routinely, in this weight group.[4]

Also used by pharmacists to compound ointments.

MECHANISM OF ACTION

Aquaphor is an emollient, also called an occlusive agent or a moisturizer. Emollients act primarily by leaving an oily film on the skin surface; the film acts as an occlusive barrier, promoting water retention because the moisture in the skin cannot readily pass through it. Emollients make the skin feel soft and smooth by helping to re-establish the integrity of the stratum corneum. The lipid materials they contain make the scales on the skin translucent and flatten them against the underlying skin. This eliminates the air between the scales and the skin surface, which is responsible for skin's dry, flaky appearance.[5]

Aquaphor contains petrolatum, mineral oil, ceresin (a mineral wax), and lanolin alcohol (wool wax alcohol). Lanolin is a natural product derived from sheep wool. Aquaphor contains no preservatives or fragrances. It is miscible with water (unlike petroleum jelly) or with aqueous solutions, forming a smooth, creamy water-in-oil emulsion.

ADVERSE EFFECTS

Dermatologic: Rarely causes allergic reactions.

Local: Decreased adhesiveness of monitor leads, temperature probes, and tape used for securing IV catheters. Nopper and associates suggest alleviating this problem by using limb leads and by gently cleansing the designated area with a skin cleanser (pHisoDerm Gentle Cleansing Bar) and water.[3]

NURSING IMPLICATIONS

Skin condition can be scored using a numeric grading scale from 0 to 9, with a score of 0 signifying normal skin without dryness and 9 indicating severe dermatitis (Table 1-10).[6]

Monitor for skin rash or local irritation.

TABLE 1-10 ◆ SKIN CONDITION GRADING SCALE

Grade	Skin Condition
0	Normal, no sign of dry skin
1	Dry skin with few visible scales
2	Dry skin with moderate visible scales
3	Dry skin with many visible scales
4	Dry skin with thicker, darker scales and areas of mild erythema
5	Dry skin with thicker, darker scales, increased areas of mild erythema, and having a rough texture
6	Dry skin with thicker, darker scales, increased areas of mild erythema, having a rough texture, and with visible superficial fissures
7	Dry skin with thicker, darker scales, increased areas of mild erythema, and having a rough texture, with deeper fissures
8	Dry, crusted skin on erythematous base with dark scales, fissures, and occasional areas of erythematous, crusting, oozing
9	Erythematous, crusting, oozing skin involving the entire area

Adapted from: Lane AT, and Drost SS. 1993. Effect of repeated application of emollient cream to premature neonates' skin. *Pediatrics* 92(3): 416. Reprinted by permission.

Each infant should have his own small jar or tube of ointment, to reduce the risk of bacterial contamination. Sharing is not advised.

REFERENCES

1. Medical Economics Data. 1998. *Physicians' Desk Reference.* Montvale, New Jersey: Medical Economics, 1667.

2. Pabst RC, et al. 1999. The effect of application of Aquaphor on skin condition, fluid requirements, and bacterial colonization in very low birth weight infants. *Journal of Perinatology* 19(4): 278–283.

3. Nopper AJ, et al. 1996. Topical ointment therapy benefits premature infants. *Journal of Pediatrics* 128(5): 660–669.

4. Edwards WH, et al. 2000. The effect of Aquaphor Original Emollient Ointment on nosocomial sepsis rates and skin integrity in infants of birth weight 501 to 1,000 grams. Abstract. Presented at Hot Topics in Neonatology, Washington, D.C., December 4.

5. Billow JA. 1993. Dermatologic products. In *Handbook of Nonprescription Drugs,* 10th ed., Covington TR, ed. Washington, DC: American Pharmaceutical Association, 521–541.

6. Lane AT, and Drost SS. 1993. Effect of repeated application of emollient cream to premature neonates' skin. *Pediatrics* 92(3): 415–419.

ARGININE HYDROCHLORIDE (R-GENE 10)
(AR-ji-neen)

**ELECTROLYTE:
ACIDIFYING AGENT**

DOSE

Treatment of Alkalosis:

- *To calculate the dose of arginine in mEq:*

  mEq =

   $0.2 \times$ Patient's Weight (kg) $\times$ (103 − Serum Chloride) (in mEq/liter) **or**

   $0.3 \times$ Patient's Weight (kg) $\times$ Base Excess (in mEq/liter)

  Give 1/3 to 1/2 of the calculated dose, then re-evaluate.

- *To calculate the dose of arginine in grams:*

  grams =

   Patient's Weight (in kg) $\times 0.1 \times$ (Serum HCO_3^- − 24) (in mEq/liter) **or**

   (Desired Decrease in Serum HCO_3^- [in mEq/liter]) $\times$ (Patient's Weight [in kg]) $\div$ 9.6

  Give 1/3 to 1/2 of the calculated dose, then re-evaluate.

Growth Hormone Reserve Test: 500 mg/kg (= 5 ml/kg of the 10 percent solution) infused IV over 30 minutes.

- *Note:* Must be given IV; oral administration is ineffective for this test.

Neonatal-onset Urea Cycle Disorders

- *For maintenance management:*

  - *Carbamoyl phosphate synthetase (CPS) or ornithine transcarbamylase (OTC):* Sodium phenylbutyrate (0.45–0.6 gm/kg/day PO in 4–6 divided doses taken with meals or feedings) and citrulline or arginine (0.17 gm/kg/day) PO.

  - *Argininosuccinic acid synthetase (AS):* Sodium phenylbutyrate 0.45–0.6 gm/kg/day and arginine (free base) 0.4–0.7 gm/kg/day PO.

  - *Argininosuccinase (AL):* Arginine (free base) 0.4–0.7 gm/kg/day PO.[1] Patients with AL deficiency can usually be managed with protein restriction and arginine alone.[1,2]

- *For management of intercurrent hyperammonemia episodes:*

  - *CPS, OTC, AS:* Sodium benzoate 0.25 gm/kg/dose, sodium phenylacetate 0.25 gm/kg/dose, and 10 percent arginine HCl 0.21 gm/kg/dose (= 2 ml/kg/dose). Dilute drugs in 25–35 ml/kg of 10 percent glucose. Give a priming infusion of these doses IV over 90 minutes. Follow with a sustaining infusion of the same doses infused IV over 24 hours.

  - *AL:* 10 percent arginine HCl 0.66 gm/kg (= 6 ml/kg) diluted in 25–35 ml/kg of 10 percent glucose. Give a priming infusion of this dose IV over 90 minutes. Follow with a sustaining infusion of the same dose infused IV over 24 hours.[2–5]

Caution: All orders for these drugs should be independently verified and double-checked at each step (ordering, dispensing, administering); there have been several cases of overdose because of improperly written orders or computation errors.[1]

ADMINISTRATION

Supplied as:

- *Injection:* 10 percent = 100 mg/ml (with 0.475 mEq chloride/ml).
- Available only in 300 ml bottles; should be repackaged in unit-dose by pharmacy for the NICU.

IV—*Rate:*

- *Metabolic alkalosis:* Infuse over at least 30 minutes. May be added to maintenance IV and infused over 24 hours. Although the maximum rate of infusion is 1 gm/kg/hour (= 10 ml/kg/hour of 10 percent solution), slower rates of infusion are recommended, if possible, to avoid vein irritation and risk of extravasation injury.
- *Growth hormone test:* Infuse IV over 30 minutes. Do not infuse more slowly or quickly than recommended because doing so may alter the test results. Give IV, not PO, for this indication.
- *Neonatal-onset urea cycle disorders:* See above under **DOSE.**

IV—*Concentration:* May use undiluted or diluted with saline or dextrose.

PO: Use the injectable form of the drug orally. Dilute before use. May dilute in feedings.

CAUTIONS/CONTRAINDICATIONS

Arginine HCl is not a first-line agent for treating uncompensated hypochloremic metabolic alkalosis. Try sodium, potassium, or ammonium chlorides first.

Arginine HCl should not be used as an alternative to chloride supplementation. Use only for infants unresponsive to management with chloride supplements.

Arginine HCl may be hazardous to patients with hyperchloremic acidosis because of its chloride content (about 0.5 mEq chloride/ml in arginine HCl 10 percent).

High-dose arginine HCl may cause *hyperchloremic* metabolic acidosis. Monitor plasma levels of chloride and bicarbonate, and administer appropriate amounts of bicarbonate.

Arginine HCl may shift potassium from cells, resulting in elevated serum potassium concentrations in patients with renal dysfunction.

Do not use in patients sensitive to arginine HCl or in those with hepatic or renal failure.

Arginine HCl is metabolized to nitrogen-containing products for excretion. Evaluate effects of a high nitrogen load on kidneys prior to use.

Arginine HCl may be toxic in infants with arginase deficiency or with liver failure.

- Because arginine HCl is a potent stimulator of insulin, excess intake may promote hypoglycemia.

- *Spironolactone* with arginine HCl in patients with severe hepatic disease may cause severe, potentially fatal, hyperkalemia. This probably results from an arginine-induced shift of potassium from cells, impaired hepatic metabolism of arginine, and/or a spironolactone-induced decrease in renal excretion of potassium. The effect of spironolactone on potassium lasts for several days after the drug is discontinued. Avoid concomitant use of arginine HCl and spironolactone or spironolactone-containing drugs such as Aldactazide (hydrochlorothiazide with spironolactone in combination).

USE

Arginine HCl is used as a source of supplemental chloride ion, as an acidifying agent, as a treatment in infants and children with errors of the urea cycle, as a dietary constituent, and as a diagnostic agent for growth disorders.

Metabolic Alkalosis: Arginine HCl is an acidifying agent used to treat refractory uncompensated hypochloremic metabolic alkalosis that has not responded to treatment with sodium chloride, potassium chloride, or ammonium chloride supplementation.

Alkalosis results from a gain of base or a loss of acid. It may lead to tissue hypoxia, CNS changes, and muscular irritability and may cause seizures and arrhythmias. Alkalemia depresses respiration, causing hypercapnia and hypoxemia, and makes it difficult to wean patients from mechanical ventilation. Hypokalemia usually accompanies alkalemic disorders. Alkalemia stimulates anaerobic glycolysis and increases production of lactic acid and ketoacids.[6,7] (Other adverse effects are listed in Table 1-11.)

The most common causes of metabolic alkalosis include prolonged nasogastric suctioning (causes excessive loss of hydrogen ions from the extracellular fluid) and excessive diuretic therapy, particularly use of loop diuretics such as furosemide in preterm infants with chronic lung disease (see Figure 1-8 in the monograph on furosemide, page 266). The volume contraction that results from prolonged suctioning and/or diuretic use decreases renal bicarbonate excretion and increases regeneration of bicarbonate. If potassium depletion also develops, even more renal bicarbonate conservation occurs. Metabolic alkalosis may also be caused by excess alkali administration (sodium bicarbonate, acetate, citrate, lactate). Metabolic alkalosis may occur with exchange transfusion because of delayed clearing of citrate buffer from the donated blood by the liver.

Symptoms of metabolic alkalosis include severe hypoventilation, weakness, cardiac arrhythmias, and occasionally clinical tetany. Plasma pH, bicarbonate, and $PaCO_2$ are all increased, and serum potassium and chloride are decreased.

Management includes correction of severe volume contraction by expanding the extracellular fluid volume with IV fluid replacement and correction of hypokalemia, if present. Nasogastric suction should be replaced milliliter for milliliter each shift with $1/2$ normal saline with 20 mEq potassium/liter. If the

TABLE 1-11 ◆ ADVERSE EFFECTS OF SEVERE ALKALEMIA

Cardiovasular	Arrhythmias
Respiratory	Tissue hypoxia, hypoventilation leading to CO_2 retention and hypoxemia, difficulty in weaning patient from ventilator
Metabolic	Hypokalemia; increased anaerobic glycolysis with increased production of organic acids, such as lactic acid and ketoacids; decreased plasma concentration of ionied calcium; tetany; hypomagnesemia and hypophosphatemia
Cerebral	CNS changes, such as lethargy, neuromuscular irritability, seizures, and reduction in cerebral blood flow

Adapted from: Adrogue HJ, and Madias NE. 1998. Management of life-threatening acid-base disorders. Part 2. *New England Journal of Medicine* 338(2): 107–111; and Jospe N, and Forbes G. 1996. Fluids and electrolytes: Clinical aspects. *Pediatrics in Review* 17(11): 395–403.

cause of the metabolic alkalosis is excess alkali administration, reduce the dose of or discontinue administration of sodium bicarbonate, THAM, or citrate (Bicitra). If the infant is receiving acetate salts of sodium and/or potassium in the parenteral nutrition solution, change back to the chloride salts of these electrolytes. If the infant is receiving furosemide or another loop diuretic, consider changing to a thiazide diuretic; consider decreasing the dose and/or frequency of diuretic administration. Chronic alkalosis may require treatment with an acidifying agent such as arginine HCl or ammonium chloride.[8]

Growth Hormone Test: Arginine HCl is also used as a diagnostic aid to evaluate pituitary growth hormone reserve in patients with such known or suspected disorders as problems of growth and stature, pituitary dwarfism, gigantism, postsurgical craniopharyngioma, and panhypopituitarism. Because of individual variability in the response to arginine HCl, diagnosis should not be made on the basis of a single test. Additional tests using other methods or a second test with arginine HCl should be conducted to confirm the diagnosis.

Neonatal-onset Urea Cycle Disorder: Arginine HCl is one of the medications used to reduce ammonium in patients with inborn errors of urea synthesis.[9] Brusilow and Maestri state that symptomatic hyperammonemia approaches the seriousness of uncontrolled hemorrhage as a medical emergency.[1] If untreated, hyperammonemic coma can lead to death. Treated, surviving infants can develop seizures, developmental delays, and severe neurologic handicaps. The urea cycle disorders are enzyme deficiencies of carbamoyl phosphate synthetase (CPS), ornithine transcarbamylase (OTC), argininosuccinic acid synthetase (AS), argininosuccinase (AL), or arginase (AR). The most common is OTC deficiency.[1] (Figure 1-2 illustrates the activities of these enzymes in the urea cycle.)

Brain damage from hyperammonemia occurs secondary to cerebral edema and increased intracranial pressure. The mechanism of cerebral edema in hyperammonemic states can be accounted for by increased whole-brain glutamine levels. Glutamine accumulates within astrocytes, causing an increase in osmolarity within the cells. This leads to large shifts of water into the cell, resulting in astrocyte swelling and cerebral edema.

FIGURE 1-2 ◆ UREA CYCLE ENZYME ACTIVITIES IN THE NEWBORN INFANT, SHOWING ARGININE.

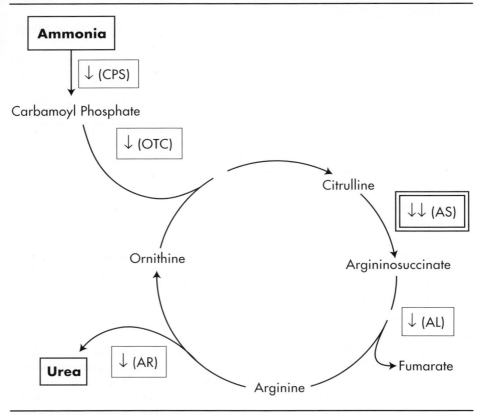

Key to urea cycle enzyme abbreviations in figure

AL: Argininosuccinate lyase (argininosuccinase)

AR: Arginase. Arginase converts this reaction sequence from a one-way synthetic system to a cyclic process, with one urea molecule fabricated for each turn of the cycle. Arginase catalyzes the hydrolysis of arginine to ornithine.

AS: Argininosuccinic acid synthetase

CPS: Carbamoylphosphate synthetase

OTC: Ornithine transcarbamoylase

↓ = Decreased enzyme activity

↓↓ = Markedly decreased enzyme activity

Adapted from: Motil KJ. 1988. Protein needs for term and preterm infants. In *Nutrition During Infancy*, Tsang RC, and Nichols BL, eds. Philadelphia: Hanley & Belfus, 107. Reprinted by permission.

- ***Diagnosis:*** Urea cycle disorders are characterized by encephalopathy, respiratory alkalosis, and hyperammonemia. (Normal plasma ammonium level is <35 micromol/liter.) A very low serum urea nitrogen concentration (such as

1 mg/dl) in a sick infant should raise the suspicion of a urea cycle disorder as well.[1]

- Hyperammonemic encephalopathy is manifested in infants by progressive lethargy, vomiting, and irritability. Plasma ammonium level and blood gases (to rule out respiratory alkalosis) should be included in the initial evaluation. If a urea cycle disorder is suspected, consult specialists in metabolic disorders and specialized references.[1,10]

- *Management:* The goal of therapy for urea cycle disorders is to prevent the development of hyperammonemia and its consequences and thus improve the long-term developmental outcome. Two strategies are used to reduce nitrogen accumulation and the need for urea nitrogen waste production: (1) Reduce dietary protein intake. (2) Give medications (see **Dose**, above) that can utilize latent biochemical pathways to synthesize and excrete waste nitrogen products. Because arginine (normally a nonessential amino acid) is an intermediate substrate in the urea cycle, it is an essential amino acid for patients who have deficiencies of CPS, OTC, AS, and AL (see Figure 1-2).

  For enteral feedings, infant formula manufacturers produce products specific for urea cycle disorders. Hemodialysis is used and may be the initial treatment of choice for very severe hyperammonemic encephalopathy. (Peritoneal dialysis and hemofiltration are not nearly as effective, and exchange transfusion offers little benefit.) Orthotopic liver transplant may be required if no other treatment is available.[1,5]

- *Nutrition:* Arginine HCl is an important dietary or intravenous constituent for preterm infants. Arginine is traditionally considered a nonessential amino acid in adults (one that need not be supplemented because it can be synthesized by the body), but it is considered essential for preterm infants (it must be supplemented because enzyme immaturity prevents synthesis of adequate amounts).[11]

  Historical note: In 1972, Heird and colleagues found that hyperammonemia occurred in infants on parenteral nutrition even though they were receiving a negligible amount of ammonia. They found that supplementing the amino acid solution of the parenteral nutrition with 0.5–1 mmol/kg/day of arginine HCl corrected these elevated blood ammonium levels.[12] Amino acid solutions are now manufactured with significantly more arginine HCl than was found in the protein hydrolysates or earlier crystalline amino acid (CAA) preparations described in Heird's study. Neonatal CAA solutions contain more arginine HCl than do adult solutions. (For the arginine contents of CAA solutions, see Table 2-5: Comparison of Neonatal CAA Solutions, page 614.)

Solubilizing Agent: Arginine is used in the product formulation of aztreonam to improve its solubility and stability. One gram of aztreonam contains 780 mg of arginine. (Aztreonam is a parenteral monobactam antibiotic having a β-lactam nucleus, with a spectrum of activity similar to the anti-Pseudomonas aminoglycosides such as amikacin.) The amount of arginine provided by aztreonam is approximately 0.3 mmol/kg/day, depending on the dose of aztreonam used, compared with 2.5–3 mmol/kg in growth hormone studies and

0.3 mmol/kg/day from human milk. High doses of arginine HCl are also given in parenteral nutrition.

Uauy and colleagues studied the metabolic tolerance to arginine HCl in preterm neonates receiving aztreonam. Serum arginine concentrations after 3 or more days of treatment with aztreonam were approximately four times higher than those in gentamicin-treated infants. A modest rise in both bilirubin and insulin blood levels occurred. The authors caution that exogenous glucose must be supplied in adequate amounts to prevent hypoglycemia when an arginine-containing antibiotic is used in preterm neonates. They concluded that the drug was well tolerated metabolically and could be used safely in the neonatal period with monitoring of serum glucose and bilirubin; however, it should be used cautiously in extremely low birth weight infants and in patients with congenital or acquired arginase deficiency or other conditions when tolerance to arginine HCl may be limited.[13]

MECHANISM OF ACTION

Arginine HCl is a dibasic amino acid essential for infant growth. The liver forms endogenous arginine from citrulline, ammonia, and aspartate in a series of steps known as the urea cycle (see Figure 1-2). In early life, arginine plays an important regulatory role in priming the urea cycle. CPS, OTC, AS, and AR are present at 16–20 weeks gestation and increase one- to threefold at birth. AS has the lowest relative activity and is the rate-limiting enzyme of the urea cycle in infants. The activities of the urea cycle enzymes are lower in infants at birth than in adults. Low enzyme activity leads to ammonium accumulation. Excess arginine HCl administration can lead to elevated urea (BUN).[11,14]

Arginine stimulates pancreatic release of glucagon and insulin and thus may play a role in anabolism. It increases blood glucose concentrations: The higher the dose of arginine HCl infused, the more glucose is released from the liver. It may also cause hypoglycemia due to release of insulin.[5]

Hypotensive Effect: Arginine is a precursor of nitric oxide (endothelium-derived relaxing factor). Nitric oxide acts as an intracellular signal that leads to smooth muscle relaxation, which has been cited as an explanation for the hypotensive effect that occurs with arginine HCl administration.[15]

Treatment of Metabolic Alkalosis: Arginine corrects severe metabolic alkalosis because of its chloride content (contains 0.475 mEq chloride/ml).

Growth Hormone Test: Arginine stimulates pituitary release of growth hormone and prolactin release that probably originates in the hypothalamus. Patients with impaired pituitary function show lower or no increases in plasma concentrations of growth hormone after administration of arginine HCl.

ADVERSE EFFECTS

Cardiovascular: Flushing with rapid IV administration.

Endocrine and Metabolic: Hyperglycemia; hypoglycemia; hyperkalemia (especially in patients with renal and/or hepatic dysfunction); hyperchloremic metabolic acidosis; elevated gastrin, glucagon, and growth hormone.

GI: GI upset with rapid IV administration; gastric irritation, abdominal pain, and bloating with oral administration.

Hematologic: Thrombocytopenia (rare).

Hypersensitivity: Rash, anaphylaxis, allergic reactions.

Infusion Site: Irritation of the vein with rapid IV administration. May cause tissue necrosis on extravasation.[16]

Renal: Elevated BUN and creatinine.

PHARMACOKINETICS/PHARMACODYNAMICS

Absorption: Well absorbed from GI tract.

Peak Effect: Peak elevations in plasma growth hormone concentrations occur at:

- *IV:* 1–2 hours after a 30-minute IV infusion.[17]
- *PO:* Approximately 2 hours after oral administration.

Metabolism: Hepatic.

Elimination: Filtered by the glomerulus and is almost completely reabsorbed by the renal tubules.[17]

NURSING IMPLICATIONS

Monitor IV site carefully to avoid IV extravasation injury. Monitor blood glucose and blood pressure.

Follow electrolyte and acid-base balance.

Monitor:

- *Treatment of metabolic alkalosis:* Monitor acid-base status (arterial or capillary blood gases), serum electrolytes, BUN, glucose.
- *Growth hormone test:* The plasma growth hormone level should rise after arginine HCl administration to >7 ng/ml in patients with normal pituitary function usually 60 minutes after the arginine HCl infusion is started (control range 0–6 ng/ml). Plasma growth hormone concentrations of <3 ng/ml in response to several stimuli may indicate severe pituitary growth hormone deficiency; concentrations of 3–7 ng/ml indicate partial growth hormone deficiency.[17]
- *Neonatal-onset urea cycle disorders:* Monitor urea, ammonium, and serum electrolytes.

COMMENTS

- Osmolarity is 950 mOsmol/liter.
- 1 mmol of arginine HCl = 210 mg; 1 mmol of arginine = 174 mg.

Interactions:

Spironolactone with arginine HCl in patients with severe hepatic disease may cause severe, potentially fatal, hyperkalemia. This probably results from an arginine-induced shift of potassium from cells, impaired hepatic metabolism of arginine, and/or a spironolactone-induced decrease in renal excretion of potassium. The effect of spironolactone on potassium lasts for several days after the drug is discontinued. Avoid concomitant use of arginine HCl and spironolactone or spironolactone-containing drugs such as Aldactazide (hydrochlorothiazide with spironolactone in combination).

References

1. Brusilow SW, and Maestri NE. 1996. Urea cycle disorders: Diagnosis, pathophysiology, and therapy. *Advances in Pediatrics* 43: 127–170.

2. Brusilow SW, et al. 1984. Treatment of episodic hyperammonemia in children with inborn errors of urea synthesis. *New England Journal of Medicine* 310(25): 1630–1634.

3. Parfite K, ed. 1999. *Martindale: The Complete Drug Reference,* 32nd ed. London: Pharmaceutical Press, 334.

4. Walter JH, and Leonard JV. 1987. Inborn errors of the urea cycle. *British Journal of Hospital Medicine* 38(3): 176–183.

5. Maestri NE, et al. 1991. Prospective treatment of urea cycle disorders. *Journal of Pediatrics* 119(6): 923–928.

6. Adrogue HJ, and Madias NE. 1998. Management of life-threatening acid-base disorders. Part 2. *New England Journal of Medicine* 338(2): 107–111.

7. Jospe N, and Forbes G. 1996. Fluids and electrolytes: Clinical aspects. *Pediatrics in Review* 17(11): 395–403.

8. Travis LB. 1996. Disorders of water, electrolyte, and acid-base physiology. In *Rudolph's Pediatrics,* 20th ed., Rudolph AM, Hoffman JIE, and Rudolph CD, eds. Stamford, Connecticut: Appleton & Lange, 1319–1331.

9. Urea Cycle Disorders Conference Group. 2001. Consensus statement from a conference for the management of patients with urea cycle disorders. *Journal of Pediatrics* 138(1 supplement): S1–S5.

10. Brusilow SW, and Horwich AL. 1994. Urea cycle enzymes. In *The Metabolic Basis of Inherited Disease,* Scriver C, et al., eds. New York: McGraw-Hill, 1187–1232.

11. Uauy R, Greene HL, and Heird WC. 1993. Conditionally essential nutrients: Cysteine, taurine, tyrosine, arginine, glutamine, choline, inositol, and nucleotides. In *Nutritional Needs of the Preterm Infant: Scientific Basis and Practical Guidelines,* Tsang RC, Lucas A, and Uauy R, eds. Baltimore: Lippincott Williams & Wilkins, 267–280.

12. Heird WC, et al. 1972. Hyperammonemia resulting from intravenous alimentation using a mixture of synthetic l-amino acids: A preliminary report. *Journal of Pediatrics* 81(1): 162–165.

13. Uauy R, et al. 1991. Metabolic tolerance to arginine: Implications for the safe use of arginine salt–aztreonam combination in the neonatal period. *Journal of Pediatrics* 118(6): 965–970.

14. Motil KJ. 1988. Protein needs for term and preterm infants. In *Nutrition During Infancy,* Tsang RC, and Nichols BL, eds. Philadelphia: Hanley & Belfus, 100–121.

15. Pedrinelli R, et al. 1995. Pressor, renal and endocrine effects of L-arginine in essential hypertensives. *European Journal of Clinical Pharmacology* 48(3-4): 195–201.

16. Bowlby HA, and Elanjian SI. 1992. Necrosis caused by extravasation of arginine hydrochloride (letter). *Annals of Pharmacotherapy* 26(2): 263–264.

17. McEvoy GK. 2000. *AHFS Drug Information.* Bethesda, Maryland: American Society of Health-System Pharmacists, 2306–2307.

ATRACURIUM (TRACRIUM)
(a-tra-KYUR-ee-um)

CENTRAL NERVOUS SYSTEM: NEUROMUSCULAR BLOCKER

DOSE

0.3 mg/kg/dose initially; then 0.1 mg/kg/dose every 15–25 minutes prn. Individualize dose.

Continuous Infusion: Has been given to neonates receiving anesthesia. After an initial IV dose of 0.4 mg/kg, infuse at 5–9 mcg/kg/minute.[1,2]

ADMINISTRATION

Rate: IV push slowly over at least 1 minute to minimize adverse cardiovascular side effects. May be given by continuous infusion.

Concentration: May give undiluted (10 mg/ml) or dilute in D_5W or 0.9 percent sodium chloride solution to 0.2 or 0.5 mg/ml.

Compatibility: Do not mix with alkaline solutions such as sodium bicarbonate. Flush line and needle between these two drugs to avoid inactivation and precipitation. See Appendix E: Y-Site Compatibility of Common NICU Drugs.

Storage: Refrigerate. When taken on transport, refrigerate immediately upon return. Discard diluted solution after 24 hours.

CAUTIONS/CONTRAINDICATIONS

Mechanical ventilation must be provided during use.

Drug does not provide analgesia or sedation, only paralysis.

USE

A neuromuscular blocking agent for skeletal muscle relaxation (paralysis) during surgical procedures such as PDA ligation and for severe, unresponsive seizures such as neonatal tetanus.

Significant changes in mechanical ventilator settings are sometimes required to prevent serious complications, such as a pneumothorax or pulmonary interstitial edema (PIE), in infants undergoing this therapy.

MECHANISM OF ACTION

Atracurium is a bisquaternary ammonium compound. It is a competitive non-depolarizing muscle relaxant.

ADVERSE EFFECTS

May cause histamine release at higher doses, but less than with tubocurarine or metocurine. Histamine response is more likely in older children than in infants.

Bradycardia is more common with atracurium than with other muscle relaxants. Tachycardia and hypotension occur uncommonly.

The greatest risk is hypoxemia from inadequate mechanical ventilation.[3]

A

PHARMACOKINETICS/PHARMACODYNAMICS

Onset of Action: 3–5 minutes.

Duration: 20–35 minutes of sufficient neuromuscular blockade. Duration of action is longer in infants than in children. Table 1-12 compares duration of action of various neuromuscular blockers. Also see monographs on pancuronium, succinylcholine, and vecuronium.

Recovery: 35–45 minutes.

Metabolism: A portion (40 percent) is degraded spontaneously by plasma esterases and Hofmann elimination (spontaneous alkaline hydrolysis); 60 percent is cleared by excretion and/or metabolism by the liver and/or other nonspecified routes.[4] Half-life is short, and accumulation does not occur. Infants are more sensitive to atracurium than are children.[5]

NURSING IMPLICATIONS

Mechanical ventilation must be provided during use.

Have reversal agents such as neostigmine and atropine at bedside.

Provide all paralyzed infants analgesia and/or sedation in conjunction with paralyzation. Consider concomitant infusion of fentanyl, morphine, or midazolam.

Provide range of motion, position changes, and eye lubrication to avoid side effects of paralyzation.

Consider need for bladder catheterization or Credé if urine output decreases.

Monitor for movement and side effects, including bradycardia.

COMMENTS

Reversal of Neuromuscular Blockade:

- *Mechanism of Reversal:* Neostigmine inhibits acetylcholinesterase at the neuromuscular junction, allowing the accumulation of acetylcholine, which

TABLE 1-12 ◆ DURATION OF ACTION OF NEUROMUSCULAR BLOCKERS

Drug	Short	Intermediate	Long
Depolarizing			
Succinylcholine	X		
Nondepolarizing			
Atracurium		X	
Tubocurarine			X
Metocurine			X
Pancuronium			X
Vecuronium		X	

Short: 5–10 minutes. *Intermediate:* About 1 hour. *Long:* About 2 hours.

Adapted from: Lerman J. 1993. Anesthesia. In *Pediatric Pharmacology and Therapeutics,* 2nd ed., Radde IC, and MacLeod SM, eds. St. Louis: Mosby-Year Book, 475–497.

TABLE 1-13 ◆ FACTORS AFFECTING NEUROMUSCULAR BLOCKING ACTION OF NONDEPOLARIZING DRUGS

Potentiators (Prolongation)	Antagonists (Shortening)
Acidosis	Alkalosis
Hypothermia	Epinephrine, norepinephrine
Neuromuscular disease	Increased potassium
Tetanus	Ranitidine
Hepatic disease	Theophylline
Cardiovascular disease	Corticosteroids
Other neuromuscular blockers	Carbamazepine
Aminoglycosides	
Magnesium sulfate	
Ketamine	
Clindamycin	
Decreased potassium (diuretics)	

Adapted from: Roberts RJ. 1984. *Drug Therapy in Infants: Pharmacologic Principles and Clinical Experience.* Philadelphia: WB Saunders, 310. Reprinted by permission.

can successfully compete with the neuromuscular blocker at the neuromuscular junction, thus restoring muscle activity. Atropine is also given to avert the non-neuromuscular effects of neostigmine, such as increased secretions, bronchoconstriction, and bradycardia.[2]

- *Dose:* Neostigmine 0.06 mg/kg/dose IV plus atropine 0.02 mg/kg/dose IV.
- *Onset of Reversal:* Approximately 10 minutes.

Interactions: Table 1-13 lists factors, including drugs, that both prolong and shorten the action of nondepolarizing drugs.

REFERENCES

1. Goudsouzian NG. 1988. Atracurium infusion in infants. *Anesthesiology* 68(2): 267–269.

2. Kalli I, and Meretoja OA. 1988. Infusion of atracurium in neonates, infants and children: A study of dose requirements. *British Journal of Anaesthesia* 60(6): 651–654.

3. Roberts RJ. 1984. *Drug Therapy in Infants: Pharmacologic Principles and Clinical Experience.* Philadelphia: WB Saunders, 308–312.

4. Fisher DM, et al. 1986. Elimination of atracurium in humans: Contributions of Hofmann elimination and ester hydrolysis versus organ-based elimination. *Anesthesiology* 65(1): 6–12.

5. Meakin G, et al. 1988. Comparison of atracurium-induced neuromuscular blockade in neonates, infants and children. *British Journal of Anaesthesia* 60(2): 171–175.

ATROPINE
(A-troe-peen)

CARDIOVASCULAR: ANTIARRHYTHMIC, ANTICHOLINERGIC; RESPIRATORY: BRONCHODILATOR

DOSE

0.01–0.03 mg/kg/dose every 4–6 hours prn. Usual dose is 0.01 mg/kg/dose.

With neostigmine for reversal of neuromuscular blockade: Neostigmine 0.06 mg/kg/dose with atropine 0.02 mg/kg/dose.

Advanced life support: 0.02 mg/kg/dose every 5 minutes.

- *Minimum:* Doses <0.1 mg may cause paradoxical bradycardea.
- *Maximum:* 0.5 mg.[1]

Respiratory dose via nebulization: 0.03–0.05 mg/kg/dose every 6–8 hours.[2]

ADMINISTRATION

IV preferred. May also be given IM, SC, ET, nebulization.

IV—*Rate:* Infuse over at least 1 minute to prevent tachycardia.

IV—*Concentration:* Use of the neonatal strength, 0.05 mg/ml, is preferred to improve accuracy in measurement of dose volume.

Nebulization: Dilute to a final total volume of 3 ml with normal saline or other concurrent medications and give by nebulization.

CAUTIONS/CONTRAINDICATIONS

Not effective for acute bronchospasm. Use faster-acting agents like β_2-adrenergic agent albuterol. Atropine inhibits mucociliary clearance in the respiratory tract for several hours after administration.

Do not use in patients with narrow-angle glaucoma (increased intraocular pressure can persist for up to 6 days), tachycardia, thyrotoxicosis, or obstructive GI or GU disease.

Infants and young children are especially susceptible to the toxic effects of anticholinergics like atropine. Increased response requiring dose adjustments has been reported in infants and children with spastic paralysis or brain damage. When environmental temperature is high, children are at increased risk for rapid rise in body temperature because of atropine's suppression of sweat gland activity.[3]

Paradoxical hyperexcitability may occur in children given large doses.[3]

Infants with Down syndrome have both an increased sensitivity to cardio-accelerator effects and are more suseptible to mydriasis.

USE

Used for older infants and children in advanced cardiac life support to treat bradycardia accompanied by poor perfusion or hypotension, although epinephrine may be more effective. Also used in the uncommon event of symptomatic bradycardia with AV block and vagally mediated bradycardia during attempts at intubation. Atropine should be used for bradycardia only after adequate oxygenation and ventilation have been ensured (because their lack can often cause bradycardia).[1] There is no evidence that atropine is useful in the acute phase of neonatal resuscitation in the delivery room.[4]

Used with neostigmine for reversal of nondepolarizing neuromuscular blocking agents such as atracurium or pancuronium.

Effective in preventing bradycardia after succinylcholine or during instrumentation of the airway.

Reduces respiratory tract secretions, although glycopyrrolate is usually used for this indication because it has fewer CNS side effects.

As an anticholinergic agent, may inhibit vagal activity, leading to relaxation of bronchial smooth muscle tone and bronchodilation of the airways. Logvinoff and colleagues reported improved lung function using atropine, suggesting that increased vagal activity may contribute to high airway resistance in BPD.[5]

Also see monograph on a related agent available for oral inhalation, ipratropium (a quaternary ammonium compound chemically related to atropine, but with fewer systemic side effects).

MECHANISM OF ACTION

Atropine is a competitive inhibitor of acetylcholine on muscarinic receptors (exocrine or secretory glands, smooth and cardiac muscle, and postganglionic cholinergic nerve terminals). Its actions are anticholinergic (parasympatholytic). Atropine antagonizes histamine and serotonin.

In advanced cardiac life support, atropine accelerates sinus or atrial pacemakers and increases atrioventricular conduction.[1]

Anticholinergics prevent increases in intracellular cyclic guanosine monophosphate (cyclic GMP), which are caused by interaction of acetylcholine with muscarinic receptors on bronchial smooth muscle.[1] Atropine causes greater dilation in larger than in smaller airways (improved airway conductance). It has its effect primarily on the central airways, whereas the β-adrenergics (metaproterenol) affect mainly the small airways. Kao and colleagues found that the bronchodilator effect of atropine was of similar magnitude and duration to that of metaproterenol and that there was no demonstrable synergy when the two were combined.[6]

ADVERSE EFFECTS

Usually well tolerated when given as a respiratory treatment in recommended doses. Kao and colleagues found no pupillary dilation, dry mouth, jitteriness, tremor, vomiting, or change in heart rate during their study.[6] Adverse effects are usually dose related.

Cardiovascular: Tachycardia and shortening of the PR interval; changes in rate, however, are less in infants than in the elderly, possibly because of diminished vagal tone.[7] The time to peak tachycardia is about 15 minutes, lasting about

6 hours.[8] Atropine has been shown *in vitro* to block the constricting effect of oxygen on the ductus arteriosus.[9] Arrhythmias may occur, particularly during the first 2 minutes after IV administration. Infants with Down syndrome have increased sensitivity to the cardioaccelerator effects, possibly because of a pharmacogenetic abnormality affecting autonomic receptors.

Dermatologic: Rash over upper trunk after administration, thought to result from release of histamine.[10]

GI: Reduced GI motility and constipation; abdominal distention with absent bowel activity; lowered esophageal sphincter tone with increased risk for regurgitation.

Ophthalmic: Mydriasis (especially in infants with Down syndrome) and cycloplegia.

PHARMACOKINETICS/PHARMACODYNAMICS

Absorption: Well absorbed. The pharmacologic activity of IM or IV atropine is two to three times greater than that of PO atropine. Some atropine is systemically absorbed when given by the respiratory route. The effects of atropine are more delayed and more prolonged than those of sympathomimetics such as isoetharine or isoproterenol.

Distribution: Well distributed throughout the body, including the CNS.

Peak Effect: Maximum clinical response (increased heart rate) at 12–16 minutes after IV administration.

Protein Binding: 20 percent.

Half-life: Half-life 4 hours (adults).

Elimination: Urine (80 percent unchanged).[11]

NURSING IMPLICATIONS

Monitor heart rate carefully before and after administration; continuous cardiac monitoring is required to detect arrhythmias and to monitor for tachycardia.

Follow abdominal exam carefully because drug decreases GI motility; if abdominal distention and decreased bowel sounds are noted, notify physician.

COMMENTS

Overdose: Symptoms are dose related: dilated pupils; dry mucous membranes; blurred vision; flushed, dry skin with rash (upper trunk, neck, and face); and fever (a serious problem in infants). Other symptoms include tachycardia, abdominal distention, reduced urine output, absent bowel activity, sedation followed by excitation, and cardiac arrhythmias.[11]

Interactions: May antagonize the actions of cisapride and metoclopramide because it has opposite pharmacologic effects on the GI tract.

As a Respiratory Aerosol Treatment:

- *Monitoring:* Monitor heart rate before, during, and after treatments. Reassess daily to taper to lowest effective dose.

- ***Dose Titration:*** Reduce dose to the next smaller dose and/or increase to the next longer interval when heart rate exceeds 180 bpm (if baseline heart rate was <150 bpm) or 200 bpm (if baseline heart rate was >150 bpm).

  Reduce dose or discontinue drug if excessive increase in heart rate or other adverse effects occur. Increase dose to the next larger dose and/or decrease interval to the next shorter interval if infant is still in respiratory distress after a trial of one to three doses. Do not increase dose if infant is experiencing adverse effects from current dose.

- ***Discontinuation of Treatment:*** Assess daily the effectiveness of and need for the drug. It there has been no improvement in respiratory status as measured by pulmonary mechanics, change in respiratory support, or clinical status after 24 hours, discontinue the drug. If heart rate continues above 180–200 bpm despite reduction in dose and lengthening of dosage interval, consider discontinuing drug or changing to another agent.

REFERENCES

1. American Heart Association, Emergency Cardiac Care Committee and Subcommittees. 1992. Guidelines for cardiopulmonary resuscitation and emergency cardiac care. Part VI: Pediatric advanced life support. *JAMA* 268(16): 2262–2275. (Comment in *JAMA,* 1992, 268[16]: 2297–2298; and *JAMA,* 1993, 269[20]: 2626.)

2. Taketomo CK, Hodding JH, and Kraus DM. 1993. *Pediatric Dosage Handbook.* Hudson, Ohio: Lexi-Comp.

3. United States Pharmacopeial Convention/USP DI. 1996. *Drug Information for the Health Care Professional,* 16th ed. Rockville, Maryland: United States Pharmacopeial Convention, 222.

4. American Heart Association, Emergency Cardiac Care Committee and Subcommittees. 1992. Guidelines for cardiopulmonary resuscitation and emergency cardiac care. Part VII: Neonatal resuscitation. *JAMA* 268(16): 2276–2281. (Comment in *JAMA,* 1992, 268[16]: 2297–2298.)

5. Logvinoff MM, et al. 1985. Bronchodilators and diuretics in children with BPD. *Pediatric Pulmonology* 1(4): 198–203.

6. Kao LC, Durand DJ, and Nickerson BG. 1989. Effects of inhaled metaproterenol and atropine on the pulmonary mechanics of infants with BPD. *Pediatric Pulmonology* 6(2): 74–80.

7. Shutt LE, and Bowes JB. 1979. Atropine and hyoscine. *Anesthesia* 34(5): 476–490.

8. Adams RG, et al. 1982. Plasma pharmacokinetics of intravenously administered atropine in normal human subjects. *Journal of Clinical Pharmacology* 22(10): 477–481.

9. Oberhansli-Weiss I, et al. 1972. The pattern and mechanism of response to oxygen by the ductus arteriosus and umbilical artery. *Pediatric Research* 6(9): 693–700.

10. Lerman J. 1993. Anesthesia. In *Pediatric Pharmacology and Therapeutics,* 2nd ed., Radde IC, and MacLeod SM, eds. St. Louis: Mosby-Year Book, 475–497.

11. Roberts RJ. 1984. *Drug Therapy in Infants: Pharmacologic Principles and Clinical Experience.* Philadelphia: WB Saunders, 284–287.

AZTREONAM (AZACTAM)
(az-TREE-oh-nam)

ANTI-INFECTIVE:
ANTIBIOTIC

DOSE

<1.2 kg: 60 mg/kg/day divided every 12 hours. Continue this interval until >4 weeks postnatal age.

1.2–2 kg:
- 0–7 days of age: 60 mg/kg/24 hours divided every 12 hours
- >7 days of age: 90 mg/kg/24 hours divided every 8 hours

>2 kg:
- 0–7 days of age: 90 mg/kg/24 hours divided every 8 hours
- >7 days of age: 120 mg/kg/24 hours divided every 6 hours[1]

Give half the usual dose in moderate renal dysfunction and one-fourth the usual dose in severe renal dysfunction.[2]

ADMINISTRATION

IV—*Rate:* May infuse over 3–5 minutes; however, infusion over 20–60 minutes by retrograde or syringe pump is preferred.

IV—*Concentration:* Maximum concentration is 20 mg/ml.

IV—*Compatibility:* See Appendix E: Y-Site Compatibility of Common NICU Drugs.

IM: Use the IM route only if necessary; IV administration is preferred in neonates. Give by deep IM. Reconstitute each gram of drug with 3 ml of normal saline or sterile water for injection.

USE

A parenteral monobactam antibiotic having a β-lactam nucleus, aztreonam is bactericidal, having a narrow antibacterial spectrum with an activity similar to the anti-Pseudomonas aminoglycosides.

Effective against Gram-negative aerobic bacteria, including most enteric bacilli, such as *Escherichia coli* and *Serratia marcescens, Pseudomonas aeruginosa, Klebsiella pneumoniae,* and *Haemophilus influenzae.*[3]

MECHANISM OF ACTION

Aztreonam acts by inhibiting bacterial cell wall synthesis and causing destruction of the bacterial cell wall.

ADVERSE EFFECTS

Hematologic: Transient eosinophilia (11 percent), leukopenia, thrombocytopenia, neutropenia, leukocytosis.

Hepatic: Transient increase in AST (SGOT), ALT (SGPT), and alkaline phosphatase.

Hypersensitivity Reactions: Rash.

Rare Effects: Phlebitis, hypotension, transient EKG changes (VPCs, PVCs, brady-cardia), seizures; transient increases in BUN/serum creatinine.

PHARMACOKINETICS/PHARMACODYNAMICS

Volume of Distribution: Largest in small preterm neonates <1 week postnatal age (0.29 liter/kg); decreases with increased postnatal and gestational ages and birth weight. Penetration into the CSF is higher at the beginning of therapy, suggesting increased penetration with meningeal inflammation.

Half-life: 3.12–9.9 hours in neonates.

Elimination: Directly correlated with postnatal age and birth weight.[4–6] Mostly excreted unchanged in the urine.

NURSING IMPLICATIONS

Monitor for hypotension and seizures.

If renal function deteriorates, adjust dose.

COMMENTS

Arginine is used in the product formulation of aztreonam to improve its solubility and stability (see arginine monograph).

REFERENCES

1. Nelson JD. 1996. *1996–1997 Pocketbook of Pediatric Antimicrobial Therapy*, 12th ed. Baltimore: Lippincott Williams & Wilkins, 16–17.

2. Manufacturer's product literature. Squibb, Princeton, New Jersey.

3. McEvoy GK. 1994. *AHFS Drug Information.* Bethesda, Maryland: American Society of Hospital Pharmacists, 164–172.

4. Likitnukul S, et al. 1987. Pharmacokinetics and plasma bactericidal activity of aztreonam in low-birth-weight infants. *Antimicrobial Agents and Chemotherapy* 31(1): 81–83.

5. Stutman HR, Marks MI, and Swabb EA. 1984. Single-dose pharmacokinetics of aztreonam in pediatric patients. *Antimicrobial Agents and Chemotherapy* 26(2): 196–199.

6. Bosso JA, and Black PG. 1991. The use of aztreonam in pediatric patients: A review. Pharmacotherapy 11(1): 20–25.

A

TABLE OF CONTENTS

B

B

BERACTANT (SURVANTA)
(ber-AKT-ant)

**RESPIRATORY:
SURFACTANT**

DOSE

Intratracheal: 4 ml/kg/dose. Use birth weight to calculate dose.

- Give in 4 increments, repositioning the infant with each dose. Inject each quarter-dose gently into the catheter over 2–3 seconds. Ventilate the infant after each quarter-dose for at least 30 seconds or until stable.

- 4 doses of 4 ml/kg can be given in the first 48 hours of life, no more frequently than every 6 hours.[1]

ADMINISTRATION

Supplied as: Intratracheal suspension 25 mg phospolipids/ml. Available in 4 or 8 ml vials.

Use a #5 French end-hole catheter and administer intratracheally.

Let warm to room temperature before use (but do not use artificial measures to warm Survanta). Unopened, unused vials warmed to room temperature may be returned to the refrigerator within 8 hours of warming and stored for future use. However, warmed, unopened vials should not be returned to the refrigerator more than once.

Do not shake. Swirl gently to resuspend.

Storage: Protect from light. Refrigerate unopened vials. Single use only. Discard unused portion.[1]

USE

A lung surfactant used to reduce the morbidity and mortality associated with respiratory distress syndrome (RDS) of the newborn. Deficiency of pulmonary surfactant is the main cause of RDS.[1,2]

MECHANISM OF ACTION

Beractant is a natural bovine lung extract containing phospholipids, neutral lipids, fatty acids, and surfactant-associated proteins to which dipalmitoylphosphatidylcholine (DPPC), palmitic acid, and tripalmitin are added to mimic the surface tension–lowering properties of natural human lung surfactant. Surfactant lowers surface tension on alveolar surfaces during respiration and stabilizes the alveoli against collapse.[3]

ADVERSE EFFECTS

Usually very well tolerated. Benefits exceed risks.

Most adverse effects occur during administration: transient bradycardia, oxygen desaturation. See **NURSING IMPLICATIONS.** Other less frequent effects: endotracheal tube reflux, pallor, vasoconstriction, hypotension, endotracheal tube blockage, hypertension, hypocarbia, hypercarbia, apnea, and pulmonary hemorrhage.

No increased incidence of intracranial hemorrhage is reported, based on pooled study results.[1,3]

PHARMACOKINETICS/PHARMACODYNAMICS

Metabolism: Beractant rapidly (within minutes) affects oxygenation and lung compliance.

NURSING IMPLICATIONS

Monitor the following during dosing: Heart rate, color, chest expansion, breath sounds, oxygen saturation, and ETT patency and position before and for 30 minutes after each dose.

Rapid improvements in lung function may require immediate reductions in peak inspiratory pressure, ventilator rate, and/or FiO$_2$.

If the infant becomes dusky or agitated or if the heart rate slows, oxygen saturation falls, or surfactant backs up the ETT, the rate of surfactant administration may need to be slowed, and ventilator settings may need to be increased. Monitor blood gases.

Avoid suctioning infant for 6–8 hours, if possible.

COMMENTS

Must be used in a neonatal center with neonatologists and others capable of neonatal intubation, mechanical ventilation, and medical management of unstable preterm infants. Qualified nurses and respiratory therapists should be available on-site when surfactant is administered, as should equipment, laboratory support, and radiology support for managing and monitoring preterm infants.[1,4]

REFERENCES

1. Manufacturer's product literature.

2. Dunn MS, et al. 1991. Bovine surfactant replacement therapy in neonates of less than 30 weeks' gestation: A randomized controlled trial of prophylaxis versus treatment. *Pediatrics* 87(3): 377–386.

3. Gomella TL, Cunningham MD, and Eyal FG. 1994. *Neonatology: Management, Procedures, On-call Problems, Diseases and Drugs,* 3rd ed. Norwalk, Connecticut: Appleton & Lange, 59–60.

4. American Academy of Pediatrics, Committee on Fetus and Newborn. 1991. Surfactant replacement therapy for respiratory distress syndrome. *Pediatrics* 87(6): 946–947.

BRETYLIUM (BRETYLOL)

(bre-TIL-ee-um)

CARDIOVASCULAR:
ANTIARRHYTHMIC

DOSE

Acute Emergencies:

- *IV: First dose:* 5 mg/kg/dose.
  Second dose: 10 mg/kg/dose may be given if ventricular fibrillation persists after an additional defibrillation attempt. May repeat every 15–30 minutes. *Maximum total dose:* 30 mg/kg.[1]
- *IM:* 2–5 mg/kg/dose as a single dose.

Maintenance: 5 mg/kg/dose IV or IM given every 6 hours.

Increase dosage interval in patients with renal dysfunction.

ADMINISTRATION

Supplied as: Injection: 50 mg/ml. Slight discoloration does not mean loss of potency.

IV—*Rate:* Rapid IV push over approximately 1 minute for life-threatening ventricular arrhythmias. For maintenance therapy, administer over 8 minutes or more.

IV—*Concentration:* May give undiluted for life-threatening emergencies. For maintenance therapy, dilute to 8 mg/ml with D_5W or normal saline.

IM: Give undiluted.

USE

An antiarrhythmic that has been used in treating ventricular tachycardia, ventricular fibrillation, or other serious ventricular arrhythmias if lidocaine and defibrillation are ineffective. The current Pediatric Advanced Life Support (PALS) recommendations, however, state that bretylium is no longer considered an appropriate agent because of the risk of hypotension, the lack of demonstrable effectiveness in ventricular tachycardia, and the absence of published studies of its use in children.[2]

Use in digitalized patients only if they have a life-threatening arrhythmia that is not caused by cardiac glycoside toxicity and is unresponsive to other antiarrhythmic drugs.[3]

MECHANISM OF ACTION

Bretylium is a Class III antiarrhythmic. An adrenergic blocking agent, it acts by inhibiting norepinephrine release by depressing adrenergic nerve terminal excitability, thereby chemically inducing a sympathectomy-like state.

ADVERSE EFFECTS

Cardiovascular: Hypotension, orthostatic hypotension, flushing, bradycardia. Possibility of transient hypertension and initial increase in arrhythmias, as well

B

as increased premature ventricular contraction due to initial release of nor-epinephrine from adrenergic postganglionic nerve terminals.

CNS: Dizziness.

GI: Rapid IV infusion often causes nausea and vomiting.

GU: Renal dysfunction.[3]

Local: Muscle necrosis, fibrosis, and atrophy with repeated IM injections at same site.

PHARMACOKINETICS/PHARMACODYNAMICS

IM: Peak plasma concentration is about 1 hour after IM administration; however, peak suppression of premature ventricular beats occurs about 6–9 hours after the IM dose.

IV: Antifibrillatory effect occurs within minutes; suppression of ventricular tachy-cardia and other ventricular arrhythmias occurs 20 minutes to 2 hours after IV dose. Duration of antiarrhythmic effect ranges from 6 to 24 hours.

Half-life: Half-life increases with decreasing renal function.

Elimination: Eliminated intact by the kidneys.

NURSING IMPLICATIONS

Monitor blood pressure and EKG continuously.

Keep patient supine to reduce risk of orthostatic hypotension, particularly during the first hour after dose.

If giving IM, rotate injection sites and do not administer near a major nerve.

COMMENTS

For short-term use only; change to an oral agent for maintenance therapy as soon as medical condition warrants.

Interactions: Bretylium increases the pressor effects of catecholamines such as dopamine and norepinephrine. Digoxin toxicity may be aggravated by the initial release of norepinephrine caused by bretylium.

REFERENCES

1. American Heart Association, Emergency Cardiac Care Committee and Subcommittees. 1992. Guidelines for cardiopulmonary resuscitation and emergency cardiac care. Part VI: Pediatric advanced life support. *JAMA* 268(16): 2262–2275. (Comment in *JAMA*, 1992, 268[16]: 2297–2298; and *JAMA*, 1993, 269[20]: 2626.)

2. The American Heart Association in collaboration with the International Committee on Resuscitation. 2000. Guidelines 2000 for cardiopulmonary resuscitation and emergency cardiovascular care. Part 10: Pediatric Advanced Life Support. *Circulation* 102(8supplement): I291–I342.

3. McEvoy GK. 1994. *AHFS Drug Information.* Bethesda, Maryland: American Society of Hospital Pharmacists, 982–984.

BUMETANIDE (BUMEX)
(byoo-MET-a-nide)

**CARDIOVASCULAR:
DIURETIC**

DOSE

0.02–0.2 mg/kg/dose every 8–12 hours. *Maximum:* 0.3 mg/kg/day.

Maintenance: Give on an intermittent schedule (every other day for 2–3 days, alternating with 1- to 2-day drug-free periods).[1–3]

Till and Rigby recommend 10–20 mcg/kg/dose 2–3 times daily IV or 10–60 mcg/kg/dose 2–3 times daily PO.[4]

ADMINISTRATION

PO: The injectable form has been given PO.

IV—*Rate:* Infuse slowly over 1–2 minutes.

IV—*Concentration:* May give undiluted.

IM: May give undiluted.

Compatibility: See Appendix E: Y-Site Compatibility of Common NICU Drugs.

USE

A potent loop diuretic used in infants with congenital heart disease and volume overload.[5,6]

MECHANISM OF ACTION

Bumetanide acts on the proximal tubule as well as on the ascending limb of the loop of Henle. Its action is similar to that of furosemide; however, it is 40 times more active than furosemide with regard to urinary excretion of sodium, chloride, potassium, and water. It has a more powerful inhibitory effect on sodium and water reabsorption than does furosemide.

ADVERSE EFFECTS

Electrolyte imbalances, such as hypokalemia, hyponatremia, hypochloremia, metabolic alkalosis.

Excessive volume depletion (dehydration, hemoconcentration).

Possible association with blood dyscrasias or hepatotoxicity.

Ototoxicity may occur, but is less likely than with furosemide.[6]

PHARMACOKINETICS/PHARMACODYNAMICS

Protein Binding: 96 percent.

Half-life: 2.5 hours in infants <6 months old.

Elimination: Renal clearance accounts for 30 percent of total plasma clearance.

NURSING IMPLICATIONS

Monitor for dehydration (fluid balance, urine output).

Monitor for electrolyte imbalances.

REFERENCES

1. Ward OC, and Lam LKT. 1977. Bumetanide in heart failure in infancy. *Archives of Disease in Childhood* 52(11): 877–882.

2. Benitz WE, and Tatro DS. 1995. *The Pediatric Drug Handbook,* 3rd ed. St. Louis: Mosby-Year Book, 233.

3. Greene MG. 1991. *The Harriet Lane Handbook,* 12th ed. St. Louis: Mosby-Year Book, 159.

4. Till JA, and Rigby ML. 1991. Treatment of cardiac disorders in the neonate. In *Neonatal Clinical Pharmacology and Therapeutics,* Rylance G, Harvey D, and Aranda JV, eds. Linacre House, Jordan Hill, Oxford: Butterworth-Heinemann, 126–152.

5. Chemtob S, et al. 1989. Pharmacology of diuretics in the newborn. *Pediatric Clinics of North America* 36(5): 1231–1250.

6. Witte MK, Stork JE, and Blumer JL. 1986. Diuretic therapeutics in the pediatric patient. *American Journal of Cardiology* 57(2): 44A–53A.

Table of Contents

CAFFEINE
(KAF-een)
(CAFCIT)

RESPIRATORY: APNEA/BRADYCARDIA

DOSE

Loading: 10 mg *caffeine base*/kg/dose. Reduce loading dose to 5 mg *caffeine base*/kg/dose if infant has received theophylline in previous 3–4 days.

Maintenance: 2.5 mg *caffeine base*/kg/dose every 24 hours. Begin 24 hours after loading dose.

Oral and IV doses are the same.

Write orders in terms of caffeine base. Caffeine citrate is 50 percent caffeine base; therefore, doses expressed as caffeine citrate are two times the dose of caffeine base (10 mg/kg caffeine base = 20 mg/kg caffeine citrate).

In 1992, Scanlon and associates recommended a higher dose because they considered that it would be safe to do so and because of greater efficacy: a loading dose of 25 mg caffeine base/kg, then a single daily dose of 6 mg caffeine base/kg/day. When the loading dose was given PO, it was given in two divided doses, 1 hour apart, to avoid GI upset.[1]

ADMINISTRATION

Supplied as: Injection: caffeine base 10 mg/ml (= caffeine citrate 20 mg/ml). Package labeling may lead to confusion; labeled as caffeine citrate 20 mg/ml, caffeine base 10 mg/ml, and 60 mg caffeine citrate per 3 ml vial. Read the label carefully.[2]

May be administered PO or IV. Not for IM use.

IV—*Rate:* Infuse over 30 minutes.

IV—*Concentration:* 10 mg/ml or less.

Preparation: An oral solution or an injection for use in neonates can be compounded by the pharmacist. Instructions for both solutions follow:

Pharmacist Compounding Directions

Caffeine Citrate Oral Solution (10 mg Caffeine Base/ml)[3,4]

Weigh 10 gm citrated caffeine powder (purified, Mallinckrodt). Dissolve in 250 ml sterile water for irrigation; then, using a 2:1 simple syrup/cherry syrup mixture, add a quantity sufficient to make a 500 ml solution and shake well.

Stability: 90 days at room temperature.

Caffeine Citrate Injection (10 mg Caffeine Base/ml)[3,5]

Prepare under laminar flow hood using aseptic technique. Weigh 20 gm citrated caffeine powder (purified, Mallinckrodt). Dissolve in 200 ml sterile water for injection. Filter twice with a 0.5 micron filter. Filter again using a 0.22 micron filter, and add enough sterile water for injection to equal 1,000 ml of solution. Transfer to 10 ml vials, autoclave, and seal. Send to laboratory to assay caffeine concentration. Send for sterility and pyrogen testing.

Stability: 90 days.

USE

Reduces the frequency and severity of neonatal apnea/bradycardia.[6]

MECHANISM OF ACTION

Caffeine stimulates the respiratory center, blocks adenosine receptors, and improves respiratory muscle contraction (see Table 1-8, page 42). It also increases neuromuscular transmission, which may increase muscle tone. Improved respiratory muscle tone has been related to increased functional residual capacity and better oxygenation in the newborn. Caffeine increases metabolic rate, which may lead to improved oxygenation and increased cardiac output. Improved metabolic rate may increase blood glucose. A release of catecholamines and an alteration in sleep-wake states may occur.[7] Both caffeine and theophylline have produced bronchodilation in preterm infants with BPD.[8]

ADVERSE EFFECTS

Usually very well tolerated in neonates whose serum concentrations are <50 mcg/ml. Above that level, jitteriness, tachycardia, and mild glycosuria have occurred.

The diuretic effect of caffeine is much weaker than that of theophylline; caffeine appears to have no effect on renal loss of fluid and electrolytes in the neonate.[7]

PHARMACOKINETICS/PHARMACODYNAMICS

Absorption: Rapidly and completely absorbed from GI tract. Peak levels are attained 30 minutes to 2 hours after dosing.

Metabolism: Metabolized by hepatic microsomal mixed-function mono-oxygenase system.

Half-life: 100 hours.

Elimination: Excreted largely unchanged in the urine.[9]

NURSING IMPLICATIONS

Monitor serum levels.

Monitor for signs of toxicity, such as jitteriness, poor sleep patterns, and tachycardia.

Hold dose and notify physician if heart rate is >180 bpm.

Monitor for GI upset and feeding intolerance.

COMMENTS

Drawing Caffeine Plasma Concentrations: Wait at least 30 minutes after completion of IV infusion and 1–2 hours after an oral dose; otherwise, blood may be drawn at any time during the dosing interval.

Therapeutic Range: 5–20 mcg/ml.

TABLE 1-14 ◆ COMPARISON OF CAFFEINE AND THEOPHYLLINE

Variable	Caffeine	Theophylline
Efficacy	+++	+++
Peripheral side effects	+/−	+++
Drug clearance	Very slow ($t_{1/2}$ = 100 hours)	Slow ($t_{1/2}$ = 30 hours)
Plasma level at steady state	Stable	Fluctuating
Need for drug monitoring	+/−	+++
Dosing interval	Once a day	1–3 times per day
Drug monitoring	HPLC/EMIT	HPLC/EMIT

+++ = very high; +/− = little to none; HPLC = high-performance liquid chromatography; EMIT = enzyme multiplied immunoassay technique; $t_{1/2}$ = half-life

Adapted from: Aranda JV, et al. 1991. Treatment of neonatal apnoea. In *Neonatal Clinical Pharmacology and Therapeutics,* Rylance G, Harvey D, and Aranda J, eds. Linacre House, Jordan Hill, Oxford: Butterworth-Heinemann Publishers, a division of Reed Educational & Professional Publishing Ltd., 98. Reprinted by permission.

Interactions:

- Infants given theophylline and phenobarbital have been shown to require higher doses of theophylline to control apnea and higher doses of phenobarbital to control seizures.[10]
- Cimetidine increases caffeine serum levels.
- Caffeine reduces the effectiveness of adenosine.

Discontinuing the Drug: Consider discontinuing caffeine when the infant is 34–36 weeks gestational age and has not had apneic spells for 1 week or more.

Comparison of Caffeine and Theophylline: Table 1-14 compares caffeine to theophylline for use in the treatment of apnea of prematurity. Some advantages of caffeine include:

- Higher therapeutic index (i.e., caffeine levels up to 50 mcg/ml have been reported with no side effects, whereas theophylline levels >15 mcg/ml may be associated with tachycardia).
- Once-daily dosing.
- Fewer adverse effects.
- Less need for drug level monitoring.
- Theophylline is methylated to caffeine, with plasma theophylline to caffeine ratios sometimes reaching 0.3 to 0.4 at steady state. Thus, the overall methylxanthine effect results from the sum of the activity of the two drugs because both drugs are pharmacologically active.[6,11]

REFERENCES

1. Scanlon JEM, et al. 1992. Caffeine or theophylline for neonatal apnoea? *Archives of Disease in Childhood* 67(4): 425–428.

2. Institute for Safe Medication Practices. February 9, 2000. *ISMP Medication Safety Alert!* www.ismp.org.

3. Eisenberg MG, and Kang N. 1984. Stability of citrated caffeine solutions for injectable and enteral use. *American Journal of Hospital Pharmacy* 41(11): 2405–2406.

4. American Society of Hospital Pharmacists, Committee on Extemporaneous Formulations. 1987. *Handbook on Extemporaneous Formulations.* Bethesda, Maryland: American Society of Hospital Pharmacists, 6.

5. Nahata MC, and Roberts DL. 1987. Formulation of caffeine injection for IV administration (letter). *American Journal of Pharmacy* 44(6): 1308, 1312.

6   Aranda JV, et al. 1977. Efficacy of caffeine in treatment of apnea in the low-birth-weight infant. *Journal of Pediatrics* 90(3): 467–472.

7. Aranda JV, et al. 1991. Treatment of neonatal apnea. In *Neonatal Clinical Pharmacology and Therapeutics,* Rylance G, Harvey D, and Aranda J, eds. Linacre House, Jordan Hill, Oxford: Butterworth-Heinemann, 95–115.

8. Davis JM, et al. 1989. Changes in pulmonary mechanics following caffeine administration in infants with bronchopulmonary dysplasia. *Pediatric Pulmonology* 6(1): 49–52.

9. Roberts RJ. 1984. *Drug Therapy in Infants: Pharmacologic Principles and Clinical Experience.* Philadelphia: WB Saunders, 119–137.

10. Yazdani M, et al. 1987. Phenobarbital increases theophylline requirement of premature infants being treated for apnea. *American Journal of Diseases of Children* 141(1): 97–99.

11. Aranda JV, et al. 1979. Metabolism of theophylline to caffeine in human fetal liver. *Science* 206(4424): 1319–1321.

CALCITRIOL

(kal-si-TRYE-ole)

(ROCALTROL, CALCIJEX)

NUTRITION: MINERAL SUPPLEMENT

DOSE

0.01–0.05 mcg/kg/24 hours PO or IV as a single daily dose

For Hypocalcemic Tetany of Preterm Infants: 0.05 mcg/kg IV daily for 5–12 days[1]

ADMINISTRATION

Supplied as: 1 and 2 mcg/ml ampoules; 0.25 and 0.5 mcg capsules.

IV—*Rate:* Infuse over at least 1 minute.

IV—*Concentration:* May give undiluted.

IV—*Compatibility:* No data exist on compatibility in parenteral nutrition solutions. Therefore, admixture in parenteral nutrition solutions cannot be recommended.

PO: No oral liquid is commercially available; instead, the oral dose may be prepared in one of three ways:

- Puncture capsule with an 18-gauge needle and squeeze contents into a syringe. Note the total volume; then give the appropriate dose increment (i.e., for a dose of 0.125 mcg, give half the volume drawn from a 0.25 mcg capsule).
- Parenteral calcitriol (Calcijex) may be given PO.
- The pharmacist can compound an oral liquid (calcitriol in oil) as follows:

Pharmacist Compounding Directions
Calcitriol Oral Liquid (Calcitriol in Oil 50 mcg/ml)[2]

Puncture 10 Rocaltrol 50 mcg capsules with an 18-gauge needle.

Squeeze capsule contents into a small conical graduate. (***Note:*** Do ***not*** use a needle and syringe to withdraw contents of each capsule because more drug can be removed by squeezing the capsules than by attempting to draw out the contents with a needle and syringe.) Add enough corn oil to equal 10 ml total volume.

Stability: 7 days at room temperature.

Storage: Store in a small amber glass bottle. Wrap in foil to protect completely from light.

CAUTIONS/CONTRAINDICATIONS

Do not use if patient has hypercalcemia.

USE

Used to treat rickets of prematurity (nutritional rickets, osteopenia of prematurity), along with calcium and phosphorus supplementation, as needed.[3]

Also used to manage hypocalcemia associated with hypoparathyroidism or pseudohypoparathyroidism and to manage hypocalcemia in patients undergoing chronic renal dialysis.

The vitamin D needs of preterm infants are similar to those of term infants. Because calcitriol is more expensive than ergocalciferol (vitamin D_2, Drisdol drops, Calciferol drops) and because calcitriol is not commercially available as an oral liquid, it should be reserved for infants who cannot adequately metabolize ergocalciferol[1] or for those who need an IV vitamin D analog.

MECHANISM OF ACTION

Calcitriol is an activated form of vitamin D (1,25-dihydroxycholecalciferol) and therefore does not require hepatic or renal activation. Vitamin D is a fat-soluble vitamin. It undergoes hydroxylation in the liver to 25-hydroxyvitamin D, which is used as a serum indicator of vitamin D status. The 25-hydroxyvitamin D metabolite is further converted to 1,25-dihydroxyvitamin D, the most physiologically active form of vitamin D, in the kidney.

Preterm infants appear to have adequate 25-hydroxylase activity.[4] It acts on intestine, bone, and kidney to ensure calcium and phosphorus homeostasis. It increases serum calcium and phosphate concentrations principally by increasing intestinal absorption of calcium and phosphate.[1,5]

For calcitriol to be effective, the patient should have an adequate calcium intake. Deficiency of vitamin D in infancy results in rickets.

ADVERSE EFFECTS

Hypercalcemia, hyperphosphatemia, hypercalciuria.

Mild pain at injection site.

Early and late signs and symptoms of vitamin D intoxication associated with hypercalcemia include:[6]

- *Early:* Weakness, somnolence, GI upset, constipation, muscle and bone pain.
- *Late:* Polyuria, anorexia, weight loss, growth retardation, conjunctivitis, pancreatitis, rhinorrhea, hyperthermia, elevated BUN, albuminuria, elevated SGOT and SGPT, ectopic calcification, hypertension, cardiac arrhythmias.

May increase cardiac arrhythmias in patients on digoxin because of the increased serum calcium concentration.

PHARMACOKINETICS/PHARMACODYNAMICS

Absorption: Well absorbed from the GI tract if fat absorption is normal. Oral absorption of vitamin D analogs requires bile. Increased calcium absorption from the GI tract occurs approximately 2 hours after oral absorption of calcitriol.

Maximum Hypercalcemic Effect: 10 hours.

Duration: 3–5 days.

Elimination: The metabolites of vitamin D analogs are excreted primarily in the bile and feces.

NURSING IMPLICATIONS

Measure dose carefully.

Monitor serum calcium and phosphorus twice weekly initially. If hypercalcemia occurs, withhold dose until calcium blood level is normal, then reinstitute at a lower dose. Hypercalcemia usually resolves within 2–7 days.[6]

REFERENCES

1. McEvoy GK. 1994. *AHFS Drug Information.* Bethesda, Maryland: American Society of Hospital Pharmacists, 2412–2413.

2. American Society of Hospital Pharmacists, Committee on Extemporaneous Formulations. 1987. *Handbook on Extemporaneous Formulations.* Bethesda, Maryland: American Society of Hospital Pharmacists, 7.

3. Chan GM, et al. 1978. The effect of 1,25 (OH) vitamin D supplementation in premature infants. *Journal of Pediatrics* 93(1): 91–96.

4. Glorieux F, et al. 1981. Vitamin D metabolism in preterm infants: Serum calcitriol values during the first five days of life. *Journal of Pediatrics* 99(4): 640–643.

5. Specker BL, Greer F, and Tsang RC. 1988. Vitamin D. In *Nutrition During Infancy,* Tsang RC, and Nichols BL, eds. Philadelphia: Hanley & Belfus, 264–276.

6. Manufacturer's product literature.

CALCIUM CASEINATE

(KAL-see-um KAY-see-in-ate)

(CASEC)

**NUTRITION:
PROTEIN SUPPLEMENT**

DOSE

1–2.5 gm/kg/day. *Maximum:* 4 gm/kg/day including protein from other sources, such as infant formula.

Order in increments of measuring spoons (e.g., 1/8, 1/4, 1/2 teaspoon) per 24-hour feeding volume. One packed level teaspoonful of casec powder contains 1.4 gm protein.

ADMINISTRATION

Supplied as: 2.5 ounce (70.88 gm) can.

PO: For enteral use only.

Preparation:

- Measure powder with measuring spoon. Pack powder in spoon of appropriate size and level off (Table 1-15). When adding to liquids, mix powder with a small amount of the liquid to make a smooth paste. Gradually stir in the rest of the liquid.

- Alternatively, powder may be measured in an empty syringe with the plunger removed (Table 1-15). Add powder to back of syringe, pack down with plunger to correct volume. Then remove plunger and pour powder from back of syringe into liquid, as above.

- May be mixed with infant formula, breast milk, or foods such as cereals, vegetables, or meats.

CAUTIONS/CONTRAINDICATIONS

Should not be used as the sole source of nutrition.

USE

An oral protein hydrolysate powder used to supplement enterally fed infants with inadequate intake or increased loss of protein. May be useful in chronically fluid-restricted infants and as a breast milk supplement. Also provides additional calcium and phosphorus.

TABLE 1-15 ◆ CASEC POWDER MEASURING INSTRUCTIONS

Measure	Protein (gm)	ml (Using a Syringe to Measure Dry Powder)
1 tsp =	1.4	5
½ tsp =	0.7	2.5
¼ tsp =	0.35	1.25
⅛ tsp =	0.18	0.63

TABLE 1-16 ◆ COMPOSITION OF CALCIUM CASEINATE

Component*	100 gm Powder	1 gm Powder	1 Tablespoon	1 Teaspoon
Protein (gm)	88	0.88	4.1	1.4
Calcium (mg)	1,600	16	80	27
Phosphorus (mg)	800	8	40	13
Calories	370	3.7	17	5.7

* Also contains negligible amounts of sodium and potassium; 100 gm contains 120 mg (5 mEq) sodium and 10 mg (0.25 mEq) potassium.

ADVERSE EFFECTS

Renal solute load is 520 mOsm/100 gm. Increases the solute load of the feeding; excessive dose may exceed the renal capacity of the infant and cause dehydration. High renal solute loads increase the amount of water obligated for renal excretion.

NURSING IMPLICATIONS

Store in a cool, dry place. Do not refrigerate. Cover opened can with plastic overcap provided. Once opened, use can within 1 month.

When mixed with feedings, cover, refrigerate, and use within 24 hours.

COMMENTS

Source: Derived from skim milk curd and lime water (calcium carbonate). See Table 1-16 for composition.[1]

Addition of up to 4 gm/100 ml to an Isocal-type formula causes no measurable increase in osmolality.

REFERENCE

1. Mead Johnson. 1994. *Mead Johnson Nutritional Pediatric Products Handbook.* Evansville, Indiana: Mead Johnson, 2.

CALCIUM CHLORIDE
(KAL-see-um KLOR-ide)

ELECTROLYTE BALANCE: ELECTROLYTE SUPPLEMENT

DOSE

Doses are expressed as calcium chloride, not as elemental calcium.

Cardiac Arrest with Hypocalcemia or Hyperkalemia, Magnesium Toxicity, or Calcium Agonist Toxicity: 20 mg/kg/dose. May repeat in 10 minutes as needed.[1,2]

ADMINISTRATION

Supplied as: Injection: 100 mg/ml (10 percent).

IV—*Rate:* May infuse over at least 1 minute for cardiac resuscitation, but administration over 1 hour or by continuous infusion over 24 hours is preferred.

IV—*Concentration:* Maximum concentration for peripheral line (to reduce risk of extravasation injury): 1 mg calcium chloride/ml. For central IV infusion, dilute to a maximum concentration of 20 mg/ml.[1] Infusion via a central line is preferred.

IV—*Compatibility:* Avoid mixing calcium salts with sodium bicarbonate because precipitation will occur. Flush line before and after doses to avoid catheter occlusion. Dilute calcium bolus with D_5W, sterile water, or saline—***not*** with parenteral nutrition—to avoid precipitation and to minimize osmolality. See Appendix E: Y-Site Compatibility of Common NICU Drugs.

USE

Cardiac resuscitation in the presence of hypocalcemia or hyperkalemia, magnesium toxicity, or calcium agonist toxicity. Calcium gluconate, rather than calcium chloride, is usually used for other indications in neonates because:

- Calcium chloride increases the amount of chloride being given to the infant, thereby increasing the risk of acidosis.

- The higher concentration of calcium in calcium chloride (calcium chloride = 27 percent, calcium gluconate = 9 percent) makes it more risky in case of overdose and more caustic in case of extravasation.

- Calcium chloride is less compatible with parenteral nutrition because calcium chloride dissociates in solution to a greater extent than calcium gluconate to yield free calcium, which is then available for precipitation with phosphate. See **Conversion Factors** under **COMMENTS.**

Neonatal Resuscitation: There is no evidence that calcium is useful in the acute phase of neonatal resuscitation in the delivery room. In hyperkalemia or severe hypocalcemia, calcium and sodium bicarbonate are required, but these conditions are not common immediately after birth.[2]

TABLE 1-17 ◆ **CONVERSION OF CALCIUM SALTS**

Calcium Salt 1 gm	Product	% Elemental Calcium	mg of Elemental Calcium/gm	mEq of Elemental Calcium/gm*
Calcium carbonate	Calcium carbonate oral suspension (Roxane)	40	400	20
Calcium chloride	10% injection	27	270	13.5
Calcium glubionate	Neo-Calglucon syrup	6.4	64	3.2
Calcium gluconate	10% injection	9	93	4.6
Calcium lactate	325 and 650 mg tabs	13	130	6.5

* One mEq of elemental calcium is equivalent to 20 mg of elemental calcium.

MECHANISM OF ACTION

Calcium has a structural function as the major component of bone mineral. Trace amounts are also present in soft tissue, where calcium plays important roles in cellular metabolism: activation of synaptic transmitter substances, mitochondrial function, the formation of cyclic AMP, modulation of the excitatory threshold, blood coagulation, and sodium permeability of cells.[3,4]

ADVERSE EFFECTS

Bradycardia, hypotension, cardiac arrhythmias with too-rapid infusion. Patient should be on a cardiorespiratory monitor and observed closely during bolus dose infusions.

Extravasation causes severe tissue damage with sloughing. Observe IV site frequently. (See Appendix G: Guidelines for Management of Intravenous Extravasations.)

Hypercalcemia, hypomagnesemia.

PHARMACOKINETICS/PHARMACODYNAMICS

Elimination: In urine and feces.[3]

NURSING IMPLICATIONS

Monitor IV site closely for early signs of infiltration.

Monitor vital signs continuously; rapid IV administration can cause bradycardia and arrhythmias.

Monitor calcium levels (ionized calcium preferred).

COMMENTS

Conversion Factors: Calcium chloride 10 percent (100 mg/ml) provides 1.35 mEq/ml or 27 mg/ml of elemental calcium. 1 mEq of elemental calcium is equivalent to 20 mg of elemental calcium (Table 1-17).

Interactions: High serum calcium increases the risk of cardiac arrhythmias in infants on digoxin.

REFERENCES

1. Taketomo CK, Hodding JH, and Kraus DM. 1997. *Pediatric Dosage Handbook.* Hudson, Ohio: Lexi-Comp, 114–115.

2. American Heart Association, Emergency Cardiac Care Committee and Subcommittees. 1992. Guidelines for cardiopulmonary resuscitation and emergency cardiac care. Part VII: Neonatal resuscitation. *JAMA* 268(16): 2276–2281. (Comment in *JAMA,* 1992, 168[16]: 2297–2298.)

3. Koo WK, and Tsang RC. 1993. Calcium, magnesium, phosphorus, and vitamin D. In *Nutritional Needs of the Preterm Infant: Scientific Basis and Practical Guidelines,* Tsang RC, et al., eds. Baltimore: Lippincott Williams & Wilkins, 135–155.

4. American Academy of Pediatrics, Committee on Nutrition. 1993. Calcium, phosphorus, and magnesium. In *Pediatric Nutrition Handbook,* Barness LA, ed. Elk Grove Village, Illinois: American Academy of Pediatrics, 115–124.

CALCIUM GLUBIONATE
(KAL-see-um gloo-BY-oh-nate)
(NEO-CALGLUCON)

ELECTROLYTE BALANCE: MINERAL SUPPLEMENT

DOSE

600–2,000 mg/kg/day PO divided every 3–6 hours (**Maximum:** 9 gm/day)[1]
   (Dose is expressed in terms of calcium glubionate, which is 6.4 percent
   elemental calcium; note that calcium gluconate is 9 percent elemental calcium
   [see Table 1-17, page 101].)

ADMINISTRATION

PO: For oral use only.

Concentration: 360 mg of calcium glubionate/ml. This drug is a thick, sugary
   syrup that is hyperosmolar; therefore, dilute it before use. May be administered
   in a small amount of infant feeding.

USE

Hypocalcemia, osteopenia of prematurity (nutritional rickets).

Because of its lower osmolality, calcium gluconate in the injectable form
   (see calcium gluconate monograph) is preferred over calcium glubionate for
   PO administration (use the injectable form, but give PO).

MECHANISM OF ACTION

Calcium has a structural function as the major component of bone mineral.[2] Trace
   amounts are also present in soft tissue, where calcium plays important roles in
   cellular metabolism: activation of synaptic transmitter substances, mitochondrial function, the formation of cyclic AMP, modulation of the excitatory
   threshold, blood coagulation, and sodium permeability of cells.[3,4]

ADVERSE EFFECTS

May cause diarrhea, especially if given undiluted, because the vehicle in Neo-
   Calglucon is sucrose 20 percent.

Excessive doses may cause hypercalcemia and hypercalciuria. Monitor serum
   calcium concentration.

PHARMACOKINETICS/PHARMACODYNAMICS

Absorption: Ranges from 21 percent to 70 percent. Influenced by parathyroid
   hormone, vitamin D, and other factors.

Elimination: Eliminated in the urine and feces.[2]

NURSING IMPLICATIONS

Dilute in formula.

Monitor for GI upset because calcium glubionate may cause feeding intolerance as
   a result of its extreme hyperosmolarity.

Monitor for response to therapy by noting calcium, phosphorus, and alkaline phosphatase levels weekly.

COMMENTS

Provides 4.14 kcal/5 ml.

REFERENCES

1. Taketomo CK, Hodding JH, and Kraus DM. 1996. *Pediatric Dosage Handbook,* 3rd ed. Hudson, Ohio: Lexi-Comp, 110.

2. Seeley RR, et al. 1992. *Anatomy and Physiology.* St. Louis: Mosby-Year Book, 171.

3. American Academy of Pediatrics, Committee on Nutrition. 1993. Calcium, phosphorus, and magnesium. In *Pediatric Nutrition Handbook,* Barness LA, ed. Elk Grove Village, Illinois: American Academy of Pediatrics, 115–124.

4. Tsang RC, Donovan EF, and Steichen JJ. 1976. Calcium physiology and pathology in the neonate. *Pediatric Clinics of North America* 23(4): 611–626.

CALCIUM GLUCONATE

(KAL-see-um GLOO-coh-nate)

ELECTROLYTE BALANCE: ELECTROLYTE SUPPLEMENT

DOSE

Doses are expressed as mg of calcium gluconate.

Maintenance: 200–800 mg/kg/day.

Cardiac Arrest with Hypocalcemia or Hyperkalemia, Magnesium Toxicity, or Calcium Agonist Toxicity: 100 mg/kg/dose every 10 minutes, but see **Neonatal Resuscitation** below under USE.[1] (See also Appendix O: Neonatal Cardiopulmonary Resuscitation and Postresuscitation Drug Doses.)

Exchange Transfusion: Citrated whole blood may bind calcium and cause hypocalcemia. Supplement with 100 mg (0.45 mEq of elemental calcium) of calcium gluconate per 100 ml of citrated blood transfused.

ADMINISTRATION

IV—*Rate:* For maintenance, give by continuous infusion over 24 hours (preferred). For bolus doses, infuse over at least 30 minutes. For cardiac resuscitation, infuse slowly over at least 1 minute.

IV—*Concentration:* Maximum for peripheral line (to reduce risk of extravasation injury): 3 mg calcium gluconate/ml for continuous infusion in the 24-hour fluid volume (preferred). For a bolus infusion, usually over one hour, 100 mg/ml concentration may be used in a peripheral line. However, the line must be observed very closely while calcium is infusing because the risk of tissue damage if it infiltrates is much greater with the 100 mg/ml than the 3 mg/ml concentration. Higher concentrations may be given via a central line.

IV—*Compatibility:* Avoid mixing calcium salts with sodium bicarbonate because precipitation will occur. Flush lines before and after doses to avoid catheter occlusion. Dilute calcium bolus with D_5W, sterile water, or saline—***not*** with parenteral nutrition—to avoid precipitation and minimize osmolality. See Appendix E: Y-Site Compatibility of Common NICU Drugs.

PO: Calcium gluconate injection may be given PO.

USE

For provision of maintenance calcium,[2] to treat hypocalcemia, to prevent hypocalcemia during exchange transfusion, to treat cardiac disturbances of hypokalemia, as an antidote for acute adverse effects of calcium channel blockers or overdose of the same, and for cardiac resuscitation when other agents have failed.

Neonatal Resuscitation: There is no evidence that calcium is useful in the acute phase of neonatal resuscitation in the delivery room. In hyperkalemia or severe hypocalcemia, calcium and sodium bicarbonate are required, but these conditions are not common immediately after birth.[1] The chloride salt of calcium (calcium chloride 20 mg/kg) is preferred over calcium gluconate for use in cardiac resuscitation. (See monograph on calcium chloride.)

MECHANISM OF ACTION

Calcium has a structural function as the major component of bone mineral. Trace amounts are also present in soft tissue, where calcium plays important roles in cellular metabolism: activation of synaptic transmitter substances, mitochondrial function, the formation of cyclic AMP, modulation of the excitatory threshold, blood coagulation, and sodium permeability of cells.[3]

ADVERSE EFFECTS

Bradycardia, hypotension, cardiac arrhythmias with too-rapid infusion. Patient should be on a cardiorespiratory monitor and observed closely during bolus dose infusions.

Extravasation causes severe tissue damage with sloughing. Observe IV site frequently. (See Appendix G: Guidelines for Management of Intravenous Extravasations.)

Hypercalcemia, hypomagnesemia.

Interactions: High serum calcium increases the risk of cardiac arrhythmias in infants on digoxin.

PHARMACOKINETICS/PHARMACODYNAMICS

Elimination: In urine and feces.[3]

NURSING IMPLICATIONS

Monitor IV sites closely for early signs of infiltration.

Monitor vital signs continuously; rapid IV administration can cause bradycardia and arrhythmias.

Monitor calcium levels. Ionized calcium preferred.

PO dosing may cause GI upset.

COMMENTS

Conversion Factors: Calcium gluconate 10 percent (100 mg/ml) provides 0.46 mEq/ml or 9.3 mg/ml of elemental calcium. 1 mEq of elemental Ca is equivalent to 20 mg elemental calcium (see Table 1-17, page 101).

REFERENCES

1. American Heart Association, Emergency Cardiac Care Committee and Subcommittees. 1992. Guidelines for cardiopulmonary resuscitation and emergency cardiac care. Part VII: Neonatal resuscitation. *JAMA* 268(16): 2276–2281. (Comment in *JAMA,* 1992, 268[16]: 2297–2298.)

2. Koo WK, and Tsang RC. 1993. Calcium, magnesium, phosphorus, and vitamin D. In *Nutritional Needs of the Preterm Infant,* Tsang RC, et al, eds. Baltimore: Lippincott Williams & Wilkins, 135–155.

3. American Academy of Pediatrics, Committee on Nutrition. 1993. Calcium, phosphorus, and magnesium. In *Pediatric Nutrition Handbook,* Barness LA, ed. Elk Grove Village, Illinois: American Academy of Pediatrics, 115–124.

CALFACTANT (INFASURF)

(cal-FAC-tant)

RESPIRATORY:
SURFACTANT

DOSE

Intratracheal: 3 ml/kg body weight at birth for the first dose (administered as two 1.5 ml aliquots). 3 ml contain 105 mg of phospholipids.

- A total of 3 doses given at 12-hour intervals has been used in clinical trials when the patient was still intubated.[1]
- **Prophylactic Dose:** Give as soon as possible after birth. Immediate care and stabilization of the infant born with hypoxemia and/or bradycardia is usually recommended prior to initiating calfactant prophylaxis.

ADMINISTRATION

Supplied as: Intratracheal suspension: 35 mg total phospholipids per ml. (The 35 mg of total phospholipids includes 26 mg phosphatidylcholine [of which 16 mg is disaturated phosphatidylcholine], and 0.65 mg protein, including 0.25 mg of surfactant-associated protein B [SP-B].)

Allow to warm to room temperature before administration.

Do not shake. The vial may be gently swirled to resuspend any particles that have settled. Visible flecks in the suspension and foaming at the surface of the suspension are normal.

Draw up the dose using a 20 gauge or larger bore needle, taking care to avoid excess foaming. Remove the needle before instilling the surfactant into the endotracheal tube.

Intratracheal (instilled into the endotracheal tube [ETT]): May administer via side-port adapter or via catheter. The total dose (3 ml) is divided into two aliquots (1.5 ml) to assure homogeneous distribution in the lungs. Following the instillation of each aliquot, the infant should be positioned with either the right or the left side dependent.

- Two attendants, one to instill the calfactant, the other to monitor the patient and assist in positioning and facilitating the dosing, are present. After each dose, the infant is placed in the appropriate position with either the right or left side dependent. Ventilation is continued during administration over 20 to 30 breaths for each aliquot, with small bursts timed only during the inspiratory cycles. The two aliquots should be separated by a pause, during which the respiratory status of the infant is evaluated and the infant is repositioned.[1,2]

Storage:

- Store in the refrigerator at temperatures between 2°C and 8°C (36°F and 46°F).
- Protect from light.
- Contains no preservatives. Single use vial. Do not dilute or sonicate. Does not require reconstitution. Discard unused portion.

- Unopened, unused vials that have warmed to room temperature may be returned to the refrigerator within 24 hours of warming and stored for future use. However, warmed, unopened vials should not be returned to the refrigerator more than once.

CAUTIONS/CONTRAINDICATIONS

If adverse effects occur, interrupt administration, stabilize the infant, then resume administration with proper monitoring.[1]

Rapid improvements in lung function, substantial increases in blood oxygenation and improved lung compliance may require immediate reduction in peak inspiratory pressure, ventilator rate, and/or FiO_2. Close clinical monitoring is necessary following administration.

Endotracheal suctioning or reintubation is sometimes needed when there are signs of airway obstruction during the administration of calfactant.[1]

USE

Used for prevention and treatment of neonatal respiratory distress syndrome (RDS) in preterm infants at high risk for RDS. It is indicated for infants 72 hours of age or less who have RDS (confirmed by clinical and radiologic findings) and requiring endotracheal intubation.[1]

- **Infasurf vs Exosurf:**
  - *Treatment.* A multicenter trial comparing synthetic surfactant (Exosurf Neonatal) with calf lung surfactant extract (Infasurf) for the treatment of RDS showed that Infasurf-treated infants had fewer air leaks and a significant reduction in severity of respiratory disease.[3]
  - *Prevention.* Hudak and colleagues showed significant reductions in the incidence of RDS, the severity of early respiratory disease, and the incidence of pulmonary leaks associated with RDS. The study also showed decreased mortality attributable to RDS in infants treated with Infasurf as compared with Exosurf Neonatal. In this study, surfactant was given at birth, and if still intubated, at 12 and 24 hours of age. Infasurf prophylaxis was associated with a greater risk of total but not severe (grades 3 and 4) intraventricular hemorrhage (IVH).[4]
- **Infasurf vs Survanta:**
  - *Treatment and prevention.* In a comparison of Infasurf to Survanta (beractant) for the treatment and prevention of RDS, Bloom and colleagues found that Infasurf had a longer duration of action than Survanta and a modest benefit over Survanta in the acute phase of RDS.[5]

MECHANISM OF ACTION

Calfactant is a natural surfactant produced by an extract of calf lung lavage. It contains phospholipids, neutral lipids, and hydrophobic surfactant-associated proteins B and C (SP-B and SP-C). The SP-B level is close to that of natural surfactant.

Calfactant restores surface activity to the lungs of preterm infants who have RDS caused by a deficiency of lung surfactant. It decreases the incidence of RDS, mortality due to RDS, and air leaks associated with RDS.

Deficiency of pulmonary surfactant is the main cause of RDS. Surfactant lowers surface tension on alveolar surfaces during respiration and stabilizes the alveoli against collapse which makes it essential for effective ventilation.

ADVERSE EFFECTS

Cardiovascular/Respiratory: Transient cyanosis (65 percent), airway obstruction (39 percent), bradycardia (34 percent), reflux of surfactant into the endotracheal tube (21 percent), requirement for manual ventilation (16 percent) and reintubation (3 percent). These are usually not associated with serious complications or death.[2]

CNS: Intraventricular hemorrhage, periventricular leukomalacia (PVL).[1]

PHARMACOKINETICS/PHARMACODYNAMICS

Onset of Action: Significant improvements in FiO_2 and mean airway pressure (MAP) occur during the first 24 to 48 hours following initiation of therapy.[2]

No pharmacokinetic studies on absorption, biotransformation, and elimination have been done.

NURSING IMPLICATIONS

Rapid improvements in lung function may require immediate reduction in peak inspiratory pressure, ventilator rate, and/or FiO_2.

Monitor the following during dosing: Heart rate, color, chest expansion, breath sounds, oxygen saturation, and ETT patency and position before and for 30 minutes after each dose.

The rate of surfactant administration may need to be slowed and ventilator settings may need to be increased if:

> The infant becomes dusky or agitated
>
> The heart rate slows
>
> The oxygen saturation falls
>
> Surfactant backs up the ETT

Monitor blood gases.

Because the drug works at the alveolar level, suctioning should not affect efficacy. Minimize suctioning as dictated by clinical necessity. No specific waiting period before suctioning after calfactant administration has been established.[1,6]

COMMENTS

Must be used in a neonatal center with personnel capable of neonatal intubation, mechanical ventilation, and medical management of unstable preterm infants. Qualified nurses and respiratory therapists should be available on-site when surfactant is administered, as should equipment, laboratory support, and radiology support for managing and monitoring preterm infants.[7]

REFERENCES

1. Medical Economics Data. 2000. *Physicians' Desk Reference.* Montvale, New Jersey: Medical Economics, 1080–1081.

2. United States Pharmacopeial Convention/USP DI. 2000. *Drug Information for the Health Care Professional,* 20th ed. Rockville, Maryland: United States Pharmacopeial Convention, 764–765.

3. Hudak ML, et al. 1996. A multicenter randomized, masked comparison trial of natural versus synthetic surfactant for the treatment of respiratory distress syndrome. *Journal of Pediatrics* 128(3): 396–406.

4. Hudak ML, et al. 1997. A multicenter randomized masked comparison trial of synthetic surfactant versus calf lung surfactant extract in the prevention of neonatal respiratory distress syndrome. *Pediatrics* 100(1): 39–50.

5. Bloom BT, et al. 1997. Comparison of Infasurf (calf lung surfactant extract) to Survanta (Beractant) in the treatment and prevention of respiratory distress syndrome. *Pediatrics* 100(1): 31–38.

6. Murali Sundar. February 28, 2000. Personal communication. Forest Pharmaceuticals, Inc. St. Louis, Missouri, 63045.

7. American Academy of Pediatrics, Committee on Fetus and Newborn. 1991. Surfactant replacement therapy for respiratory distress syndrome. *Pediatrics* 87(6): 946–947.

CAPTOPRIL (CAPOTEN)
(KAP-toe-pril)

CARDIOVASCULAR: ANTIHYPERTENSIVE

DOSE

Initial: 0.05 mg/kg/dose. This low dose may be required for the initial 24-hour period because of the initial dramatic drop in blood pressure that occurs in some infants.

- Sinaiko recommends starting treatment with 0.01 mg/kg and increasing rapidly over a 24- to 48-hour period until adequate blood pressure control is reached.[1]

Maintenance: 0.5 mg/kg/dose (range: 0.1–1 mg/kg/dose) given every 8–12 hours prn. (*Maximum:* 2 mg/kg/dose in children; lower doses are usually effective in neonates.)[2]

- O'Dea and associates reported normal blood pressure with doses of 0.01 mg/kg in preterm and term infants.[3]
- Use the lowest effective dose. Reduce dose in renal impairment.

ADMINISTRATION

PO: Administer 1 hour before or 2 hours after feedings, if possible (food reduces absorption by 35–55 percent). Maximal blood pressure reduction is at 60–90 minutes after oral administration.

Preparation: Captopril is not available as an oral liquid. One of the following methods may be used to prepare the dose:

- *Solution:* Conflicting data have been published on the stability of captopril in solution.[4,5] It is therefore safest to prepare each dose when needed. Dissolve a 25 mg tablet in 25 ml water to make a 1 mg/ml concentration; use the appropriate volume for the dose prescribed; then discard the unused portion within approximately 30 minutes.

- *Powder Papers:* The pharmacist may weigh out individual doses as powder papers that are stable for 12 weeks at room temperature.[6] These are then dispensed to the nurse to mix with a small amount of formula, breast milk, or water. Administer to baby PO immediately after dilution.

CAUTIONS/CONTRAINDICATIONS

Use with caution in patients with low renal perfusion pressure.

Do not use in patients with bilateral renal artery stenosis—causes *severe reduction in glomerular filtration rate (GFR).*

USE

Antihypertensive: Used to treat hypertension associated with renovascular abnormalities and hyperreninemia. Captopril is particularly useful in infants. Both the potency and duration of action of the drug are greater in this age group than in older children, probably because of significantly higher renin-angiotensin

FIGURE 1-3 ◆ THE RENIN-ANGIOTENSIN SYSTEM AND SITE OF ACTION OF CAPTOPRIL.

Illustrates the factors controlling renin release, angiotensin II formation (vasoconstriction), and bradykinin (vasodilator) inactivation, as well as the consequences of converting-enzyme inhibition by captopril.

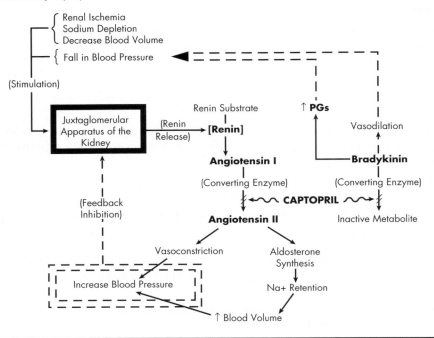

From: Roberts RJ. 1984. Cardiovascular drugs: Antihypertensives and vasodilators. In *Drug Therapy in Infants: Pharmacologic Principles and Clinical Experience*. Philadelphia: WB Saunders, 203. Reprinted by permission.

system activity in the newborn or because conditions associated with hypertension in this age group (such as renal emboli from umbilical artery catheters, steroid administration, and BPD) are reported to stimulate angiotensin formation.[1,2,7]

Cardiac: Doses up to 3.5 mg/kg/day have been used to treat severe congestive cardiac failure caused by left-to-right shunting with pulmonary hypertension. Use resulted in a fall in heart and respiratory rates and an increase in plasma sodium and improved feeding. Hypotension and increased BUN and creatinine occurred in 10 percent of patients.[8] Captopril benefits patients with dilated cardiomyopathies and hypertensive patients following coarctation surgery.[8–10]

MECHANISM OF ACTION

Captopril is a potent inhibitor of angiotensin-converting enzyme, which converts angiotensin I to angiotensin II, the major vasoconstrictor in most vascular beds.

When this conversion is inhibited, vasodilation occurs, aldosterone secretion is diminished, renal blood flow increases, and sodium excretion occurs (Figure 1-3). Captopril also prevents degradation of bradykinin and enhances the production of dilator prostaglandins.[1,3] It also lowers ventricular filling pressures and increases cardiac output in patients with low-output cardiac failure.

ADVERSE EFFECTS

Most adverse effects are dose related. Usually well tolerated if blood pressure is monitored. The incidence and severity of adverse effects are lower in children than in adults.[1]

GI disturbances (2–4 percent); proteinuria (1 percent); increased BUN and creatinine; rash; fever; eosinophilia (14 percent); taste impairment (6 percent); neutropenia (0.3 percent) (severe neutropenia has been reported in infants and children); hyperkalemia (secondary to reduced aldosterone production), especially in patients with severe renal dysfunction; chronic, dry cough; angioedema.[11,12]

Hypotension and tachycardia. First dose may cause a severe drop in blood pressure. Oliguria with blood pressure drop of 60 percent below pretreatment levels was reported in preterm infants given captopril 0.3 mg/kg.[13] Seizures were observed with episodes of sudden decreases in blood pressure during treatment.[14] Monitor blood pressure.

Severe reduction in GFR in patients with bilateral renal artery stenosis.

Additive hyperkalemia can occur with K^+ sparing diuretics.

Serum digoxin levels increase 15–30 percent.[15,16]

PHARMACOKINETICS/PHARMACODYNAMICS

Absorption: Drug is 70 percent absorbed. Absorption is reduced 35–55 percent if drug is given with a meal.

Protein binding: 25–30 percent.

Metabolism: Renal and hepatic.

Half-life: 2 hours (longer in renal dysfunction).

Elimination: Urinary.

NURSING IMPLICATIONS

Monitor BP immediately prior to first dose and frequently thereafter, in case first dose causes a precipitous drop in BP. If infant tolerates drug, BP then may be monitored per routine.

Monitor for oliguria and seizures. Feeding intolerance may occur due to GI upset.

REFERENCES

1. Sinaiko AR. 1992. Antihypertensive agents. In *Pediatric Pharmacology: Therapeutic Principles in Practice,* 2nd ed., Yaffe SJ, and Aranda JV, eds. Philadelphia: WB Saunders, 425–436.

2. Roberts RJ. 1984. *Drug Therapy in Infants: Pharmacologic Principles and Clinical Experience.* Philadelphia: WB Saunders, 203–205.

3. O'Dea RF, et al. 1988. Treatment of neonatal hypertension with captopril. *Journal of Pediatrics* 113(2): 403–406.

4. Pereira CM, and Tam YK. 1992. Stability of captopril in tap water. *American Journal of Hospital Pharmacy* 49(3): 612–615.

5. Anaizi NH, and Swenson C. 1993. Instability of aqueous captopril solutions. *American Journal of Hospital Pharmacy* 50(3): 486–488.

6. Taketomo CK, et al. 1990. Stability of captopril in powder papers under three storage conditions. *American Journal of Hospital Pharmacy* 47(8): 1799–1801.

7. Zenk KE, et al. 1984. Captopril and minoxidil for malignant hypertension in an infant. *Clinical Pharmacology* 3(3): 311–313.

8. Scammell AM, Arnold R, and Wilkinson JL. 1987. Captopril in treatment of infant heart failure: A preliminary report. *International Journal of Cardiology* 16(3): 295–301.

9. Shaddy RE, Teitel D, and Brett C. 1988. Short-term hemodynamic effects of captopril in infants with congestive heart failure. *American Journal of Diseases of Children* 142(1): 100–105.

10. Stern H, et al. 1990. Captopril in children with dilated cardiomyopathy: Acute and long-term effects in a prospective study of hemodynamic and hormonal effects. *Pediatric Cardiology* 11(1): 22–28.

11. Weismann D, et al. 1983. Captopril treatment (letter). *American Journal of Diseases of Children* 137(9): 917–919.

12. Manufacturer's product literature.

13. Tack ED, and Perlman JM. 1988. Renal failure in sick hypertensive premature infants receiving captopril therapy. *Journal of Pediatrics* 112(5): 805–810.

14. Perlman JM, and Volpe JJ. 1989. Neurologic complications of captopril treatment of neonatal hypertension. *Pediatrics* 83(1): 47–52.

15. Brogden RN, Todd PA, and Sorkin EM. 1988. Captopril. An update of its pharmacodynamic and pharmacokinetic properties, and therapeutic use in hypertension and congestive heart failure. *Drugs* 36(5): 540–600.

16. McEvoy GK. 1994. *AHFS Drug Information.* Bethesda, Maryland: American Society of Hospital Pharmacists, 985–992.

CARNITINE (CARNITOR)

(KAR-ni-teen)

NUTRITION: SUPPLEMENT

Synonyms: L-carnitine, levocarnitine, β-hydroxy-γ-trimethylaminobutyric acid

DOSE

PO: 50–100 mg/kg/day divided bid to tid. Begin with 50 mg/kg/day divided bid to tid while assessing tolerance and therapeutic response. Increase dose slowly. *Maximum:* 1 gm/dose and 3 gm/day.[1–5]

IV: 50 mg/kg loading dose. Then, in patients with severe metabolic crisis, administer 50 mg/kg over the following 24 hours divided every 3–4 hours, but never at intervals longer than every 6 hours. Subsequent daily doses: 50 mg/kg/day in divided doses. The manufacturer states that the highest dose administered has been 300 mg/kg. Individualize the dose based on clinical response.[2,5]

Preterm Infants Receiving Parenteral Nutrition (PN): 8–16 mg/kg/day continuous IV infusion[6–9] (8–16 mg/kg = 50–100 micromoles/kg). Carnitine is stable in and compatible with neonatal PN solutions.[10]

Infants with Epilepsy and Certain Metabolic Disorders: A consensus panel of nine pediatric neurologists convened to review the present state of knowledge about carnitine supplementation in infants and children with epilepsy and to develop guidelines for the appropriate use of carnitine replacement for these patients. The panel recommends these doses:[11]

- *Maintenance:* 100 mg/kg/day, up to 2 gm/day, whichever is less, PO divided into three or four doses. Carnitine is used PO for maintenance conditions such as primary carnitine transporter defect.[11]

- *"Metabolic Rescue" of Acutely Ill Patients:* 150–500 mg/kg/day IV. Parenteral carnitine is used for the acute treatment of patients with an inborn error of metabolism that results in secondary carnitine deficiency, for valproate-associated hepatotoxicity, overdose, and other acute metabolic crises associated with carnitine deficiency.[5,11]

ADMINISTRATION

Supplied as:

- *Oral Solution:* 1 gm/10 ml (= 100 mg/ml).
- *Injection:* 1 gm/5 ml and 500 mg/2.5 ml (= 200 mg/ml). Protect from light.

IV—Rate: May infuse over 2–3 minutes by direct IV infusion or by continuous infusion as when admixed in parenteral nutrition.

IV—Concentration: May give undiluted.

PO: Give during or immediately following feedings. Dilute in formula or other liquid, and give slowly to reduce gastrointestinal reactions. Space doses evenly throughout the day (every 3 or 4 hours) to increase tolerance.

CAUTIONS/CONTRAINDICATIONS

D,L-carnitine, sold in health food stores without a prescription as vitamin B_T, may cause mild myasthenia in uremic patients. Toxicity is probably caused by the D-carnitine component, which is biologically inactive and competitively inhibits L-carnitine (levocarnitine) and can cause deficiency. Discontinuation of D-carnitine quickly returns fatty acid oxidation to normal. Ensure that only L-carnitine is administered to avoid potential side effects. The prescription form of carnitine, either oral or parenteral, is in the form of L-carnitine.

USE

Parenteral Nutrition in Preterm Infants: Carnitine can be added to PN for preterm infants to improve utilization of exogenous fat. Preterm infants have limited free fatty acid oxidative capacity, which may relate to their low acylcarnitine and free carnitine levels. Reduced ability to oxidize fats could lead to deleterious effects on energy-dependent processes, increasing the risk of hypothermia, hypoglycemia, respiratory distress, infection, and delayed growth.

Failure to supplement parenteral nutrition with carnitine may lead to carnitine deficiency. Preterm infants can't synthesize enough carnitine while on PN, despite the presence of the precursors lysine and methionine in the PN fluid. Preterm infants are at greater risk than term infants for developing carnitine deficiency because they do not benefit from placental transfer of carnitine during the third trimester of pregnancy. Infants have a reduced capacity for biosynthesis of carnitine secondary to low activity of several enzymes and limited tissue reserves. Infants must rely on dietary intake of carnitine to maintain adequate stores.[6–8,12]

Carnitine stores are depleted in preterm infants after about 15 days of PN without carnitine.[6] Bonner and colleagues found carnitine deficiency with impaired ketogenesis in very low birth weight infants requiring prolonged PN. Administration of carnitine in the PN appeared to alleviate this metabolic disturbance. Supplemented infants weighing 1–1.5 kg tolerated more fat and had greater weight gain than did control infants of the same weight. However, infants weighing 0.75–1 kg did not show improvement in these factors with supplementation. The authors suggest that additional studies are needed in smaller neonates to see whether more pronounced benefits are achieved with larger doses of intravenously administered carnitine.[6] Carnitine supplementation is recommended for all neonates receiving PN for more than 2 weeks.[3,6]

Conflicting results have been reported regarding improved fat utilization with carnitine supplementation during PN in neonates. Beneficial effects on fat oxidation have been shown by some investigators, but not by others.[1] Larsson and colleagues documented only a minor, temporary influence of carnitine supplementation on the fat metabolites.[9] In a large, double-blind, placebo-controlled study, Shortland and colleagues failed to show any beneficial effect from carnitine supplementation on growth or morbidity in preterm infants.[13]

Childhood Epilepsy: Carnitine is used to prevent and treat carnitine deficiency secondary to valproic acid (VPA) toxicity.[2] VPA is a branched, medium-chain fatty acid that forms acyl derivatives with both coenzyme A and carnitine and undergoes limited mitochondrial β-oxidation. VPA causes disturbances in mitochondrial β-oxidation. VPA therapy is associated with two phenomena: mild to moderately decreased carnitine levels and a rare hepatoencephalopathy resembling both Reye's syndrome and medium-chain acyl-CoA dehydrogenase (MCAD) deficiency crisis. This association prompted the recommendation that treatment of patients on VPA with carnitine may prevent the development of Reye's-like encephalopathy, as well as preventing other nonspecific complaints, such as weakness and irritability.[14]

A consensus statement of a panel of pediatric neurologists asserts that carnitine is clearly indicated to treat valproic acid–induced hepatotoxicity or overdose. The panelists further strongly recommend carnitine administration for the following:

- Symptomatic VPA-associated hyperammonemia.

- Infants and young children receiving VPA, especially those younger than 2 years with a complex neurologic disorder who are receiving multiple anticonvulsants.

- Patients who have multiple risk factors for hepatotoxicity (e.g., neurologic impairments, poor nutrition, failure to thrive, chronic illness, multiple anticonvulsants).[11]

There is some controversy about the results of carnitine treatment. Carnitine did not prevent development of fatal liver disease in one child who developed Reye's-like encephalopathy, even though the child was receiving both VPA and carnitine.[15] Further, in a double-blind, crossover study to determine if carnitine improves the symptoms attributed to anticonvulsant medications, Freeman and colleagues concluded that the use of carnitine prophylactically for children on anticonvulsant medications improved children's well-being scores about the same degree as a placebo.[4] The researchers state that the expense of using carnitine to alleviate common, nonspecific symptoms may not be warranted (about $0.30/kg of body weight per day, or $3/day for a 10 kg child).[1,4,14]

Metabolic Disorders:

- *Carnitine Transport Defect.* Carnitine therapy is critical and lifesaving for primary carnitine transport defect, a defect of carnitine uptake across cellular membranes. The efficacy of carnitine in the treatment of this disorder has been clearly established. Carnitine treatment resolves cardiomyopathy and prevents further episodes of hypokinetic hypoglycemia. Carnitine treatment is continued indefinitely as a maintenance medication at 100 mg/kg/day PO in divided doses.[1,11]

- *Long-Chain Fatty Acid Transfer Disorders.* Three disorders of transfer of long-chain fatty acids from the cytoplasm into the mitochondria have been treated with carnitine. They are carnitine palmitoyltransferase (CPT) I deficiency, CPT II deficiency, and carnitine/acylcarnitine translocase. Clinical presentation of these disorders includes nonketotic hypoglycemia, encephalopathy, myopathy with myoglobinuria, and cardiomyopathy. Treatment with carnitine probably doesn't significantly alter the course of these diseases in most cases.[1]

- *Organic Acidemias.* Clinical benefit has been claimed after treatment of a number of organic acidemias (propionic acidemia, methylmalonic acidemia, isovaleric acidemia, and glutaryl-CoA dehydrogenase deficiency). No large-scale studies have been done to confirm a beneficial effect, but oral carnitine is used as a regular maintenance medication, and IV carnitine is used during periods of decompensation of these disorders.[1]

- *Medium-Chain Acyl-CoA Dehydrogenase Deficiency.* MCAD deficiency is an inherited fatty acid β-oxidation disorder. The efficacy of carnitine in the treatment of this disorder has been questioned.[16,17] The substance may even have detrimental effects.[1] However, there are also advocates for its use, particularly if the carnitine levels are very low, to attempt to prevent the potential toxicity of medium-chain fatty acid metabolites and secondary carnitine deficiency.[18,19] There are few clinical data either to support or to refute its use in treating this condition.[1]

- *Urea Cycle Disorders.* Carnitine has been advocated in disorders of the urea cycle, where it may protect the brain from some of the toxic effects of hyperammonemia.[1]

Ketogenic Diet: Physicians have shown renewed interest in recent years in using the ketogenic diet for seizure control, especially in patients whose seizures are refractory to antiepileptic drug (AED) therapy or who experience unacceptable side effects from AEDs. The mechanism(s) by which the ketogenic diet exerts its anticonvulsant effect is (are) not fully understood. The ketogenic diet is high in fat and low in carbohydrates and protein. It causes the main source of fuel used by the brain to shift from carbohydrates to fats and produces a state of ketosis that mimics the fasting state. Even in biblical times, fasting was observed to have a beneficial effect on seizures.[12] The metabolic shift resulting from the diet somehow causes the seizure threshold to rise. The protective effect is rapidly reversed when the diet is discontinued.

Carnitine supplementation may be needed in patients with epilepsy using the ketogenic diet. The diet may deplete carnitine stores by decreasing the intake of carnitine or increasing the demand on carnitine utilization or urinary excretion of carnitine acyl conjugates. Carnitine would be expected to facilitate ketogenesis, thus contributing to the anticonvulsant effect of the diet. The patient's carnitine profile should be evaluated before the ketogenic diet is started. Prior carnitine deficiency, presumably as a result of long-term AED therapy, may be associated with adverse sequelae such as hypoglycemia, particularly during fasting before initiation of the ketogenic diet.[11,20]

Dialysis: In patients undergoing hemodialysis, excessive clearance of carnitine may occur, leading to disordered lipid and protein metabolism. In a multicenter, double-blind, placebo-controlled trial on the use of carnitine in patients on hemodialysis, patients in the carnitine group did have decreased muscle cramps;

decreased hypotension; increased exercise capacity; decreased urea nitrogen, creatinine, and phosphorus; and an improved sense of well-being; however, there was no effect on the lipid profile.[21]

MECHANISM OF ACTION

Carnitine is necessary for normal fat utilization and energy metabolism. It facilitates entry of long-chain fatty acids into cellular mitochondria, where they are used during oxidation and energy production in the form of adenosine triphosphate (ATP). Carnitine also exports acyl groups from subcellular organelles and from cells to the urine before they accumulate to toxic concentrations.[2,5,6]

Carnitine is present in most human tissue. It is supplied both by the diet and by endogenous biosynthesis from lysine and methionine. Most individuals can synthesize carnitine from its amino acid precursors through a complex process that is dependent on at least five enzymes.

A few individuals lack at least one of these enzymes and are thus identified as genetically carnitine deficient. Carnitine deficiency or insufficiency may occur in renal disease, disorders of metabolism, and certain drug therapy.[12] Dietary sources of carnitine include red meat and dairy products. Carnitine is added to most infant formulas, and it is a component of human milk. Carnitine is not a component of parenteral nutrition but can be added to it.

ADVERSE EFFECTS

Usually well tolerated.

Nausea, diarrhea, and abdominal cramping may occur.

Large doses may cause an unpleasant fishy body odor.

To reduce or eliminate adverse GI effects and body odor, reduce the carnitine dose.

PHARMACOKINETICS/PHARMACODYNAMICS

Absorption: 16 percent.

Metabolism: Carnitine is synthesized from methionine and lysine primarily in the liver. Carnitine is metabolized to trimethylamine-N-oxide and acylcarnitine. Carnitine is not protein bound.

Half-life: 17.4 hours.

Elimination: Carnitine is excreted intact by the kidneys either as free carnitine or as acylcarnitine. Plasma carnitine concentrations may be increased in patients with renal failure. Hemodialysis removes carnitine, and a deficiency may occur.[2]

NURSING IMPLICATIONS

Dilute oral dose and give slowly to reduce GI side effects.

Consider reducing the carnitine dose if the patient has diarrhea, abdominal cramping, or body odor.

Monitoring:

- Monitor periodic blood chemistries, vital signs, plasma carnitine, and over-all clinical condition to assess efficacy of carnitine therapy. Monitor plasma carnitine levels before therapy begins, then weekly for about 1 month, and then monthly.[1,2,5]

- Consider measurement of plasma and occasionally tissue carnitine in infants with hypoketotic hypoglycemia, cardiomyopathy, or skeletal myo-pathy where very low concentrations may indicate carnitine transport defect or other disorders.

COMMENTS

Therapeutic Range: Plasma free–carnitine level should be between 35 and 60 micromoles/liter. Carnitine deficiency is defined as abnormally low plasma levels of free carnitine (<20 micromoles/liter at more than 1 week postdelivery) and may be associated with low tissue and/or urine levels. This condition may be associated with a ratio of plasma ester to free carnitine levels (acylcarnitine:free carnitine ratio) greater than 0.4 or abnormally elevated levels of esterified carnitine in the urine.[5]

Interactions: Requirements for carnitine may be increased in patients receiving valproic acid.

REFERENCES

1. Walter JH. 1996. L-Carnitine. *Archives of Disease in Childhood* 74(6): 475–478.

2. United States Pharmacopeial Convention/USP DI. 1996. *Drug Information for the Health Care Professional,* 16th ed. Rockville, Maryland: United States Pharmacopeial Convention, 1891–1893.

3. Tibboel D, et al. 1990. Carnitine deficiency in surgical neonates receiving total parenteral nutrition. *Journal of Pediatric Surgery* 25(4): 418–421.

4. Freeman JM, et al. 1994. Does carnitine administration improve the symptoms attributed to anticonvulsant medications? A double-blinded, crossover study. *Pediatrics* 93(6 part 1): 893–895.

5. Medical Economics Data. 1998. *Physicians' Desk Reference.* Montvale, New Jersey: Medical Economics, 2781–2783.

6. Bonner CM, et al. 1995. Effects of parenteral L-carnitine supplementation on fat metabolism and nutrition in premature neonates. *Journal of Pediatrics* 126(2): 287–292.

7. Helms RA, et al. 1990. Effect of intravenous L-carnitine on growth parameters and fat metabolism during parenteral nutrition in neonates. *Journal of Parenteral and Enteral Nutrition* 14(5): 448–453.

8. Schmidt-Sommerfeld E, Penn D, and Wolf H. 1983. Carnitine deficiency in premature infants receiving total parenteral nutrition: Effect of L-carnitine supplementation. *Journal of Pediatrics* 102(6): 931–935.

9. Larsson LE, et al. 1990. Parenteral nutrition in preterm neonates with and without carnitine supplementation. *Acta Anaesthesiologica Scandinavica* 34(6): 501–505.

10. Borum PR. 1993. Is L-carnitine stable in parenteral nutrition solutions prepared for preterm neonates? *Neonatal Intensive Care* September/October: 30–32.

11. De Vivo DC, et al. 1998. L-carnitine supplementation in childhood epilepsy: Current perspectives. *Epilepsia* 39(11): 1216–1225.

12. Boehm KA, et al. 1993. Carnitine: A review for the pharmacy clinician. *Hospital Pharmacy* 28(9): 843, 847–850.

13. Shortland GJ, et al. 1998. Randomised controlled trial of L-carnitine as a nutritional supplementation in preterm infants. *Archives of Disease in Childhood. Fetal and Neonatal Edition* 78(3): F185–F188.

14. Kelley RI. 1994. The role of carnitine supplementation in valproic acid therapy. *Pediatrics* 93(6): 891–892.

15. Murphy JV, Groover RV, and Hodge C. 1993. Hepatotoxic effects in a child receiving valproate and carnitine. *Journal of Pediatrics* 123(2): 318–320.

16. Treem WR, Stanley CA, and Goodman SI. 1989. Medium-chain acyl-CoA dehydrogenase deficiency: Metabolic effects and therapeutic efficacy of long-term L-carnitine supplementation. *Journal of Inherited Metabolic Diseases* 12(2): 112–119.

17. Rinaldo P, et al. 1993. Effect of treatment with glycine and L-carnitine in medium-chain coenzyme A dehydrogenase deficiency. *Journal of Pediatrics* 122(4): 580–584.

18. Van Hove JL, et al. 1994. Intravenous L-carnitine and acetyl-L-carnitine in medium-chain acyl-coenzyme A dehydrogenase deficiency and isovaleric acidemia. *Pediatric Research* 35(1): 96–101.

19. Marsden D, Sege-Petersen K, and Nyhan WL. 1992. An unusual presentation of medium-chain acyl coenzyme A dehydrogenase deficiency. *American Journal of Diseases in Children* 146(12): 1459–1462.

20. Nordli DR Jr, and De Vivo DC. 1997. The ketogenic diet revisited: Back to the future. *Epilepsia* 38(7): 743–749.

21. Golper TA, et al. 1990. Multicenter trial of L-carnitine in maintenance hemodialysis patients. Part I: Carnitine concentrations and lipid effects. *Kidney International* 38(5): 904–911.

CEFAZOLIN (ANCEF, KEFZOL)
(sef-A-zoe-lin)

**ANTI-INFECTIVE:
ANTIBIOTIC**

DOSE

<1.2 kg (0–4 weeks): 20 mg/kg/dose every 12 hours[1]

1.2–2 kg:

- 0–7 days: 20 mg/kg/dose every 12 hours
- >7 days: 20 mg/kg/dose every 12 hours

>2 kg:

- 0–7 days: 20 mg/kg/dose every 12 hours
- >7 days: 20 mg/kg/dose every 8 hours[2]

Reduce dose in renal impairment.

ADMINISTRATION

IV—*Rate:* May infuse over 3–5 minutes, but infusion over 30 minutes is preferred.

IV—*Concentration:* Maximum: 100 mg/ml.

IM: Add sterile water or sodium chloride for injection: 2 ml to a 500 mg vial for 225 mg/ml.[3]

USE

A first-generation cephalosporin that is effective against Gram-positive aerobic cocci but that has limited activity against Gram-negative bacteria. Other antibiotics are usually used to treat Gram-negative bacterial infections.

Susceptible Organisms: Streptococci, penicillin-susceptible and penicillin-resistant staphylococci, and penicillin-susceptible pneumococci.

Resistant Organisms: Enterococci, methicillin-resistant staphylococci and *Listeria monocytogenes,* Pseudomonas species, *Serratia marcescens,* Enterobacter species, indole-positive Proteus and *Bacteroides fragilis.*[4]

MECHANISM OF ACTION

Interferes with cell wall synthesis in bacteria, resulting in cell lysis. Bactericidal.

ADVERSE EFFECTS

Infrequent: Pain on IM injection. Cefazolin is the preferred first-generation cephalosporin to use if IM administration is required.

PHARMACOKINETICS/PHARMACODYNAMICS

The **clearance** of cefazolin increases and the **volume of distribution** decreases with postnatal and gestational age, resulting in a decrease in **half-life** from 4.5–5 hours in the first week of life to approximately 3 hours by 3–4 weeks of age. The half-life is twice as long as for cephalothin (see monograph). CSF penetration is poor. Cefazolin's relatively high **protein binding** (74–86 percent) reduces available bilirubin binding sites by 6 percent.[5,6]

NURSING IMPLICATIONS

Infuse slowly.

Monitor urine output.

Monitor for adverse reactions.

REFERENCES

1. Prober CG, Stevenson DK, and Benitz WE. 1990. The use of antibiotics in neonates weighing less than 1,200 grams. *Pediatric Infectious Disease Journal* 9(2): 111–121.

2. Nelson JD. 1996. *1996-1997 Pocketbook of Pediatric Antimicrobial Therapy*, 12th ed. Baltimore: Lippincott Williams & Wilkins, 16–17.

3. Manufacturer's product literature.

4. Sáez-Llorens X, and McCracken GH Jr. 1995. Clinical pharmacology of antimicrobial agents. In *Infectious Diseases of the Fetus and Newborn Infant*, 4th ed., Remington JS, and Klein JO, eds. Philadelphia: WB Saunders, 1287–1336.

5. Paap CM, and Nahata MC. 1990. Clinical pharmacokinetics of antibacterial drugs in neonates. *Clinical Pharmacokinetics* 19(4): 280–318.

6. Deguchi Y, et al. 1988. Interindividual changes in volume of distribution of cefazolin in newborn infants and its prediction based on physiologic physiological pharmacokinetic concepts. *Journal of Pharmaceutical Sciences* 77(8): 674–678.

CEFOPERAZONE (CEFOBID)
(sef-oh-PER-a-zone)

**ANTI-INFECTIVE:
ANTIBIOTIC**

DOSE

Neonates (to 28 days of age): 100 mg/kg/day divided every 12 hours[1-3]

Older Infants (>28 days of age): 100–150 mg/kg/day divided every 8–12 hours[4]

ADMINISTRATION

IV—*Rate:* May give IV push over 3–5 minutes, but infusion over 15–60 minutes is preferred.

IV—*Concentration*: Maximum: 50 mg/ml.[5]

IM: Add 2.6 ml sterile water to 1 gm vial (= 333 mg/ml). May instead use 1.3 ml sterile water plus 1.3 ml lidocaine 0.5 percent (without epinephrine) to minimize pain of IM injection.

USE

A third-generation cephalosporin.

Susceptible Organisms: *Haemophilus influenzae,* gonococci, meningococci, and many Gram-negative enteric bacilli. Both cefoperazone and ceftazidime (see monograph) have activity against Pseudomonas, but ceftazidime is usually used in neonates when anti-Pseudomonas activity is required. Susceptibility of Gram-positive organisms to third-generation cephalosporins is lower than to first- or second-generation cephalosporins.

Resistant Organisms: *Listeria monocytogenes* and enterococci.

MECHANISM OF ACTION

Interferes with cell wall synthesis in bacteria, resulting in cell lysis.

Bactericidal.

ADVERSE EFFECTS

Intestinal side effects, such as abdominal cramps and diarrhea (20 percent).

Disulfiram (Antabuse)-like reactions (nausea, vomiting, diarrhea) may occur in patients concurrently taking medications containing alcohol (e.g., phenobarbital).

Antiprothrombin effects with hemorrhagic phenomena have occurred in adults. Monitor prothrombin time and administer vitamin K if needed.

PHARMACOKINETICS/PHARMACODYNAMICS

Elimination: 70 percent biliary in adults, but less in neonates. Newborns excrete a greater proportion of the drug in the urine because of reduced hepatic funciton.[1-3,6] Because cefoperazone is excreted in the bile, minimal dosage adjustment is required in renal dysfunction.[3,6]

NURSING IMPLICATIONS

Monitor for prolonged bleeding from previous puncture sites and notify physician. Monitor platelets closely.

Observe for adverse reactions.

COMMENTS

Limited experience with use in neonates.

REFERENCES

1. Bosso JA, Chan GM, and Matsen JM. 1983. Cefoperazone pharmacokinetics in preterm infants. *Antimicrobial Agents and Chemotherapy* 23(3): 413–415.

2. Rosenfeld WN, et al. 1983. Pharmacokinetics of cefoperazone in full-term and premature neonates. *Antimicrobial Agents and Chemotherapy* 23(6): 866–869.

3. Roberts RJ. 1994. *Drug Therapy in Infants: Pharmacologic Principles and Clinical Experience.* Philadelphia: WB Saunders, 59–60.

4. Benitz WE, and Tatro DS. 1995. *The Pediatric Drug Handbook,* 3rd ed. St. Louis: Mosby-Year Book, 70.

5. Manufacturer's product literature.

6. Paap CM, and Nahata MC. 1990. Clinical pharmacokinetics of antibacterial drugs in neonates. *Clinical Pharmacokinetics* 19(4): 280–318.

CEFOTAXIME (CLAFORAN)
(sef-oh-TAX-eem)

ANTI-INFECTIVE:
ANTIBIOTIC

DOSE

<1.2 kg (0–4 weeks): 50 mg/kg/dose every 12 hours[1]
1.2–2 kg:
- 0–7 days: 50 mg/kg/dose every 12 hours
- >7 days: 50 mg/kg/dose every 8 hours

>2 kg:
- 0–7 days: 50 mg/kg/dose every 12 hours
- >7 days: 50 mg/kg/dose every 8 hours[2]

Use same dose for meningitis.[2,3]
Reduce dose in severe renal dysfunction.

ADMINISTRATION

IV—*Rate:* May infuse by IV push over at least 3–5 minutes, but infusion over 30 minutes is preferred.

IV—*Concentration:* Maximum: 200 mg/ml.[4]

IV—*Compatibility:* See Appendix E: Y-Site Compatibility of Common NICU Drugs.

IM: Reconstitute 1 gm vial with 3 ml sterile water (= 300 mg/ml).

USE

A third-generation cephalosporin used to treat suspected or proven bacterial infections in newborns, with good CSF penetration and a proven record of safety and tolerability.

Susceptible Organisms: *Haemophilus influenzae,* gonococci, meningococci, and many Gram-negative enteric bacilli. Susceptibility of Gram-positive organisms to third-generation cephalosporins is lower than to first- or second-generation cephalosporins.

Resistant Organisms: *Listeria monocytogenes* and enterococci; therefore, cefotaxime must be used in combination with ampicillin for initial treatment of neonatal infections. Routine use may lead to rapid emergence of cefotaxime-resistant, Gram-negative bacteria.[4]

MECHANISM OF ACTION

Interferes with cell wall synthesis in bacteria, resulting in cell lysis.
Bactericidal.

ADVERSE EFFECTS

Very few significant side effects reported.

Rare Effects (in adults): Rashes, phlebitis, diarrhea, leukopenia or granulocyto-penia, and eosinophilia.

Seizures can occur with massive doses.

Alterations of bowel flora may occur, including antibiotic-associated colitis.[4]

PHARMACOKINETICS/PHARMACODYNAMICS

Distribution: Distributes well into most body fluids and tissues, including the CSF.

Protein Binding: 25–50 percent.

Metabolism: Metabolized to diacetyl-cefotaxime, which retains 10–100 percent of the antimicrobial activity of cefotaxime, depending on the pathogen.

Elimination: Half-life decreases with postnatal and gestational age.[5–8]

NURSING IMPLICATIONS

Monitor urine output closely, along with renal function.

Monitor for onset of diarrhea or loose stools that might indicate bacterial overgrowth.

REFERENCES

1. Prober CG, Stevenson DK, and Benitz WE. 1990. The use of antibiotics in neonates weighing less than 1,200 grams. *Pediatric Infectious Disease Journal* 9(2): 111–121.

2. Nelson JD. 1996. *1996–1997 Pocketbook of Pediatric Antimicrobial Therapy,* 12th ed. Baltimore: Lippincott Williams & Wilkins, 16–17.

3. American Academy of Pediatrics, Committee on Infectious Diseases. 1988. Treatment of bacterial meningitis. *Pediatrics* 81(6): 904–907. (Published erratum in *Pediatrics,* 1988, 82[6]: 869.)

4. Manufacturer's product literature.

5. Roberts RJ. 1984. *Drug Therapy in Infants: Pharmacologic Principles and Clinical Experience.* Philadelphia: WB Saunders, 57–59.

6. Kafetzis DA, et al. 1982. Treatment of severe neonatal infections with cefotaxime: Efficacy and pharmacokinetics. *Journal of Pediatrics* 100(3): 483–489.

7. Paap CM, and Nahata MC. 1990. Clinical pharmacokinetics of antibacterial drugs in neonates. *Clinical Pharmacokinetics* 19(4): 280–318.

8. McCracken GH Jr, Threlkeld NE, and Thomas ML. 1982. Pharmacokinetics of cefotaxime in newborn infants. *Antimicrobial Agents and Chemotherapy* 21(4): 683–684.

Cefoxitin (Mefoxin)
(se-FOX-i-tin)

Anti-Infective:
Antibiotic

Dose

Neonates: 90–100 mg/kg/day divided every 8 hours[1,2]

Infants >3 months of age: 80–160 mg/kg/day divided every 4–6 hours[3]

Reduce dose in renal impairment.

Administration

IV—*Rate:* May infuse by IV push over 3–5 minutes, but infusion over 30 minutes is preferred.

IV—*Concentration:* Maximum: 200 mg/ml.[4]

IV—*Compatibility:* See Appendix E: Y-Site Compatibility of Common NICU Drugs.

IM: Reconstitute 1 gm vial with 2 ml sterile water (= 400 mg/ml). May reconstitute instead with 1 ml sterile water plus 1 ml lidocaine 0.5 percent (without epinephrine) to minimize pain of IM injection.

Use

A second-generation cephalosporin with activity against many Gram-negative enteric organisms, as well as ampicillin-resistant *Haemophilus influenzae.*

Is much less active against Gram-positive cocci than are first-generation cephalosporins.

Noted for its *in vitro* activity against anaerobic bacteria, including *Bacteroides fragilis.*[1,4,5]

Mechanism of Action

Interferes with cell wall synthesis in bacteria, resulting in cell lysis.

Bactericidal.

Adverse Effects

Very few significant side effects reported.

Rare Effects (in adults): Rashes, phlebitis, diarrhea, leukopenia or granulocytopenia, and eosinophilia.

Seizures can occur with massive doses.

Alterations of bowel flora may occur, including antibiotic-associated colitis.[4]

Pharmacokinetics/Pharmacodynamics

Distribution: Does not achieve sufficient concentration in CSF to treat meningitis.

Protein Binding: 73 percent.

Elimination: Half-life decreases with postnatal age and body weight. Excreted in the urine, 85–99 percent unchanged.[2,6,7]

NURSING IMPLICATIONS

Infuse drug over 30 minutes.

Monitor for rash.

Observe for signs of adverse reactions.

REFERENCES

1. Sáez-Llorens X, and McCracken GH Jr. 1995. Clinical pharmacology of antimicrobial agents. In *Infectious Diseases of the Fetus and Newborn Infant*, 4th ed., Remington JS, and Klein JO, eds. Philadelphia: WB Saunders, 1287–1336.

2. Roos R, et al. 1980. Pharmacokinetics of cefoxitin in premature and newborn infants studied by continuous serum level monitoring during combination therapy with penicillin and amikacin. *Infection* 8: 301–308.

3. Nelson JD. 1996. *1996–1997 Pocketbook of Pediatric Antimicrobial Therapy,* 12th ed. Baltimore: Lippincott Williams & Wilkins, 70.

4. Manufacturer's product literature.

5. Roberts RJ. 1984. *Drug Therapy in Infants: Pharmacologic Principles and Clinical Experience.* Philadelphia: WB Saunders, 55–57.

6. Regazzi MB, et al. 1983. Cefoxitin in newborn infants: A clinical and pharmacokinetic study. *European Journal of Clinical Pharmacology* 25(4): 507–509.

7. Paap CM, and Nahata MC. 1990. Clinical pharmacokinetics of antibacterial drugs in neonates. *Clinical Pharmacokinetics* 19(4): 280–318.

CEFTAZIDIME (FORTAZ)
(SEF-tay-zi-deem)

**ANTI-INFECTIVE:
ANTIBIOTIC**

DOSE

<1.2 kg (0–4 weeks): 50 mg/kg/dose every 12 hours[1]
1.2–2 kg:
- 0–7 days: 50 mg/kg/dose every 12 hours
- >7 days: 50 mg/kg/dose every 8 hours

>1.2 kg:
- 0–7 days: 50 mg/kg/dose every 12 hours
- >7 days: 50 mg/kg/dose every 8 hours[2]

Reduce dose in renal impairment.

ADMINISTRATION

IV—*Rate:* May infuse over 3–5 minutes, but infusion over 30 minutes is preferred.

IV—*Concentration:* Maximum: 180 mg/ml. A more dilute solution is preferred.[3]

IV—*Compatibility:* See Appendix E: Y-Site Compatibility of Common NICU Drugs.

IM: May be given IM if necessary (i.e., near the end of a course of therapy when IV access is impossible or very difficult). IV is preferred.

IM—*Concentration:* Add 1.5 ml sterile water to a 500 mg vial for 280 mg/ml concentration.[3]

USE

A third-generation cephalosporin.

Susceptible Organisms: *Haemophilus influenzae,* gonococci, meningococci, and many Gram-negative enteric bacilli. Both cefoperazone (see monograph) and ceftazidime have activity against Pseudomonas, but ceftazidime is usually used in neonates when anti-Pseudomonas activity is required. Gentamicin works synergistically with ceftazidime against Pseudomonas. Susceptibility of Gram-positive organisms to third-generation cephalosporins is lower than to first- or second-generation cephalosporins.

Resistant Organisms: *Listeria monocytogenes* and enterococci.[4–5]

MECHANISM OF ACTION

Interferes with cell wall synthesis in bacteria, resulting in cell lysis.

Bactericidal.

ADVERSE EFFECTS

Adverse effects are infrequent: diarrhea, rash, pain on intramuscular injection, candidiasis and alteration of bowel flora, slight elevation of hepatic enzymes, transient increase in BUN/creatinine.

Rare Effects: Transient leukopenia, eosinophilia, granulocytopenia.

Seizures can occur with massive doses.[5]

PHARMACOKINETICS/PHARMACODYNAMICS

Distribution: Penetrates well into the CSF, especially in meningitis. Serum levels are higher in neonates than in older infants receiving identical doses. Serum levels are lower after IM than after IV administration.

Elimination: Half-life is inversely related to gestational age and varies from 4.2 to 6.7 hours. Excreted 70–90 percent unchanged in the urine.[6–8]

NURSING IMPLICATIONS

Monitor for rash, diarrhea.

Monitor for effectiveness of drug therapy, such as improvement in clinical sepsis.

REFERENCES

1. Prober CG, Stevenson DK, and Benitz WE. 1990. The use of antibiotics in neonates weighing less than 1,200 grams. *Pediatric Infectious Disease Journal* 9(2): 111–121.

2. Nelson JD. 1996. *1996–1997 Pocketbook of Pediatric Antimicrobial Therapy,* 12th ed. Baltimore: Lippincott Williams & Wilkins, 16–17.

3 Manufacturer's product literature.

4. American Academy of Pediatrics, Committee on Infectious Diseases. 1988. Treatment of bacterial meningitis. *Pediatrics* 81(6): 904–907. (Published erratum in *Pediatrics,* 1988, 82[6]: 869.)

5. Sáez-Llorens X, and McCracken GH Jr. 1995. Clinical pharmacology of antimicrobial agents. In *Infectious Diseases of the Fetus and Newborn Infant,* 4th ed., Remington JS, and Klein JO, eds. Philadelphia: WB Saunders, 1287–1336.

6. Mulhall A, and de Louvois J. 1985. The pharmacokinetics and safety of ceftazidime in the neonate. *Journal of Antimicrobial Chemotherapy* 15(1): 97–103.

7. Paap CM, and Nahata MC. 1990. Clinical pharmacokinetics of antibacterial drugs in neonates. *Clinical Pharmacokinetics* 19(4): 280–318.

8. McCracken GH Jr, Threlkeld N, and Thomas ML. 1984. Pharmacokinetics of ceftazidime in newborn infants. *Antimicrobial Agents and Chemotherapy* 26(4): 583–584.

CEFTRIAXONE (ROCEPHIN)
(sef-trye-AX-one)

ANTI-INFECTIVE:
ANTIBIOTIC

DOSE

<1.2 kg (0–4 weeks): 50 mg/kg/dose given every 24 hours[1]

1.2–2 kg:

- 0–7 days: 50 mg/kg/dose given every 24 hours
- >7 days: 50 mg/kg/dose given every 24 hours

>2 kg:

- 0–7 days: 50 mg/kg/dose given every 24 hours
- >7 days: 75 mg/kg/dose given every 24 hours[2]

Gonococcal Infections:

- *Nondisseminated Infections (including ophthalmia neonatorum caused by N. gonorrhoeae):* 25–50 mg/kg IV or IM as a single daily dose for 7 days. *Maximum dose:* 125 mg.[3]

- *Disseminated Gonococcal Infection (including meningitis, arthritis, and sepsis):* 25–50 mg/kg IV or IM as a single daily dose for 10–14 days.[3]

- *Infants Born to Mothers with Gonococcal Infections:* In term infants, use a single dose of 125 mg IV or IM; for preterm infants, use a single dose of 25–50 mg/kg IV or IM. *Maximum dose:* 125 mg.[3]

Use cefotaxime instead of ceftriaxone in hyperbilirubinemic infants (see monograph on cefotaxime).

It is not usually necessary to reduce the dose in patients with renal or hepatic dysfunction.

ADMINISTRATION

IV—*Rate:* May infuse over at least 2–4 minutes, but administration over 10–30 minutes is preferred.

IV—*Concentration:* Maximum: 40 mg/ml.

IM: Reconstitute 250 mg vial with 0.9 ml diluent for a concentration of 250 mg/ml. Stable for 24 hours at room temperature and for 3 days refrigerated. The IM dose may need to be divided and given in two sites to avoid exceeding the usual maximum infant IM volume of 0.5 ml.

The IM route is painful; use only if IV access is unavailable. Discomfort can be minimized by using lidocaine, rather than sterile water or normal saline, as a diluent. In infants, use *lidocaine 0.5 percent without epinephrine,* rather than the 1 percent recommended by the manufacturer (for adults). Avoid exceeding a dose of 4 mg/kg of lidocaine in the volume of injection given (lidocaine 0.5 percent contains 5 mg/ml of lidocaine).

USE

A third-generation cephalosporin that can be administered IV or IM as a single daily dose.

Effective against Gram-negative aerobic bacteria, including *Neisseria gonorrhoeae, N. meningitidis, Escherichia coli,* and *Haemophilus influenzae.*[4] Also effective against Gram-positive cocci. Distributes well into the CSF when meninges are inflamed and can be used to treat meningitis.

Not effective against Pseudomonas species, *Listeria monocytogenes,* enterococci, methicillin-resistant staphylococci, or anaerobic organisms.

Because it can be given as a once-daily IM injection, it is useful when a third-generation cephalosporin is needed but IV access is not available.

MECHANISM OF ACTION

Interferes with cell wall synthesis in bacteria, resulting in cell lysis.

Bactericidal.

ADVERSE EFFECTS

Displacement of bilirubin from albumin binding sites. Use with caution in infants, particularly preterm infants, with hyperbilirubinemia.[5]

Diarrhea.

Sludging in the gall bladder, which may cause symptoms and jaundice (reversible).

Hypersensitivity reactions, such as rash, may occur.

PHARMACOKINETICS/PHARMACODYNAMICS

IM Absorption: Levels are detectable after 15 minutes and peak in approximately 1.5 hours. Bioavailability of IM is equal to IV.[6]

Volume of Distribution: Larger in infants <7 days postnatal age than in older infants because of more extracellular water and lower protein binding. CSF: Serum concentration percentage ratio was 17 percent with inflamed meninges and 4.1 percent without inflammation.[7]

Protein Binding: Decreases bilirubin binding to albumin by 43 percent, more than any other cephalosporin. Thus, it should be used with caution in infants, particularly preterm infants, with hyperbilirubinemia.[5]

Half-life: 8.5–19 hours.[8]

NURSING IMPLICATIONS

Monitor for diarrhea and jaundice.

REFERENCES

1. Prober CG, Stevenson DK, and Benitz WE. 1990. The use of antibiotics in neonates weighing less than 1,200 grams. *Pediatric Infectious Disease Journal* 9(2): 111–121.
2. Nelson JD. 1996. *1996–1997 Pocketbook of Pediatric Antimicrobial Therapy,* 10th ed. Baltimore: Lippincott Williams & Wilkins, 16–17.

3. American Academy of Pediatrics, Committee on Infectious Diseases. 1994. *Red Book: Report of the Committee on Infectious Diseases*. Elk Grove Village, Illinois: American Academy of Pediatrics, 197.

4. Manufacturer's product literature.

5. Gulian JM, et al. 1987. Bilirubin displacement by ceftriaxone in neonates: Evaluation by determination of "free" bilirubin and erythrocyte-bound bilirubin. *Journal of Antimicrobial Chemotherapy* 19(6): 823–829.

6. McCracken GH Jr, et al. 1983. Ceftriaxone pharmacokinetics in newborn infants. *Antimicrobial Agents and Chemotherapy* 23(2): 341–343.

7. Martin E, et al. 1984. Pharmacokinetics of ceftriaxone in neonates and infants with meningitis. *Journal of Pediatrics* 105(3): 475–481.

8. Paap CM, and Nahata MC. 1990. Clinical pharmacokinetics of antibacterial drugs in neonates. *Clinical Pharmacokinetics* 19(4): 280–318.

CEFUROXIME

(se-fyoor-OX-eem)

(ZINACEF, KEFUROX)

ANTI-INFECTIVE: ANTIBIOTIC

DOSE

Neonates: 20–100 mg/kg/day divided every 12 hours[1–4]

Older Infants: 100–150 mg/kg/day divided every 8 hours[5]

Reduce dose in renal impairment.

Not recommended for meningitis.

ADMINISTRATION

IV—*Rate:* May infuse by IV push over 3–5 minutes, but infusion over 30 minutes is preferred.

IV—*Concentration:*

- ***Zinacef:*** Adding 8 ml fluid to a 750 mg vial gives a concentration of 90 mg/ml.
- ***Kefurox:*** Adding 9 ml fluid to a 750 mg vial gives a concentration of 100 mg/ml.

IM: IV route is preferred. Cefuroxime is a suspension at IM concentrations and may not appear clear. May reconstitute with sterile water, dextrose 5 percent, or normal saline for injection. Stable for 24 hours at room temperature and for 48 hours when refrigerated.[6]

- ***Zinacef:*** Adding 3 ml fluid to a 750 mg vial gives a concentration of 220 mg/ml (suspension).
- ***Kefurox:*** Adding 3.6 ml fluid to a 750 mg vial gives a concentration of 220 mg/ml (suspension).

USE

A second-generation cephalosporin that is more active than cephalothin (a first-generation cephalosporin) against Group B streptococci, pneumococci, and Gram-negative enteric bacilli. Also active against *Haemophilus influenzae,* meningococci, gonococci, and staphylococci.

Not for use in neonatal meningitis because its activity against strains of *Escherichia coli* is unreliable and it is ineffective against Listeria and enterococci.[6,7]

MECHANISM OF ACTION

Interferes with cell wall synthesis in bacteria, resulting in cell lysis.

Bactericidal.

ADVERSE EFFECTS

Very few significant side effects reported.

Rare Effects (in adults): Rashes, phlebitis, diarrhea, leukopenia or granulocytopenia, and eosinophilia.

Seizures can occur with massive doses.

Alterations of bowel flora may occur, including antibiotic-associated colitis.[6,7]

Pharmacokinetics/Pharmacodynamics

Serum Levels: Inversely related to birth weight. CSF levels are 12–25 percent of corresponding serum levels in infants with meningitis.

Half-life: 3.6–5.6 hours. Repeated use does not lead to accumulation.

Elimination: Excreted in the urine.[1,2,7,8]

Nursing Implications

Monitor urine output closely.

References

1. Renlund M, and Pettay O. 1977. Pharmacokinetics and clinical efficacy of cefuroxime in the newborn period. *Proceedings of the Royal Society of Medicine* 70(9 supplement): S179–S182.

2. de Louvois J, Mulhall A, and Hurley R. 1982. Cefuroxime in the treatment of neonates. *Archives of Disease in Childhood* 57(1): 59–62.

3. Taketomo CK, Hodding JH, and Kraus DM. 1996. *1996–1997 Pediatric Dosage Handbook,* 3rd ed. Hudson, Ohio: Lexi-Comp, 138–140.

4. Gomella TL, Cunningham MD, and Eyal FG. 1994. *Neonatology: Management, Procedures, On-call Problems, Diseases and Drugs,* 3rd ed. Norwalk, Connecticut: Appleton & Lange, 476.

5. Nelson JD. 1996. *1996–1997 Pocketbook of Pediatric Antimicrobial Therapy,* 12th ed. Baltimore: Lippincott Williams & Wilkins, 71.

6. Manufacturers' product literature.

7. Sáez-Llorens X, and McCracken GH Jr. 1995. Clinical pharmacology of antimicrobial agents. In *Infectious Diseases of the Fetus and Newborn Infant,* 4th ed., Remington JS, and Klein JO, eds. Philadelphia: WB Saunders, 1287–1336.

8. Paap CM, and Nahata MC. 1990. Clinical pharmacokinetics of antibacterial drugs in neonates. *Clinical Pharmacokinetics* 19(4): 280–318.

CEPHALOTHIN (KEFLIN)
(sef-A-loe-thin)

ANTI-INFECTIVE:
ANTIBIOTIC

DOSE
<1.2 kg (0–4 weeks): 20 mg/kg/dose given every 12 hours[1]
1.2–2 kg:
- 0–7 days: 20 mg/kg/dose given every 12 hours
- >7 days: 20 mg/kg/dose given every 8 hours

>2 kg:
- 0–7 days: 20 mg/kg/dose given every 8 hours
- >7 days: 20 mg/kg/dose given every 6 hours[2]

Reduce dose in renal impairment.

ADMINISTRATION
IV: May infuse over 3–5 minutes, but infusion over 30 minutes by retrograde technique or syringe pump is preferable. Maximum concentration: 100 mg/ml.[3]

IM: Not recommended in neonates, particularly preterm infants, because of pain on injection and the small muscle mass.

USE
The prototype of first-generation cephalosporins, with activity against Gram-positive and some Gram-negative bacteria.

Ineffective against methicillin-resistant staphylococci.

ADVERSE EFFECTS
Phlebitis.

Pain on IM injection.

Additive nephrotoxicity with gentamicin.

PHARMACOKINETICS/PHARMACODYNAMICS
Distribution: Does not distribute well into the CSF, even with inflamed meninges.

Metabolism: Metabolized to deacetylcephalothin. This metabolite is 20 percent as active as cephalothin.

Half-life: About 1.5 hours in newborns.

Elimination: About 50 percent is excreted unchanged in the urine, primarily by tubular secretion.[4,5]

NURSING IMPLICATIONS
Give deep IM.

Monitor renal function and urine output.

COMMENTS

Because of their poor ability to penetrate the blood-brain barrier, first-generation cephalosporins should never be used as initial therapy for suspected or proven neonatal bacterial diseases unless meningitis has first been ruled out.

REFERENCES

1. Prober CG, Stevenson DK, and Benitz WE. 1990. The use of antibiotics in neonates weighing less than 1,200 grams. *Pediatric Infectious Disease Journal* 9(2): 111–121.

2. Nelson JD. 1996. *1996–1997 Pocketbook of Pediatric Antimicrobial Therapy,* 12th ed. Baltimore: Lippincott Williams & Wilkins, 16–17.

3. Manufacturer's product literature.

4. Hallberg T, and Svenningsen NW. 1970. Cephalothin in neonatal infections. *Acta Paediatrica Scandinavica* 206(supplement): S110.

5. Sáez-Lorenz X, and McCracken GH Jr. 1995. Clinical pharmacology of antimicrobial agents. In *Infectious Diseases of the Fetus and Newborn Infant,* 4th ed., Remington JS, and Klein JO, eds. Philadelphia: WB Saunders, 1287–1336.

CEPHAPIRIN (CEFADYL)

(sef-a-PYE-rin)

**ANTI-INFECTIVE:
ANTIBIOTIC**

DOSE

Infants <3 months of age: Not recommended because of poor CSF levels and lack of studies available in this age group. See **COMMENTS**.

Infants >3 months of age: 40–80 mg/kg/24 hours divided every 6 hours.[1]

Reduce dose in renal impairment.

ADMINISTRATION

IV: May infuse over 3–5 minutes, but infusion over 30 minutes by retrograde or syringe pump is preferred. Maximum concentration: 200 mg/ml.

IM: Add 1 ml sterile water for injection to a 500 mg vial (= 500 mg/1.2 ml or 417 mg/ml).[2] IV administration is preferred, but the IM route may be used for a few doses if necessary (i.e., to avoid restarting an IV).

USE

A first-generation cephalosporin with activity against Gram-positive and some Gram-negative bacteria.

Ineffective against methicillin-resistant staphylococci.

ADVERSE EFFECTS

Additive nephrotoxicity with gentamicin.

NURSING IMPLICATIONS

Monitor I & O and renal function.

COMMENTS

The safety of cephapirin in infants <3 months of age has not been established. Use is not recommended in this age group because of poor CSF levels and because of lack of studies in this age group. If cephapirin must be used, refer to the monograph on cephalothin (Keflin), and follow the dosages given there for weight and gestational age. (The pharmacokinetics of cephapirin and cephalothin are similar.)

Because of their poor ability to penetrate the blood-brain barrier, first-generation cephalosporins should never be used as initial therapy for suspected or proven neonatal bacterial diseases unless meningitis has first been ruled out.

REFERENCES

1. Nelson JD. 1996. *1996–1997 Pocketbook of Pediatric Antimicrobial Therapy,* 12th ed. Baltimore: Lippincott Williams & Wilkins, 71.

2. Manufacturer's product literature.

CHLORAL HYDRATE

(KLOR-al HYE-drate)

(NOCTEC)

(CONTROLLED SUBSTANCE SCHEDULE IV)

CENTRAL NERVOUS SYSTEM: SEDATIVE

DOSE

Maintenance of desired sedative state: 20–40 mg/kg/dose every 4–6 hours as required.

Single sedative dose: 30–75 mg/kg/dose. Prior to procedures such as MRI, CT scan, EEG, or ophthalmologic exam.[1]

ADMINISTRATION

PO: *Dilute with water before use.* Infants seem to prefer the cherry-flavored syrup brand to the anise-flavored brands. Give approximately 1 hour before procedure.

PR: Although chloral hydrate is also available as a suppository, it is difficult to cut the suppository (325 mg) accurately to the prescribed dose, and release of the drug from the suppository may be unreliable.

CAUTIONS/CONTRAINDICATIONS

Use with caution in patients with hepatic or renal disease (and therefore in very low birth weight infants because of their immature renal and liver functions; effects may be more prolonged and risk of accumulation is greater in these infants).

Avoid large doses in infants with severe cardiac disease.

Repetitive dosing may cause accumulation of metabolites, which may produce excessive CNS depression, predispose newborns to conjugated and nonconjugated hyperbilirubinemia, decrease albumin binding of bilirubin, and contribute to metabolic acidosis. Use for the shortest period possible at the lowest effective dose.[2,3]

USE

For short-term sedation of infants on assisted ventilation or prior to procedures.

Does not interfere with EEG results, whereas barbiturates and benzodiazepines do.

MECHANISM OF ACTION

Unknown. Produces mild cerebral depression and quiet, deep sleep. Increases tidal volume and O_2 consumption. Has no effect on CO_2 chemoreceptor response in infants.

ADVERSE EFFECTS

Usually well tolerated in neonates. An effective sedative with a low incidence of acute toxicity when administered orally in the recommended dose for short-term sedation.[2]

Reported adverse effects include gastric irritation; paradoxical excitation; and, with large doses, vasodilation, hypotension, respiratory depression, cardiac arrhythmias, and myocardial depression. May cause laryngospasm if aspirated. Withdrawal may occur when drug is discontinued suddenly after prolonged use (2 weeks). Tolerance may develop. Overdose can be fatal.

The trichloroethanol metabolite may accumulate in neonates after several days, particularly with hepatic dysfunction, causing risk of excessive blood levels and paradoxical agitation.[1,4]

Trichloroethanol is a carcinogen in laboratory animals, but has not been reported as such in humans.[2]

PHARMACOKINETICS/PHARMACODYNAMICS

Absorption: Readily absorbed from the GI tract.

Onset of Action: Approximately 15 minutes; deep sleep usually occurs within 30 to 45 minutes.

Duration: Most infants are fully awake in 2 hours.[1]

Protein Binding: 35–41 percent trichloroethanol and 71–88 percent trichloroacetic acid.

Metabolism: Metabolized to the active hypnotic metabolite trichloroethanol in the liver by alcohol dehydrogenase. Some drug is oxidized to trichloroacetic acid, which is excreted as a glucuronide in the urine.

NURSING IMPLICATIONS

Monitor infant appropriately and record data in a time-based record as per the American Academy of Pediatrics guidelines.[5]

Monitor vital signs continuously, especially noting occurrence of respiratory depression, to permit early intervention in case of apnea.

Additional dosing may be necessary if the procedure lasts longer than 2 hours.

REFERENCES

1. Roberts RJ. 1984. *Drug Therapy in Infants: Pharmacologic Principles and Clinical Experience.* Philadelphia: WB Saunders, 304–305.

2. Committee on Drugs and Committee on Environmental Health. 1993. Use of chloral hydrate for sedation in children. *Pediatrics* 92(3): 471–473.

3. Lambert GH, et al. 1990. Direct hyperbilirubinemia associated with chloral hydrate administration in the newborn. *Pediatrics* 86(2): 277–281.

4. Gershanik JJ, et al. 1981. Monitoring levels of trichloroethanol (TCE) during chloral hydrate (CH) administration to sick neonates. *Clinical Research* 29(5): 895A.

5. American Academy of Pediatrics, Committee on Drugs. 1992. Guidelines for monitoring and management of pediatric patients during and after sedation for diagnostic and therapeutic procedures. *Pediatrics* 89(6 part 1): 1110–1115.

CHLORAMPHENICOL
(klor-am-FEN-i-kole)
(CHLOROMYCETIN)

ANTI-INFECTIVE:
ANTIBIOTIC

DOSE

<2 kg: 25 mg/kg/day as a single dose
>2 kg:

- 0–7 days: 25 mg/kg/day as a single dose
- >7 days: 25 mg/kg/dose given every 12 hours[1]

Reduce dose in renal and/or hepatic dysfunction.

ADMINISTRATION

IV—*Rate:* May infuse IV push over 5 minutes, but infusion over 30 minutes is preferred.

IV—*Concentration:* Maximum: 100 mg/ml; 20 mg/ml preferred.

PO: Available suspension: 150 mg/5 ml. The oral route cannot be relied upon for treatment of neonates. Absorption is poor and erratic.

IM: Not for IM use.[2]

USE

Use has decreased as a result of the availability of third-generation cephalosporins with excellent CSF penetration and greater safety. Should be considered for use in newborns as an alternative to aminoglycosides for therapy of neonatal meningitis caused by Gram-negative enteric bacilli only in developing areas of the world, where third-generation cephalosporins are cost-prohibitive.[3]

The use of chloramphenicol may be considered in cases of infection with multi-drug-resistant bacteria when indicated by culture and sensitivities. Serum chloramphenicol levels should be monitored.

Susceptible Organisms: *Haemophilus influenzae, Streptococcus pneumoniae, Neisseria meningitidis,* Group B streptococci, coliform bacteria, *Staphylococcus aureus, Listeria monocytogenes, Bacteroides fragilis,* Salmonella.

Resistant Organisms: *Serratia marcescens, Pseudomonas aeruginosa.* Check sensitivities.

MECHANISM OF ACTION

Competes with messenger RNA for binding sites on the ribosome, thus inhibiting bacterial ribosomal protein synthesis.

Bacteriostatic.[3]

ADVERSE EFFECTS

Gray Baby Syndrome: Shock-like syndrome of vomiting, refusal to suck, pallid cyanosis, loose green stools, abdominal distention, respiratory distress, metabolic acidosis, and vasomotor collapse with progression to death. Onset at 3–4 days of therapy, but may occur within hours. Excessive doses (100–200 mg/kg/day) lead to very high (50–70 mcg/ml) serum levels. Older children can tolerate these doses, but infants have immature hepatic glucuronyl transferase and reduced glomerular and tubular function that impair their ability to metabolize and excrete the drug. The high serum levels are thought to cause inhibition of mitochondrial protein synthesis and inhibition of myocardial contractility.[3] Treatment of gray baby syndrome includes exchange transfusions (preferred) and charcoal hemoperfusion.[4] *If chloramphenicol is discontinued when early evidence of symptoms occur, the process may be reversible with complete recovery.*

Bone Marrow Suppression: Dose-related suppression is reversible and can be minimized by keeping serum level <25 mcg/ml. Anemia (most common), thrombocytopenia, leukopenia. Non-dose-related suppression is irreversible and often appears after the drug has been discontinued.

Pharmacokinetics/Pharmacodynamics

Absorption: Erratic and unreliable in neonates. Many neonates do not produce the pancreatic lipases required to metabolize chloramphenicol palmitate and therefore cannot de-esterify the oral preparation.[5,6]

Distribution: CSF levels are 35–90 percent of concurrent serum levels, even without inflamed meninges. There is a large variability in serum concentrations in preterm infants for a given dose.

Metabolism: Chloramphenicol succinate is hydrolyzed to free, active chloramphenicol, then conjugated in the liver to the glucuronide salt.

Half-life: Variable, 10–48 hours. There is an inverse correlation between half-life and postnatal age and weight.[3,5–8]

Elimination: The free drug is excreted by glomerular filtration, and the conjugated drug is excreted by tubular secretion.

Nursing Implications

Do not administer IM.

Monitor for symptoms of gray baby syndrome, such as vomiting, diarrhea, and abdominal distention.

Monitor for anemia.

Follow serum drug levels and liver and renal function tests.

Comments

Therapeutic Range: 15–25 mcg/ml.[3] Monitoring of chloramphenicol serum levels during therapy is especially important in neonates to prevent subtherapeutic levels or toxicity and because of the unpredictability of pharmacokinetics in this age group.

Interactions: Phenobarbital given concurrently may cause chloramphenicol levels to fall by increasing glucuronidation and elimination. Higher doses of chloramphenicol may be required. May also occur with concurrent use of rifampin. Phenytoin may increase chloramphenicol concentration.

REFERENCES

1. Nelson JD. 1996. *1996–1997 Pocketbook of Pediatric Antimicrobial Therapy,* 12th ed. Baltimore: Lippincott Williams & Wilkins, 16–17.

2. Manufacturer's product literature.

3. Sáez-Llorens X, and McCracken GH Jr. 1995. Clinical pharmacology of antimicrobial agents. In *Infectious Diseases of the Fetus and Newborn Infant,* 4th ed., Remington JS, and Klein JO, eds. Philadelphia: WB Saunders, 1287–1336.

4. Freundlich M, et al. 1983. Clinical and laboratory observations: Management of chloramphenicol intoxication in infancy by charcoal hemoperfusion. *Journal of Pediatrics* 103(3): 485–487.

5. Mulhall A, de Louvois J, and Hurley R. 1983. The pharmacokinetics of chloramphenicol in the neonate and young infant. *Journal of Antimicrobial Chemotherapy* 12(6): 629–639.

6. Paap CM, and Nahata MC. 1990. Clinical pharmacokinetics of antibacterial drugs in neonates. *Clinical Pharmacokinetics* 19(4): 280–318.

7. Roberts RJ. 1994. *Drug Therapy in Infants: Pharmacologic Principles and Clinical Experience.* Philadelphia: WB Saunders, 70–74.

8. Nahata MC, and Powell DA. 1983. Comparative bioavailability and pharmacokinetics of chloramphenicol after intravenous chloramphenicol succinate in premature infants and older patients. *Developmental Pharmacology and Therapeutics* 6(1): 23–32.

CHLOROTHIAZIDE (DIURIL)

(klor-oh-THYE-a-zide)

**CARDIOVASCULAR:
DIURETIC**

DOSE

10–30 mg/kg/day divided every 12 hours or as a single daily dose.[1–3]

Reduce dose in renal impairment.

ADMINISTRATION

PO (preferred): Available in an oral liquid 250 mg/5 ml.

IV—*Rate:* Infuse over at least 1 minute.

IV—*Concentration:* Reconstitute to 28 mg/ml. Do not refrigerate reconstituted solution. Discard unused portion after 24 hours. Reconstitute 500 mg vial with 18 ml of sterile water. This yields a 28 mg/ml concentration. The osmolality is 344 mOsm/kg. Can be diluted further with D_5W, $D_{10}W$, or NS, based on fluid status of infant.

IV—*Compatibility:* See Appendix E: Y-Site Compatibility of Common NICU Drugs.

CAUTIONS/CONTRAINDICATIONS

Use caution in severe liver disease.

USE

Mild to moderate edema (including pulmonary edema); hypertension.

An advantage of thiazides over furosemide is that they do not increase urinary excretion of calcium.

MECHANISM OF ACTION

Thiazides act primarily by inhibiting sodium reabsorption in the distal tubules. They increase chloride, potassium, magnesium, phosphate, water, and bicarbonate excretion and decrease calcium and uric acid excretion.[4] The antihypertensive effect is probably the result of sodium depletion.

ADVERSE EFFECTS

Dehydration and possibly prerenal azotemia; reduced serum sodium, chloride, potassium, magnesium; hyperglycemia; hypercalcemia; metabolic alkalosis as a result of chloride loss; hyperuricemia; bone marrow depression (rarely); syndrome of inappropriate antidiuretic hormone excretion.

May cause hyperlipidemia with effects on triglycerides and cholesterol.

PHARMACOKINETICS/PHARMACODYNAMICS

Absorption: Incomplete from GI tract (10–21 percent).[3] Absorption is increased if the drug is taken with food.

Onset of Action: Diuretic effect after IV administration occurs in 15 minutes, with peak at 30 minutes. Onset of antihypertensive effects takes several days; optimal effect is after 2–4 weeks.[3]

NURSING IMPLICATIONS

Monitor for dehydration and electrolyte imbalances.

Strictly monitor input and output.

Monitor for response to therapy, including reduced pulmonary edema and improved oxygenation.

COMMENTS

May need sodium or potassium supplements during therapy.

Doses higher than those recommended do not increase pharmacologic effect.

Not effective in severe renal disease. May cause increased BUN and reduced GFR. Use a loop diuretic such as furosemide instead.

May decrease urine volume in nephrogenic diabetes insipidus.

REFERENCES

1. Till JA, and Rigby ML. 1991. Treatment of cardiac disorders in the neonate. In *Neonatal Clinical Pharmacology and Therapeutics*, Rylance G, Harvey D, and Aranda JV, eds. Linacre House, Jordan Hill, Oxford: Butterworth-Heinemann, 126–152.

2. Witte MK, Stork JE, and Blumer JL. 1986. Diuretic therapeutics in the pediatric patient. *American Journal of Cardiology* 57(2): 44A–53A.

3. Olin BR. 1994. *Drug Facts and Comparisons*. St. Louis: Facts and Comparisons, 566.

4. Roberts RJ. 1984. *Drug Therapy in Infants: Pharmacologic Principles and Clinical Experience*. Philadelphia: WB Saunders, 244–246.

CIMETIDINE (TAGAMET)
(sye-MET-i-deen)

GASTROINTESTINAL: HISTAMINE (H$_2$) ANTAGONIST

DOSE

Neonates: 5–10 mg/kg/day divided every 8–12 hours

Infants: 10–20 mg/kg/day divided every 6–12 hours[1,2]

⬭ Reduce dose in renal and/or hepatic dysfunction.

⬭ Individualize dose. Adjust to lowest dose that will maintain pH of gastric secretions above 5.

ADMINISTRATION

IV—*Rate:* Infuse over 15–30 minutes, preferably. May inject over 5 minutes, but rapid IV injection has been associated with cardiac arrhythmias and hypotension. May give by continuous infusion. May admix in parenteral nutrition solution.

IV—*Concentration:* Maximum: 15 mg/ml.

IV—*Compatibility:* See Appendix E: Y-Site Compatibility of Common NICU Drugs.

IM: May give undiluted.

PO: Available as a suspension 60 mg/ml.[3]

Storage: Do not refrigerate the injection because it may precipitate. Store at room temperature.

CAUTIONS/CONTRAINDICATIONS

⬭ Use cautiously in patients concurrently receiving theophylline, phenytoin, or caffeine because cimetidine may prolong the half-life of those drugs.

USE

Treatment of gastric ulcers, gastroesophageal reflux, esophagitis, and upper GI bleeding suspected to be caused by stress or steroid treatment; prevention of pulmonary injury from gastric aspiration.[2,4,5]

Control of malabsorption in patients with short-gut syndrome by decreasing duodenal acid load, improving fat and nitrogen absorption, and reducing fecal volume.[6]

MECHANISM OF ACTION

Cimetidine is an antisecretory agent that antagonizes histamine at the H$_2$ receptor. Its primary action is to inhibit gastric acid secretion. It reduces both volume of gastric juice secreted and its hydrogen ion concentration.[7]

ADVERSE EFFECTS

Usually well tolerated.

May cause confusion, agitation (not seen with ranitidine), and seizures with excessive doses; diarrhea; bradycardia, hypotension with rapid IV push; rash; endocrine side effects, such as gynecomastia and galactorrhea (disappears if ranitidine is substituted), as a result of an antiandrogenic effect—dihydro-testosterone is displaced from androgen binding sites, causing a rise in serum testosterone; increased serum prolactin; neutropenia, agranulocytosis; elevated AST and ALT, elevated serum creatinine.[2,3]

PHARMACOKINETICS/PHARMACODYNAMICS

Absorption: Nearly completely absorbed after oral administration, with a large hepatic first-pass effect resulting in a systemic bioavailability of 60–70 percent. Administration with food does not reduce extent of absorption, only delays time to peak.

Peak Effect: After oral administration, 45–90 minutes.

Protein Binding: 20 percent.

Half-life: 2.6 hours in preterm infants.[1,4]

Elimination: Via kidney, unchanged; some in bile and feces.

NURSING IMPLICATIONS

Monitor for agitation. If seizures occur, consider that excessive dosing of cimetidine may have inadvertently occurred. Double-check dose.

May administer with food.

COMMENTS

Interactions: Binds to cytochrome P-450 and reduces the activity of hepatic microsomal drug-metabolizing enzymes, increasing the half-life and serum concentrations of theophylline, caffeine, and other drugs metabolized by the liver. Onset of inhibition is within 24 hours; inhibition subsides within 2 days after the last dose. These interactions are not likely to occur with ranitidine, although idiosyncratic reactions have occurred in some patients.[8]

REFERENCES

1. Aranda JV, Outerbridge EW, and Schentag JJ. 1983. Pharmacodynamics and kinetics of cimetidine in a premature newborn. *American Journal of Diseases of Children* 137(12): 1207.

2. Roberts RJ. 1984. *Drug Therapy in Infants: Pharmacologic Principles and Clinical Experience.* Philadelphia: WB Saunders, 295–296.

3. Manufacturer's product literature.

4. Chhattriwalla Y, Colon AR, and Scanlon JW. 1980. The use of cimetidine in the newborn. *Pediatrics* 65(2): 301–302.

5. Lambert J, Mobassaleh M, and Grand RJ. 1992. Efficacy of cimetidine for gastric acid suppression in pediatric patients. *Journal of Pediatrics* 120(3): 474–478.

6. Roberts EA. 1993. Drug therapy used in gastrointestinal diseases. In *Pediatric Pharmacology and Therapeutics,* Radde IC, and MacLeod SM, eds. St. Louis: Mosby-Year Book, 220–242.

7. Goudsouzian N, et al. 1981. The dose-response effects of oral cimetidine on gastric pH and volume in children. *Anesthesiology* 55(5): 533–536.

8. Kehoe WA, et al. 1996. Effect of ranitidine on theophylline metabolism in healthy Koreans living in China. *Annals of Pharmacotherapy* 30(2): 133–137.

CISAPRIDE (PROPULSID)
(SIS-a-pride)

**GASTROINTESTINAL:
PROKINETIC AGENT**

> *Cisapride is available only via a Limited Access Protocol because serious cardiac arrhythmias and fatalities have been reported with its use. Available only for patients with severe debilitating conditions who meet specific criteria directly through Janssen Pharmaceutical Company at 1-800-Janssen.*

DOSE

0.15–0.3 mg/kg/dose given every 6 to 8 hours at least 15 minutes prior to feedings.

Do not exceed recommended dose. Use half of the recommended dose in severe hepatic dysfunction.

ADMINISTRATION

PO: For oral use only. Supplied commercially as 1 mg/ml suspension and 10 mg tablets. One of these methods may be used to prepare a liquid form of the drug from the tablets:

- Crush a 10 mg tablet and dissolve in 10 ml water (= 1 mg/ml). Withdraw dose needed. Refrigerate remainder. Discard unused portion after 24 hours.

Pharmacist Compounding Directions
Cisapride 1mg/ml Suspension[1]

Crush 20 cisapride 10 mg tablets in a mortar. Add small volumes of simple syrup slowly while mixing to create a paste. Transfer to a graduated cylinder and add additional syrup to make a total volume of 100 ml. Add methylcellulose 1 percent to the cylinder to make a total volume of 200 ml, to yield a final concentration of 1 mg/ml. Shake well before measuring each dose.

Stability: 91 days at 4°C (32°F) and 28 days at 25°C (77°F) in amber plastic prescription bottles.

Storage: Protect from light.

CAUTIONS/CONTRAINDICATIONS

The safety of cisapride has been questioned. Cisapride administration in children may cause torsades de pointes and heart block associated with a prolonged QT interval.[2] (Also see **COMMENTS** below.)

Risk factors for serious cardiac arrhythmias include other drugs that cause QT prolongation, drugs that inhibit the enzymes that metabolize cisapride, or deplete serum electrolytes (see **Interactions** under **COMMENTS** below), or presence of disorders that predispose to arrhythmias.

Serious adverse effects (cardiovascular events including third degree heart block and ventricular tachycardia) including death have been reported in infants and children treated with cisapride. Obtain EKG before administration. Do not give cisapride if the QT interval is prolonged. Discontinue if rapid or irregular heartbeat develops.

- Do not use in patients with GI hemorrhage, mechanical obstruction, GI perforation, or other problems where stimulation of GI motility is dangerous.

- Cisapride is contraindicated with hypokalemia, hypocalcemia, and hypomagnesemia.

- Pediatric deaths have been associated with seizures and at least one case of sudden unexplained death in a 3-month-old infant.

- In Canadian labeling, cisapride is contraindicated for use in premature (i.e., born at <36 weeks gestational age) infants during the first 3 months after delivery.

USE

A prokinetic agent that increases motility in the stomach, small intestine, and colon.

Used in infants for GI motility disorders, such as delayed gastric emptying, GE reflux, excessive regurgitation, and vomiting.

Has been used to treat constipation.[3–6]

MECHANISM OF ACTION

Cisapride is a motility-stimulating agent that increases the release of acetylcholine from the myenteric plexus. This release of acetylcholine increases esophageal activity and clearance and decreases reflux of gastric contents into the esophagus. Cisapride also enhances gastric and duodenal emptying. It improves transit in both small and large bowel. Tolerance may develop to its use.

Cisapride has a chemical structure similar to metoclopramide (Reglan). Cisapride differs from metoclopramide in having no effect at the dopaminergic receptor and no extrapyramidal and antiemetic effects. Cisapride does not increase prolactin levels, as metoclopramide does.

ADVERSE EFFECTS

Cardiovascular: tachycardia, cardiac arrhythmias (see **CAUTIONS/ CONTRAINDICATIONS** above and **Interactions** under **COMMENTS** below)

May cause abdominal cramping, diarrhea (14 percent), and drowsiness. Diarrhea is dose dependent.[3] Some babies quiet after use, possibly as a result of smoother digestion.

Seizures have occurred rarely and only in patients with a history of seizures.[3]

Other potentially serious adverse effects reported in pediatric patients that may apply to infants include presence of antinuclear antibodies (ANA), anemia, hemolytic anemia, methemoglobinemia, hyperglycemia, hypoglycemia with acidosis, unexplained apneic episodes, and severe photosensitivity reaction.

PHARMACOKINETICS/PHARMACODYNAMICS

Absorption: Well absorbed.

Onset of Action: 30–60 minutes. Peak levels are at 1–2 hours. Bioavailability is 40–50 percent as a result of extensive first-pass metabolism.

Protein Binding: 98 percent.

Metabolism: Mainly in the liver via the P450 3A4 enzyme.

Half-life: Serum elimination half-life is 7–10 hours.

Elimination: 50 percent each in urine and feces.

NURSING IMPLICATIONS

Give 15–30 minutes prior to feeding.

Prepare carefully from tablet form if a suspension is not prepared by the pharmacist.

COMMENTS

Interactions:

- Anticholinergic drugs may antagonize the effects of cisapride.
- Cisapride may enhance the absorption of benzodiazepines.
- Cisapride accelerates the absorption of cimetidine and ranitidine.
- Do not give cisapride in patients receiving drugs that inhibit the hepatic cytochrome P450 3A4 enzyme because elevated cisapride serum levels may result—macrolide antibiotics (erythromycin, clarithromycin), certain antifungals (fluconazole, itraconazole, ketoconazole), protease inhibitors (indinavir, ritonavir), drugs that prolong the QT interval—phenothiazines (promethazine), Class IA (quinidine, procainamide) and Class III (sotalol) antiarrhythmics. The preceding list is not comprehensive.
- Concurrent use of potassium-wasting diuretics (bumetanide, ethacrynic acid, furosemide, thiazides) may deplete serum electrolytes and predispose to cardiac arrhythmias. Assess serum electrolytes before initiating cisapride and periodically thereafter.[3,7]

REFERENCES

1. Nahata MC, Morosco RS, and Hipple TF. 1995. Stability of cisapride in a liquid dosage form at two temperatures. *Annals of Pharmacotherapy* 29(2): 125–126.

2. Khongphatthanayothin A, Lane J, and Thomas D. 1998. Effects of cisapride on QT interval in children. *Journal of Pediatrics* 133(1): 51–56.

3. United States Pharmacopeial Convention/USP DI. 2000. *Drug Information for the Health Care Professional,* 20th ed. Rockville, Maryland: United States Pharmacopeial Convention, 899–902.

4. Van Eygen M, and Van Ravensteyn H. 1989. Effect of cisapride on excessive regurgitation in infants. *Clinical Therapeutics* 11(5): 669–677.

5. Cucchiara S, et al. 1987. Cisapride for gastroesophageal reflux and peptic esophagitis. *Archives of Disease in Childhood* 62(5): 454–457.

6. Saye ZN, Forget PP, and Geubelle F. 1987. Effect of cisapride on gastroesophageal reflux in children with chronic bronchopulmonary disease: A double-blind cross-over pH-monitoring study. *Pediatric Pulmonology* 3(1): 8–12.

7. Manufacturer's product literature. 2000. Propulsid (Cisapride). Janssen Pharmaceutica. Titusville, New Jersey.

CITRATE AND CITRIC ACID

(SIT-rayt and SIT-rik A-sid)

SOLUTIONS (BICITRA)

ELECTROLYTE BALANCE: SYSTEMIC ALKALINIZER

Synonyms: Shohl's Solution, Modified Citrate Mixtures, Citrate Salts, Sodium Citrate and Citric Acid, Citrates

DOSE

Renal Tubular Acidosis (RTA): 2–3 mEq/kg/day divided 3 or 4 times/day. Larger doses may be required. Adjust dose to maintain desired urine pH.[1,2]

ADMINISTRATION

Supplied as: Various oral liquids. See Table 1-42, page 483: Content of Oral Citrate Products.

PO: Dilute with water before administration to lessen GI pain or injury associated with oral administration of concentrated potassium. Give immediately after feedings or within 30 minutes after feedings to avoid saline laxative effect. Follow dose with additional water if infant's fluid status allows.

CAUTIONS/CONTRAINDICATIONS

Sodium Salts: Patients with oliguria or severe renal dysfunction, heart failure, hypertension, sodium restriction, or hypernatremia.

Potassium Salts: Patients with hyperkalemia, especially with renal dysfunction, or dehydration.

Use with caution in infants already on other sodium and/or potassium supplements. Include mEq of sodium and/or potassium in the citrate mixture when calculating daily maintenance electrolytes.

Avoid use in patients with aluminum toxicity because citrate salts increase aluminum absorption and may exacerbate the condition, especially in renal insufficiency.

USE

Urinary and systemic alkalinizers used in the management of chronic metabolic acidosis associated with renal tubular acidosis or renal insufficiency. Growth retardation associated with RTA is usually corrected with adequate alkali replacement, especially when treatment is begun early.[1] Citrate mixtures are more palatable than giving sodium bicarbonate orally.

1 mEq of citrate is equivalent to 1 mEq of bicarbonate.

See Table 1-42, page 483: Content of Oral Citrate Products, for mEq of sodium, potassium, and/or citrate in the various citrate-mixture products. Select a product from the table based on the patient's serum electrolyte status and the amount of citrate desired. Products containing potassium citrate are preferred in patients requiring potassium or those with sodium restriction. Products containing sodium citrate are preferred when potassium is undesirable or contraindicated.[3,4]

Mechanism of Action

Sodium citrate and potassium citrate are metabolized to bicarbonates, which increase urinary pH by increasing the excretion of free bicarbonate ions.[4]

Sodium citrate forms an undissociated calcium citrate complex, making calcium unavailable to the clotting mechanism. Sodium citrate is used as an anticoagulant for banked blood for transfusion and to prepare citrated human plasma and blood for fractionation. It has also been used to prevent curdling of milk by renin. It alters cow's milk so that large, hard curds are not formed in the stomachs of feeding infants.[3]

Adverse Effects

Usually well tolerated in infants with normal renal function and urine output when given at usual doses.

Cardiovascular: Excessive doses depress the heart.

Electrolytes:

- May cause tetany by decreasing ionized calcium concentration.
- Metabolic alkalosis, especially in patients with renal dysfunction.
- *Sodium salts:* Hypernatremia.
- *Potassium salts:* Hyperkalemia may occur, especially in patients with renal dysfunction.

GI: Saline laxative effect. GI irritation with potassium salts.

GU: Citrate mobilizes calcium from bones and increases its renal excretion; this, along with the increased urine pH, may increase the risk of urolithiasis.

See monographs on potassium, sodium bicarbonate, and sodium chloride.

Pharmacokinetics/Pharmacodynamics

Onset of Action: Within 1 hour.

Duration of Action: Up to 24 hours.

Metabolism: Metabolized by oxidation in the liver to potassium bicarbonate or sodium bicarbonate. The citrate is converted to CO_2 and water. Conversion not as complete in very ill patients, those with hepatic dysfunction, or those in shock.

Elimination: Excreted in the urine. If oxidative activity is intact, less than 5 percent is excreted unchanged.[4]

Nursing Implications

Monitor serum electrolytes, bicarbonate, urinary pH, acid-base balance.

Monitor for diarrhea.

COMMENTS

Interactions: Urinary excretion of salicylates is increased with alkaline urine; urinary excretion of quinidine, flecainide, and sympathomimetics decreases with alkaline urine. Concurrent use of aluminum-containing antacids can increase aluminum absorption, possibly leading to aluminum toxicity, particularly in infants with renal insufficiency.[4]

REFERENCES

1. Balfe JW, and Steele BT. 1993. Pharmacology in renal disease. In *Pediatric Pharmacology and Therapeutics,* 2nd ed., Radde IC, and MacLeod SM, eds. St. Louis: Mosby, 295–313.

2. Benitz WE, and Tatro DS. 1995. *The Pediatric Drug Handbook,* 3rd ed. St. Louis: Mosby-Year Book, 308–309.

3. United States Pharmacopeial Convention/USP DI. 1996. *Drug Information for the Health Care Professional,* 16th ed. Rockville, Maryland: United States Pharmacopeial Convention, 855–858.

4. McEvoy GK. 1994. *AHFS Drug Information.* Bethesda, Maryland: American Society of Hospital Pharmacists, 1642–1644.

CLINDAMYCIN (CLEOCIN)
(klin-da-MYE-sin)

**ANTI-INFECTIVE:
ANTIBIOTIC**

DOSE

<1.2 kg (0–4 weeks): 5 mg/kg/dose given every 12 hours
1.2–2 kg:

- 0–7 days: 5 mg/kg/dose given every 12 hours
- >7 days: 5 mg/kg/dose given every 8 hours

>2 kg:

- 0–7 days: 5 mg/kg/dose given every 8 hours
- >7 days: 20 mg/kg/day divided every 6–8 hours[1,2]

Reduce dose in severe hepatic and/or renal dysfunction.

ADMINISTRATION

IV administration is preferred.

IV—*Rate:* Infuse over 30–60 minutes.

IV—*Concentration:* Maximum: 18 mg/ml.

IV—*Compatibility:* See Appendix E: Y-Site Compatibility of Common NICU Drugs.

IM: May give undiluted (150 mg/ml) IM.

PO: Available as an oral suspension, 75 mg/5 ml. Shake well.

CAUTIONS/CONTRAINDICATIONS

Cardiac arrest has occurred after rapid IV administration.

Clindamycin phosphate contains benzyl alcohol.

USE

Antibacterial agent.

Susceptible Organisms: Gram-positive cocci such as *Staphylococcus aureus, Streptococcus pneumoniae;* anaerobic bacteria, especially Bacteroides species.

Resistant Organisms: Aerobic Gram-negative bacteria.

MECHANISM OF ACTION

Inhibits protein synthesis by binding to bacterial ribosomes.

Usually bacteriostatic.

ADVERSE EFFECTS

Diarrhea, including pseudomembranous colitis (20 percent of healthy neonates are colonized with *Clostridium difficile,* the causative organism in this condition;

limit the use of clindamycin in this age group whenever possible). ***Management:*** Discontinue clindamycin and opiates immediately. Treat colitis with vancomycin PO.[3,4]

Local erythema, pain, swelling, and thrombophlebitis.

Rash, including Stevens-Johnson syndrome.

Elevated hepatic enzymes, granulocytopenia, thrombocytopenia.

PHARMACOKINETICS/PHARMACODYNAMICS

Absorption: 90 percent absorption from GI tract following hydrolysis of clindamycin palmitate HCl to active clindamycin. The presence of food does not decrease absorption.

Distribution: Does not penetrate well into the CSF.

Protein Binding: 93 percent.

Metabolism: Mostly metabolized by the liver.

Half-life: Serum elimination half-life is inversely related to gestational age and birth weight. Preterm neonates: 8.7 hours; term newborns: 3.6 hours.

Elimination: About 10 percent excreted unchanged in the urine.[2,3,5]

NURSING INTERVENTIONS

Monitor for feeding intolerance and colitis.

Hematest all stools.

Monitor CBCs and liver function tests.

COMMENTS

Interactions: May enhance and prolong the action of neuromuscular blocking agents such as pancuronium.

REFERENCES

1. Nelson JD. 1996. *1996–1997 Pocketbook of Pediatric Antimicrobial Therapy,* 12th ed. Baltimore: Lippincott Williams & Wilkins, 16–17.

2. Bell MJ, et al. 1984. Pharmacokinetics of clindamycin phosphate in the first year of life. *Journal of Pediatrics* 105(3): 482–486.

3. Roberts RJ. 1984. *Drug Therapy in Infants: Pharmacologic Principles and Clinical Experience.* Philadelphia: WB Saunders, 74–75.

4. Donta ST, and Myers MG. 1982. *Clostridium difficile* toxin in asymptomatic neonates. *Journal of Pediatrics* 100(3): 431–434.

5. Koren G, et al. 1986. Pharmacokinetics of intravenous clindamycin in newborn infants. *Pediatric Pharmacology* 5(4): 287–292.

CLONIDINE (CATAPRES)
(KLOE-ni-deen)

**ANTIHYPERTENSIVE:
ALPHA-ADRENERGIC AGONIST**

DOSE

Use the lowest effective dose.

Reduce dose in renal dysfunction.

Hypertension (not commonly used in infants for this purpose):

- *PO:* 5–10 mcg/kg/day divided every 8–12 hours. May increase dose gradually, if needed, allowing 5–7 days between dose adjustments. *Maximum:* 20 mcg/kg/day divided every 6 hours.[1,2]

Opioid Withdrawal:

- *PO:* 2 mcg/kg/day divided every 6 hours. *Maximum:* 4 mcg/kg/day divided every 6 hours.[2–6]

Weaning: Wean gradually over 1–2 weeks.[6,7] Adjust the dose to avoid hypotension and oversedation; individualize dose by patient tolerance. One suggested regimen is to give the full dose for 10 days; 50 percent of the dose on days 11, 12, and 13; and no medication on day 14.[8]

Growth Hormone Provocation Test: 0.1–0.15 mg/m^2 PO as a single dose. Blood samples for growth hormone levels are usually drawn 30, 60, and 90 minutes after clonidine is given PO. Monitor patient for drowsiness, pallor, and hypotension. Use this test only after careful clinical assessment confirms inadequate growth velocity, other potential causes of growth failure have been excluded, and there is a real possibility of hypothalamic or pituitary hormone deficiency. The test should be conducted only by centers experienced in performing the procedure and interpreting the results.[9] (For information on average weight and body surface area by age, see Table M-6, page 736.

ADMINISTRATION

Supplied as:

- *Tablet:* 0.1 mg, 0.2 mg.
- *Transdermal delivery system (TDS) or patch (Catapres-Transdermal Therapeutic System [TTS]):* 0.1 mg (100 mcg/day released at an approximately constant rate for 7 days).

PO: May administer with feedings or water to decrease GI upset.

- *Preparation:* Clonidine is not supplied as an oral liquid; however, a suspension can be prepared by the pharmacist:

Pharmacist Compounding Directions
Clonidine Oral Suspension 20 mcg/ml

Crush ten 0.2 mg tablets (= 2 mg = 2,000 mcg) to a fine powder in a glass mortar. Add a small amount of purified water and triturate to form a paste. Then gradually mix with simple syrup to yield a final volume of 100 ml (= 2,000 mcg/100 ml = 20 mcg/ml). Store in an amber glass bottle.

Stability: 28 days (based on 28-day stability of a 0.1 mg/ml suspension).[10]

Storage: Refrigerate. Shake well.

- *Preparation of a liquid dose by the nurse (A liquid dosage form should usually be prepared by the pharmacy. If this is not possible, these instructions may be followed in the interim.)*

- *Pharmacy:* For each dose, dispense a unit-dose clonidine 0.2 mg tablet, an empty 30 ml amber prescription bottle, a 1 ml oral syringe with cap, and instructions for dose preparation by the nurse stating the appropriate volume for the dose prescribed.

- *Nurse:*

  - For each dose, crush tablet in the unit-dose package, transfer to the bottle provided, and add water 10 ml (= 0.2 mg/10 ml = 200 mcg/10 ml = 20 mcg/ml).

  - Shake well. Draw up the appropriate volume for the dose prescribed using the oral syringe provided. Administer immediately. Discard the unused portion. **Note:** Particles that quickly settle to the bottom are insoluble tablet excipients, not drug. Clonidine has an aqueous solubility of about 77 mg/ml.[11]

TDS/Patch: *Do not cut.* Cutting damages the integrity of the semipermeable membrane and may affect the rate of drug delivery. Reservoir contents could leak. Cutting could compromise the TDS's ability to adhere to the skin as well. Lee and Anderson suggest that placing a piece of impermeable material, such as an adhesive bandage, on the skin below a portion of the TDS may be effective in giving a partial dose. The surface area of the TDS that is blocked should be proportionate to the intended reduction in the amount of drug delivered to the skin. Lee and Anderson also recommend that the impermeable material and the TDS be secured to the skin by placing another adhesive bandage over the whole system.[12]

CAUTIONS/CONTRAINDICATIONS

- Transdermal patches cannot be recommended for routine use in neonates; more study of their efficacy and safety is needed.

- Discontinue drug gradually over 2–7 days (see **ADVERSE EFFECTS**). Use with caution in infants susceptible to vomiting or feeding intolerance that may require the infant to be NPO, leading to abrupt discontinuation of clonidine.

- Do not use if patient is hypersensitive to clonidine or any component of the product.

- Tolerance may develop to the antihypertensive effects because of fluid retention and expanded plasma volume. Concurrent use of a diuretic may make tolerance less likely and may enhance the antihypertensive effect of the drug.[8]

- If clonidine must be interrupted for surgery, give the last dose no later than 4–6 hours before surgery and give a parenteral hypotensive drug throughout the procedure, if needed. Reinstitute clonidine as soon as possible.[8]

- Numerous reports describing accidental clonidine overdose in pediatrics seem to indicate that neonates, infants, and children are especially sensitive to the effects of clonidine.[8,13]

- Retinal degeneration has been observed in laboratory animals receiving clonidine for 6 months or longer, especially with strong exposure to light. Although this has not been reported in humans, consider periodic eye exams.

Use

Management of Hypertension: Clonidine is *not* commonly used to treat hypertension in infants and children.[14] More commonly used are diuretics, hydralazine, captopril, and, for severe hypertension, sodium nitroprusside.[15]

- **Neonatal Abstinence Syndrome and Iatrogenic Narcotic Dependency:** Clonidine produces a dramatic reduction in the severity of neonatal and adult withdrawal symptoms.[5,6,8] It has been used to alleviate symptoms of iatrogenic narcotic dependency.[16] However, controlled clinical trials, pharmacokinetic studies, and more experience are needed before clonidine is routinely used to treat opioid withdrawal in infants.[3,7] Use with caution, and monitor infant for hypotension.

  - In a 1984 report, Hoder and colleagues used clonidine 3–4 mcg/kg/day PO to treat seven infants with narcotic withdrawal from maternal methadone use. Infants were given an initial dose of 0.5–1 mcg/kg orally; the dosage was increased over 1–2 days to 3–4 mcg/kg/day in divided doses. The total length of treatment ranged from 6 to 17 days. Clonidine improved major withdrawal symptoms in six of the seven infants; the one infant who did not respond was born to a mother who had also received haloperidol, desipramine, and theophylline. No toxic effects were observed.[6] More research needs to be done using clonidine in neonatal abstinence syndrome, however, because its use today is based on studies conducted in the 1980s; newer studies are not available.

  - **Use of Transdermal Delivery System:** Use of the TDS in infants should be considered experimental because documentation of its safety and efficacy, controlled clinical trials, and pharmacokinetic studies are lacking and because accurate measurement and titration of the dose are difficult. Advantages of the TDS include consistent serum concentrations, ability to give the drug when the patient is NPO, and gradual dose tapering when the TDS is removed.

- *Partial doses:* The TDS should not be cut or trimmed to adjust the dose.[17] However, adhesive tape may be used to block off a partial dose.[12] (See **ADMINISTRATION**, above.)

- *Use in older children:* Transdermal clonidine (4.2–8.5 mcg/kg/day) was successfully used in eight 2- to 8-year-old children postsurgically to prevent narcotic and benzodiazepine withdrawal after sedation of more than 7 days. The TDS was applied before the children were extubated and before sedative infusions were stopped. When the TDS was removed prematurely in two of the ten patients, both experienced withdrawal symptoms within hours; symptoms subsided in the one patient whose TDS was reinstituted. No significant side effects necessitated discontinuation of therapy. No rebound withdrawal was seen.[16]

Growth Hormone Provocation Test: Clonidine is used as a pituitary function test for the presence or absence of growth hormone. Single doses of the drug produce a pronounced increase in growth hormone concentration in normal, but not in growth-hormone-deficient, children. This increase does not occur with chronic administration of the drug.[9]

Other Uses: Other uses for clonidine in older children are treatment of autism, attention deficit hyperactivity disorder (ADHD), Tourette's syndrome, sedation,[18,19] epidural use for pain control, and for the diagnosis of pheochromocytoma.

MECHANISM OF ACTION

Antihypertensive Effect: Clonidine stimulates α_2-adrenergic receptors in the central nervous system, decreasing sympathetic outflow from the brain to the heart, kidneys, and peripheral vasculature and decreasing peripheral vascular resistance, systolic and diastolic blood pressure, and heart rate.[1,8] Clonidine reduces circulating plasma renin levels.

Anti-withdrawal Effect in Neonatal Abstinence Syndrome: α_2-adrenoceptors and μ-opioid receptors activate the same potassium channel, but by different guanine nucleotide-binding proteins.[7] Effect may result from α-adrenergic inhibiting activity in the brain.[8]

Transdermal Delivery: In the TDS, the drug diffuses through a semipermeable membrane to the skin.[12]

ADVERSE EFFECTS

Cardiovascular: Hypotension, bradycardia.

Severe *rebound hypertension* may occur if chronic therapy is abruptly discontinued (or several consecutive doses are missed), especially in patients on high doses and/or who are receiving a concomitant β-adrenergic blocking agent such as propranolol. This rebound effect is caused by a surge of adrenergic activity as central suppression of adrenergic nerve conduction stops.[14] Symptoms may include tachycardia, tremors, and agitation; rarely, hypertensive encephalopathy, cerebrovascular accidents, and death have occurred.[17] Rebound hypertension can be treated by resuming oral clonidine or by giving phentolamine or diazoxide IV.[8,17]

CNS: Drowsiness, weakness, anxiety, hypothermia.

Dermatologic: Rash, localized skin reactions (dermatitis) with use of the TDS.

GI: Dry mouth, constipation, anorexia, GI upset.

Hematologic: Thrombocytopenia (rare).

Metabolic: Transient weight gain due to sodium and water retention.

Renal: Urine retention, decrease in plasma renin activity in hyperreninemic patients.[1]

Overdose: Symptoms include CNS depression, apnea, bradycardia, arrhythmia, profound hypotension, hyporeflexia, hypothermia, miosis (pinpoint pupils), transient hypertension, irritability, and dry mouth.[13,20–22] Clonidine overdose resembles opioid intoxication. Toxicity may occur with ingestion of 0.1 mg in children.[8]

Treatment of Overdose: Treatment includes continuous cardiac/apnea monitoring and symptomatic and supportive care; atropine for severe bradycardia; IV fluids and dopamine for hypotension; furosemide, phentolamine (α-adrenergic blocking agent), diazoxide, or nitroprusside for hypertension; and rewarming if hypothermic. Naloxone is sometimes helpful.[20] Call the regional poison control center for current recommendations.[8,23]

PHARMACOKINETICS/PHARMACODYNAMICS

Absorption: Well absorbed, with bioavailability of about 65 percent.

Metabolism: Hepatic.

Protein Binding: 20–40 percent.

Peak Plasma Level: Oral: 3–5 hours and 41 hours in patients with severe renal impairment. Patch: 2–3 days.[8,17]

Half-life: 12–16 hours; up to 41 hours in renal dysfunction (adults).[8]

Elimination: 40–60 percent renal; 20 percent excreted in feces, probably via enterohepatic circulation.

When Used to Treat Hypertension:

- *Onset of Action:* Oral: 30–60 minutes; transdermal: 2–3 days.
- *Peak of Action:* 2–4 hours.
- *Duration of Action:* Oral: 8 (usually) to 36 hours.[8] Patch: 8 hours after TDS removal; then slow decline over several days.

NURSING IMPLICATIONS

Observe for excessive CNS and/or respiratory depression.

Monitor blood pressure, heart rate, and heart rhythm.

Ensure that the drug is not discontinued abruptly.

Monitor for therapeutic effects.

COMMENTS

Interactions:

✎ Concurrent *β-adrenergic blocking agent* increases risk of clonidine-withdrawal hypertensive crisis if clonidine is abruptly discontinued. Discontinue the β-blocker several days before discontinuing the clonidine. Concurrent β-blockers also impair blood pressure control.[8]

✎ Concurrent *CNS depressants* enhance clonidine-caused CNS depression.

✎ Concurrent *indomethacin* reduces clonidine's antihypertensive effects, possibly by inhibiting renal prostaglandin synthesis and/or as a result of sodium and fluid retention.[8]

✎ Concurrent *drugs that decrease heart rate* (such as *digoxin* and *β-adrenergic blocking agents*) enhance bradycardia. Because clonidine may produce bradycardia, additive effects should be considered when given concomitantly with other drugs that affect sinus node function or AV nodal conduction. Concurrent use may exacerbate bradycardia and AV block.

REFERENCES

1. Go RM, et al. 1993. Cardiovascular pharmacology. In *Pharmacology and Therapeutics*, Radde IC, and MacLeod SM, eds. St. Louis: Mosby-Year Book, 460, 582, 585.

2. Roberts RJ. 1984. *Drug Therapy in Infants: Pharmacologic Principles and Clinical Experience.* Philadelphia: WB Saunders, 197–198.

3. Levy M, and Spino M. 1993. Neonatal withdrawal syndrome: Associated drugs and pharmacologic management. *Pharmacotherapy* 13(3): 202–211.

4. Theis JG, et al. 1997. Current management of the neonatal abstinence syndrome: A critical analysis of the evidence. *Biology of the Neonate* 71(6): 345–356.

5. Hoder EL, et al. 1981. Clonidine in neonatal narcotic-abstinence syndrome (letter). *New England Journal of Medicine* 305(21): 1284.

6. Hoder EL, et al. 1984. Clonidine treatment of neonatal narcotic abstinence syndrome. *Psychiatry Research* 13(3): 243–251.

7. Anand KJ, and Arnold JH. 1994. Opioid tolerance and dependence in infants and children. *Critical Care Medicine* 22(2): 334–342.

8. United States Pharmacopeial Convention/USP DI. 2000. *Drug Information for the Health Care Professional*, 20th ed. Rockville, Maryland: United States Pharmacopeial Convention, 943–946.

9. Hindmarsh PC, and Swift PG. 1995. An assessment of growth hormone provocation tests. *Archives of Disease in Childhood* 72(4): 362–368.

10. Levinson ML, and Johnson CE. 1992. Stability of an extemporaneously compounded clonidine hydrochloride oral liquid. *American Journal of Hospital Pharmacy* 49(1): 122–125.

11. Trissel LA. 1996. *Trissel's Stability of Compounded Formulations.* Washington, DC: American Pharmaceutical Association, 73–74.

12. Lee HA, and Anderson PO. 1997. Giving partial doses of transdermal patches. *American Journal of Health-System Pharmacy* 54(15): 1759–1760.

13. Reed MT, and Hamburg EL. 1986. Person-to-person transfer of transdermal drug-delivery systems: A case report. *New England Journal of Medicine* 314(17): 1120.

14. Temple ME, and Nahata MC. 2000. Treatment of pediatric hypertension. *Pharmacotherapy* 20(2): 140–150.

15. Goble MM. 1993. Hypertension in infancy. *Pediatric Clinics of North America* 40(1): 105–122.

16. Deutsch ES, and Nadkarni VM. 1996. Clonidine prophylaxis for narcotic and sedative withdrawal syndrome following laryngotracheal reconstruction. *Archives of Otolaryngology and Head and Neck Surgery* 122(11): 1234–1238.

17. Medical Economics Data. 2000. *Physicians' Desk Reference.* Montvale, New Jersey: Medical Economics, 794–797.

18. Golianu B, et al. 2000. Pediatric acute pain management. *Pediatric Clinics of North America* 47(3): 559–587.

19. Ambrose C, et al. 2000. Intravenous clonidine infusion in critically ill children: Dose-dependent sedative effects and cardiovascular stability. *British Journal of Anaesthesia* 84(6): 794–796.

20. Wiley JF, et al. 1990. Clonidine poisoning in young children. *Journal of Pediatrics* 116(4): 654–658.

21. Corneli H, et al. 1989. Toddler eats clonidine patch and nearly quits smoking for life (letter). *JAMA* 261(1): 42.

22. Nichols M, et al. 1997. Clonidine poisoning in Jefferson County, Alabama. *Annals of Emergency Medicine* 29(4): 511–517.

23. Olson KR, and McGuigan MA. 1996. Toxicology and accidents. 11.4.8 Clonidine and antihypertensive agents. In *Rudolph's Pediatrics,* 20th ed., Rudolph AM, Hoffman JIE, and Rudolph CD, eds. Stamford, Connecticut: Appleton & Lange, 824–825.

CODEINE
ACETAMINOPHEN WITH CODEINE
(a-seat-a-MIN-oh-fen/KOE-deen)
(TYLENOL WITH CODEINE)
(CONTROLLED SUBSTANCE
SCHEDULE II FOR CODEINE
SCHEDULE V FOR ACETAMINOPHEN WITH CODEINE)

CENTRAL NERVOUS SYSTEM:
NARCOTIC
ANALGESIC

DOSE

Codeine:

- *Analgesic:* 0.5–1 mg/kg/dose given every 6–8 hours.
- *Antitussive:* 1–1.5 mg/kg/day PO divided every 4–6 hours. (Codeine has cough-suppressant effects at lower doses than those required for analgesia.)

Acetaminophen with Codeine: Acetaminophen with codeine liquid is available as 120 mg acetaminophen and 12 mg codeine/5 ml. The dose of this combination should be based on the codeine content. Using a codeine dose of 3 mg/kg/day, the dose of the combination liquid can be rounded off as follows (to reduce risk of error and facilitate preparation by the pharmacy of standardized oral unit-dose syringe):

Weight (kg)	ml/dose	Codeine Content (mg/dose)
2–3	0.5	1.2
3.1–6	1	2.4
6.1–8	1.5	3.6
8.1–10	2	4.8

Example: An analgesic order for a 2.3 kg infant in moderate pain would be written as:

Acetaminophen with codeine 0.5 ml PO every 4 hours prn for pain.

Remember that the acetaminophen component is an antipyretic and therefore masks fever. If you wish to monitor for fever, use codeine alone for pain, rather than acetaminophen with codeine.

ADMINISTRATION

Supplied as:

- *Codeine:* Oral solution: 3 mg/ml; injection: 30 mg/ml.
- *Acetaminophen with codeine:* Codeine is also available in combination with acetaminophen (Tylenol with codeine): acetaminophen 120 mg and codeine 12 mg/5 ml with alcohol 7 percent.

PO (preferred), IM, SC. (Not for IV use because of histamine release and cardio-vascular effects.)

PO: Give with feedings or water to decrease GI upset.

IM, SC: May give undiluted.

USE

Treatment of moderate pain.

Used to treat cough in older children, but not usually in infants.

MECHANISM OF ACTION

Codeine stimulates opioid receptors in the central nervous system that mimic the actions of endogenous ligands, enkephalins, and β-endorphins, thus altering perception of and response to pain. Codeine causes respiratory depression by its direct effect on the brain's respiratory center. It also causes CNS depression.[1]

ADVERSE EFFECTS

Increasing the dose increases the adverse effects, such as respiratory and CNS depression. *Antidote:* Naloxone 0.1 mg/kg/dose IV. (See Appendix J: Antidotes for Drugs That Cause Loss of Respiratory Effort.)

Cardiovascular: Hypotension, especially in patients with inadequate blood volume (due to histamine release), bradycardia.

CNS: CNS depression, increased intracranial pressure, sedation.

Endocrine: Antidiuretic hormone release.

GI: Nausea, vomiting (give with food to reduce GI upset), cramping, constipation, biliary tract spasm, delays gastric emptying.[1]

GU: Urinary tract spasm.

Ophthalmic: Pupillary contraction (miosis).

Respiratory: Respiratory depression. In general, neonates are more susceptible to the depressant effects of opioids than are older children or adults.[2]

Patients unable to tolerate codeine may be able to tolerate another narcotic agent, particularly if in a different pharmacologic class (codeine and morphine: phenanthrenes; meperidine and fentanyl: phenylpiperidines; methadone: a diphenylheptane).

Codeine, like other opioids, causes physiologic dependency; do not discontinue abruptly after prolonged use. Tolerance develops to the drug.

PHARMACOKINETICS/PHARMACODYNAMICS

Bioavailability: Codeine given orally is about two-thirds as potent as when it is administered parenterally (oral bioavailability is about 60 percent).[2]

Absorption: Moderately well absorbed from the GI tract.

Onset of Action: 20 minutes after PO administration, with maximum effect about 60–120 minutes after the dose.

Duration of Action: 4–6 hours.

Metabolism: Metabolized in the liver to morphine.

Half-life: 2–4 hours.

Elimination: Eliminated by the kidneys.

NURSING IMPLICATIONS

Observe for excessive sedation.

Monitor blood pressure and heart rate.

Observe the infant to see that pain is relieved adequately.

Watch for withdrawal after long-term administration.

COMMENTS

See Table 1-37, page 412: Narcotic Conversion Chart.

Interactions: Additive CNS depression with concurrent CNS depressants.

REFERENCES

1. Roberts RJ. 1984. *Drug Therapy in Infants: Pharmacologic Principles and Clinical Experience.* Philadelphia: WB Saunders, 302–303.

2. Bhatt-Mehta V, and Rosen DA. 1991. Management of acute pain in children. *Clinical Pharmacy* 10(9): 667–685.

COLFOSCERIL PALMITATE WITH CETYL ALCOHOL AND TYLOXAPOL

RESPIRATORY: SURFACTANT

(co-FOS-er-ill)
(EXOSURF NEONATAL)

DOSE

5 ml/kg/dose. The number of doses varies.[1]

ADMINISTRATION

Steps:

- Suction infant. Select adapter that fits infant's ETT size.
- Administer 2 half-doses (2.5 ml/kg each) intratracheally via sideport of special adapter provided. Do not interrupt mechanical ventilation. Instill each dose slowly over 5–10 minutes in small bursts timed with inspirations.
- Administer doses with baby in midline position. After the first half-dose, turn the infant's head and body 45 degrees to the right for 30 seconds while the infant remains on the ventilator.

  Return infant to midline and instill the second half-dose. Then turn the infant's head and body 45 degrees to the left for 30 seconds. Return to midline. Turning the infant helps gravity distribute surfactant evenly throughout the lungs.
- Do not suction for 2 hours after each dose, except when dictated by clinical necessity.

Preparation: Using a large-bore needle, inject 8 ml of preservative-free sterile water for injection into Exosurf vial. Vacuum will draw water into vial. Without removing needle, withdraw suspension back into syringe. Quickly release plunger to mix. Repeat three to four times or more until no large flakes or particulate matter are present. Do not vigorously shake; shaking will cause foaming.

Stability: May be used for 12 hours after reconstitution. Refrigerate (preferred—contains no preservative) or store at room temperature.[1]

USE

An artificial lung surfactant used to reduce the morbidity and mortality associated with respiratory distress syndrome of the newborn (RDS).

Rescue Regimen: For infants with established RDS.

Prophylactic Regimen: Given before the infant's first breath or within minutes of delivery to modify the course of RDS in infants at high risk for RDS.[1,2]

MECHANISM OF ACTION

Exosurf Neonatal is composed of colfosceril palmitate (dipalmitoylphosphatidyl-choline [DPPC]), which reduces surface tension; cetyl alcohol (hexadecanol), which acts as a spreading agent for the DPPC on the air-fluid interface; and tyloxapol, a nonionic surfactant that acts to disperse the DPPC and the cetyl alcohol.

ADVERSE EFFECTS

Usually very well tolerated. Benefits exceed risks.

Hyperoxia: Be prepared to reduce FiO_2 incrementally if baby becomes pink and oxygen saturation is in excess of 95 percent.

Hypocarbia: Be prepared to reduce ventilator rate immediately if CO_2 is <30 torr. Low CO_2 may reduce brain blood flow and impair cerebral oxygen delivery.

Pulmonary Air Leaks/Pneumothorax: Be prepared to reduce ventilatory pressures immediately if lung compliance improves.

Pulmonary Hemorrhage: Potentially protective measures include treating PDA during the first 2 days of life, reducing FiO_2 preferentially over ventilator pressures during the first 24–48 hours after dosing, and attempting to reduce PEEP at least minimally for at least 48 hours after dosing.

Mucus plugs.

Increased apnea requiring use of caffeine or aminophylline.

PHARMACOKINETICS/PHARMACODYNAMICS

Half-life: Alveolar half-life of DPPC is about 12 hours.

NURSING IMPLICATIONS

Monitor the following during dosing: Heart rate, color, chest expansion, breath sounds, oxygen saturation, and ETT patency and position before and for 30 minutes after each dose.

Rapid improvements in lung function may require immediate reductions in peak inspiratory pressure, ventilator rate, and/or FiO_2.

If the infant becomes dusky or agitated or if the heart rate slows, oxygen saturation falls, or surfactant backs up the ETT, the rate of surfactant administration may need to be slowed, and ventilator settings may need to be increased. Monitor blood gases.

Avoid suctioning infant for 6–8 hours, if possible.

COMMENTS

Must be used in centers with personnel capable of neonatal intubation, mechanical ventilation, and medical management of unstable preterm infants. Qualified nurses and respiratory therapists should be available on site when surfactant is administered, as should equipment for managing and monitoring preterm infants as well as laboratory and radiology support equipped to manage the needs of preterm infants.[1,3]

REFERENCES

1. Manufacturer's product literature.

2. Corbet A, et al. 1991. Decreased mortality rate among small premature infants treated at birth with a single dose of synthetic surfactant: A multicenter controlled trial. *Journal of Pediatrics* 118(2): 277–284.

3. American Academy of Pediatrics, Committee on Fetus and Newborn. 1991. Surfactant replacement therapy for respiratory distress syndrome. *Pediatrics* 87(6): 946–947.

Cosyntropin (Cortrosyn)

(koe-sin-TROE-pin)

**Diagnostic Agent:
Adrenocortical
Insufficiency**

Dose

40 mcg/kg[1-3]

Although 40 mcg/kg is more commonly used, a lower dose—3.5 mcg/kg IV—has also been used. Serum cortisol was drawn before and 30 minutes after administration of the dose. Watterberg and Scott state that although neonates may not have established a diurnal response, testing was done in the afternoon for maximal potential response because maximum adult amplitude of response was at this time.[4]

Testing Adequacy of the Adrenal Pituitary Axis: This ACTH stimulation test can be used to determine if it is safe to discontinue steroid hormone treatment or stress hormone coverage in infants who have received steroids for 7 or more days. Procedure:

- Draw blood for morning plasma cortisol concentration.
- Administer cosyntropin.
- Draw blood for serum cortisol 1 hour later.[1,2]

Congenital Adrenal Hyperplasia Evaluation: 1 mg/m^2/dose (*Maximum:* 1 mg). See Appendix M, Table M-6, to calculate the body surface area of the infant in m^2.

A normal baseline cortisol is greater than 5 mcg/dl. An adequate ACTH response is a doubling of the baseline cortisol value or an absolute 1-hour cortisol exceeding 18 mcg/dl.[1]

Administration

IV—*Rate:* Infuse IV over at least 2 minutes.

IV—*Concentration:* Reconstitute vial with 1 ml normal saline (= 0.25 mg/ml or 250 mcg/ml). The reconstituted solution is stable for 24 hours at room temperature and for 21 days under refrigeration. The drug is supplied as a 0.25 mg vial with 1 ml of sterile normal saline diluent.

IM: Administer the drug as reconstituted above by the IM route.

Use

A diagnostic agent used in the ACTH stimulation test to assess recovery of normal adrenal responsiveness after steroid hormone treatment. The ACTH stimulation test is used as a rapid assessment of adrenal function to differentiate between primary (adrenal gland) and secondary (pituitary) adrenocortical insufficiency.[1,5] The ACTH stimulation test is also used in the differential diagnosis of congenital adrenal hyperplasia.

Figure 1-4 ◆ Pituitary-Adrenal Cortex Control and the Action of Cosyntropin.

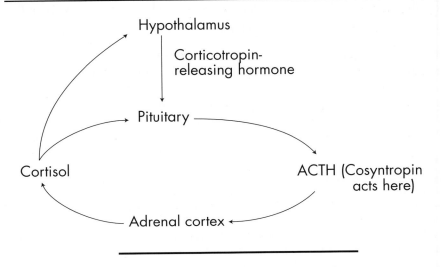

Mechanism of Action

Cosyntropin is a synthetic polypeptide, identical to the first 24 of the 39 amino acids in endogenous corticotropin. It exhibits the full corticosteroidogenic activity of natural ACTH.

Cosyntropin stimulates the adrenal cortex to secrete steroid hormones such as cortisol (hydrocortisone) as well as the steroid hormone precursor 17-hydroxyprogesterone, which can be increased in congenital adrenal hyperplasia (Figure 1-4).

In patients with primary adrenocortical insufficiency (Addison's disease), cosyntropin does not substantially increase plasma cortisol.

Cosyntropin is more potent and less allergenic than natural ACTH. A dose of 0.25 mg of cosyntropin is pharmacologically equivalent to 25 units of natural ACTH.[6]

Adverse Effects

Unlikely with short-term use.

Rarely, hypersensitivity reactions.

Possibility of decreased glucose tolerance.

Pharmacokinetics/Pharmacodynamics

Onset of Action: Following an IV push injection, plasma cortisol concentrations begin to increase within 5 minutes and approximately double within 15–30 minutes.

Peak Effect: Peak plasma cortisol concentrations are achieved within 1 hour and begin to decrease after 2–4 hours.[6]

Nursing Implications

Do not administer steroids or spironolactone (aldactazide) on the day of the test. Observe correct timing of test and blood draws.

Comments

Interactions: Falsely elevated cortisol levels may occur with concurrent spironolactone and with elevated plasma bilirubin concentrations (when fluorometric analysis is used). The patient should not receive dexamethasone, methylprednisolone, or other corticosteroids on the day of the test because these drugs will alter ACTH stimulation test results.

References

1. Strauss A, et al. 1992. Adrenal responsiveness in very-low-birth-weight infants treated with dexamethasone. *Developmental Pharmacology and Therapeutics* 19(2–3): 147–154.

2. Hingre RV, et al. 1994. Adrenal steroidogenesis in very low birth weight preterm infants. *Journal of Clinical Endocrinology and Metabolism* 78(2): 266–270.

3. Hanna CE, et al. 1993. Hypothalamic pituitary adrenal function in the extremely low birth weight infant. *Journal of Clinical Endocrinology and Metabolism* 76(2): 384–387.

4. Watterberg KL, and Scott SM. 1995. Evidence of early adrenal insufficiency in babies who develop bronchopulmonary dysplasia. *Pediatrics* 95(1): 120–125.

5. Manufacturer's product literature.

6. McEvoy GK. 1994. *AHFS Drug Information.* Bethesda, Maryland: American Society of Hospital Pharmacists, 1549–1551.

CROMOLYN (INTAL)

(KROE-moe-lin)

RESPIRATORY: ANTIHISTAMINE

DOSE

Nebulization: 20 mg every 6–8 hours. Dilute to a final total volume of 3 ml with normal saline or other concurrent medications.

Metered Dose Inhaler (MDI): 2 puffs every 6–8 hours.[1]

⟋Adjust dose in infants with significant hepatic or renal dysfunction.[2,3]

ADMINISTRATION

Supplied as:

- *Solution for Nebulization:* 20 mg/2 ml ampoules.
- *Aerosol Spray (MDI):* 800 mcg/actuation.

⟋Via nebulization or MDI.

Watterberg and associates showed that approximately 50–100 mcg of cromolyn were delivered to the lung when this configuration was used: 20 mg of cromolyn delivered by jet nebulizer placed in the ventilator circuit in place of the humidifier, driven by a gas flow of 5 liters/minute. Pressure-limited, time-cycled neonatal ventilators (Bear Cub) were used.[4]

USE

Not a bronchodilator, but may prevent triggering of airway hyperresponsiveness in infants with BPD, thereby improving lung function.[5] Results of studies have been inconsistent.[1,5]

Prevents release of inflammatory mediators such as histamine and leukotrienes from mast cells in the lung. May reduce pulmonary leukocyte concentrations and improve pulmonary mechanics when used with β-adrenergic therapy.[6]

An antiasthmatic, antiallergic, and mast cell stabilizer. A prophylactic agent; not helpful for episodes of acute bronchospasm because it has no bronchodilator activity.

MECHANISM OF ACTION

Cromolyn inhibits degranulation of mast cells. It inhibits the release of histamine and SRS-A (a slow-reacting substance of anaphylaxis, a leukotriene) from the mast cell and blocks protein kinase C and decreases PMN chemotaxis.[2] Cromolyn indirectly blocks calcium from entering mast cells, thus inhibiting mediator release.

Cromolyn has been shown to inhibit antigen-induced leukotriene release from the lung, to inhibit the inflammatory effects of platelet-activating factor (PAF), to block the late asthmatic response, and to inhibit hypoxic pulmonary hypertension (Figure 1-5).[7] Pathophysiologic abnormalities of BPD that correlate with actions of lipid mediators (arachidonic acid metabolites and PAF) are

FIGURE 1-5 ◆ **POTENTIAL ROLE OF INFLAMMATION AND LIPID MEDIATORS OF INFLAMMATION IN THE PATHOPHYSIOLOGY OF BPD—AND THE ROLE OF CROMOLYN.**

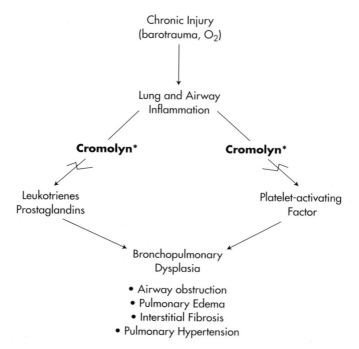

* Chromolyn inhibits the pathway at these points to relieve symptoms in infants with BPD.

Adapted from: Stenmark KR, et al. 1987. Potential role of eicosanoids and PAF in the pathophysiology of bronchopulmonary dysplasia. *American Review of Respiratory Disease* 136(3): 770–772. Reprinted by permission.

pulmonary edema, high airway resistance, increased mucus, inflammation, and pulmonary hypertension.[7]

ADVERSE EFFECTS

Usually well tolerated.

May cause dry, irritated throat, cough, nasal congestion, bronchoconstriction, lacrimation.

Rare Effects: Swollen parotid gland, dysuria, urinary frequency, dizziness, headache, rash, angioedema, joint swelling and pain, nausea.

PHARMACOKINETICS/PHARMACODYNAMICS

Absorption: Cromolyn acts locally on the lung. About 8–10 percent of the dose is absorbed from the lung.

Onset of Action: May be as long as 2–4 weeks.

Half-life: 80 minutes.

Elimination: Absorbed portion is excreted in the bile and urine. The rest is either exhaled or swallowed and excreted in the GI tract.[2]

Nursing Implications

Monitor for adverse effects on the respiratory tract, such as nasal congestion and bronchoconstriction.

Comments

Monitoring, Dose Titration, and Discontinuation of Treatments: Reassess weekly and discontinue the drug under the following conditions:[2]

- Adverse effects occur.
- The drug is no longer needed.
- There has been no improvement in respiratory status as measured by pulmonary mechanics or no change in respiratory support or clinical status after 2–4 weeks.

References

1. Watterberg KL, Murphy S, and the Neonatal Cromolyn Study Groups. 1993. Failure of cromolyn sodium to reduce the incidence of bronchopulmonary dysplasia: A pilot study. *Pediatrics* 91(4): 803–806.

2. Shook LA, et al. 1988. Improved lung resistance and compliance during cromolyn therapy in infants with bronchopulmonary dysplasia (abstract #1937). *Pediatric Research* 23(4): 524A.

3. Davis JM, Sinkin RA, and Aranda JV. 1990. Drug therapy for bronchopulmonary dysplasia. *Pediatric Pulmonology* 8(2): 117–125.

4. Watterberg KL, et al. 1991. Delivery of aerosolized medication to intubated babies. *Pediatric Pulmonology* 10(2): 136–141.

5. Rush MG, and Hazinski TA. 1992. Current therapy of bronchopulmonary dysplasia. *Clinics in Perinatology* 19(3): 563–590.

6. Stenmark KR, et al. 1985. Recovery of platelet activating factor and leukotrienes from infants with severe bronchopulmonary dysplasia: Clinical improvement with cromolyn treatment. *American Review of Respiratory Disease* 131(4 part 2, supplement): 236A.

7. Stenmark KR, et al. 1987. Potential role of eicosanoids and PAF in the pathophysiology of bronchopulmonary dysplasia. *American Review of Respiratory Disease* 136(3): 770–772.

CYCLOPENTOLATE 0.2 PERCENT AND PHENYLEPHRINE 1 PERCENT (CYCLOMYDRIL)

OPHTHALMIC: MYDRIATIC

(sye-klo-PEN-to-late and fen-ill-EF-rin)

DOSE

Instill 1 drop into each eye every 5 minutes 3 times.

Order Should Read: "Cyclomydril ophthalmic solution. 1 drop into each eye every 5 minutes × 3. Begin 1 hour prior to eye exam."

Delay in Eye Exam: If the eye exam is delayed but rescheduled for within 4 hours after the dose is given, the drops probably need not be repeated. If the delay is longer than 4 hours, discuss with ophthalmologist whether the dose should be repeated.

ADMINISTRATION

Instill topically into each eye.

CAUTIONS/CONTRAINDICATIONS

- Glaucoma.
- Narrow-angle glaucoma.

USE

For pupillary mydriasis (dilation) prior to routine ophthalmic examinations scheduled in preterm infants <1,800 gm at birth with a postnatal age of 4–6 weeks and older.

Preferred to other agents for use in infants because it contains low concentrations of the mydriatic (phenylephrine) and mydriatic cycloplegic (cyclopentolate) agents, thereby reducing the risk of hypertension (phenylephrine) and atropine-like adverse effects (cyclopentolate).

MECHANISM OF ACTION

Phenylephrine is an adrenergic agonist. This drug activates the dilator muscle of the pupil to cause contraction.

Cyclopentolate is an anticholinergic drug. It blocks the response of the muscle of the ciliary body and the sphincter muscle of the iris to cholinergic stimulation, causing pupillary dilation (mydriasis) and paralysis of accommodation (cycloplegia).

The combination of these two drugs induces mydriasis that is considerably greater than that of either drug alone.

ADVERSE EFFECTS

Systemic toxicity can occur in neonates after ophthalmic instillation of atropine-like drugs.

May cause increased intraocular pressure and stinging.

Although unlikely at this low dose, may cause signs of atropine toxicity, such as flushing and dryness of the skin and mouth or rash, tachycardia, fever, abdominal distention, bladder distention, urine retention, decreased GI motility, and behavioral disturbances.

Isenberg and associates compared the GI effects of cyclopentolate 0.25 percent, 0.5 percent, and a placebo. They reported that the 0.5 percent eyedrops significantly decreased gastric volume and acid secretion compared to the 0.25 percent and the placebo. Because this effect may predispose infants to the development of gastroenteritis, they recommend that the 0.5 percent concentration be avoided in preterm infants, but a weaker concentration can be used.[1]

May cause hypertension, especially in a traumatized, diseased eye.[2] Laws and associates studied the effects on blood pressure in screening for retinopathy of prematurity (ROP). They reported that the initial increase in blood pressure may represent a side effect of topical mydriatic, but the later increase, after the physical exam, may be a response to the stress of the ROP screening.[3]

Adverse effects of the cyclopentolate component of cyclomydril are atropine-like. See monograph on atropine.

PHARMACOKINETICS/PHARMACODYNAMICS

Onset of Action: 45–60 minutes.

Duration of Action: Approximately 4 hours (up to 12 hours in infants with blue eyes).

Onset and duration of action are partially dependent upon eye pigment. Dark-eyed infants have a longer time to onset of action and a shorter duration of action than blue-eyed infants. The pupils of very premature infants (i.e., 24- to 26-week gestational age infants in the first 2 weeks of life) do not dilate well, particularly if their eyes are dark.[4]

NURSING IMPLICATIONS

Monitor for tachycardia, hypertension, and cyanosis after administration.

Keep eyes covered or darken room for infant's comfort.

Assess vital signs, including blood pressure, observe for abdominal distention (caused by the atropine-like effect of slowing GI motility), which may occur after administration, and listen for bowel sounds before feeding.

Hold feeding for 2 hours before and 1 hour after the eye exam.

Do not repeat dose within 4 hours—and usually not within 24 hours—to reduce risk of adverse effects from systemic absorption and possible drug accumulation.

The ophthalmologist will also instill 1 drop of a local anesthetic (i.e., proparacaine 0.5 percent) into each eye just prior to the exam (onset: 15–20 seconds, duration 15–20 minutes). Because the anesthetic temporarily eliminates the "blink" reflex, protect the infant's eyes during the exam when physician is not immediately present and afterwards.

REFERENCES

1. Isenberg SJ, Abrams C, and Hyman PE. 1985. Effects of cyclopentolate eyedrops on gastric secretory function in preterm infants. *Ophthalmology* 92(5): 698–700.

2. Manufacturer's product literature.

3. Laws DE, et al. 1996. Systemic effects of screening for retinopathy of prematurity. *British Journal of Ophthalmology* 80(5): 425–428.

4. Bauer CR, Trottier MCT, and Stern L. 1973. Systemic cyclopentolate (Cyclogyl) toxicity in the newborn infant. *Journal of Pediatrics* 82(3): 501–505.

CYSTEINE HCL
(SIS-tuh-een)

NUTRITION:
AMINO ACID

DOSE

60–120 mg/kg/day IV (= 0.5–1 mmol/kg/day)

May also be calculated as 100 mg cysteine for every 2.5 gm crystalline amino acids.

ADMINISTRATION

Supplied as: 50 mg/ml concentration in 10 ml vials and in additive syringes.

Admix in daily parenteral nutrition (PN) solution.

Cysteine should be admixed by the pharmacist when the daily PN solution is prepared because it is unstable in solution, converting to cystine (insoluble) within approximately 24 hours. Therefore, cysteine would precipitate out if the manufacturer were to add it to the crystalline amino acid solution.

USE

An amino acid used as a component of PN.

An essential amino acid for infants, particularly preterm infants, because of an immaturity in the transsulfuration pathway of methionine to cysteine and taurine (Figure 1-6). Removal of cysteine from an otherwise adequate diet in 2- to 4-month-old preterm infants has resulted in lower rates of weight gain and nitrogen retention as well as lower plasma cysteine concentrations.[1,2]

Addition of cysteine to neonatal PN lowers the pH of the solution and increases calcium and phosphorus solubility. This allows a larger amount of these minerals to be added.

ADVERSE EFFECTS

Usually very well tolerated.

Metabolic Acidosis: Because it is available as the hydrochloride salt, cysteine adds to the chloride load of the infant. The risk of metabolic acidosis is greater in infants <1,250 gm. Metabolic acidosis may be managed by using the lower end of the dosage range and/or by use of acetate salts.[1]

FIGURE 1-6 ◆ TRANSSULFURATION OF METHIONINE.

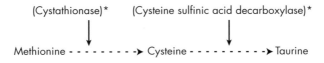

(Cystathionase)*   (Cysteine sulfinic acid decarboxylase)*

Methionine - - - - - - - -> Cysteine - - - - - - - - -> Taurine

---

* The enzyme cystathionase helps to convert methionine to cysteine. Cysteine sulfinic acid decarboxylase helps to convert cysteine to taurine. Low activity of these enzymes results in an accumulation of methionine and an insufficient amount of cysteine and taurine.

COMMENTS

When infants have reached about 1 year of age, they can adequately metabolize methionine to cysteine, so cysteine no longer needs to be added to the PN solution.[1,2]

REFERENCES

1. Zenk KE. 1985. Crystalline amino acid solutions for infants. *Infusion* 9(7/8): 104–108, 143.

2. Uauy R, Greene HL, and Heird WC. 1993. Conditionally essential nutrients: Cysteine, taurine, tyrosine, arginine, glutamine, choline, inositol, and nucleotides. In *Nutritional Needs of the Preterm Infant: Scientific Basis and Practical Guidelines,* Tsang RC, et al., eds. Baltimore: Lippincott Williams & Wilkins, 267–280.

TABLE OF CONTENTS

D

DEXAMETHASONE (DECADRON)

(dex-a-METH-a-sone)

HORMONE:
GLUCOCORTICOID

DOSE

As an Anti-inflammatory and Immunosuppressive: 0.03–0.15 mg/kg/day in divided doses every 6–12 hours.[1]

To Prevent Extubation Failure: 0.25 mg/kg/dose every 8 hours × 3. Begin 4–6 hours prior to extubation.[1–3]

With BPD: A suggested regimen is 0.05–0.1 mg/kg/dose given every 12 hours for 2–3 days. *Maximum:* 7 days.

Lower dexamethasone doses and shorter durations of therapy are now more commonly used than high-dose (initial dose ≥0.5 mg/kg/day), long-duration regimens because of adverse effects such as hyperglycemia, hypertension, growth suppression, and concerns for neurodevelopmental compromise. Even infants on moderate doses have experienced adverse effects. Stark and colleagues studied prophylactic early use of dexamethasone in extremely low birth weight infants beginning 24 hours after birth at a dose of 0.15 mg/kg/day for 3 days, followed by 0.1 mg/kg/day for 3 days, 0.05 mg/kg/day for 2 days, and 0.02 mg/kg/day for 2 days (= a total of 10 days). The daily doses were divided every 12 days IV or PO. Infants on dexamethasone were less likely to be receiving oxygen supplementation 28 days after birth. Dexamethasone in this study had no effect on death or chronic lung disease, and the infants were more likely than those not receiving dexamethasone to have decreased growth, spontaneous GI perforation, and hypertension and were more likely to be receiving insulin for hyperglycemia.[3]

Steroid trials are not routine in patients with BPD. When giving steroids, use the lowest dose for the shortest period of time.

Inhaled Glucocorticoid Therapy. Inhaled beclomethasone (Vanceril) has been used to reduce the need for systemic glucocorticoid therapy (such as oral or intravenous dexamethasone) with its attendant side effects in preterm infants.[4] Budesonide by inhalation has also been used in this age group.[5]

Caution: In patients dependent on systemic steroids, taper the systemic steroids gradually after transferring to inhaled steroids; do not discontinue abruptly. Inhaled glucocorticoids may control respiratory symptoms due to local effects, but do not provide systemic corticosteroid in amounts needed to treat patients with major stress such as trauma, surgery, or severe infection who have adrenal suppression. During major stress, patients will require supplementary systemic (IV, PO) steroids.

As a Physiologic Replacement: 0.03–0.15 mg/kg/day or 0.6–0.75 mg/m²/day divided every 6–12 hours.[2]

Base dose on severity of disease and response of patient. Reduce dose gradually to the lowest effective level.

TABLE 1-18 ◆ COMPARISON OF RELATIVE POTENCY OF CORTICOSTEROIDS
(GLUCOCORTICOIDS)

Drug	Equivalent Dose	Biologic Half-life (hours)	Anti-inflammatory Potency	Relative Mineralocorticoid Potency
Dexamethasone (Decadron)	0.75 mg	36–54	20–30	0
Hydrocortisone (Solu-Cortef)	20 mg	8–12	1	2
Methylprednisolone (Solu-Medrol)	4 mg	18–36	5	0
Prednisone	5 mg	18–36	4	1

ADMINISTRATION

IV—*Rate:* May give IV push over 1–2 minutes (usually preferred because of ease of administration) or may infuse more slowly over 30 minutes.

IV—*Concentration:* May give undiluted or diluted with saline or dextrose, as patient's fluid status warrants.

IV—*Compatibility:* See Appendix E: Y-Site Compatibility of Common NICU Drugs.

IM: May give undiluted.

PO: Available as an oral solution 0.1 mg/ml and 1 mg/ml.

USE

Has been used in neonates to reduce airway edema prior to extubation and to shorten respirator dependency in infants with BPD.[2,6,7]

MECHANISM OF ACTION

Dexamethasone is a long-acting (biologic activity of 36–54 hours), potent corticosteroid with no mineralocorticoid properties. See Table 1-18 for a comparison of dexamethasone with other corticosteroids.

ADVERSE EFFECTS

Acute: Hyperglycemia, glycosuria, hypertension may occur.

With Prolonged Use: Numerous adverse effects occur with long-term use: Adrenal suppression, severe growth retardation,[3] protein catabolism,[8] hypertrophic cardiomyopathy (57 percent of infants on dexamethasone for longer than 26 days),[9,10] hypokalemic alkalosis, sodium retention, hypertension,[3] hyperglycemia,[3] increased susceptibility to infections, intestinal hemorrhage, perforation[3] or NEC,[11] cataracts, myopathy, hypocalcemia, osteoporosis with bone fractures, nephrocalcinosis, nephrolithiasis, acute pancreatitis, and increase in intracranial pressure (pseudotumor cerebri), especially following dose reduction.[12] Use every-other-day treatment to minimize adverse effects in patients on chronic corticosteroid therapy.

Stopping after Prolonged Use (>3 days): Acute pituitary-adrenal insufficiency results from too-rapid withdrawal of corticosteroids. Taper dose gradually. Monitor infant closely for signs of adrenal crisis, which may include a decrease in serum sodium, a decrease in blood pressure, an increase in heart rate, oliguria, and signs of clinical deterioration. Reinstitute steroids immediately if these signs appear. A cortisol stimulation test can be done to assess whether it is safe to stop steroid therapy (see monograph on cosyntropin).

PHARMACOKINETICS/PHARMACODYNAMICS

Absorption: Well absorbed from the GI tract. The same dose may be given PO as IV.

Onset of Action: With IV use, 4–6 hours.

NURSING IMPLICATIONS

Monitor for hypertension, hyperglycemia after dose.

Monitor for glucose spillage in urine.

Monitor for signs and symptoms of infection.

Consider the use of H_2-antagonist therapy (e.g., ranitidine) to decrease the risk of gastric hemorrhage in infants who are at increased risk of peptic ulcer formation (e.g., those receiving other ulcerogenic drugs). Routine concomitant use of H_2-antagonist therapy does not appear to be warranted because steroid-induced ulcers occur infrequently and the efficacy of antiulcer therapy in preventing these ulcers has not been established.[12]

Monitor growth parameters (such as head circumference, length, and weight) weekly and plot on growth curve.

REFERENCES

1. Benitz WE, and Tatro DS. 1995. *The Pediatric Drug Handbook,* 3rd ed. St. Louis: Mosby-Year Book, 434–435.

2. Couser RJ, et al. 1992. Effectiveness of dexamethasone in preventing extubation failure in preterm infants at increased risk for airway edema. *Journal of Pediatrics* 121(4): 591–596.

3. Stark AR, et al. 2001. Adverse effects of early dexamethasone treatment in extremely low-birth-weight infants. *New England Journal of Medicine* 344(2): 95–101.

4. Cole CH, et al. 1999. Early inhaled glucocorticoid therapy to prevent bronchopulmonary dysplasia. *New England Journal of Medicine* 340(13): 1005–1010.

5. Arnon S, Grigg J, and Silverman M. 1996. Effectiveness of budesonide aerosol in ventilator-dependent preterm babies: A preliminary report. *Pediatric Pulmonology* 21(4): 231–235.

6. Avery GB, et al. 1985. Controlled trial of dexamethasone in respirator-dependent infants with bronchopulmonary dysplasia. *Pediatrics* 75(1): 106–111.

7. Collaborative Dexamethasone Trial Group. 1991. Dexamethasone therapy in neonatal chronic lung disease: An international placebo-controlled trial. *Pediatrics* 88(3): 421–427.

8. Van Goudoever JB, et al. 1994. Effect of dexamethasone on protein metabolism in infants with bronchopulmonary dysplasia. *Journal of Pediatrics* 124(1): 112–118.

9. Werner JC, et al. 1992. Hypertrophic cardiomyopathy associated with dexamethasone therapy for bronchopulmonary dysplasia. *Journal of Pediatrics* 120(2 part 1): 286–291.

10. Israel BA, Sherman FS, and Guthrie RD. 1993. Hypertrophic cardiomyopathy associated with dexamethasone therapy for chronic lung disease in preterm infants. *American Journal of Perinatology* 10(4): 307-310.

11. O'Neil EA, et al. 1992. Dexamethasone treatment during ventilator dependency: Possible life threatening gastrointestinal complications. *Archives of Disease in Childhood* 67(1 spec. no.): 10–11.

12. McEvoy GK. 2000. *AHFS Drug Information.* Bethesda, Maryland: American Society of Hospital Pharmacists, 2738–2757.

DEXTROSE

(DEX-trose)

NUTRITION:
CALORIC SUPPLEMENT

DOSE

Hypoglycemia: 1–2 ml/kg (= 0.1–0.2 gm/kg) of $D_{10}W$; then begin $D_{10}W$ infusion at 4–6 mg/kg/minute (60–85 ml/kg/day).[1] Higher and repeated doses may be required in some cases. If the infant does not respond, consider glucagon, steroids, or epinephrine.

Hyperkalemia: 0.4 gm/kg dextrose with 0.1 unit/kg insulin.

Insulin-induced Hypoglycemia:
0.5–1 gm/kg/dose (= 5–10 ml/kg/dose) of $D_{10}W$.

Calculating Glucose Load: The following equation is used to calculate glucose load:[2]

$$Glucose\ load = \frac{Percent\ dextrose \times Rate\ (in\ ml/hour) \times 0.167}{Body\ weight\ (in\ kg)}$$

The most precise way to monitor and regulate dextrose infusions is in mg/kg/minute. The concentration of dextrose alone does not really indicate how much the infant receives per unit of time if rate and body weight are not also considered. Typical rates:

- Preterm infants may tolerate only 3–5 mg/kg/minute initially.
- Term newborns usually tolerate an initial rate of 6–7 mg/kg/minute ($D_{10}W$ at 85–100 ml/kg/day).[1]
- Infants on parenteral nutrition may gradually increase their tolerance to 12–16 mg/kg/minute or more.
- Infants of diabetic mothers with hypoglycemia at birth may require 16–18 mg/kg/minute or more.
- Infants usually tolerate changes of 1–2 mg/kg/minute well.

TABLE 1-19 ◆ OSMOLARITY OF VARIOUS DEXTROSE CONCENTRATIONS

Dextrose Concentration in Water (%)	Osmolarity (mOsm/liter)
2.5	126
5	253
10	505
11.5	580
20	1,010
25	1,330
30	1,515

TABLE 1-20 ◆ DEXTROSE CONCENTRATION OF VARIOUS DEXTROSE SOLUTIONS

% dextrose	mg/ml*
D_3W	30
D_5W	50
$D_{7.5}W$	75
$D_{10}W$	100
$D_{12.5}W$	125
$D_{15}W$	150
$D_{17.5}W$	175
$D_{20}W$	200
$D_{25}W$	250
$D_{30}W$	300

* To convert mg/ml to gm/ml, divide by 1,000. For example, 100 mg/ml = 0.1 gm/ml.

ADMINISTRATION

May administer IV or PO. Not for SC or IM use.

IV—*Rate:* Rapid infusion of high concentrations of dextrose may cause hyper-glycemia or hyperosmolar syndrome. The osmolarity of dextrose solutions is proportional to the dextrose concentration (Table 1-19).

IV—*Concentration:*

- $D_{10}W$ is commonly used as the maintenance dextrose concentration for neonates because of their low glucose stores. Lower concentrations—D_3W and D_5W—are sometimes needed in infants, particularly very low birth weight infants, because of glucose intolerance and high fluid requirements (Table 1-20). Hypotonic solutions may cause hemolysis.
- **The maximum dextrose concentration for peripheral lines is $D_{12.5}W$.** Higher concentrations may cause vein irritation and thrombosis.
- Concentrations up to $D_{25}W$ and, rarely, $D_{30}W$ can be infused via central lines, including percutaneously placed central lines.
- Limit concentration in umbilical arterial lines to $D_{15}W$.

Preparation: Use the guidelines in Table 1-21 to prepare urgently needed non-standard concentrations of dextrose. These guidelines are for preparation of 50 ml of the desired dextrose concentration using commercially available D_5W, $D_{10}W$, $D_{25}W$, $D_{50}W$, and sterile water for injection.

USE

Provision of fluids and calories.

Treatment of hypoglycemia.

Also used with insulin to treat hyperkalemia.

TABLE 1-21 ◆ PREPARATION INSTRUCTIONS FOR NONSTANDARD CONCENTRATIONS OF DEXTROSE

Percent Dextrose Desired	For 50 ml of Solution
2.5	Dilute 25 ml of D_5W with 25 ml sterile water for injection
7.5	Dilute 6 ml of $D_{25}W$ to 50 ml with D_5W
12.5	Dilute 8.5 ml of $D_{25}W$ to 50 ml with $D_{10}W$
15	Dilute 17 ml of $D_{25}W$ to 50 ml with $D_{10}W$
17.5	Dilute 25 ml of $D_{25}W$ to 50 ml with $D_{10}W$
20	Dilute 33.5 ml of $D_{25}W$ to 50 ml with $D_{10}W$
30	Dilute 30 ml of $D_{50}W$ with 20 ml sterile water for injection

MECHANISM OF ACTION

Dextrose is a monosaccharide. It provides 3.4 kcal/gm of D-glucose monohydrate. The 5 percent concentration is isotonic. Dextrose can induce diuresis. It may decrease body protein and nitrogen losses, promote glycogen deposition, and prevent ketosis.[3]

ADVERSE EFFECTS

Rapid infusion of hyperosmolar solutions can cause hyperglycemia, glycosuria, and shifts in fluids/electrolytes, resulting in dehydration, hyperosmolar coma, and death if the infant's underlying condition goes undetected. (These are hypertonic solutions with osmolarity much higher than blood, which is about 300 mOsm/liter. For example, $D_{20}W$ is 1,010 mOsm/liter.)

Rapid changes in osmolality may produce profound effects on the brain, including intraventricular hemorrhage, particularly in preterm infants. Intracranial pressure and volume changes occur, followed by capillary dilation and possibly hemorrhage with death or residual damage.[4] This may be related to the rate of infusion and/or the concentration of the solution. Avoid rapid infusion of high concentrations of dextrose.

Pain at injection site.

Sudden appearance of glucose intolerance may be a sign of sepsis in infants. Monitor infant carefully. Decrease rate of dextrose infusion, monitor blood and urine glucose, and, if necessary, administer insulin.

Concentrated dextrose solutions may cause extravasation injuries. Limit dextrose concentration in peripheral lines to $D_{12.5}W$.

Rebound hypoglycemia may occur with sudden decreases in dextrose infusion. Taper gradually.

PHARMACOKINETICS/PHARMACODYNAMICS

Absorption: Absorbed rapidly from the small intestine by an active mechanism. Hyperosmolar solutions of dextrose given orally can cause diarrhea.

Metabolism: Oxidized to CO_2 and water.

NURSING IMPLICATIONS

Monitor blood glucose closely, especially if infant is being treated for hypoglycemia or hyperglycemia.

Monitor urine glucose at least once a day—more frequently, if necessary.

COMMENTS

Interactions: Do not administer dextrose and blood simultaneously through the same infusion set because pseudoagglutination of red cells may occur.[3]

REFERENCES

1. Gomella TL, Cunningham MD, and Eyal FG. 1994. *Neonatology: Management, Procedures, On-call Problems, Diseases and Drugs.* Norwalk, Connecticut: Appleton & Lange, 217–220.

2. Zenk KE. 1984. Calculating dextrose infusion rates in mg/kg/min. *PeriScope* (August): 5–6.

3. Olin BR. 1994. *Drug Facts and Comparisons.* St. Louis: Facts and Comparisons, 122–124.

4. Finberg L. 1967. Dangers to infants caused by changes in osmolal concentration. *Pediatrics* 40(6): 1031–1034.

DIAZEPAM (VALIUM)
(dye-AZ-e-pam)
(CONTROLLED SUBSTANCE SCHEDULE IV)

CENTRAL NERVOUS SYSTEM: SEDATIVE, ANTICONVULSANT

DOSE

The therapeutic dosage of diazepam varies widely; individualize dose.

Neonatal Abstinence (Withdrawal) Syndrome:

- *PO or IV:* 0.1–0.3 mg/kg/dose given every 6–8 hours, as needed. *Maximum:* 1 mg/kg/within an 8-hour period.[1]

- *Tapering the dose:* Maintain the effective dose for 3–5 days before attempting to wean. Reduce every 1–2 days, as tolerated. The infant should sleep well, eat effectively, and gain weight. Irritability and tremors should not be the only criteria for titrating the dose.[1]

Neonatal Tetanus:

- *IV (preferred) or IM:* 1–2 mg/dose. May repeat every 3–4 hours, as needed.[2]

- *IV recommendations:* Give in increments of 0.25 mg/kg/dose every 15–30 minutes up to three times, as needed. If condition does not improve, consider adjuvant therapy.[3] Just enough drug should be given to prevent spasms and induce adequate sedation.[4]

- Because the doses of IV diazepam needed to treat tetanus are so large and because of the adverse effects caused by the large volumes of solvents and preservatives in the product, consider changing to NG administration (using crushed tablets) as soon as the medical condition allows.[4]

- Various other doses have been used to treat neonatal tetanus:[1,5–8]

  - *For immediate control of spasms:* Diazepam 1–2 mg/kg/dose IM or slowly IV with paraldehyde 0.3 mg/kg/dose. *For continued sedation:* Diazepam 1–2 mg/kg/dose with phenobarbital 5 mg/kg/dose and chlorpromazine 2 mg/kg/dose all given via nasogastric or nasotranspyloric tube every 6 hours. Additional intermittent doses may be needed.[5]

  - 0.25 mg/kg/dose and increase incrementally, if needed, to a maximum of 4 mg/kg/dose as continuous IV infusion over 6 hours. Pancuronium, flunitrazepam (not available in the U.S.), and/or phenobarbital were used in addition.[6]

  - Up to 50 mg/kg/day given in divided doses every 2 hours in neonates with nine or more spasms/hour. Prolonged sedation and drowsiness occurred. Mean diazepam blood levels when the spasms stopped were 3,150 ng/ml in neonates, compared with 447 ng/ml in children.[7]

  - A combination of diazepam continuous IV infusion 20–40 mg/kg/day with intragastric phenobarbital 10–15 mg/kg/day in four divided doses in 19 cases of neonatal tetanus. Adverse effects were severe but reversible: drowsiness, coma, and apneic spells.[8]

Nonketotic Hyperglycinemia: Alemzadeh and colleagues used diazepam 0.4 mg/kg/day PO (in combination with sodium benzoate 400 mg/kg/day, arginine 400 mg/kg/day, folic acid 1 mg/day, carnitine 25 mg/kg/day, phenobarbital 5 mg/kg/day, and dextromethorphan 0.25 mg/kg/day).[9]

Premedication for Procedures: 0.1–0.3 mg/kg/dose IV or PO given 45–60 minutes before the procedure. (For painful procedures, an analgesic is also required.)

Sedation:

- *PO:* 0.2–0.8 mg/kg/day divided every 6–8 hours.
- *IV (preferred), IM:* 0.05–0.3 mg/kg/dose every 2–4 hours as needed. *Maximum:* 0.6 mg/kg per 8 hours.

Status Epilepticus:

- *IV:* 0.05–0.3 mg/kg/dose. May repeat every 15–30 minutes as needed. *Maximum cumulative dose:* 2 mg. Regimen may be repeated in 2–4 hours.[3]
- *IV continuous infusion:* 0.1–0.3 mg/kg/hour. Monitor for drug accumulation
- *Rectal* (for outpatient breakthrough seizures):
  - *Initial:* 0.2–0.5 mg/kg/dose. May repeat in 4–12 hours. *Maximum per dose:* 5 mg. *Treatment frequency:* Five episodes per month or one episode every 5 days. IV is preferred; use PR if no IV access.[2,10,11]

ADMINISTRATION

Supplied as:

- *Injection:* 5 mg/ml.
- *Oral liquid:* 1 mg/ml and 5 mg/ml; *Tablet:* 2 mg.
- *Rectal gel (Diastat):* 2.5 mg/0.5 ml syringe.

Both the injection and the rectal gel contain benzyl alcohol, ethyl alcohol 10 percent, propylene glycol 40 percent, and sodium benzoate.[2] Protect from light.

IV—Rate: Infuse over 3–5 minutes (*Maximum:* 1.5 mg/minute).

- Infuse slowly with continuous monitoring of the infant for respiratory depression and hypotension. Assist ventilation if necessary.

IV—Concentration:

- *IV push:* Use undiluted. Precipitates in dextrose or saline.
- *Continuous infusion:* Dilute to 0.1 mg/ml with normal saline. (The manufacturer does not recommend dilution, but a dilution of 10 mg/100 ml (= 0.1 mg/ml) normal saline has been used.[12] If a dilution must be made or if line must be flushed, normal saline is the best choice of diluent. Compatibility depends on a number of factors; consult specialized references[12] and your pharmacist.)

IM: Use undiluted (painful, poorly absorbed).

PO: May administer with feedings or with water. May mix with a small amount of infant formula, applesauce, or other soft food for immediate administration; do not store for later use. If large doses of the oral liquid are causing diarrhea in the infant, crushed tablets may be mixed with water for immediate administration PO or NG.

PR (for outpatient breakthrough seizures): For rectal administration, a dilution of diazepam injection (5 mg/ml) with propylene glycol to make a solution containing 1 mg of diazepam per ml has been used. Use a filter when drawing up the dose from a glass ampoule. Minimize use of propylene glycol–diluted product (See **USE,** below).[3] Draw up dose into a 0.5 ml oral syringe. Lubricate syringe tip before use. Hold buttocks closed to prevent rectal evacuation. For rectal use only.

The rectal gel (Diastat) is not intended for small infants because accurate neonatal doses cannot be measured with the concentration available, the product contains preservatives, and the rectal tip (4.4 cm) provided is too large.[2] In general, use caution with rectal administration of drugs in neonates, particularly preterm infants, because of the danger of rectal perforation.

CAUTIONS/CONTRAINDICATIONS

Rapid IV infusion may cause apnea, hypotension, bradycardia, or cardiac or respiratory arrest.[3]

Do not use in patients with a hypersensitivity to diazepam, any component in the product, or other benzodiazepines; patients with narrow-angle glaucoma because benzodiazepines may have anticholinergic effects;[3] infants <30 days old (injection and rectal gel) because of the preservatives in the products.[2]

Use with caution in infants with severe hepatic and/or renal dysfunction; preexisting CNS depression or respiratory depression because diazepam may compromise respiratory function; myasthenia gravis because diazepam may exacerbate the disease; or on other CNS depressants and with low serum albumin because the incidence of sedative side effects may be increased.

Does not provide analgesia: If painful procedures are anticipated, administer analgesics. If a narcotic and diazepam are used concurrently, reduce the dose of each because combined use increases the risk of adverse effects such as respiratory depression and hypotension.[13]

Physical dependence and tolerance may occur, especially with high-dose or prolonged use. Discontinue gradually after prolonged (several weeks) use to avoid withdrawal and seizures, especially in patients with epilepsy.[3]

Use care not to inject intra-arterially: Arteriospasm and necrosis may occur.

Use

Diazepam is not recommended as a first-line drug in neonates because of:

- Its long half-life and long-acting metabolites, as well as its extremely variable therapeutic dose.[13]

- The preservatives and solubilizers in the injection and the rectal gel. *Benzyl alcohol,* an antibacterial agent, has been associated with the fatal "gasping syndrome" consisting of metabolic acidosis, CNS depression, hypotension, renal failure, and intracranial hemorrhage in preterm infants. *Propylene glycol,* a solubilizer, can cause hyperosmolality in preterm infants, resulting in cardiovascular and respiratory instability and seizures.[14,15] *Sodium benzoate* may increase the risk of kernicterus because of displacement of bilirubin from albumin binding sites.[13] *Ethyl alcohol* can cause undesirable interactions, neuronal dysfunction, lethargy with poor feeding, hypoglycemia, and liver dysfunction.[16]

- Its incompatibility with aqueous solutions such as dextrose and its incompatibility with many concentrations of saline.[12]

- Accurate dose measurement of both the injection and the rectal gel is not possible for small preterm infants (for example, the dose volume for a 1 kg infant receiving 0.1 mg/kg/dose is 0.02 ml, using the 5 mg/ml concentration). The incompatibility of diazepam with aqueous solutions such as dextrose and with many concentrations of saline makes flushing the line to ensure that the dose reaches the patient risky.

- Rapid clearance of the drug from the brain, resulting in short-acting seizure control. This makes it a poor choice for maintenance seizure management. Although lorazepam is less lipid soluble than diazepam and CSF concentrations of lorazepam rise more slowly than do those of diazepam, a double-blind, randomized comparison of these two drugs found both to be equally fast-acting and equally effective in controlling seizures.[17] Lorazepam has a longer duration of antiseizure action (12–24 hours) than does diazepam (15–30 minutes), making lorazepam the preferred drug for treatment of status epilepticus.[3,18]

Diazepam is used to treat status epilepticus, to reduce anxiety, for sedation of infants on a ventilator, for preoperative sedation, and for:

- ***Neonatal tetanus:*** Diazepam is useful as an adjunct in the treatment of neonatal tetanus to relax tetanic spasms and rigidity (with tetanus immune globulin and parenteral penicillin G).[19] Diazepam has been the most used benzodiazepine for neonatal tetanus, but lorazepam is preferred because of its longer duration of action. Continuous IV infusion of midazolam may become the treatment of choice because this product does not contain propylene glycol as a solvent.[4] Neonatal tetanus, a common cause of neonatal mortality in developing countries, occurs rarely in the U.S.[20,21]

- ***Neonatal abstinence syndrome:*** Infants treated for opioid withdrawal with diazepam exhibit more sedation, reduced or no nutritive sucking, and poorer control of the GI and autonomic symptoms of opioid withdrawal than infants treated with paregoric. Studies indicate that infants treated with diazepam for methadone withdrawal may have less seizure control than infants treated with paregoric. Diazepam may be used for treatment of withdrawal from benzodiazepines and also possibly for the hyperexcitable phase following cocaine exposure. Diazepam can be used as an adjunctive agent for controlling symptoms such as tremulousness, irritability, and seizures associated with opioid withdrawal.[22,23] Its use should probably be restricted to cases refractory to other agents.[1]

- *Nonketotic hyperglycinemia (NKH):* Diazepam treats the seizures of NKH, an inborn error of glycine degradation that causes muscular hypotonia, seizures, apnea, and lethargy.

MECHANISM OF ACTION

Diazepam, like other benzodiazepines, depresses the CNS, producing levels of depression from mild sedation to coma, depending on the dose. Benzodiazepines facilitate the action of the inhibitory neurotransmitter γ-aminobutyric acid (GABA) in the CNS by acting as agonists at benzodiazepine receptor sites.[3] Benzodiazepines, particularly diazepam and lorazepam, are potent, fast-acting antiseizure drugs.[11]

Tetanus: Benzodiazepines are $GABA_A$ agonists, thereby functioning as indirect antagonists of the effects of the toxin on inhibitory systems. Their amnestic effect is another advantage.[4]

Nonketotic Hyperglycinemia: In NKH, elevated glycine concentrations in the brain are thought to be responsible for the symptoms of intractable seizures, hiccuping, muscular hypotonia, and apnea. Glycine stimulates the *N*-methyl D-aspartate (NMDA) receptors, leading to increased excitatory activity. Diazepam is a competitive inhibitor of glycine binding sites on NMDA receptors.[9,24] Other benzodiazepines (clonazepam, lorazepam) have been used in combination with dextromethorphan and benzoate to treat NKH.[25]

ADVERSE EFFECTS

Cardiovascular: Hypotension (especially with rapid IV administration), bradycardia.

CNS: Drowsiness and (rarely) paradoxical excitement. CNS depression may be prolonged in the neonate compared with older children and adults because of the infant's inability to biotransform the benzodiazepine into inactive metabolites.[3] Hypotonia after repeated doses.

Dermatologic: Pain and irritation at injection site (IV and IM), phlebitis. Infuse slowly to minimize these adverse effects.

GI: Diarrhea may occur with large enteral doses of benzodiazepine oral solutions (lorazepam, diazepam) containing the carriers propylene glycol and polyethylene glycol, probably because of their osmotic effects. This adverse effect can be avoided by substituting crushed tablets. Marshall and colleagues reported that when diazepam crushed tablets (given through a gastrostomy tube in 30 ml of water) were substituted for the oral liquid, diarrhea resolved in 36 hours.[26]

Respiratory: Respiratory depression (especially with rapid IV administration), apnea, laryngospasm. Be prepared to assist ventilation. Increased salivation and bronchial secretions may occur.

PHARMACOKINETICS/PHARMACODYNAMICS

Absorption:

- *PO:* Well absorbed, usually in 1–2 hours.[3]
- *IM:* Slow and erratic absorption.
- *Rectal gel:* 90 percent absorbed.

Onset of Action: *IV:* 1–3 minutes. *Rectal:* 15 minutes.

Duration of Action: 15–30 minutes.

Time to Peak Plasma Concentration: *PO:* 0.5–2 hours.

Protein Binding: 86 percent.

Metabolism: Hepatic demethylation primarily to the active metabolite, desmethyl-diazepam, followed by glucuronidation. Neonates have decreased metabolism of diazepam and desmethyldiazepam, which can accumulate with repeated dosing and cause toxicity.

Half-life: 40–400 hours (preterm infants) and 20–50 hours (term neonates).[27] Half-life may be prolonged in severe hepatic dysfunction.

Elimination: Urine.

NURSING IMPLICATIONS

Monitor blood pressure, heart rate, respirations, level of consciousness, and therapeutic effect.[28]

Diazepam adheres to plastic infusion tubing; inject as close to the patient as possible.[3] Even though diazepam is incompatible with aqueous solutions, if a line must be flushed after a diazepam injection, normal saline is the best choice for a flush solution.

COMMENTS

Interactions:

Other CNS depressants, such as phenobarbital and narcotics, have additive CNS and respiratory depressant effects. Use of diazepam with phenobarbital may increase the risk of apnea. Dose reduction is recommended. Increased pharmacologic effects of phenytoin may occur when diazepam is administered concurrently.

- Rifampin may enhance elimination of diazepam, resulting in decreased diazepam concentrations.
- Cimetidine, erythromycin, isoniazid, ketoconazole, or ranitidine may decrease the metabolism of diazepam.[1]

Antidote: Flumazenil (Romazicon) 2–10 mcg/kg IV every minute × 3 as needed. Monitor for return of sedation. May induce seizures in epileptics treated with diazepam.

REFERENCES

1. Roberts RJ. 1984. *Drug Therapy in Infants: Pharmacologic Principles and Clinical Experience.* Philadelphia: WB Saunders, 110–112, 340.

2. Medical Economics Data. 2000. *Physicians' Desk Reference.* Montvale, New Jersey: Medical Economics, 1012–1016, 2676–2678.

3. United States Pharmacopeial Convention/USP DI. 2000. *Drug Information for the Health Care Professional,* 20th ed. Rockville, Maryland: United States Pharmacopeial Convention, 581–584.

4. Bleck TP. 1991. Tetanus: Pathophysiology, management, and prophylaxis. *Disease-a-Month* 37(9): 545–603.

5. Dear P. 1999. Infection in the newborn. In *Textbook of Neonatology,* 3rd ed., Rennie JM, and Roberton NRC, eds. London: Churchill Livingstone, 1109–1202.

6. Simental PS, et al. 1993. Neonatal tetanus experience at the National Institute of Pediatrics in Mexico City. *Pediatric Infectious Disease Journal* 12(9): 722–725.

7. Tekur U, et al. 1983. Blood concentrations of diazepam and its metabolites in children and neonates with tetanus. *Journal of Pediatrics* 102(1): 145–147.

8. Khoo BH, Lee EL, and Lam KL. 1978. Neonatal tetanus treated with high-dosage diazepam. *Archives of Disease in Childhood* 53(9): 737–739.

9. Alemzadeh R, Gammeltoft K, and Matteson K. 1996. Efficacy of low-dose dextromethorphan in the treatment of nonketotic hyperglycinemia. *Pediatrics* 97(6 part 1): 924–926.

10. Hoppu K, and Santavuori P. 1981. Diazepam rectal solution for home treatment of acute seizures in children. *Acta Paediatrica Scandinavica* 70(3): 369–372.

11. Lowenstein DH, and Allredge BK. 1998. Status epilepticus. *New England Journal of Medicine* 338(14): 970–976.

12. Trissel LA. 1998. *Handbook on Injectable Drugs,* 10th ed. Bethesda, Maryland: American Society of Health-System Pharmacists, 378–386.

13. American Academy of Pediatrics, Committee on Fetus and Newborn, and Committee on Drugs, Section on Anesthesiology, Section on Surgery. 2000. Prevention and management of pain and stress in the neonate. *Pediatrics* 105(2): 454–461.

14. Glasgow AM, et al. 1983. Hyperosmolality in small infants due to propylene glycol. *Pediatrics* 72(3): 353–355.

15. MacDonald MG, et al. 1987. Propylene glycol: Increased incidence of seizures in low birth weight infants. *Pediatrics* 79(4): 622–625.

16. American Academy of Pediatrics, Committee on Drugs. 1984. Ethanol in liquid preparations intended for children. *Pediatrics* 73(3): 405–407.

17. Leppik IE, et al. 1983. Double-blind study of lorazepam and diazepam in status epilepticus. *JAMA* 249(11): 1452–1454.

18. Working Group on Status Epilepticus. 1993. Treatment of convulsive status epilepticus. Recommendations of the Epilepsy Foundation of America's Working Group on Status Epilepticus. *JAMA* 270(7): 854–859.

19. American Academy of Pediatrics, Committee on Infectious Diseases. 1997. *Red Book: Report of the Committee on Infectious Diseases,* 24th ed. Elk Grove Village, Illinois: American Academy of Pediatrics, 458–463.

20. Centers for Disease Control and Prevention. 1998. Neonatal tetanus—Montana, 1998. *MMWR* 47(43): 928–930.

21. Craig AS, et al. Neonatal tetanus in the United States: A sentinel event in the foreign-born. *Pediatric Infectious Disease Journal* 16(10): 955–959.

22. Anand KJ, and Arnold JH. 1994. Opioid tolerance and dependence in infants and children. *Critical Care Medicine* 22(2): 334–342.

23. Theis JG, et al. 1997. Current management of the neonatal abstinence syndrome: A critical analysis of the evidence. *Biology of the Neonate* 71(6): 345–356.

24. Matalon R, et al. 1983. Nonketotic hyperglycinemia: Treatment with diazepam—a competitor for glycine receptors. *Pediatrics* 71(4): 581–584.

25. Hamosh A, et al. 1998. Long-term use of high-dose benzoate and dextromethorphan for the treatment of nonketotic hyperglycinemia. *Journal of Pediatrics* 132(4): 709–713.

26. Marshall JD, Farrar HC, and Kearns GI. 1995. Diarrhea associated with enteral benzodiazepine solutions. *Journal of Pediatrics* 126(4): 657–659.

27. Morselli PL, Franco-Morselli R, and Bossi L. 1980. Clinical pharmacokinetics in newborns and infants: Age-related differences and therapeutic implications. *Clinical Pharmacokinetics* 5(6): 485–527.

28. American Academy of Pediatrics, Committee on Drugs. 1992. Guidelines for monitoring and management of pediatric patients during and after sedation for diagnostic and therapeutic procedures. *Pediatrics* 89(6): 1110–1115.

DIAZOXIDE
(HYPERSTAT I.V., PROGLYCEM [ORAL])
(dye-az-OX-ide)

**CARDIOVASCULAR:
ANTIHYPERTENSIVE
VASODILATOR;
ANTIHYPOGLYCEMIC**

DOSE

Reduce dose in severe renal dysfunction.

Hypertensive Crisis: 1–3 mg/kg/dose IV. May repeat every 5–15 minutes until desired blood pressure is reached (minibolus regimen).
Maximum dose: 5 mg/kg/dose. May repeat effective dose every 2–24 hours as needed. *Maximum total dose:* 150 mg/dose.[1–5]

Persistent Hyperinsulinemic Hypoglycemia (such as nesidioblastosis):

- *Initial:* 10 mg/kg/day PO divided every 8–12 hours.
  (Range: 3–20 mg/kg/day.)[4,6] Individualize dose based on plasma glucose concentration. Discontinue if not effective after 2–3 weeks. Responders continue the drug for several years.

ADMINISTRATION

Supplied as:

- *Injection:* 15 mg/ml.
- *Suspension:* 50 mg/ml.

IV—*Rate:* Infuse quickly in 30 seconds or less with close monitoring of blood pressure.[7] May also be infused over 20–30 minutes.[1,5,8]

- *The rate controversy:* Rapid IV bolus (<30 seconds) is thought to result in maximum effectiveness because of the drug's high degree of protein binding; because only unbound drug is active, rapid IV administration appears necessary to attain high plasma concentrations before most of the drug becomes protein bound.[4] However, infusion over 20–30 minutes may produce a similar but usually smaller, more gradual, and sustained fall in blood pressure. This helps to avoid precipitous falls in blood pressure and reduces the risk of impaired perfusion of vital organs that may occur with a sudden fall in blood pressure. Some investigators report no improvement in blood pressure when diazoxide is given slowly. Further study is needed.[1,8,9]

IV—*Concentration:* May give undiluted (15 mg/ml).

Inject into an established peripheral vein and avoid extravasation.

PO: Shake suspension before administration.

Storage: Protect from light. Light causes the suspension and injection to darken. Do not use if the color has darkened because the product may be subpotent.

CAUTIONS/CONTRAINDICATIONS

⬭ Do not use in infants hypersensitive to diazoxide, thiazides (such as chlorothiazide), or other sulfonamide drugs or in infants with aortic coarctation,
arteriovenous shunts, or dissecting aortic aneurysms.

⬭ Not for hypertension resulting from pheochromocytoma.[7]

⬭ Oral diazoxide is not used to treat chronic hypertension because of its adverse
effects (sodium retention and hyperglycemia).[9]

⬭ Use with caution in patients with renal or hepatic dysfunction.

⬭ Not for IM or SC use because of the irritating nature of the drug.

Treatment of overdose:

- *For hyperglycemia:* Fluids, electrolytes, insulin.
- *For hypotension:* Dopamine.

USE

Persistent Hyperinsulinemic Hypoglycemia of Infancy (PHHI): Oral diazoxide
(Proglycem) is the drug of choice for PHHI in neonates who cannot be weaned
from IV glucose. It is effective in 22–50 percent of infants with PHHI, but is less
likely to work in infants presenting with PHHI in the immediate newborn period.[6,10] Also used for the management of hypoglycemia from leucine sensitivity,
nesidioblastosis, islet cell hyperplasia, extrapancreatic malignancy, islet cell ade-
noma, and adenomatosis.[9]

Hypertensive Crisis: The parenteral form (Hyperstat I.V.) is for short-term (<10
days) treatment of acute life-threatening hypertension in hospitalized
patients.[1–3] One review of the treatment of childhood hypertension states that
diazoxide is no longer recommended because of its potential for abruptly
decreasing blood pressure[11] (see **IV—*Rate,* above**).

MECHANISM OF ACTION

Diazoxide is related chemically to thiazide diuretics.[5]

Mechanism of Antihypoglycemic Effect: Diazoxide increases plasma glucose by
inhibiting insulin release from the pancreas; by increasing epinephrine secretion
through extrapancreatic effects; and, directly, by increasing glucose production
and inhibiting glucose uptake.[5,9]

Mechanism of Antihypertensive Effect: Diazoxide acts directly on arteriolar
smooth muscle, causing vasodilation and decreased peripheral resistance. This
results in a decrease in blood pressure and a reflex increase in heart rate and cardiac output.

ADVERSE EFFECTS

Cardiovascular: Tachycardia; frequently, sodium and water retention (concurrent
chlorothiazide helps to manage this and also reduces insulin secretion);
hypotension (mainly with IV use);[6] flushing; hypertrophic cardiomyopathy;
congestive heart failure.

CNS: Extrapyramidal symptoms (reversible; treated with lorazepam, anticholinergic), seizures, transient weakness, sleepiness.

Dermatologic: Hirsutism (common, but does not always occur; Darendeliler treated a patient for $4^1/2$ years without adverse effects, including hypertrichosis[10]); rash.

Endocrine: Hyperglycemia (frequent, reversible), ketoacidosis during intercurrent illness or significant stress;[6] nonketotic hyperosmolar coma (rare).

GI: GI discomfort, vomiting, anorexia, diarrhea, ileus, constipation.[4]

GU: Mild hyperuricemia.

Hematologic: Rarely: leukopenia, thrombocytopenia.

Local: Pain at injection site (frequent); severe burning and/or phlebitis on extravasation.[4,9] (The 11.6 pH of the parenteral product makes it very irritating.)

Other: With long-term use (>4 years), coarse facial changes may occur that can be quite striking. This is managed by decreasing the dose or discontinuing the drug.[6] Fever, advanced bone age, and decreased IgG level.[9,12]

PHARMACOKINETICS/PHARMACODYNAMICS

Absorption: Readily absorbed from the GI tract.

Onset and Duration of Action—*Oral*:

- *Onset:* 1 hour.[9]
- *Duration:* 8 hours. Prolonged in renal dysfunction.

Onset and Duration of Action—*IV*:

- *Onset:* Minutes.
- *Duration:* 6 hours (range: 2–36 hours).[5]

McCrory and colleagues studied diazoxide in 36 infants and children. A marked decrease in blood pressure occurred within 10 minutes of diazoxide 5 mg/kg IV given over 30 seconds or less, with a maximum effect at 30 minutes and a duration of about 6 hours.[13]

Protein Binding: Very high (>90 percent).

Metabolism: Hepatic.

Half-life: Approximately 9–24 hours in infants and children (shorter than in adults).[5,14]

Elimination: About 50 percent excreted unchanged in the urine.

NURSING IMPLICATIONS

Observe IV site carefully to avoid extravasation.

Monitor blood glucose, blood pressure, and CBC. If the infant will be managed with long-term oral diazoxide for the treatment of hypoglycemia at home, consider advising parents to monitor blood glucose once daily, if necessary, and to report abnormalities or unusual symptoms to the physician as soon as possible.[4]

Life-threatening adverse effects—such as ketoacidosis, congestive heart failure, and nonketotic hyperosmolar coma—can be avoided by appropriate monitoring of plasma glucose, urinary ketones, and fluid balance.[12]

COMMENTS

Interactions:

Concurrent use of other *hypotension-producing agents* (such as alprostadil, antihypertensives such as hydralazine or propranolol, diuretics, and fentanyl) enhances hypotensive effects. Concurrent use of *peripheral vasodilators* (such as papaverine) may result in undesirable additive hypotension, requiring dose adjustment. Monitor patient continually for several hours after concurrent administration.[5,7,9]

Concurrent use of *phenytoin* may decrease the efficacy of phenytoin or diazoxide.[9]

Diazoxide may displace *bilirubin, warfarin,* and other highly protein bound drugs from serum proteins, resulting in higher blood levels of these substances.[7]

Concurrent *thiazide diuretics* (such as chlorothiazide) may potentiate diazoxide's hyperglycemic, hyperuricemic, and hypotensive effects.[7]

Concurrent *sympathomimetics or indomethacin* may reduce the hypotensive effects of diazoxide.

Concurrent β-adrenergic blocking agents may block the tachycardia caused by diazoxide and may increase its hypotensive effects.

REFERENCES

1. Sinaiko AR. 1993. Pharmacologic management of childhood hypertension. *Pediatric Clinics of North America* 40(1): 195–212.

2. Goble MM. 1993. Hypertension in infancy. *Pediatric Clinics of North America* 40(1): 105–122.

3. Rasoulpour M, and Marinelli KA. 1992. Systemic hypertension. *Clinics in Perinatology* 19(1): 121–137.

4. McEvoy GK. 2000. *AHFS Drug Information.* Bethesda, Maryland: American Society of Health-System Pharmacists, 1667–1670.

5. Roberts RJ. 1984. *Drug Therapy in Infants: Pharmacologic Principles and Clinical Experience.* Philadelphia: WB Saunders, 178–179.

6. Schwitzgebel VM, and Gitelman SE. 1998. Neonatal hyperinsulinism. *Clinics in Perinatology* 25(4): 1015–1038.

7. Medical Economics Data. 2000. *Physicians' Desk Reference.* Montvale, New Jersey: Medical Economics, 2806–2807.

8. Garrett BN, and Kaplan NM. 1982. Efficacy of slow infusion of diazoxide in the treatment of severe hypertension without organ hypoperfusion. *American Heart Journal* 103(3): 390–394.

9. United States Pharmacopeial Convention/USP DI. 2000. *Drug Information for the Health Care Professional,* 20th ed. Rockville, Maryland: United States Pharmacopeial Convention, 1232–1237.

10. Darendeliler F, et al. 1997. Long-term diazoxide treatment in persistent hyperinsulinemic hypoglycemia of infancy: A patient report. *Journal of Pediatric Endocrinology and Metabolism* 10(1): 79–81.

11. Bartosh SM, and Aronson AJ. 1999. Childhood hypertension: An update on etiology, diagnosis, and treatment. *Pediatric Clinics of North America* 46(2): 235–252.

12. Haymond MW. 1996. Hypoglycemia in infants and children. In *Rudolph's Pediatrics,* 20th ed., Rudolph AM, Hoffman JIE, and Rudolph CD, eds. Stamford, Connecticut: Appleton & Lange, 1828–1837.

13. McCrory WW, et al. 1979. Safety of intravenous diazoxide in children with severe hypertension. *Clinical Pediatrics* 18(11): 661–663, 666–667, 671.

14. Pruitt AW, Dayton PG, and Patterson JH. 1973. Disposition of diazoxide in children. *Clinical Pharmacology and Therapeutics* 14(1): 73–82.

DIGOXIN (LANOXIN)

(di-JOX-in)

DOSE

- For infants with normal renal function, doses are given in Table 1-22.
- Reduce dose in renal dysfunction:
  - *Loading Dose:* 50–75 percent of the standard loading dose because the half-life is prolonged and volume of distribution is smaller.
  - *Maintenance Dose:* 50 percent of the usual maintenance dose in instances of severe renal dysfunction.[1]
- Also reduce dose in the presence of hypokalemia, hypercalcemia, hyper- or hypo-magnesemia, hypothyroidism, myocarditis, and hypoxemia.
- Dose may need to be increased in the presence of hyperthyroidism.
- Tips for avoiding digoxin dosage errors are given in Table 1-23.
- See **Interactions** under **COMMENTS**.

ADMINISTRATION

IV—*Rate:* Infuse IV over at least 5 minutes.

IV—*Concentration:* Use the pediatric concentration of 100 mcg/ml. May be given undiluted.

TABLE 1-22 ◆ DIGOXIN DOSES* (WITH NORMAL RENAL FUNCTION)[3,12–15]

Age	Intravenous/Oral	
	Total Digitalizing (Loading) Dose (mcg/kg)[†]	Daily Maintenance Dose (mcg/kg/day)[‡]
Preterm Infants[‡]		
<1.5 kg	10–20	4
1.5–2.5 kg	10–20	8
Term Neonates[§]	30	10
Infants (1–12 months)	35	12

* The oral dose is traditionally 20 percent higher than the IV dose because bioavailability is lower with PO administration. Because the clinical significance of the increased dose is not known, equal IV and PO doses are shown to simplify dosing and to help to prevent dosage errors.

† Give digitalizing dose in increments of ½, ¼, ¼ at 8-hour intervals.

‡ The maintenance dose may be given as a single daily dose (every 24 hours) in preterm infants because half-life is prolonged in these infants. Change to divided doses (every 12 hours) at 1 month of age. Begin maintenance dose 24 hours after completion of digitalizing dose if every-24-hour dosing is used, and 12 hours after completion of digitalization for every-12-hour dosing.

§ Increase dose at 1 month of age to that of infants (1–12 months of age).

- Individualize dose.

IV—*Compatibility:* See Appendix E: Y-Site Compatibility of Common NICU Drugs.

IM: Poorly absorbed; therefore, not usually recommended in preterm infants.

PO: Available as a 50 mcg/ml elixir.

USE

For congestive heart failure refractory to diuretics.

To control arrhythmias such as atrial fibrillation or flutter and supraventricular tachycardia (SVT).

Probably has no beneficial effect for preterm infants with PDA.[2]

Should be used only if clearly indicated because of the toxic nature of the drug and its narrow therapeutic range.

MECHANISM OF ACTION

Digoxin increases cardiac output, decreases cardiac filling pressures, and decreases heart size and venous and capillary pressure.

Its positive inotropic action (increased myocardial contractility) inhibits Na^+-K^+ ATPase, which increases intracellular Ca^{++}, enhancing contractile activity.

Its negative chronotropic action (antiarrhythmic action/decrease in heart rate) results from slowing of conduction through the SA and AV nodes caused by vagal stimulation.[3]

ADVERSE EFFECTS

Cardiac: Arrhythmias—many types, including PVCs, bigeminy, trigeminy, tachycardia, AV dissociation, atrial fibrillation, and AV-block bradycardia (especially in preterm infants).

GI: Feeding intolerance, decreased appetite, vomiting.

Other: Lethargy.[3]

TABLE 1-23 ◆ TIPS FOR AVOIDING IATROGENIC DIGOXIN ERRORS

Digoxin has a very narrow therapeutic range. Small dosage errors can cause toxicity.

To help prevent errors:

- Require that two physicians sign digoxin chart orders and prescriptions.
- Require that physician orders state dose in mcg, corresponding volume and concentration.
- Require that a pharmacist double-check dose and dose volume. Digoxin should be packaged as unit doses by the pharmacy, if possible.
- Require that two nurses check dose and dose volume before administration.
- Use a digoxin physician order sheet that delineates signatures required and appropriate order format.
- Avoid verbal or phone orders for digoxin.
- Schedule maintenance digoxin administration times so as **not** to correspond with shift changes.

TABLE 1-24 ◆ PREPARING A 1:10 DIGOXIN DILUTION

For dose volumes <0.1 ml, prepare a 1:10 dilution to improve measurement accuracy:

1. Dilute 0.1 ml of digoxin (100 mcg/ml) with 0.9 ml of saline to make a 10 mcg/ml concentration.

2. Use the two-syringe technique to make the dilution: Draw up the drug in one syringe and the diluent in another. Inject drug into diluent syringe and mix well. This technique avoids "syringe dead space overdose," which can occur when additional fluid is drawn into a drug-containing syringe. This causes the drug in the dead space to be drawn up also, and it can result in a significantly higher dose than intended (5 mcg versus 12–18 mcg for digoxin).

Adapted from: Berman W Jr, et al. 1978. Inadvertent overadministration of digoxin to low-birth-weight infants. *Journal of Pediatrics* 92(6): 1024–1025. Reprinted by permission.

PHARMACOKINETICS/PHARMACODYNAMICS

Absorption: Oral absorption of elixir is 70–85 percent.

Volume of Distribution: Very large: 3.3 liters/kg; only 1 percent of the drug is in the serum.

Onset of Action: Within 30 minutes IV.[4]

Half-life:

- *Preterm Newborns:* 57 hours (range 38–88 hours).
- *Term Newborns:* 35 hours (range 17–52 hours).[5]

Elimination: By glomerular filtration and tubular secretion. Also eliminated in bile and undergoes enterohepatic circulation.

NURSING IMPLICATIONS

Hold drug dose if heart rate is <100 bpm or if PR interval is prolonged for age (normal PR interval is 0.07–0.14 seconds).

Monitor for arrhythmias, hypokalemia, and renal function.

Double-check dose with another RN.

Store drug in tightly covered, light-resistant containers to ensure effectiveness.

May be given with feeding.

Table 1-24 provides instructions for preparing a 1:10 dilution for dose volumes of <0.1 ml, to improve measurement accuracy.

COMMENTS

Monitoring:

- *Clinical Assessment:* Hold drug if heart rate is <100 bpm and/or PR interval is prolonged for age (normal PR interval: 0.07–0.14 seconds) or for any arrhythmia. Obtain rhythm strip before giving the third increment of the digitalizing dose and as needed to assess toxicity or clinical efficacy. Signs of improvement as a result of digoxin therapy include: increased PR interval, decreased QT interval, increased blood pressure, and improved urine and cardiac outputs.

- *Laboratory:* Follow BUN, serum creatinine, calcium, potassium, magnesium.

Serum Digoxin Levels:

- Not useful for titrating the dose, for two reasons: (1) Therapeutic levels are not well defined. (2) Accurate measurement of levels is difficult because endogenous digoxin-like substances (EDLS) may falsely elevate serum levels. In a group of newborns not treated with digoxin, levels were in the therapeutic range in most infants. During treatment, levels in infants may appear toxic because of EDLS. Also, preterm infants and those in renal failure have higher levels of EDLS.[6,7]

- *Indications for Drawing Levels:* Suspected toxicity, to assess compliance, and sometimes to tailor optimum dose (if level is low, for example, the dose can safely be increased).

- *Timing of Draws:* Draw blood for digoxin concentration at least 8 hours after the dose to avoid falsely high levels. Trough level is preferred.

- *Therapeutic Range:* 0.5–2 ng/ml; there is increased risk of toxicity with levels above 2 ng/ml. Serum levels >3.5 ng/ml during maintenance therapy are considered toxic and may be extremely hazardous.[3] However, the relationship between serum level and toxicity or clinical effect varies from patient to patient. Koren and Parker found that about one-third of pediatric patients in their study did not show symptoms or signs of toxicity even at serum levels above 5 ng/ml.[8] Digoxin levels in very severe agonal states antemortem are very high, presumably as a result of EDLS, redistribution of digoxin, and renal failure. Significant digoxin levels are frequently recorded after death in patients not receiving digoxin, probably because of EDLS.[4,9]

- *Adjusting the Dose:* If serum level is <1 ng/ml, increase dose; if 2.5–3.5 ng/ml, observe and assess the next day; if >3.5 ng/ml, hold dose for two days.[4]

Treatment of Digoxin Toxicity:

- *Stop the drug.* Most patients will excrete the excess digoxin over time. If arrhythmias are present, other treatments may be required.

- *Give phenytoin for ventricular arrhythmias.* Because mortality in digoxin overdose is high, prophylactic phenytoin may be indicated before there is evidence of serious ventricular ectopy.

- *Use atropine for bradycardia.* Transvenous pacing should be available, and appropriate venous access should be ready.

- *Give insulin with dextrose for hyperkalemia or begin dialysis (see* Dose *in dextrose monograph).* Because digoxin inhibits the sodium pump, intracellular potassium is released and may rise to fatal levels. Hyperkalemia may respond to insulin or dialysis.

- *For life-threatening acute digoxin intoxication, use digoxin immune Fab (Fab antibody fragments [Digibind]) to neutralize digoxin.*[10]

- *Use oral activated charcoal to remove digoxin.*[11] For oral or IV overdose, give 1 gm/kg/dose activated charcoal every 4–6 hours. May use charcoal in sorbitol for the first dose; if multiple doses are given, use charcoal in water because of the hyperosmotic laxative action of sorbitol. Charcoal is effective even for IV digoxin overdose because of significant enterohepatic circulation.[4]

- Peritoneal dialysis, hemodialysis, and exchange transfusion are not helpful in removing digoxin from the body because of the small percentage of the drug in the serum compared with the amount in the tissues.

Interactions:

- Decrease in digoxin dose may be needed when given concurrently with quinidine, verapamil, erythromycin, indomethacin, amiodarone, and possibly spironolactone.
- Use of β-blockers may increase *or* decrease dose requirements.
- Dose of digoxin may need to be increased with concurrent administration of antacids, cisapride, sucralfate, and metoclopramide because of decreased digoxin absorption.
- Dose may need to be decreased with concurrent administration of drugs that decrease renal function (e.g., aminoglycosides, amphotericin B, indomethacin) because digoxin elimination may decrease.

REFERENCES

1. Milner LS, Al-Mugeiren M, and Kaplan BS. 1992. Therapeutic agents and the kidney: Pharmacokinetics and complications. In *Pediatric Pharmacology: Therapeutic Principles in Practice,* Yaffe SJ, and Aranda JV, eds. Philadelphia: WB Saunders, 510–523.

2. Lundell BPW, and Boreus LO. 1983. Digoxin therapy and left ventricular performance in premature infants with patent ductus arteriosus. *Acta Paediatrica Scandinavica* 72(3): 339–343.

3. Roberts RJ. 1984. *Drug Therapy in Infants: Pharmacologic Principles and Clinical Experience.* Philadelphia: WB Saunders, 138–156.

4. Koren G, and Gorodischer R. 1992. Digoxin. In *Pediatric Pharmacology: Therapeutic Principles in Practice,* Yaffe SJ, and Aranda JV, eds. Philadelphia: WB Saunders, 355–364.

5. Lang D, and Von Bernuth G. 1977. Serum concentrations and serum half-life of digoxin in premature and mature newborns. *Pediatrics* 59(6): 902–906.

6. Koren G, et al. 1984. Significance of the endogenous digoxin-like substance in infants and mothers. *Clinical Pharmacology and Therapeutics* 36(6): 759–764.

7. Valdes R Jr, et al. 1983. Endogenous substance in newborn infants causing false positive digoxin measurements. *Journal of Pediatrics* 102(6): 947–950.

8. Koren G, and Parker R. 1985. Interpretation of excessive serum concentrations of digoxin in children. *American Journal of Cardiology* 55(9): 1210–1214.

9. Koren G, et al. 1989. Interpretation of excessive postmortem concentration of digoxin. *Archives of Pathology and Laboratory Medicine* 113(7): 758–761.

10. Hickey AR, et al. 1991. Digoxin immune Fab therapy in the management of digitalis intoxication: Safety and efficacy results of an observational surveillance study. *Journal of the American College of Cardiology* 17(3): 590–598.

11. Lalonde RL, et al. 1985. Acceleration of digoxin clearance by activated charcoal. *Clinical Pharmacology and Therapeutics* 37(4): 367–371.

12. Pinsky WW, et al. 1979. Dosage of digoxin in premature infants. *Journal of Pediatrics* 94(4): 639–642.

13. Warburton D, Bell EF, and Oh W. 1980. Pharmacokinetics and echocardiographic effects of digoxin in low-birth-weight infants with left-to-right shunting due to patent ductus arteriosus. *Developmental Pharmacology and Therapeutics* 1(2-3): 189–200.

14. Wettrell G, and Andersson KE. 1977. Clinical pharmacokinetics of digoxin in infants. *Clinical Pharmacokinetics* 2(1): 17–31.

15. Nyberg L, and Wettrell G. 1980. Pharmacokinetics and dosage of digoxin in neonates and infants. *European Journal of Clinical Pharmacology* 18(1): 69–74.

Digoxin Immune Fab (Digibind)

(di-JOX-in i-MUNE fab)

**Antidote:
Digoxin Toxicity**

Dose

Basis for Calculating Dose: Use either (1) the known digoxin overdose in milligrams or (2) the serum digoxin concentration (SDC) postdistribution (>6–10 hours after the overdose).

- **Determining Total Body Load (TBL) of Digoxin:** Use *one* of these equations:
  - TBL = mg digoxin ingested as elixir × 0.8
  - TBL = SDC in ng/ml × 0.0056 × body weight in kg
- **Determining Amount of Digoxin Immune Fab to Give:**
  - *mg digoxin immune Fab = TBL × 76*

Dose may be repeated after several hours if toxicity recurs or is not adequately resolved.[1] Table 1-25 gives the dose of digoxin immune Fab when SDC is known.

Administration

IV—*Rate:* Infuse by rapid IV push (if cardiac arrest is imminent) or by infusion over 15–30 minutes (preferred). Filter with an in-line 0.22-micron filter to remove protein aggregates.[1]

IV—*Concentration:* Reconstitute 40 mg vial with 4 ml normal saline to equal 10 mg/ml. For smaller doses, dilute further with 36 ml more of sterile water (= 1 mg/ml). If kept refrigerated, may be used up to 4 hours after reconstitution.

Use

An antigen-binding agent used as an antidote for life-threatening acute digoxin intoxication.[1–6]

Mechanism of Action

Digoxin immune Fab binds molecules of digoxin, making them unavailable for binding at their site of action and preparing them for renal elimination.

Adverse Effects

Allergic reactions are theoretically possible.

Hypokalemia: Monitor serum potassium, especially for the first few hours after treatment. Correct serum potassium cautiously to avoid hyperkalemia.

Cardiovascular:

- *Rapid Ventricular Rate:* In patients with pre-existing atrial fibrillation because of reversal of digoxin effects on AV node.
- *Worsening of CHF:* A result of the decreased concentration of digoxin.

Giving too large a dose of digoxin immune Fab is probably not dangerous, but it increases the risk of allergic, febrile, and serum-sickness reactions and prolongs the time until the infant can be redigitalized.

TABLE 1-25 ◆ DIGOXIN IMMUNE FAB DOSES (IN MG) FOR VARIOUS SERUM DIGOXIN
CONCENTRATIONS (SDCS) IN NG/ML AND BODY WEIGHTS

Body Weight (kg)	Dose (mg) for Serum Digoxin Concentration (ng/ml)				
	4 ng/ml	8 ng/ml	12 ng/ml	16 ng/ml	20 ng/ml
1	1.5	3	5	6	8
2	3	6	10	12	16
3	5	9	13	18	22
4	7	12	17	24	29
5	8	15	22	30	40
6	10	18	26	36	48
7	11	21	31	42	56
8	12	24	32	48	64
9	14	27	36	54	72
10	15	30	40	60	80

Adapted from: Medical Economics Data. 1993. *Physicians' Desk Reference*. Montvale, New Jersey: Medical Economics, 780. Reprinted by permission.

PHARMACOKINETICS/PHARMACODYNAMICS

Distribution: Large distribution in extracellular space. Improvement of symptoms is within a few to 30 minutes.

Half-life: 15–20 hours.

Elimination: Via the kidneys.[1]

NURSING IMPLICATIONS

Monitor serum digoxin and serum potassium levels carefully.

Monitor BP and continuous EKG.

Draw digoxin levels postdistribution. A blood sample drawn before 6–10 hours after the digoxin overdose (i.e., postdistribution) will show a markedly (and falsely) high serum digoxin concentration.

Draw digoxin level before administering immune Fab. Most assays measure total digoxin. Because the volume of distribution of digoxin is lower after digoxin immune Fab, the serum digoxin level may appear to skyrocket (a 10- to 20-fold increase) as the patient improves. The immune Fab/digoxin complex is pharmacologically inactive. Further, immune Fab interferes with the digoxin assay (falsely increasing or decreasing the levels).

COMMENTS

Signs of Effectiveness of Treatment: Decreased serum potassium; improvement in arrhythmias; decreased nausea, vomiting, and drowsiness.

Redigitalize only after digoxin immune Fab has been completely eliminated from the body—after several days in patients with normal renal function, a week or longer in patients with renal impairment.

REFERENCES

1. Manufacturer's product literature.

2. Zucker AR, et al. 1982. Fab fragments of digoxin-specific antibodies used to reverse ventricular fibrillation induced by digoxin ingestion in a child. *Pediatrics* 70(3): 468–471.

3. Hickey AR, et al. 1991. Digoxin immune Fab therapy in the management of digitalis intoxication: Safety and efficacy results of an observational surveillance study. *Journal of the American College of Cardiology* 17(3): 590–598.

4. Smith TW, et al. 1982. Treatment of life-threatening digitalis intoxication with digoxin-specific Fab antibody fragments: Experience in 26 cases. *New England Journal of Medicine* 307(22): 1357–1362.

5. Presti S, et al. 1985. Digoxin toxicity in a premature infant: Treatment with Fab fragments of digoxin-specific antibodies. *Pediatric Cardiology* 6(2): 91–93.

6. Kaufman J, et al. 1990. Use of digoxin Fab immune fragments in a seven-day-old infant. *Pediatric Emergency Care* 6(2): 118–121.

DOBUTAMINE (DOBUTREX)

(doh-BYU-ta-meen)

CARDIOVASCULAR:
VASOPRESSOR

DOSE

Initial: 1–2 mcg/kg/minute. Increase to 3–5 mcg/kg/minute as needed.

Usual Range: 1–10 mcg/kg/minute.[1–4]

Maximum: 15–40 mcg/kg/minute.[5]

When discontinuing infusion, taper the dose gradually.

ADMINISTRATION

Supplied as: 250 mg/20 ml vial.

IV—*Rate:* Continuous IV infusion.

IV—*Concentration:* Must be diluted prior to use. Determine concentration based on dose prescribed and infant's fluid requirements. Maximum: 5 mg/ml.

IV—*Compatibility:* See Appendix E: Y-Site Compatibility of Common NICU Drugs.

CAUTIONS/CONTRAINDICATIONS

Correct hypovolemia prior to administration.

USE

For low-output heart failure.

MECHANISM OF ACTION

Dobutamine is a catecholamine (sympathomimetic amine) related to dopamine. It primarily affects β_1 receptors, causing inotropic effects on the heart, and affects α receptors in a minor way, causing some vasoconstriction. It has fewer chronotropic (increased rate), arrhythmogenic, and vascular side effects than dopamine or isoproterenol. It does not stimulate dopaminergic receptors in the kidney as dopamine does.

At high doses, dobutamine's β_2 effects cause a decrease in total peripheral resistance (vasodilation), unlike dopamine, which increases peripheral resistance at high doses.[5]

ADVERSE EFFECTS

Tachycardia.

Arrhythmias (incidence is less than with other sympathomimetic amines such as dopamine and isoproterenol).

Increase or decrease in blood pressure. Manage by titrating infusion rate.

May cause pulmonary edema related to unexplained increase in pulmonary capillary wedge pressure.[6]

Pharmacokinetics/Pharmacodynamics

Onset of Action: 2 minutes.

Half-life: 2 minutes.

Nursing Implications

Administer carefully via syringe pump and titrate based on blood pressure response.

Monitor blood pressure, heart rate, and respiratory rate continuously.

Monitor for tachycardia and for hypertension or hypotension.

Monitor urine output.

Comments

Tolerance may develop with long-term (72 hours) use.[7]

References

1. Bohn DJ, et al. 1980. Hemodynamic effects of dobutamine after cardiopulmonary bypass in children. *Critical Care Medicine* 8(7): 367–371.

2. Schranz D, et al. 1982. Hemodynamic effects of dobutamine in children with cardiovascular failure. *European Journal of Pediatrics* 139(1): 4–7.

3. Driscoll DJ, et al. 1979. Hemodynamic effects of dobutamine in children. *American Journal of Cardiology* 43(3): 581–585.

4. Perkin RM, and Levin DL. 1982. Shock in the pediatric patient. Part II: Therapy. *Journal of Pediatrics* 101(3): 319–332.

5. Roberts RJ. 1984. *Drug Therapy in Infants: Pharmacologic Principles and Clinical Experience.* Philadelphia: WB Saunders, 169–171.

6. Perkin RM, et al. 1982. Dobutamine: A hemodynamic evaluation in children with shock. *Journal of Pediatrics* 100(6): 977–983.

7. Unverferth DA, et al. 1980. Tolerance to dobutamine after a 72-hour continuous infusion. *American Journal of Medicine* 69(2): 262–266.

DOPAMINE (INTROPIN)

(DOH-pa-meen)

**CARDIOVASCULAR:
VASOPRESSOR**

DOSE

Low (Dopamine Receptor): 0.5–2 mcg/kg/minute. Look for improved urine output.

Pressor: 5–20 mcg/kg/minute. Look for improved cardiac and urine output, peripheral perfusion, and blood pressure.

When discontinuing infusion, taper the dose gradually.

ADMINISTRATION

Supplied as: 40 mg/ml, 80 mg/ml.

IV—*Rate:* Continuous IV infusion. ***Do not*** administer via the umbilical arterial catheter or any other artery.

IV—*Concentration:* Determine concentration based on the dose and fluid requirements of the infant.[1]

IV—*Compatibility:* See Appendix E: Y-Site Compatibility of Common NICU Drugs.

CAUTIONS/CONTRAINDICATIONS

Concomitant administration with phenytoin has led to seizures, severe hypotension, and bradycardia. **Use phenytoin with extreme caution, if at all, in patients on dopamine.**

Do not administer via the umbilical artery catheter or any other arterial access.

USE

For refractory heart failure and shock.

At low doses, to increase renal perfusion.

Increase mean arterial pressure and improve ventricular function and urine output.[2–4]

MECHANISM OF ACTION

Dopamine is a catecholamine and the immediate precursor of norepinephrine and epinephrine. It directly stimulates β_1 and β_2 receptors, dopaminergic receptors, and α receptors at high doses. It indirectly causes release of norepinephrine from sympathetic nerve terminals.

Low doses of dopamine (<2 mcg/kg/minute) increase GFR, renal blood flow, and sodium excretion. Dopaminergic stimulation decreases vascular resistance in the mesenteric, renal, coronary, and cerebral vessels.[2]

Higher doses (2–10 mcg/kg/minute) increase cardiac output. The positive inotropic effect on the myocardium is caused by release of norepinephrine from nerve terminals and secondarily by direct stimulation of β_1 receptors.[2]

Doses >10 mcg/kg/minute cause α-adrenergic stimulation, which in turn causes vasoconstriction and an increase in blood pressure and peripheral and renal vascular resistance. Renal blood flow may decrease.[2]

The sympathetic innervation of the heart and other tissues is incomplete at birth (decreased density of synaptic terminations, decreased neurotransmitter release, and decreased number of β receptors); therefore, inotropic and other effects of dopamine may be reduced in neonates, particularly preterm infants, compared with older children and adults. Higher doses may be required for similar effects.[5–8]

Adverse Effects

Usually well tolerated at doses <10 mcg/kg/minute. Temporarily decrease the dose or stop the infusion if adverse effects occur. Because dopamine has a short half-life, adverse effects will usually be reversed within minutes.

Hypertension and cardiac arrhythmias with overdose. Adverse effects are most likely with doses >20 mcg/kg/minute.[8]

Treatment of Overdose: Treat massive overdose by stopping the infusion. No further treatment may be required because of the short duration of action of the drug. When this is not effective, consider using phentolamine (Regitine) IV, an α-adrenergic blocking agent.[9]

Pharmacokinetics/Pharmacodynamics

Distribution: Does not cross the blood-brain barrier.

Onset of Action: 5 minutes.

Duration of Action: <10 minutes.

Metabolism: Metabolized in the liver. Some researchers report decreased dopamine clearance in neonates,[10] whereas others do not.[11] Clearance is decreased with hepatic and renal dysfunction.[12]

Half-life: 2 minutes.

Nursing Implications

Administer carefully via syringe pump and titrate according to blood pressure response; monitor blood pressure, heart rate, and respiratory rate continuously as well as urine output.

Monitor for tachycardia, hypertension or hypotension, and dysrhythmias.[13]

Use caution when interrupting infusion, changing IV administration set, and/or flushing line. Sudden bolus may markedly increase blood pressure.

Avoid extravasation. Area of extravasation will be blanched, hard, and cold. Severe extravasation may cause local gangrene with tissue sloughing.[9] Antidote is local treatment with phentolamine (Regitine), which will cause immediate hyperemia. (See Appendix G: Guidelines for Management of Intravenous Extravasations.)

Blanching seen along vein into which dopamine is infusing is not harmful. Excessive vein blanching may be managed by rotation of infusion site.

COMMENTS

Interactions:

- Concomitant administration with phenytoin has led to seizures, severe hypotension, and bradycardia. **Use phenytoin with extreme caution, if at all, in patients on dopamine.**

- Concomitant use of β-blockers, such as propranolol, blocks the cardiac effects of dopamine.

- Concomitant use of α-blockers, such as phentolamine, blocks the peripheral vasoconstrictor effects of high-dose dopamine.

- Renal or mesenteric vasodilating effects are not blocked by either α- or β-blocking agents.[1]

REFERENCES

1. McEvoy GK. 1994. *AHFS Drug Information.* Bethesda, Maryland: American Society of Hospital Pharmacists, 765–767.

2. Roberts RJ. 1984. *Drug Therapy in Infants: Pharmacologic Principles and Clinical Experience.* Philadelphia: WB Saunders, 165–169.

3. Keeley SR, and Bohn DJ. 1988. The use of inotropic and afterload-reducing agents in neonates. *Clinics in Perinatology* 15(3): 467–489.

4. Drummond WH, et al. 1981. The independent effects of hyperventilation, tolazoline, and dopamine on infants with persistent pulmonary hypertension. *Journal of Pediatrics* 98(4): 603–611.

5. Gootman N, et al. 1983. Maturation-related differences in regional circulatory effects of dopamine infusion in swine. *Developmental Pharmacology and Therapeutics* 6(1): 9–22.

6. Driscoll DJ, et al. 1979. Comparative hemodynamic effects of isoproterenol, dopamine and dobutamine in the newborn dog. *Pediatric Research* 13(9): 1006–1009.

7. Whitsett JA, Noguchi A, and Moore JJ. 1982. Developmental aspects of alpha-and beta-adrenergic receptors. *Seminars in Perinatology* 6(2): 125–141.

8. DiSessa TG, et al. 1981. The cardiovascular effects of dopamine in the severely asphyxiated neonate. *Journal of Pediatrics* 99(5): 772–776.

9. Maggi JC, Angelats J, and Scott JP. 1982. Gangrene in a neonate following dopamine therapy. *Journal of Pediatrics* 100(2): 323–325.

10. Seri I, et al. 1984. Cardiovascular response to dopamine in hypotensive preterm neonates with severe hyaline membrane disease. *European Journal of Pediatrics* 142(1): 3–9.

11. Padbury JF, et al. 1987. Dopamine pharmacokinetics in critically ill newborn infants. *Journal of Pediatrics* 110(2): 293–298.

12. Notterman DA, et al. 1990. Dopamine clearance in critically ill infants and children: Effect of age and organ system dysfunction. *Clinical Pharmacology and Therapeutics* 48(2): 138–147.

13. Arant BS Jr. 1981. Nonrenal factors influencing renal function during the perinatal period. *Clinical Perinatology* 8(2): 225–240.

DOXAPRAM (DOPRAM)

(DOX-a-pram)

RESPIRATORY:
RESPIRATORY STIMULANT

DOSE

Loading: 2.5–3 mg/kg IV infused over 30 minutes.

Maintenance: 1–1.5 mg/kg/hour. Reduce to 0.5–0.8 mg/kg/hour as tolerated. May increase to 2–2.5 mg/kg/hour, but incidence of adverse effects is greater at higher doses.[1–3]

Some patients can respond to a dose as low as 0.25 mg/kg/hour.[4]

ADMINISTRATION

IV—*Rate (Loading Dose):* Infuse over 30 minutes.

IV—*Rate (Maintenance Dose):* Continuous.

IV—*Concentration:* 1 mg/ml or less is preferred because of the irritant nature of the drug. The recommended maximum concentration is 2 mg/ml; however, in fluid-restricted infants, it may not be possible to adhere to this maximum. If higher concentrations are used, observe IV site frequently for signs of extravasation or give via a central line.

IV—*Compatibility:* See Appendix E: Y-Site Compatibility of Common NICU Drugs.

PO: Enteral dose and frequency are not well defined. Bairam and colleagues concluded that no more than 24 mg/kg/dose given every 6 hours should be used.[5] They cautioned that oral doxapram should not be used routinely in preterm neonates with apnea because of poor absorption (10 percent), vomiting, blood pressure changes, and marked interindividual differences in plasma drug concentrations.[5–7]

CAUTIONS/CONTRAINDICATIONS

Use with caution, if at all, in patients at risk for seizures.

USE

Idiopathic apnea of prematurity that is unresponsive to theophylline. May be used concurrently with theophylline or alone.[8–10]

Has also been used for central sleep apnea, weaning from mechanical ventilation, and obstructive apnea.[1,11]

MECHANISM OF ACTION

At low doses, doxapram probably acts at the peripheral carotid chemoreceptors to mediate a respiratory response and, at higher doses, stimulates the central respiratory centers.

Doxapram causes a fall in PCO_2 and an increase in minute ventilation, tidal volume, and occlusion pressure, but no change in respiratory rate or inspiratory and expiratory times.[1,12]

ADVERSE EFFECTS

If adverse effects appear, temporarily stop infusion or decrease dose. Adverse effects usually subside 2–3 hours after discontinuation of infusion.[1]

Cardiovascular: Increased blood pressure (as a result of increased cardiac output and increased release of catecholamines), especially at doses >1.5 mg/kg/hour. Avoid giving drug during first few days of life when risk of intracranial hemorrhage is increased.

CNS: Stimulates CNS. Use with caution, if at all, in patients at risk for seizures, although an increased incidence of seizures has not been reported.[1,12] Excessive crying, disturbed sleep, irritability, jitteriness, and hyperactivity may also be seen.

GI: Abdominal distention, increased gastric residuals, vomiting, excessive salivation. A few cases of NEC have been reported in infants treated with doxapram, although direct cause has not been established.[1,2]

Local Effects: Thrombophlebitis; irritation of the skin, especially with use of a single injection site over an extended period of time. Tissue damage may occur with extravasation.

Thermoregulation: Hypothermia.

Other: Hyperglycemia may occur at higher doses.

Overdose causes seizures and cardiac arrhythmias.

Rapid infusion can cause hemolysis.

PHARMACOKINETICS/PHARMACODYNAMICS

Absorption: Oral absorption is 50–60 percent in adults, 10 percent in neonates.[5–7]

Onset of Action: 6 hours (without a loading dose).[2]

Metabolism: Metabolized in the liver to three or more metabolites, including keto-doxapram, a strong respiratory stimulant with fewer adverse effects than doxapram.[13]

Serum Half-life: 6.6–8.2 hours in neonates. The half-life decreases with age.

Elimination: Fecal (primarily) and renal.

NURSING IMPLICATIONS

Monitor vital signs continuously.

Monitor for response to therapy, such as improvement in apnea and bradycardia spells.

Monitor for side effects, including hypertension, irritability, jitteriness, and hyperactivity.

Solution contains benzyl alcohol.

COMMENTS

Benzyl Alcohol Content: Doxapram made in the U.S. contains 0.9 percent benzyl alcohol. A dose of 2.5 mg/kg/hour of doxapram gives 27 mg/kg of benzyl alcohol in 24 hours. Use the lowest effective dose because benzyl alcohol is associated with the fatal gasping syndrome of metabolic acidosis as well as CNS, respiratory, circulatory, and renal impairment.[14] A toxic benzyl alcohol dose is approximately 100–400 mg/kg/day. Benzyl alcohol is excreted in the kidney; therefore, risk increases with renal dysfunction.

Therapeutic Range: 1.5–3 mcg/ml. Toxicity has been associated with levels above 5 mcg/ml. Assays are not available at most centers, but have been described in the literature. Assay techniques include high-pressure liquid chromatography (HPLC) and gas chromatography.[1,2,10,15]

REFERENCES

1. Aranda JV, et al. 1992. Drug treatment of neonatal apnea. In *Pediatric Pharmacology: Therapeutic Principles in Practice*, Yaffe SJ, and Aranda JV, eds. Philadelphia: WB Saunders, 193–204.

2. Beaudry MA, et al. 1988. Pharmacokinetics of doxapram in idiopathic apnea of prematurity. *Developmental Pharmacology and Therapeutics* 11(2): 65–72.

3. Jamali F, et al. 1988. Doxapram dosage regimen in apnea of prematurity based on pharmacokinetic data. *Developmental Pharmacology and Therapeutics* 11(5): 253–257.

4. Bairam A, and Vert P. 1986. Low-dose doxapram for apnea of prematurity (letter). *Lancet* 1(8484): 793–794.

5. Bairam A, et al. 1991. Gastrointestinal absorption of doxapram in neonates. *American Journal of Perinatology* 8(2): 110–113.

6. Bairam A, et al. 1988. Enteral absorption of doxapram in premature newborns (abstract #323). *Pediatric Research* 23(4): 255A.

7. Bairam A, et al. 1988. Oral doxapram in premature newborns: Plasma levels and clinical effects (abstract #1195). *Pediatric Research* 23(4): 400A.

8. Sagi E, et al. 1984. Idiopathic apnoea of prematurity treated with doxapram and aminophylline. *Archives of Disease in Childhood* 59(3): 281–283.

9. Eyal F, et al. 1985. Aminophylline versus doxapram in idiopathic apnea of prematurity: A double-blind controlled study. *Pediatrics* 75(4): 709–713.

10. Hayakawa F, et al. 1986. Doxapram in the treatment of idiopathic apnea of prematurity: Desirable dosage and serum concentrations. *Journal of Pediatrics* 109(1): 138–140.

11. Weesner KM, and Boyle RJ. 1985. Successful management of central sleep hypoventilation in an infant using enteral doxapram. *Journal of Pediatrics* 106(3): 513–515.

12. Barrington KJ, et al. 1986. Physiologic effects of doxapram in idiopathic apnea of prematurity. *Journal of Pediatrics* 108(1): 125–129.

13. Bairam A, et al. 1989. Metabolism of doxapram in human fetal liver organ culture (abstract #368). *Pediatric Research* 25(4 part 2): 64A.

14. American Academy of Pediatrics, Committee on Drugs. 1985. "Inactive" ingredients in pharmaceutical products. *Pediatrics* 76(4): 635–643.

15. Barrington KJ, et al. 1987. Dose-response relationship of doxapram in the therapy for refractory idiopathic apnea of prematurity. *Pediatrics* 80(1): 22–27.

TABLE OF CONTENTS

E

ENALAPRIL [PO] AND
(e-NAL-a-pril & e-NAL-a-pril-ate)
ENALAPRILAT [IV] (VASOTEC)

**CARDIOVASCULAR:
ANTIHYPERTENSIVE**

DOSE

IV (for Hypertension): 5–10 mcg/kg/dose every 8–24 hours. Frequency depends on blood pressure response.

- Sluysmans and associates administered enalaprilat 20 mcg/kg IV over 1 minute as a single dose prior to angiography in infants with left-to-right ventricular shunt and CHF to assess clinical response. In those who responded, treatment was continued as oral enalapril 0.16 mg/kg (160 mcg/kg) as a single daily dose for 7 days.[1]

PO (for Severe Congestive Heart Failure):

- *Initial:* 0.1 mg/kg/day (= 100 mcg/kg/day) PO as a single daily dose. May increase to 0.43 mg/kg/day (= 430 mcg/kg/day) PO gradually as tolerated over a 2-week period. Mean maximal dose required was 0.3 mg/kg/day in one study.[2]
- *Maximum:* 0.5 mg/kg/day (= 500 mcg/kg/day) PO.[3]
- The oral dose should be lower in infants with CHF <20 days of age than in those >20 days of age.[4]

Reduce dose in renal impairment.

ADMINISTRATION

IV—*Rate:* Infuse over at least 5 minutes.

IV—*Concentration:* Supplied as 1.25 mg/ml (1,250 mcg/ml). May administer undiluted. ***However,*** calculated volume to administer to a small infant will probably be too small to measure accurately. Prepare a 1:10 dilution before administration: Dilute 0.1 ml of drug in 0.9 ml of saline or sterile water to equal a volume of 1 ml with a concentration of 0.125 mg/ml or 125 mcg/ml. (See Appendix A: Simplified Neonatal Calculations for instructions for making safe, accurate neonatal dilutions.)

IV—*Compatibility:* Compatible with dextrose and sodium chloride.

PO: Food does not interfere with absorption.

- *Compounding Instructions:* Prepare suspension immediately before use because period of stability is short. Dissolve 2.5 mg (half a 5 mg tablet) with 25 ml sterile water (= 100 mcg/ml). Draw up appropriate dose using a calibrated oral syringe. Discard unused portion.

CAUTIONS/CONTRAINDICATIONS

Use a low initial dose. Discontinue diuretics. A profound drop in blood pressure may occur with the initial dose, especially in patients on diuretics who are hyponatremic and/or hypovolemic. Monitor blood pressure hourly for the first 12 hours.

Reduce dose in renal impairment.

Use

For management of hypertension and heart failure because of ability to lower both left ventricular preload and afterload.

For infants with large left-to-right shunts and CHF.

An angiotensin converting enzyme (ACE) inhibitor in the same pharmacologic class as captopril, enalapril has advantages over captopril in that it has a longer duration of action, allowing once-daily dosing, and is available in parenteral form.[5–8]

Mechanism of Action

Enalapril, an ACE inhibitor, acts by inhibiting the conversion of angiotensin I to angiotensin II and by inhibiting the breakdown of bradykinin, a potent vasodilator. It suppresses the renin-angiotensin-aldosterone system. Angiotensin II is a potent vasoconstrictor and also stimulates the release of aldosterone from the adrenal cortex. Enalapril thus leads to a decrease in aldosterone, vasodilation, a loss of sodium and fluid, and an increase in serum potassium.

Adverse Effects

Hypotension. Reverse with IV fluids.

Increased serum potassium levels (1 percent of patients).

Decreased renal function; oliguria. Renal failure is more common in infants less than 4 months old with left-to-right shunts.[2]

May decrease hemoglobin and hematocrit (1 percent of patients) and may cause (rarely) bone marrow depression, neutropenia, and thrombocytopenia.

Pharmacokinetics/Pharmacodynamics

Absorption: The oral tablets are 60 percent absorbed. Therefore, when converting from IV to PO, a higher dose may be required.

Onset of Action: Within a few to 15 minutes.

Duration of Action (adult data): 6 hours (IV) and 24 hours (PO).[9]

Nursing Implications

Monitor serum potassium, blood pressure, heart rate, renal function, and blood count.

Monitor vital signs frequently before, during, and after administration (up to 1–2 hours following infusion).

COMMENTS

Interactions: Enalapril may increase digoxin levels. Rifampin may decrease enalapril effects. Indomethacin may decrease antihypertensive effect. Diuretics and/or other antihypertensives may increase enalapril effects.

REFERENCES

1. Sluysmans T, et al. 1992. Intravenous enalaprilat and oral enalapril in congestive heart failure secondary to ventricular septal defect in infancy. *American Journal of Cardiology* 70(9): 959–962.

2. Leversha AM, et al. 1994. Efficacy and dosage of enalapril in congenital and acquired heart disease. *Archives of Disease in Childhood* 70(1): 35–39.

3. Eronen M, et al. 1991. Enalapril in children with congestive heart failure. *Acta Paediatrica Scandinavica* 80(5): 555–558.

4. Nakamura H, et al. 1994. The kinetic profiles of enalapril and enalaprilat and their possible developmental changes in pediatric patients with congestive heart failure. *Clinical Pharmacology and Therapeutics* 56(2): 160–168.

5. Rheuban KS, et al. 1990. Acute hemodynamic effects of converting enzyme inhibition in infants with congestive heart failure. *Journal of Pediatrics* 117(4): 668–670.

6. Frenneaux M, et al. 1989. Enalapril for severe heart failure in infancy. *Archives of Disease in Childhood* 64(2): 219–223.

7. Wells TG, Bunchman TE, and Kearns GL. 1990. Treatment of neonatal hypertension with enalaprilat. *Journal of Pediatrics* 117(4): 664–667.

8. Marcadis ML, et al. 1991. Use of enalaprilat for neonatal hypertension. *Journal of Pediatrics* 119(3): 505–506.

9. Olin BR. 1994. *Drug Facts and Comparisons.* St. Louis: Facts and Comparisons, 801.

EPINEPHRINE

(ep-i-NEF-rin)

CARDIOVASCULAR: VASOPRESSOR
RESPIRATORY: BRONCHODILATOR

Synonyms: Epinephrine: adrenaline
Racemic epinephrine: Racepinephrine

DOSE

IV, intratracheal, intraosseous, SC.

IV push, Intratracheal, Intraosseous (IO): 0.1–0.3 ml/kg/dose of 1:10,000 (= 0.01–0.03 mg/kg/dose). May repeat every 3–5 minutes as needed.

Continuous Infusion: 0.05–1 mcg/kg/minute. Titrate dose to desired hemo-dynamic effect. Stop or decrease infusion if there are any adverse effects.

- Use a neonatal syringe pump to accurately control rate of infusion.
- Calculate the infusion using the following equation:

$C \ (mg/25ml) = 1.5 \times Dose \ (mcg/kg/minute) \times Weight \ (kg) \div Rate \ (ml/hour)$
(See Appendix A: Simplified Neonatal Calculations.)

Nebulization: Use racemic epinephrine (Vaponefrin 2 percent) 0.25 ml/dose diluted to 3 ml with normal saline.

SC: 0.01–0.03 ml/kg/dose of 1:1,000 (= 0.01–0.03 mg/kg/dose). May repeat every 20 minutes to every 4 hours as needed.

ADMINISTRATION

Supplied as:

- *Epinephrine Injection:* 1:10,000 (= 0.1 mg/ml) and 1:1,000 (= 1 mg/ml).
- *Solution for Inhalation:* Vaponefrin (Racepinephrine 2 percent [= epineph-rine base 1 percent]).

An epinephrine suspension (Sus-Phrine) 5 mg/ml (1:200) is available for a more prolonged effect; however, its high concentration and low dose (0.004–0.005 ml/kg/dose SC given every 6 hours, prn) make it difficult to measure accurately and make delivery of an overdose in small infants more likely. Therefore, its use in small infants is discouraged.

IV—*Rate:* IV push: Infuse over 1 minute.

Concentration:

- *IV Push:* May give the 1:10,000 concentration undiluted. The 1:1,000 concen-tration must be diluted before giving IV.
- *Continuous Infusion:* Determine the concentration based on the dose and fluid requirements of the infant. Use the 1:1,000 concentration to prepare the drip.
- *Intratracheal:* Use the 1:10,000 and dilute to 1–2 ml with normal saline. ET route is used for emergency resuscitation when the IV route is not immediately available.

- *IO:* May give the 1:10,000 concentration undiluted.
- *SC:* Use the 1:1,000 concentration to minimize injection volume. (Maximum pediatric injection volume is 0.5 ml.)

IV—*Compatibility:* See Appendix E: Y-Site Compatibility of Common NICU Drugs.

Protect from light. Exposure to light and air gradually causes the solution to darken—a pink coloration first, then brown. Do not use the injection if it contains a precipitate or if the solution has a pinkish or darker than slightly yellow color. Because of its instability, epinephrine expires quickly; always check the expiration date before use.

CAUTIONS/CONTRAINDICATIONS

Adverse effects are most likely to occur in hypertensive or hyperthyroid patients.

Do not use in shock (other than anaphylactic shock), angle-closure glaucoma, organic brain damage, or cardiac dilation.

Do not use with local anesthetics in certain areas such as fingers and toes because of the danger of vasoconstriction producing sloughing of tissue.

Epinephrine should not be used to counteract hypotension from phenothiazines (chlorpromazine) because it may lead to further lowering of blood pressure.

Epinephrine should not be given intra-arterially because marked vasoconstriction may result in gangrene.

USE

During cardiopulmonary resuscitation for asystole or heart rate remaining at <60 bpm after a minimum of 30 seconds of effective assisted ventilation and chest compressions.[1]

To relieve bronchospasm, respiratory distress, and wheezing.

For acute hypersensitivity or anaphylactoid reactions in older infants.

Epinephrine is added to some local anesthetics to decrease the rate of vascular absorption of the anesthetic, thereby localizing and prolonging the duration of anesthesia.[2]

MECHANISM OF ACTION

Epinephrine is an adrenergic agonist agent with both α- and β-adrenergic stimulating properties. The primary actions of epinephrine are to relax smooth muscle of the bronchial tree, stimulate the heart, and dilate skeletal muscle vasculature.[3] It also increases blood pressure, the strength of ventricular contractions, and heart rate and constricts the arterioles in the skin, mucosa, renal vascular bed, and splanchnic areas of circulation. Epinephrine increases myocardial oxygen consumption, antagonizes histamine, and causes pupillary dilation (mydriasis).

Racemic epinephrine (Racepinephrine) is about one-half as active as the levorotatory isomer (epinephrine).

ADVERSE EFFECTS

Severe reactions include cardiac arrhythmias (most commonly, premature ventricular beats and ventricular tachycardia), renal vascular ischemia, and severe hypertension with cerebral hemorrhage. Syncope has occurred in asthmatic children.

Pallor and coldness of the skin, tremor, decreased splanchnic blood flow, nausea, vomiting, transient elevation in blood sugar, hypokalemia.

After prolonged use or overdose, epinephrine may cause elevated serum lactic acid, and severe metabolic acidosis may occur.

Tolerance can occur with prolonged use.

Local: Blanching, tissue ischemia and necrosis on extravasation. Repeated local injections can cause necrosis from vascular constriction at the injection site.

Adverse effects following absorption of large doses from the respiratory tract when epinephrine is given by oral inhalation or nebulization are similar to those occurring after IV administration.

PHARMACOKINETICS/PHARMACODYNAMICS

Absorption: Epinephrine cannot be given PO because it is rapidly metabolized in the GI tract and liver, and therapeutic serum concentrations are not reached.

Onset and Duration of Action: Epinephrine has a rapid onset and short duration:

- *IV:* Onset of action after IV administration is immediate, with peak occurring at 1–2 minutes after the IV dose is administered.

- *Inhalation and SC:* Onset of bronchodilation after inhalation is about 3–5 minutes and after SC administration is 6–15 minutes; the peak effect is at about 20 minutes after the dose; duration is 1–3 hours for inhalation and 1–4 hours or less after SC administration.

Metabolism: Epinephrine is rapidly inactivated, being metabolized by catechol-*O*-methyltransferase (COMT) and monoamine oxidase (MAO) in the liver and other tissues. The drug is also deactivated by reuptake at synaptic receptor sites.

Elimination: Eliminated in the urine.

NURSING IMPLICATIONS

Monitor heart rate and rhythm, and blood pressure continuously.

Avoid extravasation. Area of extravasation will be blanched, hard, and cold. Severe extravasation of α-adrenergic drugs may cause local gangrene with tissue sloughing.[4] Antidote is local treatment with phentolamine (Regitine), which will cause immediate hyperemia. (See Appendix G: Guidelines for Management of Intravenous Extravasations and the monograph on phentolamine.)

Observe proper technique to avoid administration of epinephrine bolus during tubing change; do not give other drugs IV push into the epinephrine line to avoid inadvertently giving an epinephrine bolus.

COMMENTS

When used during cardiopulmonary resuscitation, provide adequate ventilation and cardiac compressions, and correct hypovolemia to enhance effectiveness of epinephrine.

Interactions:

- β-adrenergic blockers such as propranolol may block the β-adrenergic effects of epinephrine, causing hypertension. Vasoconstriction and hypertension are antagonized by α-adrenergic blocking agents such as phentolamine.

- Epinephrine given concurrently with bretylium may potentiate its action on adrenergic receptors and possibly cause arrhythmias.

- Epinephrine given concurrently with isoproterenol or other sympathomimetic agents may cause serious arrhythmia due to combined β-stimulating effects.

REFERENCES

1. American Heart Association in collaboration with the International Committee on Resuscitation. 2000. Part 11: Neonatal resuscitation. In Guidelines 2000 for cardiopulmonary resuscitation and emergency cardiovascular care. *Circulation* 102(supplement I): I-343–I-357.

2. McEvoy GK. 1994. *AHFS Drug Information.* Bethesda, Maryland: American Society of Hospital Pharmacists, 771–776.

3. Roberts RJ. 1984. *Drug Therapy in Infants: Pharmacologic Principles and Clinical Experience.* Philadelphia: WB Saunders, 159–163.

4. Maggi JC, Angelats J, and Scott JP. 1982. Gangrene in a neonate following dopamine therapy. *Journal of Pediatrics* 100(2): 323–325.

ERYTHROMYCIN (E-MYCIN)

(eh-rith-roe-MYE-sin)

Synonym: erythromycin lactobionate

DOSE

For Infection: IV, PO.[1]

- *<1.2 kg, 0–4 weeks:* 20 mg/kg/day divided every 12 hours
- *>1.2 kg:*
  - <7 days: 20 mg/kg/day divided every 12 hours
  - >7 days: 30 mg/kg/day divided every 8 hours

For GI Motility Disorders:

- 10 mg/kg/day divided every 8 hours, 30 minutes before feedings given IV or PO.[2]
- 3 mg/kg IV has been used for postpyloric intubation.[3]

Diagnostic: Doses of 1 and 3 mg/kg IV infused over 1 hour have been used to stimulate gastric antral contractions in children undergoing manometric studies of the upper GI tract. Both doses were equally effective, but the lower dose resulted in less nausea, vomiting, and abdominal pain.[4,5]

For Ophthalmia Neonatorum Prophylaxis: Apply 1–2 cm of ophthalmic ointment to the lower conjunctival sac of each eye once at birth. Use single-dose containers to prevent cross-contamination from one infant to another. Document in the medical record.[6]

For Acute Eye Infection: Apply 1–2 cm of ophthalmic ointment to the lower conjunctival sac every 6 hours.

ADMINISTRATION

IV—*Rate:* Infuse slowly over 60 minutes.

IV—*Concentration:* 5 mg/ml; more dilute if fluid status allows.

IV—*Compatibility:* See Appendix E: Y-Site Compatibility of Common NICU Drugs.

PO: Oral suspension may be administered with a small amount of the infant's feeding to minimize GI upset.

Ophthalmic Ointment: Apply to lower conjunctival sac of each eye. Massage eyelids gently to distribute the ointment.

CAUTIONS/CONTRAINDICATIONS

Some forms of IV erythromycin lactobionate contain the preservative benzyl alcohol, associated with the gasping syndrome in neonates.

FIGURE 1-7 ◆ **SITES OF ACTION OF FOUR PROKINETIC AGENTS.**

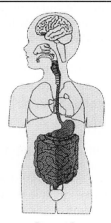
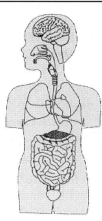
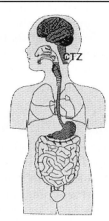
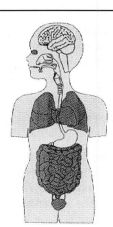

Cisapride	Erythromycin	Metoclopramide	Bethanechol
Cisapride stimulates gastrointestinal motility by enhancing the release of acetylcholine at the myenteric plexus without inducing muscarinic or nicotinic stimulation or inhibiting acetylcholinesterase activity.	**Erythromycin** stimulates gastric emptying by its action on the gastric antrum.	**Metoclopramide** is a dopamine receptor antagonist that stimulates motility of the upper gastrointestinal tract and possesses antiemetic properties by its action on dopamine receptors in the medullary chemoreceptor trigger zone (CTZ) and brain.	**Bethanechol** action on gastrointestinal motility is a result of its stimulation of all muscarinic receptors.

From: Hyman PE. 1994. Gastroesophageal reflux: One reason why baby won't eat. *Journal of Pediatrics* 125(6 part 2, supplement): S107. Reprinted by permission.

USE

A macrolide antibiotic used in neonates for *Chlamydia trachomatis* pneumonitis[7] and *Ureaplasma urealyticum* infections.[8] Its spectrum also includes staphylococci, streptococci, and *Listeria monocytogenes*. Not effective for Gram-negative bacterial infections.

Prokinetic agent for GI motility disorders. May be helpful when placement of nasojejunal (NJ) feeding tube is difficult.[4,5]

Ophthalmic Ointment: Routine eye prophylaxis for gonococcal ophthalmia in all infants at birth. Also effective in treatment (but **not** prophylaxis) of *C. trachomatis* eye infection.[6]

MECHANISM OF ACTION

Erythromycin suppresses protein synthesis.

Its prokinetic effect on the GI tract results from its action as a potent motilin receptor agonist, binding to motilin receptors on GI smooth muscle and inducing a burst of contractions migrating from the stomach to the small bowel when administered during fasting in doses 10–20 percent of those used to treat infection.[2,4,9] Other prokinetic agents are metoclopramide, cisapride, and bethanechol. Figure 1-7 identifies the sites of action of all four of these prokinetic agents.

ADVERSE EFFECTS

Usually well tolerated, but the adverse effects listed below may occur.

Cardiovascular: Cardiac toxicity requiring cardiopulmonary resuscitation temporally associated with IV erythromycin lactobionate has been reported in two preterm infants treated for Ureaplasma infection. There is a possible relationship between serum concentration and cardiac arrhythmias. The risk of arrhythmias may be reduced by utilizing a slow infusion over 1 hour and by not rapidly flushing the line after the infusion. Erythromycin given orally results in lower serum levels than doses given by the intravenous route. Arrhythmias have not been reported with oral erythromycin—perhaps for this reason.[10]

GI: Abdominal pain, nausea, vomiting.[4] Loose stools are the most frequent adverse effect reported in neonates (2.5 percent). Infantile hypertrophic pyloric stenosis (IHPS) may occur.

Hepatic: In adults, reversible intrahepatic cholestasis. Commonly associated with the estolate and ethylsuccinate salts.

Ototoxicity: High-frequency sensorineural deafness in patients older than 50 years and in patients with renal and/or hepatic dysfunction or receiving high doses.

Relatively Common: Vein irritation, thrombophlebitis, and pain on infusion. Can be minimized by dilution and slow infusion.

PHARMACOKINETICS/PHARMACODYNAMICS

Absorption: Well absorbed orally.[11] Oral suspension may be given with infant's formula without reducing absorption.

Distribution: Poorly distributed into CSF, making the drug levels there inadequate to treat infection.

Elimination: Excreted in bile.

NURSING IMPLICATIONS

Monitor IV site carefully.

Monitor for diarrhea.

Flush line *slowly* after administration.

COMMENTS

Interactions: May increase serum theophylline, digoxin, methylprednisolone, carbamazepine, and anticoagulant levels or effects.

REFERENCES

1. Nelson JD. 1996. *1996–1997 Pocketbook of Pediatric Antimicrobial Therapy,* 12th ed. Baltimore: Lippincott Williams & Wilkins, 16–17.

2. Janssens J, et al. 1990. Improvement of gastric emptying in diabetic gastroparesis by erythromycin: Preliminary studies. *New England Journal of Medicine* 322(15): 1028–1031.

3. Di Lorenzo C, Lachman R, and Hyman PE. 1990. Intravenous erythromycin for postpyloric intubation. *Journal of Pediatric Gastroenterology and Nutrition* 11(1): 45–47.

4. Di Lorenzo C, et al. 1994. Effect of erythromycin on antroduodenal motility in children with chronic functional gastrointestinal symptoms. *Digestive Diseases and Sciences* 39(7): 1399–1404.

5. Hyman PE. 1994. Gastroesophageal reflux: One reason why baby won't eat. *Journal of Pediatrics* 125(6 part 2): S103–S109.

6. Poland RL. 1993. Consultation with the specialist: Eye prophylaxis in the newborn infant. *Pediatrics in Review* 14(11): 423.

7. Harrison HR, et al. 1978. *Chlamydia trachomatis* infant pneumonitis: Comparison with matched controls and other infant pneumonitis. *New England Journal of Medicine* 298(13): 702–708.

8. Cassell GH, Waites KB, and Crouse DT. 1991. Perinatal mycoplasmal infections. *Clinics in Perinatology* 18(2): 241–262.

9. Tomomasa T, et al. 1986. Erythromycin induces migrating motor complex in human gastrointestinal tract. *Digestive Diseases and Sciences* 31(2): 157–161.

10. Farrar HC, et al. 1993. Cardiac toxicity associated with intravenous erythromycin lactobionate: Two case reports and a review of the literature. *Pediatric Infectious Disease Journal* 12(8): 688–691.

11. Ginsburg CM. 1986. Pharmacology of erythromycin in infants and children. *Pediatric Infectious Disease* 5(1): 124–129.

ERYTHROPOIETIN/EPOETIN ALFA (EPOGEN, PROCRIT)

(eh-rith-roe-POH-ee-tin/eh-POH-ee-tin)

BLOOD MODIFIER: COLONY-STIMULATING FACTOR

Synonyms: EPO, HuEPO, recombinant human erythropoietin, r-HuEPO, rEpo

DOSE

Various regimens have been used. These range from 500 to 1,400 units/kg/week, given in divided doses over the week or as a single dose each week, SC or IV. Table 1-26 shows some of the dosage regimens that have been used.

- *Need for Iron Supplementation:* Iron supplementation is needed when EPO is given, to support increased erythropoiesis. Iron depletion resulting from incorporation of iron into hemoglobin may cause a functional iron deficiency leading to a decrease or loss of epoetin efficacy. Iron supplementation is important in preterm infants receiving EPO; in fact, optimal iron supplementation can increase the effect of EPO.[1] EPO is usually administered with iron; however, some clinicians express concern about the use of iron in the first 2 weeks of life because of its potential for oxidation and because the long-term effects of giving iron in the first 2 weeks of life are not known.

- Iron supplementation is given PO as ferrous sulfate drops if tolerated or IV as iron dextran.

  - *Ferrous sulfate drops:* 6 mg elemental iron/kg/day PO.[2,3] Adjust iron dose to serum ferritin. Higher doses may be needed.

  - *Iron dextran:* Infants receiving parenteral nutrition (PN) may receive iron dextran in the PN solution 1 mg/kg/day (or 3–5 mg/kg/dose once a week). Iron dextran may also be infused by Y-site injection into the line.

- *Need for Vitamin E Supplementation:* Used in most studies. Is probably also needed to prevent hemolytic anemia when iron and EPO are administered together.[2–6]

  - *Vitamin E drops:* 25 units/day PO. (See monographs on ferrous sulfate and vitamin E.)

ADMINISTRATION

Supplied as: Injection: 2,000; 3,000; 4,000 units/ml (and others). Do not shake the vial because this may denature the glycoprotein, rendering the drug biologically inactive.

May be given SC (preferred) or IV.

IV—*Rate:* Infuse over 1–3 minutes.

IV—*Concentration:* May give undiluted or dilute with an equal volume of normal saline.

IV—*Continuous Infusion by Admixing in Parenteral Nutrition* (only limited data available on this method): Ohls and colleagues reported that EPO given by PN admixture resulted in EPO concentrations, clearance, and effectiveness similar to

TABLE 1-26 ◆ ERYTHROPOIETIN/EPOETIN (EPOGEN) DOSE REGIMEN COMPARISON

Reference	Dose per Day	Dose per Week	Other Supplements
Shannon et al. 1995[4]	100 units/kg/day SC, 5 days per week for 6 weeks	500 units/kg/week SC for 6 weeks	• 3 mg elemental iron/kg/day PO, increasing to 6 mg/kg/day PO when on full feedings • Vitamin E 15 units/day PO • Multivitamins 1 ml/day PO
Kumar et al. 1998[5]	300 units/kg/dose twice a week for 6 weeks	600 units/kg/week	6 mg elemental iron/kg/day PO
Ohls et al. 1999[2]	400 units/kg/dose IV or SC three times a week until the infant was 36 weeks PCA	1,200 units/kg/week	• IV iron 5 mg/kg/week or PO 6 mg elemental iron/kg/day adjusted to serum ferritin
Donato et al. 2000[3]		1,250 units/kg/week IV for 2 weeks; then 750 units/kg/week SC	• 6 mg elemental iron/kg/day PO • Folic acid 2 mg/day
Calhoun et al. 2000[6]	400 units/kg/dose SC three times a week for 2 weeks or 200 units/kg/day IV for 2 weeks Monitor serum ferritin as needed.	1,200 units/kg/week SC or 1,400 units/kg/week IV Note: Iron dextran and EPO were both admixed in the parenteral nutrition solution.	Iron dextran 1 mg/kg/day IV or a 3–5 mg/kg/dose once a week or 3 mg elemental iron/kg/day PO if feedings equalled at least 60 ml/kg/day and 6 mg elemental iron/kg/day PO when infant was on full feedings

those achieved with SC dosing. The dose used was EPO 200 units/kg/day for 10 consecutive days, plus iron supplementation as iron dextran 1 mg/kg/day. Both drugs were admixed in the PN solution. Cited advantages are reduced discomfort from repeated SC injections, repeated breaks of the skin are not made, and there is no leakage of medication from the SC injection site (this had been observed).[1]

SC: May give undiluted, or dilute with an equal volume of normal saline. Recommended injection site is the lateral thigh; alternate thighs with each injection.[6]

Storage: Refrigerate.

Cautions/Contraindications

Do not use in patients with uncontrolled hypertension.

Follow restrictive transfusion guidelines and minimize phlebotomy losses.[4,6]

EPO is not a substitute for an emergency blood transfusion.

Use

Anemia of Prematurity. Anemia of prematurity is characterized by low hematocrit, decreased reticulocyte index, and an inappropriately low serum erythropoietin concentration relative to the severity of the anemia. EPO may increase the hematocrit and decrease the need for RBC transfusions.[2,4–8] EPO is designated an orphan drug by the FDA for use in the treatment of anemia of prematurity.

Used in older children and adults for anemia of chronic renal failure, chemotherapy-induced anemia, and anemia in zidovudine-treated HIV-infected patients.[9]

Cost: Costs of the transfusions that use of EPO may have avoided have been compared with the cost of the drug. If the efficacy of EPO permits elimination of two transfusions, or if two doses of EPO can be obtained when a vial is opened, then the cost of EPO therapy is similar to the cost of transfusions. Use of strategies to reduce the need for transfusions (such as the use of microtechniques for laboratory tests and institution of stricter transfusion guidelines) is less expensive than EPO administration and can help minimize its use.[6,7,10–12] Smaller, sicker infants; need for mechanical ventilation; sepsis; increased risk for chronic lung disease; lower birth hematocrit; and increased phlebotomy losses have been identified as predictors of transfusion need.[6] Infants at increased risk for transfusion—and who are thus the most likely to benefit from EPO therapy—should be identified in the first week of life.[13]

EPO has also been used successfully for other neonatal anemias, including anemia of bronchopulmonary dysplasia[14] and the late anemia at 1–3 months of life caused by Rh hemolytic disease of the newborn, especially in infants who received intrauterine transfusions.[15] Also, infants with congenital heart disease often experience prolonged hospitalization, multiple invasive procedures, and significant phlebotomy losses requiring multiple transfusions.[10] In one study, these infants showed a significant increase in hematocrit and a decrease in transfusions with the use of EPO.[16]

Mechanism of Action

Erythropoietin is a colony-stimulating factor. It stimulates red blood cell production by stimulating the division and differentiation of erythroid progenitors in the bone marrow and inducing the release of reticulocytes from the bone marrow into the bloodstream, where they mature to erythrocytes.

EPO is produced by mammalian cells into which the human erythropoietin gene has been introduced. The product contains the identical amino acid sequence of natural erythropoietin.

ADVERSE EFFECTS

Hypertension when circulating red cell mass is increased too rapidly. Do not use in patients with uncontrolled hypertension.

Edema, fatigue, fever, rash, nausea, diarrhea, cough, and hypersensitivity reactions.

Seizures have occurred; however, their relationship to EPO treatment is uncertain.[9]

May cause transient early thrombocytosis and late neutropenia.[8] May cause poly-cythemia—monitor the hematocrit and adjust dose if needed.

May cause local skin reaction at the injection site.

PHARMACOKINETICS/PHARMACODYNAMICS

Bioavailability and Excretion: The bioavailability of EPO after SC administration in preterm infants was 42 percent.[17] Higher doses of EPO given less frequently, especially with IV administration, may result in increased EPO excretion and decreased bioavailability. Methods of administration that achieve lower peak serum concentrations over a longer period of time, such as admixing EPO in the PN solution and infusing it over 24 hours, may be more efficacious.[10,18] One study compared giving 100 units/kg/dose 5 times weekly with giving 500 units/kg/week as a single dose. More frequent dosing (100 units/kg/day) produced a more significant and sustained increase in stimulated erythropoiesis in very low birth weight infants than did the higher weekly dose. The authors suggest that infants at risk for greater phlebotomy losses receive more frequent dosing and that those at lower risk receive less frequent dosing to enhance cost-effectiveness.[19]

Volume of Distribution and Clearance: Neonates, including preterm infants, have a larger volume of distribution and a more rapid clearance of EPO than adults, necessitating the use of higher doses per kilogram of body weight than are required for adults.[6,17,18]

Response Time: A reticulocyte response may occur within 72 to 96 hours after initiation of EPO therapy, but a change in hematocrit may not occur for 5–7 days, depending on the volume of ongoing phlebotomy losses. Consider measuring the reticulocyte count, venous hematocrit, and absolute neutrophil count after 1–2 weeks of EPO therapy.[6]

NURSING IMPLICATIONS

Monitor blood pressure, hematocrit, reticulocyte count.

Rotate injection sites.

Monitor for signs and symptoms of cellulitis.

Keep track of doses. Knowledge of the number of doses given minimizes errors and ensures discontinuation of the drug when the course is completed.

Monitoring: Check reticulocyte count and venous hematocrit after 1–2 weeks of EPO therapy. Consider monitoring absolute neutrophil count (although this has not turned out to be a problem in neonatal studies despite researchers' initial concerns). Monitoring of serum ferritin may be necessary to determine adequacy of iron supplementation.[6]

REFERENCES

1. Bader D, et al. 1996. Decreased ferritin levels, despite iron supplementation, during erythropoietin therapy in anaemia of prematurity. *Acta Paediatrica* 85(4): 496–501.

2. Ohls RK, et al. 1999. A multi-centered, randomized, double-blind, placebo-controlled trial of erythropoietin and iron administration to preterm infants. *Pediatric Research* 45(4): 216A.

3. Donato H, et al. 2000. Effect of early versus late administration of human recombinant erythropoietin on transfusion requirements in premature infants: Results of a randomized, placebo-controlled, multi-center trial. *Pediatrics* 105(5): 1066–1072.

4. Shannon KM, et al. 1995. Recombinant human erythropoietin stimulates erythropoiesis and reduces erythrocyte transfusions in very low birth weight preterm infants. *Pediatrics* 95(1): 1–8. (Comment in *Pediatrics*, 1995, 95[1]: 9–10.)

5. Kumar P, Shankaran S, and Krishnan RG. 1998. Recombinant human erythropoietin therapy for treatment of anemia of prematurity in very low birth weight infants: A randomized, double-blind, placebo-controlled trial. *Journal of Perinatology* 18(3): 173–177.

6. Calhoun DA, et al. 2000. Consistent approaches to procedures and practices in neonatal hematology. *Clinics in Perinatology* 27(3): 733–753.

7. Wandstrat TL, and Wolfe M. 1996. Hematopoietic growth factors. Part 2. *Neonatal Network* 15(7): 25–28.

8. Halperin DS, et al. 1990. Effects of recombinant human erythropoietin in infants with the anemia of prematurity: A pilot study. *Journal of Pediatrics* 116(5): 779–786.

9. Kastrup EK. 2001. *Drug Facts and Comparisons.* St. Louis: Facts and Comparisons, 139–142.

10. Ohls RK. 2000. The use of erythropoietin in neonates. *Clinics in Perinatology* 27(3): 681–696.

11. Meyer MP. 1997. Anaemia of prematurity: Epidemiology, management and costs. *Pharmacoeconomics* 12(4): 438–445.

12. Ohls RK, Osborne KA, and Christensen RD. 1995. Efficacy and cost analysis of treating very low birth weight infants with erythropoietin during their first two weeks of life: A randomized, placebo controlled trial. *Journal of Pediatrics* 126(3): 421–426.

13. Al-Kharfy T, et al. 1996. Erythropoietin therapy in neonates at risk of having bronchopulmonary dysplasia and requiring multiple transfusions. *Journal of Pediatrics* 129(1): 89–96.

14. Ohls RK, Hunter DD, and Christensen RD. 1993. A randomized, placebo-controlled trial of recombinant erythropoietin in treatment of the anemia of bronchopulmonary dysplasia. *Journal of Pediatrics* 123(6): 996–1000.

15. Scaradavou A, et al. 1993. Suppression of erythropoiesis by intrauterine transfusions in hemolytic disease of the newborn: Use of erythropoietin to treat the late anemia. *Journal of Pediatrics* 123(2): 279–284.

16. Shaddy RE, et al. 1995. Epoetin alfa therapy in infants awaiting heart transplantation. *Archives of Pediatrics and Adolescent Medicine* 149(3): 322–325.

17. Brown MS, et al. 1993. Single-dose pharmacokinetics of recombinant human erythropoietin in preterm infants after intravenous and subcutaneous administration. *Journal of Pediatrics* 122(4): 655–657.

18. Ohls RL, Veerman MW, and Christensen RD. 1996. Pharmacokinetics and effectiveness of recombinant erythropoietin administered to preterm infants by continuous infusion in total parenteral nutrition solution. *Journal of Pediatrics* 128(4): 518–523.

19. Brown MS, and Keith JF III. 1999. Comparison between two and five doses a week of recombinant human erythropoietin for anemia of prematurity: A randomized trial. *Pediatrics* 104(2 part 1): 210–215.

ETHYL ALCOHOL (ETHANOL)

(ETH-il AL-koe-hol)

ANTIDOTE:
CENTRAL OCCLUDED CATHETERS

DOSE

Instill 0.3–0.6 ml of 70 percent ethyl alcohol solution into catheter.

ADMINISTRATION

Instill catheter-specific volume into the catheter and allow to dwell for 1–2 hours; then aspirate.[1,2]

Concentration: 70 percent.

Pharmacist Compounding Directions
70 Percent Ethyl Alcohol Solution[2]

Draw up 3.5 ml of 98 percent ethyl alcohol (dehydrated alcohol injection, USP) using appropriate aseptic technique. Add 1.5 ml sterile water for injection to make 5 ml. Filter with a 0.22-micron filter.

USE

Re-establishment of central venous catheter patency for occlusions caused by IV fat emulsion. Successful in restoring patency in 80 percent of catheters occluded with lipids.[3,4]

See Appendix F: Restoring Patency to Occluded Central Venous Catheters for an algorithm for choosing the correct pharmacologic agent for clearing an occluded central line.

MECHANISM OF ACTION

Ethyl alcohol acts as a lipid solvent. The mechanism of a dextrose–amino acid–lipid occlusion is not known, but it may result from aggregation of the lipid particles by divalent and trivalent cations and formation of a lipid-protein complex.[3,4]

ADVERSE EFFECTS

Systemic toxicity should not occur as long as the alcohol is instilled into the catheter and aspirated back out.

If alcohol is inadvertently injected systemically, however, the following may occur: sedation, alcohol intoxication, increased liver function tests, increased urine uric acid, alcohol odor to breath, vein irritation, extravasation injury, fever.

May cause hypoglycemia in diabetic patients.[5]

PHARMACOKINETICS/PHARMACODYNAMICS

Metabolism: Metabolized in the liver to acetaldehyde or acetate.

Nursing Implications

Procedure is usually performed by a physician.

Monitor patient closely for adverse effects.

References

1. Holcombe BJ, Forloines-Lynn S, and Garmhausen LW. 1992. Restoring patency of long-term central venous access devices. *Journal of Intravenous Nursing* 15(1): 36–41.

2. Holcombe BJ, Forloines-Lynn S, and Garmhausen LW. 1993. Erratum for corrected algorithm. Restoring patency of long-term central venous access devices. *Journal of Intravenous Nursing* 16(1): 55.

3. Pennington CR, and Pithie AD. 1987. Ethanol lock in the management of catheter occlusion. *Journal of Parenteral and Enteral Nutrition* 11(5): 507–508.

4. Pennington CR. 1990. Management of catheter occlusion (letter). *Journal of Parenteral and Enteral Nutrition* 14(5): 551.

5. Olin BR. 1994. *Drug Facts and Comparisons.* St. Louis: Facts and Comparisons, 125–126.

TABLE OF CONTENTS

F

FAMOTIDINE (PEPCID)
(fa-MOE-ti-deen)

GASTROINTESTINAL: HISTAMINE (H_2) ANTAGONIST

DOSE

PO: 1–2 mg/kg/day divided every 8 hours.

IV: 0.3 mg/kg/dose given every 8 hours
(*Maximum:* 2.4 mg/kg/day).[1–6]

IV Continuous Infusion: 1–2 mg/kg/day. The daily dose can be given by continuous infusion over 24 hours. May be admixed in parenteral nutrition solution.

Monitor gastric fluid pH to keep it above 3.5 for the majority of the dosing interval.

Reduce dose or give at longer intervals in severe renal dysfunction. Reduced renal function may result in increased plasma concentrations of famotidine, thus increasing the risk of side effects.

ADMINISTRATION

Supplied as:

- *PO:* Powder for oral suspension 8 mg/ml. Reconstituted suspension is stable for 30 days at room temperature; shake well.
- *Injection:* 10 mg/ml.

PO: May administer with food.

IV—*Rate:* May infuse over 2–3 minutes, but infusion over 30 minutes is preferred.

IV—*Concentration:* Dilute with saline or dextrose to 0.2–4 mg/ml.

IV—*Compatibility:* See Appendix E: Y-Site Compatibility of Common NICU Drugs.

USE

For treatment of gastroesophageal reflux, reflux esophagitis, gastric hypersecretory states, upper GI mucosal lesions. Also used for prophylaxis of stress-induced gastric mucosal injury.

Comparison with other H_2 blockers: More potent than cimetidine (40–60 times) or ranitidine (10–15 times) and has a longer duration of action because of its greater affinity for the histamine H_2 receptor. Can be given every 8–12 hours, whereas ranitidine is given every 6–12 hours in adults. More frequent dosing may be required in critically ill infants and children to achieve target gastric fluid pH; therefore, the every-8-hour dosing interval is recommended under **DOSE** in this monograph. The efficacy and safety profile is similar to that of ranitidine.[2] Experience with famotidine in infants and children is limited.

MECHANISM OF ACTION

Famotidine is an H_2 blocker that is a reversible, competitive antagonist of the action of histamine on H_2 receptors. It inhibits gastric acid secretion and reduces the volume of gastric juice and its hydrogen ion concentration.

ADVERSE EFFECTS

Extremely potent and relatively free of side effects.

Cardiovascular: Rapid IV administration increases the risk of hypotension and cardiac arrhythmias. Other adverse effects reported are bradycardia, tachycardia, hypertension, and AV block.

CNS: Seizures (one report), insomnia, drowsiness, fever.

Dermatologic: Rarely, rash, flushing, dry mouth or skin.

GI: May cause abdominal symptoms such as constipation, vomiting, diarrhea, abdominal discomfort, flatulence, and alterations in taste.

Hematologic: Rarely, thrombocytopenia.

Hepatic: Increased liver enzymes.

Ophthalmic: Orbital edema.

Otic: Ringing or buzzing in the ears.

Renal: Increased BUN/creatinine, proteinuria.

Respiratory: Rarely, bronchospasm.

PHARMACOKINETICS/PHARMACODYNAMICS

Time to Peak Plasma Concentration: 1–3 hours.

Bioavailability: Oral administration results in a bioavailability of about 40 percent. Bioavailability is slightly increased when the drug is given with food and slightly decreased when it is coadministered with antacids. When changing from the IV route to PO, increase the dose by about 60 percent because of the drug's incomplete bioavailability.[2]

Protein Binding: 15–20 percent.

Metabolism: 30 percent hepatic.

Half-life: 3.3 hours (variable).[3] The half-life is increased with renal dysfunction, requiring dose reduction.

Elimination: Primarily unchanged in the urine.[4–6]

NURSING IMPLICATIONS

Monitor gastric fluid pH.

Monitor renal and hepatic function and platelets.

Shake suspension well before administration.

COMMENTS

Interactions: Famotidine does not inhibit cytochrome P-450; therefore, concurrent administration with theophylline or other drugs metabolized in the liver should not cause elevated serum concentrations. Decreases absorption of keto-conazole, itraconazole, and cefpodoxime. Concurrent use with sucralfate may reduce absorption of famotidine.

REFERENCES

1. Miyake S, et al. 1987. Effect of a new H$_2$ blocker, famotidine, in reflux esophagitis among severely handicapped children. *Clinical Therapeutics* 9(5): 548–558.

2. Reed MD, Sutphen JL, and Blumer JL. 1992. Drugs used to modulate gastrointestinal function. In *Pediatric Pharmacology: Therapeutic Principles in Practice,* Yaffe SJ, and Aranda JV, eds. Philadelphia: WB Saunders, 437–465.

3. Kraus G, et al. 1990. Famotidine: Pharmacokinetic properties and suppression of acid secretion in paediatric patients following cardiac surgery. *Clinical Pharmacokinetics* 18(1): 77–81.

4. Lauritsen K, Laursen LS, and Rask-Madsen J. 1990. Clinical pharmacokinetics of drugs used in the treatment of gastrointestinal diseases. *Clinical Pharmacokinetics* 19(1 part 1): 11–31.

5. Lauritsen K, Laursen LS, and Rask-Madsen J. 1990. Clinical pharmacokinetics of drugs used in the treatment of gastrointestinal diseases. *Clinical Pharmacokinetics* 19(2 part 2): 94–125.

6. Treem WR, Davis PM, and Hyams JS. 1991. Suppression of gastric acid secretion by intravenous administration of famotidine in children. *Journal of Pediatrics* 118(5): 812–816.

FENTANYL (SUBLIMAZE)
(FEN-ta-nil)
(CONTROLLED SUBSTANCE SCHEDULE II)

CENTRAL NERVOUS SYSTEM: NARCOTIC ANALGESIC

DOSE

PDA Ligation:

- *IV Push over 1–2 minutes:* 5–10 mcg/kg/dose.
- *Maximum:* 30 mcg/kg/dose.[1]

Adjunct to Anesthesia in Neonatal Surgery: 12.5 mcg/kg provided adequate analgesia for 90 minutes in neonates with increased intra-abdominal pressure, whereas a dose of 25–50 mcg/kg was required for neonates with normal intra-abdominal pressure. Most infants resumed respiratory efforts within 2 hours after a dose of 25–50 mcg/kg. Most neonates who receive fentanyl as the primary analgesic should be ventilated postoperatively because of the drug's variable and prolonged half-life in neonates.[2–4]

Sedation/Analgesia:

- *IV Push:* 1–4 mcg/kg/dose given every 2–4 hours or as needed on an individual basis.
- *Continuous Infusion:* IV bolus of 1 mcg/kg; then start infusion of 0.5 mcg/kg/hour up to 4 mcg/kg/hour.
- Start with a low dose and increase gradually as tolerance develops or as needed, based on individual response.

ADMINISTRATION

IV Push:

- *Concentration:* May give undiluted.
- *Rate:* Infuse IV push doses over at least 1–2 minutes.

Continuous Infusion: *Sample calculation for a dose of 1 mcg/kg/hour infused at a rate of 0.5 ml/hour:* How many micrograms of fentanyl should be added to 25 ml D_5W to give a 900 gm infant a dose of 1 mcg/kg/hour? The starting infusion rate for the fentanyl is 0.5 ml/hour to allow for dose increase, if needed, without overloading the infant with fluid.

For drugs dosed in mcg/kg/hour (also see Appendix A: Simplified Neonatal Calculations):

$$C \ (= mcg/25\ ml) = \frac{25 \times D \ (= mcg/kg/hour) \times W \ (kg)}{R \ (= ml/hour)}$$

$$C = \frac{25 \times 1 \times 0.9}{0.5} = 45\ mcg$$

where: C = mcg of fentanyl per 25 ml fluid
                D = dose of fentanyl in mcg/kg/hour
                W = baby's body weight in kg
                R = rate of the fentanyl drip in ml/hour

Write the order as follows:

Fentanyl 45 mcg in 25 ml D_5W to run at 0.5 ml/hour (= 1 mcg/kg/hour)

Compatibility: See Appendix E: Y-Site Compatibility of Common NICU Drugs.

USE

Used as an adjunct to anesthesia, for analgesia, or for sedation in infants on
mechanical ventilation.[1,5,6]

MECHANISM OF ACTION

Fentanyl is a synthetic narcotic analgesic, 50–100 times as potent as morphine.
Narcotic agonists have activity at the mu (μ), kappa (K), and possibly at the
delta (Δ) opioid receptors, and they occupy the same receptors as endogenous
opioid peptides (enkephalins or endorphins). Unlike morphine, fentanyl does
not cause histamine release and, *when administered properly,* is not usually associated with hypotension.[7,8]

ADVERSE EFFECTS

Dose-dependent respiratory depression (***Antidote:*** Naloxone 0.1 mg/kg/dose IV
[see Appendix J: Antidotes for Drugs That Cause Loss of Respiratory Effort]),
seizures, hypotension (uncommon), reduced GI motility, and urinary retention
may occur.

Rapid IV push administration is associated with an increased risk of hypotension,
bradycardia, and respiratory muscle paralysis. Chest wall (truncal muscle) rigidity, sometimes called "wooden chest syndrome" can occur; it is reversed with
atracurium 0.3 mg/kg/dose infused IV over 1 minute.

Tolerance may develop, requiring increased dose or dose frequency. Tolerance
developed in 5 days in one group of newborns on ECMO; the infants required
approximately double the dose requirement on day 6 as on day 1 to maintain the
same degree of sedation.[9]

Physical dependence can occur. Discontinue the drug slowly over a few days to
prevent withdrawal symptoms. Narcotic withdrawal may occur with continuous
fentanyl infusion; the effect is both dose- and duration-dependent.[10] The
Neonatal Withdrawal Score Sheet (Appendix K) may be used to guide dose
tapering.[11]

PHARMACOKINETICS/PHARMACODYNAMICS

Onset of Action: Immediate when given IV, with full sedative effect in several minutes. Has a faster onset of action than morphine.

Duration of Action: 1–2 hours.[2,3] Has a shorter duration of action than
morphine.[12]

Protein Binding: 80–89 percent.[4]

Metabolism: Hepatic by mixed-function oxidase enzyme system. Conditions that decrease hepatic perfusion, such as increased intra-abdominal pressure, increase the elimination half-life.

Half-life: In neonates, 18 hours (range: 6–32 hours).[1,13] Half-life is 25 percent longer than in adults because of a larger volume of distribution in neonates.

NURSING IMPLICATIONS

When giving to a nonintubated patient in preparation for a procedure, use conscious sedation precautions and monitoring, including frequent continuous vital sign monitoring and pulse oximetry. Have naloxone at bedside for reversal; monitor for hypotension.

If weaning after prolonged use, titrate by utilizing the Neonatal Withdrawal Score Sheet (Appendix K) to assess tolerance of the weaning procedure.

COMMENTS

Fentanyl transdermal patches cannot be cut for smaller doses and cannot be used on neonates.

REFERENCES

1. Collins C, et al. 1985. Fentanyl pharmacokinetics and hemodynamic effects in preterm infants during ligation of patent ductus arteriosus. *Anesthesia and Analgesia* 64(11): 1078–1080.

2. Yaster M. 1987. The dose response of fentanyl in neonatal anesthesia. *Anesthesiology* 66(3): 433–435.

3. Robinson S, and Gregory GA. 1981. Fentanyl-air-oxygen anesthesia for ligation of patent ductus arteriosus in preterm infants. *Anesthesia and Analgesia* 60(5): 331–334.

4. Lerman J. 1993. Anesthesia. In *Pediatric Pharmacology and Therapeutics,* Radde IC, and MacLeod SM, eds. St. Louis: Mosby-Year Book, 483–484.

5. Bell SG, and Ellis LJ. 1987. Use of fentanyl in mechanically ventilated neonates. *Neonatal Network* 6(2): 27–31.

6. Anand KJ, Sippell WG, and Aynsley-Green A. 1987. Randomised trial of fentanyl anaesthesia on preterm babies undergoing surgery: Effects on the stress response. *Lancet* 1(8524): 62–66.

7. Hickey PR, et al. 1985. Pulmonary and systemic hemodynamic responses to fentanyl in infants. *Anesthesia and Analgesia* 64(5): 483–486.

8. Maguire DP, and Maloney P. 1988. A comparison of fentanyl and morphine use in neonates. *Neonatal Network* 7(1): 27–32.

9. Arnold JH, et al. 1991. Changes in the pharmacodynamic response to fentanyl in neonates during continuous infusion. *Journal of Pediatrics* 119(4): 639–643.

10. Katz R, Kelly HW, and Hsi A. 1994. Prospective study on the occurrence of withdrawal in critically ill children who receive fentanyl by continuous infusion. *Critical Care Medicine* 22(5): 763–767.

11. Finnegan LP. 1985. Neonatal abstinence. In *Current Therapy in Neonatal Perinatal Medicine,* Nelson N, ed. Toronto: BC Decker, 262–270.

12. Singleton MA, Rosen BA, and Fisher DM. 1987. Plasma concentrations of fentanyl in infants, children and adults. *Canadian Journal of Anesthesia* 34(2): 152–155.

13. Truog R, and Anand KJS. 1989. Management of pain in the post-operative neonate. *Clinics in Perinatology* 16(1): 61–78.

FERROUS SULFATE
(FER-us SUL-fate)
(FER-IN-SOL DROPS)

NUTRITION: IRON SUPPLEMENT

Synonyms: iron sulfate, iron

DOSE

Prophylactic Iron Supplementation for Preterm Infants: Doses for supplementation in preterm infants are typically 0.1–0.2 ml/day of Fer-In-Sol Drops (= 2.5–5 mg elemental iron/day). Administer as a single daily dose beginning at 1–2 months of age and continue until 6–12 months of age. *Maximum dose:* 15 mg elemental iron/day (= 0.6 ml of Fer-In-Sol Drops). Base dosage on birth weight:

- *<1 kg:* A total of 4 mg elemental iron/kg/day starting at about 1 month of age and continuing for 6 months, then 2 mg/kg/day until 12 months of age. The dose is larger for very low birth weight infants during the first 6 months to accommodate their greater need for iron for growth.
- *1–1.5 kg:* A total of 3 mg elemental iron/kg/day for 6 months, then 2 mg/kg/day until 12 months of age.
- *1.5–2.5 kg:* 2 mg elemental iron/kg/day until 12 months of age.

Treatment of Established Iron Deficiency: 3 mg/kg/day PO.[1]

Iron-fortified formula (containing 12 mg iron/liter) can provide 2 mg/kg/day of the dose requirement for the previous dose recommendations.

Iron Supplementation with Administration of Erythropoietin (Epoetin Alfa, Epogen): Shannon and colleagues used 3 mg/kg/day elemental iron, increasing to 6 mg/kg/day when infants tolerated full caloric feedings enterally.[2] Infants also received vitamin E and multivitamins. They conclude that a supplemental iron dose of 6 mg/kg/day is adequate to support erythropoiesis in infants given 500 units of erythropoietin per week. Ohls and associates supplemented infants receiving EPO by continuous infusion in their parenteral nutrition solution with iron dextran 1 mg/kg/day.[3]

ADMINISTRATION

PO: Iron is best absorbed when given before or between feedings. However, the dose may be diluted in a small amount of infant formula immediately prior to administration to ease administration and reduce GI upset.

Concentration: Fer-In-Sol Drops contain 25 mg elemental iron/ml (125 mg ferrous sulfate/ml). Many other concentrations of iron are available. When ordering, specify exact product and concentration desired to prevent over- or underdose.

USE

An iron supplement used to prevent and treat iron deficiency anemia in preterm infants. Preterm infants require iron supplementation until 12 months of age.

Iron supplementation is not required for term infants on high-iron formula.

MECHANISM OF ACTION

Iron is an essential mineral. It is a component of hemoglobin, myoglobin, and many enzymes.

ADVERSE EFFECTS

Iron supplementation at the doses listed is usually very well tolerated.

May cause dark stools, constipation, or diarrhea.

May cause temporary darkening of membrane covering infant's teeth upon contact. Reduce this risk by diluting iron drops in formula or other liquid and by preventing contact with erupted teeth. Tooth stain can be removed by gentle brushing.

Overdose: Use precautions to avoid iron overdose. Pharmacy should dispense iron as unit dose, rather than as bulk bottles, to avoid iatrogenic overdose that could be fatal. Counsel parents regarding risk of accidental ingestion for infants discharged on this medication. Iron intoxication may cause diarrhea, vomiting, leukocytosis, hyperglycemia, dehydration, rapid pulse, hypotension, convulsions, anuria, and hyperthermia and can lead to death.
Antidote: Induce emesis, sodium bicarbonate lavage, and chelation with deferoxamine for serum iron concentrations >300 mg/dl. Refer to specialized texts and your regional poison center for further assistance.

Possible Increased Infections: Although very controversial, there is some animal and *in vitro* evidence of increased infections with iron supplementation. The increase is attributed to saturation of transferrin and lactoferrin, which have bacteriostatic properties.[4,5]

PHARMACOKINETICS/PHARMACODYNAMICS

Absorption: Absorbed from the duodenum and upper jejunum by active transport. Food can decrease absorption by 40–66 percent, but GI intolerance may require administration with feedings. Transported in the blood bound to transferrin.

Onset of Action: Red blood cell form and color changes within 3–10 days.

Peak Effect: Peak reticulocytosis in 5–10 days and an increase in hemoglobin values within 2–4 weeks.[6]

Elimination: Urine, sweat, sloughing of intestinal mucosal cells.

NURSING IMPLICATIONS

Monitor for constipation or diarrhea.

Carefully check order for dose. Order may be written in mg or ml; these are sometimes inadvertently interchanged.

When checking total iron dose, include mg of iron in infant's formula as well as iron supplement.

Educate parents on safe storage of this drug, as well as what to do in case of accidental ingestion.

COMMENTS

Interactions:

- ***Vitamin E and Iron:*** Preterm infants weighing <1.5 kg at birth have marginal supplies of vitamin E as a result of low placental transfer of the vitamin, decreased tissue stores, and impaired absorption. Even a dose of 2 mg of iron/kg/day at 2 weeks of age can predispose the infant to vitamin E deficiency, increased red cell hemolysis, and hemolytic anemia. Vitamin E may not be well absorbed from the GI tract in these infants, and oral iron may reduce vitamin E absorption. Delay giving iron-fortified formula or iron supplements until 1 month of age.[7] Improved composition of infant formulas has resolved most of this problem by decreasing unsaturated fatty acids and increasing vitamin E content.[7,8]

  Infants weighing <1.5 kg can be supplemented with oral vitamin E, 50 units daily for approximately the first month, until their digestive system matures, tocopherol absorption improves, and blood vitamin E levels rise. Vitamin E supplementation can then be discontinued and iron supplementation begun.[1]

- ***Antacids, Caffeine, and Milk:*** May decrease iron absorption.

- ***Vitamin C:*** Because it maintains iron in the ferrous state, vitamin C may increase iron absorption.

Iron Content of Cow's Milk Formula:

- ***Unfortified:*** Supplies at least 1.5 mg of iron per reconstituted liter.

- ***Fortified:*** Supplies at least 12 mg of iron as ferrous sulfate per reconstituted liter. Because term infants who are fed unfortified formula may deplete their iron stores as early as 6 months of age, it is advisable to change to iron-fortified formula before about 3 months of age.[1]

REFERENCES

1. Dallman PR. 1993. Nutritional anemias in childhood: Iron, folate, and vitamin B$_{12}$. In *Textbook of Pediatric Nutrition,* 2nd ed., Suskind RM, and Lewinter-Suskind L, eds. New York: Raven Press, 96.

2. Shannon KM, et al. 1995. Recombinant human erythropoietin stimulates erythropoiesis and reduces erythrocyte transfusions in very low birth weight preterm infants. *Pediatrics* 95(1): 1–8.

3. Ohls RK, Veerman MW, and Christensen RD. 1996. Pharmacokinetics and effectiveness of recombinant erythropoietin administered to preterm infants by continuous infusion in total parenteral nutrition solution. *Journal of Pediatrics* 128(4): 518–523.

4. American Academy of Pediatrics, Committee on Nutrition. 1978. Relationship between iron status and incidence of infection in infancy. *Pediatrics* 62(2): 246–250.

5. Weinberg ED. 1984. Iron withholding: A defense against infection and neoplasia. *Physiological Reviews* 64(1): 65–102.

6. Taketomo CK, Hodding JH, and Kraus DM. 1996. *Pediatric Dosage Handbook,* 3rd ed. Hudson, Ohio: Lexi-Comp, 291–293.

7. Zipursky A, et al. 1987. Oral vitamin E supplementation for the prevention of anemia in premature infants: A controlled trial. *Pediatrics* 79(1): 61–68.

8. Gross SJ, and Gabriel E. 1985. Vitamin E status in preterm infants fed human milk or infant formula. *Journal of Pediatrics* 106(4): 635–639.

FLECAINIDE (TAMBOCOR)   ANTIARRHYTHMIC
(fle-KAY-nide)

DOSE

Starting dose:

- *<6 months of age:* 50 mg/m^2/day divided every 8–12 hours.
- *≥6 months of age:* 100 mg/m^2/day divided every 8–12 hours.[1]

Average effective dose: 140 mg/m^2/day (range 100–200 mg/m^2/day) divided every 8–12 hours.[2,3]

Maximum dose: 200 mg/m^2/day (8 mg/kg/day). It is not recommended that clinicians exceed this dose because in some children given doses of >200 mg/m^2/day, plasma levels have risen rapidly to far above therapeutic values. Plasma drug concentrations in these patients is labile. Small changes in dose may lead to disproportionate increases in plasma levels.[1,4]

Dosing interval: Base choice of dosing interval (8 hours versus 12 hours) on age and serum trough concentration. See information on elimination half-life and patient age under **PHARMACOKINETICS/PHARMACODYNAMICS** below.[2,5]

- The dose of this drug can be expressed either on a body-surface-area (mg/m^2) or a body-weight (mg/kg) basis. Dosing is most often calculated on a body-weight basis. However, dosing based on body surface area (in m^2) was found to correlate with flecainide serum trough levels somewhat better than dosing based on body weight.[2,5]
- Adjust dose no more frequently than every 4 days because of flecainide's long half-life.
- Reduce dose by 25–50 percent in patients with severe renal impairment.[1,4] Use with caution in those with severe hepatic impairment. Monitor serum trough concentrations.

ADMINISTRATION

PO: Flecainide may be administered with food; however, milk, infant formula, and possibly yogurt interfere with the drug's absorption. The serum concentration of flecainide may increase dramatically when an infant is switched from a milk formula to dextrose feedings. Consider reducing the flecainide dose when milk is removed from the diet (such as during gastroenteritis or weaning) to reduce the chance of flecainide toxicity. Monitor trough flecainide levels during major changes in milk intake.[1,2,6]

Supplied as: Tablets: 50 mg, 100 mg.

Preparation of an oral liquid by the pharmacist: Flecainide is not available commercially as an oral liquid; however, one can be prepared by the pharmacist.

Pharmacist Compounding Directions
Flecainide Oral Liquid 20 mg/ml[7]

Pulverize 24 100-mg tablets in a mortar to a fine powder. Add 20 ml of cherry syrup, and mix to a uniform paste. Add cherry syrup to the mortar gradually to almost 120 ml, mixing well after each addition. Transfer to a calibrated amber plastic prescription bottle, and add enough cherry syrup to bring to a final volume of 120 ml (= 2,400 mg/120 ml = 20 mg/ml).

Label: "Shake well before using. Protect from light."

Expiration: 60 days.

Storage: Room temperature (25°C [77°F]) or under refrigeration (5°C [41°F]).

CAUTIONS/CONTRAINDICATIONS

- Avoid in children with structurally abnormal hearts (after surgery for treatment of congenital heart disease)[2] because cardiac arrest and sudden death have occurred. Flecainide may not be safe in infants with atrial flutter or ventricular arrhythmias and abnormal hearts,[2] myocardial depression, primary cardiomyopathies, pre-existing second- or third-degree atrioventricular (AV) block, chronic atrial fibrillation, or in patients hypersensitive to the drug.[1,2]

- Can cause proarrhythmia (new or worsening supraventricular or ventricular arrhythmias).

- Flecainide should be started in the hospital and accompanied by rhythm monitoring because most proarrhythmias occur during initiation of therapy.[2] A cardiologist skilled in the treatment of arrhythmias in infants and children should directly supervise use of this drug in these patients.[1]

- The probability of adverse effects, especially cardiac, increases with higher plasma drug concentrations. There is a high risk of toxicity in infants who seem to require doses in excess of 200 mg/m^2/day (8 mg/kg/day) but have persistently low serum trough levels because of unclear pharmacokinetics.[2]

- Correct pre-existing hypokalemia or hyperkalemia before administration of flecainide.[1,8]

- For the first year of flecainide treatment, a 12-lead ECG and plasma trough flecainide concentration are suggested whenever the infant is seen for clinical follow-up.[1,4] Close supervision is warrented. (See **COMMENTS** for further information on when to check plasma flecainide concentrations.)

USE

Treatment of supraventricular tachycardias (SVTs) in children with structurally normal hearts.[2] Reserve the drug for life-threatening arrhythmias unresponsive to conventional therapy.[4]

Shown to be effective for prophylaxis of SVT in a small number of infants, with no adverse effects.[9]

SVT with hydrops in a 27-week preterm infant unresponsive to adenosine and amiodarone was successfully treated with flecainide.[10]

Perry and Garson reviewed all published experience with flecainide in infants, children, and fetuses. The 704 case references they reviewed showed flecainide to be safe (no deaths with usual oral dosing, <1 percent serious proarrhythmia) and effective (73–100 percent control, depending on mechanism) in infants and children with SVT. The authors concluded that the drug may not be safe for children with structurally abnormal hearts and atrial flutter or ventricular arrhythmias.[2]

Control of recurrent episodes of SVT in ongoing therapy with flecainide has been proven to be effective.[11]

In combination with other antiarrhythmics, flecainide has been used to successfully treat a number of patients with arrhythmias:

- The combination of flecainide and sotalol safely and effectively controlled SVT in infants <1 year of age. The median flecainide dose was 100 mg/m^2/day (range: 40–150 mg/m^2/day), and the median sotalol dose was 175 mg/m^2/day (range: 100–250 mg/m^2/day). No proarrhythmia occurred.[3]

- The combination of flecainide and amiodarone was safe and effective in controlling refractory tachyarrhythmias in infants using an initial dose of 70 mg/m^2/day and increasing to 110 mg/m^2/day if needed. Flecainide trough levels were monitored and ranged from 0.35 to 0.73 mcg/ml (= 350–731 ng/ml) during combined therapy. No proarrhythmias occurred.[12]

- The combination of flecainide and propranolol therapy was successful in treating five children with permanent junctional reciprocating tachycardia. There were no side effects.[13]

MECHANISM OF ACTION

Flecainide is a Class IC antiarrhythmic agent. It acts by blocking sodium channels involved in cardiac depolarization. Marked suppression of the cardiac conduction system and a moderate negative inotropic effect occur with its use. Increased PR, QRS, and QT intervals are seen on ECG.[1]

ADVERSE EFFECTS

Cardiovascular: New or exacerbated ventricular or supraventricular arrhythmias; new or exacerbated congestive heart failure; second- or third-degree AV block; and, rarely, sinus bradycardia, sinus pause, or sinus arrest.[3] Hypertension or hypotension may occur (rare).

CNS: Tiredness, weakness.[8]

Dermatologic: Rash.[4]

GI: Nausea, swollen lips and tongue, possible hepatic dysfunction (rare), constipation, loss of appetite.[8]

Hematologic: Leukopenia, thrombocytopenia (rare). Discontinue drug if bone marrow depression occurs.[4,8]

Neuromuscular: Tremor.

Ophthalmic: Photophobia, nystagmus (<1 percent of patients).[4]

Respiratory: Dyspnea.[4]

Monitoring: Blood counts, ECG, plasma trough flecainide concentrations.[8] Monitoring of plasma levels is required in patients with renal failure or severe hepatic disease because elimination is much slower in these patients.[1]

Overdose: Effects of overdose may include acute nausea; bradycardia; hypotension; AV block, widened QRS interval, polymorphic ventricular tachycardia, and ventricular fibrillation; asystole; and electromechanical dissociation, coma, and death from respiratory failure or asystole.[4,14,15]

Treatment is symptomatic and supportive care, with ECG, blood pressure, and respiratory monitoring.[4] Treatment may include evacuation of the stomach; oxygen; mechanical respiratory assistance; and inotropic agents such as dopamine, dobutamine, or isoproterenol. Refer to the package insert, and contact a poison control center for treatment recommendations. Sodium bicarbonate may be useful for the treatment of widened QRS and ventricular ectopy resulting from flecainide toxicity. Sodium bicarbonate and sodium chloride probably work by increasing the extracellular concentration of sodium displacing flecainide from its receptor sites, either inside the selectivity filter of the fast sodium channel or at an external anesthetic receptor site.[15,16]

Zeigler and Peterson describe flexanide toxicity in a 2.8 kg, 38-week-gestation infant receiving flecainide at approximately 4 mg/kg/day (100 mg/m[2]/day) plus amiodarone 10 mg/kg/day. On day 18 of life, the nurse caring for the infant noted that he was pale and lethargic, slightly hypotensive, and developing feeding difficulty. The infant developed bradycardia, widened QRS, complete AV block, and ventricular rates ranging from 40 to 50 beats/minute. Flecainide levels were markedly elevated at 2.1 mcg/ml and 1.59 mcg/ml (usual therapeutic levels for infants and children are 0.2–0.5 mcg/ml). The infant was treated with supportive care, sodium bicarbonate IV, oxygen, and calcium gluconate. He recovered from the toxic reaction within 48 hours.[17]

PHARMACOKINETICS/PHARMACODYNAMICS

Absorption: Nearly complete after oral administration. Food does not affect absorption; however, milk products decrease absorption in infants. See **ADMINISTRATION,** above.

Peak Effect: About 2–3 hours[2] (range: 1–6 hours).

Time to Steady State: 3–5 days.[8]

Metabolism: Hepatic.[1]

Protein Binding: 40 percent.[1]

Elimination: Primarily in the urine, with only 5 percent eliminated in feces. About 30 percent (range: 10–50 percent) is eliminated as unchanged drug and the rest as metabolites.[1] Elimination may be prolonged with alkaline urine (pH 8 or higher), in renal dysfunction, with hepatic dysfunction, and in hydropic infants.[1]

Half-life: *Half-life is age dependent. <1 month: 29 hours; 1 month–1 year: 11–12 hours; 1–12 years: 8 hours.*[12] The half-life is prolonged in patients with renal dysfunction.[1]

NURSING IMPLICATIONS

- Monitor trough levels and ECG. Run an ECG strip daily until levels are established or if dose is being changed.
- Inform physician of changes in milk intake. Suggest monitoring flecainide levels.
- Act quickly when ECG changes, such as an increased QRS duration, are noted.[17]

COMMENTS

Interactions:

- Concurrent use of flecainide and digoxin may increase plasma digoxin levels by 13–19 percent.[1]
- Concurrent use of flecainide and amiodarone may increase plasma flecainide twofold or more; reduce the flecainide dose by 50 percent, and monitor serum flecainide concentrations.[1,8]
- Concurrent use of flecainide and cimetidine may increase flecainide serum concentrations. Flecainide dose reduction may be needed.[4]
- Concurrent use of propranolol and flecainide may increase serum levels of both drugs by about 20–30 percent. Negative inotropic effects of both drugs may be additive.[1,8]
- Concurrent urinary acidifiers may increase elimination of flecainide; urinary alkalination may decrease flecainide elimination. Dose adjustment may be needed.[8]

Reference Range:

- The usual therapeutic level of flecainide in infants and children is 0.2–0.5 mcg/ml (= 200–500 ng/ml).[2] In some cases, levels as high as 0.8 mcg/ml (= 800 ng/ml) may be required for control.[1]
- Plasma trough (drawn <1 hour before the dose) should be obtained at presumed steady state (after at least five doses) after initiation or change in dose and when the diet changes.[2,4]
- *Range:* 350–731 ng/ml trough during combined therapy with amiodarone.[12]

Laboratory Interaction: Concurrent propranolol caused falsely high flecainide levels in one case. Inform laboratory of all drugs being administered at the time of sampling.[18]

REFERENCES

1. Medical Economics Data. 2000. *Physicians' Desk Reference,* 54th ed. Montvale, New Jersey: Medical Economics, 1667–1670.

2. Perry JC, and Garson A Jr. 1992. Flecainide acetate for treatment of tachyarrhythmias in children: Review of world literature on efficacy, safety, and dosing. *American Heart Journal* 124(6): 1614–1621.

3. Price JF, et al. 2002. Flecainide and sotalol: A new combination therapy for refractory supraventricular tachycardia in children <1 year of age. *Journal of the American College of Cardiology* 39(3): 517–520.

4. McEvoy GK. 2000. *AHFS Drug Information.* Bethesda, Maryland: American Society of Health-System Pharmacists, 1526–1534.

5. Perry JC, et al. 1989. Flecainide acetate for resistant arrhythmias in the young: Efficacy and pharmacokinetics. *Journal of the American College of Cardiology* 14(1): 185–191.

6. Russell GAB, and Martin RP. 1989. Flecainide toxicity. *Archives of Disease in Childhood* 64(6): 860–862.

7. Allen LV, and Erickson MA. 1996. Stability of baclofen, captopril, diltiazem hydrochloride, dipyridamole, and flecainide acetate in extemporaneously compounded oral liquids. *American Journal of Health-System Pharmacists* 53(18): 2179–2184.

8. United States Pharmacopeial Convention/USP DI. 2000. *Drug Information for the Health Care Professional,* 20th ed. Rockville, Maryland: United States Pharmacopeial Convention, 1539–1541.

9. O'Sullivan JJ, Gardiner HM, and Wren C. 1995. Digoxin or flecainide for prophylaxis of supraventricular tachycardia in infants. *Journal of the American College of Cardiology* 26(4): 991–994.

10. Abraham P. 2001. Supraventricular tachycardia with hydrops in a 27-week premature baby. *International Journal of Clinical Practice* 55(8): 569–570.

11. Moak JP. 2000. Supraventricular tachycardia in the neonate and infant. *Progress in Pediatric Cardiology* 11(1): 25–38.

12. Fenrich AL Jr, Perry JC, and Friedman RA. 1995. Flecainide and amiodarone: Combined therapy for refractory tachyarrhythmias in infancy. *Journal of the American College of Cardiology* 25(5): 1195–1198.

13. Drago F, et al. 2001. Permanent junctional reciprocating tachycardia in infants and children: Effectiveness of medical and non-medical treatment. *Italian Heart Journal* 2(6): 456–461.

14. Hanley NA, Bourke JP, and Gascoigne AD. 1998. Survival in a case of life-threatening flecainide overdose. *Intensive Care Medicine* 24(7): 740–742.

15. Goldman MJ, Mowry JB, and Kirk MA. 1997. Sodium bicarbonate to correct widened QRS in a case of flecainide overdose. *Journal of Emergency Medicine* 15(2): 183–186.

16. Ranger S, et al. 1993. Modulation of flecainide's cardiac sodium channel blockade actions by extracellular sodium: A possible cellular mechanism for the action of sodium salts in flecainide cardiotoxicity. *Journal of Pharmacology and Experimental Therapeutics* 264(3):1160–1167.

17. Zeigler VL, and Peterson J. 1991. Flecainide toxicity in a neonate with supraventricular tachycardia. *Heart & Lung* 20(6): 689–691.

18. De Giovanni JV. 1997. Flecainide levels—a cautionary note (letter). *Heart* 78(3): 319.

FLUCONAZOLE (DIFLUCAN)

(floo-KOE-na-zole)

**ANTI-INFECTIVE:
ANTIFUNGAL**

DOSE

<29 weeks gestational age during first 2 weeks of life: 6 mg/kg/dose given every 72 hours.

- *After 2 weeks of life:* 6 mg/kg/day as a single daily dose.

>29 weeks gestational age: 6 mg/kg/day as a single daily dose.[1–3]

Candida UTI: 3–6 mg/kg/day as a single daily dose.

Reduce dose in renal dysfunction: In moderate dysfunction, give 50 percent of dose; in severe dysfunction, give 25 percent of dose.

ADMINISTRATION

IV—*Rate:* Infuse IV over 1 hour.

IV—*Concentration*: May administer undiluted (2 mg/ml).

IV—*Compatibility:* See Appendix E: Y-Site Compatibility of Common NICU Drugs.

PO: Suspensions of 10 mg/ml and 40 mg/ml are available commercially. The injectable form of the drug has been given PO.

CAUTIONS/CONTRAINDICATIONS

Administration to infants receiving cisapride can result in life-threatening arrhythmias.[4]

Use with caution in pre-existing renal dysfunction.

USE

An antifungal agent for systemic candidiasis and meningitis. Also effective against Cryptococcus, Coccidioides, and dermatophytes.

Advantages over amphotericin B and flucytosine are a longer half-life, allowing once-daily dosing; good distribution characteristics with similar CSF and serum levels; distribution into the eye; ease of administration; good oral bioavailability as well as IV dosage form; and fewer adverse effects.

More data in neonates are needed.[1,2,5,6]

MECHANISM OF ACTION

Fluconazole inhibits fungal cytochrome P-450 and sterol C-14 α-demethylation, resulting in a fungistatic effect.

ADVERSE EFFECTS

Usually well tolerated.

May cause vomiting, diarrhea, rash, and elevations in liver function tests, particularly in patients on concomitant phenytoin, isoniazid, valproic acid, or rifampin (adult data). Mild and transient elevation in liver function tests was reported in a preterm infant.[6]

Pharmacokinetics/Pharmacodynamics

Absorption: Well absorbed orally (>90 percent).

Distribution: Wide, including into the CSF.

Protein Binding: Low (12 percent).

Half-life: 30 hours; prolonged with renal dysfunction.

Elimination: Excreted primarily (80 percent) in the kidneys.

Nursing Implications

Monitor for diarrhea, feeding intolerance.

Monitor liver function tests.

Comments

Interactions:

- Cimetidine and rifampin decrease fluconazole levels by 40 percent and 25 percent, respectively.
- Hydrochlorothiazide increases fluconazole levels by 40 percent.
- Fluconazole increases phenytoin levels by 75 percent.

References

1. Witman MN, and Johnson GM. 1990. Fluconazole treatment of disseminated candidiasis in a very low birth weight infant (abstract #1653). *Pediatric Research* 27(4 part 2): 287A.

2. Miller MJ. Fungal infections. In *Infectious Disease of the Fetus and Newborn,* 4th ed., Remington JS, and Klein JO, eds. Philadelphia: WB Saunders, 731.

3. Nelson JD. 1996. *1996–1997 Pocketbook of Pediatric Antimicrobial Therapy,* 10th ed. Baltimore: Lippincott Williams & Wilkins, 56.

4. Medical Economics Data. 1998. *Physicians' Desk Reference,* 52nd ed. Montvale, New Jersey: Medical Economics, 1308–1309.

5. Wiest DB, et al. 1991. Fluconazole in neonatal disseminated candidiasis. *Archives of Disease in Childhood* 66(8): 1002.

6. Viscoli C, et al. 1989. Fluconazole therapy in an underweight infant. *European Journal of Clinical Microbiology and Infectious Diseases* 8(10): 925–926.

FLUCYTOSINE (ANCOBON)

(flu-SI-toh-seen)

ANTI-INFECTIVE:
ANTIFUNGAL

Synonyms: 5-fluorocytosine, 5-FC*

DOSE

100–150 mg/kg/24 hours, divided every 6 hours.[1]

Reduce dose in renal impairment to avoid accumulation and resultant bone marrow toxicity:

- *Moderate:* 25–50 mg/kg/dose every 12 hours
- *Severe:* 25–50 mg/kg/dose as a single daily dose[2]

Duration of therapy is usually 2–4 weeks.

ADMINISTRATION

PO: For oral use only. To reduce GI upset, administer a little at a time over 15 minutes.

Concentration: 10–20 mg/ml, prepared per Pharmacist Compounding Directions below.

Compounding: An oral liquid is not commercially available.

Pharmacist Compounding Directions
Flucytosine Oral Liquid 10 mg/ml[3]

Empty two 500 mg capsules into a conical graduate. Dilute to 100 ml with distilled water. Pour into an amber glass bottle. Shake vigorously. Adjust pH to neutral to acidic (5–6.5) with dilute sodium hydroxide. May filter to remove talc; however, some active drug may be removed.

Stability: 7 days.

Storage: Protect from light.

IV: Flucytosine 1 percent (2.5 gm in 250 ml normal saline) can be obtained by special request on a compassionate-use basis from the Hoffman-LaRoche Company. Mina and associates found that parenteral flucytosine was well tolerated in a group of 304 patients (55 neonates).[4]

USE

For treatment of severe systemic fungal infections, usually in combination with another antifungal agent—particularly amphotericin B—because of rapid development of resistance when used alone and the synergistic effects of the combination against Candida and Cryptococcus.

Penetrates well into the CSF, an advantage over amphotericin B.

---

* Avoid using the abbreviation "5-FC" for flucytosine; it can be inadvertently confused with "5-FU," which is an antineoplastic agent.

A lower dose of amphotericin B can be used if flucytosine is used concomitantly because concurrent use enhances antifungal activity.[1,5,6]

MECHANISM OF ACTION

Flucytosine is transformed in the fungal cell to 5-fluorouracil, which is an inactive pyrimidine substitute and also inhibits thymidylate synthetase, thus interfering with DNA synthesis and fungal cell growth.

ADVERSE EFFECTS

CNS: Sedation.

GI: Nausea, vomiting, diarrhea.

Hematologic: Bone marrow depression (anemia, thrombocytopenia, leukopenia).

Liver: Hepatocellular damage.

Renal: Increased BUN and serum creatinine.

The incidence of adverse effects is increased in infants on combined amphotericin/flucytosine therapy.

PHARMACOKINETICS/PHARMACODYNAMICS

Absorption: Well absorbed orally. Peak serum levels occur between 2 and 6 hours after administration. Protein binding is low. After a dose of 25 mg/kg, levels were 40 mcg/ml at 2 hours and 27 mcg/ml at 4 and 6 hours.[7]

Distribution: Distributes well into the CSF (65–90 percent of serum levels).

Elimination: Primarily (90 percent) excreted unchanged in the urine by glomerular filtration.[8]

NURSING IMPLICATIONS

Monitor for diarrhea or feeding intolerance.

Monitor hepatic, renal, and hematologic status.

Monitor serum levels, especially with renal dysfunction.

COMMENTS

Therapeutic Range: 50–75 mcg/ml. Maximum therapeutic level: <100 mcg/ml. Bone marrow suppression is more frequent with levels >100–125 mcg/ml. Follow serum concentrations, especially in renal dysfunction.

Interactions: Amphotericin B may increase the effectiveness and toxicity of flucytosine. Flucytosine causes false elevation of serum creatinine when determined by the Kodak Ektachem analyzer.

REFERENCES

1. Miller MJ. 1995. Fungal infections. In *Infectious Diseases of the Fetus and Newborn Infant*, 4th ed. Remington JS, and Klein JO, eds. Philadelphia: WB Saunders, 729–730.

2. Daneshmend TK, and Warnock DW. 1983. Clinical pharmacokinetics of systemic antifungal drugs. *Clinical Pharmacokinetics* 8(1): 17–42.

3. Committee on Extemporaneous Formulations. 1987. *Handbook on Extemporaneous Formulations.* Bethesda, Maryland: American Society of Hospital Pharmacists, 24.

4. Mina FA, Hopkins SJ, and Richelo B. 1988. Parenteral 5-fluorocytosine in the therapy of systemic mycoses. *Annals of the New York Academy of Sciences* 544: 571–574.

5. Johnson DE, et al. 1984. Systemic candidiasis in very low-birth-weight infants (<1500 grams). *Pediatrics* 73(2): 138–143.

6. Faix RG. 1984. Systemic Candida infections in infants in intensive care nurseries: High incidence of central nervous system involvement. *Journal of Pediatrics* 105(4): 616–622.

7. Hill HR, et al. 1974. Recovery from disseminated candidiasis in a premature neonate. *Pediatrics* 53(5): 748–752.

8. Baley JE. 1990. Pharmacokinetics, outcome of treatment and toxic effects of amphotericin B and 5-fluorocytosine in neonates. *Journal of Pediatrics* 116(5): 791–797.

FLUDROCORTISONE (FLORINEF)   HORMONE:
(floo-droe-KOR-tis-ohne)   MINERALOCORTICOID

Synonym: 9α-fluorocortisol

DOSE

0.05–0.2 mg/day (= 50–200 mcg/day) as a single daily dose.[1,2]

Note: The dose is the same irrespective of the size (weight) or age of the patient. Newborns are quite insensitive to mineralocorticoids and may require larger doses than adults.

ADMINISTRATION

Supplied as:

- *Tablet:* 0.1 mg/tablet (= 100 mcg/tablet). Tablet is scored (= 0.05 mg or 50 mcg/half-tablet).

PO: May administer with feedings to reduce GI upset.

Note: No parenteral mineralocorticoid is commercially available now that desoxycorticosterone acetate (DOCA) has been removed from the market (see COMMENTS below).

CAUTIONS/CONTRAINDICATIONS

Use with caution in patients with sensitivity to fludrocortisone, pre-existing renal dysfunction, cardiac disease, congestive heart failure, hypertension, impaired hepatic function, or peripheral edema.

USE

As partial replacement therapy for adrenocortical insufficiency and to treat salt-losing forms of congenital adrenogenital syndrome. To treat these disorders, fludrocortisone is administered along with appropriate glucocorticoid therapy, such as hydrocortisone. (See monograph on hydrocortisone. Also see Table 1-18: Comparison of Relative Potency of Corticosteroids [Glucocorticoids], page 182.) Sodium chloride supplementation is usually also required.[1–4]

MECHANISM OF ACTION

Fludrocortisone acts on the distal tubule of the kidney to increase excretion of potassium and hydrogen ions and enhance reabsorption of sodium, with subsequent water retention. The drug also has high glucocorticoid activity—it is 15 times more potent than hydrocortisone (see Table 1-18: Comparison of Relative Potency of Corticosteroids [Glucocorticoids], page 182, and the monograph on hydrocortisone)—but is used only for its mineralocorticoid effects.[5] Fludrocortisone inhibits endogenous steroid production.

ADVERSE EFFECTS

Because fludrocortisone has glucocorticoid activity, it may cause adverse effects and require precautions similar to those for glucocorticoids.[5] (See monograph on hydrocortisone. Also see Table 1-18: Comparison of Relative Potency of Corticosteroids [Glucocorticoids], page 182.)

Cardiovascular: Hypertension, congestive heart failure, peripheral edema.

Endocrine/Metabolic: Hypokalemic alkalosis, growth suppression, hyperglycemia, suppression of endogenous steroid production (hypothalamic-pituitary-adrenal suppression), sodium and water retention, glucose intolerance, osteoporosis, poor wound healing, excessive weight gain. Muscle weakness may occur as a result of excessive potassium loss.[5] Taper dose gradually after long-term therapy, as for glucocorticoids such as hydrocortisone, to prevent adverse effects.

GI: GI upset.

Hypersensitivity: Anaphylaxis (rare), rash.

PHARMACOKINETICS/PHARMACODYNAMICS

Absorption: Well absorbed from the GI tract.

Duration of Action: 1–2 days.

Protein Binding: High.

Metabolism: Hepatic, renal.

Half-life: The plasma half-life is about 3.5 hours; the biological half-life is 18–36 hours.

Elimination: Renal.

NURSING IMPLICATIONS

Monitor the patient for signs that indicate the need for dose adjustment, such as remission or exacerbation of the disease and stress (surgery, infection, trauma). Reduce the dose of fludrocortisone if blood pressure becomes elevated.

Monitor serum electrolytes (particularly sodium and potassium), blood pressure, and urine output.

Monitor for edema, too-rapid weight gain.

Monitor blood glucose.

Monitor growth and development in infants on prolonged therapy.

COMMENTS

Equivalents: Fludrocortisone 0.1 mg has a sodium retention activity equal to DOCA 1 mg.

- *Providing a mineralocorticoid for patients who are NPO for surgery and therefore cannot take oral fludrocortisone:* Fludrocortisone is the only mineralocorticoid available, and it is available only for oral administration. However, as Table 1-18 (page 182) indicates, hydrocortisone (Solu-Cortef) has significant mineralocorticoid activity. Approximately 20 mg of hydrocortisone (Solu-Cortef) IV has a mineralocorticoid action equivalent to that of 0.1 mg of fludrocortisone. Thus, when hydrocortisone (Solu-Cortef) is given at the higher doses (stress doses) (see monograph on hydrocortisone) during surgery, it provides adequate mineralocorticoid activity and permits interruption of mineralocorticoid replacement with fludrocortisone.[6]

Interactions:

- *Digoxin:* Fludrocortisone-induced hypokalemia may increase the risk of digoxin toxicity or arrhythmias.

- *Enzyme inducers:* Phenytoin and rifampin and other cytochrome P-450 hepatic enzyme inducers (barbiturates, carbamazepine, primidone) may increase the metabolism of fludrocortisone. An increase in the fludrocortisone dose may be required.

- *Hepatic dysfunction:* Fludrocortisone clearance may be decreased.

- *Hypokalemia-causing medications:* Albuterol, amphotericin B, carbenicillin, diuretics such as furosemide and chlorothiazide, insulin, mezlocillin, piperacillin, sodium polystyrene sulfonate (Kayexalate), and ticarcillin may, in combination with fludrocortisone, increase the risk of severe hypokalemia. Monitor serum potassium; supplementation may be required.

- *Thyroid dysfunction:* Fludrocortisone clearance may be increased in hyperthyroidism and decreased in hypothyroidism.[5]

REFERENCES

1. Speiser PW, and New MI. 1994. Prenatal diagnosis and management of congenital adrenal hyperplasia. *Clinics in Perinatology* 21(9): 631–645.

2. Merke DP, and Cutler GB Jr. 1997. New approaches to the treatment of congenital adrenal hyperplasia. *JAMA* 277(13): 1073–1076.

3. Hochberg Z, et al. 1986. Requirement of mineralocorticoid in congenital adrenal hyperplasia due to 11 beta-hydroxylase deficiency. *Journal of Clinical Endocrinology and Metabolism* 63(1): 36–40.

4. Zenk KE. 2000. Advances in the treatment of congenital adrenal hyperplasia. *Mother Baby Journal* 5(1): 50–55.

5. United States Pharmacopeial Convention/USP DI. 2000. *Drug Information for the Health Care Professional,* 20th ed. Rockville, Maryland: United States Pharmacopeial Convention, 1548–1549.

6. Miller WL. 1996. The adrenal cortex. In *Rudolph's Pediatrics,* 20th ed., Rudolph AM, Hoffman JIE, and Rudolph CD, eds. Stamford, Connecticut: Appleton & Lange, 1711–1742.

FLUMAZENIL (ROMAZICON)
(FLU-may-zee-nil)

ANTIDOTE:
BENZODIAZEPINE OVERDOSE

DOSE

2–10 mcg/kg every minute × 3 as needed.[1–3] Usual total dose required in children: 24 mcg/kg.[1] Use several small doses, rather than one large injection, to better control reversal and possible adverse effects.

If resedation occurs, may repeat dose every 20 minutes as needed.

A 20 mcg/kg loading dose, then 50 mcg/kg/hour for 6 hours was used to treat one neonate for transplacental diazepam overdose manifested as recurrent apnea.[2]

ADMINISTRATION

Supplied as: 0.1 mg/ml in 5 ml and 10 ml multidose vials.

IV—*Rate:* May give IV push over 30 seconds to 1 minute.

IV—*Concentration:* May give undiluted.

IV—*Compatible with:* Dextrose and saline solutions.

USE

An antagonist for benzodiazepines (e.g., diazepam, lorazepam, midazolam).

Use as a diagnostic screening method for patients with excessive respiratory and/or CNS depression is controversial.

MECHANISM OF ACTION

Flumazenil competitively inhibits the activity at the benzodiazepine recognition site on the GABA/benzodiazepine receptor complex. It is used to reverse benzodiazepine-induced conscious sedation and for benzodiazepine overdose. This is analogous to reversal of narcotic effects by naloxone.

ADVERSE EFFECTS

May cause abrupt withdrawal and provoke seizures in infants on chronic benzodiazepine therapy.

Vomiting, tremor and involuntary movements, cutaneous vasodilation, pain at injection site, and agitation may occur.

Resedation may occur as a result of the long half-life of some benzodiazepines (such as diazepam) and their metabolites, as well as the immaturity of metabolic pathways in the neonate. Observe the infant for several hours after reversal with flumazenil. Administer repeat doses of flumazenil if necessary.

PHARMACOKINETICS/PHARMACODYNAMICS

Onset of Action: 1–2 minutes.

Half-life: Varies from 41 to 79 minutes in adults. Half-life in neonates has not been reported.

Nursing Implications

 Monitor for resedation and need for repeat flumazenil dose.

Monitor blood pressure and respiratory status.

References

1. Jones RD, et al. 1991. Antagonism of the hypnotic effect of midazolam in children: A randomized, double-blind study of placebo and flumazenil administered after midazolam-induced anaesthesia. *British Journal of Anaesthesia* 66(6): 660–666.

2. Richard P, et al. 1991. The use of flumazenil in a neonate. *Journal of Toxicology. Clinical Toxicology* 29(1): 137–140.

3. Collins S, and Carter JA. 1991. Resedation after bolus administration of midazolam to an infant and its reversal by flumazenil. *Anaesthesia* 46(6): 471–472.

FOLIC ACID (FOLVITE)

(FOE-lik A-sid)

NUTRITION:
VITAMIN SUPPLEMENT

Synonyms: Folate, pteroylglutamic acid

DOSE

Nutritional Maintenance for Preterm Infants: 50 mcg/day[1] (approximately 15 mcg/kg/day) given as a single daily dose. Begin supplementation of preterm infants when enteral feedings are started, and continue until the infant weighs about 2 kg or is 40 weeks PCA.

Folic Acid Deficiency: 0.5–1 mg/day.

ADMINISTRATION

Supplied as:

- Injection: 5 mg/ml
- Tablets: 100 mcg/tablet (= 0.1 mg/tablet). Also available: 400 mcg, 800 mcg, and 1 mg/tablets.

PO: May give crushed half-tablet (50 mcg/half-tablet) mixed in small amount of feeding.

Folic acid is not available as an oral liquid; however, the pharmacist can compound the following preparation from the injection:

Pharmacist Compounding Directions
Folic Acid Oral Solution 50 mcg/ml[2–4]

Mix 1 ml of folic acid injection (5 mg/ml) and 90 ml purified water USP. Adjust pH to 9 with 2.8 ml of sodium hydroxide 0.1 normal solution (N). (The NaOH is added because folic acid may precipitate after varying lengths of time below a pH of about 5.) Add purified water USP to make 100 ml volume.

Stability: 30 days.

Storage: Refrigerate. Protect from light and excessive heat.

IV—*Rate:* Infuse over at least 1 minute.

IV—*Concentration:* May give undiluted, or dilute with sterile water to 100 mcg/ml (= 0.1 mg/ml).

IV—*Continuous Infusion in Parenteral Nutrition (PN):* Folic acid is physically compatible with and stable in PN solutions prepared daily.[5]

IM, SC: May give undiluted. May dilute with sterile water to 100 mcg/ml (= 0.1 mg/ml).

Protect from light.

Oral liquid multivitamin drops (Vi-Daylin, Poly-Vi-Sol) do not contain folic acid because folic acid is relatively unstable at the pH in these formulations.

CAUTIONS/CONTRAINDICATIONS

Use with caution in patients who have anemia but the cause has not yet been diagnosed. Large doses of folic acid may mask the hematologic effects of vitamin B_{12} deficiency (pernicious anemia), but will not prevent progression of irreversible neurologic abnormalities, despite absence of anemia. Adequate doses of vitamin B_{12} may prevent, halt, or improve neurologic changes caused by pernicious anemia.

USE

Anemias of nutritional origin or prematurity. Preterm infants are predisposed to folate deficiency because of limited intrauterine hepatic stores and because of their rapid postnatal growth. The risk is increased if their diet is deficient in folic acid or because of medications they may be taking.[6] Infant formulas designed for preterm infants contain more folic acid than standard formulas; supplementation with folic acid may not be required.

Treatment of megaloblastic and macrocytic anemias due to folate deficiency.

Does not treat pernicious, aplastic, or normocytic anemias.

Manifestations of Folic Acid Deficiency: Disturbance in DNA synthesis that may alter cell division in many tissues, especially those with high rates of cell multiplication (bone marrow, intestine). Folic acid deficiency is diagnosed by assessing blood smears and serum and blood folate concentrations. Serum folate of 3 ng/ml and RBC folate of 140 ng/ml are lower limits of normal. Hypersegmentation of neutrophils and megaloblastic changes on blood smears are apparent. The infant may experience poor growth. In severe cases, macrocytic anemia and neurologic manifestations, such as hypotonia, occur.[6]

MECHANISM OF ACTION

Folic acid is a water-soluble vitamin. It is required for nucleoprotein synthesis and maintenance of normal erythropoiesis. Tetrahydrofolic acid is the metabolically active form of folic acid and functions as a coenzyme, serving as an acceptor and donor of one-carbon units in amino acid and nucleotide metabolism.[6] Folic acid stimulates production of red and white blood cells and platelets in certain megaloblastic anemias. Resistance to treatment may be the result of depressed hematopoiesis, presence of antimetabolic (see **Interactions** under **COMMENTS** in this monograph) drugs, or deficiencies of vitamins B_6, B_{12}, C, and E.

ADVERSE EFFECTS

Usually well tolerated. Allergic reactions such as rash, bronchospasm (rarely).

Overdose: High doses of folic acid are generally considered nontoxic.

PHARMACOKINETICS/PHARMACODYNAMICS

Absorption: Rapidly and completely absorbed from the proximal small intestine. Patients with absorption problems are usually able to absorb folic acid.

Onset of Action: Reticulocytosis usually begins 2–5 days following initiation of therapy.

Metabolism: Hepatic. Only a small amount of folic acid is stored in the liver; therefore, daily supplementation is desirable.[6]

Elimination: Renal, feces.

NURSING IMPLICATIONS

Monitor reticulocyte response and rise in hemoglobin and hematocrit.

Monitor serum phenytoin concentration when given concurrently.

COMMENTS

Interactions:

- Folic acid given concurrently with phenytoin may result in lowered phenytoin levels and increased seizure frequency because of increased metabolic clearance of phenytoin and/or redistribution of phenytoin in the CSF and brain. Monitor serum phenytoin concentrations and seizure frequency.

- Phenytoin and primidone may decrease serum folate levels and produce symptoms of folic acid deficiency on long-term therapy.

- Phenytoin interferes with folate absorption, and antibiotics interfere with colonic bacterial production of folate.

- Chloramphenicol antagonizes the hematopoietic action of folic acid in folate-deficient patients.

- Trimethoprim (in Bactrim, Septra) and pyrimethamine inhibit dihydrofolate reductase, an enzyme required for the production of the active form of this vitamin, tetrahydrofolic acid.

REFERENCES

1. Specker BL, DeMarini S, and Tsang RC. 1992. Vitamin and mineral supplementation. In *Effective Care of the Newborn Infant,* Sinclair JC, and Bracken MB, eds. Oxford: Oxford University Press, 162–177.

2. Nahata MC, and Hipple TF. 1992. *Pediatric Drug Formulations,* 2nd ed. Cincinnati: Harvey Whitney Books, 37.

3. Woods D. 1993. Extemporaneous formulation in pharmacy practice. Part 1: Folic acid oral solution. *New Zealand Pharmacy* 13: 34.

4. Trissel LA. 1996. *Trissel's Stability of Compounded Formulations.* Washington, DC: American Pharmaceutical Association, 118–119.

5. Trissel LA. 1994. *Handbook on Injectable Drugs,* 8th ed. Bethesda, Maryland: American Society of Hospital Pharmacists, 464–466.

6. Ehrenkranz RA. 1993. Iron, folic acid, and vitamin B_{12}. In *Nutritional Needs of the Preterm Infant: Scientific Basis and Practical Guidelines,* Tsang RC, et al., eds. Baltimore: Lippincott Williams & Wilkins, 177–194.

FUROSEMIDE (LASIX)
(fur-OH-se-mide)

CARDIOVASCULAR:
DIURETIC

DOSE

Emergency: 1–2 mg/kg/dose as a single dose.

Maintenance: 1–2 mg/kg/dose given daily every 12 hours.[1,2] In infants <31 weeks postconceptional age, dose every 24 hours or longer to prevent accumulation to toxic serum concentrations.[3]

Maximum: 2 mg/kg/day in preterm infants.[4] Use the minimum effective dose.

A higher oral than IV dose may be required because bioavailability is reduced when furosemide is given orally.

ADMINISTRATION

PO: Oral suspensions of 8 mg/ml and 10 mg/ml are available. The low-alcohol-content product is preferred (Roxane: <1 percent alcohol; Hoechst-Roussel: 11.5 percent alcohol). Give with feedings to reduce GI irritation.

IV—*Rate:* Infuse slowly over 1–2 minutes. Rapid IV infusion may increase ototoxic effects. Maximum: 0.5 mg/kg/minute.

IV—*Concentration:* May give undiluted.

IV—*Compatibility:* See Appendix E: Y-Site Compatibility of Common NICU Drugs.

IM: May give undiluted.

CAUTIONS/CONTRAINDICATIONS

Thiazide diuretics are preferred for chronic therapy. Furosemide should not be used routinely for prolonged periods in preterm infants for the following reasons:

- Metabolic alkalosis may occur. This can lead to compensatory hypoventilation, resulting in increased $PaCO_2$. Therefore, excessive furosemide use can lead to high ventilator settings with their attendant problems (Figure 1-8).[5]

- Incidence of patent ductus arteriosus increases. Furosemide stimulates renal production of prostaglandin E_2 and may increase the incidence of PDA in infants with respiratory distress syndrome.[6]

- Calcium wasting occurs. Furosemide causes calcium wasting, leading to three problems in the neonate:
  - Nephrocalcinosis (kidney stones).[7]
  - Cholelithiasis (gall stones).[8]
  - Osteopenia. Added to the predisposition of neonates for nutritional rickets, osteopenia caused by furosemide places infants at great risk for bone fractures.

FIGURE 1-8 ◆ **A RESULT OF PROLONGED FUROSEMIDE USE IN PRETERM INFANTS—CASCADING EVENTS LEADING TO LUNG INJURY.**

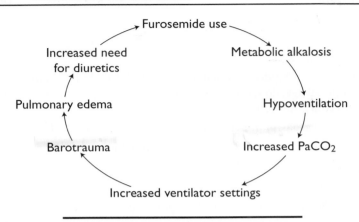

USE

A potent loop diuretic used to treat edema associated with heart, renal, pulmonary, and hepatic disease.

Also used to treat hypertension, fluid overload, and hypercalcemia.

Because of its potency, indicated only when a greater diuretic effect than that produced by thiazide diuretics is needed.[1,2]

MECHANISM OF ACTION

Furosemide acts on the proximal and distal tubules as well as on the loop of Henle. The drug enhances excretion of sodium, potassium, chloride, calcium, magnesium, hydrogen, ammonium, bicarbonate, and possibly phosphate.

ADVERSE EFFECTS

Electrolyte imbalances such as hypokalemia, hyponatremia, and hypochloremia.

Chronic furosemide use may cause hypercalciuria, leading to several potentially serious complications (see **CAUTIONS/CONTRAINDICATIONS** above).

Excessive volume depletion, producing dehydration, hemoconcentration.

Ototoxicity (especially in patients with renal dysfunction and/or on concomitant aminoglycosides).

Hyperglycemia and glycosuria.

Rash.

Rare association with blood dyscrasias (anemia, leukopenia, purpura, aplastic anemia).

Because oral furosemide contains sorbitol, it may cause diarrhea at higher doses.

See also **CAUTIONS/CONTRAINDICATIONS** above regarding long-term use of furosemide.

PHARMACOKINETICS/PHARMACODYNAMICS

Oral Bioavailability: 20 percent in preterm infants <20 days old (60 percent in adults).

Peak Effect after Oral Dose: 1 hour.

Duration of Action: 6 hours.

Protein Binding: 94 percent.

Half-life: 20 hours.[4]

NURSING IMPLICATIONS

Monitor for dehydration and electrolyte imbalance; monitor I & O, urine specific gravity.

Handle infant with care to prevent bone fractures (prolonged use in preterm infants, may cause bone demineralization).

COMMENTS

With Supplements: Potassium and/or sodium supplementation in patients on furosemide should be as the chloride salt (KCl, NaCl).

Interactions:

- Concomitant indomethacin may reduce sodium-excreting and antihypertensive effects because indomethacin inhibits prostaglandin synthesis.
- Concomitant aminoglycosides may increase the risk of ototoxicity.
- Furosemide may increase the duration of nondepolarizing neuromuscular blocking agents (atracurium, pancuronium).
- Furosemide may increase the risk of digoxin toxicity, possibly as a result of potassium and magnesium loss.

REFERENCES

1. Chemtob S, et al. 1989. Pharmacology of diuretics in the newborn. *Pediatric Clinics of North America* 36(5): 1231–1250.

2. Guignard JP, and Gouyon JB. 1988. Body fluid homeostasis in the newborn infant with congestive heart failure: Effects of diuretics. *Clinics in Perinatology* 15(3): 447–466.

3. Mirochnick MH, et al. 1988. Furosemide pharmacokinetics in very low birth weight infants. *Journal of Pediatrics* 112(4): 653–657.

4. Peterson RG, et al. 1980. Pharmacology of furosemide in the premature newborn infant. *Journal of Pediatrics* 97(1): 139–143.

5. Hazinski TA. 1985. Furosemide decreases ventilation in young rabbits. *Journal of Pediatrics* 106(1): 81–85.

6. Green TP, et al. 1983. Furosemide promotes patent ductus arteriosus in premature infants with the respiratory distress syndrome. *New England Journal of Medicine* 308(13): 743–748.

7. Hufnagle KG, et al. 1982. Renal calcifications: A complication of long-term furosemide therapy in preterm infants. *Pediatrics* 70(3): 360–363.

8. Randall LH, et al. 1992. Cholelithiasis in infants receiving furosemide: A prospective study of the incidence and one-year follow-up. *Journal of Perinatology* 12(2): 107–111.

TABLE OF CONTENTS

G

G

GANCICLOVIR (CYTOVENE)   ANTIVIRAL
(gan-SYE-kloe-veer)

Synonyms: DHPG, GCV

DOSE

IV: Although the pediatric dose has not been established, the following doses are those most frequently used:

- *Induction:* 10 mg/kg/day divided every 12 hours for 14–21 days, then...

- *Maintenance:* 5 mg/kg/day or 6 mg/kg/day as a single dose five times a week.[1–8] If retinitis progresses during maintenance therapy, re-treat with the twice-a-day induction regimen.[2]

- Some experts have used ganciclovir with cytomegalovirus immune globulin IV (CMV-IGIV).[3] Tajiri and colleagues administered ganciclovir with CMV-IGIV 130–260 mg/kg/dose weekly in immunocompetent infants with CMV hepatitis.[7]

- *Other doses have been used:* Nigro and colleagues compared two dosing regimens for the treatment of symptomatic congenital CMV in infants: 5 mg/kg/dose given twice daily for 2 weeks versus 7.5 mg/kg/dose given twice daily for 2 weeks and continuing with a maintenance dose of 10 mg/kg/dose three times a week for 3 months. Their study indicated the higher dose and more prolonged therapy to be more effective in otherwise immunocompetent infants.[9]

PO: Frenkel and associates studied the pharmacokinetics, safety, tolerance, and antiviral effects of ganciclovir PO in infants and children and reported that a dose of 30 mg/kg/dose given PO every 8 hours was efficacious and safe.[10]

Reduce dose or increase dosing interval in renal dysfunction.[1–3]

ADMINISTRATION

IV—*Rate:* Infuse over 1–2 hours.[1]

IV—*Concentration:* Maximum: 10 mg/ml.[1]

- *Stability:* Reconstitute with nonbacteriostatic sterile water. Bacteriostatic water is not used because the paraben preservatives may cause precipitation. The reconstituted solution must be further diluted with D_5W or NS before administration.

- Administer with an inline filter, preferably 0.22 micron.[11]

IM or SC: Do not administer IM or SC. Severe tissue irritation may result from the high pH (pH 11) of ganciclovir.[1]

PO: Administer with feedings for improved absorption. Do not open or crush capsules.[2]

Supplied as:

- Powder for injection, lyophilized, as sodium: 500 mg. Each 500 mg vial contains 2 mEq of sodium.[11]
- *PO:* Capsule: 250 mg.

Because of the risk of teratogenicity, precautionary measures such as using a vertical laminar airflow hood and wearing latex gloves are recommended while compounding this drug. If the hood is not available, wear a surgical mask and minimize the creation of dust from the drug.

No oral liquid is commercially available; however, a suspension can be prepared by the pharmacy as follows:

Pharmacist Compounding Directions
Ganciclovir Suspension 25 mg/ml1[1,12]

1. Reconstitute each of 5 vials of ganciclovir for injection 500 mg (Cytovene-IV) with 3 ml sterile water for injection. Shake well until dissolved.
2. Transfer the contents of the vials (total volume: approximately 15 ml) to a graduated cylinder and add the following, shaking well:
   - Ora-Sweet cherry-flavored syrup (Paddock Laboratories, Minneapolis): 50 ml
   - Hydrogen peroxide 3 percent: 1 ml
3. Add additional Ora-Sweet syrup to reach a final volume of 100 ml (= 2,500 mg/100 ml = 25 mg/ml).
4. Dispense in an amber prescription bottle. Label "Shake well before each use. Use Cytotoxic Drug Precautions."

Stability: 28 days. Store at room temperature.

Note: Hydrogen peroxide was chosen as a preservative to enhance the antimicrobial properties of the suspending vehicle.

Preparation of Oral Suspension from Capsules: Ganciclovir 100 mg/ml prepared from capsule contents combined with Ora-Sweet or Ora-Sweet SF was stable for 123 days at room temperature.[13]

CAUTIONS/CONTRAINDICATIONS

Do not use in infants having absolute neutrophil counts (ANCs) <500 cells/mm^3 and/or platelet counts of <25,000 cells/mm^3.

Hypersensitivity to ganciclovir or acyclovir.[1]

Infuse through a vein with good blood flow to allow rapid dilution and distribution of the drug. This may reduce risk of phlebitis and pain at injection site.[1]

Use with caution in pediatric patients and only after weighing potential benefits and risks. Data documenting safety, efficacy, and pharmacokinetics in pediatric use are limited. However, adverse effects and efficacy in infants and children reported to date appear to be similar to those seen in adults. The probability of long-term carcinogenicity and reproductive toxicity (seen in animal studies) should also be considered before using ganciclovir in pediatrics.[1,2]

Maintain good hydration.

Monitoring: Complete blood count, platelet count, urine output, blood urea nitrogen, serum creatinine, and liver function tests. For treatment of CMV retinitis: ophthalmologic exams. Monitoring of serum ganciclovir concentrations has not been shown to be useful for ensuring efficacy or avoiding toxicity.[2]

USE

Treatment of cytomegalovirus (CMV) retinitis in immunocompromised patients; treatment of CMV enterocolitis,[14] encephalitis, pneumonitis, hepatitis,[7,15] prevention of CMV disease in transplant patients.

Although ganciclovir has been used to treat congenital CMV infection,[4–6,9] it is not recommended routinely because of insufficient efficacy data.[3] Its use to treat congenital infection may result in only temporary improvement, without having an ameliorating effect on long-term clinical outcome.[4]

MECHANISM OF ACTION

Ganciclovir is active against cytomegalovirus. Human CMV, a DNA virus, is a member of the herpesvirus group.[1,3] Ganciclovir is structurally related to acyclovir. It is a prodrug whose antiviral activity results from its conversion within the cell to the triphosphate form. Ganciclovir is thought to be rapidly phosphorylated in CMV-infected cells to the monophosphate form by a CMV-encoded enzyme, then converted to the diphosphate and triphosphate. Levels of ganciclovir triphosphate are as much as 100-fold greater in CMV-infected cells than in uninfected cells. The ganciclovir triphosphate competitively inhibits DNA polymerase by acting as a substrate and becoming incorporated into the DNA. This inhibits DNA synthesis by suppressing DNA chain elongation. Chain elongation resumes when ganciclovir is discontinued.[2]

The virus may develop resistance to ganciclovir, probably by decreased ability to form the active triphosphate.[2] Possible signs of viral resistance are poor clinical response or persistent viral excretion during therapy. Ganciclovir is mostly virustatic rather than virucidal in action—that is, it appears to suppress virus activity, not eradicate the virus.[4]

ADVERSE EFFECTS

Hypersensitivity (rash, fever), photosensitivity, phlebitis and pain at site of injection.[2]

Cardiovascular: Arrhythmias, hypertension.

CNS: Seizures, sedation.

GI: Loss of appetite, diarrhea, vomiting.[2]

Hematologic: Granulocytopenia (17 percent),[9] thrombocytopenia (10 percent),[5] anemia. Cell counts usually begin to recover within 3–7 days after the drug is discontinued.[1]

Hepatic: Abnormal liver function tests.[9]

Ophthalmic Retinal detachment in patients with CMV retinitis.

Renal: Hematuria, increased serum creatinine and BUN.

Respiratory: Dyspnea.

Management of Overdose: Hemodialysis may be useful in reducing serum concentrations. Maintain adequate hydration. Consider use of hematopoietic growth factors.[1]

PHARMACOKINETICS/PHARMACODYNAMICS

Absorption: Oral absorption of ganciclovir is poor—about 5 percent fasting and 6–9 percent following food.[1] Bioavailability of oral ganciclovir in children is slightly lower than in adults.[10]

Distribution: Widely distributed to all tissues, fluids, and organs, including the cerebrospinal fluid and the eye.[2]

Protein Binding: 1–2 percent.[2]

Elimination: Renal excretion of unchanged drug is the major route of elimination.[1] *Dialysis:* Plasma concentrations are reduced by about 50 percent after a single 4-hour hemodialysis.[1,2]

Half-life: Neonates 2–49 days of age: 2.4 hours after a single-dose 1-hour IV infusion. Ganciclovir exhibited linear pharmacokinetics in neonates.[16] Zhou and colleagues investigated the population pharmacokinetics of ganciclovir in newborns with congenital CMV. Pharmacokinetic parameters of total clearance from plasma and apparent total volume of distribution were 0.428 ± 0.079 liters/hour and 1.773 ± 0.320 liters, respectively.[17] Half-life is prolonged with renal dysfunction.

NURSING IMPLICATIONS

Handle and dispose of drug following some or all guidelines issued for antineoplastic drugs because ganciclovir shares some of the properties of antitumor agents (carcinogenicity and mutagenicity). Use gloves when handling. Check with hospital pharmacy for additional handling and disposal policies.

Avoid inhalation, ingestion, and direct contact with skin or mucous membranes of the powder contained in capsules or the IV solution. Ganciclovir solution is alkaline (pH 11). In case of contact, wash area thoroughly with soap and water; rinse eyes thoroughly with plain water.[1]

Do not administer by rapid IV bolus because high plasma levels may increase toxicity.[1]

Observe IV site carefully to avoid extravasation injury.

COMMENTS

Interactions:

- Concurrent zidovudine may cause severe hematologic toxicity.[1,2]

- Concurrent imipenem-cilastatin may cause generalized seizures.[1,2]
- Concurrent bone marrow depressants (e.g., flucytosine, vincristine, amphotericin B) or radiation therapy may cause additive suppression of bone marrow.[1,2]
- Concurrent nephrotoxic agents, such as amphotericin B or cyclosporine, may increase serum creatinine and the risk of renal-function impairment. Decreased elimination and increased risk of ganciclovir toxicity may occur.[2]

REFERENCES

1. Medical Economics Data. 2000. *Physicians' Desk Reference,* 54th ed. Montvale, New Jersey: Medical Economics, 2623–2629.

2. United States Pharmacopeial Convention/USP DI. 2000. *Drug Information for the Health Care Professional,* 20th ed. Rockville, Maryland: United States Pharmacopeial Convention, 1618–1622.

3. American Academy of Pediatrics, Committee on Infectious Diseases. 2000. Cytomegalovirus infection. In *Red Book: Report of the Committee on Infectious Diseases,* 25th ed., Pickering LK, ed. Elk Grove Village, Illinois: American Academy of Pediatrics, 227–230.

4. Reigstad H, et al. 1992. Ganciclovir therapy of congenital cytomegalovirus disease. *Acta Paediatrica* 81(9): 707–708.

5. Hocker JR, et al. 1990. Ganciclovir therapy of congenital cytomegalovirus pneumonia. *Pediatric Infectious Disease Journal* 9(10): 743–745.

6. Attard-Montalto SP, et al. 1993. Ganciclovir treatment of congenital cytomegalovirus infection: A report of two cases. *Scandinavian Journal of Infectious Disease* 25(3): 385–388.

7. Tajiri H, et al. 2001. Cytomegalovirus hepatitis confirmed by in situ hybridization in three immunocompetent infants. *Scandinavian Journal of Infectious Disease* 33(10): 790–793.

8. Rohrer T, et al. 1999. Combined treatment with zidovudine, lamivudine, nelfinavir, and ganciclovir in an infant with human immunodeficiency virus type 1 infection and cytomegalovirus encephalitis: Case report and review of the literature. *Pediatric Infectious Disease Journal* 18(4): 382–386.

9. Nigro G, Scholz H, and Bartmann U. 1994. Ganciclovir therapy for symptomatic congenital cytomegalovirus infection in infants: A two-regimen experience. *Journal of Pediatrics* 124(2): 318–322.

10. Frenkel LM, et al. 2000. Oral ganciclovir in children: Pharmacokinetics, safety, tolerance, and antiviral effects. *Journal of Infectious Disease* 182(6): 1616–1624.

11. Trissel LA. 1998. *Handbook on Injectable Drugs.* Bethesda, Maryland: American Society of Health-System Pharmacists, 556–559.

12. Data on file at Roche Pharmaceuticles Service Center, 800-526-6367.

13. Anaizi NH, Swenson CF, and Dentinger PJ. 1999. Stability of ganciclovir in extemporaneously compounded oral liquids. *American Journal of Health-System Pharmacists* 56(17): 1738–1741.

14. Fox LM, Gerber MA, and Penix L. 1999. Intractable diarrhea from cytomegalovirus enterocolitis in an immunocompetent infant. *Pediatrics* 103(1): 145 (e10). (Electronic abstracts: www.pediatrics.org).

15. Stronati M, et al. 1995. Ganciclovir therapy of congenital human cytomegalovirus hepatitis. *Acta Paediatrica* 84(3): 340–341.

16. Trang JM, et al. 1993. Linear single-dose pharmacokinetics of ganciclovir in newborns with congenital cytomegalovirus infections. NIAID Collaborative Antiviral Study Group. *Clinical Pharmacology and Therapeutics* 53(1): 15–21.

17. Zhou XJ, et al. 1996. Population pharmacokinetics of ganciclovir in newborns with congenital cytomegalovirus infections. *Antimicrobial Agents and Chemotherapy* 40(9): 2202–2205.

GENTAMICIN (GARAMYCIN)

(jen-ta-MYE-sin)

**ANTI-INFECTIVE:
ANTIBIOTIC**

DOSE

<1.2 kg (0–4 weeks): 2.5 mg/kg/dose given every 18–24 hours*

1.2–2 kg:

- 0–7 days: 2.5 mg/kg/dose given every 12–18 hours*
- >7 days: 2.5 mg/kg/dose given every 8–12 hours

>2 kg:

- 0–7 days: 2.5 mg/kg/dose given every 12 hours
- >7 days: 2.5 mg/kg/dose given every 8 hours[1–3]

Reduce dose in renal impairment.

Individualize dose based on serum concentrations.

Alternate Dosing Approaches:

- *Loading Dose:* 4 mg/kg has been used.[4] (Based on limited data.)

- *Once-daily Dosing:* 4 mg/kg as a single daily dose has been used in a few studies for term infants and for infants >34 weeks gestation with normal renal function.[5–7] Once-daily dosing takes advantage of the postantibiotic effect of aminoglycosides, reduces the cost of therapy, and may offer equal efficacy with decreased nephrotoxicity and vestibular and auditory (cochlear) ototoxicities.[5–7] The postantibiotic effect refers to a period of time after complete removal of an antibiotic during which there is no growth of the target organism. The fall in the level in serum below the MIC does not appear to impair antibacterial efficacy. In fact, the higher peak level in serum may enhance drug efficacy early in the dosing interval.[8,9] Chuck and colleagues reported that a once-daily aminoglycoside regimen was used, at least some of the time, in 11 percent of neonatal units and 23 percent of pediatric services.[10] Actual daily dosage and monitoring policies in infants and children were highly variable in the hospitals surveyed. An editorial by response to this report by Brown and colleagues cautions that extended-interval dosing (EID) has not eliminated aminoglycoside nephrotoxicity and ototoxicity. Some factors of concern to the authors are the use of EID methods for patients with reduced renal function, for prolonged therapy, against pathogens for which aminoglycoside MICs are relatively high, and/or in instances where the aminoglycoside does not readily achieve therapeutic concentrations at the site of infection.[11] Although EID is used in many units, Nelson and McCracken caution that there are no well-controlled, prospective studies of infants and children in adequate numbers to know whether single-dose aminoglycoside therapy is safe or effective and that such studies are required before this regimen can be recommended for routine use in pediatrics.[12]

---

* See Appendix B: Every-18-Hour Medication Worksheet.

- *With Renal Dysfunction:* After the initial dose, measure two or three serum concentrations to determine half-life and to establish frequency of subsequent doses.[2] Reimche and associates adjusted dosage regimens based on serum creatinine concentrations (<0.67 mg/dl—no change; 0.67–1.1—change interval to every 24 hours; 1.1–1.32—change interval to every 36 hours; >1.33—change interval to every 48 hours).[13]

- *For Obese (LGA) Infants:* Gentamicin can be dosed on actual weight for obese infants. Lean body weight (e.g., the infant's weight at the 50th percentile) need not be used.[14]

- *For Term Neonates on Extracorporeal Membrane Oxygenation (ECMO):* Begin with an empiric dose and interval of 2.5 mg/kg every 18 hours. Adjust dose based on serum concentrations. Dose modifications may again be required after discontinuation of ECMO.[15] Gentamicin has a higher volume of distribution, lower clearance, and longer half-life in infants on ECMO.[16]

- *With Exchange Transfusion:* Double-volume exchange transfusion reduces serum concentrations by 20–60 percent. If possible, schedule exchange to precede scheduled dose.

Other methods of gentamicin dosing have been published based on postconceptional age.[17]

ADMINISTRATION

IV (preferred)—*Rate:* Infuse over 30 minutes. Infusion over less than 20 minutes may cause excessive (>12 mcg/ml) peak serum levels.

IV—*Concentration:* No maximum concentration is specified. Volume of diluent depends on the fluid status of the patient.

IV—*Compatibility:* See Appendix E: Y-Site Compatibility of Common NICU Drugs.

IM: Use undiluted. May be given IM for a few doses for infants with difficult IV access.

IM administration of drugs is discouraged in neonates because of their small muscle mass and poor perfusion, as well as trauma to the infant.

Intrathecal or intraventricular administration of gentamicin does not improve outcome and may increase fatalities, possibly as a result of rapid Gram-negative bacterial lysis and release of higher amounts of endotoxin.[18]

CAUTIONS/CONTRAINDICATIONS

Interactions: Aminoglycosides (i.e., gentamicin, tobramycin) have a potential curare-like effect on neuromuscular function:

- Use with caution in newborns of mothers who have received magnesium sulfate. Hypermagnesemic infants are more likely to have apnea after receiving aminoglycosides.[19,20]

- Infants with botulism are more likely to become apneic when given aminoglycosides. Muscle weakness may be aggravated in infants with myasthenia gravis.

- Respiratory paralysis may occur when aminoglycosides are given soon after anesthesia or muscle relaxants.
- Do not admix penicillins or cephalosporins in the same IV solution with gentamicin because doing so will cause gradual inactivation of the gentamicin. Inactivation may also occur *in vivo*, but only in patients with severe renal dysfunction.
- Indomethacin reduces gentamicin clearance and prolongs half-life.[21]

USE

An aminoglycoside antibiotic for treatment of infections caused by Gram-negative organisms—*Escherichia coli, Pseudomonas aeruginosa,* and Serratia species. Used in combination with ampicillin for Streptococcus Group D (enterococcal) infections. Also commonly used in combination with ampicillin to treat suspected infection in the newborn. Synergistic bactericidal activity has been demonstrated with aminoglycosides and penicillins against Streptococcus Group B, *Staphylococcus aureus, Listeria monocytogenes,* and enterococcal infections despite resistance of the microorganisms to the aminoglycosides alone.

Comparison with Tobramycin Therapy: The pharmacology, dosage, and therapeutic serum levels of tobramycin and gentamicin are the same. Tobramycin is less nephrotoxic than gentamicin in adult studies. Tobramycin has greater activity against Pseudomonas than does gentamicin.[22]

MECHANISM OF ACTION

Gentamicin is an aminoglycoside antibiotic. Aminoglycosides act on microbial ribosomes to irreversibly inhibit protein synthesis.

ADVERSE EFFECTS

May cause rash (uncommon).

Ototoxicity: Both auditory (cochlear) and vestibular toxicity can occur. The risk is greater in patients with renal impairment, with pre-existing hearing loss, with duration of therapy >10 days, with concurrent furosemide therapy, and when large amounts of the drug are administered. Avoid concurrent use of other ototoxic drugs, if possible.

Renal Toxicity: Uncommon in neonates, but characterized by decreased creatinine clearance, cells or casts in the urine, decreased urine specific gravity, oliguria, proteinuria, and increasing BUN and serum creatinine. Renal toxicity is usually reversible if the drug is discontinued promptly. Avoid concurrent use of other nephrotoxic drugs.

PHARMACOKINETICS/PHARMACODYNAMICS

Absorption: Poor oral absorption, but excessive levels may accumulate in neonates receiving concomitant oral and parenteral aminoglycosides.[23] Peak blood level after IM administration is at 0.5–1 hour.

Distribution: CSF levels are 0.3–3.7 mcg/ml after a 2.5 mg/kg dose. Concentration correlates with degree of meningeal inflammation. Preterm infants with left-to-right patent ductus arteriosus shunts had a significantly larger gentamicin volume of distribution, which may have been caused by the increased extracellular fluid volume resulting from pulmonary shunting.[24] The volume of distribution of gentamicin in various neonatal studies ranges from 0.35 to 0.78 liters/kg.

Half-life: ≤2 kg and ≤7 days old = 10.5–14 hours; >2 kg and ≤7 days = 4.5–5.5 hours; all infants >7 days = 3.2 hours. Half-life correlates inversely with creatinine clearance, gestational age, birth weight, postnatal age, and postconceptional age.

Elimination: Renal.[25–27]

NURSING IMPLICATIONS

Monitor urine output and BUN, serum creatinine, and renal function tests carefully to avoid renal toxicity.

Monitor serum gentamicin concentrations carefully. Hold dose if trough is >2 mcg/ml and notify physician.

COMMENTS

Therapeutic Range:

- **Peak:** 4–10 mcg/ml, drawn 30 minutes after the completion of a 30-minute infusion.

- **Trough:** 0.5–2 mcg/ml, drawn just before the dose.

If penicillins and aminoglycosides are both present in serum samples being assayed for gentamicin, falsely low gentamicin concentrations may result, leading to unnecessary upward dose adjustment and increased risk of toxicity. To reduce the risk of this interaction, administer the penicillin/cephalosporin after the gentamicin level is drawn.[28]

REFERENCES

1. Nelson JD. 1996. *1996–1997 Pocketbook of Pediatric Antimicrobial Therapy,* 12th ed. Baltimore: Lippincott Williams & Wilkins, 16–17.

2. Taketomo CK, Hodding JH, and Kraus DM. 1996. *Pediatric Dosage Handbook,* 3rd ed. Hudson, Ohio: Lexi-Comp.

3. Prober CG, Stevenson DK, and Benitz WE. 1990. The use of antibiotics in neonates weighing less than 1,200 grams. *Pediatric Infectious Disease Journal* 9(2): 111–121.

4. Watterberg KL, et al. 1989. The need for a loading dose of gentamicin in neonates. *Therapeutic Drug Monitoring* 11(1): 16–20.

5. Skopnik H, and Heimann G. 1995. Once daily aminoglycoside dosing in full term neonates. *Pediatric Infectious Disease Journal* 14(1): 71–72.

6. Hayani KC, et al. 1994. Single daily dosing of gentamicin in neonates (abstract #1771). *Pediatric Research* 35(4 part 2): 298A.

7. Gresores A, et al. 1994. A once-daily gentamicin dosing regimen for neonates >34 weeks postconceptional age (abstract #1768). *Pediatric Research* 35(4 part 2): 297A.

8. Gilbert DN. 1991. Once-daily aminoglycoside therapy. *Antimicrobial Agents and Chemotherapy* 35(3): 399–405.

9. Zhanel GG, Hoban DJ, and Harding GK. 1991. The postantibiotic effect: A review of *in vitro* and *in vivo* data. *DICP: Annals of Pharmacotherapy* 25(2): 153–163.

10. Chuck SK, Raber SR, and Rodvold KA. 2000. National survey of extended-interval aminoglycoside dosing. *Clinical Infectious Diseases* 30(3): 433–439.

11. Brown GH, Bertino JS, and Rotschafer JC. 2000. Editorial response: Single daily dosing of aminoglycosides—A community standard? *Clinical Infectious Diseases* 30(3): 440–441. (Comment on *Clinical Infectious Diseases*, 2000, 30[3]:433–439.)

12. Nelson JD, and McCracken GH Jr. 2000. Extended-interval aminoglycoside dosing. *Pediatric Infectious Disease Journal Newsletter* 19(6, Yellow Pages): 1–2.

13. Reimche LD, et al. 1987. An evaluation of gentamicin dosing according to renal function in neonates with suspected sepsis. *American Journal of Perinatology* 4(3): 262–265.

14. Zenk KE, et al. 1984. Effect of body weight on gentamicin pharmacokinetics in neonates. *Clinical Pharmacology* 3(2): 170–173.

15. Bhatt-Mehta V, Johnson CE, and Schumacher RE. 1992. Gentamicin pharmacokinetics in term neonates receiving extracorporeal membrane oxygenation. *Pharmacotherapy* 12(1): 28–32.

16. Cohen P, et al. 1990. Gentamicin pharmacokinetics in neonates undergoing extracorporal membrane oxygenation. *Pediatric Infectious Disease Journal* 9(8): 562–566.

17. Paap CM, and Nahata MC. 1990. Clinical pharmacokinetics of antibacterial drugs in neonates. *Clinical Pharmacokinetics* 19(4): 280–318.

18. Mustafa MM, et al. 1989. Increased endotoxin and interleukin-1 beta concentrations in cerebrospinal fluid of infants with coliform meningitis and ventriculitis associated with intraventricular gentamicin therapy. *Journal of Infectious Disease* 160(5): 891–895.

19. L'Hommedieu CS, Huber PA, and Rasch DK. 1983. Potentiation of magnesium–induced neuromuscular weakness by gentamicin. *Critical Care Medicine* 11(1): 55–56.

20. L'Hommedieu CS, et al. 1983. Potentiation of magnesium sulfate–induced neuromuscular weakness by gentamicin, tobramycin and amikacin. *Journal of Pediatrics* 102(4): 629–631.

21. Dean RP, Domanico RS, and Covert RF. 1994. Prophylactic indomethacin alters gentamicin pharmacokinetics in preterm infants <1,250 grams (abstract #481). *Pediatric Research* 35(4 part 2): 83A.

22. Sáez-Llorens X, and McCracken GH Jr. 1995. Clinical pharmacology of antimicrobial agents. In *Infectious Diseases of the Fetus and Newborn Infant*, 4th ed., Remington JS, and Klein JO, eds. Philadelphia: WB Saunders, 1288–1335.

23. Miranda JC, et al. 1984. Gentamicin absorption during prophylactic use for necrotizing enterocolitis. *Developmental Pharmacology and Therapeutics* 7(5): 303–306.

24. Watterberg KL, et al. 1987. Effect of patent ductus arteriosus on gentamicin pharmacokinetics in very low birth weight (less than 1,500 g) babies. *Developmental Pharmacology and Therapeutics* 10(2): 107–117.

25. Kildoo C, et al. 1984. Developmental pattern of gentamicin kinetics in very low birth weight (VLBW) sick infants. *Developmental Pharmacology and Therapeutics* 7(6): 345–356.

26. Landers S, et al. 1984. Gentamicin disposition and effect on development of renal function in the very low birth weight infant. *Developmental Pharmacology and Therapeutics* 7(5): 285–302.

27. Kasik JW, et al. 1985. Postconceptional age and gentamicin elimination half-life. *Journal of Pediatrics* 106(3): 502–505.

28. Riff LJ, and Jackson GG. 1972. Laboratory and clinical conditions for gentamicin inactivation by carbenicillin. *Archives of Internal Medicine* 130(6): 887–891.

GLUCAGON

(GLOO-ka-gon)

HORMONE:
GLUCOSE-ELEVATING AGENT

DOSE

Intermittent: 0.3 mg/kg/dose given every 4 hours as needed.
   Maximum: 1 mg/dose.

Continuous Infusion: Begin with 0.5 mg/kg/day; increase every 30 minutes to 1 hour as needed to maintain normoglycemia. Wean gradually over 24–36 hours after normoglycemia is achieved.[1]

Conversion: 1 USP unit of glucagon = 1 International Unit (IU) = approximately 1 mg.

ADMINISTRATION

Supplied as: Injection: As a lyophilized powder 1 mg (1 unit)/vial with 1 ml diluent.

IV (preferred), IM, SC: Dilute powder with 1 ml of diluent provided to make a 1 mg/ml solution. Immediate use after reconstitution is recommended; however, may be kept up to 48 hours in the refrigerator (temperature 5°C), if necessary.

IV Continuous Infusion: Reconstitute powder with diluent provided, then dilute with $D_{10}W$ to a volume based on the dose and the infant's fluid requirements.

CAUTIONS/CONTRAINDICATIONS

Use with caution in patients with pheochromocytoma because glucagon stimulates catecholamine release, causing hypertension.

Use with caution in patients with insulinoma because glucagon may paradoxically decrease blood glucose.

USE

Treatment of severe neonatal hypoglycemia.

Some causes of hypoglycemia in the newborn include: infant of a diabetic mother, large for gestational age (LGA) infant, nesidioblastosis, and maternal drug treatment (such as with chlorpropamide, β-sympathomimetic tocolytic therapy, and thiazides).

Treatment Options: Dextrose infusion (4–6 mg/kg/minute and may exceed 15–20 mg/kg/minute) is the initial treatment of choice for hypoglycemia. If this is insufficient or if IV access is not readily available, glucagon, diazoxide (10–15 mg/kg/day), steroids (hydrocortisone 5 mg/kg/day or prednisone 2 mg/kg/day),[2,3] or octreotide (Sandostatin) (see octreotide monograph)[4,5] also have been used to treat severe hypoglycemia. Subtotal pancreatectomy may be necessary for infants with hyperinsulinism whose condition cannot be controlled medically.[5]

G

MECHANISM OF ACTION

Glucagon is a polypeptide hormone produced by the α cells of the pancreatic islets of Langerhans. The source is beef or porcine pancreas. Glucagon:

- Promotes hepatic glycogenolysis and gluconeogenesis.
- Stimulates adenylate cyclase to produce increased cyclic-AMP, which is involved in a series of enzymatic activities that result in increased plasma glucose, relaxation of smooth muscle, and inotropic effect on the heart.[6]

The intensity of effect of glucagon depends on glycogen reserve in the liver and the presence of phosphorylases.

ADVERSE EFFECTS

Nausea and vomiting may occur occasionally. This adverse effect is dose and rate dependent (for IV).

Hypersensitivity reactions may occur because glucagon is a protein. Patients who are allergic to beef or pork may also be allergic to glucagon. Serum potassium may be decreased with large doses of glucagon.[6]

Severe, intractable hypoglycemia may follow rapid dose reduction. Taper continuous infusion gradually.

PHARMACOKINETICS/PHARMACODYNAMICS

Absorption: Cannot be given orally because it is destroyed in the GI tract.

Peak Effect: Maximum hyperglycemic effects occur by about 30 minutes.

Duration of Action: 1 to 2 hours.

Metabolism and Elimination: Degraded primarily in the liver and kidney by enzymatic proteolysis.

Half-life: Plasma half-life is 3–10 minutes.

NURSING IMPLICATIONS

Monitor blood glucose.

Infuse IV glucagon slowly, over at least 1 minute, to decrease risk of nausea and vomiting.

COMMENTS

Interactions:

- Phenytoin inhibits the stimulant effect of glucagon on insulin release by the pancreatic islet cells.
- Propranolol partially inhibits the hyperglycemic effect of glucagon.
- Epinephrine increases and prolongs the hyperglycemic effect of glucagon.
- Glucagon and dextrose may be used together without decreasing the effects of either.

REFERENCES

1. Benitz WE, and Tatro DS. 1995. *Pediatric Drug Handbook,* 3rd ed. St. Louis: Mosby, 261.

2. Kien CL. 1993. Carbohydrates. In *Nutritional Needs of the Preterm Infant: Scientific Basis and Practical Guidelines,* Tsang RC, et al., eds. Baltimore: Lippincott Williams & Wilkins, 47–63.

3. Cowett RM. 1985. Pathophysiology, diagnosis, and management of glucose homeostasis in the neonate. *Current Problems in Pediatrics* 15(3): 1–47.

4. Tauber MT, Harris AG, and Rochiccioli P. 1994. Clinical use of the long acting somatostatin analogue octreotide in pediatrics. *European Journal of Pediatrics* 153(5): 304–310.

5. Stanley CA. 1997. Hyperinsulinism in infants and children. *Pediatric Clinics of North America* 44(2): 363–374.

6. United States Pharmacopeial Convention/USP DI. 1996. *Drug Information for the Health Care Professional,* 16th ed. Rockville, Maryland: United States Pharmacopeial Convention, 1541–1543.

G

GLUCOSE POLYMERS
(GLOO-kos POL-ih-mer)
(POLYCOSE, MODUCAL)

**NUTRITION:
CALORIC SUPPLEMENT**

DOSE

Use amount needed to increase caloric density of formula.

Liquid product provides 2 kcal/ml; powdered product, 8 kcal/level tsp.

ADMINISTRATION

PO: Mix with formula. First mix with small amount of formula to form a slurry; then add remainder of formula. Shake feeding well to assure additive is mixed.

Storage:

- *Dissolved Powder and Opened Liquid:* Refrigerate. Discard unused portion after 24 hours.

- *Dry Powder:* Write the date opened on the can label. Discard unused portion after one month. Reseal with its plastic cover after each use.

- Avoid contamination of powder with measuring spoon/scoop. Use clean measuring spoon for each measurement. Do not store spoon/scoop inside can.

USE

A caloric supplement from a carbohydrate source. Used to increase the caloric density of feedings. Glucose polymers have a low osmolality and are readily digestible and well tolerated by infants. May be used as a carbohydrate source in patients with gastroenteritis and other conditions where lactose and sucrose digestion may be impaired.[1]

May be used in infants with galactosemia, whereas lactose should be avoided. (Lactose is broken down by lactase to glucose and galactose. See Figure 2-3, page 604, in the **Nutrition** section.)

May need to give MCT oil concurrently to balance fat and carbohydrate intakes. Modular protein supplement (Casec) may be added as well. The percentages of fat and carbohydrate should be approximately equal as in human milk (52 percent fat, 42 percent carbohydrate, 6 percent protein).

MECHANISM OF ACTION

Polycose and Moducal consist primarily of glucose polymers with chain lengths of from 5 to 10 glucose units and contain only small amounts of the simple sugars glucose, maltose, and isomaltose. The osmolality of these products is approximately one-fifth that of a glucose solution of comparable caloric value.

ADVERSE EFFECTS

High glucose loads may be detrimental to infants with decreased pulmonary reserve. Glucose metabolism increases carbon dioxide production, minute ventilation, and O_2 consumption, which may compromise infants with poor respiratory status. Although respiratory compromise has been demonstrated specifically with IV glucose administration, caution should be exercised with high levels of oral glucose products as well. Balancing glucose with fat intake is associated with reduced CO_2 production.[2,3]

Addition of glucose polymers increases osmolality of formula only minimally.

PHARMACOKINETICS/PHARMACODYNAMICS

Absorption: Well absorbed.

Metabolism: Cornstarch is hydrolyzed to glucose polymers (see Figure 2-2, page 603, in the **Nutrition** section). Compared with a dextrose solution (glucose), the higher molecular weight of glucose polymers results in a lower osmolality and helps reduce the potential for osmotic diarrhea.

NURSING IMPLICATIONS

Shake feeding well to ensure that additive is mixed.

Monitor infant's respiratory status and blood gases to ensure tolerance.

REFERENCES

1. Manufacturers' product literature.

2. Van Aerde JE, et al. 1989. Effect of replacing glucose with lipid on the energy metabolism of newborn infants. *Clinical Science* 76(6): 581–588.

3. Van Aerde JE. 1991. Acute respiratory failure and bronchopulmonary dysplasia. In *Neonatal Nutrition and Metabolism,* Hay WW Jr, ed. St. Louis: Mosby-Year Book, 476–506.

GLYCERIN 80 PERCENT
(GLI-ser-in)
[GLYCERIN MICROENEMA]

GASTROINTESTINAL:
LAXATIVE

DOSE

0.2 ml per rectum daily as needed if no stool output for more than 24 hours.

ADMINISTRATION

Rectal: Place surgical lubricant on the syringe tip; insert the tip into the rectum.

Pharmacist Compounding Directions
Glycerin 80 Percent Microenema for Neonates[1]

Measure 80 ml glycerin USP in a conical graduate; then add sufficient sterile water for irrigation to bring the volume to 100 ml. Mix; then pour into an amber glass bottle and shake well. This volume is sufficient to prepare approximately 500 doses. Draw up 0.2 ml into 0.5 ml oral syringes and label: Lubricate syringe tip before use. For rectal use only. Refrigerate. Do not add overfill.

Stability: 3 months.

Storage: Refrigerate syringes in labeled zippered plastic bag.

USE

Laxative to promote bilirubin excretion by reducing enterohepatic circulation, decreasing gastrointestinal transit time, and encouraging passage of meconium. In healthy preterm infants, full intestinal motile function may not occur until 29–31 weeks postconceptional age.

May improve feeding tolerance, particularly in infants who have gastric residuals, emesis, and abdominal distention from gastrointestinal hypomotility.

Glycerin enemas are as effective and safe as glycerin suppository chips in stimulating bowel movements in neonates. The enemas offer the advantages of dose consistency as well as cleanliness, convenience, and staff safety (see COMMENTS below).[1,2]

MECHANISM OF ACTION

Glycerin acts as a hyperosmotic agent, pulling water into the GI tract and thereby stimulating evacuation by reflex.

ADVERSE EFFECTS

Usually very well tolerated.

Overdose could result in diarrhea and dehydration.

PHARMACOKINETICS/PHARMACODYNAMICS

Absorption: Poorly absorbed from rectal mucosa.

Onset of Action: 90 minutes (range: 10–180 minutes).

Nursing Implications

Allow to warm to room temperature before administration.

Administer carefully to avoid injuring the rectal mucosa.

Monitor for stool result.

Comments

Advantages of Enema over Suppository-chip Administration:

- Reduces nursing time required for dose preparation and administration.
- Standardized dose saves pharmacy preparation time.
- *Warning:* To prepare suppository chips, a sharp blade is often used to cut small pieces from pediatric glycerin suppositories. This results in nonstandardized sizes and possible contamination of the material. Use of a blade presents a risk of injury to nurses, is cumbersome, and is time-consuming.

References

1. Zenk KE, Koeppel RM, and Liem LA. 1993. Comparative efficacy of glycerin enemas and suppository chips in neonates. *Clinical Pharmacy* 12(11): 846–848.

2. Morriss FH. 1991. Neonatal gastrointestinal motility and enteral feeding. *Seminars in Perinatology* 15(6): 478–481.

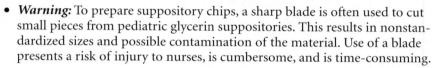

GLYCOPYRROLATE (ROBINUL)

(glye-koe-PYE-roe-late)

DOSE

IV or IM: 4–10 mcg/kg/dose given every 4–8 hours

PO: 40–100 mcg/kg/dose given every 8–12 hours

In Reversal of Neuromuscular Blockade: 0.2 mg for each 1 mg neostigmine given

ADMINISTRATION

Supplied as: Injection: 0.2 mg/ml (= 200 mcg/ml); Tablets: 1 mg, 2 mg.

IV—*Rate:* Maximum: 20 mcg/minute.

IV—*Concentration:* May give undiluted.

IM: May give undiluted.

PO: An oral liquid is not commercially available. May use the injectable form of the drug and give PO, or an oral liquid can be prepared by the pharmacist.

Pharmacist Compounding Directions
Glycopyrrolate Oral Suspension 100 mcg/ml[1]

Crush tablets in syrup at 100 mcg/ml.

Stability: 2 weeks refrigerated.

Incompatible with: Drugs having an alkaline pH such as phenobarbital and sodium bicarbonate.

CAUTIONS/CONTRAINDICATIONS

Note that the ***PO dose is 10 times the parenteral dose;*** be sure to recalculate the dose when changing routes of administration.

Should not be used in patients with narrow-angle glaucoma, urinary tract obstruction, ileus.

Infants, patients with Down syndrome, and children with spastic paralysis or brain damage may be hypersensitive to the antimuscarinic effects (e.g., mydriasis, tachycardia).

USE

An anticholinergic drug used to reduce excessive respiratory and salivary secretions.

Used as an adjuvant in neuromuscular blockade reversal, glycopyrrolate protects against the peripheral muscarinic effects (e.g., bradycardia and excessive secretions) of cholinergic agents such as neostigmine. Given to reverse neuromuscular blockade caused by nondepolarizing muscle relaxants (e.g., atracurium).

Glycopyrrolate 8 mcg/kg IV was used successfully to treat eosphageal spasm associated with apnea and bradycardia in a 3-week-old infant.[2]

MECHANISM OF ACTION

Glycopyrrolate is a quaternary ammonium anticholinergic (antimuscarinic) drug. This chemical structure limits its diffusion across the blood-brain barrier, so it produces fewer CNS side effects than atropine. It also causes less tachycardia than does atropine, but is more effective in drying oral and tracheal secretions. Glycopyrrolate may decrease the volume and acidity of gastric secretions better than atropine.[3]

ADVERSE EFFECTS

May delay gastric emptying.

May cause drowsiness, nervousness, tachycardia, rash, dry mouth, constipation, urinary retention, impaired sweating, and blurred vision.

PHARMACOKINETICS/PHARMACODYNAMICS

Absorption: Incompletely absorbed from the GI tract.

Onset of Action: After IV administration, about 1 minute. Following IM injection, onset is delayed until 15–30 minutes and peaks at about 30–45 minutes.

Duration of Action: Anticholinergic effects following parenteral administration last 7 hours and, after oral administration, up to 8–12 hours.

Elimination: Primarily in feces via biliary elimination and in urine.

NURSING IMPLICATIONS

Monitor heart rate.

Observe for constipation and urine retention.

COMMENTS

Interactions: Additive adverse effects (xerostomia, blurred vision, constipation) may occur when drugs with anticholinergic effects (e.g., antihistamines, disopyramide, meperidine, procainamide, quinidine) are used with glycopyrrolate.

REFERENCES

1. Taketomo CK, Hodding JH, and Kraus DM. 1997. *Pediatric Dosage Handbook,* 4th ed. Hudson, Ohio: Lexi-Comp, 347–349.

2. Fontan JP, et al. 1984. Esophageal spasm associated with apnea and bradycardia in an infant. *Pediatrics* 73(1): 52–55.

3. Lerman J. 1993. Anesthesia. In *Pediatric Pharmacology and Therapeutics,* 2nd ed., Radde IC, and MacLeod SM, eds. St. Louis: Mosby-Year Book, 475–497.

G

TABLE OF CONTENTS

HEPARIN SODIUM (LIQUAEMIN)
(HEP-a-rin SOE-dee-um)

BLOOD MODIFIER: ANTICOAGULANT

DOSE

Systemic Anticoagulation:

- *Loading Dose:* 50 units/kg IV (*Maximum:* 100 units/kg).[1]
- *Continuous Infusion:* 20–35 units/kg/hour. Increase or decrease dose by 5 units/kg/hour, depending on results of clotting studies. Dose requirements decrease as the clot resolves. McDonald and Hathaway reported clinical resolution of thrombi with heparin doses of 16–35 units/kg/hour (mean = 27 units/kg/hour).[2]
- *Intermittent Dosing:* 100 units/kg given every 4 hours IV. (Continuous infusion is preferred over intermittent dosing.)
- *Duration of Therapy:* Usually 5–7 days. Continue for 48 hours after resolution of thrombus.[2] If clinical improvement is not seen in 24 hours or if the infant continues to worsen over the next 6–12 hours after beginning therapy, thrombolysis (urokinase) should be considered.[1]

Line Flush: 0.3–0.5 ml of a heparin/saline solution. A concentration of heparin of 2 units/ml in 1/2 NS is preferred. Flush heparin locks every 1–4 hours.[3,4]

- Occlusions are more likely to occur in catheters with smaller lumens; therefore, flush more frequently in smaller infants.[3,5]
- A heparin dose for flushing is usually safe if it is well below the dose needed for systemic heparinization. Table 1-27 lists heparin flush doses for infants of various weights. Table 1-28 gives heparinized and nonheparinized flush solutions by infant weight.

Heparinized IV Solutions to Maintain Line Patency: 0.5–1 unit/ml.

- If central line infusion rate is >10 ml/hour, heparin is probably not required to maintain line patency.
- Minimize the total heparin load by using the 0.5 unit/ml concentration for infants on high fluid loads. For example, very low birth weight infants may receive more than 200 ml/kg/day in the first few days of life and have multiple lines containing heparin, plus receive multiple heparinized flushes.
- The dose of heparin used to maintain line patency (1 unit/ml) in one study averaged between 2.4 and 4.1 units/kg/hour and resulted in heparin levels averaging less than 0.05 unit/ml.[6]

ADMINISTRATION

IV (preferred); SC.

IV—*Rate:* Over 1 minute for initial loading dose, then by continuous infusion.

IV—*Concentration:* May give undiluted.

IV—*Compatibility:* See Appendix E: Y-Site Compatibility of Common NICU Drugs.

TABLE 1-27 ◆ DAILY HEPARIN LOCK FLUSH

Central Venous Catheters (Broviacs)

• Heparin dose in table is based on 40 units/kg.

• Select dose of heparin for daily flushing of central line that is locked off.

• Fill adapter plug with appropriate heparin concentration, then attach to line and flush.

• For single-lumen catheter, dilute to a total of 2 ml. A bifuse or trifuse infusion set does not constitute a double- or triple-lumen catheter.

• For double-lumen catheters that are both locked off, dilute to a total of 4 ml and give 2 ml in each lumen.

• If locked-off central line is used for administration of medication or for withdrawal of blood for lab specimens, follow with 0.3–0.5 ml of a heparin solution of 10 units/ml. Daily flush using this table is not required when locked-off catheter is being used more than three times per shift: Infants on multiple medications could receive an excessive daily dose of heparin with daily flushing.

Percutaneous Lines

• Once-daily flushing may be insufficient for percutaneous lines because of their smaller diameter and may cause them to clot off. For this reason, more frequent flushing, as follows, is being used by some units for percutaneous lines.

  • Body weight ≤1,200 gm: 5 units of heparin in 0.5–1 ml preservative-free saline every 8 hours.

  • Body weight >1,200 gm: 10 units of heparin in 0.5–1 ml preservative-free saline every 8 hours.

Infant Weight (kg)	Heparin (units)	Heparin (ml of 100 units/ml)	Concentration after Dilution to 2 ml with Normal Saline (units/ml)
1	40	0.4	20
1.2	48	0.48	24
1.5	60	0.6	30
2	80	0.8	40
2.5	100	1	50
3	120	1.2	60
3.5	140	1.4	70
4	160	1.6	80
4.5	180	1.8	90
5	200	2	100*
5.5	200	2	100*
6	200	2	100*

* Maximum

Note: Use preservative-free heparin.

TABLE 1-28 ◆ IV FLUSH SOLUTIONS: HEPARINIZED AND NONHEPARINIZED

Guidelines for use:

- Select flush solution that corresponds to the infant's weight.
- Use heparinized flushes for starting IVs and peripheral IV locks.
- Use nonheparinized solutions for flushing between medications.
- Dextrose, rather than saline, flushes are specified in the very low birth weight category to reduce the sodium and chloride load, which minimizes the risk of hyperchloremia and hypernatremia. If an infant is glucose intolerant, saline flushes can be substituted.

Infant's Weight	Nonheparinized Solution	Heparinized Solution*
<800 gm	D$_5$W	D$_5$W with heparin 2 units/ml[†]
800–1,500 gm	NaCl 0.45%	NaCl 0.45% with heparin 2 units/ml[†]
>1,500 gm	NaCl 0.9%	NaCl 0.9% with heparin 10 units/ml[‡]

* Use preservative-free heparin.

[†] Prepared by pharmacy.

[‡] Commercially available.

From: Romanowski GL, and Zenk KE. 1991. Intravenous flush solutions for neonates (abstract P-227). Presented at the 26th Annual ASHP Midyear Clinical Meeting. Reprinted by permission. (R2011)

CAUTIONS/CONTRAINDICATIONS

Do not use for systemic anticoagulation in infants with evidence of intracranial or GI bleeding or platelet count <50,000/mm^3.

USE

For prophylaxis and treatment of large-vessel thromboembolic disease, to maintain patency of IV or arterial catheters,[7] and to prevent clotting during ECMO.

Continuous heparin (1 unit/ml of IV fluid) helps reduce serum triglycerides during infusion of IV fat emulsion. Heparin helps release lipoprotein lipase (LPL) from the surface of the vascular endothelium into the circulation. LPL hydrolyzes triglycerides to glycerol and free fatty acids. Free fatty acid concentrations remain low enough not to interfere with albumin-bilirubin binding, and no adverse effect on unbound bilirubin occurs.[8,9]

Alpan and associates showed that heparinization of parenteral nutrition (1 unit/ml) reduces the incidence of phlebitis and increases the duration of peripheral catheter patency.[10]

Continuous heparin infusion is better than intermittent flushes for maintaining patency of umbilical arterial catheters.[5]

Mechanism of Action

Prepared from beef lung or porcine intestinal mucosa, heparin inhibits reactions that lead to clotting. It potentiates the action of antithrombin-III, thereby inactivating thrombin, activated coagulation factors IX, X, XI, XII, and plasmin. It prevents the conversion of fibrinogen to fibrin. Heparin has no fibrinolytic activity and will not lyse clots, but will prevent their extension.

Adverse Effects

Possibility of serious bleeding, such as pulmonary hemorrhage or intracranial hemorrhage, as a result of overanticoagulation. Increased risk of intraventricular hemorrhage in preterm infants.[11]

Allergic reactions such as fever and urticaria, increased liver enzymes, osteoporosis.

Pharmacokinetics/Pharmacodynamics

Absorption: PO administration does not alter coagulation because it is not absorbed. Heparin must be used parenterally.

Onset of Action: Immediate.

Clearance: *Variable:* greater in newborns (1.49 ml/kg/minute) than in adults (0.43 ml/kg/minute). Clearance increases in infants with thrombosis.[12] Infant levels of Antithrombin-III antigen are 26.5 percent of normal adult values.[12] Newborns require larger amounts of heparin than adults to achieve heparinization.[2]

Metabolism: Liver.

Half-life: 24–28 weeks gestation: 42 minutes; 29–36 weeks gestation: 36 minutes; adults: 63 minutes. Volume of distribution varied inversely with gestational age (37 ml/kg for adults; 81 ml/kg for 25–28 weeks gestation).[12] Half-life may be prolonged in hepatic dysfunction and at higher doses.

Elimination: Kidney.

Nursing Implications

During heparin therapy, monitor for bleeding from previous puncture sites (heel-sticks/IV sites).

Carefully calculate and measure all doses and double-check with another RN.

Check all urine and stools for occult blood.

Monitor platelet count and CBC. Monitor activated partial thromboplastin time (aPTT) or activated clotting time (ACT) prior to initiation of heparinization, 6–8 hours after initiation of continuous infusion with loading dose, and 6–8 hours after changes in dose.[1] ACT is preferred by some centers for neonates because it is inexpensive, requires small blood volumes (0.2–0.4 ml), and can be done rapidly at the bedside. aPTT requires more blood, and baseline values are usually prolonged in newborns compared with normal adult values.[1,2,6,13]

Titrate to keep aPTT or whole-blood ACT at 1.5–2.5 times baseline. The target ACT is 180–250 seconds.[1]

COMMENTS

Therapeutic Range: 0.3–0.5 units/ml.[2]

Antidote: Protamine (see protamine monograph).

REFERENCES

1. Gal P, and Ransom JL. 1991. Neonatal thrombosis: Treatment with heparin and thrombolytics. *DICP: The Annals of Pharmacotherapy* 25(7–8): 853–856.

2. McDonald MM, and Hathaway WE. 1982. Anticoagulant therapy by continuous heparinization in newborn and older infants. *Journal of Pediatrics* 101(3): 451–457.

3. Zenk KE. 1988. Heparin locks and children: Think small. *Nursing88* 18(11): 100–101.

4. Romanowski GL, and Zenk KE. 1991. Intravenous flush solutions for neonates (abstract P-227). Presented at the 26th Annual ASHP Midyear Clinical Meeting.

5. Bosque E, and Weaver L. 1986. Continuous versus intermittent heparin infusion of umbilical artery catheters in the newborn infant. *Journal of Pediatrics* 108(1): 141–143.

6. Edwards MS, et al. 1983. Effect of continuous heparin infusion on bactericidal activity for group B streptococci in neonatal sera. *Journal of Pediatrics* 103(5): 787–790.

7. Roberts RJ. 1984. *Drug Therapy in Infants: Pharmacologic Principles and Clinical Experience.* Philadelphia: WB Saunders, 299–301.

8. Zaidan H, et al. 1982. Effect of continuous heparin administration on Intralipid clearing in very low-birth-weight infants. *Journal of Pediatrics* 101(4): 599–602.

9. Spear ML, Stahl GE, and Hamosh M. 1988. Effect of heparin dose and infusion rate on lipid clearance and bilirubin binding in premature infants receiving intravenous fat emulsions. *Journal of Pediatrics* 112(1): 94–98.

10. Alpan G, et al. 1984. Heparinization of alimentation solutions administered through peripheral veins in premature infants: A controlled study. *Pediatrics* 74(3): 375–378.

11. Lesko SM, et al. 1986. Heparin use as a risk factor for intraventricular hemorrhage in low-birth-weight infants. *New England Journal of Medicine* 314(18): 1156–1160.

12. McDonald MM, et al. 1981. Heparin clearance in the newborn. *Pediatric Research* 15(7): 1015–1018.

13. Green TP, et al. 1990. Whole blood activated clotting time in infants during extracorporeal membrane oxygenation. *Critical Care Medicine* 18(5): 494–498.

HYALURONIDASE (WYDASE)

(hye-a-loo-ROE-ni-dase)

**ANTIDOTE:
EXTRAVASATION**

DOSE

15 units SC. Dose may be repeated in 30–60 minutes, if needed, for severe swelling.
Sample physician's order: Hyaluronidase 15 units SC to IV extravasation site,
per protocol.[1,2]

Hyaluronidase (see also Appendix G: Guidelines for Management of Intravenous
Extravasations) has also been given and saline flushing used to remove the
harmful substance.[3–5] Davies and colleagues used the following technique in two
preterm infants with serious extravasation injuries from parenteral nutrition to
prevent major scarring:

- Under aseptic conditions, the affected area was cleaned and infiltrated with
  lidocaine. Hyaluronidase 500–1,000 units was injected into the subcutaneous
  tissue beneath the damaged skin. Four small punctures were made with a
  scalpel blade in the tissue plane around the area. The area was flushed with
  copious amounts of saline using a Veress (blunt) needle inserted into one of
  the incisions. Excess fluid was able to flow freely out of, or was gently mas-
  saged out of, the other three incisions. Careful massage of the fluid toward the
  incisions prevented a compression effect on the underlying structures. The
  flushing process was repeated through each incision.[3]

ADMINISTRATION

Supplied as: Wydase Lyophilized, 150 units/vial/ml. (Hyaluronidase is not commercially available. See **COMMENTS** below.)

SC: *Concentration:* 15 units/ml.

Preparation:

- *Reconstitute:* 150-unit vial with 1 ml of normal saline injection
  (= 150 units/ml).
- *Prepare a 1:10 Dilution:* Using a tuberculin syringe, withdraw 0.1 ml of the
  150 unit/ml solution and add to 0.9 ml of normal saline injection to equal a
  total of 1 ml (= 15 units/ml).

Administration Procedure:[1]

- *Stop* infusion.
- *Elevate* the extremity (can use a skin traction stockinette dressing with a window). Do not apply heat[6] or cool compresses.
- *Inject* hyaluronidase locally by the subcutaneous or intradermal route using a
  25 gauge needle. The dose is 15 units given in four 0.2 ml aliquots into the
  periphery or leading edge of the site, changing the needle after each injection.
- The additional 0.2 ml may be injected into the needle through which the IV
  was running before removing it from the extravasation site. This delivers
  hyaluronidase directly into the tissue plane in which the extravasation
  occurred.

- **Wrap** the extremity loosely for approximately 2 hours. Do not apply heat, especially moist heat, because heat can damage and macerate the tissue even further.[6]
- **Observe** and document the appearance of the lesion (induration, swelling, discoloration, blanching, and blister formation) every 15 minutes for approximately 2 hours.
- **Care for open wounds.** Apply silver sulfadiazine cream. Consult plastic surgery and the burn unit services, if available, early in the course of treatment. Smaller lesions will slough and heal spontaneously, whereas larger ulcers will require excision and grafting.

Storage: Reconstituted 150 units/vial is stable for 24 hours if refrigerated.

Use

Used to treat extravasation of dextrose 10 percent, calcium salts,[7] potassium salts, sodium bicarbonate, aminophylline,[8] radiocontrast media,[9] hypertonic saline,[9,10] nafcillin,[2] blood, parenteral nutrition,[3,8] and many other drugs such as higher concentrations of dextrose. These drugs and/or solutions can sometimes cause severe tissue necrosis and sloughing on infiltration. Hyaluronidase may markedly reduce the amount of local tissue damage and destruction caused by infiltration. Promoting rapid absorption decreases the degree and duration of pain associated with the extravasation. It can reduce pressure necrosis from mechanical compression of tissues by large amounts of IV fluids trapped in a limited tissue space.[1]

Administer within 1 hour after the toxic insult, if possible. **There is little or no advantage if the drug is given 3 or more hours after extravasation.**[8]

Small areas of extravasation caught early may not require hyaluronidase treatment.

Mechanism of Action

Hyaluronidase is an enzyme that reduces or prevents tissue injury by temporarily destroying the normal tissue barrier (tissue cement, hyaluronic acid). This causes the rapid diffusion of extravasated fluids through tissues, increasing the absorptive surfaces and the resultant rate of absorption. Paradoxically, even though the irritating material is spread over a larger area, tissue reaction is minimized as a result of rapid absorption and dilution in tissue fluids.[11]

Adverse Effects

Usually very well tolerated. Rarely, has caused allergic reactions in adults (urticaria). Inadvertent IV injection during local administration is not dangerous because hyaluronidase is rapidly inactivated by inhibitors in the blood.

Do not inject into infected or cancerous tissue; doing so might promote the spread of these conditions.

Pharmacokinetics/Pharmacodynamics

Onset of Action: Almost instantaneous; there is usually a marked decrease in swelling within 10–30 minutes after administration. Extravasated fluid diffuses over an area three to five times larger than if untreated.

Duration: Depolymerization of hyaluronic acid by hyaluronidase lasts for 24–48 hours, when the mesenchymal cells regenerate the cement substance.

Metabolism: Rapidly inactivated by a thermolabile hyaluronidase inhibitor in the plasma.

Nursing Implications

Document condition of site and treatment on medical record.

Observe site for improvement (i.e., less swelling and redness).

Comments

Hyaluronidase is no longer commercially available. Directions for aseptic compounding of hyaluronidase injection 150 units/ml by pharmacy have been published.[12] The Pediatric Pharmacy Advocacy Group, Inc. stated that availability of hyaluronidase injection is vital to the proper care of patients with extravasation injuries. They also state that individual practitioners should investigate the availability of hyaluronidase injection from compounding pharmacies that exhibit good manufacturing practices and comply with state board of pharmacy regulations in their state.[13]

References

1. Zenk KE. 1981. Management of intravenous extravasations. *Infusion* 5(4): 77–79.

2. Zenk KE, Dungy CL, and Greene GR. 1981. Nafcillin extravasation injury: Use of hyaluronidase as an antidote. *American Journal of Diseases of Children* 135(12): 1113–1114.

3. Davies J, Gault D, and Buchdahl R. 1994. Preventing the scars of neonatal intensive care. *Archives of Disease in Childhood. Fetal and Neonatal Edition* 70(1): F50–F51.

4. Murphy PM, and Gault DT. 1990. Treatment of extravasation injury (letter). *Anaesthesia* 45(7): 600.

5. Gault DT. 1993. Extravasation injuries. *British Journal of Plastic Surgery* 46(2): 91–96.

6. Brown AS, Hoelzer DJ, and Piercy SA. 1979. Skin necrosis from extravasation of intravenous fluids in children. *Plastic and Reconstructive Surgery* 64(2): 145–150.

7. Raszka WV Jr, Kueser TK, and Smith FR. 1990. The use of hyaluronidase in the treatment of intravenous extravasation injuries. *Journal of Perinatology* 10(2): 146–149.

8. Laurie SWS, et al. 1984. Intravenous extravasation injuries: The effectiveness of hyaluronidase in their treatment. *Annals of Plastic Surgery* 13(3): 191–194.

9. Elam EA, et al. 1991. Cutaneous ulceration due to contrast extravasation: Experimental assessment of injury and potential antidotes. *Investigative Radiology* 26(1): 13–16.

10. Zimmet SE. 1993. The prevention of cutaneous necrosis following extravasation of hypertonic saline and sodium tetradecyl sulfate. *Journal of Dermatologic Surgery and Oncology* 19(7): 641–646.

11. Bertelli G, et al. 1994. Hyaluronidase as an antidote to extravasation of Vinca alkaloids: Clinical results. *Journal of Cancer Research and Clinical Oncology* 120(8): 505–506.

12. Allen LV Jr. 2001. Hyaluronidase 150 U/ml injection. (Contemporary Compounding). *U.S. Pharmacist* 26(6): 69–71.

13. Pediatric Pharmacy Advocacy Group. 2001. Position Statement on hyaluronidase injection (Wydase) availability. *Journal of Pediatric Pharmacology and Therapeutics* 6(6): 522–524.

HYDRALAZINE (APRESOLINE)
(hye-DRAL-a-zeen)

CARDIOVASCULAR: ANTIHYPERTENSIVE

DOSE

Hypertension:[1]

- *IV, IM (for hypertensive emergencies):* 0.1–0.4 mg/kg/dose (IV preferred) every 4–6 hours. *Maximum:* 3.5 mg/kg/day divided every 4–6 hours.
- *PO:* 0.75–7.5 mg/kg/day in two to four divided doses.

Heart Failure:[2,3]

- *IV, IM:* 0.1–0.5 mg/kg/dose every 6–8 hours. A dose of 0.1–1 mg/kg/dose every 6 hours IV has also been recommended.[4]
- *Continuous Infusion:* 1–2 mcg/kg/minute.
- *PO:* 0.25–1 mg/kg/dose. *Maximum:* 7 mg/kg/day. Usual range: 1–4 mg/kg/day.

Double the dose when changing from IV to PO because of decreased bioavailability.

ADMINISTRATION

Supplied as: Injection: 20 mg/ml. An oral liquid is not commercially available; however, the injectable dosage form may be given PO or an oral solution may be prepared by the pharmacist.

May give IV, IM, or PO.

IV—*Rate:* Infuse IV over at least 1 minute.

IV—*Concentration:* May give undiluted.

IV—*Compatibility:* See Appendix E: Y-Site Compatibility of Common NICU Drugs.

Pharmacist Compounding Directions
Hydralazine Oral Solution 4 mg/ml[5]

Withdraw 20 ml hydralazine (20 mg/ml) from ampoule. Mix with 8 ml propylene glycol. Transfer to a graduate and add water to a total volume of 100 ml.

Stability: 30 days.

Storage: Refrigerate.

USE

An antihypertensive.

Has also been used in cardiac failure for afterload reduction in infants with left-to-right intracardiac shunts.[1,2,6,7]

MECHANISM OF ACTION

Hydralazine is a direct-acting arterial vasodilator. Its mechanism of action is unknown. It acts primarily on precapillary arterioles. It reduces systemic vascular resistance.

ADVERSE EFFECTS

Usually well tolerated in infants; however, diarrhea, emesis, and rare bone marrow depression may occur. Antinuclear antibody and lupuslike syndrome have developed in some children, including one 12-month-old infant after 3 months of therapy.[2,3,8]

Numerous other side effects reported in adults include tachycardia, dizziness, sweating, flushing, sodium retention, edema, and lupuslike syndrome. Rare complications are drug fever, urticaria, and bone marrow depression.

Many side effects can be controlled by concurrent administration of a β-blocker (propranolol). Markedly lower hydralazine doses are required when combined with propranolol. Sodium and water retention can be counteracted with a diuretic.

Avoid precipitous drops in blood pressure because of hypotension-related adverse effects on the CNS.[1]

PHARMACOKINETICS/PHARMACODYNAMICS

Absorption: Rapidly absorbed. Bioavailability is 30–50 percent because of extensive first-pass clearance by the liver. Enhanced absorption if taken with food.

Onset and Duration of Action: *PO:* Onset: 30–60 minutes; duration: up to 8 hours. *IV:* Onset: 5–10 minutes; peak: 30 minutes; duration: 2–4 hours.

Protein Binding: 87 percent.

Metabolism: Genetically determined by acetylator phenotype as slow or fast acetylators. Slow acetylators have higher plasma levels of hydralazine, require lower doses, and are more likely to experience adverse effects. Metabolized in the liver.

Elimination: In urine, as active drug (12–14 percent) and metabolites.

NURSING IMPLICATIONS

Monitor blood pressure closely.

Monitor for diarrhea.

REFERENCES

1. Sinaiko AR. 1992. Antihypertensive agents. In *Pediatric Pharmacology: Therapeutic Principles in Practice*, 2nd ed., Yaffe SJ, and Aranda JV, eds. Philadelphia: WB Saunders, 425–436.
2. Artman M, and Graham TP. 1987. Guidelines for vasodilator therapy of congestive heart failure in infants and children. *American Heart Journal* 113(4): 994–1005.
3. Artman M, et al. 1987. Hemodynamic effects of hydralazine in infants with idiopathic dilated cardiomyopathy and congestive heart failure. *American Heart Journal* 113(1): 144–150.

4. Till JA, and Rigby ML. 1991. Treatment of cardiac disorders in the neonate. In *Neonatal Clinical Pharmacology and Therapeutics,* Rylance TG, Harvey D, and Aranda J, eds. Linacre House, Jordan Hill, Oxford: Butterworth-Heinemann, 126–152.

5. Nahata MC, and Hipple TF. 1992. *Pediatric Drug Formulations,* 2nd ed. Cincinnati: Harvey Whitney Books, 40.

6. Manufacturer's product literature.

7. Pruitt AW. 1981. Pharmacologic approach to the management of childhood hypertension. *Pediatric Clinics of North America* 28(1): 135–144.

8. Rao PS. 1986. Chronic afterload reduction in infants and children with primary myocardial disease. *Journal of Pediatrics* 108(4): 530–534.

HYDROCHLORIC ACID [HCL] 0.1 N
(hye-droe-KLOR-ik A-sid)

**ANTIDOTE:
OCCLUDED CENTRAL
CATHETERS**

DOSE

0.2 ml/dose IV per procedure described under **ADMINISTRATION.**

ADMINISTRATION

IV—*Concentration:* 0.1 Normal (N).

**Procedure for Restoring Patency to Occluded Central Catheters
Using 0.1 N HCl:**[1,2]

1. Draw up 0.2 ml 0.1 N HCl in a syringe.

2. Instill into a secure central venous catheter, including percutaneous lines, positioned in the superior vena cava.

3. If the catheter will not irrigate or aspirate, instill HCl with gentle repeated push-pull action. The pressure may cause the catheter to balloon. Care must be taken to permit only a *small amount* of ballooning, or the catheter may crack and/or rupture.

4. If the catheter does not clear, allow the HCl to dwell in the catheter for 60 minutes.

5. Attempt to aspirate. When patency is restored, as determined by the ability to aspirate blood freely, withdraw the HCl and 0.5–1 ml of blood to remove residual clot or precipitate and the HCl. It is preferable not to push the HCl into the bloodstream; however, Shulman and colleagues state that if the occlusion resolves as the HCl is injected, the excess HCl can be either injected into the patient or withdrawn.[3]

6. Irrigate with normal saline; then flush with 2 ml of heparin/saline; then resume infusion. **Note:** Before resuming infusion, reassess solution or medications being infused through the central line to determine cause of occlusion so that it may be corrected. If the cause may have been a calcium/phosphorus precipitation, reduce the concentration in parenteral nutrition solution.

7. If first attempt is unsuccessful, repeat the procedure.

8. If second attempt is unsuccessful, allow HCl to dwell in catheter overnight.

Compounding: HCl 0.1 N can be compounded by the pharmacy as follows using appropriate sterile technique:[1,2,4–7]

Pharmacist Compounding Directions
HCl 0.1 Normal[1,2,4-7]
Using a glass syringe for transfer, add 4.3 ml of 37 percent weight to volume (w/v) HCl to 500 ml sterile water; filter through a filter suitable for strong acids. Use caution in preparing this solution accurately. Concentrated HCl is highly corrosive and should be handled as such. Filtration with a 0.22-micron filter has been considered adequate cold sterilization, but pyrogens are not removed. Package in 3 ml aliquots in sterile 10 ml evacuated glass vials.
Storage: Refrigerate at 4°C (39°F).
Stability: 6 months.

Use

Clearance of central venous catheter occlusions caused by insoluble precipitates, such as calcium and phosphorus, or drugs. Occlusions from drugs that are incompatible with the solution infusing (see Appendix E: Y-Site Compatibility of Common NICU Drugs) or minerals usually occur rapidly (within 1 day), whereas thrombosis is gradual, over 2–4 days. HCl 0.1 N has been used to clear occlusions from sequential administration of amikacin, piperacillin, vancomycin, and heparin.[3] Salvage of catheters is preferable to premature removal and replacement.[8] (Other agents used to clear occluded catheters are urokinase, ethyl alcohol, and sodium bicarbonate.[1,2] See Appendix F: Restoring Patency to Occluded Central Venous Catheters for an algorithm to assist in selecting the appropriate agent.)

Treatment of severe metabolic alkalosis in a neonate and in adults.[4,9]

Mechanism of Action

HCl lowers the pH of a solution, thereby dissolving mineral and certain drug precipitates. It is not effective if the occlusion is caused by IV fat emulsion because acid is not a good solvent for fat. HCl contains 0.1 mEq/ml of hydrogen and chloride ion. Its pH is 1.1.[7]

Adverse Effects

Administered by the route and in the concentration and volume recommended, HCl is unlikely to cause adverse effects.

Hyperchloremia or metabolic acidosis may occur, but they are unlikely using the 0.2 ml dose recommended. For example, 9 ml of 0.1 N HCl must be given to a 3 kg infant to change the serum bicarbonate level by 1 mmol/liter.[3,10]

Possible effects include pain and irritation at injection site, thrombophlebitis if used in a peripheral line, and tissue necrosis at extravasation sites. Use only in well-placed central venous catheters. Infiltration into the mediastinum could result in potentially lethal complications. Not for use in umbilical or arterial lines.

Transient febrile reactions have occurred when large volumes (4–17 ml) were infused into the systemic circulation during attempts to clear a line.[8] This has not been reported in other studies where the HCl was aspirated, rather than injected systemically.

Hemolysis is possible with rapid infusion of large amounts.

PHARMACOKINETICS/PHARMACODYNAMICS

Onset of Action: Often immediate, or may take a number of hours. If the catheter has not cleared after 24 hours, further efforts with HCl will not be useful.[3]

NURSING IMPLICATIONS

Generally injected by a physician.

Monitor patient for side effects.

REFERENCES

1. Holcombe BJ, Forloines-Lynn S, and Garmhausen LW. 1992. Restoring patency of long-term central venous access devices. *Journal of Intravenous Nursing* 15(1): 36–41.

2. Holcombe BJ, Forloines-Lynn S, and Garmhausen LW. 1993. Erratum for corrected algorithm. Restoring patency of long-term central venous access devices. *Journal of Intravenous Nursing* 16(1): 55.

3. Shulman RJ, et al. 1988. Use of hydrochloric acid to clear obstructed central venous catheters. *Journal of Parenteral and Enteral Nutrition* 12(5): 509–510.

4. Pilla S, and Muller RJ. 1985. Use of intravenous hydrochloric acid in severe metabolic alkalosis. *Hospital Pharmacy* 20(10): 725–729.

5. Duffy LF, et al. 1989. Treatment of central venous catheter occlusions with hydrochloric acid. *Journal of Pediatrics* 114(6): 1002–1004.

6. Phelps SJ, and Cochran EB. 1993. *Guidelines for Administration of Intravenous Medications to Pediatric Patients,* 4th ed. Bethesda, Maryland: American Society of Hospital Pharmacists, 60.

7. Budavari S. 1996. *The Merck Index,* 12th ed. Rahway, New Jersey: Merck, 4821.

8. Breaux CW Jr, et al. 1987. Calcium phosphate crystal occlusion of central venous catheters used for total parenteral nutrition in infants and children: Prevention and treatment. *Journal of Pediatric Surgery* 22(9): 829–832.

9. Unger A, et al. 1985. Treatment of severe metabolic alkalosis in a neonate with hydrochloric acid infusion. *Clinical Pediatrics* 24(8): 444–446.

10. Benitz WE, and Tatro DS. 1995. *The Pediatric Drug Handbook,* 3rd ed. St. Louis: Mosby-Year Book, 305.

HYDROCHLOROTHIAZIDE WITH SPIRONOLACTONE (ALDACTAZIDE)

CARDIOVASCULAR: DIURETIC

(hye-droe-klor-oh-THYE-a-zide
speer-on-oh-LAK-tone)

DOSE

Hydrochlorothiazide 1–3 mg/kg/day and spironolactone 1–3 mg/kg/day given as a single daily dose or divided every 12 hours PO.

ADMINISTRATION

PO (only): An oral liquid is not commercially available. One can be compounded by the pharmacist as described below. **Dilute the prepared suspension before use by mixing with a small amount of infant formula.**

Pharmacist Compounding Directions
Aldactazide Suspension
(4 mg Hydrochlorothiazide/ml and 4 mg Spironolactone/ml)[1]

Pulverize 20 Aldactazide tablets (25 mg spironolactone and 25 mg hydrochlorothiazide/tablet), and add a sufficient quantity of simple syrup to make 125 ml. May wet tablets with a small amount of sterile water for irrigation to dissolve coating. Shake well. State order in terms of ml and concentration. For example, for a 2 kg infant requiring 2 mg/kg/day of hydrochlorothiazide with spironolactone, write order as follows: Aldactazide (4 mg/ml) 0.5 ml PO every 12 hours.
Stability: 60 days.
Storage: Refrigerate.

CAUTIONS/CONTRAINDICATIONS

Use with caution in patients with decreased renal and/or liver function.

USE

To reduce pulmonary fluid accumulation in chronic lung disease, mild hypertension, and heart failure. Thiazides cause only moderate diuresis compared with furosemide.

Aldactazide contains hydrochlorothiazide and spironolactone in a 1:1 fixed-dose combination. The hydrochlorothiazide is a diuretic, and spironolactone is a competitive antagonist of aldosterone that helps to prevent potassium loss and hypokalemia.

An advantage of thiazides over furosemide is that they do not increase urinary excretion of calcium.[2–6]

MECHANISM OF ACTION

Thiazides inhibit sodium reabsorption in the distal nephron. More sodium in the lumen of this segment leads to more exchange of sodium for potassium and to increased potassium loss. Chloride is lost in association with inhibition of sodium reabsorption.[5,6]

ADVERSE EFFECTS

Hypovolemia, hyponatremia, hypercalcemia, hypophosphatemia, and magnesium deficiency.[6]

Hyperkalemia could occur if infant is also receiving potassium supplements; however, hypokalemia occurs in some infants despite the spironolactone component of the drug and may require potassium chloride supplementation.

The thiazide component (hydrochlorothiazide) may cause hyperglycemia or impairment of glucose tolerance.[2,5,6]

PHARMACOKINETICS/PHARMACODYNAMICS

Absorption: Well absorbed PO.

Onset of Action: The onset of action of the diuretic effect of hydrochlorothiazide is 1–2 hours. The onset of the potassium sparing effect of spironolactone is 3–5 days.

Elimination: Excreted in the urine.

NURSING IMPLICATIONS

Monitor for signs of dehydration, including decreased urine output, tachycardia, fluid balance, and elevated urine specific gravity.

Monitor electrolytes closely; may need sodium or potassium supplements during drug therapy.

COMMENTS

Aldactazide is available in oral form only; if a parenteral thiazide diuretic is needed, use chlorothiazide (see monograph for this drug).

REFERENCES

1. ASHP, Committee on Extemporaneous Formulations. 1987. *Handbook on Extemporaneous Formulations.* Bethesda, Maryland: American Society of Hospital Pharmacists, 47.

2. Chemtob S, et al. 1989. Pharmacology of diuretics in the newborn. *Pediatric Clinics of North America* 36(5): 1231–1250.

3. Kao LC, et al. 1987. Oral theophylline and diuretics improve pulmonary mechanics in infants with bronchopulmonary dysplasia. *Journal of Pediatrics* 111(3): 439–444.

4. Albersheim SG, et al. 1989. Randomized, double-blind, controlled trial of long-term diuretic therapy for bronchopulmonary dysplasia. *Journal of Pediatrics* 115(4): 615–620.

5. Roberts RJ. 1984. *Drug Therapy in Infants: Pharmacologic Principles and Clinical Experience.* Philadelphia: WB Saunders, 226–249.

6. Sherbotie JR, and Kaplan BS. 1992. Diuretics. In *Pediatric Pharmacology: Therapeutic Principles in Practice,* 2nd ed., Yaffe SJ, and Aranda JV, eds. Philadelphia: WB Saunders, 524–534.

HYDROCORTISONE
(hye-droe-KOR-ti-sone)
(SOLU-CORTEF)

HORMONE:
GLUCOCORTICOID

Synonym: cortisol

DOSE

Anti-inflammatory and Immunosuppressive: 0.8–4 mg/kg/day or
25–120 mg/m^2/day divided every 6 hours.[1] (See Appendix M: Normal Neonatal
Laboratory and Other Values to calculate the infant's body surface area in m^2.)

Acute Adrenal Insufficiency: 1–2 mg/kg/dose IV, then 25–150 mg/day divided
every 6 hours.[1,2] Also begin cortisone acetate 2 mg/kg/day IM daily immediately
to allow tapering of IV hydrocortisone over several days.

Congenital Adrenal Hyperplasia:

- *Initial:* 1–1.2 mg/kg/day or 30–36 mg/m^2/day PO divided to give one-third of
  the daily dose every AM and two-thirds every PM or one-quarter in the morning, one-quarter at noon, and one-half the daily dose at night. This regimen
  will achieve a serum cortisol level more closely reflecting diurnal variation.

- *Maintenance:* 0.7–0.8 mg/kg/day or 20–25 mg/m^2/day PO divided as above.
  Titrate dose to suppress ACTH secretion but to allow normal bone development and growth.[1] The patient may be converted to cortisone acetate
  25 mg/m^2/day IM.

Neonatal Hypoglycemia: 1–2 mg/kg/dose IV every 8 hours.
Maximum: 5 mg/kg/day IV divided every 6–8 hours.[3,4]

Chronic Adrenal Insufficiency:

- *Standard Replacement:* 10–15 mg/m^2/day (approximately 0.3–0.5 mg/kg/day)
  PO with fludrocortisone 0.1–0.2 mg/day PO.[1,5]

- *Minor Surgery (day of surgery):* Two times the standard replacement divided
  bid.[5]

- *Major Surgery (day before surgery, day of surgery, postoperative day 1):* Five
  to ten times the standard replacement dose divided tid.[5]

**Base dose on severity of disease and response of patient. Reduce dose gradually
to the lowest effective level.**

ADMINISTRATION

Salts of Hydrocortisone: The *sodium phosphate* and *sodium succinate* salts are for
IV use; the *acetate* salt is a long-acting parenteral suspension for repository use
and should not be given IV.

IV—Rate: Infuse over at least 1 to several minutes.

IV—Concentration: Dilute to 0.1–1 mg/ml.[6]

IV—Compatibility: See Appendix E: Y-Site Compatibility of Common NICU
Drugs.

IM: May give undiluted.

PO: A suspension is commercially available for oral use (Cortef: hydrocortisone cypionate, 10 mg/5 ml).

Topical: Use the 0.5 percent cream or ointment to avoid adrenal suppression. Avoid use of potent topical steroids in infants.

Use

Glucocorticoids have been used in neonates for congenital adrenal hyperplasia, for hypoglycemia, for BPD to shorten weaning from respirator (dexamethasone), for hemangiomatosis, and prior to extubation to reduce laryngeal edema and stridor.[3,7–10]

Mechanism of Action

Hydrocortisone is a short-acting corticosteroid with glucocorticoid, anti-inflammatory, and mineralocorticoid effects. Corticosteroids have anti-inflammatory capabilities; reduce capillary permeability; stabilize lysosomal enzymes; are immunosuppressive; and affect carbohydrate, protein, and fat metabolism to maintain metabolic homeostasis. Corticosteroids induce fetal lung surfactant.

Adverse Effects

Use every-other-day treatment to minimize adverse effects and to reduce growth retardation in patients on chronic corticosteroid therapy.

Acute: Acute adverse effects usually do not occur (except in cases of too-rapid withdrawal after prolonged use; see **Acute Adrenal Insufficiency** below).

With Prolonged Use: Adrenal suppression, including severe growth retardation; hypokalemic alkalosis; sodium retention; hypertension; hyperglycemia; increased susceptibility to infections; cataracts; myopathy; hypocalcemia; osteoporosis with bone fractures; nephrocalcinosis; nephrolithiasis; acute pancreatitis; and pseudotumor cerebri.

Acute Adrenal Insufficiency: Acute pituitary-adrenal insufficiency results from too-rapid withdrawal of corticosteroids after prolonged (>7–10 days) use.[3] Taper dose gradually if infant has received steroids for longer than 7–10 days.

Pituitary-adrenal integrity can be assessed by checking the morning cortisol levels before and 1 hour after cosyntropin (ACTH) administration (cosyntropin 0.063 mg IV/IM if baby weighs <1 kg or 0.13 mg IV/IM if weight is >1 kg). An adequate ACTH response is a doubling of the baseline cortisol value or an absolute one hour cortisol >18 mcg/dl. (See cosyntropin monograph.)

With Topical Use: Percutaneous absorption is much greater in neonates than in older infants, children, and adults. Use the lowest concentration of topical hydrocortisone (0.5 percent) and only for limited periods of time, especially in the warm, moist diaper area. Particularly with a plastic covering, a diaper behaves like an occlusive dressing and markedly enhances systemic absorption. Observe infants on prolonged topical steroids for signs of adrenal suppression and other adverse effects listed above. Avoid use of high-potency topical steroids; use only the low-potency hydrocortisone.

PHARMACOKINETICS/PHARMACODYNAMICS

Absorption: Oral absorption is about 50 percent.

Onset of Action: 4–6 hours with IV use. For planned extubation, begin corticosteroid therapy 12–24 hours prior to extubation.

Metabolism: Metabolized in the liver.

Biologic Half-life: 8–12 hours.

NURSING IMPLICATIONS

Monitor blood pressure, serum electrolytes, and fluid status (I & O).

Monitor for signs and symptoms of infection.

Monitor growth parameters such as head circumference, length, and weight weekly and plot on growth curve.

Monitor for hyperglycemia after dose and glucose spillage in the urine.

COMMENTS

Sodium Content: Hydrocortisone sodium succinate contains 2 mEq sodium/gm of drug.[6]

Relative potencies of various corticosteroids are given in Table 1-18, page 182.

REFERENCES

1. Benitz WE, and Tatro DS. 1995. *The Pediatric Drug Handbook,* 3rd ed. St. Louis: Mosby-Year Book, 429–433.

2. Taketomo CK, Hodding JH, and Kraus DM. 1993. *Pediatric Dosage Handbook,* 2nd ed. Hudson, Ohio: Lexi-Comp, 349–351.

3. Roberts RJ. 1984. *Drug Therapy in Infants: Pharmacologic Principles and Clinical Experience.* Philadelphia: WB Saunders, 296–299.

4. Gomella TL, Cunningham MD, and Eyal FG. 1994. *Neonatology: Management, Procedures, On-Call Problems, Diseases and Drugs,* 3rd ed. Norwalk, Connecticut: Appleton & Lange, 217–220.

5. Liapi C, and Chrousos GP. 1992. Glucocorticoids. In *Pediatric Pharmacology,* 2nd ed., Yaffe SJ, and Aranda JV, eds. Philadelphia: WB Saunders, 466–475.

6. Trissel LA. 1994. *Handbook on Injectable Drugs,* 8th ed. Bethesda, Maryland: American Society of Hospital Pharmacists, 545–558.

7. Avery GB, et al. 1985. Controlled trial of dexamethasone in respirator-dependent infants with bronchopulmonary dysplasia. *Pediatrics* 75(1): 106–111.

8. Young MC, and Hughes IA. 1990. Response to treatment of congenital adrenal hyperplasia in infancy. *Archives of Disease in Childhood* 65(4): 441–444.

9. Helbock HJ, Insoft RM, and Conte FA. 1993. Glucocorticoid-responsive hypotension in extremely low birth weight newborns. *Pediatrics* 92(5): 715–717.

10. Sandrini R, Jospe N, and Migeon CJ. 1993. Temporal and individual variations in the dose of glucocorticoid used for the treatment of salt-losing congenital virilizing adrenal hyperplasia due to 21-hydroxylase deficiency. *Acta Paediatrica* 388(supplement): S56–S61.

TABLE OF CONTENTS

IBUPROFEN (ADVIL, MOTRIN)
(eye-byoo-PROE-fen)

ANALGESIC:
ANTIPYRETIC, ANALGESIC

DOSE

Analgesic: 4–10 mg/kg/dose every 6–8 hours. *Maximum:* 40 mg/kg/day.

Antipyretic:

- *Temperature <102.5°F (39.2°C):* 5 mg/kg/dose.
- *Temperature ≥102.5°F (39.2°C):* 10 mg/kg/dose.
- *Maximum:* 40 mg/kg/day in divided doses given every 4–8 hours.

The manufacturers state that neither the safety nor the efficacy of ibuprofen has been established in infants younger than 6 months of age; however, some clinicians are giving this drug to younger infants—for example, to 2-month-old term infants with their first immunizations, to reduce fever and discomfort.

ADMINISTRATION

Supplied as: Suspension: 100 mg/5 ml (= 20 mg/ml). Drops: 40 mg/ml.

PO: Give with feedings to reduce GI upset and risk of GI bleeding.

Shake well before use.

CAUTIONS/CONTRAINDICATIONS

Cautions:

- Use caution when administering to infants receiving anticoagulants or to those with decreased hepatic or renal function.
- The antipyretic, analgesic, and anti-inflammatory actions of ibuprofen may mask symptoms of or worsening of infections.
- Use with caution postoperatively.[1]

Contraindications:

- Hypersensitivity to ibuprofen or aspirin.
- Active GI bleeding.
- Do not use in patients with a ductal-dependent lesion because ibuprofen may close the ductus arteriosus. For example, an infant receiving alprostadil (PGE) to maintain ductal patency should not receive ibuprofen.

USE

A nonsteroidal anti-inflammatory drug agent (NSAID), a non-narcotic analgesic, and an antipyretic. Can be considered for mild to moderate pain, such as from fractured ribs from nutritional osteopenia (rickets of prematurity) or fractured clavicle.

Used perioperatively, can decrease or eliminate the need for opiates postoperatively for mild to moderate pain, thus eliminating or reducing opiate-induced side effects (sedation, respiratory depression, emesis, urinary retention, constipation). NSAIDs may enhance the quality of analgesia by combining an analgesic having central effects (narcotic analgesics such as morphine) with an analgesic having peripheral effects (ibuprofen). However, there are concerns regarding impaired hemostasis. Romsing and Walther-Larsen's review of the literature confirms that hemorrhagic events occur in the postoperative period in patients who have received NSAIDs, but it cannot be said for certain that the bleeding is caused by the NSAIDs. The authors recommend caution in using NSAIDs in surgical procedures that involve considerable dissection of tissues or where reduction in hemostatic function is a risk—for example, in patients with a pre-existing coagulation defect or in those whose outcome would be adversely affected by increased bleeding.[1]

Comparison of Non-opioid Analgesics/Antipyretics:

- The antipyretic effect of ibuprofen is at least as effective as that of aspirin and acetaminophen.[2] The incidence of severe adverse reactions to ibuprofen appears to be less than that to aspirin. *(Note: Aspirin is discussed here for comparison purposes only; it is not recommended for antipyretic or analgesic use in infants.)*

- According to a study by Lesko and Mitchell, the safety profiles of acetaminophen and ibuprofen appear to be similar. (See Table 1-2: Comparison of Acetaminophen, Ibuprofen, and Aspirin Given at Normal Doses, page 4.) Lesko and Mitchell compared short-term acetaminophen and ibuprofen on their incidence of serious adverse effects among 27,065 febrile children younger than 2 years of age in a practitioner-based, randomized clinical trial. There were no hospital admissions for acute renal failure or anaphylaxis. However, 3 children in the ibuprofen group were admitted for acute GI bleeding. The risk of hospitalization for GI bleeding from ibuprofen was 17 per 100,000. This was not significantly greater than the risk among children in the acetaminophen group. The authors concluded that the risk of severe adverse effects among children less than 2 years old was small and did not vary by choice of medication.[3]

Closure of Ductus Arteriosus (Investigational Use): Van Overmeire and colleagues found that intravenous ibuprofen (www.FDA.Gov/orphan) (starting on day 3 of life, 10 mg/kg IV, followed at 24-hour intervals by two doses of 5 mg/kg IV each) therapy is as efficacious as indomethacin for treatment of patent ductus arteriosus in preterm infants with RDS and is significantly less likely to induce ologuria.[4] More study is needed before ibuprofen can be used routinely in place of indomethacin for PDA in preterm infants.

Patel and colleagues found that ibuprofen, unlike indomethacin, has no adverse effects on cerebral hemodynamics.[5] In another study, ibuprofen did not significantly reduce mesenteric and renal blood flow velocity when compared with indomethacin.[6] Both indomethacin and ibuprofen inhibit cyclooxygenase I (COX I) and cyclooxygenase II (COX II). Ibuprofen is a less potent inhibitor of COX I and possibly for that and other reasons has less effect on cerebral, mesenteric, and renal blood flow.

In a study by De Carolis and colleagues using ibuprofen prophylactically, no patent
ductus arteriosus was demonstrated at 72 hours of life in 20 of 23 infants given
prophylactic IV ibuprofen 10 mg/kg, followed by 5 mg/kg after 24 hours and 48
hours. Ibuprofen was not associated with any significant adverse effects except
for food intolerance in this study.[7] Dani and colleagues also found that prophylactic treatment with ibuprofen reduced PDA occurrence at 3 days of life compared with rescue treatment, but both rescue and prophylaxis were effective in
closing the ductus without significant adverse effects.[8]

MECHANISM OF ACTION

Ibuprofen is an NSAID. It has pharmacologic actions similar to other NSAIDs,
such as aspirin and indomethacin. Its anti-inflammatory effect may result from
its inhibition of prostaglandin synthesis. Its antipyretic effect probably results
from its action on the hypothalamus, increasing heat dissipation by vasodilation
and increased peripheral blood flow.

Ibuprofen is a peripherally acting, not a centrally acting, analgesic.

Ibuprofen inhibits platelet aggregation and prolongs bleeding time, but does not
affect prothrombin time or whole-blood clotting time.[9]

The renal toxicity of NSAIDs (seen in decreased renal perfusion, sodium and fluid
retention, and decreased renal function) may be caused by their inhibition of
renal prostaglandins, which are directly involved in the maintenance of renal
hemodynamics and sodium and fluid balance.[10]

ADVERSE EFFECTS

Usually well tolerated; most adverse effects occur with chronic use.

Cardiovascular: Fluid retention and peripheral edema; congestive heart failure;
increased blood pressure.

CNS: Drowsiness.

Dermatologic: Rarely, nonspecific dermatitis, pruritus, and urticaria.

GI: Nausea, vomiting, abdominal pain, gastritis, GI bleeding, GI perforation.

Hematologic: Neutropenia, anemia, inhibition of platelet aggregation, prolongation of bleeding time, thrombocytopenia.

Hepatic: Elevated liver function tests, especially serum ALT (SGPT).

Renal: Acute renal failure (rare). Patients at greatest risk of renal decompensation
with ibuprofen include those with renal dysfunction, heart failure, or hepatic
dysfunction; those with fluid depletion, such as patients on diuretics; and those
receiving nephrotoxic drugs concomitantly. With short-term use, the risk of
increased BUN and creatinine is small and not significantly greater than with
acetaminophen.[11]

Other: Hypersensitivity reactions, anaphylaxis, bronchospasm.

Overdose: May cause nystagmus, hypotension, apnea, acute renal failure, and
coma. A 21-month-old child developed acute renal failure and tonic clonic
seizures with significant hypocalcemia and hypomagnesemia after ingestion of

8 gm of ibuprofen. Al-Harbi and colleagues suggest that, although the mechanism is unclear, the electrolyte imbalance was probably aggravated by the use of sodium polystyrene sulfonate and furosemide as part of the overdose management.[12]

PHARMACOKINETICS/PHARMACODYNAMICS

Absorption: Well absorbed from GI tract.

Onset of Antipyretic Effect: About 70 minutes in infants 1 year of age and younger. The degree of effect on temperature reduction appears to increase until at least 2 hours after administration.

Peak Effect: 2–4 hours; peak serum concentrations are at 1 hour after a dose of the suspension.

Duration of Action: 6–8 hours. Ibuprofen has a longer duration of action than does aspirin (4 hours) or acetaminophen (4 hours).

Metabolism: The major metabolites are carboxylated-hydroxylated compounds. Because of high (99 percent) protein binding, ibuprofen may compete with other drugs for protein binding sites.

Half-life: 0.9–2.3 hours.

Elimination: Excreted in the urine as inactive metabolites or their conjugates; some biliary excretion.

NURSING IMPLICATIONS

Monitoring:

- Temperature, if treating fever.
- For signs of pain relief, if treating pain. (See Table 1-38: Neonatal Pain Relief/Sedation Assessment Scale, page 413.)
- BUN, creatinine, and serum potassium periodically, especially with hepatic or renal dysfunction; in patients being given diuretics concurrently; or with signs of renal toxicity, such as increased blood pressure, fluid retention, or rapid weight gain.
- Periodic hemoglobin/hematocrit; occult blood loss in the stool with prolonged therapy.
- Liver function tests (AST [SGOT]; ALT [SGPT]) if signs and symptoms of hepatotoxicity occur.
- Periodic ophthalmologic exam for patients on long-term treatment for juvenile rheumatoid arthritis (JRA).

If ibuprofen is prescribed for infants outside the hospital, advise parents of the correct dose for the infant's weight; which concentration to use; and to call a health care practitioner if there is no improvement or the condition worsens in 24 hours, if they must give ibuprofen for longer than 3 days, or if inadvertent overdose occurs.

Sponging with tepid water should be considered along with antipyretic medication.

COMMENTS

Interactions:

- Coadministration of NSAIDs and digoxin may increase serum digoxin concentrations.

- NSAIDs may increase serum phenytoin levels.

- NSAIDs may decrease the effects of loop diuretics such as furosemide.

- Coadministration of other GI irritants, such as oral potassium, may increase adverse GI effects.

- Coadministration of NSAIDs and anticoagulants (e.g., warfarin) or thrombolytic agents (e.g., urokinase, alteplase) may cause bleeding. Coadminister with caution and monitor carefully.

- Concurrent administration of aspirin or of another NSAID increases the risk of adverse GI effects and is probably not desirable.

- Concurrent ibuprofen and aminoglycoside therapy has caused transient renal failure in four children, two of whom were twin 23-month-old brothers hospitalized simultaneously for exacerbations of chronic lung disease. In one twin, this drug combination caused vomiting, lethargy, generalized edema, oliguria, and a rise in serum creatinine from 0.2 to 5.2 mg/dl 16 days after admission. He required peritoneal dialysis for 8 days before his condition returned to normal. The other twin had a much milder course, with a transient asymptomatic increase in serum creatinine from 0.6 to 1.5 mg/dl.[13]

REFERENCES

1. Romsing J, and Walther-Larsen S. 1997. Peri-operative use of nonsteroidal drugs in children: Analgesic efficacy and bleeding. *Anaesthesia* 52(7): 673–683.

2. Walson PD, et al. 1989. Ibuprofen, acetaminophen and placebo treatment of febrile children. *Clinical Pharmacology and Therapeutics* 46(1): 9–17.

3. Lesko SM, and Mitchell AA. 1999. The safety of acetaminophen and ibuprofen among children younger than 2 years old. *Pediatrics* 104(4): e39.

4. Van Overmeir B, et al. 2000. A comparison of ibuprofen and indomethacin for closure of patent ductus arteriosus. *New England Journal of Medicine* 343(10): 674–681.

5. Patel J, et al. 2000. Randomized double-blind controlled trial comparing the effects of ibuprofen with indomethacin on cerebral hemodynamics in preterm infants with patent ductus arteriosus. *Pediatric Research* 47(1): 36–42.

6. Pezzati M, et al. 1999. Effects of indomethacin and ibuprofen on mesenteric and renal blood flow in preterm infants with patent ductus arteriosus. *Journal of Pediatrics* 135(6): 733–738.

7. De Carolis MP, et al. 2000. Prophylactic ibuprofen therapy of patent ductus arteriosus in preterm infants. *European Journal of Pediatrics* 159(5): 364–368.

8. Dani C, et al. 2000. Prophylaxis of patent ductus arteriosus with ibuprofen in preterm infants. *Acta Paediatrica* 89(11): 1369–1374.

9. McEvoy GK. 1994. *AHFS Drug Information.* Bethesda, Maryland: American Society of Hospital Pharmacists, 1233–1236.

10. United States Pharmacopeial Convention/USP DI. 1996. *Drug Information for the Health Care Professional,* 16th ed. Rockville, Maryland: United States Pharmacopeial Convention, 386–434.

11. Lesko SM, and Mitchell AA. 1997. Renal function after short-term ibuprofen use in infants and children. *Pediatrics* 100(6): 954–957.

12. Al-Harbi NN, Domrongkitchaiporn S, and Lirenman DS. 1997. Hypocalcemia and hypomagnesemia after ibuprofen overdose. *Annals of Pharmacotherapy* 31(4): 432–434.

13. Kovesi TA, Swartz R, and MacDonald N. 1998. Transient renal failure due to simultaneous ibuprofen and aminoglycoside therapy in children with cystic fibrosis (letter). *New England Journal of Medicine* 338(1): 65–66.

IMIPENEM-CILASTATIN (PRIMAXIN)
(i-mi-PEN-em—sye-la-STAT-in)

**ANTI-INFECTIVE:
ANTIBIOTIC**

DOSE

<1.2 kg: 20 mg/kg/dose given every 18–24 hours.* Continue this dose for first 4 weeks of life.

1.2–2 kg:
- 0–7 days: 20 mg/kg/dose given every 12 hours
- >7 days: 20 mg/kg/dose given every 12 hours

>2 kg:
- 0–7 days: 20 mg/kg/dose given every 12 hours
- >7 days: 20 mg/kg/dose given every 8 hours[1,2]

Reduce dose in renal dysfunction:
- *Moderate (creatinine clearance 21–30 ml/minute/1.73 m²):* 20 mg/kg/dose given at the next longer dosing interval than listed above for age and weight (i.e., if every 12 hours above, give every 18 hours;* if every 8 hours above, give every 12 hours).
- *Severe (creatinine clearance 6–20 ml/minute/1.73 m²):* 10 mg/kg/dose given at two interval increments greater than listed above for weight and age (i.e., if every 12 hours above, give every 24 hours; if every 8 hours above, give every 18 hours*).
- If creatinine clearance is 0–5 ml/minute/1.73 m², use imipenem-cilastatin only if dialysis is instituted within 48 hours.[3]

ADMINISTRATION

IV (Use Primaxin IV):
- *Rate:* May infuse over 30–60 minutes by retrograde or syringe pump.
- *Concentration:* Maximum: 5 mg/ml.

IM (Use Primaxin IM):
- The IM formulation is not for IV use.
- The IM route is painful; use only if IV access is unavailable. Discomfort can be minimized by using lidocaine (without epinephrine), rather than sterile water or normal saline, as a diluent. Use lidocaine 0.5 percent, rather than the 1 percent recommended by the manufacturer because the 0.5 percent reduces the risk of a toxic amount of lidocaine being given. The 1 percent is intended for use in adults. If the infant were to receive lidocaine by another route (e.g., for a procedure) excessive doses could result because the dose of lidocaine given with IM imipenem is close to the infant's therapeutic dose. Avoid exceeding a

---

* See Appendix B: Every-18-Hour Medication Worksheet.

dose of 4 mg/kg of lidocaine in the volume of injection given (lidocaine 0.5 percent contains 5 mg/ml of lidocaine).

Compatible with: Saline or dextrose solutions.

Use

A very broad spectrum bactericidal antibiotic active against most Gram-positive and Gram-negative aerobic and anaerobic bacteria, including *Bacteroides fragilis.*

Effective against streptococci, *Escherichia coli*, Enterobacter, *Haemophilus influenzae*, Serratia species, *Pseudomonas aeruginosa*, *Listeria monocytogenes*, *Staphylococcus aureus*, and *Staphylococcus epidermidis*, including penicillinase-producing strains (methicillin-resistant staphylococci are resistant) and enterococci.[4]

Has a high degree of stability in the presence of β-lactamases.

Not active against Chlamydia, Mycoplasma, fungi, and viruses.

Overturf has stated that imipenem-cilastatin should be reserved for the most serious infections unresponsive to better established and cheaper therapeutic agents.[5] It may be useful in certain cases to provide a simpler (i.e., monotherapy) or less toxic alternative for treatment of the occasional complex, mixed infection.

Mechanism of Action

Imipenem-cilastatin inhibits mucopeptide synthesis in the bacterial cell wall. Compared with penicillins and cephalosporins, it has increased antibacterial activity and stability against hydrolysis by most β-lactamases. Imipenem is a carbapenem antibiotic in fixed combination with cilastatin. Cilastatin is an inhibitor of dehydropeptidase I (DHP I), an enzyme present in the proximal renal tubular cells that inactivates imipenem by hydrolyzing the β-lactam ring. Inhibition of DHP I increases urinary imipenem concentrations.[3]

Adverse Effects

Ahonkhai and colleagues reported the following adverse effects from nine centers in 178 infants and children 26 days to 18 years of age: diarrhea alone or with vomiting (5.1 percent); irritation of IV infusion site (3.3 percent); rash (2.2 percent); changes in laboratory tests: thrombocytosis (8.9 percent), elevations in aspartate aminotransferase (7.9 percent) and alanine aminotransferase (5.6 percent), and eosinophilia (8.4 percent). They concluded that the adverse effects were generally mild and reversible.[6]

Freij and colleagues reported that the 30 newborn infants in their study tolerated the drug well without any apparent clinical or laboratory adverse effects.[2]

CNS: Wong and associates reported that 33 percent of infants and children with meningitis treated with imipenem-cilastatin developed seizures after antibiotic therapy was administered. They concluded that the usefulness of this drug for the treatment of bacterial meningitis in pediatrics may be limited by a possible increased incidence of drug-related seizure activity. Patients with impaired renal function and/or underlying CNS abnormalities, such as a previous history of seizures, may be predisposed to development of seizures with this drug.[7]

Pharmacokinetics/Pharmacodynamics

Volume of Distribution: Larger in infants <4 days postnatal age than in older infants. The CSF:serum concentration percentage ratio was 4–10 percent.[8]

Half-life: The half-life of imipenem is 2.1 hours, and that of cilastatin is 3.9–6.3 hours.[2] Because the half-life of cilastatin is 2–3 times that of imipenem and because dosing must be based on the active imipenem component, cilastatin may accumulate in neonates.[2,8–10]

Nursing Implications

Monitor for seizure activity.

Monitor blood pressure.

Inspect IV site for signs of irritation.

Comments

Sodium Content: 3.2 mEq sodium/gm.

References

1. Nelson JD. 1996. *1996–1997 Pocketbook of Pediatric Antimicrobial Therapy*, 12th ed. Baltimore: Lippincott Williams & Wilkins, 16–17.

2. Freij BJ, et al. 1985. Pharmacokinetics of imipenem-cilastatin in neonates. *Antimicrobial Agents and Chemotherapy* 27(4): 431–435.

3. McEvoy GK. 1994. *AHFS Drug Information*. Bethesda, Maryland: American Society of Hospital Pharmacists, 182–190.

4. Neu HC, and Labthavikul P. 1982. Comparative *in vitro* activity of N-formimidoyl thienamycin against Gram-positive and Gram-negative aerobic and anaerobic species and its beta-lactamase stability. *Antimicrobial Agents and Chemotherapy* 21(1): 180–187.

5. Overturf GD. 1989. Use of imipenem-cilastatin in pediatrics. *Pediatric Infectious Diseases Journal* 8(11): 792–794.

6. Ahonkhai VI, et al. 1989. Imipenem-cilastatin in pediatric patients: An overview of safety and efficacy in studies conducted in the United States. *Pediatric Infectious Diseases Journal* 8(11): 740–744.

7. Wong VK, et al. 1991. Imipenem/cilastatin treatment of bacterial meningitis in children. *Pediatric Infectious Diseases Journal* 10(2): 122–125.

8. Gruber WC, et al. 1985. Single-dose pharmacokinetics of imipenem-cilastatin in neonates. *Antimicrobial Agents and Chemotherapy* 27(4): 511–514.

9. Begue PC, et al. 1987. Pharmacokinetic and clinical evaluation of imipenem/cilastatin in children and neonates. *Scandinavian Journal of Infectious Disease Supplementum* 52: 40–45.

10. Paap CM, and Nahata MC. 1990. Clinical pharmacokinetics of antibacterial drugs in neonates. *Clinical Pharmacokinetics* 19(4): 280–318.

IMMUNE GLOBULIN INTRAVENOUS

(i-MUNE GLOB-yoo-lin in-tra-VE-nas)

(SANDOGLOBULIN)

BIOLOGIC:
IMMUNE SERUM

Synonyms: gamma globulin, IGIV, IVIG

DOSE

Neonatal Sepsis: 500–800 mg/kg/dose as a single daily dose for 2 days[1]

> *(= 16.7–26.7 ml/kg/dose of 3 percent [= 30 mg/ml] concentration or*
> *8.3–13.3 ml/kg/dose of 6 percent [= 60 mg/ml] concentration).*

Idiopathic Thrombocytopenic Purpura (ITP): 400 mg/kg/dose for 2–5 consecutive days is one regimen for treating ITP.[2]

ADMINISTRATION

Supplied as: A single-dose vial containing no preservative.

IV—*Rate:* Infuse IV over 3 hours via syringe pump (preferred). One study reported safe infusion in neonates at a rate of 0.08–0.1 ml/kg/minute (4.8–6 ml/kg/hour).

IV—*Concentration:* Use the 1 gm vial. For a 3 percent (30 mg/ml) concentration, use *all* of the diluent using the double-ended transfer needle; to prepare a 6 percent (60 mg/ml) concentration, use only half of the diluent (16.5 ml). Use of the 6 percent concentration is preferred in neonates because of their limited fluid requirements.[3]

IV—*Maximum Concentration:* 12 percent (not for use in peripheral lines).

Compatibility: Do not mix with other drugs or IV solutions, except dextrose. The manufacturer states that IVIG may be administered by Y-site injection with parenteral nutrition; however, the resultant osmolality is very high and may not be appropriate for peripheral veins.[3]

CAUTIONS/CONTRAINDICATIONS

Acute renal failure may occur, particularly patients with compromised renal function. IGIV preparations containing sucrose (Sandoglobulin, Panglobulin, Gammar-P IV) may present a greater risk. Patients at increased risk for developing acute renal failure include those with pre-existing renal insufficiency, volume depletion, sepsis, concomitant administration of nephrotoxic drugs, and others.

Renal function, including urine output, blood urea nitrogen (BUN), and serum creatinine, should be assessed prior to infusion of IGIV, particularly in patients with increased risk for developing acute renal failure. Assess again at appropriate intervals.

Do not exceed recommended dose. Reduction in dose, concentration and/or rate of infusion in patients at risk for acute renal failure has been proposed to reduce the risk of this event. Also, assuring that the infant is not volume depleted prior to IGIV infusion may be beneficial.

The maximum recommended rate of infusion for sucrose-containing products is 2 mg immune globulin/kg/minute for Sandoglobulin and Panglobulin; 1 mg immune globulin/kg/minute for Gammar-P IV. If renal dysfunction develops, consider discontinuing IGIV.[4,5]

USE

Used in severe infections in newborn infants to provide immediate blood levels of IgG.

Trials are still ongoing to determine if there is efficacy for routine use and to determine the optimal dose.[6–8] There is no consensus as yet on the efficacy of prophylactic use to reduce the incidence of nosocomial infections in neonates.

MECHANISM OF ACTION

IVIG provides passive immunity by increasing the infant's antibody titer and antigen-antibody reaction potential. IgG antibodies help to prevent or modify certain infections in susceptible individuals.[2] Most placental transfer of IgG occurs after approximately 32 weeks gestation, and very preterm infants are deficient in total IgG and specific antibodies. Further, neonates become functionally hypogammaglobulinemic compared with adults as a result of catabolism of transplacentally acquired maternal IgG.

IVIG has improved complement activation and chemotaxis by neonatal sera and hastened resolution of neutropenia in animals with Group B Streptococcus and neonates with sepsis.[1,7,9]

ADVERSE EFFECTS

Acute renal failure may occur (see **CAUTIONS/CONTRAINDICATIONS** above).[4,5]

Usually well tolerated in neonates. If hypotension, sweating, fever, and flushing occur, slow or stop the infusion for 15–30 minutes, then resume. Anaphylaxis and hypotension are more frequent in children with IgA immunodeficiency who have been sensitized to certain immunoglobulin components such as IgA as a result of multiple immunoglobulin infusions. Monitor blood pressure and have epinephrine ready.

Risk of transmission of viral infections (including hepatitis B and HIV) in IVIG is extremely small because of the Cohn ethanol method of fractionating human plasma, which eliminates the infectivity of viruses. A few cases of non-A non-B hepatitis have been reported, however.

PHARMACOKINETICS/PHARMACODYNAMICS

Increase in antibodies is transient; dose may need to be repeated. Terminal elimination half-life is 30.7 days. IgG is significantly elevated for 14 days after a 500 mg/kg infusion.[6]

NURSING IMPLICATIONS

Monitor for potential anaphylaxis symptoms, including hypotension.

Monitor for response to therapy, such as improved clinical picture.

Comments

IVIG is obtained from the purified, standardized, pooled human plasma of several hundred to several thousand donors. There may be variation in antibody content and levels between lots and between manufacturers.

References

1. Baker CJ, and Edwards MS. 1995. Group B streptococcal infections. In *Infectious Diseases of the Fetus and Newborn Infant,* 4th ed., Remington JS, and Klein JO, eds. Philadelphia: WB Saunders, 980–1054.

2. McEvoy GK. 1994. *AHFS Drug Information.* Bethesda, Maryland: American Society of Hospital Pharmacists, 2154–2161.

3. Manufacturer's product literature.

4. Centers for Disease Control. 1999. Renal insufficiency and failure associated with immune globulin intravenous therapy—United States, 1985–1998. *MMWR* 48(24): 518–521.

5. United States Pharmacopeial Convention/USP DI. 2000. *Drug Information for the Health Care Professional,* 20th ed. Rockville, Maryland: United States Pharmacopeial Convention, 1759–1765.

6. Weisman LE, et al. 1986. Pharmacokinetics of intravenous immunoglobulin (Sandoglobulin) in neonates. *Pediatric Infectious Disease* 5(3 supplement): S185–S188.

7. Whitelaw A. 1990. Treatment of sepsis with IgG in very low birthweight infants. *Archives of Disease in Childhood* 65(4 spec. no.): 347–348.

8. Hill HR, et al. 1986. Intravenous IgG in combination with other modalities in the treatment of neonatal infection. *Pediatric Infectious Disease* 5(3 supplement): S180–S184.

9. Christensen RD, et al. 1991. Effect on neutrophil kinetics and serum opsonic capacity of intravenous administration of immune globulin to neonates with clinical signs of early-onset sepsis. *Journal of Pediatrics* 118(4 part 1): 606–614.

INAMRINONE (INOCOR)
(eye-NAM-ri-nohn)

CARDIOVASCULAR: INOTROPIC AGENT

DOSE

Loading: 3–4.5 mg/kg in divided doses IV over 5 or more minutes.[1]

Maintenance:

- *Neonates:* 3–5 mcg/kg/minute
- *Infants >4 weeks of age:* 10 mcg/kg/minute

ADMINISTRATION

Loading Dose: Infuse by IV push over at least 3 minutes.

Maintenance Dose: Continuous IV infusion by syringe pump (see **DOSE** above).

Concentration: May give undiluted (5 mg/ml) or diluted to 1–3 mg/ml with saline or 0.45 percent saline.

Compatibility: See Appendix E: Y-Site Compatibility of Common NICU Drugs.

CAUTIONS/CONTRAINDICATIONS

Name Change: The drug *inamrinone* was formerly called *amrinone*. The name was changed to inamrinone because the former name was easy to confuse with amiodarone, another cardiac drug. During the changeover and for some time thereafter, stock of drug labeled with the old name may still be on pharmacy shelves. Use caution when dispensing or administering inamrinone.

USE

A positive inotropic agent with vasodilator activity. Reduces afterload and preload by direct relaxant effect on smooth muscle.

Indicated for short-term management of patients with CHF who are not controlled by diuretics and digoxin. Also used for pulmonary hypertension and postoperative low cardiac output.[2,3]

MECHANISM OF ACTION

This bipyridine derivative acts by inhibiting phosphodiesterase subfraction III and increasing c-AMP in myocytes and peripheral vasculature. It is thought to increase the sensitivity of contractile proteins in the heart to calcium, resulting in an increased inward flux of calcium and enhanced contractility. It increases heart rate and decreases pulmonary and systemic vascular resistance.

ADVERSE EFFECTS

Thrombocytopenia—reversible (2.4 percent).

Arrhythmias (3 percent); may be related to rate of infusion.

Hypotension (1.3 percent).

Hepatotoxicity (0.2 percent).

GI effects (nausea, vomiting, abdominal pain).

Pharmacokinetics/Pharmacodynamics

Onset of Action: 2–5 minutes after administration; duration is 30 minutes to 2 hours, depending on the dose.

Metabolism: In the liver by conjugation.

Elimination: Primarily in the urine.

Nursing Implications

Perform continuous cardiac monitoring for tachycardia.

Continuously monitor blood pressure for hyper- or hypotension.

Strictly monitor I & O.

Monitor for improvement in heart function, such as improved urine output, stable blood pressure, and improved oxygenation.

Comments

Interactions: Inotropic effects are additive with digoxin.

References

1. United States Pharmacopeal Convention/USP DI. 2000. *Drug Information for the Health Care Professional,* 20th ed. Rockville, Maryland: United States Pharmacopeal Convention, 123–124.

2. Berner M, et al. 1990. Hemodynamic effects of amrinone in children after cardiac surgery. *Intensive Care Medicine* 16(2): 85–88.

3. Lawless S, et al. 1989. Amrinone in neonates and infants after cardiac surgery. *Critical Care Medicine* 17(8): 751–754.

INDOMETHACIN (INDOCIN IV)
(in-doe-METH-a-sin)

CARDIOVASCULAR: DUCTUS ARTERIOSUS

DOSE

A course of indomethacin is defined as three IV doses given at 12- to 24-hour intervals (Table 1-29). If anuria or marked oliguria (urine output <0.6 ml/kg/hour) is seen at the time of the second or third dose, no additional doses should be given until laboratory studies indicate that renal function has returned to normal.[1] Use 12-hour dosing interval if urine output is ≥1 ml/kg/hour after prior dose; use 24-hour interval if urine output is <1 ml/kg/hour.

If one 3-dose course is not effective, or if the ductus arteriosus reopens, a second course of 1–3 doses may be given as described above, each dose separated by a 12- to 24-hour interval.

If the infant remains unresponsive after two courses, surgery may be necessary to close the ductus arteriosus.

Prevention of Intraventricular Hemorrhage (IVH): Ment and associates reported that indomethacin significantly lowered the incidence and severity of IVH, particularly the severe form (Grade IV IVH), closed the patent ductus arteriosis, and was not associated with significant adverse drug events in very low birth weight neonates. Indomethacin 0.1 mg/kg IV was given at 6–12 postnatal hours and every 24 hours for two more doses.[2]

ADMINISTRATION

IV—Rate: Infuse over 30 minutes.[3–6]

Do not administer via the umbilical arterial catheter (UAC) because blood flow to the intestines may be compromised. Not for intra-arterial use.

Although the manufacturer recommends infusion over 5–10 seconds, rapid administration may cause significant decrease in mesenteric artery[7] and cerebral blood flow, which may contribute to development of NEC or cerebral ischemia. Hammerman and associates found that slow, continuous infusion at 11 mcg/kg/hour for 36 hours (= 396 mcg/kg) was effective in closing the ductus and minimized the potential adverse effects of reduction in cerebral blood flow velocity and increase in serum creatinine, compared with an equivalent dose of

TABLE 1-29 ◆ INDOMETHACIN DOSING BY AGE

| | Dose | | |
| | First | Second | Third |
Age at First Dose		(mg/kg/dose)	
<48 hours	0.2	0.1	0.1
2–7 days	0.2	0.2	0.2
>7 days	0.2	0.25	0.25

0.2 mg/kg, then 0.1 mg/kg, 0.1 mg/kg every 12 hours IV, by rapid 1-minute injection for 2 additional doses (= 400 mcg/kg).[8] Further study is needed, however, because this study had a small number of patients.

IV—*Concentration:* The 1 mg vial is usually diluted to 1 ml (1 mg/ml) with preservative-free normal saline or sterile water for injection. May be diluted to 2 ml (= 0.5 mg/ml). Indomethacin may precipitate if diluted further because it is not buffered and pH values below 6 may result in precipitation of the insoluble indomethacin free acid moiety.[1]

IV—*Compatibility:* See Appendix E: Y-Site Compatibility of Common NICU Drugs.

CAUTIONS/CONTRAINDICATIONS

The manufacturer cautions that the drug should not be given if the infant has proven or suspected untreated infection, bleeding (especially active intracranial hemorrhage or GI bleeding), thrombocytopenia, coagulation defects, NEC, or significant renal impairment.

Do not administer to congenital heart disease patients in whom patency of the ductus arteriosus is necessary for satisfactory pulmonary or systemic blood flow (e.g., pulmonary atresia, severe tetralogy of Fallot, severe coarctation of the aorta).

USE

Pharmacologic closure of the patent ductus arteriosus.[9] Used when usual medical management (e.g., fluid restriction, diuretics, respiratory support) is ineffective. Clear-cut evidence of a hemodynamically significant patent ductus may not be present (respiratory distress, continuous murmur, hyperactive precordium, cardiomegaly). Pulmonary plethora on chest x-ray is a more reliable sign of a left-to-right shunt.

Prevention of intraventricular hemorrhage.[2]

MECHANISM OF ACTION

Indomethacin is a potent inhibitor of prostaglandin synthesis. Although the exact mechanism that causes closure of the patent ductus arteriosus is not known, it is thought to be through inhibition of prostaglandin synthesis. The E-type prostaglandins (PGE_1) maintain patency of the ductus, and indomethacin causes its constriction. Indomethacin is effective in approximately 75–80 percent of patients.

ADVERSE EFFECTS

GI: GI distention, bleeding, and perforation.

Hematologic: Inhibition of platelet aggregation, with increased tendency to bleeding. Extension of intracranial hemorrhages has not been seen despite the effects on platelet aggregation.[10]

Renal: Reduced renal function (41 percent of infants): decreased urine output, elevations of BUN and creatinine, reduced GFR and creatinine clearance associated with hyponatremia and hyperkalemia, and a fall in renin activity.[11] These effects are transient in most infants.

Other: IV extravasation causes tissue irritation.

PHARMACOKINETICS/PHARMACODYNAMICS

Absorption: In neonates, <15 percent oral absorption.

Protein Binding: 99 percent (adults).

Metabolism: Clearance in preterm infants is 10–20 times slower than in adults. This results from reduced hepatic drug metabolism and conjugating enzyme activity.

Half-life: Varies inversely with postnatal age and weight. Infants <7 days: 20 hours; >7 days: 12 hours. Infants <1 kg: 21 hours; >1 kg: 15 hours.

Elimination: Renal and biliary excretion. Undergoes enterohepatic circulation.[1,12,13]

NURSING IMPLICATIONS

Monitor urine output, BUN, serum creatinine, and serum electrolytes prior to initiating therapy and throughout regimen. Withhold drug if BUN is >30 mg/dl, if serum creatinine is >1.8 mg/dl, or if infant is oliguric (≤1 ml/kg/hour). Strictly monitor I & O.

Withhold drug if there is abdominal distention or a change in the abdominal exam, and notify physician.

Withhold dose if infant is thrombocytopenic (platelets <50,000/mm^3) or there is a bleeding diathesis. Monitor CBC.

COMMENTS

Be sure an echocardiogram has been done and ductal-dependent congenital heart disease has been ruled out prior to the first dose. As a precaution, precalculate dosage of alprostadil in the event that it must be quickly administered after the first indomethacin dose.

There may be an apparent volume discrepancy among vials of Indocin IV; however, assay has confirmed the vials contain 1 mg, as labeled.[6]

Interactions:

- Drugs that rely on renal function for elimination may require dose reduction while the infant is treated with indomethacin. Serum amikacin and gentamicin peak and trough may be elevated, for example. Infants on digoxin should be monitored for arrhythmias and may require digoxin serum concentrations because of possible digoxin accumulation.

- Concomitant furosemide therapy may have a beneficial effect on the renal function of infants on indomethacin. Infants on both furosemide and indomethacin have been shown to have higher urine output, urinary excretion of sodium and chloride, and GFR than those who receive indomethacin alone, without altering the efficacy of indomethacin in closing the ductus arteriosus.[14] However, because indomethacin does not seem to cause permanent renal injury, use of furosemide in combination routinely is not needed.

- The diuretic effects of furosemide may be reduced when the patient is on indomethacin because the latter inhibits prostaglandin synthesis, which may result in fluid retention. Conversely, giving furosemide before indomethacin may cause the indomethacin to be ineffective because furosemide stimulates the renal synthesis of PGE_2 (thiazides do not).[15]

- Indomethacin may decrease the antihypertensive effects of hydralazine, thiazide diuretics, furosemide, or β-blocking agents such as propranolol.

REFERENCES

1. Manufacturer's product literature.

2. Ment LR, et al. 1994. Low-dose indomethacin and prevention of intraventricular hemorrhage: A multicenter randomized trial. *Pediatrics* 93(4): 543–550.

3. Colditz P, et al. 1989. Effect of infusion rate of indomethacin on cerebrovascular responses in preterm neonates. *Archives of Disease in Childhood* 64(1 spec. no.): 8–12.

4. Simko A, et al. 1994. Effects on cerebral blood flow velocities of slow and rapid infusion of indomethacin. *Journal of Perinatology* 14(1): 29–35.

5. Austin N, et al. 1992. Regional cerebral blood flow velocity changes after indomethacin infusion in premature infants. *Archives of Disease in Childhood* 67(7 spec. no.): 851–854.

6. Zenk KE, Barnes J, and Sarandis S. 1986. Apparent volume discrepancy among vials of Indocin I.V. (letter). *American Journal of Hospital Pharmacy* 43(4): 874–878.

7. Coombs RC, et al. 1990. Gut blood flow velocities in the newborn: Effects of patent ductus arteriosus and parenteral indomethacin. *Archives of Disease in Childhood* 65(10 spec. no.): 1067–1071.

8. Hammerman C, et al. 1995. Continuous versus multiple rapid infusions of indomethacin: Effects on cerebral blood flow velocity. *Pediatrics* 95(2): 244–248.

9. Halliday HL, Hirata T, and Brady JP. 1979. Indomethacin therapy for large patent ductus arteriosus in the very low-birth-weight infant: Results and complications. *Pediatrics* 64(2): 154–159.

10. Maher P, et al. 1985. Does indomethacin cause extension of intracranial hemorrhages: A preliminary study. *Pediatrics* 75(3): 497–500.

11. Seyberth H, et al. 1983. Effect of prolonged indomethacin therapy on renal function and selected vasoactive hormones in very-low-birth-weight infants with symptomatic patent ductus arteriosus. *Journal of Pediatrics* 103(6): 979–984.

12. Yaffe SJ, et al. 1980. The disposition of indomethacin in preterm babies. *Journal of Pediatrics* 97(6): 1001–1006.

13. Thalji AA, et al. 1980. Pharmacokinetics of intravenously administered indomethacin in premature infants. *Journal of Pediatrics* 97(6): 995–1000.

14. Yeh TF, et al. 1982. Furosemide prevents the renal side effects of indomethacin therapy in premature infants with patent ductus arteriosus. *Journal of Pediatrics* 101(3): 433–437.

15. Green TP, et al. 1983. Furosemide promotes patent ductus arteriosus in premature infants with the respiratory-distress syndrome. *New England Journal of Medicine* 308(13): 743–748.

INSULIN, REGULAR HUMAN
(IN-su-lin)
(HUMULIN R)

HORMONE: HYPOGLYCEMIC AGENT

Synonyms: regular insulin, crystalline insulin

DOSE

IV—*Push:* 0.05–0.1 unit/kg over 15–20 minutes (insulin administered subcutaneously is not well absorbed in preterm infants).

IV—*Continuous Infusion:* Initial dose: 0.04 unit/kg/hour.
Maximum: 0.1 unit/kg/hour.

- Change of the insulin infusion rate requires a doctor's order.
- ***Titration:*** If blood glucose is ≥180 mg/dl, increase insulin infusion in increments of 0.01 unit/kg/hour.
- If hypoglycemia occurs, stop the insulin infusion and administer $D_{10}W$ at 2 ml/kg (= 0.2 gm/kg).
- May resume insulin infusion at a lower rate when blood glucose normalizes.

Reduce dose in renal dysfunction.

For Hyperkalemia:

- Give dextrose and insulin to shift potassium into cells and lower serum potassium.
- Malone reported that a dextrose/insulin combination was more effective than Kayexalate in treating hyperkalemia in his study of preterm infants of 28 weeks gestation or less. Insulin, 0.05–0.1 units/kg/hour, was concomitantly infused with dextrose; then the dose was titrated to maintain the desired serum glucose concentration. The glucose load was approximately 5 mg/kg/minute. He measured serum potassium every 6 hours and discontinued therapy when concentrations were <6 mEq/liter. He monitored serum glucose by test strip every 20 minutes for the first hour, every 30 minutes for the second hour, and every 2–4 hours thereafter while the infant was receiving insulin.[1]
- If appropriate, discontinue blood products, foods, and medications that contain potassium (i.e., potassium supplements, potassium-sparing diuretics, potassium in IV fluids).
- Sodium bicarbonate (see monograph) used to correct acidosis facilitates a shift of potassium into cells.
- Furosemide (see monograph) can be used to increase urinary potassium excretion. Maintain high urine output with IV fluids as medical condition warrants.
- Sodium polystyrene sulfonate (Kayexalate) (see monograph) is used to bind potassium in the GI tract to remove potassium from the body.

- Calcium gluconate (see monograph) can be used to antagonize the cardio-toxic effects of potassium in patients whose ECGs show absent P waves or a broad QRS complex. Usually not indicated for patients on digoxin.
- Hemodialysis or peritoneal dialysis can lower serum potassium; this may be needed in patients with renal dysfunction.

In digitalized patients, use caution not to lower serum potassium too rapidly because it may induce digitalis toxicity.

Calculations and Ordering: The order should be written so that 0.04 unit/kg/hour is infused at 0.2 ml/hour. At that rate, a 20 ml volume is sufficient for a 24-hour supply of insulin. D_5W (preferred) or 1/2 NS may be used as a diluent, depending on the infant's status. The units of insulin to dilute in 20 ml can be calculated as in Figure 1-9.

ADMINISTRATION

Continuous IV Infusion: Use a neonatal syringe pump with high accuracy and infusion consistency.

- Infusion should be prepared by the pharmacy, if possible.
- *Guard against dilution errors:* **Avoid using the commercially available 100 unit/ml concentrations. Nurses should prepare doses using a special dilution of regular human insulin 1 unit/ml. This concentration can be prepared by the pharmacy using the special insulin diluent available from the manufacturer. Human insulin is preferred.**
- Use a two-syringe technique when diluting insulin to prevent overdose that can occur if insulin in syringe dead space is drawn into the actual delivery volume.
- Flush 10 ml or more of the insulin solution through and out of the tubing to saturate insulin binding sites. (Albumin can also be used to minimize insulin adsorption to tubing; however, this is not necessary and adds to the cost of treatment.)
- Insulin solution should be attached at a stopcock to the parenteral nutrition (PN) line.

Compatibility: See Appendix E: Y-Site Compatibility of Common NICU Drugs.

CAUTIONS/CONTRAINDICATIONS

Avoid interrupting the insulin infusion for lab sampling.

USE

To improve the body's ability to deliver calories and accelerate rate of weight gain in preterm infants who are glucose intolerant (i.e., serum glucose >180 mg/dl with caloric intake <120 kcal/kg/day).[2-4] Consider insulin infusion if blood glucose by bedside whole blood monitoring is ≥180 mg/dl (verified with laboratory) or if there is glycosuria.

Used with dextrose to treat hyperkalemia.

FIGURE 1-9 ◆ INSULIN CALCULATIONS AND ORDERING.

Calculation of units needed:

$$\frac{\text{units/kg/hour} \times \text{weight (kg)} \times \text{volume to prepare (ml)}}{\text{rate of infusion (ml/hour)}} = \begin{array}{l}\text{units of insulin to} \\ \text{dilute in 20 ml volume}\end{array}$$

Then, 0.02 unit/kg/hour = 0.1 ml/hour
  0.04 unit/kg/hour = 0.2 ml/hour
  0.06 unit/kg/hour = 0.3 ml/hour
  0.08 unit/kg/hour = 0.4 ml/hour
  0.1 unit/kg = 0.5 ml/hour

Example:

You need to order an insulin infusion for a 1.8 kg hyperglycemic infant. How many units of insulin should you order for a 20 ml volume of D$_5$W at a dose of 0.02 unit/kg/hour?

Step 1: Select the rate of infusion of 0.1 ml/hour that corresponds to the insulin dose of 0.02 unit/kg/hour from the list above.

Step 2: Calculate the number of units to dilute in 20 ml volume:

$$\frac{0.02 \text{ unit/kg/hour} \times 1.8 \text{ kg} \times 20 \text{ ml}}{0.1 \text{ ml/hour}} = 7.2 \text{ units of insulin for 20 ml volume}$$

Or, using the simplified version of the equation above, multiply 4 times the infant's weight to get the number of units for a 20 ml volume; then infuse it at the rate corresponding to the dose you want from the list above:

  $4 \times 1.8 \text{ kg} = 7.2 \text{ units per 20 ml}$

Step 3: Write the order as:

Regular human insulin 7.2 units in 20 ml D$_5$W to run at 0.1 ml/hour = 0.02 unit/kg/hour).
  Wt = 1.8 kg.

Step 4: Titrating the dose.

If you need to increase the insulin unit/kg/hour dose, select the new rate in ml/hour corresponding to the dose needed from the list above. The concentration in units of insulin per 20 ml remains the same.

Suggested format of physician order:

• Regular human insulin _____ units in 20 ml D$_5$W to run at 0.2 ml/hour (= 0.04 unit/kg/hour).
  Wt = _____ kg.

• Monitor blood glucose at bedside initially every 15 minutes, then every hour until stable, then every 4 hours.

• Double-check whole blood glucose at the bedside if <80 or >180 mg/dl, and call MD or NNP. Draw serum glucose and send to lab if glucose ≤60 mg/dl.

MECHANISM OF ACTION

Insulin is required for proper glucose utilization in normal metabolic processes. It is synthesized by the β-cells in the pancreatic islets. Regular insulin is rapid acting. Insulin is affected by the counterregulatory hormones, growth hormone, cortisol, glucagon, epinephrine, and somatostatin. Insulin is required for normal growth and development.

For treatment of hyperkalemia, insulin with glucose shifts potassium into the cells and lowers serum potassium levels.

ADVERSE EFFECTS

May cause severe hypoglycemia, hypokalemia.

Overdose may cause seizures and death from hypoglycemia.

PHARMACOKINETICS/PHARMACODYNAMICS

Onset of Action: 30–60 minutes.

Duration of Action: 5–7 hours. The onset of action and time of peak level of human insulin may be earlier than for beef or pork insulin.

Metabolism: Metabolized in the liver.

Elimination: Excreted in the kidney; therefore, reduce dose in renal dysfunction.

NURSING IMPLICATIONS

Monitor blood glucose at the bedside every 15 minutes after starting infusion until values are stable.

Avoid infusing in the line used for blood sampling (i.e., UVC/UAC). Infant may need a peripheral IV site.

Infuse solution through a port as close to the infant as possible. Avoid inadvertent boluses of insulin.

Prior to administration, flush 10 ml of solution through the tubing to reduce insulin adsorption to the plastic tubing.

Spell out "units." Do not use the abbreviation "U," which can be mistaken for "0" (e.g., 8 U might be mistaken for 80).

Have two RNs check calculations and preparation of insulin.

COMMENTS

Insulin should not be ordered as an additive in the PN solution because the PN solution would have to be discarded if hypoglycemia were to occur. Also, because insulin binds to plastic bags and tubing, the dose of insulin received might not be as accurate and predictable as when it is infused via syringe pump.

Interactions:

- Dobutamine, epinephrine, thiazide diuretics, and thyroid hormone decrease the hypoglycemic effects of insulin.
- β-blockers (e.g., propranolol) increase the hypoglycemic effects of insulin.

REFERENCES

1. Malone TA. 1991. Glucose and insulin versus cation-exchange resin for the treatment of hyperkalemia in very low birth weight infants. *Journal of Pediatrics* 118(1): 121–123.

2. Collins JW Jr, et al. 1991. A controlled trial of insulin infusion and parenteral nutrition in extremely low birth weight infants with glucose intolerance. *Journal of Pediatrics* 118(6): 921–927.

3. Kanarek KS, Santeiro ML, and Malone JI. 1991. Continuous infusion of insulin in hyperglycemic low-birth weight infants receiving parenteral nutrition with and without lipid emulsion. *Journal of Parenteral and Enteral Nutrition* 15(4): 417–420.

4. Binder ND, et al. 1989. Insulin infusion with parenteral nutrition in extremely low birth weight infants with hyperglycemia. *Journal of Pediatrics* 114(2): 273–280.

IPRATROPIUM (ATROVENT)
(I-pra-TROE-pee-um)

**RESPIRATORY:
BRONCHODILATOR**

DOSE

Metered Dose Inhaler (MDI): 2 puffs every 6 hours

Solution for Nebulization: 250 mcg every 8 hours

ADMINISTRATION

MDI: Each actuation delivers 18 mcg.

Solution for Nebulization: 0.5 mg (= 500 mcg)/2.5 ml unit dose.[1]

CAUTIONS/CONTRAINDICATIONS

Use with caution in narrow-angle glaucoma because an acute attack may be precipitated. Acute eye pain may occur.

Use with caution in bladder-neck obstruction because urinary retention may be precipitated.

Not for use as initial treatment for acute bronchospasm where a rapid response is required because ipratropium has a slower onset of action and less bronchodilation than other bronchodilators such as albuterol in acute attacks.

USE

Used to treat bronchospasm related to chronic lung disease.[2]

MECHANISM OF ACTION

Ipratropium is an anticholinergic drug similar in action to atropine (see monograph) that acts by antagonizing the actions of acetylcholine at parasympathetic effector cells, thereby inhibiting parasympathetic bronchoconstriction. Anticholinergic compounds probably act on the larger, more central airways. Ipratropium provides significant bronchodilator effect but is not as potent as albuterol (see monograph). There is some additive effect when β-agonists are used in combination with ipratropium.

ADVERSE EFFECTS

Overdose is not likely because ipratropium is not well absorbed systemically after aerosol or oral (MDI) administration.

Nervousness, dizziness, nausea, blurred vision, dry mouth, irritation from aerosol, cough, exacerbation of symptoms, palpitations, rash, and urinary difficulties and constipation may occur.

Rebound airway hyperresponsiveness may occur when drug is discontinued.

Has caused bronchoconstriction as a result of the benzalkonium chloride and edetic acid (EDTA) in the solution. Benzalkonium chloride can cause bronchoconstriction by releasing spasmogenic mediators from mast cells and EDTA by chelation of calcium ions.[3]

Pharmacokinetics/Pharmacodynamics

Onset of Action: Slow; effects may not be seen immediately.

Maximum Effect (Bronchodilation): 1–2 hours after the dose.

Duration of Action: 6–8 hours; duration is longer than that of β-agonists.

Tolerance (Tachyphylaxis): Does not occur because this drug is a receptor antagonist.

Nursing Implications

Monitor for increased bronchospasm, constipation.

May admix with albuterol in nebulizer.

Comments

Dose Titration: When respiratory status has improved, try *lengthening the interval between doses.* Taper to the lowest effective dose.

- If the infant is still in respiratory distress after a trial of one to three doses, *increase the dose* to the next larger dose and/or shorten the interval to the next shorter interval. Do not increase the dose if the infant is experiencing adverse effects from the existing dose.

Discontinuation of Treatment: If adverse effects occur or if the drug is no longer needed, discontinue it. If there has been no improvement in respiratory status as measured by pulmonary mechanics, change in respiratory support, or clinical status after three doses, discontinue the drug. As noted under **Adverse Effects,** rebound airway hyperresponsiveness may occur when the drug is discontinued.

Interactions: There is some additive effect when β-agonists are used in combination with ipratropium.

References

1. Manufacturer's product literature.

2. Brundage KL, et al. 1990. Bronchodilator response to ipratropium bromide in infants with bronchopulmonary dysplasia. *American Review of Respiratory Disease* 142(5): 1137–1142.

3. Beasley CRW, Rafferty P, and Holgate ST. 1987. Bronchoconstrictor properties of preservatives in ipratropium bromide (Atrovent) nebuliser solution. *British Medical Journal* 294(9): 1197–1198.

IRON DEXTRAN (INFeD, DexFerrum)
(EYE-ern DEKS-tran)

**NUTRITION:
IRON SUPPLEMENT**

DOSE

Test Dose:

- *IV:* Give as a test dose 10 mg elemental iron (Fe) or the first day's Fe dose, whichever is less. Infuse over 1 hour or longer.
- *IM:* Give as a test dose 10 mg Fe or the first day's Fe dose, whichever is less.
- *Monitoring during the Test Dose (IV or IM):* Monitor heart rate, blood pressure, respiration, and temperature every 15 minutes for the first hour. If no hypersensitivity reaction occurs, wait 1 hour and then give the remainder of the first day's dose.

Note: A test dose is not often used in neonates, although it is recommended in the product labeling.[1] The manufacturer recommends a test dose of 25 mg, which exceeds the appropriate infant dose above. Instead, use the 10 mg-or-less dose.[2]

Iron Deficiency Anemia (to Restore Hemoglobin and Replenish Iron Stores): Use the following formula to calculate the total deficit or required dose (in mg) of iron:[3]

$$Dose\ Fe\ (mg/kg) = [12\ (gm/dl) - Hgb\ (gm/dl)] \times 4.5$$

Divide the total dose into daily (or less frequent) increments usually not exceeding the following maximum daily doses:[1]

- *Infants weighing <5 kg:* 25 mg Fe.
- *Infants weighing 5–10 kg:* 50 mg Fe.

Provision of Daily Iron Requirement during Chronic, Long-term Parenteral Nutrition (PN): Friel and colleagues found that a total iron intake of 400 mcg/kg/day, half of it provided by IV iron (200–250 mcg Fe/kg/day IV by continuous infusion in the PN solution), was insufficient to maintain iron balance or to meet fetal accretion rates (1,000 mcg Fe/kg/day) in very low birth weight newborns receiving PN. Endogenous iron from blood transfusions did not provide an adequate supply of iron. Based on these study results, the researchers suggest an iron intake of 1,000 mcg Fe/kg/day IV for very low birth weight newborn infants on PN so intake equals fetal accretion rates.[4]

Prophylaxis for Iron Deficiency in Preterm Infants in Developing Countries: Heese and colleagues suggest administering 100 mg Fe one time IM between the ages of 6 and 8 weeks, reporting that this dose benefited the majority of infants in their trial. They comment that in developing countries, where iron deficiency is common and often severe, where diet and income are often inadequate, and where compliance with oral iron administration to the infant is poor even when iron is provided free, administration of iron dextran to preterm infants after 4 weeks of age may be of benefit for their future health.[5]

We suggest that daily dose be limited to the usual maximum, either 25 or 50 mg, depending on the infant's weight as shown above.

Infants on Erythropoietin/Epoetin Alfa and Parenteral Nutrition: Infants receiving erythropoietin/epoetin alfa have been given iron dextran admixed in the PN solution at a dose of 1 mg Fe/kg/day (or 3–5 mg Fe/kg/dose once a week).[6–8]

ADMINISTRATION

Supplied as: Injection: 50 mg Fe/ml.

IV is usually preferred over IM administration because of infants' (particularly preterm infants') small muscle mass and poor absorption from the muscle, to avoid staining of the skin, and to reduce pain and irritation at the injection site.

IV—Rate: Infuse over 1–6 hours. Or may be infused over 24 hours, as when added to the PN solution.

IV—Concentration: May inject undiluted or dilute with normal saline.
Note: Dilution with dextrose may increase local pain and cause phlebitis.

- Although the product labeling[1] does not recommend that iron dextran be added to PN, iron dextran is added to PN in current medical practice.[1,4,6–8]

- Mayhew and Quick state that a distinctive rust-colored precipitate occurred when INFeD brand iron dextran was added to PN containing low final concentrations of protein. PN solutions with final protein concentrations of 2 percent or greater were compatible with the addition of INFeD; solutions with 1.5 percent or less protein developed an iron precipitate within 12–24 hours.[9] Iron dextran may affect lipid emulsion stability.

IM: Give undiluted. Begin with a small fraction of the dose. Increase incrementally each day until the maximum daily dose is reached or until the total dose is given.

- To minimize skin staining, use Z-track technique: Displace the skin laterally prior to injection, and use a separate needle to withdraw the drug from the vial. Rotate the injection site.

CAUTIONS/CONTRAINDICATIONS

- Oral iron is much safer than parenteral iron; use the parenteral form only if enteral administration is not possible.[1]

- The product labeling states that iron dextran should not normally be given to infants younger than 4 months of age.[1] IM iron dextran has been associated with an increased incidence of Gram-negative sepsis, primarily caused by *Escherichia coli,* in neonates in other countries. However, it has been used IV in the U.S. in a limited number of neonates without evidence of unusual adverse effects or risk of sepsis.[1,2]

- Do not use in anemias not resulting from iron deficiency, in hemochromatosis, or in hemolytic anemia because iron overload may occur. Also, do not use if infant is hypersensitive to the drug or any of its components.[1]

- Hemosiderosis may result from excessive doses beyond the amounts required for restoration of hemoglobin and replenishment of iron stores.
- Excess iron may increase a patient's susceptibility to infection.
- Use with extreme care in patients with serious liver dysfunction because iron accumulation may occur.[1]
- Use with caution in infants receiving repeated blood transfusions because the addition of high RBC iron content may produce iron overload.

USE

Parenteral iron is used when iron cannot be administered orally.

Iron dextran is used to treat iron deficiency anemia. It is also used as an iron supplement for infants on erythropoietin therapy to optimize hematologic response to the drug. Infants on long-term parenteral nutrition may also need parenteral iron.

Infants on Erythropoietin/Epoetin Alfa: Iron supplementation increases the effectiveness of erythropoietin in preterm infants. Infants on erythropoietin may be undergoing active erythropoiesis while having ongoing blood loss from the collection of blood for clinical tests.[6] Erythropoietin is usually administered with iron; however, some clinicians are concerned about the use of iron in the first 2 weeks of life because of its oxidative potential[10] and because the long-term effects of giving iron in the first 2 weeks of life are not known.

MECHANISM OF ACTION

Iron dextran is a complex of ferric hydroxide and dextran in normal saline. Iron is a component in the formation of hemoglobin, and adequate amounts are necessary for erythropoiesis and to maintain the oxygen transport capacity of blood.

ADVERSE EFFECTS

With IV Administration: Usually well tolerated IV in infants.

- Anaphylaxis (usually occurs within several minutes of administration in adults; but anaphylaxis is a very unlikely occurrence in infants) is characterized by sudden respiratory difficulty and/or cardiovascular collapse. Keep epinephrine readily available.

Fever; arthralgia, myalgia; pain and redness at intravenous injection sites (osmolality is >2,000 mOsm/kg); rash; shivering.

- Rapid infusion may cause hypotension and flushing.

With IM Administration: IM injection may cause sarcomas, but the connection has not been proved. Sarcomas were produced experimentally when repeated doses were given at the same site to laboratory animals.[11] Iron dextran can stain the skin, and it can cause pain and redness or sores at the IM injection site. Large intramuscular doses have been associated with infection in infants.

Overdose: Overdose with iron dextran usually does not produce acute toxicity (however, see **CAUTIONS/CONTRAINDICATIONS** above regarding iron overload).

PHARMACOKINETICS/PHARMACODYNAMICS

Absorption: Most of an IM dose is absorbed within 72 hours and the rest, over 3–4 weeks. Iron is available much more rapidly when given IV.

Protein Binding: 90 percent or more.

Metabolism: Iron dextran is removed from the plasma by the reticuloendothelial system and is dissociated into iron and dextran. The released iron is then bound to protein to form hemosiderin or ferritin and some transferrin. This protein-bound iron replenishes depleted iron stores and incorporates into hemoglobin.

Onset of Action: An increase in reticulocyte count can be seen in a few days.[1]

Storage in the Body: Iron is stored as ferritin or hemosiderin primarily in hepatocytes and in the reticuloendothelial system, with some stored in muscle.[12]

Elimination: Small amounts are lost daily in such areas as shedding of skin, hair, nails, feces, and urine.

NURSING IMPLICATIONS

Oral iron should be discontinued before parenteral iron is initiated.

Observe for rust-colored precipitate when iron is added to PN solution.

Have epinephrine readily available.

Monitoring: Consider monitoring serum ferritin, serum iron concentration, hemoglobin, hematocrit, reticulocyte count, and total iron-binding capacity or transferrin.

COMMENTS

Interactions: May cause falsely elevated serum bilirubin values and falsely decreased serum calcium values in blood drawn 4 hours after IV iron dextran administration. The serum from blood samples will have a brown color.

The fetal accretion rate of iron is 1,000 mcg Fe/kg/day.[4]

REFERENCES

1. Medical Economics Data. 2000. *Physicians' Desk Reference,* 54th ed. Montvale, New Jersey: Medical Economics, 2775–2776.

2. McEvoy GK. 2000. *AHFS Drug Information.* Bethesda, Maryland: American Society of Health-System Pharmacists, 1306–1309.

3. Benitz WE, and Tatro DS. 1995. *The Pediatric Drug Handbook,* 3rd ed. St. Louis: Mosby-Year Book, 348–349.

4. Friel JK, et al. 1995. Intravenous iron administration to very low-birth-weight newborns receiving total and partial parenteral nutrition. *Journal of Parenteral and Enteral Nutrition* 19(2): 114–118.

5. Heese HD, et al. 1990. Prevention of iron deficiency in preterm neonates during infancy. *South African Medical Journal* 77(7): 339–345.

6. Ohls RK, Veerman MW, and Christensen RD. 1996. Pharmacokinetics and effectiveness of recombinant erythropoietin administered to preterm infants by continuous infusion in total parenteral nutrition solution. *Journal of Pediatrics* 128(4): 518–523.

7. Ohls RK. 2000. The use of erythropoietin in neonates. *Clinics in Perinatology* 27(3): 681–696.

8. Calhoun DA, et al. 2000. Consistent approaches to procedures and practices in neonatal hematology. *Clinics in Perinatology* 27(3): 733–753.

9. Mayhew SL, and Quick MW. 1997. Compatibility of iron dextran with neonatal parenteral nutrition solutions. *American Journal of Health-System Pharmacy* 54(5): 570–571.

10. Thibeault DW. 2000. The precarious antioxidant defenses of the preterm infant. *American Journal of Perinatology* 17(4): 167–181.

11. Magnusson G, Flodh H, and Malmfors T. 1977. Oncological study in rats of Ferastral, an iron-poly-(sorbitol-gluconic acid) complex, after intramuscular administration. *Scandanavian Journal of Haematology* 32(supplement): S87–S98.

12. United States Pharmacopeial Convention/USP DI. 2000. *Drug Information for the Health Care Professional,* 20th ed. Rockville, Maryland: United States Pharmacopeial Convention, 1849–1850.

ISOPROTERENOL (ISUPREL)
(eye-soe-proe-TER-e-nol)

CARDIOVASCULAR:
VASOPRESSOR;
RESPIRATORY: BRONCHODILATOR

DOSE

Continuous IV Infusion: Dosage range: 0.05–2 mcg/kg/minute.[1] Most infants require doses in the middle of this range, 0.1–1 mcg/kg/minute. Begin with 0.05 mcg/kg/minute, and increase by 0.1 mcg/kg/minute increments every 5–15 minutes until desired response is achieved or toxicity occurs.

Effectiveness is optimized if hypovolemia and acidosis are corrected prior to initiation of therapy.

Nebulization: Isoproterenol 1 percent 0.01 ml/kg/dose given every 1–2 hours.[2] The dose can be simplified and standardized as follows:

- *Preterm Infants:* Isoproterenol 1 percent 0.05 ml/dose.
- *Term Infants:* Isoproterenol 1 percent 0.1 ml/dose.
- Dilute all doses for nebulization to 3 ml with normal saline or other compatible medications for nebulization, and give every 1–2 hours, as needed.
- Give less frequently as soon as respiratory status has improved.

ADMINISTRATION

Supplied as: Injection: 0.2 mg/ml (= 0.02 percent = 1:5,000 = 200 mcg/ml). Solution for nebulization: 0.25 percent (= 2.5 mg/ml), 0.5 percent (= 5 mg/ml), 1 percent (= 10 mg/ml).

IV Continuous Infusion:

- *Concentration:* Determine concentration based on the dose and fluid requirements of the infant. (See Appendix A: Simplified Neonatal Calculations.)

$$C\ (mg/25ml) = 1.5 \times Dose\ (mcg/kg/minute) \times Weight\ (kg) \div Rate\ (ml/hour)$$

- *IV—Rate:* Determine concentration based on the dose and fluid requirements of the infant.
- Use neonatal infusion pump to accurately deliver dose.

IV—*Compatibility:* Sodium bicarbonate causes partial inactivation of isoproterenol and is therefore considered incompatible with it.

Nebulization: Dilute to 3 ml with normal saline or other compatible medications.

Isoproterenol gradually darkens (due to oxidation) when exposed to light, air, or heat. Protect from light, and do not use if the solution is pinkish to brownish in color.

CAUTIONS/CONTRAINDICATIONS

Use with caution in infants with renal or cardiovascular disease such as hypertension. Do not use in patients with pre-existing arrhythmias or digoxin toxicity.

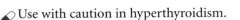 Use with caution in hyperthyroidism.

USE

Improves cardiac output; reverses bronchospasm; also used to treat bronchopulmonary dysplasia (BPD),[1] hemodynamically compromised bradyarrhythmias
or atropine-resistant bradyarrhythmias, ventricular arrhythmias due to AV
nodal blocks, low cardiac output, and vasoconstrictive shock states.

Bronchodilator: β_2-specific nebulized adrenergic agents such as albuterol are
preferred over isoproterenol. Use IV isoproterenol only for bronchospasm
refractory to inhaled β agents.

MECHANISM OF ACTION

Isoproterenol is a sympathomimetic drug that has a chemical structure related to
epinephrine, but that differs in its pharmacologic properties. Isoproterenol has
almost no action on α receptors and acts directly on β receptors, stimulating
both the β_1- and β_2 receptors. Its action results from stimulation of production
of cyclic AMP by activation of the enzyme adenyl cyclase.

Cardiovascular: Isoproterenol increases cardiac output through positive inotropic
and chronotropic action and increases venous return to the heart. It increases
the oxygen demand of most tissues, including the heart, and it increases myocardial contractility and heart rate more than dopamine or dobutamine. It reduces
peripheral resistance through vasodilation in skeletal muscle and mesenteric
vascular beds. Pulmonary artery pressure and resistance are decreased. Renal
blood flow may increase, decrease, or remain the same.

Respiratory: Isoproterenol relaxes smooth muscle of the bronchial tree.

Other Effects: Isoproterenol relaxes GI smooth muscle. It causes glycogenolysis
and insulin secretion by direct effect on the pancreatic islet cells.[3]

ADVERSE EFFECTS

Cardiac arrhythmias, focal necrosis of cardiac cells, flushing, hyperglycemia, hypoglycemia, tachycardia, restlessness, insomnia, GI distress, nausea, tremor, cough,
dyspnea, sweating. Tolerance may develop.

Risk of isoproterenol-induced arrhythmias may be reduced by maintaining adequate oxygenation and fluid status during infusion.

Most adverse effects subside rapidly when the drug is discontinued because it has a
short duration of action.

May cause rebound bronchoconstriction if IV is stopped abruptly. Therefore, discontinue gradually over 24–48 hours.

Saliva may appear to turn pink or red after oral inhalation because isoproterenol
changes to these colors on exposure to air.

Reduce infusion rate (for continuous IV infusion) or lengthen the dosing interval
(for nebulization) if heart rate exceeds 180 bpm (if baseline heart rate was <150
bpm) or 200 bpm (if baseline heart rate was >150 bpm). A moderate increase in

heart rate after nebulization treatment is expected and may indicate absorption and therapeutic response.

Monitor ECG for ischemic changes.

Tachyphylaxis may occur.

PHARMACOKINETICS/PHARMACODYNAMICS

Absorption: Cannot be administered orally because it is rapidly metabolized in the GI tract and therefore does not achieve therapeutic blood levels.

Onset of Action: Immediately after IV administration; 2–5 minutes after oral inhalation.

Duration of Action: A few minutes after IV administration; 0.5–1 hour after oral inhalation.

Metabolism: Metabolized primarily in the liver and other tissues by catechol-*O*-methyltransferase (COMT).

Half-life: 2.5–5 minutes. Isoproterenol must be given by continuous IV infusion because of its short half-life. Intermittent administration may result in decompensation of the infant.

Elimination: 50 percent is excreted unchanged in the urine.

NURSING IMPLICATIONS

Monitor for development of tolerance and need to increase the dose.

Continuously monitor blood pressure and heart rate, ECG, respiratory rate, blood gases, urine flow. Monitor blood glucose.

Observe proper technique during tubing changes to avoid administration of an isoproterenol bolus; do not administer bolus doses of other drugs into the isoproterenol line to avoid inadvertently giving an isoproterenol bolus.

Discontinue IV isoproterenol gradually over 24–48 hours to prevent rebound bronchoconstriction.

COMMENTS

Interactions:

- Additive cardiotoxicity when given concurrently with other sympathomimetic amines such as epinephrine.

- β-adrenergic blocking drugs such as propranolol reduce the action of isoproterenol due to β blockade.

- Concurrent use of bretylium may potentiate the action of vasopressors and possibly result in arrhythmias.

REFERENCES

1. Taketomo CK, Hodding JH, and Kraus DM. 1997. *Pediatric Dosage Handbook.* Hudson, Ohio: Lexi-Comp, 407–408.

2. Davis JM, Sinkin RA, and Aranda JV. 1990. Drug therapy for bronchopulmonary dysplasia. *Pediatric Pulmonology* 8(2):117–125.

3. Roberts RJ. 1984. *Drug Therapy in Infants: Pharmacologic Principles and Clinical Experience.*
    Philadelphia: WB Saunders, 171–172.

TABLE OF CONTENTS

K

KETAMINE (KETALAR)
(KEET-a-meen)
(CONTROLLED SUBSTANCE SCHEDULE III)

CENTRAL NERVOUS SYSTEM: ANESTHETIC

DOSE

IV: 0.5–1 mg/kg/dose. Average amount is 2 mg/kg/dose for 5–10 minutes of surgical anesthesia. *Maximum:* 4.5 mg/kg/dose.[1]

- *Continuous Infusion:* 10–15 mcg/kg/minute IV.
- *Alternatively:* A loading dose of 1–2 mg/kg IV, followed by a continuous infusion of 0.5–1 mg/kg/hour has been recommended.[2]

IM: 3–7 mg/kg/dose. *Maximum:* 13 mg/kg/dose.[1]

PO: 6 mg/kg/dose, diluted.

Repeat doses are half the initial dose as often as required. The larger the dose, the longer the time to recovery.

Reduce dose in hepatic dysfunction.

ADMINISTRATION

Supplied as: 10, 50, 100 mg/ml vials.

IV—*Rate:* 0.5 mg/kg/minute. Infuse over at least 1 minute.[1]

IV—*Concentration:* Dilute to 1–2 mg/ml. May dilute with D_5W, NS, or sterile water. Maximum: 2 mg/ml.

IM—*Concentration:* 100 mg/ml.

Compatibility: May dilute with sterile water, normal saline, or dextrose.

USE

An anesthetic agent for short diagnostic and minor surgical procedures (such as laser surgery) that do not require skeletal muscle relaxation.

Induces coma, analgesia, and amnesia. Patient appears to be awake but is immobile and unresponsive to pain.

Some advantages over barbiturate anesthesia: analgesic effects; lower incidence of cardiovascular and respiratory depression.

MECHANISM OF ACTION

Ketamine is a phencyclidine derivative that produces a dissociative anesthesia and profound analgesia. It dissociates the cortex from the limbic system and increases cerebral blood flow and cerebral oxygen consumption. Ketamine increases cardiac output, blood pressure and pulmonary artery pressure, and heart rate because it increases plasma norepinephrine levels. It also increases muscle tone, which may resemble seizures in appearance. Ketamine improves pulmonary compliance and relieves bronchospasm.[1–3]

K

Adverse Effects

Do not administer to patients for whom increased intracranial pressure, cerebral blood flow, CSF pressure, cerebral metabolism, or intraocular pressure may present a risk.

Cardiovascular: Elevation in systemic and pulmonary artery pressure, tachycardia, dysrhythmias. Hypotension, bradycardia, and decreased cardiac output may follow administration in critically ill patients.

CNS:

- Emergence reactions (psychic disturbances such as hallucinations, delirium) lasting up to 24 hours in older patients. Minimize by reducing verbal, tactile, and visual simulation during recovery period. Treat severe reactions with pentobarbital, thiopental, or diazepam.

- Increased muscle tone that may resemble seizures. Extensor spasm with opisthotonos in infants receiving high, repeated doses.

- Avoid use in patients at risk for intracranial hypertension because drug increases intracranial pressure as a result of cerebral vasodilation.[2]

Dermatologic: Transient erythema, morbilliform rash; pain and redness at IM injection site.

GI: Hypersalivation; GI upset.

Ophthalmic: Nystagmus; slightly increased intraocular pressure.

Respiratory: Decrease in respiratory rate and tidal volume (mechanical ventilation and oxygen may be required); apnea and enhanced pressor response following rapid IV administration; laryngospasm, stimulation of respirations, and increase in secretions. Gag and cough reflexes are generally preserved.

Prevention of Side Effects: Pretreatment with a benzodiazepine such as midazolam 15 minutes before the procedure may reduce side effects such as these: psychic, circulatory, increased ICP and cerebral blood flow, tachycardia, and jerky movements. Benzodiazepines prolong recovery time.

Pharmacokinetics/Pharmacodynamics

Loss of Consciousness: *IV:* Onset 30 seconds; duration 5–10 minutes. *IM:* Onset 3–4 minutes; duration 12–25 minutes. Analgesia lasts 30–40 minutes and amnesia lasts for 1–2 hours.[1,4]

Metabolism: Ketamine is N-methylated in the liver to norketamine, which has one-third the activity of ketamine. Very little metabolism of ketamine occurs in newborns.

Half-life: 2 hours (adults).

Elimination: Renal.

K

Nursing Implications

Initiate conscious sedation precautions and monitoring, including frequent
continuous vital sign monitoring and pulse oximetry, when used in the
nonintubated patient for a procedure.

Monitor for respiratory depression, heart rate, respiratory rate, and blood pressure
postanesthesia, especially in infants with cardiac decompensation and/or hypertension. Observe for CNS side effects during recovery period.

Have emergency equipment at bedside.

References

1. Roberts RJ. *Drug Therapy in Infants: Pharmacologic Principles and Clinical Experience.* Philadelphia: WB
   Saunders, 307.

2. Tobias JD, and Rasmussen GE. 1994. Pain management and sedation in the pediatric intensive care unit.
   Pediatric Clinics of North America 41(6): 1269–1291.

3. Gassner S, et al. 1974. The effect of ketamine on pulmonary artery pressure: An experimental and clinical study. *Anaesthesia* 29(2): 141–146.

4. Grant IS, Nimmo WS, and McNicol LR. 1983. Ketamine disposition in children and adults. *British
   Journal of Anaesthesia* 55(11): 1107–1111.

TABLE OF CONTENTS

LEVOTHYROXINE (SYNTHROID)
(lee-voe-thye-ROX-een)

HORMONE: THYROID REPLACEMENT

Synonym: T_4

DOSE

Individualize dose based on clinical response and results of thyroid function tests. (See *Follow-up* under **USE** below.)

PO: Give as a single daily dose; Table 1-30 lists amounts. Adjust dose based on clinical response and laboratory tests.[1] (See *Follow-up* under **USE** below.)

- Ehrlich suggests that the dose be rounded to the nearest 25, 37.5 (= a 25 mcg tablet plus a 12.5 mcg tablet), or 50 mcg tablet.[2] This simplifies dosing and dose preparation, and it reduces the chance for error.

- The dose based on body weight (mcg/kg/day) decreases gradually as the child grows, as Table 1-30 shows. The daily dose in the last column (mcg/day) appears to increase as the child grows, but actually does not if the child's weight is taken into account. For example, a 2-month-old infant weighing 4 kg who is given 50 mcg/day of levothyroxine (= 12.5 mcg/kg/day), compared to a 12-month-old infant weighing 10 kg given 75 mcg/day (= 7.5 mcg/kg/day).

Dose Controversy: The initial dose of levothyroxine for congenital hypothyroidism (CH) is controversial. The American Academy of Pediatrics and others recommend a higher dose of 14 mcg/kg/day initially.[3-5] Dubuis and colleagues suggest that earlier treatment and a higher initial dose of levothyroxine (11.6 mcg/kg/day) be used to improve the outcome of infants with the severe form of CH, as defined by a knee epiphysis area at diagnosis of <0.05 cm².[6] Ehrlich considers a starting dose of 10 mcg/kg/day rounded to the nearest 25, 37.5, or 50 mcg tablet to be a reasonable compromise.[2] Others consider a dose of 8 mcg/kg/day sufficient for initial treatment of the majority of infants and caution that higher initial doses could expose many infants to a high risk of

TABLE 1-30 ◆ ORAL LEVOTHYROXINE DOSING, BY AGE

Age	Daily Dose* Based on Body Weight (mcg/kg/day)	Daily Dose* (mcg/day)
Preterm infants <2 kg or infants at risk for cardiac failure	8–12[4] Transient hypothyroidism: 5–6[4]	25 mcg/day. (May increase to 50 mcg/day in 4–6 weeks.)[12]
0–3 months	10–15[11]	25–50 mcg/day (usually 37.5 mcg/day)[12]
3–6 months	8–10[11]	25–50 mcg/day (usually 37.5 mcg/day)[12]
6–12 months	6–8[11]	50–75 mcg/day[12]
1–5 years	5–6[11]	75–100 mcg/day[12]

*Adjust dose based on clinical response and laboratory tests.[1] (See *Follow-up* under **USE** below.)

overdose and dangerous hyperthyroidism.[7,8] Vogiatzi and Kirkland reported that an initial levothyroxine dose of 37.5 mcg/day required fewer dose changes than did a dose of 25 mcg/day and that their data supported the American Academy of Pediatrics' recommended frequency of thyroid function studies during the first 2 years of life.[3,9] (See *Follow-up* under **USE** below.)

Changing Routes of Administration: Use caution when switching routes of administration because the parenteral dose is lower than the oral dose. The IV or IM pediatric dose is 50–75 percent of the oral dose.[10] Example:

> **Problem:** The infant you have been caring for has been receiving levothyroxine orally at a dose of 10 mcg/kg/day. The infant is now unable to take anything by mouth. How would you calculate an equivalent dose of parenteral levothyroxine?

> **Answer:** You are aware that the IV or IM dose should be 50–75 percent (one-half to three-quarters) of the oral dose. So:

$$10 \; mcg \times 0.5 = 5 \; mcg; \; 10 \; mcg \times 0.75 = 7.5 \; mcg.$$

The equivalent parenteral dose would be 5–7.5 mcg/kg/day. When the infant is again able to take the drug PO, the dose will need to be increased back to 10 mcg/kg/day. When switching from IV to tablets, continue to give the IV dose for several days, tapering it gradually, because there is a delay of several days in the drug's onset of activity when it is given orally.

ADMINISTRATION

The routes of administration, in order of preference, are oral, then IV, then IM.

PO: Give on an empty stomach. Give at the same time each day, preferably every morning, for consistent effect.

- No oral liquid formulation is commercially available; levothyroxine suspension prepared by the pharmacy may lead to unreliable dosage and is not recommended.[3] The nurse in the unit may use one of the following methods to prepare a liquid dose:

  - *Doses corresponding to a tablet or half-tablet size (e.g., 25 mcg, 37.5 mcg):* Crush tablet(s) and mix with a few milliliters of water, breast milk, or non-soybean formula immediately prior to administration. Discard unused portion.[3,11]

  - *Doses between tablet sizes (e.g., 30 mcg):* Crush one or more 25 mcg tablets and dilute each with 2.5 ml of water, breast milk, or non-soybean formula immediately prior to administration. Shake well. Resulting concentration = 10 mcg/ml. Administer appropriate volume for dose ordered. (For example, for the 30 mcg dose, give 3 ml.) Discard unused portion.

IV—*Rate:* Infuse over 2–3 minutes.

IV—*Concentration:* Dilute lyophilized powder with normal saline to 100 mcg/ml (= 0.1 mg/ml). Use immediately after reconstituting; discard unused portion.

IM—100 mcg/ml (= 0.1 mg/ml). (See **IV**—*Concentration* above for instructions.)

Supplied as:

Oral Tablets: Dose per tablet:

Micrograms	12.5	25	50	75	88	100
Milligrams	0.0125	0.025	0.05	0.075	0.088	0.1

Note: Be careful of the decimal point with this drug. Use micrograms, rather than milligrams to order and dispense levothyroxine for infants. Using micrograms is easier and less likely to produce errors. To prevent errors in moving the decimal point, be consistent in your NICU as to how the units for this drug are expressed. For example, if physician orders are expressed in micrograms, then the unit-dose labels should also be written in micrograms.

Injection: Dose per vial of lyophilized powder:

Micrograms	200	500
Milligrams	0.2	0.5

Storage: Protect from light.

CAUTIONS/CONTRAINDICATIONS

Cautions:

- Avoid changing brands without reassessing the patient because various commercially available levothyroxine tablets (e.g., Synthroid and several generic preparations) may have different levothyroxine contents and may cause different thyroid function in patients.[10]

- Use caution in interpreting thyroid function tests in neonates: Serum T_4 (levothyroxine) is transiently elevated and serum T_3 (triiodothyronine) is transiently low in neonates, and the infant pituitary is relatively insensitive to the negative feedback effect (increased thyroid hormone levels inhibit and decreased concentrations stimulate pituitary thyroid-stimulating hormone [TSH] synthesis) of thyroid hormones. Do not use adult normal range for serum thyroxine concentration to evaluate neonatal thyroid function. Use infant reference values.[12]

Contraindications:

- Hypersensitivity to levothyroxine or any component in the product.
- Cardiovascular disease.
- Thyrotoxicosis (hypermetabolic state from excessive thyroid hormone activity, usually caused by transplacental passage of thyroid-stimulating immunoglobulin from a mother with Graves' disease).
- Hypothyroidism with adrenocortical insufficiency or panhypopituitarism. If a patient's hypothyroidism is secondary to hypopituitarism, adrenal

insufficiency is likely to be present. In that case, adrenal insufficiency must first be corrected with corticosteroids before levothyroxine is begun, to prevent precipitation of acute adrenocortical insufficiency. Thyroid agents increase metabolism and tissue demands for adrenal hormones and may precipitate an acute adrenal crisis.

Use
A thyroid hormone used as replacement therapy in the treatment of hypothyroidism, including congenital hypothyroidism, and to suppress the growth of some goiters.

Congenital Hypothyroidism:

- *Diagnosis:* Signs and symptoms include large for gestational age, lethargy, hypothermia, feeding problems, failure to gain weight, dry skin, skin mottling, thick tongue, hoarse cry, umbilical hernia, persistence of mild jaundice, respiratory problems, constipation, and large anterior and posterior fontanels.[10] Routine screening for hypothyroidism at birth is recommended in all infants because of the deleterious effects of thyroid deficiency on growth and development. A low T_4 and a serum TSH concentration >40 mIU/liter is diagnostic of primary hypothyroidism. A TSH between 20 and 40 mIU/liter should be repeated.[3]

- *Treatment:* If hypothyroidism is suspected, a pediatric endocrinologist should be consulted to facilitate diagnosis and optimize treatment. Treatment with levothyroxine should be instituted immediately and continued throughout life, unless transient hypothyroidism (see below) is suspected. If CH is suspected but laboratory results are delayed, begin treatment as soon as possible after birth while waiting for the test results to improve the chance for normal growth and development. Treatment that begins after about 3 months of age may reverse many of the physical effects but not all of the mental effects of hypothyroidism.[12]

- *Follow-up:*
  - Clinical examination, including assessment of growth and development, should be performed every few months during the first 3 years of life.[3]
  - Laboratory evaluations for serum T_4 and TSH should be done 2–4 weeks after initiation of levothyroxine treatment, every 1–2 months during the first year of life, every 2–3 months between 1 and 3 years, and then every 3–12 months thereafter until growth is complete. Tests should be done more frequently if there is a question about compliance or if values are abnormal. Evaluate 2 weeks after any change in dose.[3,9]
  - The goal of therapy is to ensure normal growth and development and to maintain the serum total T_4 or free T_4 concentration in the upper half of the normal range (10–16 mcg/dl). The normal range for free T_4 depends on the method, but approximates 1.4–2.3 ng/dl in the first year of life. In most infants, serum TSH is suppressed into the normal range (usually below 10 mIU/liter), but some infants have serum TSH concentrations between

10 and 20 mIU/liter despite T_4s being in the upper half of the normal range. If the T_4 does not increase to the upper half of the normal range by 2 weeks and/or the TSH does not decrease to less than 20 mIU/liter within 4 weeks after starting levothyroxine, the child may not be receiving enough levothyroxine regularly—because of noncompliance, inadequacy of dose, or method of administration.[3,9,10]

- Growth rate should accelerate after therapy is begun, with growth deficit usually restored within a few months. Delayed bone maturation suggests inadequate dosage when other signs of hypothyroidism have been corrected. Overtreatment for long periods of time may cause brain damage, accelerate bone age, and cause premature craniosynostosis.[3,10]

Transient Hypothyroidism: Transient hypothyroidism in the newborn may result from intrauterine exposure to antithyroid drugs such as propylthiouracil and methimazole or iodine (including iodide-containing expectorants, pre- or postnatal topical application of iodine in disinfectants such as povidone iodine, iodinated contrast materials); sulfonamides; or lithium, maternal antithyroid antibodies, or endemic iodine deficiency.[3,13] The T_4 and TSH values of infants with hypothyroidism whose mothers were receiving an antithyroid drug returned to normal within 1–3 weeks after birth without treatment. Because transient hypothyroidism is not recognized as such in some infants, initial treatment is similar to that of any infant with CH. For this reason, it is important to determine at some later time whether the hypothyroidism is permanent and if the infant needs lifelong treatment. To determine the child's status, treatment should be withdrawn for 30 days after 3 years of age; if the TSH and T_4 concentrations remain normal throughout the withdrawal period, treatment is no longer necessary. If they are abnormal, treatment can be begun again.[3]

Transient Hypothyroidism of Prematurity: Another form of transient thyroid dysfunction occurs in preterm infants. It is most likely delayed maturation of the hypothalamic-pituitary-thyroid axis. This disorder corrects spontaneously in 4–8 weeks without treatment.[1,14]

MECHANISM OF ACTION

Levothyroxine is a synthetic preparation of the monosodium salt of the natural isomer of the thyroid hormone thyroxine. Thyroid hormone increases the metabolic rate of body tissues; it also regulates cell growth and differentiation. Thyroid hormone is involved in normal metabolism, growth, and development, especially the development of the central nervous system in infants. A feedback system involving the hypothalamus, anterior pituitary, and thyroid normally regulates circulating thyroid hormone concentrations.[10,12]

Comparison of Thyroid Hormones: Several preparations of thyroid hormones (Table 1-31) are available, but levothyroxine is preferred because it is more uniform in potency than the others and is easily measured in the serum.[12] *The names of some of the thyroid hormone preparations sound and look similar; be careful not to confuse the products.*

TABLE 1-31 ◆ COMPARISON OF THYROID HORMONES

Thyroid Hormone Product	Composition	Type*	Equivalent Strength (Approximate) Based on Clinical Response
Levothyroxine	Thyroxine (T_4) Tetraiodothyronine	Synthetic	100 mcg (= 0.1 mg) or less
Liothyronine	Triiodothyronine (T_3)	Synthetic	25 mcg (= 0.025 mg)
Liotrix	Levothyroxine (T_4) and liothyronine (T_3)	Synthetic	60 mcg (= 0.06 mg) and 15 mcg (= 0.015 mg) or 50 mcg (= 0.05 mg) and 12.5 mcg (= 0.0125 mg), respectively
Thyroglobulin	Levothyroxine (T_4) and liothyronine (T_3)	Natural	60 mg Note: Thyroglobulin is an iodinated glycoprotein from which the hormones thyroxine (T_4) and triiodothyronine (T_3) are formed.
Thyroid	Levothyroxine (T_4) and liothyronine (T_3)	Natural	60 mg

* *Natural* thyroid hormones are extracts of beef or pork thyroid gland. Natural thyroid hormones are more economical than those prepared synthetically; however, the potency of the natural products is inexact because it is difficult to measure their exact hormone content. *Synthetic* products are generally preferred because they offer more uniform potency standardization.

ADVERSE EFFECTS

Adverse effects of levothyroxine are generally associated with excessive dose, vary with the individual, and correspond to symptoms of hyperthyroidism. Adverse effects usually disappear with dose reduction or temporary withdrawal of treatment.[15]

Cardiovascular: Flushing, tachycardia, arrhythmias, congestive heart failure, hypertension.

Central Nervous System: Irritability, sleeplessness, fever, sweating, tremors, pseudotumor cerebri.[16]

Dermatologic: Partial hair loss may occur during the first few months of therapy, but hair growth returns with continued treatment. Rash may occur.

GI: Diarrhea.

Other: Increased appetite, weight loss.

Treatment of Overdose:

- *Overtreatment:* Signs of overtreatment include diarrhea, sleeplessness, increased appetite, tachycardia, irritability, and excessive sweating. Excessive dosage over a longer period may cause osteoporosis, psychomotor retardation, premature cranial synostosis, and advancement of bone age.[1]

  If symptoms of overtreatment occur, withdraw levothyroxine therapy for 2–6 days; then resume at a lower dose.

- *Massive Overdose:*
  - Signs may include seizures, increased sympathetic activity (irritability, diaphoresis, tremor, tachyarrhythmias), fever, hypoglycemia, congestive heart failure, and unrecognized adrenal insufficiency. Symptoms may be delayed for several days; therefore, an extended follow-up period is required.[15] Serious toxic reaction following acute ingestions of levothyroxine is infrequent, however.
  - Golightly and associates studied 41 children with levothyroxine overdose; 11 had symptoms between 12 hours and 11 days after the overdose. The researchers reported that no adverse effect was considered severe enough to warrant specific symptomatic treatment, and all symptoms fully resolved in 14 days. The authors recommended a conservative approach to treatment in cases of levothyroxine ingestion in children because observed effects were generally mild and often unrelated to either estimated amounts of hormone consumed or serum thyroxine levels.[17]
  - If massive overdose occurs, stop the drug and institute supportive care as needed: Reduce GI absorption by emptying the stomach up to 3–4 hours after oral ingestion of a toxic dose; administer oxygen and maintain ventilation if needed; consider digoxin if congestive heart failure develops; control fever (acetaminophen), hypoglycemia, or fluid loss as appropriate; consider propranolol to counteract increased sympathetic activity; consider IV hydrocortisone to partially inhibit conversion of T_4 to T_3, the active form of the drug.[12]

PHARMACOKINETICS/PHARMACODYNAMICS

Absorption: Oral absorption is variable and incomplete (range: 50–75 percent), especially when the drug is taken with food, and may be reduced in patients with malabsorption states or diarrhea.[12] Absorption from an IM site is variable.

Onset, Peak, and Duration of Action: The onset of action for therapeutic effects is 3–5 days after oral administration and 6–8 hours after IV administration. The time to peak therapeutic effect with chronic stable oral dosing is 3–4 weeks. Therapeutic effect lasts 1–3 weeks after withdrawal of chronic therapy.[12] Response to changes in dose is slow.

Protein Binding: 99 percent bound principally to thyroxine-binding globulin (TBG) but also to a lesser extent to thyroxine-binding pre-albumin (TBPA) or to albumin.[15]

Metabolism: T_4 is metabolized by sequential monodeiodination in peripheral tissues to T_3, the active form of the drug. Small amounts are metabolized in the liver and excreted in bile.

Half-life: The half-life in euthyroidism is about 6–7 days. The half-life is decreased in patients with hyperthyroidism (3–4 days) and increased with hypothyroidism (9–10 days).

Elimination: Undergoes enterohepatic recycling and excretion in the feces. Some is also eliminated in the urine.

NURSING IMPLICATIONS

On discharge, advise parents:

- Not to discontinue the drug without contacting their health care provider, to refill the child's prescription before it runs out, to keep medical appointments as scheduled, and to give the exact amount of drug prescribed, not more or less.

- Not to change brands without contacting the physician.

- To contact the physician immediately if the child has signs of hyperthyroidism from overtreatment, such as disturbed sleep patterns, increased pulse, irritability, or excessive sweating.

COMMENTS

Interactions:

- *Thyroid function tests* may be affected by amiodarone, antithyroid drugs (propylthiouracil, methimazole), barbiturates, carbamazepine, chloral hydrate, diazepam, dopamine, glucocorticoid, heparin, insulin, methadone, metoclopramide, nitroprusside, phenytoin, propranolol, rifampin, somatostatin analogs, and thiazides.[11]

- *Cholestyramine or colestipol* decreases absorption of levothyroxine by binding to it. Administer levothyroxine 1 hour before or 4 hours after cholestyramine and monitor thyroid function tests if these drugs must be given concurrently. Sucralfate, sodium polystyrene sulfonate (Kayexalate), aluminum hydroxide, calcium carbonate, and ferrous sulfate may also reduce absorption.[15]

- Levothyroxine increases the effect of *oral anticoagulants;* the dose of the oral anticoagulant may need to be decreased.

- Levothyroxine may increase *insulin* requirements. Monitor blood glucose during concurrent therapy.

- Concurrent use with *ketamine* may cause tachycardia and hypertension.

- Concurrent administration of high doses of thyroid hormones with *human growth hormone* (somatrem or somatropin) may accelerate epiphyseal closure. However, untreated hypothyroidism may interfere with the growth response to growth hormone; concurrent or prior treatment is recommended.

- Thyroid hormones may increase receptor sensitivity to *catecholamines.*

Reference Range: See *Follow-up* under **USE** above.

REFERENCES

1. Fisher DA. The thyroid. 1996. In *Rudolph's Pediatrics,* 20th ed., Rudolph AM, Hoffman JIE, and Rudolph CD, eds. Stamford, Connecticut: Appleton & Lange, 1750–1773.

2. Ehrlich RM. 1995. Thyroxine dose for congenital hypothyroidism. Editorial. *Clinical Pediatrics* 34(10): 521–522.

3. American Academy of Pediatrics, Section on Endocrinology and Committee on Genetics, and American Thyroid Association, Committee on Public Health. 1993. Newborn screening for congenital hypothyroidism: Recommended guidelines. *Pediatrics* 91(6): 1203–1209.

4. Fisher DA. 1998. Thyroid function in premature infants: The hypothyroxinemia of prematurity. *Clinics in Perinatology* 25(4): 999–1014.

5. Fisher DA, and Foley BL. 1989. Early treatment of congenital hypothyroidism. *Pediatrics* 83(5): 785–789.

6. Dubuis J, et al. 1996. Outcome of severe congenital hypothyroidism: Closing the developmental gap with early high dose levothyroxine treatment. *Journal of Clinical Endocrinology and Metabolism* 81(1): 222–227.

7. Campos SP, et al. 1995. Outcome of lower L-thyroxine dose for treatment of congenital hypothyroidism. *Clinical Pediatrics* 34(10): 514–520.

8. Touati G, et al. 1997. A thyroxine dosage of 8 micrograms/kg per day is appropriate for the initial treatment of the majority of infants with congenital hypothyroidism. *European Journal of Pediatrics* 156(2): 94–98.

9. Vogiatzi MG, and Kirkland JL. 1997. Frequency and necessity of thyroid function tests in neonates and infants with congenital hypothyroidism. *Pediatrics* 100(3): e6.

10. McEvoy GK. 1999. *AHFS Drug Information.* Bethesda, Maryland: American Society of Health-Systems Pharmacists, 2788–2794.

11. Medical Economics Data. 1998. *Physicians' Desk Reference,* 52nd ed. Montvale, New Jersey: Medical Economics, 1374–1377.

12. United States Pharmacopeial Convention/USP DI. 1996. *Drug Information for the Health Care Professional,* 16th ed. Rockville, Maryland: United States Pharmacopeial Convention, 2876–2880.

13. Reifen RM, and Zlotkin S. 1993. Microminerals. In *Nutritional Needs of the Preterm Infant: Scientific Basis and Practical Guidelines,* Tsang RCL, et al., eds. Baltimore: Lippincott Williams & Wilkins, 195–207.

14. van Wassenaer AG, et al. 1997. Effects of thyroxine supplementation on neurologic development in infants born at less than 30 weeks' gestation. *New England Journal of Medicine* 336(1): 21–26.

15. Parfite K. 1999. *Martindale: The Complete Drug Reference,* 32nd ed. London: Pharmaceutical Press, 1497–1499.

16. Raghavan S, DiMartino-Nardi J, and Linder B. 1997. Pseudotumor cerebri in an infant after L-thyroxine therapy for transient neonatal hypothyroidism. *Journal of Pediatrics* 130(3): 478–480.

17. Golightly LK, et al. 1987. Clinical effects of accidental levothyroxine ingestion in children. *American Journal of Diseases of Children* 141(9): 1025–1027.

LIDOCAINE (XYLOCAINE)

(LYE-doe-kane)

DOSE

IV/Endotracheal/Intraosseous: 0.5–1 mg/kg/dose every 5–10 minutes. *Maximum:* 5 mg/kg. If a second or third IV dose is required, consider starting a *continuous infusion* at 10–50 mcg/kg/minute.[1,2]

Infiltration for Local Anesthesia: *Maximum:* 4.5 mg/kg/dose per 2-hour period (= 0.9 ml/kg of lidocaine 0.5 percent).

- Use the 0.5 percent (= 5 mg/ml), rather than the 1 percent, lidocaine concentration in the NICU to avoid overdose.
- Table 1-32 gives directions for buffering lidocaine for subcutaneous injection.

For Status Epilepticus: 2 mg/kg IV, followed by 2 mg/kg/hour (= 30 mcg/kg/minute) was used in one study.[3]

Topical:

- **EMLA** (eutectic mixture of local anesthetics, lidocaine with prilocaine) cream. (See lidocaine/prilocaine cream monograph.)
- **Lidocaine ointment:** *Maximum:* 3 mg/kg per 2-hour period.

Decrease dose in patients with hepatic dysfunction, congestive heart failure, decreased hepatic blood flow, and shock. Also decrease dose in asphyxiated, acidotic infants, who may also experience reduced elimination. Use the low end of the dosage range, above, in these conditions, and monitor serum concentrations.

ADMINISTRATION

Do not use lidocaine-epinephrine combination products in neonates.

For IV, endotracheal, or intraosseous route, use the product without preservatives intended for IV use.

TABLE 1-32 ◆ BUFFERING LIDOCAINE FOR SUBCUTANEOUS INFILTRATION

Directions: Add 9 ml of lidocaine to 1 ml of 1 mEq/ml sodium bicarbonate in a sterile glass vial. Mix well. Prepare immediately before administration. Discard unused portion.

- Addition of sodium bicarbonate reduces the shelf life of lidocaine, so the solution cannot be stored.
- Addition of bicarbonate hastens the onset of analgesia and reduces the stinging pain.
- If this solution is prepared in a syringe, be sure to first draw up the sodium bicarbonate, then the lidocaine. This will avoid tissue damage from injection of traces of concentrated sodium bicarbonate in the syringe hub and needle.

Adapted from: Yaster M, Tobin JR, and Fisher QA. 1994. Local anesthetics in the management of acute pain in children. *Journal of Pediatrics* 124(2): 165–176; and McKay W, Morris R, and Mushlin P. 1987. Sodium bicarbonate attenuates pain on skin infiltration with lidocaine, with or without epinephrine. *Anesthesia and Analgesia* 66(6): 572–574.

For infiltration for local anesthesia, the product with preservatives may be used.

IV—*Rate:* Infuse over 2–4 minutes.

IV—*Concentration:* May give undiluted.

IV—*Compatibility:* See Appendix E: Y-Site Compatibility of Common NICU Drugs.

CAUTIONS/CONTRAINDICATIONS

Do not use lidocaine-epinephrine combination products in neonates.

USE

To treat ventricular arrhythmias.

To relieve pain of minor surgical procedures, when given by local infiltration.

For refractory status epilepticus.

MECHANISM OF ACTION

Lidocaine is a class IB antiarrhythmic. It is thought to act by stabilizing the neuronal membrane, thereby preventing calcium uptake and blocking sodium and potassium movement, but the precise mechanism is unknown. Lidocaine is a sodium channel blocker. It has minimal slowing of phase 0 depolarization and faster repolarization.

ADVERSE EFFECTS

Myocardial depression, widened QRS, drowsiness, seizures, muscle twitching.

Transient depression of EEG.

Methemoglobinemia has followed topical application for teething discomfort and use as a laryngeal anesthetic spray. Seizures have occurred from overuse of oral lidocaine (lidocaine viscous) in children.

Pain on subcutaneous infiltration. Reduce pain by buffering the pH of the solution (see Table 1-32) and by using a small needle (26 or 30 gauge). To avoid tissue necrosis and arrhythmias, do not use a lidocaine-epinephrine combination product in neonates.[4]

Overdose: See **COMMENTS** for therapeutic range and effects of higher concentrations. In case of overdose, stop drug; institute resuscitative measures. Treat convulsions with a benzodiazepine or a short-acting barbiturate. Methemoglobinemia may be treated with methylene blue 1–2 mg/kg given slowly over several minutes.

PHARMACOKINETICS/PHARMACODYNAMICS

Absorption: Percutaneous absorption is increased in preterm infants.

Onset of Action: For local infiltration analgesia, 1–5 minutes.

Protein Binding: 20 percent (less than in adults, where it is 70 percent).

Metabolism: Extensive metabolism occurs on first pass through the liver, inactivating 60 percent of the drug before it reaches the systemic circulation. Metabolized to two active metabolites, monoethylglycinexylidide (MEGX) and glycinexylidide (GX).

Half-life: 3 hours.

Elimination: 16 percent renal (higher in neonates than in adults, where it is 2 percent). The GX metabolite may accumulate in renal dysfunction.

NURSING IMPLICATIONS

Requires continuous cardiac monitoring.

Monitor IV site carefully and frequently to avoid infiltration.

Monitor serum concentrations and hepatic function.

COMMENTS

Therapeutic Range: 1.5–5 mcg/ml.

- *>6 mcg/ml:* Significant risk for CNS and cardiovascular depression.
- *>8 mcg/ml:* Seizures, obtundation, hypotension, respiratory depression, decreased cardiac output, coma.

Interactions: β-blockers and cimetidine increase lidocaine serum concentrations. Monitor for toxicity.

REFERENCES

1. Benitz WE, and Tatro DS. 1995. *The Pediatric Drug Handbook,* 3rd ed. St. Louis: Mosby-Year Book, 183–184.

2. American Heart Association, Emergency Cardiac Care Committee and Subcommittees. 1992. Guidelines for cardiopulmonary resuscitation and emergency cardiac care. Part 6: Pediatric advanced life support. *JAMA* 268(16): 2262–2275. (Comment in *JAMA,* 1992, 268[16]: 2297–2298; and *JAMA,* 1993, 269[20]: 2627.)

3. Hellstrom-Westas L, et al. 1988. Lidocaine for treatment of severe seizures in newborn infants. Part 1: Clinical effects and cerebral electrical activity monitoring. *Acta Paediatrica Scandinavica* 77(1): 79–84.

4. Robieux IC. 1993. Treatment of pain in infants and children: The role of pharmacology. In *Pediatric Pharmacology and Therapeutics,* 2nd ed., Radde IC, and MacLeod SM, eds. St. Louis: Mosby-Year Book, 499–513.

LIDOCAINE/PRILOCAINE CREAM
(LYE-doe-kane/PRIL-oh-kane)
[5 PERCENT]
EUTECTIC MIXTURE OF LOCAL ANESTHETICS (EMLA)

LOCAL ANESTHETIC:
TOPICAL

DOSE

Infants ≥37 weeks gestational age: For small infants, <10 kg, use just enough cream to cover the site with a thick layer. Individualize the dose to the size of the baby. Limit area and duration. Table 1-33 indicates the maximum recommended dosages, application areas, and application times for EMLA based on age and body weight (for infants with normal renal and hepatic function, when the cream is applied to intact skin). Reduce amount in infants with impaired hepatic and/or renal function. If an infant older than 3 months does not meet the minimum weight requirement, restrict the maximum total dose of EMLA to that indicated by the infant's weight.[1]

Circumcision:

- Taddio and colleagues found that EMLA was efficacious and safe in preventing pain from circumcision in neonates (mean birth weight 3.6 kg at mean postnatal age of 1.3 days). None of the neonates had any clinical signs of methemoglobinemia. Serum concentrations of lidocaine and prilocaine were considerably below those considered toxic.[2] The researchers used the following procedure: 1 ml (1 gm) of cream was drawn into a 3 ml syringe. One-third of the dose was applied to the lower abdomen. The penis was extended upward and gently pressed against the abdomen. The remainder of the dose was applied to a Tegaderm dressing, which was then placed over the penis and taped to the abdomen so that the cream surrounded the penis. After 60–80 minutes, the dressing was removed, and the cream was wiped away with a tissue. The authors recommend that other interventions to comfort the infant (e.g., the use of a pacifier and the administration of sucrose) should also be used.[2]

- In another report, Taddio and colleagues note that neonatal circumcision is associated with increased pain response during vaccination 4–6 months after the surgery. However, preoperative treatment with EMLA during circumcision

TABLE 1-33 ◆ MAXIMUM EMLA DOSE, APPLICATION AREA, AND APPLICATION TIME BY AGE AND WEIGHT

Age/Body Weight	Maximum Total Dose	Maximum Area	Maximum Time
0–3 months or <5 kg	1 gm	10 cm^2	1 hour
3–12 months and >5 kg	2 gm	20 cm^2	4 hours
1–6 years and >10 kg	10 gm	100 cm^2	4 hours

From: Manufacturer's product literature.

attenuates the pain response to later vaccination. The authors recommend EMLA treatment to prevent neonatal circumcision pain.[3]

ADMINISTRATION

Supplied as: A cream—lidocaine 2.5 percent with prilocaine 2.5 percent. Two Tegaderm dressings are included. Available in 5 gm and 30 gm sizes.

Topical use only. For external use only; not for ophthalmic use; not for use on mucous membranes. Instructions for use:

1. At least 60 minutes before the procedure (venipuncture, lumbar puncture, or other procedure), apply a thick layer of EMLA to the skin site.

2. Do not rub the cream into the skin.

3. Cover with an occlusive dressing such as the Tegaderm patch provided with the cream.[1]

CAUTIONS/CONTRAINDICATIONS

Not for use in infants <37 weeks gestational age or in infants <12 months of age receiving concurrent methemoglobin-inducing agents (see **COMMENTS** below for some of these drugs).[1]

Use with caution in patients with severe hepatic disease because of their limited ability to metabolize lidocaine and prilocaine; toxic blood levels could result.[1]

Methemoglobinemia may occur,[4] especially if infants receiving EMLA are also receiving drugs with additive or synergistic effects. (See **COMMENTS** below for interactions.)

Antidote: For drug-induced methemoglobinemia, the antidote is methylene blue 1–1.5 mg/kg given slowly IV.[5–7]

USE

Produces local analgesia of intact skin for minor procedures in infants ≥37 weeks gestational age.

Has been used effectively to alleviate pain caused by insertion of intravenous catheters, venipuncture, lumbar puncture, and of vaccinations.[8–10] Has also been used during the application of split-thickness skin grafts.[1]

MECHANISM OF ACTION

EMLA stands for "eutectic mixture of local anesthetics." A eutectic mixture is one whose melting point is lower than the melting points of either of its components. The crystalline bases of lidocaine and prilocaine become fluid at room temperature when mixed.[11] Both lidocaine and prilocaine belong to the amino-amide group of local anesthetics. Local anesthetics inhibit conduction of nerve impulses from sensory nerves by changing the cell membrane's permeability to ions.

Adverse Effects

Methemoglobinemia may occur,[4] especially if EMLA is applied to infants receiving drugs with additive or synergistic effects. (See **Comments** below for interactions.) The younger the infant, the more likely this is to occur.[12] Methemoglobinemia occurred in a 5.3 kg 12-week-old boy treated preoperatively with co-trimoxazole (sulfamethoxazole-trimethoprim combinations). The infant received 5 ml of EMLA on the backs of the hands and in the antecubital area; the cream was inadvertently left on the skin for 5 hours. The infant developed a "brownish" cyanosis that did not improve after oxygen ventilation. Methylene blue (see **Comments** below) was given slowly IV, and the cyanosis disappeared within 30 minutes.[5]

Infants have lower NADH-dehydrogenase (nicotinamide adenine dinucleotide-dehydrogenase) activity and therefore develop methemoglobinemia more readily than older children and adults. Infants with G6PD deficiency are more likely to develop methemoglobinemia from EMLA. Do not use the drug in infants with congenital or idiopathic methemoglobinemia.

Initially causes blanching at the site of application; then after prolonged application, causes increased redness. These should not be considered adverse effects, but rather *normal* effects on vessels after application. Blanching or redness recedes a few hours after removal of the bandage. Avoid prolonged application times on diseased skin, however, to avoid severe inflammation or purpura.[11]

Pharmacokinetics/Pharmacodynamics

Absorption: Poor through intact skin, but the drugs are readily absorbed through mucous membranes; the genital area; and abraded, diseased, or ulcerated skin. Infants, especially preterm infants, have increased skin permeability to topically applied agents compared with children or adults.

Onset/Duration of Action: In the oral and genital areas, onset is within a few minutes after application, and duration is short (1–2 hours after removal of the cream) because the drugs are rapidly transported away from the application area by underlying vessels.[11]

Anesthetic/Analgesic Effects: The anesthesia produced is apparent at a depth of up to 5 mm. Effective analgesia is achieved 60–90 minutes after application under occlusive dressing on normal intact skin (after 5–30 minutes on diseased skin). The shortest application time recommended is 10 minutes.[13] The degree of dermal analgesia increases for up to 3 hours under an occlusive dressing.

Metabolism: Both lidocaine and prilocaine are metabolized in the liver.

Half-life: The mean half-life of lidocaine is 110 ± 24 minutes and is prolonged with cardiac or hepatic dysfunction. The mean half-life of prilocaine is 70 ± 48 minutes and is prolonged in hepatic or renal dysfunction.

Elimination: Renal for both lidocaine and prilocaine.

Nursing Implications

Place a protective cotton bandage over the EMLA dressing on older infants capable of playing with the dressing to avoid ingestion of the cream or rubbing of it into the eyes. The bandage will protect the Tegaderm from damage and can contain and absorb the cream if it leaks, preventing its spread.[14]

COMMENTS

The antidote for drug-induced methemoglobinemia is methylene blue 1–1.5 mg/kg given slowly IV.[5–7]

Refer also to the monographs on lidocaine, and methyline blue.

Interactions:

- Class I antiarrhythmic drugs such as tocainide and mexiletine may have additive or synergistic toxic effects.[1]
- Infants already being treated with drugs associated with drug-induced methemoglobinemia—such as sulfonamides (including co-trimoxazole—e.g., Bactrim and Septra),[5] acetaminophen, benzocaine, chloroquine, dapsone, nitrofurantoin, nitroglycerin, nitroprusside, nitric oxide, phenobarbital, and phenytoin—have a greater risk for developing methemoglobinemia with EMLA use.[1]

REFERENCES

1. Manufacturer's product literature.

2. Taddio A, et al. 1997. Efficacy and safety of lidocaine-prilocaine cream for pain during circumcision. *New England Journal of Medicine* 336(17): 1197–1201.

3. Taddio A, et al. 1997. Effect of neonatal circumcision on pain response during subsequent routine vaccination. *Lancet* 349(9052): 599–603.

4. Frayling IM, et al. 1990. Methaemoglobinaemia in children treated with prilocaine-lignocaine cream. *British Medical Journal* 301(6744): 153–154.

5. Jakobson B, and Nilsson A. 1985. Methemoglobinemia associated with a prilocaine-lidocaine cream and trimethoprim-sulphamethoxazole: A case report. *Acta Anaesthesiologica Scandinavica* 29(4): 453–455.

6. Engberg G, et al. 1987. Plasma concentrations of prilocaine and lidocaine and methaemoglobin formation in infants after epicutaneous application of a 5 percent lidocaine-prilocaine (EMLA). *Acta Anaesthesiologica Scandinavica* 31(7): 624–628.

7. Olson ML, and McEvoy GK. 1981. Methemoglobinemia induced by local anesthetics. *American Journal of Hospital Pharmacy* 38(1): 89–93.

8. Halperin DL, et al. 1989. Topical skin anesthesia for venous, subcutaneous drug reservoir and lumbar punctures in children. *Pediatrics* 84(2): 281–284.

9. Robieux I, et al. 1991. Assessing pain and analgesia with a lidocaine-prilocaine emulsion in infants and toddlers during venipuncture. *Journal of Pediatrics* 118(6): 971–973.

10. Uhari M. 1993. A eutectic mixture of lidocaine and prilocaine for alleviating vaccination pain in infants. *Pediatrics* 92(5): 719–721.

11. Juhlin L, and Evers H. 1990. EMLA: A new topical anesthetic. *Advances in Dermatology* 5: 75–92.

12. Nilsson A, et al. 1990. Inverse relationship between age-dependent erythrocyte activity of methaemoglobin reductase and prilocaine-induced methaemoglobinaemia during infancy. *British Journal of Anaesthesia* 64(1): 72–76.

13. de Waard-van der Spek FB, et al. 1992. EMLA cream: An improved local anesthetic. Review of current literature. *Pediatric Dermatology* 9(2): 126–131.

14. Norman J, and Jones PL. 1990. Complications of the use of EMLA (letter). *British Journal of Anaesthesia* 64(3): 403.

Loperamide (Imodium)

(loe-PER-a-mide)

Gastrointestinal: Antidiarrheal

Dose

Acute: 0.1 mg/kg/dose given bid to tid.

Usual: 0.4–0.8 mg/kg/day divided every 12 hours.

- *Maximum:* 0.8 mg/kg/day.[1]

Chronic: 0.08–0.24 mg/kg/day divided bid to tid. Reduce to the lowest effective dose.

- *Maximum:* 2 mg/dose.

Reduce dose in hepatic dysfunction.

If clinical improvement is not seen in 48 hours, discontinue use.

Administration

PO: For oral use *only*. Available in liquid form 1 mg/5 ml (= 0.2 mg/ml). Contains 5.25 percent alcohol.

Use

An antidiarrheal agent that is used as an adjunct to the management of diarrhea refractory to standard treatment, such as dietary adjustment and provision of fluids and electrolytes. Reduces daily stool output and duration of diarrhea.[1,2] Decreases volume of stool and electrolyte output in short gut syndrome and in infants with ileostomies.

Antidiarrheals are not used to treat ordinary acute watery diarrhea; they are useless against that type of diarrhea and can be dangerous for infants. Rehydration with appropriate fluids and electrolytes and prevention or correction of the cause of the diarrhea are the most important aspects of care.

Mechanism of Action

Loperamide has a chemical structure similar to meperidine and diphenoxylate. Loperamide acts by inhibiting (slowing) longitudinal and circular muscle activity, which decreases intestinal motility.

Adverse Effects

May cause constipation, vomiting, abdominal distention, ileus, dry mouth, rash (rare), nervousness, somnolence. Habituation and tolerance have not occurred.

Overdose is reversed with naloxone.

Motala and associates reported that of 30 infants with acute infectious diarrhea given loperamide 0.8 mg/kg/day for 48 hours after admission with rehydration with IV fluids, 2 infants had to be withdrawn from the trial because ileus developed in 1 and the other had persistent, severe vomiting. Transient drowsiness developed in 4 other infants.[2] These researchers and others caution that the use of this drug in infants be limited to closely monitored inpatients.[2,3]

Bhutta and Tahir reported poisoning after administration of over-the-counter loperamide caused toxic dilation and paralytic ileus in 18 young infants in Multan, Pakistan; at least 6 of the infants died. Although the label on the over-the-counter drug stated that it was not for use in infants <1 year of age, the population is 99 percent illiterate and could not read the warning.[4] The oral liquid has since been withdrawn in a number of countries, including Pakistan.[4,5]

Loperamide liquid is available without a prescription in the U.S. Caution parents not to administer it to their infants. Careful monitoring for adverse effects is required when the drug is given to hospitalized infants.

PHARMACOKINETICS/PHARMACODYNAMICS

Distribution: Does not penetrate the CNS, which explains the drug's relative lack of central opiate-like adverse effects.

Peak Action: 2.5–5 hours after administration.

Half-life: 9–14 hours.

Elimination: Enterohepatic circulation occurs; 30 percent of the drug excreted in the stool and 2 percent in the urine.

NURSING IMPLICATIONS

Monitor for abdominal distention, presence/absence of bowel sounds, and feeding intolerance.

Monitor fluid and electrolyte status carefully as in any infant with diarrhea.

Check CNS status for drowsiness.

Observe for ileus.

REFERENCES

1. Diarrhoeal Diseases Study Group (UK). 1984. Loperamide in acute diarrhoea in childhood: Results of a double-blind, placebo controlled multicentre clinical trial. *British Medical Journal (Clinical Research Edition)* 289(6454): 1263–1267.

2. Motala C, et al. 1990. Effect of loperamide on stool output and duration of acute infectious diarrhea in infants. *Journal of Pediatrics* 117(3): 467–471.

3. Hill ID, et al. 1991. Reply (letter). *Journal of Pediatrics* 119(5): 843.

4. Bhutta TI, and Tahir KI. 1990. Loperamide poisoning in children (letter). *Lancet* 335(10): 363.

5. Bhutta ZA, and Molla AM. 1991. Safety of loperamide in infants with diarrhea (letter). *Journal of Pediatrics* 119(5): 842–843.

LORAZEPAM (ATIVAN)
(lor-AZ-e-pam)
(CONTROLLED SUBSTANCE SCHEDULE IV)

CENTRAL NERVOUS SYSTEM: SEDATIVE

DOSE

Sedation: 0.05–0.1 mg/kg/dose every 4–8 hours

Status Epilepticus:

- *IV:* 0.04–0.15 mg/kg[1,2]
- *Rectal:* 0.05–0.1 mg/kg PR using the parenteral dosage form[3]

Reduce dose in renal or hepatic dysfunction.

ADMINISTRATION

IV, PO, IM, or PR. ***Do not administer via intra-arterial route because arteriospasm may occur, resulting in gangrene.***

IV—*Rate:* Infuse slowly over 2 minutes or more.

IV—*Concentration:* Dilute with an equal volume of sterile water, D_5W, or NS immediately prior to IV use.

IV—*Compatibility:* See Appendix E: Y-Site Compatibility of Common NICU Drugs.

PO: Available as an oral solution (2 mg/ml). May also give parenteral dosage form PO if the oral solution is not available.

IM (rarely used in neonates): Administer undiluted into deep muscle mass.

Rectal: The IV form of lorazepam has been given PR for seizures when an IV cannot be started. Absorption is rapid through the rectal mucosa.

USE

Management of anxiety.

Treatment of status epilepticus.

MECHANISM OF ACTION

A benzodiazepine, lorazepam increases the action of the inhibitory neurotransmitter GABA and of other inhibitory transmitters by binding to specific benzodiazepine receptor sites.

ADVERSE EFFECTS

Respiratory depression. Be prepared to assist ventilation.

Hypotension with rapid IV administration.

Paradoxical excitation has occurred in children; in infants, lorazepam has caused neurotoxicity, resulting in seizures.[4,5] Myoclonus has been associated with lorazepam use in preterm infants.[6]

L

Diarrhea with benzodiazepine oral solution thought to be due to osmotic effects of the propylene glycol and polyethylene glycol in the preparation. Diarrhea resolved with conversion to crushed tablets.[7]

Rare: Neutropenia and jaundice; abnormal liver function tests and kidney function; decreased hematocrit.

With Long-term (4–6 weeks) Use: Potential for physical dependence; taper dose gradually to prevent withdrawal symptoms.

PHARMACOKINETICS/PHARMACODYNAMICS

Absorption: Readily absorbed orally.

Onset of Action: Onset is rapid (but slower than diazepam).

Duration of Action: Long-term (>16 hours) control of convulsions after a single dose.[8,9]

Protein Binding: 70–99 percent.

Metabolism: Metabolized to inactive glucuronide conjugate in the liver.

Half-life: 10–20 hours.

Elimination: Urine.

NURSING IMPLICATIONS

Protect drug from light; store in the refrigerator.

Monitor for myoclonic jerking.

Monitor for respiratory depression and therapeutic effects; document.

COMMENTS

Interactions: Other CNS depressants such as phenobarbital and narcotics have additive CNS depressant effects. May increase digoxin levels.

Benzyl Alcohol Content: The injection contains 2 percent benzyl alcohol (= 20 mg/ml). Use of the 4 mg/ml concentration, rather than the 2 mg/ml, minimizes benzyl alcohol intake, although a serial dilution may be required for accurate measurement of small doses. Fatal gasping syndrome in neonates has been associated with 100–400 mg/kg/day of benzyl alcohol.

Antidote: Flumazenil (Romazicon) 2–10 mcg/kg IV every minute × 3 as needed, see also Appendix J: Antidotes for Drugs That Cause Loss of Respiratory Effort.

REFERENCES

1. Deshmukh A, et al. 1986. Lorazepam in the treatment of refractory neonatal seizures: A pilot study. *American Journal of Diseases of Children* 140(10): 1042–1044.

2. McDermott CA, et al. 1992. Pharmacokinetics of lorazepam in critically ill neonates with seizures. *Journal of Pediatrics* 120(3): 479–483.

3. Levin SD. 1993. Clinical pharmacology in neonatal and childhood seizure disorders. In *Pediatric Pharmacology and Therapeutics*, 2nd ed., Radde IC, and MacLeod SM, eds. St. Louis: Mosby-Year Book, 556–572.

4. Cronin CMG. 1992. Neurotoxicity of lorazepam in a premature infant. *Pediatrics* 89(6): 1129–1130.

5. Reiter PD, and Stiles AD. 1993. Lorazepam toxicity in a premature infant. *Annals of Pharmacotherapy* 27(6): 727–729.

6. Lee DS, Wong HA, and Knoppert DC. 1994. Myoclonus associated with lorazepam therapy in very-low-birth-weight infants. *Biology of the Neonate* 66(6): 311–315.

7. Marshall JD, Farrar HC, and Kearns GL. 1995. Diarrhea associated with enteral benzodiazepine solutions. *Journal of Pediatrics* 126(4): 657–659.

8. Lacey DJ, et al. 1986. Lorazepam therapy of status epilepticus in children and adolescents. *Journal of Pediatrics* 108(5 part 1): 771–774.

9. Crawford TO, Mitchell WG, and Snodgrass SR. 1987. Lorazepam in childhood status epilepticus and serial seizures: Effectiveness and tachyphylaxis. *Neurology* 37(2): 190–195.

TABLE OF CONTENTS

M

MAGNESIUM SULFATE

(mag-NEE-zee-um SUL-fate)

ELECTROLYTE BALANCE: ELECTROLYTE SUPPLEMENT

Synonyms: $MgSO_4$, Epsom salts

DOSE

Hypomagnesemia:

- *IM/IV:* 25–50 mg/kg/dose (= 0.2–0.4 mEq/kg) every 6 hours for three to four doses until symptoms resolve and serum magnesium levels return to normal.[1]
- *PO:* 100–200 mg/kg/day divided every 6 hours.

Seizures and Hypertension:

- *IM/IV:* 25–100 mg/kg/dose given every 4–6 hours (children).[2] Monitor serum magnesium concentrations.

Maintenance Requirement for Patients on Parenteral Nutrition:
30–60 mg/kg/day (= 0.25–0.5 mEq/kg/day).[1]

Persistent Pulmonary Hypertension of the Newborn (PPHN): Abu-Osba and associates treated infants with PPHN using a loading dose of 200 mg/kg (1.6 mEq/kg), then a maintenance infusion of 20–50 mg/kg/hour (0.16–0.4 mEq/kg/hour) for up to 8 hours with frequent serum magnesium determinations.[3] This treatment, however, is experimental. Other methods (such as alkalinization, tolazoline, ECMO, and nitric oxide) are more frequently used to treat this disorder.

Reduce dose and monitor serum magnesium concentrations in renal impairment.

ADMINISTRATION

Supplied as: A 50 percent solution or 500 mg $MgSO_4$/ml (= 4 mEq/ml).

IV—*Rate:* Infuse over 3–4 hours.

IV—*Concentration:* ≤30 mg/ml preferred; maximum: 200 mg/ml.

IV—*Compatibility:* See Appendix E: Y-Site Compatibility of Common NICU Drugs.

IM: Not the preferred route in neonates because of their poor muscle mass. If used, maximum concentration is 200 mg/ml.

PO: May use the parenteral form PO and dilute in feedings.

USE

Treatment of hypomagnesemia. Symptoms of hypomagnesemia are similar to tetany from hypocalcemia, usually with magnesium serum levels <1.5 mEq/liter and a normal serum calcium.[4]

Provision of maintenance magnesium requirements for patients on parenteral nutrition.

M

Mechanism of Action

Magnesium is an essential component of many enzyme reactions relating to carbo-hydrate metabolism and ATP. It is involved in neurochemical transmission and muscular excitability. Magnesium has bronchodilator effects and antihypertensive, antiarrhythmic, and anticonvulsant properties. Excess magnesium decreases the amount of acetylcholine liberated by the motor nerve impulse. When taken orally, magnesium acts as an osmotic laxative, drawing fluid into the bowel and causing colon distension, which increases peristalsis.

Adverse Effects

Hypotension with Rapid IV Administration: Monitor blood pressure. Monitor for cardiac arrhythmias and respiratory and CNS depression during infusion. Monitor serum magnesium levels.

Flushing, sweating, depressed reflexes, flaccid paralysis, hypothermia, cardiac and CNS depression, respiratory paralysis.

Diarrhea may occur with oral administration. Dilute and give in divided doses.

Treat overdose of magnesium with calcium gluconate IV, resuscitation, and assisted ventilation. Peritoneal dialysis and hemodialysis are effective.

Pharmacokinetics/Pharmacodynamics

Absorption: In the jejunum and ileum when given orally.

Onset of Action: Immediate if given IV.

Duration of Action: 30 minutes if given IV.

Elimination: In the urine if given IV at a rate proportional to serum concentration and GFR. Primarily in the feces if given PO.

Maternal magnesium sulfate crosses the placenta and accumulates in the fetus, particularly if the mother receives prolonged and high doses. The magnesium is excreted over a period of 7 days and usually has no clinical effect, but it may cause apnea and general flaccidity in the neonate, especially in those with reduced renal function.

Nursing Implications

Continuously monitor blood pressure, heart rate, and respiratory rate during infusion.

Monitor electrolyte values, especially for hypocalcemia.

Monitor for diarrhea with oral doses.

Comments

Conversion Factor: 1 gm magnesium sulfate = 8 mEq magnesium.

Interpretation of Magnesium Levels:[5]

- *Low Levels:*
  - Hypomagnesemia: <1.5 mEq/liter.

- *Normal Levels:*
  - Normal level: 1.5–2.5 mEq/liter.
  - Therapeutic level for preeclampsia, eclampsia, treatment of convulsive toxemia: 4–7 mEq/liter (anticonvulsant levels have also been expressed as 2.5–7.5 mEq/liter).
- *Toxic Levels* (see **ADVERSE EFFECTS** above for treatment):
  - Loss of deep tendon reflexes, hypotension, narcosis: 7–10 mEq/liter.
  - Respiratory paralysis: 12–15 mEq/liter.
  - Effects on cardiac conduction, with lengthened PR interval, widened QRS, and dysrhythmias, which may lead to complete heart block: >15 mEq/liter.
  - Likelihood of cardiac arrest: >25 mEq/liter.

Interactions:

- Infants with hypermagnesemia may be more resistant to the effects of indomethacin on closure of the ductus arteriosus.
- Hypermagnesemic infants may experience respiratory arrest after receiving aminoglycosides.[4,6]
- The effects of neuromuscular blocking agents (e.g., atracurium) may be increased with prolonged apnea when magnesium sulfate is given concurrently.

REFERENCES

1. Kerner JA Jr. 1983. *Manual of Pediatric Parenteral Nutrition.* New York: Wiley, 132.
2. Taketomo CK, Hodding JH, and Kraus DM. 1993. *Pediatric Dosage Handbook,* 2nd ed. Hudson, Ohio: Lexi-Comp, 422–424.
3. Abu-Osba YK, et al. 1992. Treatment of severe persistent pulmonary hypertension of the newborn with magnesium sulphate. *Archives of Disease in Childhood* 67(1 spec. no.): 31–35.
4. L'Hommedieu CS, et al. 1983. Potentiation of magnesium sulfate–induced neuromuscular weakness by gentamicin, tobramycin and amikacin. *Journal of Pediatrics* 102(4): 629–631.
5. Olin BR. 1994. *Drug Facts and Comparisons.* St. Louis: Facts and Comparisons, 142–144.
6. L'Hommedieu CS, Huber PA, and Rasch DK. 1983. Potentiation of magnesium-induced neuromuscular weakness by gentamicin. *Critical Care Medicine* 11(1): 55–56.

MEDIUM-CHAIN TRIGLYCERIDES
(tri-GLISS-er-ides)
(MCT OIL)

NUTRITION:
CALORIC SUPPLEMENT

DOSE

Initial: 0.5 ml every 6 hours (or every other feeding).

- If tolerated, may advance in 24 hours to 0.5 ml every 3 hours (every feeding).
- May increase dose volume with a corresponding reduction in dose frequency after 24 hours to 1 ml every 6 hours as tolerated to simplify administration.

MCT oil is a caloric supplement, providing 7.6 kcal/ml. *Maximum dose:* 55 percent of calories from fat.

ADMINISTRATION

PO: Mix with formula. In older infants on a more varied diet, may mix with fruit juice, vegetables, and other foods.

A significant portion of the MCT oil (about 33 percent) may adhere to the feeding tube during gavage feeding, so the infant may receive fewer than the intended calories administered.[1]

USE

Useful as a nutritional supplement in preterm infants because absorption of MCT oil is not dependent upon pancreatic lipase or bile salts, both of which are limited in quantity in preterm infants.

Also useful for other patients, such as infants with cholestasis, who have difficulty utilizing long-chain triglycerides.

MECHANISM OF ACTION

MCT oil is derived from coconut oil that has been hydrolyzed and re-esterified with glycerol. It consists of saturated fatty acids—approximately 75 percent octanoic acid (C_8) and 23 percent decanoic acid (C_{10}) and other fatty acids. Figure 2-1, page 602, found in the **Nutrition** section, illustrates the differences between absorption of LCTs and MCTs.

ADVERSE EFFECTS

Diarrhea may be an indication that the dose has exceeded the infant's tolerance for the oil. Reduce the dose.

Lipid pneumonia. Undiluted MCT oil may be aspirated; mix with formula before administration.[2]

Large amounts of MCTs may cause elevated blood and spinal fluid levels of medium-chain fatty acids in patients with advanced hepatic cirrhosis because of their impaired hepatic clearance. May lead to coma.

May exacerbate ketosis in patients with acidosis.[3,4]

M

NURSING IMPLICATIONS

Mix well into feeding.

Monitor growth parameters (head circumference, weight, length) weekly.

Monitor for diarrhea.

COMMENTS

Contains no essential fatty acids. Essential fatty acids are long-chain triglycerides (LCTs C_{16} to C_{18}).

Does not increase the osmolality of feedings.

Glucose polymers (Polycose) may need to be given concurrently to balance the fat and carbohydrate intakes. Modular protein supplement (Casec) may be added as well. The percentages of CHO and fat should be approximately equal to those in human milk (52 percent fat, 42 percent CHO, 6 percent protein).

REFERENCES

1. Mehta NR, et al. 1991. Adherence of medium-chain fatty acids to feeding tubes of premature infants fed formula fortified with medium-chain triglyceride. *Journal of Pediatric Gastroenterology and Nutrition* 13(3): 267–269.

2. Smith RM, Brumley GW, and Stannard MW. 1978. Neonatal pneumonia associated with medium-chain triglyceride feeding supplement. *Journal of Pediatrics* 92(5): 801–804.

3. Bach AC, and Babayan VK. 1982. Medium-chain triglycerides: An update. *American Journal of Clinical Nutrition* 36(5): 950–962.

4. Manufacturer's product literature.

MEPERIDINE (DEMEROL)

(me-PER-i-deen)

(CONTROLLED SUBSTANCE SCHEDULE II)

CENTRAL NERVOUS SYSTEM: NARCOTIC ANALGESIC

Synonym: pethidine

DOSE

IV, IM, SC: 0.5–1 mg/kg/dose given every 4 hours, as needed.

PO: 1–2 mg/kg/dose given every 4 hours, as needed.

Premedication with Lytic Cocktail (DPT) (*Caution:* Use of DPT is discouraged by the American Academy of Pediatrics, and its use has been decreasing with the availability of safer and more effective agents.):[1]

- Demerol (meperidine) 0.5 mg/kg/dose
- Phenergan (promethazine) 0.25 mg/kg/dose
- Thorazine (chlorpromazine) 0.25 mg/kg/dose
  - May mix all three components in the same syringe so that DPT may be given as a single IM injection.

ADMINISTRATION

Supplied as: Injection: 10 mg/ml; oral syrup: 10 mg/ml.

IV—*Rate:* Infuse over at least 1–2 minutes. Rapid IV administration increases the incidence of adverse effects.

IV—*Concentration:* May give undiluted; however, dilution with at least an equal volume of dextrose or saline is preferred.

IM, SC—*Concentration:* May give undiluted. The IV route is preferred to IM or SC in neonates because of poor absorption.

PO: Dilute oral dose in feedings or water to prevent the slight topical anesthetic effect on the mucous membranes.

USE

Management of severe pain.

MECHANISM OF ACTION

Meperidine stimulates opioid receptors in the CNS that mimic the actions of endogenous ligands, enkephalins, and β-endorphins, thus altering perception of and response to pain. It causes respiratory depression by a direct effect on the brain's respiratory center. It also causes CNS depression.

ADVERSE EFFECTS

Increasing the dose increases the adverse effects, such as respiratory and CNS depression. *Antidote:* Naloxone 0.1 mg/kg/dose IV (see Appendix J: Antidotes for Drugs That Cause Loss of Respiratory Effort).

Cardiovascular: Bradycardia, hypotension (due to histamine release), especially in patients with inadequate blood volume. Meperidine is more likely than most other opioids to cause side effects associated with histamine release.

CNS: CNS depression and arrest requiring mechanical ventilation, increased intracranial pressure, and sedation. May cause twitches, tremors, and/or seizures with prolonged, repeated use because of accumulation of normeperidine metabolite.

Endocrine: Antidiuretic hormone release.

GI: Nausea, vomiting (take with food to reduce GI upset). Delayed gastric emptying, cramping, and biliary tract spasm. Meperidine is more likely to cause constipation than most other narcotic analgesics.

GU: Urinary tract spasm.

Local: Repeated SC administration causes local tissue irritation and induration.

Ophthalmic: Pupillary contraction (miosis).

Respiratory: Respiratory depression. In general, neonates are more susceptible to the depressant effects of opioids than are older children or adults.[2] Lower doses at more frequent intervals are less likely to cause respiratory depression than are higher doses at longer intervals.

Patients unable to tolerate meperidine may be able to tolerate another narcotic agent, particularly if it is in a different pharmacologic class (codeine and morphine: phenanthrenes; meperidine and fentanyl: phenylpiperidines; methadone: a diphenylheptane).

Causes addiction; do not discontinue abruptly after prolonged use. Tolerance develops to the drug.

Pharmacokinetics/Pharmacodynamics

Absorption: Only about 25 percent of an oral dose is absorbed; therefore, the dose should be reduced when converting from oral to IV administration.

Onset of Action: *IV:* 1 minute; *PO, IM, SC:* 15 minutes; *lytic cocktail (DPT):* 30 minutes.

Peak Effect: *IV:* 5–7 minutes; *PO, IM, SC:* 30–90 minutes after the dose.

Duration of Action: 2–4 hours. The duration of action decreases as tolerance develops during chronic therapy. The duration of action of the lytic cocktail (DPT) is 2–14 hours.

Protein Binding: High.

Metabolism: Metabolized in the liver to normeperidine (an active and toxic metabolite), followed by hydrolysis and subsequent conjugation. Normeperidine can cause excitation and seizures; however, in newborns the rate of formation of normeperidine is slow, so accumulation to toxic levels is most likely to occur only with renal failure or with toxic oral doses of meperidine.[3]

Half-life: Elimination half-life in neonates is prolonged and variable, with a median of 10.7 hours.[4] It is, however, much shorter in older infants aged

3–18 months: 2.3 hours.[1] The half-life of the normeperidine metabolite is dependent on renal function.

Elimination: Renal.

NURSING IMPLICATIONS

Observe for excessive sedation.

Monitor blood pressure and heart rate.

Observe the infant to see that pain is relieved adequately.

Watch for withdrawal after long-term administration.

COMMENTS

See Table 1-37: Narcotic Conversion Chart, page 412, to convert from codeine to other narcotics.

Interactions: Additive CNS depression with concurrent CNS depressants; reduce dose proportionately (usually by 25–50 percent) when administering concomitantly with phenothiazines or other tranquilizers.

REFERENCES

1. American Academy of Pediatrics, Committee on Drugs. 1995. Reappraisal of lytic cocktail/demerol, phenergan, and thorazine (DPT) for the sedation of children. *Pediatrics* 95(4): 598–602. (Comment in *Pediatrics,* 1996, 97[5]: 779–780.)

2. Bhatt-Mehta V, and Rosen DA. 1991. Management of acute pain in children. *Clinical Pharmacy* 10(9): 667–685.

3. Roberts RJ. 1984. *Drug Therapy in Infants: Pharmacologic Principles and Clinical Experience.* Philadelphia: WB Saunders, 302–303.

4. Pokela ML, et al. 1992. Pharmacokinetics and pharmacodynamics of intravenous meperidine in neonates and infants. *Clinical Pharmacology and Therapeutics* 52(4): 342–349.

MEROPENEM (MERREM)

ANTI-INFECTIVE:
ANTIBIOTIC

(mer-oh-PEN-em)

DOSE

For Infants >3 Months of Age:

- *Intra-abdominal infections:* 20 mg/kg/dose given every 8 hours.
- *Meningitis:* 40 mg/kg/dose given every 8 hours.[1,2]

Reduce dose in renal impairment.

ADMINISTRATION

Supplied as: Powder for injection: 500 mg/vial and 1 gm/vial.

IV—*Rate:* May give over 3–5 minutes, but infusion over 30 minutes is preferred.

IV—*Concentration:* 50 mg/ml. Table 1-34 shows how many hours meropenem is stable when reconstituted in various solutions in concentrations of 2.5–50 mg/ml.

CAUTIONS/CONTRAINDICATIONS

Efficacy and tolerability have not yet been evaluated in infants less than 3 months of age, although kinetic studies have been done.[3,4]

USE

FDA-approved for treating intra-abdominal infections and meningitis in pediatric patients 3 months of age or older.

Effective as a single agent for serious infections, including meningitis, and in treating complicated infections caused by organisms that may be resistant to standard antibiotic therapy.[5]

Not for routine use because of the risk for development of bacterial resistance to meropenem: Reserve for infections resistant to other classes of antibiotics. Other antibiotics that are equally effective per culture and sensitivity, that are safe, and that exhibit a narrower spectrum of activity should be used preferentially.[5] (See Appendix H: Classification and Spectrum of Activity of Anti-Infectives.)

MECHANISM OF ACTION

Meropenem, like imipenem-cilastatin, is a carbapenem antibiotic. Meropenem has an extremely broad spectrum of activity against Gram-positive and

TABLE 1-34 ◆ STABILITY OF RECONSTITUTED MEROPENEM

Solution	Number of Hours Stable at Room Temperature of 15°C–25°C (59°F–77°F)	Number of Hours Stable Refrigerated at 4°C (39°F)
Normal saline (NS)	2	18
D₅W	1	8
Sterile water	2	12

Gram-negative bacteria, including anaerobes. Meropenem is more potent than imipenem against *Pseudomonas aeruginosa*. Whereas imipenem must be coadministered with cilastatin, an inhibitor of the renal tubular enzyme dehydropeptidase I (DHP-I), meropenem need not be because the molecule is stable against hydrolysis by DHP-I.

Meropenem's spectrum of activity includes *Staphylococcus aureus*, Group A Streptococcus and *Streptococcus pneumoniae* (including all strains of pneumococcus that have decreased susceptibility to penicillin). It is also active against *Haemophilus influenzae* and *Moraxella catarrhalis, Escherichia coli*, Klebsiella, Enterobacter and Serratia, and Pseudomonas. Meropenem is highly active against anaerobes, including *Bacteroides fragilis*.[5]

ADVERSE EFFECTS

CNS: Well tolerated. Meropenem does not appear to cause seizures in infants with bacterial meningitis, as imipenem does.[5,6]

Dermatologic: Rash (1.9 percent).[6] The rash is mostly diaper-area moniliasis.

GI: Diarrhea (4.3 percent), vomiting (1 percent), oral moniliasis, glossitis.

Hematologic: Hematologic problems such as increased or decreased platelets, increased eosinophils, prolonged prothrombin time, decreased WBC, decreased hemoglobin and hematocrit, and others occur in less than 1 percent of patients.

Hepatic: Increased liver enzymes and bilirubin (<1 percent).

Hypersensitivity: Allergic reaction may occur.

Local: Inflammation at injection site; phlebitis.

PHARMACOKINETICS/PHARMACODYNAMICS

Distribution: Most tissues, including CSF. Average CSF concentration is about 16 percent of simultaneous plasma concentration in meningitis.

Half-life:

- *Premature newborns:* 3 hours
- *Term newborns:* 2 hours
- *Infants 3 months to 2 years of age:* 1.4 hours[3,4]

Elimination: Cleared by the kidney; 70 percent eliminated unchanged in the urine. Decreased renal clearance with renal impairment.[1]

NURSING IMPLICATIONS

Observe for rash and diarrhea.

COMMENTS

Interactions: No drug interactions with meropenem for drugs used in neonates have been reported.[7]

Sodium Content: 3.9 mEq/gm.

REFERENCES

1. Bradley JS. 1997. Meropenem: A new, extremely broad spectrum beta-lactam antibiotic for serious infections in pediatrics. *Pediatric Infectious Disease Journal* 16(3): 263–268.

2. Nelson JD. 1996. *1996–1997 Pocketbook of Pediatric Antimicrobial Therapy,* 12th ed. Baltimore: Lippincott Williams & Wilkins, 77.

3. Blumer JL, et al. 1995. Sequential, single-dose pharmacokinetic evaluation of meropenem in hospitalized infants and children. *Antimicrobial Agents and Chemotherapy* 39(8): 1721–1725.

4. Martinkova J, et al. 1995. Meropenem pharmacokinetics in pre-term and full-term neonates (abstract #686). In *Program and Abstracts of the Seventh European Congress of Clinical Microbiology and Infectious Diseases,* March 26 to 30, Vienna, 133.

5. Edwards MS. 1997. Antibacterial therapy in pregnancy and neonates. *Clinics in Perinatology* 24(1): 251–266.

6. Bradley JS, Faulkner KL, and Klugman KP. 1996. Efficacy, safety and tolerability of meropenem as empiric antibiotic therapy in hospitalized pediatric patients. *Pediatric Infectious Disease Journal* 15(8): 749–757.

7. Medical Economics Data. 1998. *Physicians' Desk Reference.* Montvale, New Jersey: Medical Economics, 3170–3175.

M

METAPROTERENOL (ALUPENT)
(met-a-proe-TER-e-nol)

**RESPIRATORY:
BRONCHODILATOR**

DOSE

Nebulization: 0.01 ml (0.5 mg)/kg/dose of 5 percent (= 0.13 ml/kg of 0.4 percent) given every 3–6 hours. ***Maximum:*** 0.3 ml (15 mg) of 5 percent. Dilute to a final total volume of 3 ml with normal saline or other concurrent medications.

Some clinicians recommend a dose of 0.1–0.25 ml (5–12.5 mg) of a 5 percent solution diluted to 1.5–2 ml with half-normal or normal saline every 6 hours.

Table 1-35 lists metaproterenol volume conversions.

ADMINISTRATION

Supplied as:

- *Concentrate (usually for outpatient use):* 5 percent (50 mg/ml).
- *Unit Dose (usually for inpatient use):* 0.4 percent (4 mg/ml).

Dose Titration:

- *Reduce the dose* to the next smaller dose and/or increase the interval to the next longer interval when the heart rate exceeds 180 bpm (if baseline HR was <150 bpm) or 200 bpm (if baseline HR was >150 bpm). A moderate increase in heart rate is expected and may indicate absorption and therapeutic response. Lengthening the interval between doses should be tried when respiratory status has improved. Taper to the lowest effective dose.

- *Increase the dose* to the next larger dose and/or decrease the interval to the next shorter interval if the infant is still in respiratory distress after a trial of one to three doses. However, do not increase the dose if the infant is experiencing adverse effects from the current dose.

Discontinuation of Treatment: If adverse effects occur or if the drug is no longer needed, discontinue the drug. If there has been no improvement in respiratory status as measured by pulmonary mechanics, change in respiratory support, or clinical status after three doses, discontinue the drug.

USE

A selective β_2 sympathomimetic agent for bronchodilation in reversible airway obstruction.[1]

May improve pulmonary function in infants with BPD.[2–4]

MECHANISM OF ACTION

Metaproterenol produces β_2-adrenergic stimulation (bronchial dilation and vasodilation) with minor β_1 (increased myocardial contractility and conduction) effects. It stimulates adenyl cyclase, which converts ATP to cyclic AMP. Cyclic AMP mediates cellular responses. It also inhibits histamine release from mast cells, produces vasodilation, and increases ciliary motility.

TABLE 1-35 ◆ **METAPROTERENOL VOLUME CONVERSIONS: ml TO mg**

5% (50 mg/ml) Concentrate	0.4% (4 mg/ml) Unit Dose	mg
0.1 ml	1.3 ml	5 mg
0.15 ml	1.9 ml	7.5 mg
0.2 ml	2.5 ml (adult dose)	10 mg
0.3 ml	3.8 ml	15 mg

ADVERSE EFFECTS

Tachycardia, arrhythmias, increased blood pressure, and hyperglycemia.

May cause more cardiac stimulation than albuterol, especially in patients with hypoxia, because it is less β_2 selective.

Lower frequency of adverse effects than for isoproterenol.

Tolerance may develop after prolonged use.

PHARMACOKINETICS/PHARMACODYNAMICS

Onset of Action: 5–30 minutes.

Duration of Action: 2–6 hours. Cabal and associates reported that metaproterenol treatments lasted 3–4 hours.[2]

Metabolism: Metaproterenol is resistant to methylation by the COMT system. It undergoes extensive metabolism on first pass through the liver.

Elimination: Primarily in the urine.

NURSING IMPLICATIONS

Monitor heart rate, blood pressure, and respiratory status.

REFERENCES

1. Manufacturer's product literature.

2. Cabal LA, et al. 1987. Effects of metaproterenol on pulmonary mechanics, oxygenation, and ventilation in infants with chronic lung disease. *Journal of Pediatrics* 110(1): 116–119.

3. Davis JM, Sinkin RA, and Aranda JV. 1990. Drug therapy for bronchopulmonary dysplasia. *Pediatric Pulmonology* 8(2): 117–125.

4. Blanchard PW, Brown TM, and Coates AL. 1987. Pharmacotherapy in bronchopulmonary dysplasia. *Clinics in Perinatology* 14(4): 881–910.

METHADONE (DOLOPHINE)
(METH-a-done)

CENTRAL NERVOUS SYSTEM: NARCOTIC ANALGESIC

(CONTROLLED SUBSTANCE SCHEDULE II)

DOSE

Relief of Severe Pain, Sedation:

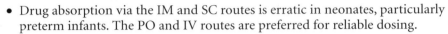

- *PO, IV, IM, SC:* 0.1 mg/kg/dose given every 4 hours for two or three doses, then every 6–12 hours, as needed. *Dose range:* 0.05–0.2 mg/kg/dose. *Maximum:* 10 mg/dose.
- Drug absorption via the IM and SC routes is erratic in neonates, particularly preterm infants. The PO and IV routes are preferred for reliable dosing.

Neonatal Narcotic Abstinence Syndrome: PO (preferred), IV, IM, SC:
0.05–0.2 mg/kg/dose every 12–24 hours or 0.5 mg/kg/day divided every 8 hours. Taper by 0.05 mg/kg/day or more slowly, as tolerated. Treatment may require 1–1.5 months. Tapering may be easier with morphine than with methadone because of methadone's long half-life.

Iatrogenic Opioid Withdrawal (such as from prolonged fentanyl or morphine infusions in the NICU):

- *Initial:* 0.05–0.1 mg/kg/dose given every 6 hours, with increases of 0.05 mg/kg/dose until symptoms are controlled.
- *Maintenance (after 24–48 hours of therapy):* Administer every 12 or 24 hours. Discontinue after weaning (see below) to doses of 0.05 mg/kg/day. Plasma concentrations decrease slowly because of methadone's prolonged half-life.[1]

Weaning from Long-term Narcotics:

- For infants on short-term (<1 week) opioids with low to moderate doses, reduce the dose by 25–50 percent initially and later by 20 percent every 6–8 hours; then discontinue as tolerated. Weaning can usually be completed in <72 hours. Increase the weaning time proportionately if opioids have been given for >1 week.[1]
- For infants on long-term (>1 week) continuous high-dose opioid infusion, gradually decrease concentration of continuous infusion—first by 20 percent and later by 10 percent every 12–24 hours, depending on patient tolerance. Then convert to intermittent IV doses of morphine or fentanyl every 2–4 hours or methadone IV every 4–6 hours. Then change to oral opioid (methadone, morphine, or codeine) when tolerated, with gradual weaning of the total daily dose as medical condition warrants. When changing from one opioid to another (such as converting from IV morphine drip to oral methadone), calculate the equianalgesic dose; then use this dose for 24 hours (observing for over- or underdosing) before starting to wean.[1,2] Monitor for recurrence of withdrawal symptoms. The infant should not be agitated or

distressed, should be able to sleep between feedings, should not be overly sedated, but may manifest mild withdrawal symptoms. Weaning may require 2–3 weeks.[1] (To convert the dose, route, or drug, use Table 1-37: Narcotic Conversion Chart, page 412.)

ADMINISTRATION

Supplied as:

- *Injection:* 10 mg/ml.
- *Oral liquid:* 1 mg/ml (preferred for infants for accurate oral dose measurement), 2 mg/ml, 10 mg/ml.

IV—*Rate:* Infuse over several minutes. Have available naloxone (see **ADVERSE EFFECTS** below) and equipment to support respiration.

IV, IM, SC—*Concentration:* Dilute the 10 mg/ml injection to a concentration of 1 mg/ml; then measure the dose prescribed (see Appendix A: Simplified Neonatal Calculations, Calculations for Preparing a 1:10 or a 1:100 Dilution, page 661). This helps prevent potential overdose that could result from the inability to measure the small neonatal dose volumes accurately.

PO: Dilute with water or a small amount of feeding just prior to administration.

Storage: Protect from light.

CAUTIONS/CONTRAINDICATIONS

Do not use in infants who are hypersensitive to methadone.

Use with caution in infants with decreased respiratory reserve, hypoxia, or hypercapnia. May increase airway resistance and decrease respiratory drive.[3]

Rapid IV injection may cause severe respiratory depression, hypotension, peripheral circulatory collapse, and cardiac arrest. Use caution in flushing the line to avoid rapid infusion of the dose during the flush.

Use the lowest effective dose for the shortest time necessary, but be certain pain is being managed adequately. Table 1-38, Neonatal Pain Relief/Sedation Assessment Scale (page 413) can be used to assess the infant's degree of pain or sedation (comfort score).[4]

Physiologic dependence (requiring the continued administration of the drug to prevent withdrawal symptoms) may develop after chronic use. Taper gradually. Finnegan's Neonatal Abstinence Score is very useful in the clinical assessment of infants and children following long-term sedation in the NICU.[1] (See Appendix K: Neonatal Withdrawal Score Sheet, page 717).

Tolerance (a decrease in the drug's pharmacologic effects with repeated administration or an increase in the dose required to achieve the same clinical effect) may develop.[1]

Drug may accumulate after repeated dosing due to its long half-life.

Titrate dose carefully to avoid excessive somnolence.

Calculate dose carefully to avoid toxic effects.

Use

A long-acting narcotic analgesic used to treat severe pain,[1,2,5] neonatal narcotic abstinence syndrome,[1,5,6] and iatrogenic opioid dependence in the NICU.[1] Advantages of methadone include its long duration of action and its ease of administration IV or PO.[1] Its prolonged half-life permits less frequent dosing after the initial loading period, but requires careful dose adjustments. For infants with limited IV access, intermittent IV boluses of methadone provide for constant analgesic effect without use of a port for a continuous infusion.[5]

Berde and colleagues reported that methadone IV provided prolonged analgesia for children after surgery; children receiving methadone required fewer supplemental doses during the following 36 hours and reported lower pain scores than did those receiving morphine.[7]

It is important to provide adequate sedation and analgesia for the infant's comfort and to reduce physiologic stress responses to critical illness and major surgical trauma that may directly influence patient outcome.[1] Use of opioid analgesia during essential treatment procedures in newborns with respiratory difficulties may reduce the duration of hypoxemia and associated distress.[8]

Mechanism of Action

Methadone is a synthetic μ-receptor agonist narcotic analgesic with actions similar to those of morphine.[9] It stimulates opioid receptors in the CNS that mimic the actions of endogenous enkephalins and β-endorphins. Like other narcotic analgesics, methadone alters both the perception of pain and the emotional response to pain. It alters intestinal motility by local and possibly central action.

Adverse Effects

Cardiovascular: Bradycardia, shock, cardiac arrest; histamine release (tachycardia, hypotension, increased sweating, facial flushing, wheezing).

CNS: Somnolence, paradoxical excitation, weakness, increased intracranial pressure.[3,10] If somnolence occurs, reduce the dose and greatly prolong the dosing interval.[5]

Dermatologic: Rash. Local tissue irritation with repeated SC administration.

GI: GI upset, vomiting, constipation (more likely with methadone than with other narcotic analgesics), biliary contraction.

GU: Urinary tract spasm, urine retention (antidiuretic effect).

Ophthalmic: Miosis (constricted pupils).

Respiratory: Respiratory depression, apnea.

Overdose: Symptoms include severe drowsiness; hypotension; severe restlessness; pinpoint pupils; bradycardia; respiratory depression; unconsciousness; weakness; cold, clammy skin.[10] **Antidote: Naloxone** (Narcan) 0.1 mg/kg/dose IV, and repeat dose every 3–5 minutes, as needed. (See monograph on naloxone.) Use other supportive measures, such as oxygen, IV fluids, and vasopressors, as indicated. Naloxone may precipitate withdrawal in physically dependent patients and may interfere with control of pain management; titrate dose carefully and use smaller than usual doses in these patients.

See Appendix J: Antidotes for Drugs That Cause Loss of Respiratory Effort.

PHARMACOKINETICS/PHARMACODYNAMICS

Absorption: About 50 percent absorbed. (An oral dose is about half as potent as the same dose given by the parenteral route.)[3,5]

Onset of Action:

- *PO:* 30–60 minutes.
- *IM:* 10–20 minutes.

Duration of Action:

- *PO:* 4–6 hours.
- *IV:* 3–4 hours. (Duration increases with chronic use, then decreases as tolerance develops during chronic therapy.)

Peak Effect:

- *PO:* 1.5–2 hours.
- *IV:* 15–30 minutes.[10]

Protein Binding: 85 percent.[9]

Metabolism: Metabolized by N-demethylation in the liver to inactive substances.

Half-life: 15–25 hours and longer with repeated administration because of accumulation.[7,9,10] Half-life is shorter in children than in adults. The mean half-life of methadone in infants exposed to methadone *in utero* was 53 hours in the postnatal period.[11]

Elimination: Urine and bile. Elimination of opioids is slower in neonates than in adults. However, the rate of elimination usually reaches and even exceeds adult values within the first year of life.[9] Renal clearance is increased at a urine pH of <6.

NURSING IMPLICATIONS

Prepare a 1:10 dilution. Measure dose carefully. Flush the line slowly. Use correct technique to avoid overdose from administration of drug left in the syringe dead space (hub). See Appendix C: IV Drug Administration Methods, Serial Dilution and Accuracy, page 673.

Monitor respirations; blood pressure; CNS status; and pain relief, if applicable.[12]

Methadone is a long-acting depressant, whereas naloxone acts for much shorter periods. Therefore, monitor the infant continuously for recurrence of respiratory or cardiovascular depression, and repeat naloxone as needed; continuous infusion of naloxone may be indicated following initial treatment.[3,10]

COMMENTS

Equivalence: Methadone 1 mg IM or 2 mg PO = morphine 1 mg IM.

Use the Finnegan Neonatal Abstinence Scoring System (see Appendix K: Neonatal Withdrawal Score Sheet, page 717) as a guide to weaning.[1,13]

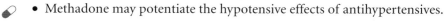 Reduce dose in renal impairment.

Interactions:

- Concurrent use of drugs that cause CNS depression potentiate CNS depressant, hypotensive, and respiratory depressant effects.

- Concurrent use with medications with anticholinergic activity (such as atropine, glycopyrrolate) may increase risk of constipation, paralytic ileus, or urinary retention.

- Methadone may counteract the effects of metoclopramide in the GI tract.

- Concurrent phenytoin or rifampin may increase methadone metabolism (probably via induction of hepatic microsomal enzyme activity), reduce blood concentrations, and precipitate withdrawal.[10]

- Methadone may potentiate the hypotensive effects of antihypertensives.

REFERENCES

1. Anand KJS, and Arnold JH. 1994. Opioid tolerance and dependence in infants and children. *Critical Care Medicine* 22(2): 334–342.

2. American Academy of Pediatrics, Committee on Fetus and Newborn, Committee on Drugs, Section on Anesthesiology, Section on Surgery. 2000. Prevention and management of pain and stress in the neonate. *Pediatrics* 105(2): 454–461.

3. Medical Economics Data. 2000. *Physicians' Desk Reference.* Montvale, New Jersey: Medical Economics, 2711–2713.

4. Chay PCW, Duffy BJ, and Walker JS. 1992. Pharmacokinetic-pharmacodynamic relationship of morphine in neonates. *Clinical Pharmacology and Therapeutics* 51(3): 334–342.

5. Berde C, et al. 1990. American Academy of Pediatrics report of the subcommittee on disease-related pain in childhood cancer. *Pediatrics* 86(5 part 2): 818–825.

6. American Academy of Pediatrics, Committee on Substance Abuse. 1995. Drug-exposed infants. *Pediatrics* 96(2 part 1): 364–367.

7. Berde CB, Beyer JE, and Bournaki MC. 1991. Comparison of morphine and methadone for prevention of postoperative pain in 3- to 7-year-old children. *Journal of Pediatrics* 119(1 part 1): 136–141.

8. Pokela M. 1994. Pain relief can reduce hypoxemia in distressed neonates during routine treatment procedures. *Pediatrics* 93(3): 379–383.

9. Olkkola KT, Hamunen K, and Maunuksela EL. 1995. Clinical pharmacokinetics and pharmacodynamics of opioid analgesics in infants and children. *Clinical Pharmacokinetics* 28(5): 385–404.

10. United States Pharmacopeial Convention/USP DI. 2000. *Drug Information for the Health Care Professional,* 20th ed. Rockville, Maryland: United States Pharmacopeial Convention, 2311–2340.

11. Olson GD, and Lees MH. 1980. Ventilatory response to carbon dioxide of infants following chronic prenatal methadone exposure. *Journal of Pediatrics* 96(6): 983–989.

12. American Academy of Pediatrics, Committee on Drugs. 1992. Guidelines for monitoring and management of pediatric patients during and after sedation for diagnostic and therapeutic procedures. *Pediatrics* 89(6): 1110–1115.

13. Levy M, and Spino M. 1993. Neonatal withdrawal syndrome: Associated drugs and pharmacologic management. *Pharmacotherapy* 13(3): 202–211.

METHYLENE BLUE (UROLENE BLUE)   ANTIDOTE:
(METH-i-leen blu)   METHEMOGLOBINEMIA

DOSE

Methemoglobinemia in Infants: *IV:* 1–1.5 mg/kg/dose (= 0.1–0.15 ml/kg/dose of a 1 percent solution) IV.[1,2] May repeat after 1 hour if methemoglobin persists. If two doses are unsuccessful, exchange transfusion may be required.

Methemoglobin Reductase Deficiency: *Oral:* 1.5–5 mg/kg/day PO. Given as a single daily dose. (May give with ascorbic acid 5–8 mg/kg/day PO given in three to four divided doses.)[3,4] This usually is sufficient to maintain the methemoglobin concentration below that which causes cyanosis. These patients usually require treatment only for cosmetic purposes.

Refractory Hypotension in Septic Shock: 1 mg/kg/dose IV infused over 1 hour. May repeat one time.[5,6]

Diagnostic Indicator Dye (such as to disclose aspirated dye in the tracheal material during suctioning in an infant with a tracheostomy): *Maximum:* 5 mg/kg/day (= 0.5 ml/kg/day of the 1 percent solution) PO divided in feedings. Mix well. Give for several feedings; then discontinue.

Caution: Excessive amounts of methylene blue (MB) can be toxic (see **CAUTIONS/CONTRAINDICATIONS** and **ADVERSE EFFECTS** below); use the smallest volume that will adequately color the feeding. MB is visible at very low concentrations.

- Blue food coloring has been used in the place of MB to color feedings for diagnostic purposes because of the lower cost of the food coloring. However, it too could have adverse effects if given in excessive amounts, such as transiently blue colored diarrhea and skin. Use only the minimum volume that will adequately color the feeding and discontinue when no longer needed.

Reduce Dose in Renal Dysfunction: Consider use of the low dose in the range in very low birth weight infants because of their immature renal function.

ADMINISTRATION

Supplied as: Injection: 10 mg/ml (= 1 percent).

IV—*Rate:*

- Infuse over 1 hour (preferred) or over 5–15 minutes.
- Do not give by rapid IV push because the high local concentration of MB may cause the formation of additional methemoglobinemia.

IV—*Concentration:* May give undiluted or dilute with normal saline.[7]

PO: Administer after meals with water, per fluid tolerance of the infant.

Intraosseous (IO) Administration: There is one report of successful use of MB by the IO route in a 6-week-old (3 kg) infant for acquired methemoglobinemia. This route was used on an emergency basis because IV access could not be established.[8] The rate of infusion and concentration recommended for IV administration are suggested for IO use.

Cautions/Contraindications

Cautions:

- Red blood cells of infants contain lower concentrations of the enzymes required to reduce methemoglobin to hemoglobin, making them transiently more susceptible to methemoglobin produced by high concentrations of MB.

- Do not exceed recommended dose or infusion rate. Rapid IV injection or large doses can produce methemoglobinemia.

- *Monitoring:* Measure blood methemoglobin concentration before MB administration if patient is symptomatic (because MB itself can produce methemoglobinemia) and then 1 to 2 hours after administration of MB to assess effectiveness of therapy. Monitor complete blood count (CBC) and reticulocyte count to assure that hemolysis has not occurred.[7]

- MB will not reverse cyanosis caused by sulfhemoglobinemia. (Dapsone and acetaminophen cause both methemoglobinemia and sulfhemoglobinemia.) Disappearance of sulfhemoglobin after withdrawal of the inciting agent parallels normal red cell life.

Contraindications:

- *Glucose-6-phosphate Dehydrogenase (G6PD) Deficiency.* Do not use in infants with G6PD deficiency who have methemoglobinemia because MB may aggravate the methemoglobinemia and precipitate acute hemolysis.

- *Cyanide Poisoning.* Do not give MB to treat excess methemoglobinemia induced by sodium nitrite during treatment of cyanide poisoning because MB will release cyanide from the cyanomethemoglobin complex, causing an increase in the blood cyanide concentration and increased toxicity. MB has been used as an antidote for cyanide poisoning; however, sodium nitrite with sodium thiosulfate is safer and more effective.[7]

- *Intraspinal/Intrathecal Injection:* Not for intraspinal or intrathecal injection because neural damage, including paraplegia, has occurred.[3]

- *Subcutaneous Injection:* Do not give by subcutaneous (SC) injection because necrotic abscess may occur.

- *Hypersensitivity to MB.*

Use

A dye used to treat methemoglobinemia. Also used in diagnostic procedures as an antiseptic and experimentally to treat refractory shock.

Methemoglobinemia. Lowers the concentration of methemoglobin in red blood cells by regenerating hemoglobin. Used to treat acquired (drug-induced) methemoglobinemia and hereditary methemoglobinemia. Chronic methemoglobinemia resulting from reduced methemoglobin reductase activity is treated by daily oral administration of methylene blue.[9]

**FIGURE 1-10 ◆ MECHANISM OF ACTION FOR THE CONVERSION OF METHEMOGLOBIN TO HEMO-
GLOBIN BY METHYLENE BLUE.**

$$\text{Step 1.} \quad \overset{(G6PD)}{NADP + G6P \longrightarrow NADPH + 6PG}$$

$$\text{Step 2.} \quad \overset{(NADPH\text{-}Flavin\ Reductase)}{\mathbf{MB} + NADPH \longrightarrow LMB + NADP^+}$$

$$\text{Step 3.} \quad HBFe^{3+} + LMB \longrightarrow HBFe^{2+} + MB$$

Key to abbreviations in figure:
   6PG: 6-phosphogluconolactone
   G6P: glucose-6-phosphate
   G6PD: glucose-6-phosphate dehydrogenase
   $HBFe^{2+}$: hemoglobin
   $HBFe^{3+}$: methemoglobin
   LMB: leucomethylene blue (white)
   MB: methylene blue
   NADP: nicotinamide-adenine dinucleotide phosphate
   $NADP^+$: oxidized NADP
   NADPH: reduced NADP

Explanation of figure:

   Step 1. NADPH is generated by G6PD.

   Step 2. The NADPH generated by this reaction is an essential cofactor for NADPH-flavin reductase, an enzyme that reduces MB to LMB. This is why red blood cells deficient in G6PD are unable to reduce MB (blue) to LMB (white).

   Step 3. LMB then catalyzes the reduction of methemoglobin to hemoglobin.

   Note: If an excessive dose of MB is given or there is a defect in the patient's methemoglobin reduction mechanism, then MB accumulates because it overwhelms the amount of enzyme available to metabolize it. The accumulated MB then functions as a hemoglobin oxidizing (rather than reducing) agent, resulting in methemoglobinemia.[15]

- Ascorbic acid IV or PO may be used as an alternative to MB in chronic, idiopathic methemoglobinemia and is usually required only for cosmetic purposes, to maintain the methemoglobin concentration below the concentration that causes a cyanotic appearance. Ascorbic acid reduces methemoglobin to hemoglobin too slowly to be of benefit in treatment of acquired methemoglobinemia.[7,10]

Diagnostic Indicator Dye. Has also been used as an indicator dye in diagnostic procedures such as fistula detection and to assess gastroesophageal reflux, endotracheal tube placement, and jejunal tube placement. In an infant with a tracheostomy, methylene blue can be diluted in the feedings for several meals to disclose aspirated dye in the tracheal material during tracheostomy suctioning.[11]

Intra-amniotic (IA) Use. IA injection of MB has been used to diagnose premature rupture of fetal membranes or to identify separate amniotic sacs in twin pregnancies.[7,12] (See **Adverse Effects from Intra-Amniotic Injection** below.)

Urinary Tract Antiseptic. Has mildly bacteriostatic and antiseptic activity. MB was used for minor urinary tract infections; however, it has been replaced by more effective agents.

M

Septic Shock. Has been used experimentally to increase vascular tone and blood pressure in septic shock unresponsive to colloid, inotropic agents, and corticosteroids.[5,6]

Mechanism of Action

MB is a thiazine dye.

Methemoglobinemia: *MB in low concentrations* acts as a cofactor to accelerate the conversion of methemoglobin to hemoglobin in the red blood cells. *MB in high concentrations* has the opposite effect, in that it oxidizes the ferrous (Fe^{2+}) iron of hemoglobin to the ferric (Fe^{3+}) state, facilitating the conversion of hemoglobin to methemoglobin.[7] The ferric iron in methemoglobin does not bind oxygen, making it unable to transport oxygen (Figure 1-10).

Shock: Septic shock may be mediated in part by excess synthesis of nitric oxide. Tsuneyoshi and colleagues studied the functional status of arteries in patients with septic shock and severe hypotension. Their results indicated that the main cause of reduced sensitivity to pressor agents may be a massive generation of nitric oxide via the L-arginine pathway.[13] Increased levels of nitrates and nitrites, metabolites of nitric oxide, have been found in newborn infants with septic shock.[5,14] Excess nitric oxide mediates hypotension by dilating vascular smooth muscle through activation of soluble guanylate cyclase to produce cyclic guanosine monophosphate (cGMP). In vascular smooth muscle cells, cGMP causes vasodilation and in myocytes may decrease contractility.[5] The hemodynamic effects of nitric oxide can be partially antagonized by MB, through inhibition of the enzyme guanylate cyclase (Figure 1-11).

Adverse Effects

Dermatologic:

- Topical exposure or IV injection of MB stains the skin. Blue staining of the skin following IV overdose may persist for 6 days.

- Inadvertent extravasation or SC administration may cause tissue necrosis.

- MB is a photosensitizing compound. A photosensitivity reaction involves the absorption of light energy by a compound, followed by the release of energy into the surrounding tissues. The energy can be released as heat, or it can be transferred, as a free electron, to a bystander molecule or molecular oxygen to form superoxide. The clinical presentation of a photosensitivity reaction manifests initially as edema and erythema of the skin similar to a sunburn. This may be followed by the formation of bullae that eventually desquamate over several days.[12] Possible photosensitization or MB-induced necrosis of the skin occurred in two full-term neonates exposed postnatally to MB. Bullae and desquamation developed.[15] Infants receiving chronic oral MB need to have their skin protected from sunlight and ultraviolet light with protective clothing and age-appropriate sunscreen until tolerance is determined.

FIGURE 1-11 ◆ MECHANISM OF ACTION OF METHYLENE BLUE IN THE TREATMENT OF SEPTIC SHOCK.

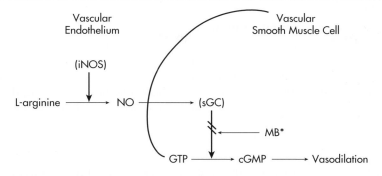

* MB blocks the pathway at this point.

Key to figure abbreviations:
    cGMP: cyclic guanosine monophosphate
    GTP: guanosine triphosphate
    iNOS: inducible nitric oxide synthase
    MB: methylene blue
    NO: nitric oxide
    sGC: soluble guanylate cyclase

Explanation of figure:

NO has been implicated as the major cause of the profound vasodilation and hypotension associated with sepsis. The figure describes its mechanism and how MB blocks this effect.

1. In septic shock, stimuli such as endotoxin (and other factors) increase the activity of the enzyme iNOS.

2. iNOS synthesizes NO from L-arginine.

3. NO then diffuses into smooth muscle cells, where it stimulates the enzyme sGC, resulting in enhanced synthesis of cGMP from GTP. cGMP then causes vascular relaxation (vasodilation), reduced blood pressure, and reduced responsiveness to vasoconstrictors.

4. MB modulates the action of NO in shock by inhibiting sGC, thereby preventing vasodilation and hypotension.[30,31]

GI: Oral administration may cause nausea, vomiting, diarrhea. Administer after meals with water to minimize these adverse GI effects. Large IV doses may also cause nausea and abdominal pain. MB causes blue-green discoloration of feces.

GU: Bladder irritation, dysuria, blue-green discoloration of urine.

Overdose: Cumulative doses of MB exceeding 7 mg/kg may cause toxicity. Signs of overdose can include:

- ***Cardiovascular:*** Chest pain, tremor, cyanosis, arrhythmias, electrocardiographic changes (diminished or inverted T wave amplitude, diminished R wave amplitude), sweating, transient but severe hypertension or hypotension.

- ***Dermatologic:*** Photosensitivity.

- **GI:** Nausea, vomiting, abdominal pain, hyperbilirubinemia.
- **Hematologic:** Hemolytic anemia (Heinz body anemia), hyperbilirubinemia,[10] methemoglobinemia.

Adverse Effects from Intra-Amniotic Injection:

- Prenatal exposure of neonates to MB in the amniotic cavity has resulted in complications including blue tracheal secretions, Heinz body hemolytic anemia with a precipitous drop in hematocrit (continuing for up to 10 days), respiratory distress, hyperbilirubinemia, methemoglobinemia, bluish-tinged urine (for 6 days after intra-amniotic injection), and deep blue skin staining that has persisted more than 2 weeks.[16] Exchange transfusion and/or phototherapy may be required to correct hyperbilirubinemia and anemia.[12,16–18]

- Porat and associates summarized the literature on the clinical characteristics and hospital course of neonates with MB toxicity. The doses of intra-amniotic MB administered ranged from 10 mg (3 kg infant) to 100 mg (1.09 kg infant), a dose that caused severe skin staining and phototoxicity. Most doses ranged from 10 to 70 mg.[12,17,19] Because MB is visible at very low concentrations, Plukett suggested that a smaller dose, such as 1.6 mg, was enough to confirm the presence of rupture of membranes without causing hemolysis.[20]

- Phototoxicity and intestinal atresia have also been reported in neonates following intra-amniotic MB.

  - *Phototoxicity:* Phototoxicity occurred in a 27-week gestation, 1.09 kg infant exposed to a large (100 mg) IA dose of methylene blue and treatment with phototherapy. Porat and colleagues thought that some or most of the initial deep blue skin staining was caused by direct absorption of the dye into the epidermis. Areas not in contact with the dye because of marked body flexion of the fetal position (inguinal folds and under the chin) were not initially stained; however, by the next day, these areas gradually became blue, probably because of systemic distribution of MB absorbed enterically (or possibly percutaneously). All areas exposed to phototherapy, about one-third of the total body surface area, blistered and desquamated followed by re-epithelialization.[12]

  - *Intestinal Atresia:* Fetal exposure to intra-amniotic MB is associated with a risk of small intestinal atresia. Van der Pol and colleagues reported that jejunal atresia occurred in 17 (19 percent) of the 86 consecutive twin pregnancies given intra-amniotic MB for prenatal diagnosis. In 15 of the affected cases, it was possible to determine that the affected fetus had been the one exposed to MB. All infants needed surgery to relieve the intestinal obstruction. They concluded that there was a strong suggestion of a causal relation between use of MB in second trimester amniocentesis and occurrence of jejunal atresia.[21] Twins have a higher rate of intestinal atresia than singletons even without having received MB.[22] McFadyen commented on the dangers of intra-amniotic MB and the risk of jejunal atresia and recommended avoidance of MB for second trimester amniocentesis.[23] The mechanism of action of intestinal atresia secondary to intra-amniotic MB may

TABLE 1-36 ◆ METHEMOGLOBIN CONCENTRATIONS IN NORMAL INFANTS

Age of Infant	Methemoglobin gm/dl Mean (Range)	Methemoglobin as Percent of Total Hemoglobin Mean (Range)
Preterm	0.38 (0.02–0.83)	2.2 (0.08–4.7)
Term newborn (1 to 10 days)	0.22 (0.00–0.58)	1.5 (0.00–2.8)
Term infant (1 month to 1 year)	0.14 (0.02–0.29)	1.2 (0.17–2.4)

Adapted from: Nathan DG, and Orkin SH. 1998. *Nathan and Oski's Hematology of Infancy and Childhood,*
5th ed., vol. 2. Philadelphia: WB Saunders, xii. Reprinted by permission.

be hemolysis or acute intestinal hypoxia secondary to MB-induced release of norepinephrine and subsequent vasoconstriction. The GI tract may be particularly sensitive in fetuses.[19,23–26]

PHARMACOKINETICS/PHARMACODYNAMICS

Absorption: About 74 percent of orally administered MB is absorbed from the GI tract.

Onset of Action: Within 30 minutes. Cyanosis should clear promptly, within 1–2 hours.

Metabolism: Rapidly metabolized by tissue to leucomethylene blue, which in turn is able to reduce methemoglobin to hemoglobin. MB is not effective to treat methemoglobinemia in patients with G6PD deficiency because these patients have a lessened ability to reduce MB to leucomethylene blue (see Figure 1-10, page 389).[26]

Elimination: Renal (about 75 percent) and biliary. Eliminated as leucomethylene blue in the urine along with some unchanged drug.[3,27]

NURSING IMPLICATIONS

Staining of skin of health care providers may be removed with a topical application of diluted sodium hypochlorite (NaClO) solution (= modified Dakin's solution, available in 0.25 percent and 0.5 percent concentrations). Avoid contact with eyes; may cause skin irritation. Avoid using diluted sodium hypochlorite to remove blue staining on neonates' skin because of the risk of skin irritation and chemical burns of their delicate skin and because there are no data on safety of this solution in this age group.

Full-strength (5 percent) sodium hypochlorite solution (= laundry bleach) is too concentrated for application to tissues.

Blue staining of skin by MB hinders assessment of hypoxia, including use of pulse oximetry.

- *Monitoring:* Measure blood methemoglobin concentration before MB administration if patient is symptomatic (because MB itself can produce methemoglobinemia) and then 1 to 2 hours after administration of MB to assess effectiveness of therapy. Monitor CBC and reticulocyte count to assure that hemolysis has not occurred.[7]

COMMENTS

Interactions:

- *Urine pH:* MB may interfere with analysis of urine pH.

- *Pulse Oximetry:* MB will temporarily cause inaccurate, artificially low (perhaps as low as 0) pulse oximetry saturation readings within 30 seconds of MB infusion. These usually return to baseline values within 4 to 5 minutes after administration. The probable mechanism of the interference is with light wave emission of the pulse oximeter; the light emission of the pulse oximeter is mostly absorbed by the light emission of methylene blue. The oximeter interprets this as an indication of the presence of reduced hemoglobin, which leads to erroneously low values for oxygen saturation.[28,29]

Reference Range: Table 1-36 gives reference values.

REFERENCES

1. Roberts RJ. 1984. *Drug Therapy in Infants: Pharmacologic Principles and Clinical Experience.* Philadelphia: WB Saunders, 345.

2. Lane PA, Nuss R, and Ambruso DR. 1999. Hematologic disorders. In *Current Pediatric Diagnosis and Treatment,* Hay WW Jr, ed. Stamford, Connecticut: Appleton & Lange, 723–773.

3. Benitz WE, and Tatro DS. 1995. *The Pediatric Drug Handbook,* 3rd ed. St. Louis: Mosby-Year Book, 11.

4. Taketomo CK, Hodding JH, and Kraus DM. 1997. *Pediatric Dosage Handbook,* 4th ed. Hudson, Ohio: Lexi-Comp, 484–485.

5. Driscoll W, et al. 1996. Effect of methylene blue on refractory neonatal hypotension. *Journal of Pediatrics* 129(6): 904–908.

6. Schreiber MD. 1996. Methylene blue: NO panacea. *Journal of Pediatrics* 129(6): 790–793.

7. United States Pharmacopeial Convention/USP DI. 1996. *Drug Information for the Health Care Professional,* 16th ed. Rockville, Maryland: United States Pharmacopeial Convention, 2036–2038.

8. Herman MI, et al. 1999. Methylene blue by intraosseous infusion for methemoglobinemia. *Annals of Emergency Medicine* 33(1): 111–113.

9. Mentzer WC. 1996. Methemoglobinemia. In *Rudolph's Pediatrics,* 20th ed., Rudolph AM, Hoffman JIE, and Rudolph CD, eds. Stamford, Connecticut: Appleton & Lange, 1220–1221.

10. Mansouri A, and Lurie AA. 1993. Concise review: Methemoglobinemia. *American Journal of Hematology* 42(1): 7–12.

11. Orenstein SR. 1996. Disorders of esophageal motility. In *Rudolph's Pediatrics,* 20th ed., Rudolph AM, Hoffman JIE, and Rudolph CD, eds. Stamford, Connecticut: Appleton & Lange, 1057–1060.

12. Porat R, Gilbert S, and Magilner D. 1996. Methylene blue-induced phototoxicity: An unrecognized complication. *Pediatrics* 97(5): 717–721.

13. Tsuneyoshi I, Kanmura Y, and Yoshimura N. 1996. Nitric oxide as a mediator of reduced arterial responsiveness in septic patients. *Critical Care Medicine* 24(6): 1083–1086.

14. Shi Y, et al. 1993. Plasma nitric oxide levels in newborn infants with sepsis. *Journal of Pediatrics* 123(3): 435–438.

15. Sills MR, and Zinkham WH. 1994. Methylene-blue-induced Heinz body hemolytic anemia. *Archives of Pediatrics and Adolescent Medicine* 148(3): 306–310.

16. Troche BI. 1989. The methylene blue baby (letter). *New England Journal of Medicine* 320(26): 1756–1757.

17. Cowett RM, Hakanson DO, and Kocon RW. 1976. Untoward neonatal effect of intra-amniotic administration of methylene blue. *Obstetrics and Gynecology* 48(1 supplement): S74–S75.

18. Crooks J. 1982. Haemolytic jaundice in a neonate after intra-amniotic injection of methylene blue. *Archives of Disease in Childhood* 57(11): 872–873.

19. Serota FT, Bernbaum JC, and Schwartz E. 1979. The methylene-blue baby (letter). *Lancet* 2(8152): 1142–1143.

20. Plukett GD. 1973. Neonatal complications. *Obstetrics and Gynecology* 41(3): 476–477.

21. van der Pol JG, et al. 1992. Fetal and neonatal medicine: Jejunal atresia related to the use of methylene blue in genetic amniocentesis in twins. *British Journal of Obstetrics and Gynaecology* 99(2): 141–143.

22. Cragan JD, Martin ML, and Waters GD. 1994. Increased risk of small intestinal atresia among twins in the United States. *Pediatric and Adolescent Medicine* 148(7): 733–739.

23. McFadyen I. 1992. The dangers of intra-amniotic methylene blue. *British Journal of Obstetrics and Gynaecology* 99(2): 89–90.

24. Nicolini U, and Monni G. 1990. Intestinal obstruction in babies exposed in utero to methylene blue (letter). *Lancet* 336(8725): 1258–1259.

25. Kidd SA, et al. 1996. Fetal death after exposure to methylene blue dye during mid-trimester amniocentesis in twin pregnancy. *Prenatal Diagnosis* 16(1): 39–47.

26. McEnerney JK, and McEnerney LN. 1983. Unfavorable neonatal outcome after intra-amniotic injection of methylene blue. *Obstetrics and Gynecology* 61(3 supplement): S35–S37.

27. Parfitt K, ed. 1999. *Martindale: The Complete Drug Reference*, 32nd ed. London: Pharmaceutical Press, 984–985.

28. Scott DM, and Cooper MG. 1991. Spurious pulse oximetry with intrauterine methylene blue injection. *Anaesthesia and Intensive Care* 19(2): 267–268.

29. Barker SJ, and Tremper KK. 1987. Pulse oximetry: Applications and limitations. *International Anesthesiology Clinics* 25(3): 155–175.

30. Moncada S, and Higgs A. 1993. The L-arginine-nitric oxide pathway. *New England Journal of Medicine* 329(27): 2002–2012.

31. Anderson MR, and Blumer JL. 1997. Advances in the therapy for sepsis in children. *Pediatric Clinics of North America* 44(1): 179–201.

METHYLPREDNISOLONE
(meth-ill-pred-NISS-oh-lone)
(SOLU-MEDROL)

HORMONE:
GLUCOCORTICOID

DOSE

As an Anti-inflammatory and Immunosuppressive: 0.16–0.8 mg/kg/day divided every 6–12 hours.[1]

For Status Asthmaticus: 1–2 mg/kg IV as a single dose, then 0.5–1 mg/kg/dose IV every 6 hours for up to 5 days, then change to oral prednisone.[1] Base dose on severity of disease and response of patient. Reduce dose gradually to the lowest effective level.

ADMINISTRATION

Supplied as:

- *Oral:* 2 mg tablets (scored) (Medrol), but not as an oral liquid. (Prednisone, hydrocortisone, and dexamethasone are available as oral liquids.)
- *Injection:* 40 mg/ml vial.

IV—*Rate:* Infuse over at least 1 to several minutes.

IV—*Concentration:* May give undiluted (40 mg/ml) or may dilute with dextrose or saline. The diluent provided in "Act-O-Vial" and "Univial" contains benzyl alcohol. Insert needle through center of plunger-stopper and withdraw this diluent; replace with nonpreserved saline.

IV—*Compatibility:* See Appendix E: Y-Site Compatibility of Common NICU Drugs.

IM: May give undiluted.

USE

An intermediate-acting corticosteroid with anti-inflammatory (glucocorticoid) and no mineralocorticoid effects. (See Table 1-18, page 182, for a comparison of various corticosteroids.) It has fewer sodium-retaining and hypertensive adverse effects than hydrocortisone or prednisone.

Uses for corticosteroids include treatment of hypoglycemia; in infants with BPD, to shorten weaning from respirator (dexamethasone);[2,3] and prior to extubation, to reduce laryngeal edema and stridor.

MECHANISM OF ACTION

Corticosteroids are anti-inflammatory and immunosuppressive; reduce capillary permeability; stabilize lysosomal enzymes; and affect carbohydrate, protein, and fat metabolism to maintain metabolic homeostasis. Corticosteroids induce fetal lung surfactant.

ADVERSE EFFECTS

Acute Adverse Effects: Usually do not occur, except with too-rapid withdrawal after long-term use.

Acute Pituitary-Adrenal Insufficiency: Results from too-rapid withdrawal of corticosteroids after prolonged use (receipt of corticosteroids for longer than 7–10 days).[1] Taper dose gradually if infant has received steroids for longer than 7–10 days.

Adverse Effects with Prolonged Use: Adrenal suppression, including severe growth retardation; hypokalemic alkalosis; sodium retention; hypertension; hyperglycemia; increased susceptibility to infections; cataracts; myopathy; hypocalcemia; osteoporosis with bone fractures; nephrocalcinosis; and nephrolithiasis. Use alternate-day treatment to minimize adverse effects in patients on chronic corticosteroid therapy.

PHARMACOKINETICS/PHARMACODYNAMICS

Absorption: Well absorbed from the GI tract. The same dose may be used as PO or IV. However, because it is not available as an oral liquid, other corticosteroids are usually used when the PO route is indicated (dexamethasone, prednisone).

Onset of Action: 4–6 hours with IV administration. For planned extubation, begin corticosteroid treatment 12–24 hours prior to procedure.

NURSING IMPLICATIONS

Monitor for hypertension, hyperglycemia after dose.

Monitor for signs and symptoms of infection.

Monitor growth parameters, such as head circumference, length, and weight, weekly, and plot on growth curve.

Monitor for serum electrolytes, glucose and fluid status, and glucose spillage in urine.

COMMENTS

Sodium Content: Methylprednisolone sodium succinate contains 2 mEq sodium/gm.

REFERENCES

1. Benitz WE, and Tatro DS. 1995. *The Pediatric Drug Handbook,* 3rd ed. St. Louis: Mosby-Year Book, 435–436.

2. Avery GB, et al. 1985. Controlled trial of dexamethasone in respirator-dependent infants with bronchopulmonary dysplasia. *Pediatrics* 75(1): 106–111.

3. Collaborative Dexamethasone Trial Group. 1991. Dexamethasone therapy in neonatal chronic lung disease: An international placebo-controlled trial. *Pediatrics* 88(3): 421–427.

METOCLOPRAMIDE
(met-oh-kloe-PRA-mide)
(REGLAN, MAXOLON)

DOSE

0.1–0.2 mg/kg/dose given every 6 hours (i.e., every other feeding) 30 minutes prior to the feeding. *Maximum:* 1 mg/kg/day.

Placement of Nasojejunal (NJ) Feeding Tube: 0.1 mg/kg 10–20 minutes prior to tube placement.[1]

ADMINISTRATION

Supplied as: 5 mg/ml.

May be given PO, IM, or IV. Administer 30 minutes prior to feedings.

PO—Available as an oral liquid at 10 mg/ml and 1 mg/ml concentrations.

IM (rarely used): May give undiluted.

IV—*Rate:* May infuse IV over 1–2 minutes, but infusion by retrograde or syringe pump over 15 minutes is preferred.

IV—*Concentration:* May be given IV undiluted (5 mg/ml); however, dilution to 0.1 mg/ml is preferred.

IV—*Compatibility:* See Appendix E: Y-Site Compatibility of Common NICU Drugs.

USE

For gastrointestinal dysmotility. Has been used to prevent GE reflux,[2,4] to promote enteral feeding in infants with feeding intolerance,[3] to facilitate intubation of the small intestine, in management of gastric stasis, and for emergency evacuation of the stomach prior to administration of anesthesia for emergency surgery. May be helpful for difficult placement of an NJ feeding tube.

Used in older children and adults at higher doses (1–2 mg/kg/dose) as an antiemetic in the treatment of chemotherapy-induced nausea and vomiting. The extrapyramidal adverse effects (see **ADVERSE EFFECTS** below) are primarily associated with these doses.

Has been given to postpartum women who delivered preterm infants and were having difficulty maintaining milk production. A dose of 10 mg every 8 hours for 7 days, tapered off over 2 days, was associated with successful maintenance of lactation.[5]

MECHANISM OF ACTION

The mechanism of action of metoclopramide probably results from both dopamine antagonism and augmentation of acetylcholine release from postganglionic nerve terminals.

Metoclopramide's chemical structure is similar to that of procainamide. It is a potent centrally acting antiemetic and gastrointestinal prokinetic (forward-motion) agent. It improves peristalsis, increases lower esophageal sphincter pressure, and improves gastric emptying.[3,6,7] (See Figure 1-7, page 227, which illustrates sites of action of four prokinetic agents, including metoclopramide.)

ADVERSE EFFECTS

Adverse effects increase with increasing dose.

High doses may cause extrapyramidal effects. Extrapyramidal syndrome in children is an oculogyric crisis with torticollis and neck pain. (The syndrome is reversed by stopping the drug; treatment with diphenhydramine 1.5 mg/kg/dose IV/IM may be needed.) Permanent extrapyramidal effects such as tardive dyskinesia have occurred.[8]

Methemoglobinemia has been reported in preterm and term infants overdosed on metoclopramide. If methemoglobinemia occurs, it is treated by withholding metoclopramide and administering methylene blue 1–2 mg/kg/dose IV over 5 minutes.

Commonly seen side effects in infants are irritability or sedation.

Nausea and diarrhea may occur. Increased serum prolactin and gynecomastia have been reported in adults.

PHARMACOKINETICS/PHARMACODYNAMICS

Absorption: Rapidly absorbed from GI tract. Bioavailability is variable (32–97 percent) because of first-pass drug metabolism.

Onset of Action: 1–3 minutes after IV, 10–15 minutes after IM, and 30–60 minutes after PO administration.

Duration of Action: 1–2 hours.

Protein Binding: 40 percent.

Metabolism: Metabolized by the liver to the sulfate and glucuronide.

Half-life: 4–5 hours.

Elimination: Mostly in the urine.[9–10]

NURSING IMPLICATIONS

For best effect, administer at least 15–30 minutes before feeding.

Monitor for irritability and diarrhea.

COMMENTS

Interactions: May increase the rate of absorption of some drugs as a result of improved gastric emptying and intestinal acceleration; however, this is not usually clinically significant. Narcotics and anticholinergics antagonize the GI effects of metoclopramide.

M

References

1. Reed MD, Sutphen JL, and Blumer JL. 1992. Drugs used to modulate gastrointestinal function. In *Pediatric Pharmacology: Therapeutic Principles in Practice,* 2nd ed., Yaffe SJ, and Aranda JV, eds. Philadelphia: WB Saunders, 437–465.

2. Machida HM, et al. 1988. Metoclopramide in gastroesophageal reflux of infancy. *Journal of Pediatrics* 112(3): 483–487.

3. Hyams JS, et al. 1986. Effect of metoclopramide on prolonged intraesophageal pH testing in infants with gastroesophageal reflux. *Journal of Pediatric Gastroenterology and Nutrition* 5(5): 716–720.

4. Meadow WL, et al. 1989. Metoclopramide promotes enteral feeding in preterm infants with feeding intolerance. *Developmental Pharmacology and Therapeutics* 13(1): 38–45.

5. Ehrenkranz RA, and Ackerman BA. 1986. Metoclopramide effect on faltering milk production by mothers of premature infants. *Pediatrics* 78(4): 614–620.

6. Hyman PE. 1994. Gastroesophageal reflux: One reason why baby won't eat. *Journal of Pediatrics* 125(6 part 2, supplement): S103–S109.

7. Hyman PE, Abrams CE, and Dubois A. 1988. Gastric emptying in infants: Response to metoclopramide depends on the underlying condition. *Journal of Pediatric Gastroenterology and Nutrition* 7(2): 181–184.

8. Putnam PE, et al. 1992. Tardive dyskinesia associated with metoclopramide use in a child. *Journal of Pediatrics* 121(6): 983–985.

9. Bateman DN. 1983. Clinical pharmacokinetics of metoclopramide. *Clinical Pharmacokinetics* 8(6): 523–529.

10. Kearns GL, et al. 1988. Metoclopramide pharmacokinetics and pharmacodynamics in infants with gastroesophageal reflux. *Journal of Pediatric Gastroenterology and Nutrition* 7(6): 823–829.

METRONIDAZOLE (FLAGYL)

(meh-troe-NI-da-zole)

ANTI-INFECTIVE: ANTIBIOTIC

DOSE

Loading: An initial loading dose of 15 mg/kg has been recommended.[1]

Maintenance: *Preterm Infants:* Begin the maintenance doses listed below 48 hours after the loading dose. *Term Infants:* Begin the maintenance doses listed below 24 hours after the loading dose.

- *<1.2 kg (0–4 weeks):* 15–35 mg/kg/day divided or 7.5 mg/kg/dose given every 48 hours[2]
- *1.2–2 kg:*
  - 0–7 days: 7.5 mg/kg/dose given every 24 hours
  - >7 days: 7.5 mg/kg/dose given every 12 hours
- *>2 kg:*
  - 0–7 days: 7.5 mg/kg/dose given every 12 hours
  - >7 days: 15 mg/kg/dose given every 12 hours
- *Older Infants and Children:* 7.5 mg/kg/dose given every 6 hours[3]

Use with caution and at lower doses in patients with severe hepatic and/or renal dysfunction.

ADMINISTRATION

IV—*Rate:* Over 1 hour.

IV—*Concentration:* Dilute to at least 8 mg/ml.

IV—*Compatibility:* See Appendix E: Y-Site Compatibility of Common NICU Drugs.

PO: Administer with feedings to reduce GI upset. An oral liquid is not commercially available, but a 50 mg/ml suspension can be compounded by the pharmacist as follows:

Pharmacist Compounding Directions
Metronidazole Suspension 50 mg/ml[4]

Pulverize 10 metronidazole 250 mg tablets; mix with a small amount of distilled water. Add cherry syrup to equal a total volume of 50 ml. Shake well.

Stability: 30 days.

Storage: Refrigerate.

USE

An antibiotic effective against anaerobic Gram-positive and anaerobic Gram-negative bacteria (e.g., *Bacteroides fragilis*) and protozoa.

Ineffective against aerobic bacteria. Must therefore be used in conjunction with other antibiotics for treating mixed infections, such as the bowel perforation of necrotizing enterocolitis.[5–9]

Used to treat *C. difficile* antibiotic-associated pseudomembranous colitis (AAPC).

MECHANISM OF ACTION

Metronidazole is a nitroimidazole. It enters cells of microorganisms, forming compounds that bind to DNA, inhibit synthesis, and cause cell death.

ADVERSE EFFECTS

CNS: Seizures, peripheral neuropathy. Discontinue if abnormal neurologic signs appear.

GI: GI upset, furry tongue, overgrowth of Candida.

GU: Dysuria. May color urine deep red/brown.

Hematologic: Mild, reversible neutropenia (leukopenia); thrombocytopenia (rare).

Other: Rash, fever, flushing, thrombophlebitis.

Based on experimental animal data, researchers have expressed concern over the carcinogenic potential of metronidazole. This has not occurred in humans, however. Two retrospective studies in adults showed no increase in cancer following exposure to this drug.[10–12]

Causes mild disulfiramlike reaction (nausea, flushing, abdominal cramps) if infant concurrently receives an alcohol-containing medication.

PHARMACOKINETICS/PHARMACODYNAMICS

Absorption: Well absorbed PO.

Distribution: Distributes well into tissues, bone, abscesses. CSF concentrations have been equal to or higher than concomitant serum concentrations.[1]

Protein Binding: <20 percent.

Metabolism: Up to 60 percent hepatic.

Half-life: Inversely related to gestational age in infants (22.5–109 hours).

Elimination: 60–80 percent in urine and 6–15 percent in feces.

NURSING IMPLICATIONS

Monitor CBC for neutropenia.

Monitor renal and liver function.

COMMENTS

Interactions:

- Barbiturates decrease metronidazole levels. Consider increasing dose to avoid therapeutic failure.
- May decrease clearance of phenytoin, resulting in excessive phenytoin levels.
- Potentiates effects of warfarin, prolonging prothrombin time.

- Flushing, GI symptoms, sweating, headache (disulfiram-like reactions). When metronidazole and alcohol are given concurrently, acetaldehyde may accumulate due to interference with the oxidation of alcohol, resulting in disulfiram-like effects. Some oral liquid medications may contain alcohol (phenobarbital; some theophylline products contain 20 percent alcohol).

References

1. Jager-Roman E, et al. 1982. Pharmacokinetics and tissue distribution of metronidazole in the newborn infant. *Journal of Pediatrics* 100(4): 651–654.

2. Prober CG, Stevenson DK, and Benitz WE. 1990. The use of antibiotics in neonates weighing less than 1,200 grams. *Pediatric Infectious Disease Journal* 9(2): 111–121.

3. Nelson JD. 1996. *1996–1997 Pocket Book of Pediatric Antimicrobial Therapy*, 12th ed. Baltimore: Lippincott Williams & Wilkins, 16–17, 78.

4. ASHP, Committee on Extemporaneous Formulations. 1987. *Handbook on Extemporaneous Formulations*. Bethesda, Maryland: American Society of Hospital Pharmacists, 32.

5. Roberts RJ. 1984. *Drug Therapy in Infants: Pharmacologic Principles and Clinical Experience*. Philadelphia: WB Saunders, 76–77.

6. Feldman WE. 1976. *Bacteroides fragilis* ventriculitis and meningitis. *American Journal of Diseases of Children* 130(8): 880–883.

7. Hall P, et al. 1983. Intravenous metronidazole in the newborn. *Archives of Disease in Childhood* 58(7): 529–531.

8. Berman BW, et al. 1978. *Bacteroides fragilis* meningitis in a neonate successfully treated with metronidazole. *Journal of Pediatrics* 93(5): 793–795.

9. Brook I. 1983. Treatment of anaerobic infections in children with metronidazole. *Developmental Pharmacology and Therapeutics* 6(3): 187–198.

10. Beard CM, et al. 1979. Lack of evidence for cancer due to use of metronidazole. *New England Journal of Medicine* 301(10): 519–522.

11. Friedman GD. 1980. Cancer after metronidazole (letter). *New England Journal of Medicine* 302(9): 519–520.

12. United States Pharmacopeial Convention/USP DI. 1996. *Drug Information for the Health Care Professional*, 16th ed. Rockville, Maryland: United States Pharmacopeial Convention, 2055–2059.

Metyrapone (Metopirone)

(meh-TER-uh-pohn)

Diagnostic Agent: Pituitary Function Test

Dose

35 mg/kg/dose for one dose[1]

Administration

PO: May give with feeding to reduce GI irritation.

Preparation: A metyrapone suspension is not commercially available. A 50 mg/ml suspension can be prepared by the pharmacist as follows:

Pharmacist Compounding Directions
Metyrapone 50 mg/ml Suspension

Crush a 250 mg tablet to a fine powder before removing from the unit-dose packaging. Transfer powdered tablet to a small empty screw-cap prescription vial. Mix powder with 5 ml water. Let sit for 15 minutes, shaking frequently. Withdraw volume for dose needed. Protect from light. Discard unused portion. (Use of simple syrup as a vehicle in this product is not recommended because of its high osmolality.)

Procedure: Figure 1-12 outlines the pituitary function testing procedure, normal responses, and actions to take based on the outcome.

Figure 1-12 ◆ Procedure for pituitary function test.

Step 1: On a day when no steroids are given, draw baseline plasma cortisol and 11-deoxycortisol at 9 AM.

Step 2: At 11 PM on the same day (the day the baseline was drawn), give metyrapone 35 mg/kg PO.

Step 3: The following morning at 9 AM, draw postmetyrapone cortisol and 11-deoxycortisol levels.

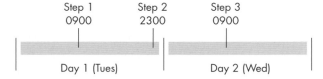

	Step 1	Step 2	Step 3
	0900	2300	0900
	Day 1 (Tues)		Day 2 (Wed)

Normal Response:
- A 4 times or greater increase in 11-deoxycortisol with a 50% or greater decrease in postmetyrapone cortisol.

Plan:
- If responses are normal, discontinue steroids.
- If responses are abnormal, continue low-dose dexamethasone (at 0.1 mg/kg/day qod) for 2 or more weeks; then repeat the test.

FIGURE 1-13 ◆ SITE OF ACTION OF METYRAPONE.

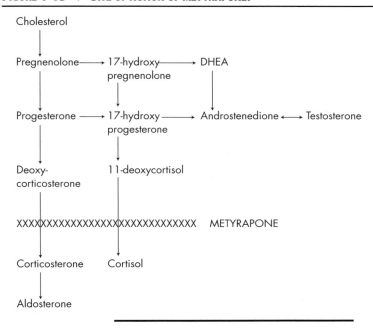

USE

Used diagnostically when infants have been on steroids for 10 days or more to determine if steroids may be discontinued. Metyrapone testing should be done only when steroids have been decreased to dexamethasone 0.05 mg/kg every 12 hours every other day *or* hydrocortisone 1.5 mg/kg every 12 hours every other day (qod) for at least a week.

The test is done to assess the capacity of the pituitary to produce ACTH in response to a physiologic stimulus. It is useful for evaluating the hypothalamic-pituitary-adrenal axis (HPAA) after long-term suppression with glucocorticoid therapy. A normal response indicates recovery of the HPAA and predicts that the patient will respond normally to stress.[1,2]

The ACTH stimulation test using cosyntropin (Cortrosyn) is a simpler, safer test for assessing recovery of adrenal suppression after steroid treatment. (See cosyntropin monograph for information on that test.)

MECHANISM OF ACTION

Metyrapone transiently blocks 11-β-hydroxylase and, therefore, the secretion of cortisol (Figure 1-13). The negative feedback control increases ACTH secretion, which stimulates increased secretion of all steroids prior to the enzyme block.

ADVERSE EFFECTS

Usually well tolerated.

May cause nausea or abdominal discomfort, which can be reduced by giving the drug with a feeding.

Metyrapone suspension compounded with simple syrup has caused transient abdominal distention and hypotension shortly after administration in small preterm infants who have been NPO, possibly as a result of their inability to tolerate the high osmolality of the product. Compounding with water, not simple syrup, is therefore recommended.

May cause acute adrenal insufficiency in patients with reduced adrenal secretory capacity.

Overdose: One 6-year-old girl died after ingesting 2 gm metyrapone. Treat overdose immediately with large doses of hydrocortisone and saline and glucose infusions. Take measures to reduce absorption. Monitor blood pressure and fluid and electrolyte balance for a few days.[3]

Pharmacokinetics/Pharmacodynamics

Absorption: Rapid, good absorption.

Half-life: 1–2.5 hours.

Elimination: In urine, primarily as glucuronides.[3]

Nursing Implications

Oral administration in syrup may cause feeding intolerance and abdominal distention.

Monitor for signs of acute adrenal insufficiency, such as hypotension and clinical deterioration.

Carefully watch timing for pituitary function test. Pass information on to the next shift that the test is in progress.

Comments

Interactions: Phenytoin (and possibly also phenobarbital) may increase metabolism of metyrapone and invalidate the response to this test. Phenytoin should be discontinued 2 weeks before the test. Some clinicians recommend doubling the metyrapone dose to increase response to metyrapone in patients in whom anticonvulsants cannot be discontinued.

References

1. Alkalay AL, et al. 1990. Hypothalamic-pituitary-adrenal axis function in very low birth weight infants treated with dexamethasone. *Pediatrics* 86(2): 204–210.

2. Edwards CRW. 1986. *Endocrinology.* Chicago: Year Book Medical Publishers, 80.

3. Olin BR. 1994. *Drug Facts and Comparisons.* St. Louis: Facts and Comparisons, 504–505.

MIDAZOLAM (VERSED)
(mid-AY-zoe-lam)
(CONTROLLED SUBSTANCE SCHEDULE IV)

CENTRAL NERVOUS SYSTEM: SEDATIVE

M

DOSE

Sedation During Mechanical Ventilation:

- *Intermittent:* 0.05–0.1 mg/kg/dose IV every 2–4 hours prn.
- *Continuous Infusion:*
  - Loading Dose: 0.05–0.2 mg/kg IV.[1]
  - Maintenance Dose: 0.2 mcg/kg/minute. May increase by 0.1 mcg/kg/minute every 30 minutes until light sleep is induced.
  - Usual range: 0.4–0.6 mcg/kg/minute.[1]
    Maximum: 6 mcg/kg/minute.
  - Booker and associates recommend a dose of 2–6 mcg/kg/minute in children requiring artificial ventilation.[2]

Premedication:

- *IV:* 0.05 mg/kg. *Maximum:* 0.2 mg/kg. Give 1–5 minutes before procedure.
- *IM:* 0.07 mg/kg. *Maximum:* 0.2 mg/kg. Give 15–30 minutes before procedure.
- *PO:* 0.2–0.4 mg/kg. Give 30–45 minutes before procedure.
- *PR:* 0.3 mg/kg. Give 20–30 minutes before procedure.
- *Intranasal:* 0.2 mg/kg. Give 5–10 minutes before procedure.[1–8]

Refractory Seizures: 0.05–0.2 mg/kg/dose IV. May be followed by continuous infusion.[9]

Dose may need to be reduced or interval lengthened in patients with severe hepatic and/or renal dysfunction or CHF; monitor carefully.

ADMINISTRATION

IV—*Rate:* Infuse over at least 2–3 minutes. For continuous infusion, use a neonatal syringe pump.

- Alternatively, others have recommended that, rather than giving a loading dose, the infusion may be run more rapidly for the first several hours to establish a therapeutic level. Infusion may begin at 0.5 mcg/kg/minute for infants <32 weeks gestation and 1 mcg/kg/minute in infants >32 weeks gestation. Then titrate to the lowest effective dose.[10]
- ***Precaution:*** Frequently reassess the rate of infusion, particularly after the first 24 hours, to administer the lowest effective dose and reduce the risk of drug accumulation.[10]

IV—*Concentration:* Use the 5 mg/ml (not 1 mg/ml) concentration to prepare the drip, to minimize fluid volume and benzyl alcohol intake. Dilute with D_5W,

$D_{10}W$, or sodium chloride for more accurate measurement of IV push doses and for preparation of continuous infusions.

IV—*Compatibility:* See Appendix E: Y-Site Compatibility of Common NICU Drugs.

IM—*Concentration:* May give undiluted.

Intranasal: Use the more concentrated formulation (5 mg/ml) to minimize fluid volume. Carefully instill the calculated dose a few drops at a time in alternate nares.

PO: The injectable form of midazolam has been given PO. The pharmacist can compound a 2.5 mg/ml midazolam solution as follows:

Pharmacist Compounding Directions
Midazolam Solution 2.5 mg/ml[11]

Dilute midazolam injection 5 mg/ml in an equal volume of Syrpalta (a flavored dye-free syrup).

Stability: 56 days refrigerated or at room temperature.

USE

An antianxiety agent for infants on assisted ventilation.

Sedation prior to short procedures.

Induction or maintenance of anesthesia.

Has a rapid onset and short duration and produces less local pain on IM or IV administration than other benzodiazepines.

Produces anterograde amnesia of perioperative events. Patients receiving larger doses have longer amnesia.

MECHANISM OF ACTION

Benzodiazepines act by facilitating GABA-mediated synaptic transmission. They bind to specific central nervous system benzodiazepine postsynaptic receptors that amplify GABA effects. Benzodiazepine receptors appear early during ontogenesis.[12] Midazolam is a water-soluble benzodiazepine with a potency about three to four times that of diazepam.

ADVERSE EFFECTS

With high doses or rapid IV infusions, particularly if fentanyl is being given concurrently: respiratory depression and arrest, hypotension. Laryngospasm, hiccups, GI upset, and excessive sedation may occur.

No serious adverse effects have been reported with oral midazolam 0.5–1 mg/kg. Dysphoria and lack of head control may occur.

Physiologic dependency. If the infant has received the drug for approximately a week, the dose must be tapered gradually to minimize withdrawal symptoms.

- To taper, use Appendix K: Neonatal Withdrawal Score Sheet as a guide.

- Decrease daily dose by about 10 percent every 1–2 days, as tolerated, using the withdrawal score sheet as a guide.
- If a dose taper fails (score is 8 or above), resume the previously effective dose for about 3–5 days as tolerated, then begin to taper again.

Myoclonus may occur. Onset was 2–48 hours after beginning the midazolam infusion, ceased a few hours after discontinuing the drug, and never recurred. The myoclonus appeared as twitches of all four limbs, sometimes rhythmic and of variable frequency.[13]

PHARMACOKINETICS/PHARMACODYNAMICS

Oral Bioavailability: About 45 percent.

Absorption: Nasal—approximately 60 percent. Rectal—40–50 percent.

Onset of Action: 10 minutes.

Protein Binding: 97 percent.

Metabolism: Hepatic.

Half-life (children): 1–4 hours; intranasal half-life is shorter.[6]

Elimination: Hydroxymethyl midazolam is eliminated in the urine. About 2–10 percent of an oral dose is eliminated in the feces.

NURSING IMPLICATIONS

Monitor respirations, CNS status, and blood pressure.[14]

When administered to nonintubated patients for a procedure, initiate conscious sedation precautions and monitor vital signs continuously, including pulse oximetry; monitor for respiratory depression and hypotension. Facilities for administration of oxygen and controlled respirations should be readily available whenever the drug is given IV.[14]

COMMENTS

Use the lowest effective dose for the shortest time necessary. Maximum duration is 2 weeks.

Midazolam contains 1 percent benzyl alcohol (10 mg benzyl alcohol/ml) as a preservative, which has been associated with the fatal "gasping baby syndrome" in neonates. Clinical signs of the gasping syndrome include metabolic acidosis, hypotension, CNS depression, and cardiovascular collapse. A midazolam dose of 1 mcg/kg/minute would give 2.88 mg/kg/day of benzyl alcohol if midazolam 5 mg/ml were used to prepare the drip (14.4 mg/kg/day BA if the 1 mg/ml midazolam were used).

Antidote: Flumazenil (Romazicon) 2–10 mcg/kg IV (see monograph for that drug).

Interactions: Concurrent use of midazolam with fentanyl potentiates both the beneficial and the adverse effects of midazolam. This combination should be used with careful monitoring and cautious dosing.[3,4] Midazolam potentiates the effects of concurrent CNS and respiratory depressants. Concurrent cimetidine or ranitidine with orally administered midazolam may increase midazolam serum concentrations.

REFERENCES

1. Silvasi DL, Rosen DA, and Rosen KR. 1988. Continuous intravenous midazolam infusion for sedation in the pediatric intensive care unit. *Anesthesia and Analgesia* 67(3): 286–288.

2. Booker PD, Beechey A, and Lloyd-Thomas AR. 1986. Sedation of children requiring artificial ventilation using an infusion of midazolam. *British Journal of Anaesthesia* 58(10): 1104–1108.

3. Yaster M, et al. 1990. Midazolam-fentanyl intravenous sedation in children: Case report of respiratory arrest. *Pediatrics* 86(3): 463–467.

4. Bailey PL, et al. 1990. Frequent hypoxemia and apnea after sedation with midazolam and fentanyl. *Anesthesiology* 73(5): 826–830.

5. Karl HW, et al. 1992. Comparison of the safety and efficacy of intranasal midazolam or sufentanil for preinduction of anesthesia in pediatric patients. *Anesthesiology* 76(2): 209–215.

6. Lerman J. 1993. Anesthesia. In *Pediatric Pharmacology and Therapeutics*, 2nd ed., Radde IC, and MacLeod SM, eds. St. Louis: Mosby-Year Book, 475–497.

7. Taketomo CK, Hodding JH, and Kraus DM. 1996. *1996–1997 Pediatric Dosage Handbook*, 3rd ed. Hudson, Ohio: Lexi-Comp, 463–466.

8. Zeltzer LK, et al. 1990. Report of the subcommittee on the management of pain associated with procedures in children with cancer. *Pediatrics* 86(5 part 2): 826–831.

9. Benitz WE, and Tatro DS. 1995. *The Pediatric Drug Handbook*, 3rd ed. St. Louis: Mosby-Year Book, 97–99.

10. Kastrup EK. 1997. Midazolam. *Drug Facts and Comparisons*. St. Louis: Facts and Comparisons, 281b–281i.

11. Steedman SL, et al. 1992. Stability of midazolam hydrochloride in a flavored dye-free oral solution. *American Journal of Hospital Pharmacy* 49(3): 615–618.

12. Aaltonen L, Erkkola R, and Kanto J. 1983. Benzodiazepine receptors in the human fetus. *Biology of the Neonate* 44(1): 54–57.

13. Magny JF, et al. 1994. Midazolam and myoclonus in neonate. *European Journal of Pediatrics* 153(5): 389–390.

14. American Academy of Pediatrics, Committee on Drugs. 1992. Guidelines for monitoring and management of pediatric patients during and after sedation for diagnostic and therapeutic procedures. *Pediatrics* 89(6): 1110–1115.

MORPHINE

(MOR-feen)

(CONTROLLED SUBSTANCE SCHEDULE II)

CENTRAL NERVOUS SYSTEM: NARCOTIC ANALGESIC

DOSE

Pain Relief and Sedation During Mechanical Ventilation: 0.05–0.1 mg/kg/dose IV repeated every 4 hours as needed.

Continuous Infusion for Pain Relief and/or Sedation:

- *Loading Dose:* 0.1 mg/kg/dose infused over 1 1/2 hours; then reduce infusion to following maintenance dose.

- *Maintenance Dose:*

  - Preterm and term infants <5–6 months: 15–20 mcg/kg/hour (= 0.015–0.020 mg/kg/hour) IV.[1–3]

  - All infants >5–6 months: 50–60 mcg/kg/hour (= 0.05–0.06 mg/kg/hour) IV.[4]

- Chay and colleagues proposed that neonates receive two consecutive continuous infusions (the loading infusion followed by the maintenance infusion) to rapidly achieve steady state concentration and pain relief while avoiding the high concentrations and potential adverse effects resulting from a bolus loading dose.[2] By this method, the plasma level will increase to a maximum at the end of the loading infusion, then slowly adjust to the steady state maintenance infusion plasma level.

Treatment of Narcotic Withdrawal: 0.5 mg/kg/dose PO repeated every 4 hours as needed. Taper gradually over days to weeks as guided by the Finnegan Neonatal Abstinence Scoring System (see Appendix K: Neonatal Withdrawal Score Sheet).[5]

General Dosing Considerations:

- *Decrease Dose:* Shock, abnormal hemodynamics, and hepatic and/or renal failure may prolong the half-life and effects of morphine, decreasing dose requirements.

- *Increase Dose:* Tolerance develops with prolonged use, possibly increasing dosage requirements. Serum concentrations decrease with time without any change in dose, suggesting improved clearance.[3,6]

- Neonates have a limited ability to conjugate morphine to morphine-6-glucuronide (M6G), an active metabolite 20 times more active than morphine. Because of this, neonates are less sensitive to the analgesic effects of morphine. Larger doses may be required in some infants.[2]

- Infants on ventilators may tolerate higher doses.

- Individualize dose.

M

ADMINISTRATION

Supplied as: Morphine is available in many concentrations. Suggest stocking preservative-free injection 1 mg/ml to accurately measure small bolus doses and 10 mg/ml for preparing drips and doses for larger babies. Astramorph PF and Duramorph PF are proprietary names for preservative-free parenteral morphine products, which are preferred for neonates.

IV—*Rate:* For IV push, infuse over at least 4–5 minutes to avoid hypotension.

IV—*Concentration:* Use only ≤1 mg/ml concentration to prevent potential overdose that could result from inability to measure the small neonatal dose volumes accurately.

IV—*Compatibility:* See Appendix E: Y-Site Compatibility of Common NICU Drugs.

USE

Treatment of severe pain, and treatment of neonatal abstinence syndrome.

MECHANISM OF ACTION

Morphine, a narcotic analgesic, stimulates opioid receptors in the CNS that mimic the actions of endogenous enkephalins and β-endorphins.[7]

ADVERSE EFFECTS

The incidence of adverse effects, including respiratory depression, of morphine is approximately the same as other narcotics such as fentanyl and meperidine

TABLE 1-37 ◆ NARCOTIC CONVERSION CHART

Narcotic	Dose (mg) Equivalent to 1 mg of Parenteral Morphine
Morphine	
IV or subcutaneous	1
Oral liquid	2–5
Meperidine	
IV or subcutaneous	7.5
Oral	30
Methadone	
IV	1
Oral	2
Codeine	
Oral	20
Fentanyl	
IV or subcutaneous	0.012

Adapted from: Robieux IC. 1993. Treatment of pain in infants and children: The role of pharmacology. In *Pediatric Pharmacology and Therapeutics,* 2nd ed., Radde IC, and MacLeod SM, eds. St. Louis: Mosby-Year Book, 505. Reprinted by permission.

when equivalent analgesic doses are used. However, differing adverse effects may be experienced by different patients; therefore, other narcotics in addition to morphine should be available for use if the patient cannot tolerate morphine (Table 1-37).[7] Adverse effects such as CNS and respiratory depression increase with increasing dose.

Antidote: Naloxone (Narcan) 0.1 mg/kg/dose IV. See Appendix J: Antidotes for Drugs That Cause Loss of Respiratory Effort.

Cardiovascular: Hypotension (especially with rapid IV push), bradycardia.

CNS: Excessive sedation, seizures. Continuous infusion of 30–40 mcg/kg/hour, which is usually well tolerated in older children, has caused seizures in neonates. Accumulation in renal failure may increase neurotoxicity.[1,3]

GI/GU: Constipation, urinary retention.

Respiratory: CO_2 retention.[2] Respiratory depression and arrest with high doses or rapid IV infusions, particularly with concurrent use of other CNS depressants.

PHARMACOKINETICS/PHARMACODYNAMICS

Absorption: Well absorbed.

Peak of Action—IV: 15–30 minutes.

Duration: 2–4 hours.

Protein Binding: 30 percent.

Metabolism: High degree of first-pass metabolism in the liver. Metabolized by conjugation with glucuronic acid. Pharmacokinetic parameters vary widely among preterm and term neonates.[2]

Half-life: In preterm neonates 35 weeks gestation = 28 hours; term neonates 0–10 days = 6.9 hours; 8–70 days = 3.9 hours; >1 year = 2 hours. Olkkola and colleagues found that morphine kinetics in children seemed to mature very early; patients aged 5–6 months had parameters similar to those in adults.[4]

Elimination: Significant amounts of unchanged morphine along with metabolites are excreted in the urine.[3,7]

TABLE 1-38 ◆ NEONATAL PAIN RELIEF/SEDATION ASSESSMENT SCALE

Score	Observed Behavior
3	Overly sedated; little or no response to handling or endotracheal suctioning.
2	No distress; patient remains quiet when undisturbed but responds to stimulation.
1	Occasional periods of distress.
0	Significant distress, including facial grimacing, excessive body movement, tachycardia, and a decrease in transcutaneous partial pressure of oxygen.

Adapted from: Chay PCW, Duffy BJ, and Walker JS. 1992. Pharmacokinetic-pharmacodynamic relationships of morphine in neonates. *Clinical Pharmacology and Therapeutics* 51(3): 334–342. Reprinted by permission.

NURSING IMPLICATIONS

When administering morphine to nonintubated patients for a procedure, initiate conscious sedation precautions, and monitor vital signs continuously, including pulse oximetry.

Monitor respirations, CNS status, and blood pressure.

Monitor adequacy of pain relief.

Have naloxone available.

COMMENTS

Use the lowest effective dose for the shortest time necessary, but be certain pain is being managed adequately. Chay and colleagues used a four-point scale (Table 1-38) to assess pain relief and sedation (comfort score). The goal was a comfort score of two.[2]

Morphine causes physiologic dependency. If the infant has received the drug for more than about 2 weeks, the dose must be tapered gradually to minimize withdrawal symptoms.

- **Long-term follow-up:** No differences in intelligence, motor function, or behavior at 5 to 6 years of age were found between neonates who received morphine for sedation during mechanical ventilation and placebo-treated neonates.[8]

Interactions: Concurrent use of benzodiazepines (i.e., midazolam, lorazepam) potentiates both the beneficial and the adverse effects of morphine. This combination should be used only with careful monitoring and cautious dosing.

REFERENCES

1. Koren G, et al. 1985. Morphine-induced seizures in newborn infants. *Veterinary and Human Toxicology* 27(6): 519–520.

2. Chay PCW, Duffy BJ, and Walker JS. 1992. Pharmacokinetic-pharmacodynamic relationship of morphine in neonates. *Clinical Pharmacology and Therapeutics* 51(3): 334–342.

3. Koren G, et al. 1985. Postoperative morphine infusion in newborn infants: Assessment of disposition characteristics and safety. *Journal of Pediatrics* 107(6): 963–967.

4. Olkkola KT, et al. 1988. Kinetics and dynamics of postoperative intravenous morphine in children. *Clinical Pharmacology and Therapeutics* 44(2): 128–136.

5. Levy M, and Spino M. 1993. Neonatal withdrawal syndrome: Associated drugs and pharmacologic management. *Pharmacotherapy* 13(3): 202–211.

6. Robieux IC. 1993. Treatment of pain in infants and children: The role of pharmacology. In *Pediatric Pharmacology and Therapeutics*, 2nd ed., Radde IC, and MacLeod SM, eds. St. Louis: Mosby-Year Book, 499–513.

7. Roberts RJ. 1984. *Drug Therapy in Infants: Pharmacologic Principles and Clinical Experience.* Philadelphia: WB Saunders, 302–303.

8. MacGregor R, et al. 1998. Outcome at 5–6 years of prematurely born children who received morphine as neonates. *Archives of Diseases in Children. Fetal and Neonatal Edition* 79(1): F40–F43.

MULTIVITAMINS

(mul-tee-VYE-ta-minz)

(VI-DAYLIN MULTIVITAMIN DROPS, POLY-VI-SOL INFANT DROPS)

DOSE

1 ml PO as a single daily dose or divided every 12 hours mixed in a small amount of the infant's feeding.

Begin with 0.5 ml PO bid in infants receiving less than 20 ml of formula per feeding, then advance to 1 ml PO as a single daily dose when feeding tolerance has improved and feeding volumes are larger.

Begin vitamin supplementation only when infant has advanced to full-strength formula to avoid GI upset.

Continue vitamin supplement in formula-fed preterm infants until the infant's intake exceeds 300 kcal/day or a body weight of 2.5 kg is achieved.[1]

ADMINISTRATION

PO: Mix in a small amount of infant's feeding to dilute and facilitate administration.

USE

Preterm infants need multivitamin supplementation because their nutritional intake is limited. Infant formula products contain the RDA of vitamins in a volume of approximately 750 ml, but preterm infants often consume much less than this amount. (Table 1-39 lists vitamin RDAs for term infants.) Nutritional rickets has been reported in infants fed proprietary formula containing 400 units of vitamin D per liter but no additional supplementation.[2] Formulas for premature infants contain a higher concentration of vitamins; however, supplementation may still be required if the infant is not receiving an adequate volume of feeding or has a condition that increases vitamin requirements. Breastfed infants should be supplemented with 400 units of vitamin D daily. This can be provided by giving 1 ml of multivitamins daily.

Multivitamins contain water-soluble and fat-soluble vitamins, including vitamins A, D, E, B-complex, and C. They contain B_{12}, but no folic acid, and they contain no vitamin K. *Trivitamins* (Tri-Vi-Sol and Vi-Daylin ADC) contain only vitamins A, D, and C. Because of their limited content, they are not the preferred vitamin supplement for preterm infants. (Table 1-40 compares multi- and trivitamin contents.)

ADVERSE EFFECTS

Usually well tolerated when given at recommended doses.

High Osmolality: Multivitamins are very hyperosmolar and may increase the risk of necrotizing enterocolitis, especially when given undiluted to an infant who is not yet tolerating feedings. The risk can be minimized by diluting before use, by

TABLE 1-39 ◆ RECOMMENDED DAILY ALLOWANCES OF VITAMINS FOR TERM INFANTS

Vitamin	Birth to 6 Months	6 Months to 1 Year
A (mcg R.E.)	375	375
D (units)	300	400
E (units)	4	6
K (mcg)	5	10
C (mg)	30	35
Thiamin (B_1) (mg)	0.3	0.4
Riboflavin (B_2) (mg)	0.4	0.5
Niacin (B_3) (mg)	5	6
Pyridoxine (B_6) (mg)	0.3	0.6
Folate (mcg)	25	35
Vitamin B_{12} (mcg)	0.3	0.5
Biotin (mcg)	35	50
Pantothenic acid (mg)	2	3

Note: The recommendations in this table are for term infants. In the absence of specific information on the vitamin requirements of preterm infants, it seems reasonable to ensure vitamin intakes compara-ble with the amounts recommended for term infants.[3,4]

R.E. = retinol equivalents.

Adapted from: National Academy of Sciences. 1989. *Recommended Dietary Allowances,* 10th ed. Washington, DC: National Academy Press; and Greene HL. 1993. Disorders of the water-soluble vitamin B-complex and vitamin C. In *Textbook of Pediatric Nutrition,* 2nd ed., Suskind RM, and Lewinter-Suskind L, eds. New York: Raven Press, 73–89.

TABLE 1-40 ◆ COMPARISON OF ORAL VITAMIN DROPS

Vitamin	Multivitamins[a,b] (per ml)	Trivitamins[c] (per ml)
A (units)	1,500	1,500
D (units)	400	400
E (units)	5,[a] 4[b]	
B_1 (mg)	0.5	
B_2 (mg)	0.6	
B_3 (mg)	8	
B_6 (mg)	0.4	
B_{12} (mcg)	2,[a] 1.5[b]	
C (mg)	35	35

[a] Poly-Vi-Sol Infant Drops (Mead Johnson)

[b] Vi-Daylin Multivitamin Drops (Ross)

[c] Vi-Daylin ADC Drops (Ross), Tri-Vi-Sol Drops (Mead Johnson)

giving in two divided doses in infants receiving small feedings, and by spacing medication administration throughout the day, rather than administering all medications in one feeding.

NURSING IMPLICATIONS

Monitor for feeding intolerance.

REFERENCES

1. American Academy of Pediatrics, Committee on Nutrition. 1980. Vitamin and mineral supplement needs in normal children in the United States. *Pediatrics* 66(6): 1015–1021.

2. Lewin PK, et al. 1971. Iatrogenic rickets in low-birth-weight infants. *Journal of Pediatrics* 78(2): 207–210.

3. Greene HL. 1993. Disorders of the water-soluble vitamin B-complex and vitamin C. In *Textbook of Pediatric Nutrition,* 2nd ed., Suskind RM, and Lewinter-Suskind L, eds. New York: Raven Press, 73–89.

4. American Academy of Pediatrics, Committee on Nutrition. 1977. Nutritional needs of low-birth-weight infants. *Pediatrics* 60(4): 519–530.

MUPIROCIN (BACTROBAN)

(myoo-PEER-oh-sin)

DOSE

Apply a small amount to the affected area three times a day.

Duration of Therapy: Continue therapy for 5–14 days. Re-evaluate if there is no improvement within 3–5 days.

Use with caution in patients with impaired renal function; see **CAUTIONS/CONTRAINDICATIONS** below.

ADMINISTRATION

Supplied as: Ointment, 2 percent.

Affected area may be covered with a gauze dressing if desired.[1]

CAUTIONS/CONTRAINDICATIONS

Hypersensitivity to mupirocin or to the polyethylene glycol (PEG) contained in the vehicle. If skin reaction develops, stop therapy and wash affected area.

Not for ophthalmic use.

The PEG in the base in which mupirocin is delivered can be absorbed into the systemic circulation, especially through open wounds and damaged skin (such as occurs in burns), in potentially toxic amounts.[1] PEG is excreted by the kidneys. Rarely, excessive absorption of PEG has resulted in renal failure and death. Do not use mupirocin where absorption of large amounts of PEG in the ointment is possible, especially in patients with moderate or severe renal impairment.[2]

Prolonged or repeated use may result in overgrowth of nonsusceptible organisms, including fungi, leading to secondary infections.

USE

A topical antibiotic used to treat superficial infections caused by *Staphylococcus aureus* (including methicillin-resistant and β-lactamase-producing strains), *Staphylococcus epidermidis* and other coagulase-negative staphylococci, *Streptococcus pyogenes*, and many Gram-negative aerobic bacteria (excluding *Pseudomonas aeruginosa*). Most active against Gram-positive aerobic bacteria. Inactive against anaerobic bacteria, Chlamydia, and fungi.

Topical vs Systemic Treatment: Some clinicians prefer topical mupirocin over systemic anti-infective therapy for treatment of superficial skin infections caused by susceptible organisms because the drug seems to be as effective as and has fewer adverse effects than systemic therapy.[3,4] In infants, however, only the most minor infections can be treated topically; systemic antibiotics must be used to treat most infections because of the immaturity of the infant's immune system.

Intravenous Catheter Sites: Mupirocin has been applied prophylactically to intravenous catheter entrance sites. However, Zakrzewska-Bode and colleagues reported increasing resistance of coagulase-negative staphylococci with routine topical application of mupirocin to the insertion sites of central venous catheters of neonates in a neonatal intensive care unit. After 5 years, mupirocin resistance was 42 percent of clinical isolates of coagulase-negative staphylococci. This decreased to 21 percent in a 5-month mupirocin-free interval, and 1 year after routine mupirocin application was discontinued, the incidence of resistance had dropped to 13 percent.[5]

Methicillin-Resistant *Staphylococcus aureus* (MRSA): Back and associates described the epidemiology of and interventions used to control two MRSA epidemics in a neonatal intensive care unit. All infants (colonized and noncolonized) and parents of and personnel working with colonized infants were treated simultaneously with 5 days of mupirocin. The investigators found that intensive microbiologic surveillance and isolation were effective in containing the spread of MRSA and that mupirocin failed to eradicate the organism in colonized infants.[6]

MECHANISM OF ACTION

Mupirocin inhibits bacterial protein synthesis by binding to bacterial isoleucyl transfer-RNA synthetase. Mupirocin shows no cross-resistance with many antibiotics, including chloramphenicol, erythromycin, gentamicin, methicillin, neomycin, and penicillin.

ADVERSE EFFECTS

Usually well tolerated.

Dermatologic: Mild, transient tenderness, burning, and stinging of skin; rash; dry skin; and erythema. Some of the adverse effects may be caused by the PEG vehicle in the drug product rather than by the mupirocin itself.

PHARMACOKINETICS/PHARMACODYNAMICS

Absorption: Minimal absorption through intact skin.

Onset of Action: Patient should show a response after 3–5 days.

Duration of Action: Probably active for at least 24 hours on intact skin.

Protein Binding: 95 percent.

Metabolism: Any mupirocin that is absorbed is inactivated mostly by conversion in the liver. A small amount is converted in the skin to monic acid.

Elimination: Metabolite is excreted in the urine.

NURSING IMPLICATIONS

Monitor for improvement in infection.

Check for signs of intolerance to mupirocin, such as erythema, increased exudate, or rash.

REFERENCES

1. United States Pharmacopeial Convention/USP DI. 1996. *Drug Information for the Health Care Professional,* 16th ed. Rockville, Maryland: United States Pharmacopeial Convention, 2114–2115.

2. McEvoy GK. 1994. *AHFS Drug Information.* Bethesda, Maryland: American Society of Hospital Pharmacists, 2261–2263.

3. Britton JW, Fajardo JE, and Krafte-Jacobs B. 1990. Comparison of mupirocin and erythromycin in treatment of impetigo. *Journal of Pediatrics* 117(5): 827–829.

4. McLinn S. 1988. Topical mupirocin vs. systemic erythromycin treatment for pyoderma. *Pediatric Infectious Disease Journal* 7(11): 785–790.

5. Zakrzewska-Bode A, et al. 1995. Mupirocin resistance in coagulase-negative staphylococci, after topical prophylaxis for the reduction of colonization of central venous catheters. *Journal of Hospital Infection* 31(3): 189–193.

6. Back NA, et al. 1996. Control of methicillin-resistant *Staphylococcus aureus* in a neonatal intensive-care unit: Use of intensive microbiologic surveillance and mupirocin. *Infection Control and Hospital Epidemiology* 17(4): 227–231.

TABLE OF CONTENTS

N

NAFCILLIN (UNIPEN)

(naf-SILL-in)

ANTI-INFECTIVE:
ANTIBIOTIC

DOSE

<1.2 kg (0–4 weeks): 25 mg/kg/dose given every 12 hours[1]

1.2–2 kg:

- 0–7 days: 25 mg/kg/dose given every 12 hours
- >7 days: 25 mg/kg/dose given every 8 hours

>2 kg:

- 0–7 days: 25 mg/kg/dose given every 8 hours
- >7 days: 25 mg/kg/dose given every 6 hours[2]

Reduce dose in combined renal and hepatic dysfunction. Dose need not be adjusted in renal dysfunction alone.

ADMINISTRATION

Supplied as: Powder in 500 mg, 1 gm, and 2 gm vials. Reconstitute 1 gm vials with 3.4 ml of sterile water for a final concentration of 250 mg/ml. Reconstituted solution is stable for 3 days at room temperature, 7 days if refrigerated.

IV—*Rate:* May infuse over 5–10 minutes, but infusion over 30–60 minutes is preferred. IV is the preferred route of administration.

IV—*Concentration:* Maximum: 30 mg/ml.

IV—*Compatibility:* See Appendix E: Y-Site Compatibility of Common NICU Drugs.

IM: Reconstitute to 250 mg/ml. A few doses may be administered IM (e.g., at the end of a course of therapy to avoid starting another IV). However, the IM route is irritating to the tissue; the IV route is preferred.

USE

Treatment of infections caused by penicillinase-producing staphylococci.

Methicillin-resistant staphylococci are also resistant to nafcillin—use vancomycin for these infections.

MECHANISM OF ACTION

Penicillins act by interrupting bacterial cell wall synthesis. Nafcillin is a penicillinase-resistant penicillin.

ADVERSE EFFECTS

Extravasation can cause severe tissue damage with necrosis. Damage may be minimized by prompt local treatment with hyaluronidase.[3,4] (See Appendix G: Guidelines for Management of Intravenous Extravasations.)

Agranulocytosis and granulocytopenia have been reported.[5,6]

May cause allergic reactions.

PHARMACOKINETICS/PHARMACODYNAMICS

Protein Binding: 90 percent.

Metabolism: Hepatic.

Half-life: 2.2–5.5 hours.

Elimination: Hepatic clearance; only 8–25 percent excreted in urine.[7-9]

NURSING IMPLICATIONS

Monitor IV site carefully—can cause severe tissue damage with extravasation. Monitor liver function tests.

COMMENTS

Sodium Content: Contains 2.9 mEq sodium/gm.

REFERENCES

1. Prober CG, Stevenson DK, and Benitz WE. 1990. The use of antibiotics in neonates weighing less than 1,200 grams. *Pediatric Infectious Disease Journal* 9(2): 111–121.
2. Nelson JD. 1996. *1996–1997 Pocketbook of Pediatric Antimicrobial Therapy*, 12th ed. Baltimore: Lippincott Williams & Wilkins, 16–17.
3. Zenk KE, Dungy CI, and Greene GR. 1981. Nafcillin extravasation injury: Use of hyaluronidase as an antidote. *American Journal of Diseases of Children* 135(12): 1113–1114.
4. Zenk KE. 1981. Management of intravenous extravasations. *Infusion* 5(4): 77–79.
5. Greene GR, and Cohen E: 1978. Nafcillin-induced neutropenia in children. *Pediatrics* 61(1): 94–97.
6. Kitzing W, Nelson JD, and Mohs E. 1981. Comparative toxicities of methicillin and nafcillin. *American Journal of Diseases of Children* 135(1): 52–55.
7. Sáez-Llorens X, and McCracken GH Jr. 1995. Clinical pharmacology of antimicrobial agents. In *Infectious Diseases of the Fetus and Newborn Infant*, 4th ed., Remington JS, and Klein JO, eds. Philadelphia: WB Saunders, 1287–1336.
8. Banner W, et al. 1980. Pharmacokinetics of nafcillin in infants with low birth weights. *Antimicrobial Agents and Chemotherapy* 17(4): 691–694.
9. Feldman WE, Nelson JD, and Stanberry LR. 1978. Clinical and pharmacokinetic evaluation of nafcillin in infants and children. *Journal of Pediatrics* 93(6): 1029–1033.

NALOXONE (NARCAN)

(nal-OK-sohn)

ANTIDOTE:
NARCOTIC OVERDOSE

DOSE

Reversal of Narcotic-induced Respiratory Depression: 0.1 mg/kg/dose. May repeat every 3–5 minutes as required.

- Consider the duration of action and elimination rate for the opiate being reversed.
- Reassess the infant every 1–2 hours because repeated doses may be needed.[1–3]
- *Continuous Infusion:* 0.04–0.16 mg/kg/hour. Base continuous infusion dose on dose required with intermittent therapy.[4,5]

Reversal of Respiratory Depression Induced by Narcotics Given to the Mother Within 4 Hours of Delivery: 0.1 mg/kg IV, ET, or if perfusion is adequate, SC or IM. Maintain adequate ventilation before administration of naloxone. Repeat every 2–3 minutes as needed. Avoid administration if mother is narcotic dependent because naloxone may precipitate withdrawal reaction in the newborn.[6]

Septic Shock: 0.02–0.05 mg/kg IV push initially, followed by a continuous infusion of 2–8 mcg/kg/minute (0.13–0.5 mg/kg/hour).[7,8]

ADMINISTRATION

Supplied as: 1 mg/ml and 0.4 mg/ml.

IV Push—*Rate:* Infuse over at least 1 minute.

IV Push—*Concentration:* May give undiluted.

Continuous IV Infusion: Use naloxone 1 mg/ml; then dilute up to 25 ml with dextrose. Discard 24 hours after diluting. To calculate continuous drip, refer to Appendix A: Simplified Neonatal Calculations.

IM and SC: May give undiluted.

ET: Dilute in 1–2 ml NS.

Incompatible with: Alkaline drugs such as sodium bicarbonate.

USE

Reversal of narcotic-induced respiratory depression and hypotension. (See Appendix J: Antidotes for Drugs That Cause Loss of Respiratory Effort.)

Diagnosis of suspected narcotic overdose.

Not effective in reversing the adverse effects of benzodiazepines (lorazepam, midazolam) or barbiturates.

At much larger doses, naloxone has been shown to have a pressor effect in shock by blocking endogenous opiates or endorphins that are released in shock. Response is better if used early, rather than in infants with long-standing shock.[7,8]

Mechanism of Action

Naloxone is a pure narcotic antagonist.

Adverse Effects

Usually well tolerated; appears to be free of adverse effects. Has been associated with agitation, hypertension, arrhythmias, convulsions, nausea, and vomiting, but these effects may have been related to the underlying disease or to induced abstinence syndrome in acutely dependent patients.[9]

Will precipitate withdrawal if given to infants of drug-addicted mothers shortly after birth. May also precipitate withdrawal in infants to whom narcotics have been administered for several or more days, and will reverse the analgesic effects of the narcotics.

The duration of action of naloxone is shorter than that of morphine; after narcotic overdose, reassess the infant periodically for relapse (coma) and other adverse effects.

Pharmacokinetics/Pharmacodynamics

Absorption: Not given orally because of almost complete metabolism to the glucuronide on first pass after oral absorption.

Onset of Action: After IV administration—1–2 minutes; when given IM—15–40 minutes.

Duration of Action: 1–4 hours.

Metabolism: Glucuronidation in the liver.

Half-life: About 3 hours in neonates.

Elimination: The metabolites are excreted in the kidney.

Nursing Implications

Monitor for response to therapy, including improved respiratory effort.

Do not use if there is a history of intrauterine narcotic exposure.

References

1. American Academy of Pediatrics, Committee on Drugs. 1980. Naloxone use in newborns. *Pediatrics* 65(3): 667–669.

2. American Academy of Pediatrics, Committee on Drugs. 1990. Naloxone dosage and route of administration for infants and children: Addendum to emergency drug doses for infants and children. *Pediatrics* 86(3): 484–485.

3. American Academy of Pediatrics, Committee on Drugs. 1988. Emergency drug doses for infants and children. *Pediatrics* 81(3): 462–465.

4. Tenenbein M. 1984. Continuous naloxone infusion for opiate poisoning in infancy. *Journal of Pediatrics* 105(4): 645–648.

5. Lewis JM, et al. 1984. Continuous naloxone infusion in pediatric narcotic overdose. *American Journal of Diseases of Children* 138(10): 944–946.

6. American Heart Association, Emergency Cardiac Care Committee and Subcommittees. 1992. Guidelines for cardiopulmonary resuscitation and emergency cardiac care. Part VII: Neonatal resuscitation. *JAMA* 268(16): 2276–2281. (Comment in *JAMA*, 1992, 268[16]: 2297–2298.)

7. Groeger JS, Carlon GC, and Howland WS. 1983. Naloxone in septic shock. *Critical Care Medicine* 11(8): 650–654.

8. Furman WL, et al. 1984. Continuous naloxone infusion in two neonates with septic shock. *Journal of Pediatrics* 105(4): 649–651.

9. United States Pharmacopeial Convention/USP DI. 1996. *Drug Information for the Health Care Professional,* 16th ed. Rockville, Maryland: United States Pharmacopeial Convention, 2127–2129.

NEOSTIGMINE
(nee-oh-STIG-meen)
(PROSTIGMIN)

ANTIDOTE: NONDEPOLARIZING NEUROMUSCULAR BLOCKING AGENT; ANTIMYASTHENIC

DOSE

Reversal of Nondepolarizing Neuromuscular Blockade After Surgery:
0.025–0.1 mg/kg/dose. Give with atropine.
- *Commonly Used Regimen:*
  - Neostigmine 0.04–0.06 mg/kg/dose IV
  - Atropine 0.02 mg/kg/dose IV
  - Atropine may be given several minutes before or concomitantly with neostigmine to prevent bradycardia.

Diagnosis of Myasthenia Gravis (MG) and Neonatal Myasthenia Gravis:
- 0.04 mg/kg/dose IM × 1 *or* 0.02 mg/kg/dose IV × 1
- Give atropine IV immediately before or IM 30 minutes before neostigmine.
- Significant improvement in muscle weakness within several minutes to 1 hour after the dose usually indicates myasthenia gravis. Observe the patient for 1–2 hours after the dose.

Symptomatic Control of Myasthenia Gravis and Neonatal Myasthenia Gravis:
Therapy is often required day and night. Give larger portions of the total daily dose at times of greater fatigue, such as in the afternoons, evenings, or at meal-times.
- *Oral:* 2 mg/kg/day divided every 3–4 hours. Individualize interval between doses.
- *IM, SC:* 0.01–0.04 mg/kg/dose given every 2–3 hours. (Atropine 0.01 mg/kg/dose IM, SC may be given with each dose or with alternate doses to counteract the muscarinic side effects of neostigmine.)[1]

ADMINISTRATION

Supplied as: Injection: 1:1,000 (= 1 mg/ml); 1:2,000 (= 0.5 mg/ml); 1:4,000 (= 0.25 mg/ml); tablet: 15 mg/tablet.

IV—*Rate:* Infuse over several minutes.

IV—*Concentration:* May give undiluted.

IM, SC: May give undiluted.

PO: Administer with feedings to decrease possibility of side effects.
- *Oral Liquid:* Neostigmine is not commercially available as an oral liquid, and no stability information on an oral liquid compounded by the pharmacist was located. The following is suggested for preparation of an oral liquid if there is no alternative:
  - Immediately prior to each dose the nurse can mix the crushed 15 mg tablet with 15 ml of water or simple syrup (= 1 mg/ml), shake well, and

administer a volume equal to the mg dose using a calibrated oral syringe. Discard unused portion. Preparation just prior to each dose obviates concern about inactivation.

- Capsules or powder papers may be prepared by the pharmacist in the appropriate milligram dose from the crushed tablets.

CAUTIONS/CONTRAINDICATIONS

Be sure to reduce the dose when converting from the oral to the parenteral route.

Overdose may cause cholinergic crisis, which can be fatal.

Do not use neostigmine in patients with GI or GU obstruction. Use with caution in patients with bradycardia, cardiac arrhythmias, epilepsy, hyperthyroidism, and asthma.

USE

Antidote for *nondepolarizing* neuromuscular blocking agents (tubocurarine, metocurine, pancuronium, atracurium) or to reverse these agents after surgery. Neostigmine does not antagonize, and may prolong, the block of *depolarizing* neuromuscular blocking agents such as succinylcholine.

Diagnosis and symptomatic control of MG.

Diagnosis of neonatal MG. Neostigmine allows reduction in secretions and more normal feeding of these infants. Neonatal MG develops with 72 hours of birth in at least 12 percent of infants born to myasthenic mothers. Signs usually subside by 12 weeks of age.

MECHANISM OF ACTION

Neostigmine is an anticholinesterase. It inhibits destruction of acetylcholine by acetylcholinesterase, thereby facilitating transmission of impulses across the myoneural junction. This produces miosis, bradycardia, increased tone of intestinal and skeletal muscle, constriction of bronchi and ureters, and stimulation of secretion by salivary and sweat glands.

Neostigmine enhances the peak effect and prolongs the duration of action of acetylcholine at the motor end plate.[1]

Neostigmine inhibits the destruction of acetylcholine by acetylcholinesterase at the neuromuscular junction, allowing the accumulation of acetylcholine, which can successfully compete with the neuromuscular blocker at the neuromuscular junction, thus restoring muscle activity. Atropine is also given to avert the non-neuromuscular effects of neostigmine, such as increased secretions, bronchoconstriction, and bradycardia.[2]

ADVERSE EFFECTS

The most common adverse effects are caused by excessive cholinergic stimulation.

Other: Bronchoconstriction; rash from the bromide component of neostigmine bromide.

Overdose: May cause cholinergic crisis, which consists of CNS, intensified muscarinic, and nicotinic effects. Cholinergic crisis can be fatal. Overdose is marked by these effects:

- *CNS:* Difficulty breathing, seizures, unusual irritability, restlessness.

- *Muscarinic:* Severe diarrhea, excessive increase in bronchial secretions or salivation, severe vomiting, troubled breathing, wheezing, bradycardia, severe stomach cramps or pain, unusual tiredness or weakness, miosis.

- *Nicotinic:* Increasing muscle weakness or paralysis, especially in arms, neck, shoulders, and tongue. Muscle cramps or twitching.

Management of Overdose: Maintain adequate respiration. Discontinue neostigmine. Administer atropine 0.01–0.04 mg/kg/dose IV to counteract the muscarinic effects of neostigmine. Atropine does *not* alleviate the skeletal muscle effects and respiratory paralysis of neostigmine overdose. In myasthenic patients, weakness beginning about 1 hour after the dose is probably overdosage, whereas weakness occurring 3 or more hours after the dose is probably underdosage or resistance.[1]

PHARMACOKINETICS/PHARMACODYNAMICS

Absorption: Poorly absorbed (1–2 percent). Oral dose must be about 30 times the parenteral dose for equivalent effect. *Be sure to reduce the dose when converting from the oral to the parenteral route.*

Onset of Action: *IV:* 4–8 minutes; *IM:* 20–30 minutes; *PO:* 45–75 minutes.

Duration of Action: *IV, IM:* 2–4 hours; *PO:* 3–6 hours.

Protein Binding: Low (15–25 percent).

Metabolism: Plasma, hepatic.

Elimination: Renal.

NURSING IMPLICATIONS

For neonatal myasthenia gravis, keep a daily record of dosing and effects on condition during initial therapy to facilitate arranging an optimal therapeutic regimen.[1]

Monitor heart rate, respiratory rate, and muscle strength.

COMMENTS

Interactions: May increase the neuromuscular blocking effects of succinylcholine, prolonging respiratory depression with extended periods of apnea.[3]

REFERENCES

1. United States Pharmacopeial Convention/USP DI. 1996. *Drug Information for the Health Care Professional,* 16th ed. Rockville, Maryland: United States Pharmacopeial Convention, 435–440.

2. Roberts RJ. 1984. *Drug Therapy in Infants: Pharmacologic Principles and Clinical Experience.* Philadelphia: WB Saunders, 308–312.

3. Benitz WE, and Tatro DS. 1995. *The Pediatric Drug Handbook,* 3rd ed. St. Louis: Mosby, 130–131.

NITRIC OXIDE (iNOMAX FOR INHALATION)
(NYE-trik OX-ide)

RESPIRATORY: VASODILATOR

Synonyms: NO, inhaled nitric oxide (iNO)

DOSE

Term Infants and Those >34 Weeks Gestational Age: Begin with 20 parts per million (ppm). Reduce dose to lowest possible level.[1] In a trial by Clark and colleagues, infants whose oxygenation improved with 20 ppm were reduced to 5 ppm as tolerated at the end of 4 hours of treatment.[1,2]

Maximum: Doses above 20 ppm are usually not used because of the increased risk of methemoglobinemia and elevated nitrogen dioxide (NO_2).[1]

Duration: Maintain treatment up to 14 days or until the underlying oxygen desaturation has resolved and the infant is ready to be weaned from iNO.[1]

ADMINISTRATION

Supplied as: Portable aluminum cylinders containing NO gas in 800 ppm and 100 ppm concentrations in nitrogen.

- iNO is given as a gas by inhalation. iNO should be administered using FDA-approved devices that are capable of administering iNO in constant concentration ranges in parts per million through the respiratory cycle.[3] The delivery system should not cause generation of excessive inhaled NO_2.[1]

Storage: Store at controlled room temperature, ideally 25°C (77°F), with a permissible range of 15°–30°C (59°–86°F).

CAUTIONS/CONTRAINDICATIONS

iNO should not be used in neonates dependent on right-to-left shunting of blood.[1]

An echocardiogram is recommended to rule out congenital heart disease.[3]

iNO therapy should be directed by physicians qualified by education and experience in its use and should be offered only at centers that are qualified to provide multisystem support, generally including onsite extracorporeal membrane oxygenation (ECMO) capability. A center that collaborates with another to provide ECMO must have the capability to transfer the infant to the collaborating center without interrupting iNO therapy.[3] iNO failure criteria should be established prospectively, as should mechanisms for the timely transfer of infants to the collaborating ECMO center.

Infants undergoing iNO are extremely sensitive to any interruption in supply,[4] possibly because iNO causes a reduction in the production of endogenous NO. In the event of a system failure or a wall-outlet power failure, a backup battery power supply and reserve NO delivery system should be available.[1]

Administration of iNO for indications other than those approved by the FDA or in other neonatal populations, including compassionate use, requires a formal protocol approved by the FDA and the institutional review board, as well as informed parental consent.[3]

It is not possible to administer 100 percent FiO_2 while providing iNO because the iNO dilutes the oxygen in the inspiratory circuit.

Occupational Exposure: Exposure limit for NO is 25 ppm and for NO_2 is 5 ppm.

USE

Term or Near-term Infants: iNO is indicated for the treatment of term and near-term (>34 weeks gestation) neonates with hypoxic respiratory failure associated with clinical or echocardiographic evidence of persistent pulmonary hypertension of the newborn (PPHN). In infants >34 weeks, iNO improves oxygenation, reduces mortality, reduces the need for ECMO, and reduces the incidence of chronic lung disease.[1–3,5,6] iNO has not been shown to be effective for infants with congenital diaphragmatic hernia.[7] iNO is used with additional therapies that may include surfactant and high-frequency oscillatory ventilation to maximize oxygen delivery. Other agents, such as vasodilators, IV fluids, and sodium bicarbonate, may be used as appropriate.[1]

Preterm Infants: iNO may improve oxygenation but not survival in preterm infants. Significant benefit has not yet been established in this age group.[5,8] Data on the use of iNO in preterm infants are preliminary. Safety, such as the risk for intraventricular hemorrhage, and efficacy have not yet been established. More study is needed in this age group because preterm infants may experience more toxic effects from the use of iNO than do more mature infants.[3]

MECHANISM OF ACTION

Inhaled nitric oxide is a selective pulmonary vasodilator without significant effects on the systemic circulation. Its short half-life limits its action to the pulmonary circulation. Excess iNO is quickly bound to hemoglobin and inactivated.[9] iNO causes vasodilation by acting on the receptors in the muscle wall of blood vessels. The mechanism of action involves guanylyl cyclase activation, leading to production of cyclic guanosine monophosphate (GMP) and subsequent smooth-muscle relaxation. iNO causes vasodilation via the same mechanism as endogenous NO.

Endogenous NO: Nitric oxide (endothelial-derived relaxing factor [EDRF]) is produced in vascular endothelial cells. Endogenous NO is generated from the amino acid L-arginine by nitric oxide synthase through a metabolic route, the L-arginine–nitric oxide pathway. The actions of NO are mediated by activation of soluble guanylyl cyclase, which increases the concentration of cyclic GMP in target cells. The actions of endogenous NO are diverse. NO plays an important part in increasing blood flow to the lungs at birth.[10] In the central nervous system, NO is a neurotransmitter; in the periphery, NO regulates various GI, respiratory, and GU tract functions; NO also inhibits platelet aggregation and adhesion and regulates cardiac contractility. The NO synthesized by vascular endothelium is responsible for vasodilator tone, which is needed to regulate blood pressure; in septic shock, endogenous NO causes persistent vasodilation and resistance to vasoconstrictors.[9,11,12] A discussion of the role of endogeous NO in septic shock can be found in the monograph on methylene blue and in Figure 1-11, page 391.

Adverse Effects

iNO does not increase neurodevelopmental, behavioral, or medical abnormalities when given to children 2 years of age or older.[13] It is possible that preterm infants may experience more toxic effects than term and near-term infants from iNO; more study is needed in this population.[8,14,15]

Hematologic: Methemoglobinemia; elevated NO_2 levels. The risk of these adverse effects increases significantly when iNO is given at doses >20 ppm. Conflicting data on inhibition of platelet aggregation and prolongation of bleeding time have been published.[16]

Pulmonary: Direct pulmonary injury (attributable to excess levels of NO_2) and contamination of ambient air.[3]

Overdose—Recognizing and Treating: iNO overdose may cause elevations in methemoglobin and NO_2. Methemoglobin may reduce the oxygen delivery capacity of the circulation. Methemoglobinemia increases with iNO dosage. Peak methemoglobin levels occur between approximately 8 and 40 hours after initiation of iNO. Methemoglobinemia that is not corrected by reduction or discontinuation of iNO therapy can be treated with methylene blue IV (see monograph on methylene blue).[1] In air, NO reacts rapidly with oxygen to form NO_2, a brown gas capable of inducing lung injury. If NO_2 levels are >3 ppm or methemoglobin levels are >5–7 percent, reduce the iNO dose or discontinue iNO.

Pharmacokinetics/Pharmacodynamics

Absorption: iNO diffuses from the alveoli to pulmonary vascular smooth muscle.

Metabolism and Elimination: iNO is rapidly inactivated by hemoglobin, producing methemoglobin.

Half-life: Less than 5 seconds. The fate of iNO in the body is complex; however, most NO is eliminated by means of rapid inactivation in the bloodstream by binding to hemoglobin and, subsequently, metabolism to nitrate.[9]

Nursing Implications

Infants on iNO require continuous monitoring of ventilatory status, vital signs, frequent blood gas measurements, and routine physical examination.

- **Monitoring:**
  - Infants receiving iNO should be monitored following institutionally derived protocols designed to avoid the potentially toxic effects associated with iNO administration.[3] Measure a baseline methemoglobin level; then repeat every 12–24 hours. Methemoglobin levels should be maintained below 2.5 percent. Monitor continuous online iNO, NO_2, and O_2 levels using a properly calibrated analysis device with alarms, such as the INOvent delivery system (INO Therapeutics, Inc., Clinton, New Jersey). Sample gas for analysis should be drawn before the Y-piece, proximal to the patient.[1]

Comments

Long-term, comprehensive medical and neurodevelopmental follow-up should be provided.[3]

Prospective data collection for treatment time, course, toxic effects, treatment failure, use of alternative therapies, and outcomes should be provided.

Interactions: No interactions have been reported; however, NO donor compounds, including sodium nitroprusside and nitroglycerin, may have an additive effect with iNO on the risk of development of methemoglobinemia.

References

1. Manufacturer's product literature.

2. Clark RH, et al. 2000. Low-dose nitric oxide therapy for persistent pulmonary hypertension of the newborn. *New England Journal of Medicine* 342(7): 469–474.

3. American Academy of Pediatrics, Committee on Fetus and Newborn. 2000. Use of inhaled nitric oxide. *Pediatrics* 106(2 part 2): 344–345.

4. Richmond SWJ. 2000. Adjunctive pharmacologic agents. In *Rational Therapeutics for Infants and Children: Workshop Summary,* Yaffe S, ed. Washington, DC: National Academy Press, 414–420.

5. Finer NN, and Barrington KJ. 2000. Nitric oxide therapy for the newborn infant. *Seminars in Perinatology* 24(1): 59–65.

6. Neonatal Inhaled Nitric Oxide Study Group (NINOS). 1997. Inhaled nitric oxide in full-term and nearly full-term infants with hypoxic respiratory failure. *New England Journal of Medicine* 336(9): 597–604.

7. Neonatal Inhaled Nitric Oxide Study Group (NINOS). 1997. Inhaled nitric oxide and hypoxic respiratory failure in infants with congenital diaphragmatic hernia. *Pediatrics* 99(6): 838–845.

8. Kinsella JP, et al. 1999. Inhaled nitric oxide in premature neonates with severe hypoxaemic respiratory failure: A randomised controlled trial. *Lancet* 354(9184): 1061–1065.

9. Moncada S, and Higgs A. 1993. The L-arginine–nitric oxide pathway. *New England Journal of Medicine* 329(27): 2002–2012.

10. Abman SH, et al. 1990. Role of endothelium-derived relaxing factor during transition of pulmonary circulation at birth. *American Journal of Physiology* 259(6 part 2): H1921–H1927.

11. Tsuneyoshi I, Kanmura Y, and Yoshimura N. 1996. Nitric oxide as a mediator of reduced arterial responsiveness in septic patients. *Critical Care Medicine* 24(6): 1083–1086.

12. Shi Y, et al. 1993. Plasma nitric oxide levels in newborn infants with sepsis. *Journal of Pediatrics* 123(3): 435–438.

13. Neonatal Inhaled Nitric Oxide Study Group (NINOS). 2000. Inhaled nitric oxide in term and near-term infants: Neurodevelopmental follow-up of the Neonatal Inhaled Nitric Oxide Study Group (NINOS). *Journal of Pediatrics* 136(5): 611–617.

14. Franco-Belgium Collaborative NO Trial Group. 1999. Early compared with delayed inhaled nitric oxide in moderately hypoxaemic neonates with respiratory failure: A randomised controlled trial. *Lancet* 354(9184): 1066–1071.

15. Van Meurs KP, et al. 1997. Response of premature infants with severe respiratory failure to inhaled nitric oxide. *Pediatric Pulmonology* 24(5): 319–323.

16. Davidson D, et al. 1998. Inhaled nitric oxide for the early treatment of persistent pulmonary hypertension of the term newborn: A randomized, double-masked, placebo-controlled, dose-response, multicenter study. *Pediatrics* 101(3): 325–334.

NITROGLYCERIN (NITRO-BID IV)

(nye-troe-GLI-ser-in)

CARDIOVASCULAR: VASODILATOR

Synonym: NTG

DOSE

IV:

- *Initial:* Try 0.1–1 mcg/kg/minute initially. If needed, increase at 1 mcg/kg/minute increments every 30–60 minutes.
- *Usual:* 1–5 mcg/kg/minute. *Maximum:* 10 mcg/kg/minute.
- Higher doses may be required if proper administration precautions are not followed.
- Titrate cautiously to desired hemodynamic effect.
- Dose has not been well established in neonates.

Topical:

- Ribbon of 2 percent ointment, up to 2.4 mg/kg (4 mm/kg).

ADMINISTRATION

Supplied as:

- *Injection* 0.5 mg/ml and 5 mg/ml.
- *Topical:* 2 percent ointment.

IV—*Rate:* Continuous IV infusion.

IV—*Concentration:* Dilute before use. Maximum: 400 mcg/ml.

IV—*Compatibility:* See Appendix E: Y-Site Compatibility of Common NICU Drugs.

Drug Loss:

- Use a glass syringe on the syringe pump with as short a segment of low-volume tubing as possible to minimize drug loss during infusion.
- Attach NTG infusion below filter. Use non-PVC tubing if possible to minimize adsorption. Once a type of syringe and tubing have been selected, continue using the same type of setup with each tubing change to avoid dangerous fluctuations in dose.
- Doses of NTG in published studies are commonly based on use of PVC administration sets and are too high when non-PVC administration sets are used. Adjust dose accordingly.
- Plastic IV containers, some IV filters, and IV administration sets may decrease NTG concentration as much as 80 percent, depending on the rate of infusion and length of exposure time. Low infusion rates, high concentrations, and long lengths of tubing increase chance of drug loss.

Topical Treatment of Extravasation of Dopamine or Other Vasoconstrictor Drugs and Peripheral Tissue Ischemia:

- Apply a ribbon of 2 percent ointment up to a total dose of 2.4 mg/kg (4 mm/kg) to affected areas. May repeat once or twice at 8-hour intervals.[1,2]
  - 2 mg measured 0.1 ml in a syringe (may use a 0.5 ml oral syringe to measure dose, then apply topically).[2]
  - 2.5 cm or 1 inch contains 15 mg of nitroglycerin as squeezed from the tube. Apply in a thin, even layer. Do not rub or massage into the skin.

Monitor blood pressure.

CAUTIONS/CONTRAINDICATIONS

Use with caution in severe hepatic or renal disease.

Contraindicated in hypotension, hypovolemia, inadequate cerebral circulation, increased intracranial pressure, constrictive pericarditis, and pericardial tamponade.

USE

A vasodilator that may be useful in newborns with depressed myocardial function, such as in congestive cardiomyopathy, because of its effects in reducing preload and improving coronary blood flow without a fall in mean arterial pressure.[3-6]

2 percent NTG ointment has been used topically to reverse dopamine extravasation injury. Onset of action was within minutes. No drop in systemic BP occurred after the application.[1] The ointment has also been used for peripheral tissue ischemia.[2]

Maynard and Oh caution against use of NTG to facilitate venous cannulation in neonates. Catheter insertion was unsuccessful in more patients treated with NTG, and more infiltration and bleeding occurred at the catheter site. Catheter duration was possibly shorter.[7]

MECHANISM OF ACTION

NTG relaxes vascular smooth muscle by stimulating intracellular cyclic GMP production. NTG is a direct vasodilator with its primary effect on large veins (capacitance vessels) and less effect on arteries. It is a direct coronary vasodilator, and it reduces pulmonary vascular resistance, left ventricular filling pressures, ventricular volume, and cardiac work (reduces preload).

Doses <2 mcg/kg/minute cause venodilation. Doses of 3–5 mcg/kg/minute cause progressive arteriolar dilation, decreased systemic vascular resistance (SVR), and increased cardiac index.

ADVERSE EFFECTS

Hypotension, flushing, hypoxemia, decreased cardiac output, tachycardia, and GI upset have been reported.

Alcohol intoxication has occurred in some patients. Consider this possibility with high-dose, long-duration therapy. Minimize risk by choosing a low-alcohol product. (Alcohol content of NTG concentrate for injection varies by brand:

Tridil 0.5 mg/ml, 10 percent alcohol; Nitro-Bid IV 5 mg/ml, propylene glycol 4.5 percent; Tridil 5 mg/ml, 30 percent propylene glycol and 30 percent alcohol.) Methemoglobinemia (cyanotic skin and mucous membranes, vomiting, shock, coma) may occur because nitrate ions liberated during metabolism of nitroglycerin can oxidize hemoglobin to methemoglobin. Methemoglobinemic blood is chocolate brown without color change on exposure to air. *Antidote:* Methylene blue 1–1.5 mg/kg IV undiluted, given slowly over several minutes.

PHARMACOKINETICS/PHARMACODYNAMICS

Absorption: Extensive first-pass deactivation occurs following oral administration.

Onset of Action: 1–2 minutes; onset 15–30 minutes after topical application to treat peripheral tissue ischemia.[2]

Duration of Action: 3–5 minutes.

Protein Binding: 60 percent.

Metabolism: Hepatic by nitrate reductase.

Half-life: 1–4 minutes.

Elimination: Metabolites are excreted in the urine.

NURSING IMPLICATIONS

Continuously monitor vital signs, especially blood pressure and heart rate.

Monitor for hypotension and tachycardia.

COMMENTS

NTG (as diluted by the manufacturer with lactose, dextrose, alcohol, propylene glycol, or other inert ingredients) is not explosive.

Interactions: Calcium channel blockers (e.g., nifedipine, verapamil), other antihypertensives, β-blockers, and alcohol potentiate NTG's hypotensive effects. NTG may decrease the pharmacologic effects of heparin.

REFERENCES

1. Denkler KA, and Cohen BE. 1989. Reversal of dopamine extravasation injury with topical nitroglycerin ointment. *Plastic and Reconstructive Surgery* 84(5): 811–813.

2. Wong AF, McCulloch LM, and Sola A. 1992. Treatment of peripheral tissue ischemia with topical nitroglycerin ointment in neonates. *Journal of Pediatrics* 121(6): 980–983.

3. Keeley SR, and Bohn DJ. 1988. The use of inotropic and afterload-reducing agents in neonates. *Clinics in Perinatology* 15(3): 467–489.

4. Butt W, Bohn DJ, and Whyte H. 1986. Clinical experience with systemic vasodilator therapy in the newborn infant. *Australian Paediatric Journal* 22(2): 117–120.

5. Hill NS, et al. 1981. Intravenous nitroglycerin: A review of pharmacology, indications, therapeutic effects and complications. *Chest* 79(1): 69–76.

6. Artman M, and Graham TP. 1987. Guidelines for vasodilator therapy of congestive heart failure in infants and children. *American Heart Journal* 113(4): 994–1005.

7. Maynard EC, and Oh W. 1989. Topical nitroglycerin ointment as an aid to insertion of peripheral venous catheters in neonates. *Journal of Pediatrics* 114(3): 474–476.

NITROPRUSSIDE SODIUM
(nye-troe-PRUSS-ide SOE-dee-um)
(NIPRIDE)

**CARDIOVASCULAR:
ANTIHYPERTENSIVE**

DOSE

0.3–6 mcg/kg/minute by continuous IV infusion using a neonatal syringe pump.
The average dose is 3 mcg/kg/minute. Begin at a low dose, usually
0.5–1 mcg/kg/minute; then increase gradually to avoid a sudden drop in blood
pressure. *Titrate dose to produce desired response.*

Attempt dose reduction of 15–25 percent every 6–12 hours. The drug can be discontinued once the dose reaches 0.5 mcg/kg/minute.[1]

Use with caution in hepatic or renal insufficiency.

ADMINISTRATION

IV Continuous Infusion—*Concentration Maximum:* 0.2 mg/ml. Must be diluted
prior to use. Dilute only in dextrose (not saline) solutions.

IV—*Compatibility:* See Appendix E: Y-Site Compatibility of Common NICU
Drugs.

May be given via central or peripheral catheter.

Protect from light. Wrap the IV bag/syringe and tubing to prevent photo-
degradation. Although manufacturer states tubing need not be wrapped,
wrapping is probably necessary in neonates because of the slow IV infusion
rate, especially when the solution in the tubing is exposed to phototherapy.[2]

Nitroprusside is normally brownish in color. If the solution turns blue, green, or
dark red, replace it. Discard solution 24 hours after preparation.

CAUTIONS/CONTRAINDICATIONS

Hepatic and/or Renal Insufficiency: Use with caution; drug may accumulate,
resulting in toxicity.

Use with caution in infants with hypothyroidism (see **ADVERSE EFFECTS** below).

USE

A potent, immediate-acting, IV, antihypertensive agent for hypertensive emergencies. Relaxes vascular smooth muscle, with consequent dilation of peripheral
arteries and (especially) veins. Useful for congestive cardiomyopathy in
newborns.

Has also been used for afterload reduction in combination with dopamine for
patients with severe refractory congestive heart failure.

Because of its balanced venous and arteriolar vasodilation, may be more valuable
than hydralazine, which produces only arteriolar vasodilation, or nitroglycerin,
which produces only venous dilation.

Increases blood flow to the lung by dilating pulmonary vessels and reducing pulmonary vascular resistance.[3–8]

MECHANISM OF ACTION

Nitroprusside reduces preload and afterload; it acts directly on arterial and venous smooth muscle to an equal extent, possibly as a result of an increase in cyclic GMP.[9] Dilation of the veins promotes peripheral pooling of blood and decreases venous return to the heart, thereby reducing left ventricular end-diastolic pressure and pulmonary capillary wedge pressure (preload). Arteriolar relaxation reduces systemic vascular resistance, systolic arterial pressure, and mean arterial pressure (afterload).

ADVERSE EFFECTS

Precipitous fall in blood pressure, treated with volume expansion.

Tachyphylaxis.

The drug's vasodilating effects increase intracranial pressure in patients whose intracranial pressure is already elevated.

Has also caused rash, flushing, irritation at the infusion site, nausea, restlessness, muscle twitching, bradycardia, ECG changes, and tachycardia.

Thiocyanate (the major metabolite of sodium nitroprusside) may inhibit uptake and binding of iodine, producing hypothyroidism. Use with caution in infants with hypothyroidism.

Elevations in cyanide ion, which can reach toxic, potentially lethal levels.

Signs and Symptoms of Cyanide Toxicity: Venous hyperoxemia with bright red venous blood, metabolic acidosis, elevated cyanide levels, marked clinical deterioration. *Antidote:* Sodium thiosulfate 10 mg/kg/minute for 15 minutes IV.

Signs and Symptoms of Methemoglobinemia: Impaired oxygen delivery despite adequate cardiac output and adequate arterial PO_2, chocolate brown–colored blood without color change on exposure to air. *Antidote:* 1–1.5 mg/kg of methylene blue IV over several minutes.

Signs and Treatment of Nitroprusside Overdose: Profound hypotension, metabolic acidosis, and increasing tolerance to the drug are early indications of overdose. Stop the infusion of nitroprusside; administer sodium nitrite 3 percent at 4–6 mg/kg IV over 2–4 minutes; then give sodium thiosulfate 20 percent, 10 mg/kg/minute for 15 minutes IV. Amyl nitrite inhalations may be given for 15–30 seconds per minute until the 3 percent sodium nitrite solution can be prepared. The nitrite-thiosulfate regimen may be repeated at half the original doses after 2 hours if needed. (Use commercially available Cyanide Antidote Kit.) RBC cyanide concentrations can also be useful in detecting toxicity.

PHARMACOKINETICS/PHARMACODYNAMICS

Onset of Action: 0.5–5 minutes.

Duration of Action: Blood pressure returns to pretreatment levels within 1–10 minutes after stopping the infusion.

Metabolism: Metabolized in the liver and kidney to thiocyanate, which requires the enzyme rhodanese.

Half-life: 2 minutes.

Elimination: The major metabolite, thiocyanate, is excreted primarily through the kidneys. The half-life of thiocyanate is approximately 4 days, which accounts for its accumulation in patients with renal dysfunction.[3]

NURSING IMPLICATIONS

Continuously monitor all vital signs, including blood pressure, during administration.

Monitor for response to therapy, including improvement in blood gases (pH and acid-base balance) and oxygenation.

Monitor hemoglobin levels daily. Plasma thiocyanate concentrations should be monitored daily in patients receiving therapy for longer than 48 hours, especially in patients with renal or hepatic dysfunction. Thiocyanate levels 35–100 mcg/ml are considered toxic; levels of >200 mcg/ml may be fatal.[10] Others state that thiocyanate levels should not exceed 12 mg/dl.[11]

Protect tubing and syringe from light by wrapping in foil.

COMMENTS

Begin oral antihypertensive agents while the patient is receiving nitroprusside so that transition can be made to oral therapy as soon as medical condition warrants.

REFERENCES

1. Benitz WE, et al. 1985. Use of sodium nitroprusside in neonates: Efficacy and safety. *Journal of Pediatrics* 106(1): 102–110.

2. Trissel LA. 1994. *Handbook on Injectable Drugs,* 8th ed. Bethesda, Maryland: American Society of Hospital Pharmacists, 971–976.

3. Roberts RJ. 1984. *Drug Therapy in Infants: Pharmacologic Principles and Clinical Experience.* Philadelphia: WB Saunders, 184–186.

4. Manufacturer's product literature.

5. Stephenson LW, et al. 1979. Effects of nitroprusside and dopamine on pulmonary arterial vasculature in children after cardiac surgery. *Circulation* 60(2 part 2): 104–110.

6. Subramanyam R, Tandon R, and Shrivastava S. 1982. Hemodynamic effects of sodium nitroprusside in patients with ventricular septal defect. *European Journal of Pediatrics* 138(4): 307–310.

7. Sinaiko AR. 1993. Pharmacologic management of childhood hypertension. *Pediatric Clinics of North America* 40(1): 195–212.

8. Kaplan S. 1990. New drug approaches to the treatment of heart failure in infants and children. *Drugs* 39(3): 388–393.

9. Till JA, and Rigby ML. 1991. Treatment of cardiac disorders in the neonate. In *Neonatal Clinical Pharmacology and Therapeutics,* Rylance G, Harvey D, and Aranda J, eds. Linacre House, Jordan Hill, Oxford: Butterworth-Heinemann, 126–152.

10. Taketomo CK, Hodding JH, and Kraus DM. 1993. *Pediatric Dosage Handbook,* 2nd ed. Hudson, Ohio: Lexi-Comp, 498–499.

11. Benitz WE, and Tatro DS. 1995. *The Pediatric Drug Handbook,* 3rd ed. St. Louis: Mosby-Year Book, 220–221.

NOREPINEPHRINE (LEVOPHED)

(nor-ep-i-NEF-rin)

CARDIOVASCULAR:
VASOPRESSOR

Synonyms: levarterenol, noradrenaline

DOSE

Begin with 0.01–0.1 mcg/kg/minute. Adjust the dose gradually to achieve the desired blood pressure. Most infants require 0.05–0.5 mcg/kg/minute. *Maximum:* 1–2 mcg/kg/minute. Continuously monitor blood pressure for hypertension and ECG for arrhythmias.

ADMINISTRATION

Supplied as: Injection: 1 mg/ml.

IV Continuous Infusion—*Concentration:* Must be diluted prior to use. Determine concentration based on the dose and fluid requirements of the infant:

$$C\ (mg/25\ ml) = 1.5 \times Dose\ (mcg/kg/minute) \times Weight\ (kg) \div Rate\ (ml/hour)$$

(See Appendix A: Simplified Neonatal Calculations.)

IV—*Rate:* Determine the rate based on the fluid requirements of the infant.

Use neonatal infusion pump to deliver dose accurately.

IV—*Compatibility:* D_5W and D_5NS are the recommended diluents because dextrose protects against loss of potency caused by oxidation. Normal saline alone (without dextrose) does not afford this protection. (See Appendix E: Y-Site Compatibility of Common NICU Drugs.)

Incompatible with: Alkaline solutions such as sodium bicarbonate.

Stability: Do not use if brown in color or if solution contains a precipitate.

CAUTIONS/CONTRAINDICATIONS

Do not give in patients with peripheral or mesenteric vascular thrombosis because the drug may increase the area of ischemia.

Do not use in patients with pheochromocytoma; severe hypertension may result.

Do not use in patients with tachyarrhythmias because of increased risk of arrhythmias.

Reduce infusion by tapering gradually.

Use a large vein to administer this drug to avoid risk of extravasation.

USE

Used in the treatment of severe hypotension that persists after adequate fluid replacement. Because norepinephrine decreases renal blood flow to already hypoperfused tissues, its value as an inotropic agent is seriously limited.[1]

MECHANISM OF ACTION

Norepinephrine is an adrenergic agonist. It is an endogenous neurotransmitter released from postganglionic adrenergic nerves. It stimulates β_1-adrenergic receptors (causing inotropic and chronotropic effects on the heart) and α-adrenergic receptors (causing vasoconstriction). The major effect of norepinephrine is to increase total peripheral resistance, which elevates blood pressure and induces reflex bradycardia. Vasoconstriction predominates over inotropic effect, so cardiac output may be unchanged or decreased; the drug may cause renal ischemia.[1]

ADVERSE EFFECTS

Cardiovascular: Arrhythmias, tachycardia, bradycardia, hypertension, pallor. Organ ischemia may occur as a result of vasoconstriction of renal and mesenteric arteries; avoid prolonged use of this drug, which causes prolonged reduction of blood flow to these areas. Norepinephrine may aggravate, rather than improve, hypoperfusion associated with hemorrhagic shock.[1] The drug may produce vasoconstriction in the mesenteric vascular bed, inducing splanchnic ischemia and facilitating bacterial translocation from the gut.

GI: Vomiting.

Local: Extravasation may cause vasospasm leading to local ischemia, necrosis, and sloughing. Treat norepinephrine extravasation with the α-blocker phentolamine infiltrated locally. (See Appendix G: Guidelines for Management of Intravenous Extravasations and monograph on phentolamine.)

Ophthalmic: Photophobia.

Other: Sweating, anxiety, respiratory distress.

Overdose: Severe hypertension, reflex bradycardia, marked increase in peripheral resistance, decreased cardiac output. For excessive hypertensive effect, slow the rate of infusion or temporarily discontinue administration until the blood pressure normalizes. This is usually all that is required because of the short duration of the drug.[2]

PHARMACOKINETICS/PHARMACODYNAMICS

Absorption: Ineffective when given orally; poorly absorbed from SC injection.

Onset of Action: Rapid.

Duration of Action: 1–2 minutes. Must be given by continuous infusion.

Metabolism: Rapidly metabolized by catechol-O-methyltransferase (COMT) and monoamine oxidase (MAO) in the liver, kidney, and plasma to inactive metabolites.

Half-life: 1 minute.

Elimination: Renal, primarily as metabolites. Less than 20 percent of dose excreted unchanged.

NURSING IMPLICATIONS

Monitor blood pressure, heart rate, urine output.

Carefully observe IV site. If blanching occurs along the course of the infused vein, change infusion site at intervals to allow the effects of local vasoconstriction to subside.

COMMENTS

Interactions:

- Concurrent use of bretylium may potentiate the action of vasopressors on adrenergic receptors possibly resulting in cardiac arrhythmias.

- α- and β-adrenergic blocking agents: α-Blocking agents such as phentolamine block the pressor effects of norepinephrine. β-Blocking agents such as propranolol block the cardiac-stimulating effects of the drug. Administration of propranolol in patients receiving norepinephrine may result in higher blood pressure because of blockade of β-mediated arteriolar dilation.

- Concurrent use of digoxin may produce additive inotropic effects and increase the risk of cardiac arrhythmias. If these two agents are given concurrently, use caution and monitor ECG closely.

- Methyldopa and diphenhydramine may potentiate the pressor effects of norepinephrine.

- Atropine may block the reflex bradycardia caused by norepinephrine, resulting in increased pressor effect.

REFERENCES

1. Roberts RJ. 1984. *Drug Therapy in Infants: Pharmacologic Principles and Clinical Experience.* Philadelphia: WB Saunders, 163–165.

2. United States Pharmacopeial Convention/USP DI. 1996. *Drug Information for the Health Care Professional,* 16th ed. Rockville, Maryland: United States Pharmacopeial Convention, 2741–2751.

NYSTATIN (MYCOSTATIN)
(nye-STAT-in)

ANTI-INFECTIVE:
ANTIFUNGAL AGENT

DOSE

Oral Candidiasis (Thrush):

- *Preterm Infants and Low Birth Weight Infants:* 0.5–1 ml/dose (of 100,000 units/ml) four times a day. Administer by applying one-half the dose to each side of the mouth (= 0.25–0.5 ml/dose to each side of the mouth).

- *Older Infants:* 2 ml/dose four times a day. Administer by applying one-half the dose to each side of the mouth (= 1 ml/dose to each side of the mouth).

Intestinal Candidiasis: Give the above doses PO. (The dose should be swallowed, rather than applied topically to the mouth.)

Candida Diaper Dermatitis: Apply to affected skin area two to four times a day after cleansing area.

Duration of Oral or Topical Therapy:

- Continue therapy for 2 weeks; however, longer courses may be needed.

- To prevent relapse, continue treatment until 2–3 days after the infection has cleared, the cultures have returned to normal, or prophylaxis is no longer desired.

ADMINISTRATION

Supplied as: Suspension, oral: 100,000 units/ml. Powder, topical: 100,000 units/gm. Cream or ointment: 100,000 units/gm. Nystatin is available in lozenge form, but lozenges are not recommended in infants because they are not capable of using them safely.

Candidiasis of the Mouth: Shake suspension well. Wipe white plaques off with gauze, if possible. Then swab the mouth, particularly candidal lesions, with nystatin suspension.

Storage: Nystatin powder should be refrigerated.

CAUTIONS/CONTRAINDICATIONS

Contraindicated in those infants with a hypersensitivity to nystatin.

Occlusive dressings (e.g., tight-fitting diaper or plastic pants, bandage, or tape) should be avoided in general and especially in infants with candidiasis because they provide conditions that favor growth of yeast and release of its irritating endotoxin.

Not for ophthalmic use.

Use caution when applying nystatin powder, to keep the infant from breathing in the nystatin and talc in airborne powder. Inhalation of toxic quantities of baby powder by infants can cause cough, dyspnea, sneezing, vomiting, cyanosis, and death. There is no adequate treatment for the pulmonary complications.[1]

Use

An antifungal agent for local treatment of skin, mucous membrane, and gastro-intestinal tract infection caused by *Candida* (Monilia) *albicans* and other Candida species. Not all strains of the organism are susceptible. Nystatin is less expensive than newer topical antifungals, and more studies have been done on its safety and effectiveness in infants than have been completed on the performance of the newer antifungals. Because other infectious agents produce lesions similar to those caused by Candida, cultures should, if possible, be obtained before nystatin therapy is begun. Prolonged parenteral nutrition and/or broad-spectrum antibiotics increase susceptibility to Candida infections; discontinue these therapies as soon as medically warranted.

Choice of Dosage Form: The suspension is used to treat oral candidiasis. The cream is preferred over the ointment for candidiasis in intertriginous areas (neck folds, creases in diaper area). Nystatin topical powder is quite useful for treating very moist lesions. Munz and colleagues found that Candida diaper dermatitis responded equally well to nystatin cream and to combined therapy with nystatin cream and oral nystatin suspension. Eradication of Candida from skin and gastrointestinal tract and incidence of recurrence were similar in both groups.[2]

With Topical Corticosteroids: Short-term combined use of nystatin and a corti-costeroid may provide earlier relief of local inflammation and pain of cutaneous infections.[3] However, the nystatin/triamcinolone product commercially available is not a good choice for infants. This high-potency steroid is more likely than hydrocortisone to cause corticosteroid-induced hypothalamic-pituitary-adrenal axis (HPAA) suppression, intracranial hypertension, and Cushing's syndrome. Manifestations of adrenal suppression include growth retardation, delayed weight gain, low plasma cortisol concentrations, and lack of response to corti-cotropin stimulation. Adrenal supression is more likely to occur in infants than in adults because of infants' greater skin surface area–to–body weight ratio.[3] If a corticosteroid cream is needed, use hydrocortisone 0.5 percent cream (a lower potency corticosteroid) as a separate product with the nystatin cream or oint-ment. Discontinue the hydrocortisone after 2–3 days. (See hydrocortisone monograph for further information.)

- Nystatin is not indicated for systemic Candida infections because it is not absorbed from the gastrointestinal tract; systemic antifungals, such as ampho-tericin B, should be used instead.

Mechanism of Action

Nystatin is a polyene antifungal agent with a chemical structure very similar to that of amphotericin B. It binds to ergosterol, a sterol in sensitive fungal cell mem-branes, resulting in increased permeability of the membrane to small molecules, thus allowing leakage of essential cellular constituents, cell lysis, and death.[4,5] Nystatin is not effective against bacterial or viral infections.

ADVERSE EFFECTS

Usually well tolerated.

Dermatologic: Rarely, local irritation or contact dermatitis with topical use.

GI (with oral use): Mild nausea, vomiting, diarrhea.

PHARMACOKINETICS/PHARMACODYNAMICS

Absorption: Very little absorption from gastrointestinal tract, intact skin, or mucous membranes.

Onset of Action: Relief in symptoms usually occurs within 24–72 hours.

Elimination: Eliminated in the feces as unchanged drug.

NURSING IMPLICATIONS

Use proper hygiene and skin care procedures to prevent spread of infection and reinfection.

Keep affected areas dry and exposed to air, if possible.

Use caution when applying nystatin powder to avoid the infant's breathing in the airborne nystatin and talc.[1] (See **CAUTIONS/CONTRAINDICATIONS** above.)

REFERENCES

1. Mofenson HC, et al. 1981. Baby powder—a hazard! *Pediatrics* 68(2): 265–266.

2. Munz D, Powell KR, and Pai CH. 1982. Treatment of candidal diaper dermatitis: A double-blind placebo-controlled comparison of topical nystatin with topical plus oral nystatin. *Journal of Pediatrics* 101(6): 1022–1025.

3. McEvoy GK. 1994. *AHFS Drug Information.* Bethesda, Maryland: American Society of Hospital Pharmacists, 2288–2290, 2316–2319.

4. United States Pharmacopeial Convention/USP DI. 1996. *Drug Information for the Health Care Professional,* 16th ed. Rockville, Maryland: United States Pharmacopeial Convention, 2199–2203.

5. Roberts RJ. 1984. *Drug Therapy in Infants. Pharmacologic Principles and Clinical Experience.* Philadelphia: WB Saunders, 81–82.

TABLE OF CONTENTS

O

OCTREOTIDE
(oak-TREE-oh-tide)
(SANDOSTATIN)

HORMONES:
GLUCOSE-ELEVATING AGENT

DOSE

Hypoglycemia:

- *Intermittent IV or SC:* Starting dose: 2–10 mcg/kg/day divided every 6–8 hours, up to 40 mcg/kg/day divided every 4–8 hours. Adjust dose to maintain symptomatic control.

- *Continuous SC Infusion:* 2–10 mcg/kg/day. (Continuous SC infusion using a portable pump has been used in two infants with nesidioblastosis.)[1]

Antidiarrheal: 2–20 mcg/kg/day divided every 12 hours. Adjust dose to maintain symptomatic control.

Postoperative Chylothorax (very limited experience): Cheung and colleagues reported successful use of 10 mcg/kg/day SC in three divided doses. The dose was increased in a stepwise manner by 5–10 mcg/kg/day every 72–96 hours, to 40 mcg/kg/day. Weaning of octreotide occurred after 3 days of insignificant chyle output (<10 ml/day). Complete resolution of chylothorax with reduction of triglyceride content in the pleural fluid was achieved with SC octreotide despite continuation of an enteral feeding MCT diet (Pregestimil and, subsequently, MCT-enriched Pepti-Junior [Nutricia, Holland]). The authors considered octreotide a promising pharmacologic therapy for chylothorax after surgery for congenital heart disease.[2]

In severe renal impairment, the half-life of octreotide may be increased. Dose adjustment may be required.

ADMINISTRATION

Supplied as: Injection: 0.05 mg/ml (= 50 mcg/ml), 0.1 mg/ml, 0.2 mg/ml, 0.5 mg/ml, and 1 mg/ml.

SC (preferred), IV.

SC: May give undiluted or may dilute with NS or D_5W.

Continuous SC Infusion: May dilute with NS or D_5W in an amount based on the dose and fluid requirements of the infant.

IV—*Rate:* Infuse over at least 3 minutes in emergencies; however, infusion over 30 minutes is preferred.

IV—*Concentration:* May give undiluted in emergencies; however, it is preferred to give diluted with NS or D_5W in an amount based on the fluid requirements of the infant for a 30-minute infusion.

IV—*Compatibility:* Not compatible with parenteral nutrition because of the formation of a glycosyl octreotide conjugate, which may decrease the effectiveness of octreotide.

Storage: Refrigerate for long-term storage; however, stable at room temperature for 14 days if protected from light. Protect from light.

USE

Used for short-term management of persistent hyperinsulinemic hypoglycemia, such as in nesidioblastosis. A few patients have been treated for as long as 5 years with little evidence of problems caused by suppression of growth hormone or thyroid-stimulating hormone.[1,3]

Also used to treat hypersecretory diarrhea and fistulae in infants. Significant reductions in stool or ileal output have been achieved with this drug.[1]

Used to treat acromegaly because of its suppressant effects on growth hormone.

MECHANISM OF ACTION

Octreotide, a long-acting analog of somatostatin, suppresses glucagon and insulin release from pancreatic islets. It inhibits insulin secretion by decreasing the influx of calcium ions and through a direct effect on secretory granules.[4] It inhibits serotonin and growth hormone release, and it suppresses thyroid-stimulating hormone.

Octreotide inhibits gall bladder contractions. It reduces splanchnic blood flow and inhibits the release of gastrin, vasoactive intestinal polypeptide (VIP), and other GI hormones. It slows gastrointestinal transit time. It inhibits intestinal epithelial secretion of electrolytes and water, increases absorption of water and electrolytes, and inhibits motor activity in the stomach and small intestine. Octreotide may act directly on vascular somatostatin receptors to reduce lymph fluid excretion. Octreotide reduces chyle output and reduces the ratio of triglyceride concentrations in the lymph to those in serum.[2]

ADVERSE EFFECTS

Tachyphylaxis may occur.

Cardiovascular: Flushing, hypertension.

CNS/Muscle: Insomnia, fever, chills, seizures, Bell's palsy, muscle weakness, increased creatine phosphokinase, muscle spasm, tremor.

Dermatologic: Hair loss, bruising, rash.

Endocrine: Possible growth retardation (suppresses growth hormone) during long-term treatment; however, in most studies, growth and development were within normal range.[1] May also cause hypoglycemia, hyperglycemia, galactorrhea, hypothyroidism (suppresses thyroid-stimulating hormone).

GI: Nausea, diarrhea, abdominal distension, abdominal pain, flatulence, constipation. Scheduling injections of octreotide between meals and at bedtime reduces the occurrence of GI side effects. Rare: GI bleed.

GU: Oliguria.

Hepatic: Gallbladder microlithiasis (reported in adolescents), hepatitis, jaundice.

Local: Local injection-site pain, stinging with redness and swelling; thrombo-phlebitis. Local reactions may be reduced by allowing the solution to reach room temperature before administration (do not heat artificially) and injecting slowly.

Respiratory: Shortness of breath, rhinorrhea.

PHARMACOKINETICS/PHARMACODYNAMICS

Absorption: Rapidly and completely absorbed from injection site.

Peak Effect: About 30 minutes after the dose.

Duration of Action: 6–12 hours.

Protein Binding: Highly protein bound.

Half-life: Elimination half-life is 1.5 hours.

Elimination: Renal.

NURSING IMPLICATIONS

Monitor blood glucose.

Monitor for thrombophlebitis.

Rotate injection sites.

Consider dose increase if tachyphylaxis occurs.

COMMENTS

Interactions: Concurrent use of glucagon, growth hormone, or insulin may result in hypo- or hyperglycemia; monitoring and dose adjustments may be necessary.

REFERENCES

1. Tauber MT, Harris AG, and Rochiccioli P. 1994. Clinical use of the long acting somatostatin analogue octreotide in pediatrics. *European Journal of Pediatrics* 153: 304–310.

2. Cheung Y, Leung MP, and Yip M. 2001. Octreotide for treatment of postoperative chylothorax. *Journal of Pediatrics* 139(1): 157–159.

3. Stanley CA. 1997. Hyperinsulinism in infants and children. *Pediatric Clinics of North America* 44(2): 363–374.

4. Wolfsdorf JI. 1998. Hyperinsulinemic hypoglycemia of infancy (editorial). *Journal of Pediatrics* 132(1): 1–3.

TABLE OF CONTENTS

P

P

PALIVIZUMAB (SYNAGIS)

(pal-i-VI-zu-mab)

**BIOLOGIC:
MONOCLONAL
ANTIBODY FOR RSV**

Synonym: MEDI-493

DOSE

15 mg/kg/dose once per month throughout respiratory syncytial virus (RSV) season. (RSV season is usually November through April, but may vary. Check with the local Health Department.)

Give monthly even if RSV infection develops.

Consider use for a second RSV season in patients with severe chronic lung disease (CLD), especially those requiring continuing medical therapy.

ADMINISTRATION

Supplied as: 100 mg/ml. Reconstitute with 1 ml of sterile water. Swirl gently for 30 seconds; then let stand to clarify for 20 minutes prior to administration.[1]

Intramuscular to anterolateral thigh. Give dose volumes >1 ml as a divided dose.

Storage: Refrigerate. Do not freeze. Opened vials should be used within 6 hours.

Cost-Saving Tip: The American Academy of Pediatrics recommends that, to minimize waste, physicians should schedule administration so that two or more eligible patients can receive the vaccine within the 6-hour period after a vial is opened.[2]

CAUTIONS/CONTRAINDICATIONS

- Palivizumab has not been studied in infants and children with congenital heart disease and is not licensed by the FDA for these patients.[2]
- As with all IM injections, do not use in patients with thrombocytopenia (platelets <40,000/mm^3) or coagulation disorders.[1]

USE

To prevent (but not to treat) serious RSV infections. Reduces RSV-related hospitalizations by 55 percent.[3] The need for and efficacy of RSV prophylaxis in an inpatient hospital setting has not been studied. Other means of preventing RSV disease (strict observance of infection control practices, including rapidly identifying and cohorting RSV-infected infants) are recommended.[2]

Consider using for:

- Children <2 years old with CLD who required medical therapy for CLD within the 6 months preceding the anticipated start of RSV season.[2]
- Preterm infants born at ≤32 weeks gestation. Both gestational age and postnatal age should be considered in deciding whether to treat the following infants. Those:
  - 28 weeks gestation or earlier may benefit from palivizumab up to 12 months of age.

- 29–32 weeks gestation may benefit from palivizumab up to 6 months of age.[2]

Comparison with respiratory syncytial virus-immune globulin ([RSV-IGIV], see monograph): Both palivizumab and RespiGam are used to prevent RSV infections.

- *Palivizumab is usually preferred over RSV-IGIV because palivizumab:*
  - Is 50–100 times more active against RSV than RSV-IGIV.[4,5]
  - Is easier to give (is given IM, whereas RSV-IGIV must be given as a 3- to 4-hour IV infusion).
  - Has fewer adverse effects.
  - Does not interfere with the MMR and varicella vaccines.
  - Is free of potential contamination by infectious agents because it is not a blood product.
  - Has a more reliable supply because its availability does not depend on the blood donor pool.[2]
  - Does not increase the risk of fluid overload, as RSV-IGIV does.
- *RSV-IGIV is preferred over palivizumab in these circumstances:*
  - For the first month of prophylaxis for premature infants about to be discharged from the hospital during RSV season because RSV-IGIV provides coverage against additional respiratory viral illnesses, whereas palivizumab protects only against RSV.[2]
  - For severely immunocompromised children who receive standard immune globulin IV (IGIV) monthly, consider substituting RSV-IGIV during the RSV season. However, RSV-IGIV is contraindicated in children with cyanotic congenital heart disease.[1,2,6]

MECHANISM OF ACTION

Palivizumab is an intramuscular monoclonal antibody preparation that inhibits RSV replication. It binds to the F glycoprotein on the surface of the virus to keep it from infecting cells. This humanized monoclonal antibody is produced by recombinant DNA technology.[5]

ADVERSE EFFECTS

Well tolerated.[2–4]

May cause mild and transient erythemia, pain, and induration at injection site (2.7 percent of patients).[3]

Mild or moderate elevations of the enzyme aspartate aminotransferase occurred in 3.6 percent of those who received palivizumab versus 1.6 percent of those receiving a placebo.[3]

Pharmacokinetics/Pharmacodynamics

Half-life: 20 days. Monthly doses of 15 mg/kg maintained trough serum concentrations of >40 mcg/ml for most patients.[4]

Nursing Implications

Advise parents that palivizumab should be accompanied by a program to prevent RSV transmission:

- Eliminate exposure to cigarette smoke
- Limit exposure to contagious settings such as child care centers
- Emphasize handwashing.[2]

Comments

Interactions: None reported

References

1. Manufacturer's product literature.

2. American Academy of Pediatrics, Committee on Infectious Diseases and Committee on Fetus and Newborn. 1998. Prevention of respiratory syncytial virus infections: Indications for the use of palivizumab and update on the use of RSV-IGIV. *Pediatrics* 102(5): 1211–1216.

3. IMpact-RSV Study Group. 1998. Palivizumab, a humanized respiratory syncytial virus monoclonal antibody, reduces hospitalization from respiratory syncytial virus infection in high-risk infants. *Pediatrics* 102(3 part 1): 531–537.

4. Subramanian KNS, et al. 1998. Safety, tolerance and pharmacokinetics of a humanized monoclonal antibody to respiratory syncytial virus in premature infants and infants with bronchopulmonary dysplasia. *Pediatric Infectious Disease Journal* 17(2): 110–115.

5. Johnson S, et al. 1997. Development of humanized monoclonal antibody (MEDI-493) with potent *in vitro* and *in vivo* activity against respiratory syncytial virus. *Journal of Infectious Diseases* 176(5): 1215–1224.

6. Meissner HC, et al. 1996. Prevention of respiratory syncytial virus infection in high-risk infants: Consensus opinion on the role of immunoprophylaxis with respiratory syncytial virus hyperimmune globulin. *Pediatric Infectious Disease Journal* 15(12): 1059–1068.

PANCURONIUM (PAVULON)
(pan-kyur-OH-nee-um)

**CENTRAL NERVOUS
SYSTEM:
NEUROMUSCULAR BLOCKER**

DOSE

0.02–0.09 mg/kg every 1–4 hours. Begin with lowest dose and titrate upward, if needed.

Dose Titration: Administration at intervals of 2 hours or less should prompt an increase in dose. Paralysis lasting beyond 4–6 hours suggests excessive dosing.[1]

ADMINISTRATION

IV only.

Rate: Over at least 1 minute IV push, or by continuous infusion.

Concentration: May give undiluted or may dilute with sodium chloride, dextrose, or lactated Ringer's.

Compatibility: See Appendix E: Y-Site Compatibility of Common NICU Drugs.

CAUTIONS/CONTRAINDICATIONS

Significant changes in mechanical ventilator settings are sometimes required to prevent serious air leak complications as the infant responds to therapy.

USE

A long-acting neuromuscular blocking agent for skeletal muscle relaxation (paralysis) during surgical procedures such as PDA ligation.[2,3]

Also used for severe, unresponsive seizures such as neonatal tetany.

MECHANISM OF ACTION

Pancuronium is a nondepolarizing neuromuscular blocking agent that acts by competitive inhibition of acetylcholine for receptor sites on the postjunctional membrane. Infants <1 month of age are especially sensitive to nondepolarizing neuromuscular blockers.

ADVERSE EFFECTS

Increased heart rate and blood pressure. Giving slow, incremental doses minimizes these cardiovascular effects.

Increased salivation.

Transient rash (occasional).

Hypersensitivity (rare) characterized by bronchospasm, flushing, redness, hypotension, tachycardia, and other reactions possibly mediated by histamine release.

Prolonged severe skeletal muscle weakness (rare), especially in patients receiving other drugs, such as aminoglycosides, that may enhance neuromuscular blockade. Use caution with prolonged use to facilitate mechanical ventilation of neonates.

Methemoglobinemia (rare).[2]

PHARMACOKINETICS/PHARMACODYNAMICS

Onset of Action: 60 seconds.

Duration of Action: 40–60 minutes.

Protein Binding: 87 percent.

Metabolism: Undergoes hepatic biotransformation via deacetylation.

Half-life: 120 minutes (adults).

Elimination: Largely excreted in the urine, 40 percent unchanged; 11 percent has been recovered in bile. In renal failure, elimination half-life is doubled, and the plasma clearance is reduced by approximately 50 percent.

NURSING IMPLICATIONS

Refrigerate drug. When taken on transport, refrigerate immediately upon return.

Have reversal agents at bedside.

All paralyzed infants need analgesia and/or sedation in conjunction with paralyzation. Consider concomitant infusion of fentanyl, morphine, or midazolam.

Provide range of motion, position changes, and eye lubrication to avoid side effects of paralysis.

Consider need for bladder catheterization or Credé if urine output decreases.

Monitor for movement and side effects, including hypertension and tachycardia.

COMMENTS

Mechanical ventilation must be provided during use.

Drug does not produce analgesia or sedation, only paralysis.

Reversal of Neuromuscular Blockade:

- *Mechanism of Reversal:* Neostigmine inhibits acetylcholinesterase at the neuromuscular junction, allowing the accumulation of acetylcholine, which can successfully compete with the neuromuscular blocker at the neuromuscular junction, thus restoring muscle activity. Atropine is also given to avert the nonneuromuscular effects of neostigmine, such as increased secretions, bronchoconstriction, and bradycardia.[1]

- *Reversal Dose:* Neostigmine 0.06 mg/kg IV plus atropine 0.02 mg/kg IV.

- *Onset of Reversal:* Approximately 10 minutes.

Interactions: See Table 1-13, page 77.

REFERENCES

1. Roberts RJ. 1984. *Drug Therapy in Infants: Pharmacologic Principles and Clinical Experience.* Philadelphia: WB Saunders, 308–312.

2. Cunliffe M, et al. 1986. Neuromuscular blockade for rapid tracheal intubation in children: Comparison of succinylcholine and pancuronium. *Canadian Anaesthetists Society Journal* 33(6): 760–764.

3. Lerman J. 1993. Anesthesia. In *Pediatric Pharmacology and Therapeutics*, Radde IC, and MacLeod SM, eds. St. Louis: Mosby-Year Book, 475–497.

PAREGORIC

(par-e-GOR-ik)

[CAMPHORATED OPIUM TINCTURE]
(CONTROLLED SUBSTANCE SCHEDULE III)

CENTRAL NERVOUS SYSTEM:
NARCOTIC
ANALGESIC;
ANTIDIARRHEAL

DOSE

0.2 ml (equivalent to 80 mcg morphine) every 3 hours. Increase dose by 0.05 ml (equivalent to 20 mcg morphine) every 3 hours until symptoms are under control.

Maximum: 0.7 ml/dose (equivalent to 280 mcg morphine/dose).

Tapering the Dose: Begin tapering when symptoms have been under control for 3–5 days, and taper gradually over 2–4 weeks, as tolerated.

Appendix K: Neonatal Withdrawal Score Sheet facilitates objective assessment of the infant's symptoms.[1]

ADMINISTRATION

Supplied as: Contains morphine equivalent of 400 mcg/ml (= 2 mg morphine equivalent per 5 ml).

PO.

CAUTIONS/CONTRAINDICATIONS

See **USE** for components of this drug that are potentially hazardous to infants.

Opium tincture contains 25 times more morphine than does paregoric (camphorated opium tincture); it is vital that these two products not be confused. If opium tincture is used, prepare a 1:25 dilution in water before use. A 1:25 dilution of opium tincture may be given at the doses shown above.[2]

USE

Neonatal narcotic withdrawal.[3] Consider use if GI symptoms such as diarrhea occur. However, other agents are preferred (see below).

The 1996 USP DI states that paregoric is not recommended for ameliorating withdrawal symptoms in opioid-dependent neonates.[1] Paregoric contains substances that are potentially hazardous to infants: camphor (a CNS stimulant), benzoic acid (a potent displacer of bilirubin from albumin binding sites and one of the metabolic products of benzyl alcohol, a preservative that has caused deaths in preterm infants), and 45 percent alcohol (a gastric irritant, a CNS depressant, may cause hepatic damage and hypoglycemia). Paregoric has been replaced for this purpose by other opioid drugs with fewer or no hazardous additional ingredients, such as morphine oral solution, benzodiazepines, barbiturates, or diluted opium tincture. Methadone has also been used, but tapering is difficult due to its long elimination half-life. These other medications should be used, whenever possible, instead of paregoric.[1]

MECHANISM OF ACTION

Because of its morphine content, opium increases smooth muscle tone of the GI tract, inhibits GI motility and propulsion, and reduces digestive secretions. The passage of intestinal contents is delayed, the feces become desiccated, and constipation results. The small doses of opium that reduce diarrhea do not have a significant analgesic effect and do not produce euphoria.[2]

ADVERSE EFFECTS

Hold dose if excessive drowsiness or respiratory depression appears. ***Antidote:*** Naloxone 0.1 mg/kg/dose IV. See Appendix J: Antidotes for Drugs That Cause Loss of Respiratory Effort. *Note:* Naloxone administration may precipitate withdrawal.

Too rapid tapering of dose may lead to recurrence of symptoms.

Opium has all the toxic potentials of narcotic agonists.

May cause respiratory depression, constipation, hypotension, bradycardia, CNS depression, increased intracranial pressure, sedation, release of antidiuretic hormone, urine retention, urinary tract spasm, histamine release, physical dependence, and tolerance.

PHARMACOKINETICS/PHARMACODYNAMICS

Absorption: Well absorbed (morphine).

Protein Binding: Low (morphine).

Metabolism: Metabolized in the liver to glucuronide metabolites.

Half-life: 2–3 hours (morphine).

Elimination: Biliary and renal as morphine-3-glucuronide.

NURSING IMPLICATIONS

Monitor for respiratory depression, lethargy.

Utilize the Appendix K: Neonatal Withdrawal Score Sheet to determine effectiveness of therapy and timing of titration.

COMMENTS

Interactions: Additive CNS depression with other CNS depressants. Naloxone reverses the effects of paregoric and will precipitate withdrawal.

REFERENCES

1. United States Pharmacopeial Convention/USP DI. 1996. *Drug Information for the Health Care Professional,* 16th ed. Rockville, Maryland: United States Pharmacopeial Convention, 2286–2290.

2. McEvoy GK. 1994. *AHFS Drug Information.* Bethesda, Maryland: American Society of Hospital Pharmacists, 1881–1882.

3. Levy M, and Spino M. 1993. Neonatal withdrawal syndrome: Associated drugs and pharmacologic management. *Pharmacotherapy* 13(3): 202–211.

PENICILLIN G AQUEOUS
(pen-i-SILL-in G)
[POTASSIUM OR SODIUM]

ANTI-INFECTIVE:
ANTIBIOTIC

DOSE

Systemic and Localized Infections (see dosing for specific indications below):

- **<1.2 kg (0–4 weeks):** 25,000 units/kg/dose given every 12 hours[1,2]
- **1.2–2 kg:**
  - 0–7 days: 25,000 units/kg/dose given every 12 hours
  - >7 days: 25,000 units/kg/dose given every 8 hours
- **>2 kg:**
  - 0–7 days: 25,000 units/kg/dose given every 8 hours
  - >7 days: 25,000 units/kg/dose given every 6 hours[2]

Meningitis (but see below for AAP recommendations for Group B streptococcal infection with meningitis):

- **<1.2 kg (0–4 weeks):** 50,000 units/kg/dose given every 12 hours[1,2]
- **1.2–2 kg:**
  - 0–7 days: 50,000 units/kg/dose given every 12 hours
  - >7 days: 75,000 units/kg/dose given every 8 hours
- **>2 kg:**
  - 0–7 days: 50,000 units/kg/dose given every 8 hours
  - >7 days: 50,000 units/kg/dose given every 6 hours[2]

Group B Streptococcal Infection with Meningitis (use with an aminoglycoside):[3]

- **0–7 days:** 100,000–150,000 units/kg/day divided every 8–12 hours IV
- **>7 days:** 200,000–250,000 units/kg/day divided every 6 hours IV
- For bacteremia, continue therapy for 10–14 days; for uncomplicated meningitis, continue for 14 days (a longer course of therapy may be required).[3]

Congenital Syphilis (proven or highly probable):

- **0–7 days:** 100,000 units/kg/day divided every 12 hours IV or IM for 10–14 days
- **>7 days:** 150,000 units/kg/day divided every 8 hours IV or IM for 10–14 days
- **>28 days:** 200,000 units/kg/day divided every 6 hours IV for 10–14 days[3]

ADMINISTRATION

IV—*Rate:* Infuse over 30 minutes.

IV—*Concentration:* 50 mg/ml preferred, to reduce vein irritation. Maximum: 100 mg/ml.

IV—*Compatibility:* See Appendix E: Y-Site Compatibility of Common NICU Drugs.

IM—*Concentration:* 100,000 units/ml. Although the IV route is preferred, penicillin may be administered IM in patients with difficult IV access. Repeated IM injections may cause muscle fibrosis and atrophy. The IV route is preferred for meningitis.

Use

A bactericidal natural penicillin used to treat congenital syphilis, tetanus neonatorum, gonococcal infection, sepsis, and meningitis with Group A or nonenterococcal Group D Streptococcus. Also used to treat Group B Streptococcus pulmonary infections and abscesses, as well as Group A Streptococcus skin infections.

Active against Gram-positive organisms such as Group B Streptococcus, Group A Streptococcus, and *Streptococcus pneumoniae.* Usually used in combination with gentamicin for neonatal Group B streptococcal disease because of synergistic effects. Effective against *Listeria monocytogenes;* however, IV ampicillin alone or with gentamicin is considered the treatment of choice.

Active against some Gram-negative organisms, such as *Neisseria meningitidis* and *N. gonorrhoeae* (disseminated gonococcal infection or gonococcal ophthalmia), that do not produce penicillinase.

Active against certain strains of anaerobic bacteria, such as Clostridium, Peptococcus, Bacteroides (*B. fragilis* is resistant, however), and *Treponema pallidum* (congenital syphilis).

Inactivated by penicillinase.[3,4]

Mechanism of Action

Penicillins act by interrupting bacterial cell wall synthesis.

Adverse Effects

Rapid IV push of penicillin G potassium may cause cardiac arrhythmias and arrest. The potassium component is the cause; the result is analogous to administering KCl by IV push. Sodium penicillin G is preferred for use in the NICU.

May cause electrolyte imbalance. Sodium penicillin G contains 2 mEq Na per million units, and penicillin G potassium contains 1.7 mEq K per million units. May need to reduce maintenance sodium or potassium while infant is on either of these drugs.

CNS: Neurotoxic reactions, including seizures with high serum levels.

Hematologic: Anemia, thrombocytopenia, eosinophilia, leukopenia, granulocytopenia, neutropenia.

Hypersensitivity Reactions: Rash and anaphylaxis; not likely to occur in neonates, however.

Renal: Acute interstitial nephritis.

PHARMACOKINETICS/PHARMACODYNAMICS

Absorption: Not recommended for oral use because it is broken down by gastric acid, resulting in only about 30 percent absorption. Penicillin V is much preferred when an oral penicillin is needed because it is acid stable, achieving blood levels 2–5 times higher than penicillin G.

Half-life: Inversely related in neonates to creatinine clearance rate; ranges between 1 and 2.5 hours.

Elimination: Excreted by the kidney, 10 percent by glomerular filtration and 90 percent by tubular secretion. Dosing interval is wide at birth (every 12 hours); as the renal function matures, the dosing interval is shortened.[4,5]

NURSING IMPLICATIONS

Administer over at least 30 minutes.

Monitor hematologic and renal systems, serum electrolytes.

COMMENTS

Conversion: Penicillin G aqueous is generally prescribed and dispensed in units, rather than by weight. Each mg of penicillin G potassium powder for injection has a potency of 1,355–1,595 units. Each mg of penicillin G sodium powder for injection has a potency of 1,420–1,667 units.

REFERENCES

1. Prober CG, Stevenson DK, and Benitz WE. 1990. The use of antibiotics in neonates weighing less than 1,200 grams. *Pediatric Infectious Disease Journal* 9(2): 111–121.

2. Nelson JD. 1996. *1996–1997 Pocketbook of Pediatric Antimicrobial Therapy,* 12th ed. Baltimore: Lippincott Williams & Wilkins, 16–17.

3. American Academy of Pediatrics, Committee on Infectious Diseases. 1994. *Red Book: Report of the Committee on Infectious Diseases,* 23rd ed. Elk Grove Village, Illinois: American Academy of Pediatrics, 445–455.

4. Roberts RJ. 1984. *Drug Therapy in Infants: Pharmacologic Principles and Clinical Experience.* Philadelphia: WB Saunders, 45–48.

5. Paap CM, and Nahata MC. 1990. Clinical pharmacokinetics of antibacterial drugs in neonates. *Clinical Pharmacokinetics* 19(4): 280–318.

PENICILLIN G BENZATHINE (BICILLIN L-A, PERMAPEN)

ANTI-INFECTIVE: ANTIBIOTIC

(pen-i-SILL-in G BENZ-a-theen)

Synonym: benzathine penicillin G

DOSE

Asymptomatic Congenital Syphilis: 50,000 units/kg IM for a single dose.[1–4]

Penicillin G benzathine may be given if the infant's evaluation (i.e., CSF examination, long-bone radiographs, and CBC with platelets) is normal and follow-up is certain. If any part of the infant's evaluation is abnormal or not done, or the CSF analysis cannot be interpreted because the CSF was contaminated with blood during the LP, then a 10-day course of aqueous penicillin G or procaine penicillin G is required.[3]

ADMINISTRATION

Supplied as:

- A viscous, opaque suspension for IM injection: 600,000 units/ml (1 ml, 2 ml, 4 ml), 300,000 units/ml (10 ml multidose vial).
- Also available as a combination product of penicillin G benzathine with penicillin G procaine (Bicillin C-R).

For deep IM administration only.

IM: Give into the midlateral muscles of the thigh in infants. Do not give IV or SC. Viscosity of the suspension requires use of a ≥23 gauge needle. A smaller bore needle such as 24 or 25 gauge is not recommended.

IM—Concentration: Give undiluted.

Caution: Prefilled syringes (TUBEX) of benzathine penicillin G are not marked with graduations, are not labeled with the total volume in the syringe, nor the concentration. The manufacturer's label indicates only the total number of units contained in the syringe (e.g., benzathine penicillin 600,000 units/syringe). Certain steps must be taken to measure a dose for an infant because only part of the syringe contents is needed.

1. ***Determine the Volume.*** Withdraw entire contents of TUBEX into another syringe and note the total volume.

2. ***Note the number of units*** of benzathine penicillin on the TUBEX label.

3. ***Determine the Concentration.*** Divide the units by the volume to determine the concentration. You can then calculate the dose volume.

- ***Example:*** Benzathine penicillin G 150,000 units has been ordered for an infant with asymptomatic congenital syphilis who is in your care. You have a TUBEX of Bicillin L-A (penicillin G benzathine suspension) labeled 1,200,000 units. The label doesn't state the concentration or volume, nor does it have any graduations. How would you proceed to figure out the dose volume?

- Withdraw the contents into another syringe. The volume measures 2 ml.
- Divide 1,200,000 units by 2 ml. The concentration is 600,000 unit/ml.
- Divide the 150,000 unit dose ordered by the concentration of 600,000 units/ml. The dose volume is 0.25 ml.

Storage: Refrigerate. Do not freeze. Shake multiple-dose vial well before using.

CAUTIONS/CONTRAINDICATIONS

Penicillin G benzathine must *not* be given IV, intravascularly, or intra-arterially.

Avoid injection into or near a nerve since permanent neurologic damage may result. If evidence of blood supply compromise occurs at proximal, or distal to, the site of injection, consult an appropriate specialist immediately.

Read the label carefully to assure you are giving the intended drug. Brand names of products that may cause confusion include:

- *Crysticillin:* This is one of the brand names for procaine penicillin for IM administration. **It is not crystalline (aqueous) penicillin G for IV administration.**

- *Bicillin C-R:* This is a combination product **for deep IM administration** containing both penicillin G benzathine and penicillin G procaine.

Spell out "units," rather than using a "U" when ordering or transcribing an order for penicillin to avoid a tenfold dosing error. The "U" could look like an additional zero.

USE

A long-acting (depot, or repository form of penicillin G) **intramuscular** penicillin G suspension used for moderately severe infections caused by penicillin G-sensitive organisms sensitive to low and persistent penicillin serum concentrations.[5] Primarily used to treat asymptomatic congenital syphilis when CNS involvement has been excluded.[6]

CNS concentrations are not high enough to treat CNS syphilis.

Choice of products: Carefully differentiate between products when ordering, dispensing, or administering penicillin. Legibly and clearly state the type of penicillin intended because products differ in duration of action, serum concentration, and route of administration:

- *Aqueous penicillin G* gives high serum penicillin concentration with short duration. *May be given either IV or IM.* (See monograph on penicillin G aqueous.)

- *Benzathine penicillin G* (Bicillin L-A, Permapen) gives very low, sustained serum penicillin concentrations for 2–3 weeks. *Given IM only.*

- *Combination product* of penicillin G benzathine and penicillin G procaine (Bicillin C-R) gives an early peak serum penicillin concentration, then a sustained low serum concentration for 2–3 weeks. *Given IM only.*

- *Procaine penicillin G* (Crysticillin AS, Wycillin, Pfizerpen-AS) gives low penicillin serum concentrations that are sustained for 1–2 days. *Given IM only.* (See monograph on penicillin G procaine.)

Mechanism of Action

Penicillins act by interrupting bacterial cell wall synthesis.

Benzathine penicillin G is prepared by reacting dibenzylethylenediamine with penicillin G aqueous.

Adverse Effects

Penicillin G benzathine is usually well tolerated without evidence of local reaction at the site of injection or of systemic reaction.[6] However, very serious adverse effects that have been fatal may occur[7] and precautions should be observed to avoid a medication error.

CNS: Neurotoxic reactions, including seizures with high serum levels.

Hematologic: Anemia, thrombocytopenia, eosinophilia, leukopenia, granulocytopenia, neutropenia.

Hypersensitivity Reactions: Rash and anaphylaxis; not likely to occur in neonates, however.

Local: Use only by deep IM. Do not administer IV, intra-arterially, subcutaneously, by fat-layer injection, or into or near a nerve. IV injection may cause embolic or toxic reactions. Intra-arterial injection may cause extensive necrosis of the extremity or organ. Subcutaneous or fat-layer injection may cause pain and induration. Injection into or near a nerve may result in permanent neurologic damage. Consult an appropriate specialist promptly if any evidence of compromise of the blood supply occurs.[5,8]

Renal: Acute interstitial nephritis.

In treatment of syphilis, a pseudoanaphylactic reaction, Jarisch-Herxheimer reaction may occur. It is thought to be caused by the release of pyrogen and/or endotoxins from phagocytized organisms. This reaction occurs 2–12 hours after initiation of penicillin and subsides within 12–24 hours. Symptoms may include fever, sweating, malaise, increased pulse rate, arthralgia, and an increase in blood pressure followed by a decrease in blood pressure.[9]

Pharmacokinetics/Pharmacodynamics

Absorption: Relatively insoluble: It forms a tissue depot from which the drug is slowly absorbed and hydrolyzed to penicillin G. Serum concentrations are lower and more prolonged than an equivalent IM dose of aqueous penicillin G or procaine penicillin G because of slow absorption and hydrolysis.[9]

Distribution: Very minimal CSF concentrations.

Peak Effect: 12–24 hours.[6]

Duration of Action: Serum concentrations of 0.07–0.09 mcg/ml are still detectable 12 days after a dose.[6] Larger doses result in a longer duration, rather than higher serum concentrations.

Half-life: 5.5–6 hours. The half-life is longer than that of aqueous penicillin G primarily because absorption from the injection site continues over a longer time period.[6]

Elimination: Excreted by the kidney, 10 percent by glomerular filtration and 90 percent by tubular secretion. Excretion is considerably delayed in neonates and young infants with impaired renal function.[5]

NURSING IMPLICATIONS

Not for IV administration.

Rotate injection sites. Repeated IM injection of the drug into the anterolateral thigh should be avoided since quadriceps femoris fibrosis and atrophy may occur.

IM injection should be made at a slow, steady rate to avoid blockage of the needle.

Discontinue injection if signs or symptoms suggest the onset of severe pain.[5,9]

COMMENTS

Conversion: Penicillin G benzathine is generally prescribed and dispensed in units, rather than by weight. Each mg of penicillin G benzathine = 1,090–1,272 units.

REFERENCES

1. Nelson JD. 1996. *1996–1997 Pocket Book of Pediatric Antimicrobial Therapy,* 12th ed. Baltimore: Lippincott Williams & Wilkins, 17.

2. American Academy of Pediatrics, Committee on Infectious Diseases. 1997. *Red Book: Report of the Committee on Infectious Diseases,* 24th ed. Elk Grove Village, Illinois: American Academy of Pediatrics, 504–514.

3. Centers for Disease Control. 1998. 1998 guidelines for treatment of sexually transmitted diseases. *MMWR* 47(No. RR-1): 41–46.

4. Paryani SG, et al. 1994. Treatment of asymptomatic congenital syphilis: Benzathine versus procaine penicillin G therapy. *Journal of Pediatrics* 125(3): 471–475.

5. Medical Economics Data. 1998. *Physicians' Desk Reference,* 52nd ed. Montvale, New Jersey: Medical Economics, 3019–3021.

6. McCracken GH Jr, and Nelson JD. 1983. *Antimicrobial Therapy for Newborns,* 2nd ed. New York: Grune & Stratton, 12–13.

7. Pearson L. 1998. Analysis of an error. *The Nurse Practitioner* 23(7): 8, 13.

8. United States Pharmacopeial Convention/USP DI. 1996. *Drug Information for the Health Care Professional,* 16th ed. Rockville, Maryland: United States Pharmacopeial Convention, 2317–2318.

9. McEvoy GK. 1998. *AHFS Drug Information.* Bethesda, Maryland: American Society of Health-System Pharmacists, 302–304.

PENICILLIN G PROCAINE (WYCILLIN)   ANTI-INFECTIVE:

(pen-i-SILL-in G PRO-cain)   **ANTIBIOTIC**

Synonym: procaine penicillin G

DOSE

Congenital Syphilis (Symptomatic and Asymptomatic): 50,000 units/kg/day given once daily IM for 10–14 days. [1–4]

ADMINISTRATION

Supplied as:

- Injection (a viscous, opaque suspension for IM injection): 600,000 units/ml (1 ml, 2 ml, 4 ml), 300,000 units/ml (10 ml vials); 500,000 units/ml (= 600,000 units/1.2 ml).
- Also available as a combination product of penicillin G benzathine with penicillin G procaine (Bicillin C-R).

For deep IM administration only.

IM: Give into the midlateral muscles of the thigh in infants. Do not give IV or SC. Viscosity of the suspension requires use of a ≥23-gauge needle. A small-bore needle such as a 24- or 25-gauge is not recommended.

IM—*Concentration:* Give undiluted.

Caution: Prefilled syringes (TUBEX) of procaine penicillin G are not marked with graduations, are not labeled with the total volume in the syringe nor the concentration. The manufacturer's label indicates only the total number of units contained in the syringe (e.g., procaine penicillin 600,000 units/syringe). Certain steps must be taken to measure a dose for an infant because only part of the syringe contents is needed.

1. ***Determine the Volume.*** Withdraw entire contents of TUBEX into another syringe and note the total volume.
2. ***Note the number of units*** of penicillin procaine on the TUBEX label.
3. ***Determine the Concentration.*** Divide the units by the volume to determine the concentration. You can then calculate the dose volume for the infant.

- ***Example:*** Procaine penicillin G 150,000 units has been ordered for an infant with congenital syphilis who is in your care. You have a TUBEX of Wycillin (penicillin G procaine suspension) labelled 1,200,000 units. The label doesn't state the concentration or volume, nor does it have any graduations. How would you proceed to figure out the dose volume?
  - Withdraw the contents into another syringe. The volume measures 2 ml.
  - Divide 1,200,000 units by 2 ml. The concentration is 600,000 units/ml.
  - Divide the 150,000 unit dose ordered by the concentration of 600,000 units/ml. The dose volume is 0.25 ml.

Storage: Refrigerate. Do not freeze.

CAUTIONS/CONTRAINDICATIONS

Penicillin G procaine must not be given IV, intravascularly, or intra-arterially.

Avoid injection into or near a nerve since permanent neurologic damage may result. If evidence of blood supply compromise occurs at, proximal, or distal to, the site of injection, consult an appropriate specialist immediately.

Contains 120 mg procaine/300,000 units, which may cause allergic reactions, CNS stimulation, seizures, myocardial depression and conduction disturbances, or systemic vasodilation.[5]

Read the label carefully to assure you are giving the intended drug. Brand names of products that may cause confusion include:

- *Crysticillin:* This is one of the brand names for procaine penicillin for IM administration. **It is not crystalline (aqueous) penicillin G for IV administration.**

- *Bicillin C-R:* This is a combination product **for deep IM administration** containing both penicillin G benzathine and penicillin G procaine.

Spell out "units," rather than using a "U" when ordering or transcribing an order for penicillin to avoid a tenfold dosing error. The "U" could look like an additional zero.

USE

Penicillin G procaine is a long-acting (depot, or repository form of penicillin G) **intramuscular** penicillin G suspension used for moderately severe infections caused by penicillin G-sensitive organisms sensitive to low and persistent penicillin serum concentrations.

Congenital Syphilis: The CDC, the American Academy of Pediatrics, and many clinicians state that symptomatic neonates or asymptomatic neonates with abnormal CSF may receive penicillin G procaine 50,000 units/kg once daily for 10–14 days.[3,4,6,7]

Choice of products: Carefully differentiate between products when ordering, dispensing, or administering penicillin. Legibly and clearly state the type of penicillin intended because products differ in duration of action, serum concentration, and route of administration:

- *Aqueous penicillin G* gives high-serum penicillin concentration with short duration. *May be given either IV or IM.* (See monograph on penicillin G aqueous.)

- *Benzathine penicillin G* (Bicillin L-A, Permapen) gives very low, sustained serum penicillin concentrations for 2–3 weeks. *Given IM only.* (See monograph on penicillin G benzathine.)

- *Combination product* of penicillin G benzathine and penicillin G procaine (Bicillin C-R) gives an early peak serum penicillin concentration, then a sustained low serum concentration for 2–3 weeks. *Given IM only.*

- *Procaine penicillin G* (Crysticillin AS, Wycillin, Pfizerpen-AS) gives low peni-cillin serum concentrations that are sustained for 1–2 days. *Given IM only.*

Mechanism of Action

Penicillins act by interrupting bacterial cell wall synthesis.

Procaine penicillin G is prepared by reacting equimolar amounts of penicillin G aqueous with procaine hydrochloride.

Adverse Effects

Procaine penicillin G is usually well tolerated without evidence of local reaction at the site of injection or of systemic reaction.[7] However, very serious adverse effects that may be fatal may occur,[8] and precautions should be carefully observed to avoid a medication error.

CNS: Neurotoxic reactions, including seizures with high serum levels.

Hematologic: Anemia, thrombocytopenia, eosinophilia, leukopenia, granulo-cytopenia, neutropenia.

Hypersensitivity Reactions: Rash and anaphylaxis; not likely to occur in neonates, however.

Local: Sterile abscesses and pain may occur at injection site. Inadvertent intravas-cular administration of penicillin G procaine, including administration directly into or immediately adjacent to an artery, has rarely resulted in occlusion, thrombosis, and severe neurovascular damage, especially in neonates and chil-dren. The severe neurovascular effects appear to occur because the repository forms of penicillin G form microemboli within arteries and can cause secondary thrombosis that occludes the vessels and eventually gives rise to peripheral gangrene.[5]

Renal: Acute interstitial nephritis.

In treatment of syphilis, a pseudoanaphylactic reaction, Jarisch-Herxheimer reaction may occur. It is thought to be caused by the release of pyrogen and/or endotoxins from phagocytized organisms. This reaction occurs 2–12 hours after initiation of penicillin and subsides within 12–24 hours. Symptoms may include fever, sweating, malaise, increased pulse rate, arthralgia, and an increase in blood pressure followed by a decrease in blood pressure.[5]

Some sources recommend that procaine penicillin G be avoided in neonates, because of the greater risk of procaine toxicity and sterile abscesses than in older children. However, the CDC, the American Academy of Pediatrics, and many clinicians state that neonates with congenital syphilis that are symptomatic, or asymptomatic neonates with abnormal CSF may receive penicillin G procaine 50,000 units/kg daily for 10–14 days.[3,4,6,7]

Pharmacokinetics/Pharmacodynamics

Absorption: Relatively insoluble: It forms a tissue depot from which the drug is slowly absorbed and hydrolyzed to penicillin G. Serum concentrations are lower and more prolonged than an equivalent IM dose of aqueous penicillin G.[5]

Distribution: CSF concentrations 4 hours after an IM dose of 50,000 units/kg of penicillin G procaine average 0.14 mcg/ml. The minimum treponemicidal concentration of penicillin G is generally defined as 0.03 units/ml (or 0.02 mcg/ml).[5]

Peak Effect: 1–4 hours.

Duration of Action: 1–2 days.

Half-life: 5.5–6 hours. The half-life is longer than with aqueous penicillin G primarily because absorption from the injection site continues over a longer time period.[7]

Elimination: Excreted by the kidney, 10 percent by glomerular filtration and 90 percent by tubular secretion.

NURSING IMPLICATIONS

Not for IV administration.

Rotate injection sites. Repeated IM injection of the drug into the anterolateral thigh should be avoided since quadriceps femoris fibrosis and atrophy may occur.

IM injection should be made at a slow, steady rate to avoid blockage of the needle.

Discontinue injection if signs or symptoms suggest the onset of severe pain.[5]

COMMENTS

Conversion: Penicillin G procaine is generally prescribed and dispensed in units, rather than by weight. Each mg of penicillin G procaine = 900–1,050 units.

REFERENCES

1. Nelson JD. 1996. *1996–1997 Pocket Book of Pediatric Antimicrobial Therapy,* 12th ed. Baltimore: Lippincott Williams & Wilkins, 8, 17.

2. Centers for Disease Control. 1998. 1998 guidelines for treatment of sexually transmitted diseases. *MMWR* 47(No. RR-1): 41–46.

3. American Academy of Pediatrics, Committee on Infectious Diseases. 1997. *Red Book: Report of the Committee on Infectious Diseases,* 24th ed. Elk Grove Village, Illinois: American Academy of Pediatrics, 504–514.

4. Paryani SG, et al. 1994. Treatment of asymptomatic congenital syphilis: Benzathine versus procaine penicillin G therapy. *Journal of Pediatrics* 125(3): 471–475.

5. Benitz WE, and Tatro DS. 1995. *The Pediatric Drug Handbook.* St. Louis: Mosby-Year Book, 488.

6. McEvoy GK. 1998. *AHFS Drug Information.* Bethesda, Maryland: American Society of Health-System Pharmacists, 308–311.

7. McCracken GH Jr, and Nelson JD. 1983. *Antimicrobial Therapy for Newborns,* 2nd ed. New York: Grune & Stratton, 11–12.

8. Pearson L. 1998. Analysis of an error. *The Nurse Practitioner* 23(7): 8, 13.

PHENOBARBITAL (LUMINOL)
(feen-oh-BAR-bi-tal)
(CONTROLLED SUBSTANCE SCHEDULE IV)

CENTRAL NERVOUS SYSTEM: ANTICONVULSANT, SEDATIVE

DOSE

Status Epilepticus:

- *Loading Dose:* 5–10 mg/kg/dose every 20–30 minutes as needed, up to a maximum of 35 mg/kg. Patients usually respond within 10 minutes. Be prepared to support respirations.
- *Maintenance Dose:* 3–8 mg/kg/24 hours divided every 12 hours or as a single daily dose. Begin maintenance dose no sooner than 12–24 hours after loading dose is given.[1–6]

Seizure Control, Treatment of Infants of Drug-Addicted Mothers, and Sedation:

- *Loading Dose:* 10 mg/kg/24 hours divided every 12 hours for 2 days (= total loading dose of 20 mg/kg) IV, PO. Does not control diarrhea. A loading dose of 20 mg/kg should result in a serum concentration of 20–33 mcg/ml (1.3–1.6 times the single dose) for infants with a volume of distribution (V_d) of 0.6–1 liter/kg.
- *Maintenance Dose:* 3–8 mg/kg/24 hours divided every 12 hours or as a single daily dose.

Cholestatic Jaundice (direct hyperbilirubinemia = conjugated hyperbilirubinemia): 4–5 mg/kg/24 hours divided every 12 hours. Titrate dose by serum concentrations. Use the same therapeutic range as for seizure management and other indications (15–40 mcg/ml). **(The use of phenobarbital is no longer routine clinical management of neonatal unconjugated hyperbilirubinemia.)**

Reduce dose in infants with severe liver and/or renal disease and in those with low urinary pH.

Use a lower dose (3–4 mg/kg/24 hours) in very low birth weight infants because of their immature hepatic and renal function. Monitor serum concentration.

Use a lower dose in infants with perinatal asphyxia.

Individualize dose based on serum concentrations.

ADMINISTRATION

IV—*Rate:* Infuse at 1 mg/kg/minute or slower.

IV—*Concentration:* May give undiluted (65 mg/ml).

IV—*Compatibility:* See Appendix E: Y-Site Compatibility of Common NICU Drugs.

IM: May be given undiluted. Absorption by IM route is unreliable; IM route should be used for status epilepticus only if IV is not available.

PO: Available as an oral liquid (contains 10–13.5 percent alcohol).

CAUTIONS/CONTRAINDICATIONS

Do not administer intra-arterially.

Do not use in intermittent porphyria.

USE

Drug of choice to control seizures in infants. Most neonates with seizures (60–85 percent) are controlled with phenobarbital alone. Seizures related to hypoxic-ischemic encephalopathy secondary to perinatal asphyxia usually do not require prolonged therapy.[5]

To control withdrawal symptoms in infants of drug-addicted mothers.

For sedation.

Has been used to reduce serum bilirubin in jaundiced infants and in chronic cholestasis.

Use for prevention of intraventricular hemorrhage has not been encouraging.[7]

MECHANISM OF ACTION

In the treatment of seizures, phenobarbital limits the spread of seizure activity and may raise seizure threshold.

In the treatment of unconjugated hyperbilirubinemia, phenobarbital induces glucuronyl transferase activity for glucuronide conjugating capacity of bilirubin. It also stimulates bile flow and increases the concentration of the Y-binding protein involved in the uptake of bilirubin by hepatocytes. Treatment of hyperbilirubinemia with phenobarbital is delayed and variable.[8,9]

ADVERSE EFFECTS

Drowsiness, paradoxical excitation, rash (rare in newborns), hepatitis, megalo-blastic anemia, and respiratory depression. Also may cause mild behavioral disturbances and decreased attention span, which can interfere with learning skills.

Extravasation may cause tissue necrosis.

Cardiovascular toxicity such as hypotension may occur with rapid IV administration.

Chronic administration can cause depletion of folic acid, pyridoxine, and changes in vitamin D homeostasis. Osteopenia may result.

Seizures may result from abrupt discontinuation of the drug; taper gradually.

Infants of mothers receiving chronic phenobarbital may have a coagulopathy at birth responsive to vitamin K.

PHARMACOKINETICS/PHARMACODYNAMICS

Absorption: 80–100 percent of oral dose absorbed. Peak levels occur between 2 and 4 hours after an oral dose.

Protein Binding: 10–30 percent.

Metabolism: Hepatic. Induces hepatic enzyme activity, thereby leading to more rapid elimination of the drug itself (autoinduction), bilirubin, and other drugs metabolized in the liver. Stimulates bile flow. Metabolism changes rapidly during newborn period secondary to hepatic maturation. Assess effectiveness and levels closely.

Half-life: 60–200 hours in preterm infants, 41–120 hours in term infants.[10]

Elimination: One-third excreted in the urine. High urine pH encourages elimination.

NURSING IMPLICATIONS

Monitor for respiratory depression and lethargy.

Closely monitor drug levels.

COMMENTS

Therapeutic Range: 15–40 mcg/ml. Draw a trough level just prior to the dose.

- Lethargy and sedation occur with serum concentrations >40 mcg/ml and severe lethargy at >70 mcg/ml.

Check for a possible cause of seizures (hypoglycemia, electrolyte imbalance) and treat cause.

Interactions:

- CNS depressants may cause additive depressant effects. Respiratory depression is more common when phenobarbital is used with benzodiazepines.

- Valproic acid decreases the metabolism of phenobarbital. Rifampin may increase phenobarbital metabolism.

- Phenobarbital decreases the effects of oral anticoagulants, corticosteroids, acetaminophen, β-blockers (propranolol), quinidine, theophylline, metronidazole, and phenytoin (may also increase levels; monitor both phenobarbital and phenytoin levels when this combination is given).[11]

REFERENCES

1. Roberts RJ. 1984. *Drug Therapy in Infants: Pharmacologic Principles and Clinical Experience.* Philadelphia: WB Saunders, 97–104.

2. Bergman I, Painter MJ, and Crumrine PK. 1982. Neonatal seizures. *Seminars in Perinatology* 6(1): 54–67.

3. Fischer JH, et al. 1981. Phenobarbital maintenance dose requirements in treating neonatal seizures. *Neurology* 31(8): 1042–1044.

4. Lockman LA, et al. 1979. Phenobarbital dosage for control of neonatal seizures. *Neurology* 29(11): 1445–1449.

5. Dodson WE. 1989. Medical treatment and pharmacology of antiepileptic drugs. *Pediatric Clinics of North America* 36(2): 421–433.

6. Gilman JT, et al. 1989. Rapid sequential phenobarbital treatment of neonatal seizures. *Pediatrics* 83(5): 674–678.

7. Morgan MEI, Massey RF, and Cooke RWI. 1982. Does phenobarbitone prevent periventricular hemorrhage in very low-birth-weight babies?: A controlled trial. *Pediatrics* 70(2): 186–189.

8. Modi N. 1991. Drugs and neonatal jaundice. In *Neonatal Clinical Pharmacology and Therapeutics*, Rylance G, Harvey D, and Aranda J, eds. Linacre House, Jordan Hill, Oxford: Butterworth-Heinemann, 166–175.

9. Wallin A, and Boreus LO. 1984. Phenobarbital prophylaxis for hyperbilirubinaemia in preterm infants: A controlled study of bilirubin disappearance and infant behavior. *Acta Paediatrica Scandinavica* 73(4): 488–497.

10. Rylance G. 1991. Pharmacological principles and kinetics. In *Neonatal Clinical Pharmacology and Therapeutics*, Rylance G, Harvey D, and Aranda J, eds. Linacre House, Jordan Hill, Oxford: Butterworth-Heinemann, 1–25.

11. Olin BR. 1994. *Drug Facts and Comparisons*. St. Louis: Facts and Comparisons, 1458.

PHENTOLAMINE (REGITINE)
(fen-TOHL-uh-meen)

**ANTIDOTE:
EXTRAVASATION;
ANTIHYPERTENSIVE**

DOSE

SC:

Treatment of extravasation of α-*adrenergic drugs:* 0.1–0.2 mg/kg/dose SC.
  Physician's Order: "Regitine ____ mg SC to IV extravasation site, per unit
  protocol."[1–4]

IV:

- *Afterload Reduction in Congestive Heart Failure/Pulmonary Hypertension:*
  2.5–15 mcg/kg/minute by IV continuous infusion.[4]

- *Pheochromocytoma:*
  - *Diagnosis:* 0.05–0.1 mg/kg/dose IV, IM (See warning under
    CAUTIONS/CONTRAINDICATIONS below.)
  - *Hypertension (prior to surgery for pheochromocytoma):* 0.05–0.1 mg/kg/dose
    given 1–2 hours prior to pheochromocytomectomy; repeat as needed to
    control blood pressure. Titrate the dose to control or prevent hypertension.
    Maximum: 5 mg/dose.

ADMINISTRATION

Supplied as: 5 mg/ml in 1 ml vial. Discard unused portion.

SC—Treatment of Extravasation of α-**adrenergic Drugs**

- *Concentration:* 0.5 mg/ml.

- *Preparation of Dilution:* Dilute 0.1 ml of commercially available phentolamine 5 mg/ml with 0.9 ml normal saline
  (= 0.5 mg/ml, 1 ml).

- *Administration Procedure:*
  - *Stop* the intravenous infusion and remove the needle.
  - *Cleanse* the site and surrounding area with a povidone-iodine solution.
  - *Inject* phentolamine (0.5 mg/ml) locally into area of extravasation in divid-
    ed increments of approximately 0.2 ml using a 25-gauge needle. Change
    needle between each dose increment.

IV—Rate: Infuse over at least 1 minute. May also be given by continuous infusion.

IV—Concentration: 5 mg/ml. May give undiluted or dilute with normal saline.

CAUTIONS/CONTRAINDICATIONS

Warning Regarding the Phentolamine Test: Although phentolamine is indicated
  as an aid in the diagnosis of pheochromocytoma, determinations of blood and
  urine catecholamine concentrations are considered safer and more reliable.

- Deaths have occurred after IV administration of phentolamine for the diagnosis of pheochromocytoma. The phentolamine test may be considered when additional confirmatory evidence of pheochromocytoma is required and the potential benefits of the test outweigh the possible risks.[5]

- The test is more reliable in detecting pheochromocytomas in patients with sustained hypertension than in those with paroxysmal hypertension. It is of no value if the patient is not hypertensive at the time of the test.

- False-negative response may occur with a pheochromocytoma that is not secreting enough epinephrine or norepinephrine to elevate the blood pressure or to sustain an elevation.

- False-positive responses to the test have occurred in patients with essential hypertension; in patients receiving sedatives, opiates, or antihypertensives; and in patients with uremia.[5]

USE

Used to treat extravasation of α-adrenergic drugs (norepinephrine, phenylephrine, dopamine, epinephrine). These drugs can sometimes cause severe tissue blanching, gangrene, and sloughing on infiltration.[1–3]

Small areas of blanching, such as those following the vein and blanching limited locally at the insertion site into which dopamine is infusing, are not harmful and will usually reverse without treatment. It may be necessary to alternate the lines into which dopamine is infusing. If blanching extends more than approximately ¼ inch (= ½ inch diameter) past the insertion site and is spreading, it should alert the nurse to a potential extravasation. Assess the entire clinical picture: Is the area large, cold, hard, edematous, or severely blanched?

May be used up to 12 hours after the extravasation occurred.

A short-acting drug, it is particularly effective for IV use when rapid and precise control of blood pressure is necessary.[6] Phentolamine has little effect on the blood pressure of healthy individuals or patients with essential hypertension.

Pheochromocytoma. Controls or prevents paroxysmal hypertension immediately prior to or during pheochromocytomectomy. Although indicated as an aid in the diagnosis of pheochromocytoma, determinations of blood and urine catecholamine concentrations are considered safer and more reliable.

Peripheral Vasospastic Disorders. Used as an adjunctive therapy in the treatment of peripheral vasospastic disorders, although efficacy has not been established.

Congestive Heart Failure. Used for afterload reduction in congestive heart failure.[4]

MECHANISM OF ACTION

In subcutaneous treatment of extravasation of α-adrenergic drugs, phentolamine blocks α-adrenergic receptors, causing vasodilation.

Hypertension: The mechanism of action in the treatment of hypertension is α-adrenergic blockade (α_1 and α_2 receptors) and antagonism of effects of circulating epinephrine and norepinephrine to cause vasodilation and reduction in peripheral resistance.[7] Phentolamine has greater α-adrenergic blocking effects than does tolazoline (Priscoline).[5]

Congestive Heart Failure: Used as a vasodilator or for congestive heart failure, phentolamine reduces afterload and pulmonary arterial pressure, increases cardiac output, and has a positive inotropic effect.[7] Cerebral blood flow is generally maintained.[5]

Adverse Effects

Marked hypotension, cardiac arrhythmias, tachycardia, and nasal congestion.

Adverse GI effects are common (nausea, vomiting, abdominal pain, exacerbation of peptic ulcer) and generally prevent long-term use of phentolamine.[4–6]

Although local SC injection is usually well tolerated, the infant should be monitored for hypotension. Blood pressure decrease may result from administration of phentolamine in addition to the temporary discontinuation of the drug that infiltrated (e.g., dopamine).

Treatment of Hypotension: Use supportive measures such as IV fluids. If drug treatment is needed, use norepinephrine. *Do not treat hypotension with epinephrine* because that drug may exacerbate the hypotension. (Epinephrine stimulates both α and β receptors. Because phentolamine is blocking the α receptors, the resultant effect is a β-effect of vasodilation and further decrease in blood pressure.)

Pharmacokinetics/Pharmacodynamics

Subcutaneous Treatment of Extravasation of α-adrenergic Drugs:

- *Onset of Action:* Within 5–20 minutes, the area around the injection will become hyperemic.

IV:

- *Onset of Action:* Immediate.
- *Peak Effect:* Within 2 minutes.
- *Duration of Action:* 15–30 minutes.
- *Half-life:* Approximately 19 minutes.
- *Elimination:* Process not completely known, but 13 percent is excreted in the urine as unmetabolized drug.[7]

Nursing Implications

Subcutaneous Treatment of Extravasation of α-adrenergic Drugs (See Appendix G: Guidelines for Management of Intravenous Extravasations):

- Document site condition and treatment in the medical record.
- Observe site carefully. Area should become hyperemic, then return to normal skin color.
- Monitor for hypotension.

IV:

- Monitor blood pressure, vital signs.

- Monitor for adverse GI effects.

COMMENTS

Interactions:

- Concurrent use of dopamine with phentolamine antagonizes the peripheral vasoconstriction produced by high doses of dopamine.
- Concurrent use of epinephrine with phentolamine may block the α-adrenergic effects of epinephrine, possibly resulting in severe hypotension and tachycardia.
- Prior administration of phentolamine may decrease the pressor response to phenylephrine.[7]

REFERENCES

1. Zenk KE. 1981. Management of intravenous extravasations. *Infusion* 5(4): 77–79.

2. Siwy BK, and Sadove AM. 1987. Acute management of dopamine infiltration injury with regitine. *Plastic and Reconstructive Surgery* 80(4): 610–612.

3. Zenk KE, and Sills J. 1985. Management of dopamine-induced perivascular blanching and extravasations in LBW infants. *Journal of Perinatology* 6(1): 82A.

4. Benitz WE, and Tatro DS. 1995. *The Pediatric Drug Handbook,* 3rd ed. St. Louis: Mosby-Year Book, 206–207.

5. McEvoy GK. 1994. *AHFS Drug Information.* Bethesda, Maryland: American Society of Hospital Pharmacists, 814–816.

6. Voorhess ML. 1996. Adrenal medulla, sympathetic nervous system, and multiple endocrine neoplasia syndromes. In *Rudolph's Pediatrics,* 20th ed., Rudolph AM, ed. Stamford, Connecticut: Appleton & Lange, 1742–1750.

7. United States Pharmacopeial Convention/USP DI. 1996. *Drug Information for the Health Care Professional,* 16th ed. Rockville, Maryland: United States Pharmacopeial Convention, 2388–2389.

PHENYTOIN (DILANTIN)
(FEN-i-toyn)

CENTRAL NERVOUS SYSTEM: ANTICONVULSANT

DOSE

Status Epilepticus:

- *IV Loading Dose:* 5–10 mg/kg/dose every 20–30 minutes as needed, up to 20 mg/kg total dose IV. This will produce a plasma concentration of approximately 16–17 mcg/ml in newborns with a V_d of 1.2 liter/kg.
- *IV Maintenance Dose:* 4–6 mg/kg/day IV divided every 12 hours or as a single daily dose.

Cardiac Arrhythmias:

- *Loading Dose:* 10–15 mg/kg IV infused over 1 hour.
- *Maintenance Dose:* 4–7 mg/kg/day divided into two doses.[1]

For PO Use in Neonates: 15–20 mg/kg/day given daily or in two divided doses. Monitor blood levels.[1,2] When giving the oral suspension, larger doses up to 20 mg/kg/day may be needed to achieve therapeutic levels.

Fosphenytoin: 75 mg is equivalent to phenytoin 50 mg. The dose of fosphenytoin is expressed as phenytoin equivalents (PE). For example, "an initial maintenance dose of 4–6 mg PE/kg/day is suggested."

Reduce dose in severe hepatic dysfunction.

Caution: The relationship between dose and serum concentrations is nonlinear because of saturation of metabolic pathways. Thus, doubling the dose may more than double the serum concentrations.

ADMINISTRATION

Supplied as:

- *Phenytoin:* Injection: 50 mg/ml. Oral suspension: 25 mg/ml and 6 mg/ml.
- *Fosphenytoin (Cerebyx):* Injection: 75 mg (= 50 mg phenytoin equivalents [PE]) per ml.

IV—*Rate:* Infuse no faster than 0.5 mg/kg/minute.

IV—*Concentration:* May give undiluted. If diluted, *use normal saline only* and administer immediately to reduce risk of precipitation.

IV—*Flush:* Use saline flush only, not heparinized saline.

IV—*Compatibility:* See Appendix E: Y-Site Compatibility of Common NICU Drugs. Heparin and dextrose are incompatible with phenytoin. Use a sodium chloride 0.9 percent flush volume of 1 ml before and after administration, if fluid status allows. Administer at the recommended rate at the hub of the catheter to minimize dead space and resultant mixing with IV solution (to reduce risk of precipitation). Do not infuse phenytoin into a central line because residual intraluminal dextrose and heparin (even after tubing flush) may cause central line occlusion. Percutaneous central venous catheters are particularly at risk for occlusion because of their small diameter.

PO: Oral-liquid dosage forms (6 mg/ml and 25 mg/ml) are available. Shake well before use. Give 1 hour before or 2 hours after feedings, if possible, to maximize absorption.

Avoid switching between products of different manufacturers because the dose-dependent clearance of phenytoin makes even small changes in availability potentially dangerous.

Storage: Phenytoin may be stored at room temperature. Fosphenytoin should be refrigerated.

Use

For acute and chronic neonatal seizures when phenobarbital has been ineffective. Used with phenobarbital for seizures refractory to phenobarbital alone.

To suppress ventricular arrhythmias. For digoxin-induced tachyarrhythmias. Phenytoin is a Class IB antiarrhythmic.[1,3]

Very limited experience with fosphenytoin in neonates; not enough experience to recommend yet.

Mechanism of Action

Phenytoin is a hydantoin anticonvulsant that acts by limiting the spread of seizures from a focus in the motor cortex. Phenytoin affects synaptic transmission.

Adverse Effects

Rapid IV administration causes hypotension, cardiovascular collapse and/or CNS depression, bradycardia, and arrhythmias and can be fatal.[4]

Lymphadenopathy, peripheral neuropathy, hepatotoxicity, hyperbilirubinemia, nausea, irritability, deterioration of mental performance, maculopapular rash (can be a severe exfoliative, Stevens-Johnson syndrome), megaloblastic anemia, thrombocytopenia, leukopenia, leukocytosis, granulocytopenia, eosinophilia, and other blood dyscrasias. In older infants and children on chronic therapy, coarsening of facial features, chronic acneiform rash, hirsutism, and gum hyperplasia.

Altered vitamin D metabolism leading to rickets and osteomalacia, particularly in patients on multiple anticonvulsants with limited sun exposure.

Causes tissue necrosis upon extravasation. Fosphenytoin produces fewer local reactions than phenytoin injection.[5]

Depletes folic acid and pyridoxine and changes vitamin D homeostasis.

Infants of mothers receiving phenytoin have reduced concentrations of vitamin K-dependent clotting factors, putting these infants at risk for hemorrhage.

IV phenytoin contains propylene glycol as a solvent. Propylene glycol has caused hyperosmolality in preterm infants, resulting in cardiovascular and respiratory instability and seizures.[6,7]

Fosphenytoin has been associated with fewer adverse effects in general than phenytoin.[5]

Pharmacokinetics/Pharmacodynamics

Absorption: Poorly absorbed PO. IM absorption of phenytoin is poor and very slow because the drug crystallizes in the muscle; IM route is not recommended. Fosphenytoin is completely bioavailable, however, after IM injection. Fosphenytoin has advantages over phenytoin injection that are related to its greater solubility, which makes unnecessary the extreme alkalinity, propylene glycol, and ethanol needed in the phenytoin formulation.[5]

Distribution: Distributes into the CSF rapidly; CSF levels exceed those in serum.

Protein Binding: 70–90 percent. Protein binding is less in preterm infants (approximately 40 percent); therefore, a lower therapeutic range is probably effective.

Metabolism:

- Metabolized to inactive metabolites. Hepatic biotransformation can be saturated at usual therapeutic concentrations, and dose-dependent kinetics occur. Doubling the dose can more than double the serum concentration. There is slower elimination at higher plasma levels. Kinetics change and are sometimes difficult to predict.[4,8–10]

- Fosphenytoin is converted to phenytoin. The conversion half-life is approximately 15 minutes. When fosphenytoin is given IM, the peak plasma concentration is reached in approximately 3 hours.

Half-life: Varies markedly: preterm infants 60–130 (average 75) hours; term infants 10–100 (average 20) hours; children 2–30 hours. Rate of metabolism increases rapidly over the first 2–3 weeks.

Nursing Implications

Monitor for hypotension and bradycardia during administration.

Monitor liver function tests closely.

Monitor serum concentrations closely.

Comments

Experience with fosphenytoin in neonates is too limited at this time to recommend its use.[5] Fosphenytoin should be prescribed and dispensed in PE units to avoid errors.

Therapeutic Range: 10–20 mcg/ml. Some clinicians recommend levels of 6–14 mcg/ml in preterm infants because of lower protein binding.

Potential for Toxicity:

- The relationship between dose and serum concentrations is nonlinear. Please see **Caution** under **Dose** above.

- *Serum Levels:* Because the signs of toxicity in older children and adults (nystagmus above 20 mcg/ml, ataxia above 30 mcg/ml, paradoxical seizures above 35 mcg/ml, mental changes above 40 mcg/ml) are more subtle or not apparent clinically in neonates, serum concentration monitoring is mandatory.[11]

Interactions:

- The following *increase* the effects of phenytoin: chloramphenicol, cimetidine, fluconazole, isoniazid, propranolol, sulfonamides, and trimethoprim. Because they inhibit phenytoin metabolism, concomitant administration may result in excessive phenytoin levels. Monitor for phenytoin toxicity.

- Phenobarbital and valproic acid may affect phenytoin metabolism; phenytoin may affect the metabolism of phenobarbital and valproic acid. Monitor serum levels of all anticonvulsants when a new one is added.

- The following *decrease* the effects of phenytoin: antacids, some antineoplastics, continuous drip feedings, rifampin, sucralfate, and theophylline. All may decrease phenytoin absorption.

- Phenytoin decreases the effects of certain other drugs by increasing hepatic microsomal enzymes, thereby increasing the metabolism of these drugs: acetaminophen, carbamazepine, corticosteroids, folic acid, metyrapone, quinidine, theophylline, valproic acid, and vitamin D.

- Phenytoin increases the effects of these drugs: primidone, warfarin.

- Fosphenytoin can be expected to interact with the same drugs that interact with phenytoin.[5]

REFERENCES

1. Benitz WE, and Tatro DS. 1995. *The Pediatric Drug Handbook,* 3rd ed. St. Louis: Mosby-Year Book, 119–121, 185.

2. Bergman I, Painter MJ, and Crumrine PK. 1982. Neonatal seizures. *Seminars in Perinatology* 6(1): 54–67.

3. Strasburger JF. 1991. Cardiac arrhythmias in childhood: Diagnostic considerations and treatment. *Drugs* 42(6): 974–983.

4. Painter MJ, et al. 1981. Phenobarbital and phenytoin in neonatal seizures: Metabolism and tissue distribution. *Neurology* 31(9): 1107–1112.

5. Fierro LS, et al. 1996. Safety of fosphenytoin sodium. *American Journal of Health-System Pharmacy* 53(11): 2707–2712.

6. MacDonald MG, et al. 1987. Propylene glycol: Increased incidence of seizures in low birth weight infants. *Pediatrics* 79(4): 622–625.

7. Glasgow AM, et al. 1983. Hyperosmolality in small infants due to propylene glycol. *Pediatrics* 72(3): 353–355.

8. Morselli PL, Franco-Morselli R, and Bossi L. 1980. Clinical pharmacokinetics in newborns and infants: Age-related differences and therapeutic implications. *Clinical Pharmacokinetics* 5(6): 485–527.

9. Rylance G. 1991. Pharmacological principles and kinetics. In *Neonatal Clinical Pharmacology and Therapeutics*, Rylance G, Harvey D, and Aranda J, eds. Linacre House, Jordan Hill, Oxford: Butterworth-Heinemann, 1–25.

10. Spino M, Rasymas A, and Radde IC. 1993. Dosing considerations and therapeutic drug monitoring. In *Pediatric Pharmacology and Therapeutics,* 2nd ed., Radde IC, and MacLeod SM, eds. St. Louis: Mosby-Year Book, 169–183.

11. Wiriyathian S, Kaojarern S, and Rosenfeld CR. 1982. Dilantin toxicity in a preterm infant: Persistent bradycardia and lethargy. *Journal of Pediatrics* 100(1): 146–149.

PHOSPHORUS
(FOS-for-us)

ELECTROLYTE BALANCE:
ELECTROLYTE SUPPLEMENT

DOSE

Severe Hypophosphatemia: 0.15–0.3 mmol/kg/dose
  (= 5–9 mg elemental phosphorus/kg/dose)
Maintenance: 0.5–2 mmol/kg/day (= 16–63 mg elemental phosphorus/kg/day)[1]
Order phosphorus in millimoles (mmol) of elemental phosphorus, not in mEq,
  because the milliequivalent content changes with the pH of the solution.

ADMINISTRATION

IV—*Rate:* Maximum: 0.05 mmol/kg/hour.[2] For potassium phosphates, the maximum rate can also be expressed in terms of potassium content: 0.3 mEq of potassium/kg/hour for an unmonitored patient and 0.5 mEq/kg/hour of potassium for a monitored patient.

IV—*Concentration:* Preferred dilution is in the 24-hour maintenance IV, rather than infusing over shorter periods of time. For potassium phosphates, the maximum potassium concentration is 0.08 mEq/ml, if possible. For sodium phosphates, the maximum sodium concentration is 0.5 mEq/ml for a peripheral line. Table 1-41 lists phosphorus and sodium or potassium contents of the phosphate injections.

IV—*Compatibility:* See Appendix E: Y-Site Compatibility of Common NICU Drugs.[3]

PO:

- Administer in 2–4 divided doses and mix with feedings.

TABLE 1-41 ◆ PHOSPHORUS AND SODIUM OR POTASSIUM CONTENTS OF VARIOUS PHOSPHATE PRODUCTS

Product	Elemental Phosphorus (mmol/ml)	(mg/ml)	Potassium (mEq/ml)	Sodium (mEq/ml)
Sodium phosphates injection	3	93 (31 mg/mmol)	0	4 (1.3 mEq Na/mmol)
Potassium phosphates injection	3	93 (31 mg/mmol)	4.4 (1.46 mEq K/mmol)	0
Fleet Phosphosoda[2] (sodium phosphate and sodium biphosphate)— PO and PR	4.1	127	0	4.82

Conversion: 1 mmol phosphorus = 31 mg elemental phosphorus (approximately).

Note: Specify the sodium or potassium salt when ordering. *Example of an oral phosphate supplement order: Sodium Phosphates—0.5 mmol elemental phosphorus PO every 6 hours with feedings.*

- The injectable form of sodium or potassium phosphates may be administered orally and mixed with feedings.

PR: The rectal route is not commonly used for phosphorus in neonates. No dosage recommendation is available.

CAUTIONS/CONTRAINDICATIONS

Use with caution in dehydration or in the presence of renal failure.[4–6]

USE

Treatment of hypophosphatemia.

Provision of maintenance phosphorus in parenteral nutrition solutions.

Treatment of nutritional rickets of prematurity.

Phosphate may be infused separately when the amount of protein and/or calcium in the parenteral nutrition solution precludes inclusion of phosphorus in the solution without precipitation.[1,7,8]

MECHANISM OF ACTION

Phosphorus is an intracellular ion required for formation of energy-transfer enzymes such as ADP and ATP. Phosphorus is also needed for bone metabolism and mineralization.

ADVERSE EFFECTS

Hyperphosphatemia, hypocalcemia.

Cardiac arrhythmias with rapid potassium phosphates IV infusion, hypotension, acute renal failure.

With oral administration, GI discomfort (greater with sodium than with potassium salt), diarrhea.

Hypocalcemia, tetany, hyperphosphatemia, dehydration, coma, and hypernatremia have been described in infants receiving sodium phosphates enema or oral solution.

Hyperkalemia, hypernatremia (depending on salt used).

PHARMACOKINETICS/PHARMACODYNAMICS

Absorption: Approximately 60 percent.

Elimination: Renal.[2]

NURSING IMPLICATIONS

Monitor for feeding intolerance with oral dosing.

Infuse IV dose slowly; monitor for hypocalcemia and hypotension.

Monitor serum phosphorus during therapy: daily during correction of hypophosphatemia and weekly during parenteral nutrition therapy, when electrolytes have stabilized.

COMMENTS

Normal Serum Phosphorus: Higher for infants than for adults; 5.4–10.9 mg/dl at 1 week; 6.2–8.7 mg/dl at 3 weeks.

References

1. Kerner JA Jr. 1983. *Manual of Pediatric Parenteral Nutrition.* New York: Wiley, 132–133.

2. Benitz WE, and Tatro DS. 1995. *The Pediatric Drug Handbook,* 3rd ed. St. Louis: Mosby-Year Book, 315–316.

3. Trissel LA. 1998. *Handbook on Injectable Drugs,* 10th ed. Bethesda, Maryland: American Society of Health-Systems Pharmacists, 1013–1018.

4. Smith MS, Feldman KW, and Furukawa CT. 1973. Coma in an infant due to hypertonic sodium phosphate medication. *Journal of Pediatrics* 82(3): 481–482.

5. Chesney RW, and Haughton PB. 1974. Tetany following phosphate enemas in chronic renal disease. *American Journal of Diseases of Children* 127(4): 584–586.

6. Davis RF, et al. 1977. Hypocalcemia, hyperphosphatemia, and dehydration following a single hypertonic phosphate enema. *Journal of Pediatrics* 90(3): 484–485.

7. Aladjem M, et al. 1980. Changes in the electrolyte content of serum and urine during total parenteral nutrition. *Journal of Pediatrics* 97(3): 437–439.

8. Knochel JP. 1981. Hypophosphatemia (nutrition in medicine). *Western Journal of Medicine* 134(1): 15–26.

POTASSIUM

(poe-TASS-ee-um)

[CHLORIDE, ACETATE]

See phosphorus monograph for potassium phosphates.

See citrate and citric acid solutions monograph for potassium citrate.

DOSE

Maintenance: 2–6 mEq/kg/day (usually 2–3 mEq/kg/day) diluted in 24-hour maintenance IV solution. Higher doses are required in infants receiving diuretics. Titrate dose with previous day's requirement and potassium serum levels.

Intermittent: 1 mEq/kg/dose.

Oral Potassium Supplement: 2–6 mEq/kg/day (usually 2–3 mEq/kg/day) divided every 6 hours and diluted in feedings.

ADMINISTRATION

IV—*Rate:*

- <0.3 mEq/kg/hour IV, cardiac monitor not required.
- 0.3–0.5 mEq/kg/hour IV, cardiac monitor required.
- *Maximum IV infusion rate:* 0.5 mEq/kg/hour.

Do not give by IV push. Intermittent doses should be administered over 6–8 hours or, preferably, diluted in the entire day's maintenance IV solution.

IV—*Concentration:*

- Peripheral line preferred: <40 mEq/liter (= 0.04 mEq/ml). Maximum: 80 mEq/liter (= 0.08 mEq/ml). Concentrations >80 mEq/liter (= 0.08 mEq/ml) should be infused via a central line because of the potential for severe vein irritation and risk of IV extravasation injury.
- Central line: >80 mEq/liter (= 0.08 mEq/ml). One investigator recommended a maximum of 150 mEq/liter (= 0.15 mEq/ml) in a central line and, in severely fluid restricted patients with central lines, 200 mEq/liter (= 0.2 mEq/ml).[1]
- Vials of KCl are commercially available at a concentration of 2 mEq/ml (= 2,000 mEq/liter). ***This must be diluted.*** It cannot be infused full strength particularly via a peripheral line because of the extremely high osmolality.
- In the infant whose IV rate is minimal, potassium added to the IV fluid in the volumetric chamber may take several hours to travel through the tubing. Mix well with solution in chamber to avoid layering, which would result in infusion of concentrated potassium. Administer via pump (at the appropriate rate and concentration) at a port close to patient if urgently needed.

IV—*Compatibility:* See Appendix E: Y-Site Compatibility of Common NICU Drugs.

PO: May use KCl injection 2 mEq/ml and give PO, mixed with the infant's formula to minimize fluid volume.

TABLE 1-42 ◆ CONTENT OF ORAL CITRATE PRODUCTS

Mixture	Each ml containes (mEq)		
	Na	K	Citrate
Polycitra	1	1	2
Polycitra-K	0	2	2
Bicitra (Shohl's)	1	0	1
Oracit	1	0	1

Note: Adjust dosage to maintain desired urine pH. One mEq of citrate is equivalent to 1 mEq bicarbonate.

From: Barone MA. 1996. *The Harriet Lane Handbook*, 14th ed. St. Louis: Mosby-Year Book, 510. Reprinted by permission.

CAUTIONS/CONTRAINDICATIONS

Do not keep potassium chloride on floor stock because of the toxicity of this drug and to protect against inadvertent overdose, which could be fatal. Doses should be prepared by pharmacy whenever possible.

Do not use the word *bolus* to refer to intermittent potassium doses because "bolus" implies an IV push, which could cause arrhythmias and cardiac arrest.

Do not give to anuric or severely oliguric patients. Be sure patient is urinating before giving potassium.

Changes in the potassium concentration of an IV solution should be made in the pharmacy, rather than on the ward. Prevent potassium layering by agitating the bag or bottle before infusing.

USE

Provision of maintenance potassium and correction of hypokalemia. The chloride salt is the usual maintenance form; the acetate can be substituted if metabolic acidosis with hyperchloremia is present.[1-3]

Potassium and/or sodium citrate mixtures are used for urinary alkalinization. Table 1-42 compares the content of some commercial citrate products. (See also citrate and citric acid solutions monograph.)

MECHANISM OF ACTION

Potassium is the main intracellular cation. It is essential for intracellular tonicity; transmission of nerve impulses; cardiac, skeletal, and smooth muscle contraction; and maintenance of normal renal function. Potassium is important in carbohydrate utilization, protein synthesis, regulation of nerve conduction, and muscle contraction.[4]

ADVERSE EFFECTS

If inadequately diluted, severe vein irritation with extravasation injury.

Hyperkalemia, hyperchloremia (chloride salt), alkalosis (acetate salt). Potassium accumulation with renal dysfunction.

Cardiac arrhythmias (peaked T waves, widened QRS, flattened P waves, bradycardia, heart block), respiratory paralysis, hypotension if infused too rapidly.

Oral potassium and/or sodium citrates may cause diarrhea. Oral KCl may cause gastric irritation.

Treatment of Overdose:

- Stop potassium infusion and monitor ECG. Infuse dextrose and insulin at a ratio of 3–4 gm dextrose to 1 unit regular insulin IV to shift potassium into the cells.
- Give sodium bicarbonate 1 mEq/kg IV to reverse acidosis and produce shift of potassium into cells.
- Give calcium gluconate 10 percent, 100 mg/kg IV to reverse ECG changes.
- Give sodium polystyrene sulfonate (Kayexalate) 1 gm/kg per rectum to remove potassium from the body.
- Hemodialysis or peritoneal dialysis is effective.[4]

PHARMACOKINETICS/PHARMACODYNAMICS

Metabolism: Potassium acetate is converted to bicarbonate in the liver. Conversion may be impaired in hepatic dysfunction.

Elimination: Urine.

NURSING IMPLICATIONS

Monitor IV site carefully because infiltration causes severe tissue damage.

Continuous cardiac monitoring is required during intermittent IV infusion.

Oral dosing may cause feeding intolerance.

COMMENTS

Correction of serum potassium concentrations of ≥3 mEq/liter is not an emergency and can be done in the next day's IV solution. There is usually cause for concern only if the infant has a serum potassium <3 mEq/liter with a normal pH, is symptomatic with marked weakness or paralysis, and is having arrhythmias on ECG.

Interactions: With potassium-sparing diuretics (spironolactone, Aldactazide), hyperkalemia may occur because of additive effect. Digoxin toxicity may occur with hypokalemia.

REFERENCES

1. Hamil RJ, et al. 1991. Efficacy and safety of potassium infusion therapy in hypokalemic critically ill patients. *Critical Care Medicine* 19(5): 694–699.

2. Khilnani P. 1992. Electrolyte abnormalities in critically ill children. *Critical Care Medicine* 20(2): 241–250.

3. Schaber DE, et al. 1985. Intravenous KCl supplementation in pediatric cardiac surgical patients. *Pediatric Cardiology* 6(1): 25–28.

4. Olin BR. 1994. *Drug Facts and Comparisons.* St. Louis: Facts and Comparisons, 134–137.

PREDNISONE

(PRED-ni-sone)

HORMONE: GLUCOCORTICOID

DOSE

As an Anti-inflammatory and Immunosuppressive: 0.5–2 mg/kg/day given as a single daily dose or divided every 6–12 hours.[1,2] Base dose on severity of disease and response of patient. Reduce dose gradually to lowest effective level.

ADMINISTRATION

For oral use only.

Supplied as:

- *Oral liquid:* 1 mg/ml (5 percent alcohol content). *Avoid the 5 mg/ml product because of its high (30 percent) alcohol content.*

- *Tablets:* 1, 2.5, 5, and 10 mg for those doses that equal these tablet or half-tablet (most are scored) sizes. Use of the solid dosage form may be preferred for fluid-restricted infants. Crush tablet and dilute in a small amount of feeding immediately prior to administration.

USE

Glucocorticoids have been used in neonates for congenital adrenal hyperplasia, for hypoglycemia, for BPD to shorten weaning from respirator,[3] for hemangiomatosis, and prior to extubation to reduce laryngeal edema and stridor.[1–4]

MECHANISM OF ACTION

Prednisone is an oral, intermediate-acting (biologic activity of 18–36 hours) corticosteroid with glucocorticoid, anti-inflammatory, and mineralocorticoid effects.

Prednisone has fewer mineralocorticoid effects than hydrocortisone, but more than dexamethasone (see Table 1-18, page 182).

ADVERSE EFFECTS

Acute: Acute adverse effects are unlikely (except in cases of too-rapid withdrawal after prolonged use; see **Acute Adrenal Insufficiency** below).

With Prolonged Use: Adrenal suppression, including severe growth retardation; hypokalemic alkalosis; sodium retention; hypertension; hyperglycemia; increased susceptibility to infections; cataracts; myopathy; hypocalcemia; peptic ulcer; osteoporosis with bone fractures; nephrocalcinosis; nephrolithiasis; acute pancreatitis; pseudotumor cerebri; and left ventricular hypertrophy. Use every-other-day treatment to reduce growth retardation and other adverse effects in patients on chronic corticosteroid therapy.

Acute Adrenal Insufficiency: Acute pituitary-adrenal insufficiency results from too-rapid withdrawal of corticosteroids after prolonged (>7–10 days) use.[4] Taper dose gradually if infant has received steroids for longer than 7–10 days.

Pituitary-adrenal integrity can be assessed by use of cosyntropin (ACTH). (See cosyntropin monograph.)

Pharmacokinetics/Pharmacodynamics

Absorption: Well absorbed.

Onset of Action: Several hours. For planned extubation, begin corticosteroid 12–24 hours prior to extubation.

Half-life: 18–36 hours.

Nursing Implications

Monitor blood pressure, serum electrolytes, and fluid status and for hyperglycemia after dose.

Monitor for signs and symptoms of infection.

Monitor growth parameters such as head circumference, length, and weight weekly and plot on growth curve.

Monitor for glucose spillage in urine.

References

1. Benitz WE, and Tatro DS. 1995. *The Pediatric Drug Handbook,* 3rd ed. St. Louis: Mosby-Year Book, 436–438.

2. Collaborative Dexamethasone Trial Group. 1991. Dexamethasone therapy in neonatal chronic lung disease: An international placebo-controlled trial. *Pediatrics* 88(3): 421–427.

3. Avery GB, et al 1985. Controlled trial of dexamethasone in respirator-dependent infants with bronchopulmonary dysplasia. *Pediatrics* 75(1): 106–111.

4. Roberts RJ. 1984. *Drug Therapy in Infants: Pharmacologic Principles and Clinical Experience.* Philadelphia: WB Saunders, 296–299.

PROPRANOLOL (INDERAL)
(proe-PRAN-oh-lole)

CARDIOVASCULAR: ANTIARRHYTHMIC; ANTIHYPERTENSIVE; BETA-ADRENERGIC BLOCKER

DOSE

Cardiac Arrhythmias:

- *IV:* 0.01–0.15 mg/kg/dose. *Usual dose:* 0.1 mg/kg/dose. Repeat every 4–8 hours, if needed. *Maximum:* 1 mg/dose.[1,2]
- *PO:* 0.05–2 mg/kg/day divided every 6–8 hours. Begin with 0.25 mg/kg/dose, with frequent monitoring of blood pressure and heart rate response.
- Use caution and begin with a low initial dose because the most dramatic cardiac effects occur at the beginning of treatment. Then increase the dose daily as needed.[1]
- *Other doses have been recommended for cardiac arrhythmias:*
  - The manufacturer states a usual oral dose of 2–4 mg/kg/day divided every 12 hours. *Maximum:* 16 mg/kg/day.[3]
  - Strasburger states that a usual oral maintenance dose for antiarrhythmia is 2–6 mg/kg/day divided every 6 hours.[2]

Hypertension:

- *IV:* 0.01–0.15 mg/kg/dose. *Usual dose:* 0.1 mg/kg/dose. Repeat every 6–8 hours, if needed. *Maximum:* 1 mg/dose.[4]
- *PO: Initial dose:* 0.5–1 mg/kg/24 hours divided every 6–12 hours. Monitor the blood pressure to see what the dosing interval should be. Infants with slow hepatic metabolism may require a dose only once or twice a day. Begin with 0.25 mg/kg/dose with frequent monitoring of blood pressure and heart rate response. Use caution when giving the first dose because the most dramatic cardiac effects occur at the beginning of treatment. The dose can then be increased daily as needed and tolerated. *Usual dose:* 2–4 mg/kg/day. *Maximum:* 16 mg/kg/day, or 60 mg/day. Up to 30 days of treatment may be required for maximum effect.[1,3,4]

Tetralogy of Fallot Hypoxemic Spells:

- *IV (acute):* 0.15–0.25 mg/kg/dose by slow push. If needed, dose may be repeated once after 15 minutes.
- *PO (maintenance):* 1–2 mg/kg/dose every 6 hours, as needed.

Garson and colleagues recommend an initial dose of 1 mg/kg/day (0.25 mg/kg every 6 hours) the first week of treatment.[5] If this is ineffective, they recommend increasing the dose in increments of 1 mg/kg/day to a maximum of 5 mg/kg/day, allowing 24 hours at each new dose. If the patient has initial control of spells and then becomes refractory, the dose may be increased slowly to a maximum of 10–15 mg/kg/day with frequent monitoring of heart size, heart rate, and cardiac contractility.

Thyrotoxicosis (Neonatal Graves' Disease):

- *PO:* 2 mg/kg/day divided every 6 hours. Begin with 0.25 mg/kg/dose given every 6 hours. May increase daily as needed. *Maximum:* 4 mg/kg/day. Use with antithyroid agents (see **CAUTIONS/CONTRAINDICATIONS** below).[1,6–10]
- Monitor the infant carefully, and individualize the dose because it may vary greatly from patient to patient and because neonatal thyrotoxicosis varies in severity.[6]

Reduce dose in hepatic dysfunction.

For infants who are NPO for surgery or other reasons, an IV propranolol dose one-tenth the current oral dose may temporarily be substituted.

ADMINISTRATION

Supplied as:

- *Injection:* 1 mg/ml.
- *Oral liquid:* 4 mg/ml, 8 mg/ml, and the concentrate at 80 mg/ml.
- *Tablets:* 10 mg.

IV—*Rate:* Infuse over 10 minutes with continuous ECG and blood pressure monitoring. *Maximum:* 1 mg/minute.

IV—*Concentration:* May give undiluted (1 mg/ml) or diluted with saline or dextrose.

PO: Administer with feedings. Dilute the concentrated oral solution (80 mg/ml) with water, juice, applesauce, or feedings just before administration. Do not store after mixing.

- Once the dose reaches 10 mg every 6 hours, propranolol tablets, rather than liquid, may be used.[6] Effectiveness of the liquid and the tablet preparations is reported to be similar.[11] The tablet may be crushed and mixed with a small amount of feeding just prior to administration.[12] Use of solid dosage forms improves accuracy, reduces errors in computation and liquid dose measurement, and eliminates spills and mess.

Storage: Protect from light.

CAUTIONS/CONTRAINDICATIONS

Do not use propranolol in patients with hyperactive airways, chronic lung disease, asthma, second- or third-degree AV block, shock, obstructive pulmonary disease, heart failure, or hypoglycemia.[13,14]

Use with caution in severe hepatic dysfunction.

Intravenous propranolol should be reserved for emergencies; use the oral route of administration whenever possible.[3]

Use caution when changing between the oral and IV routes of administration. The IV dose is approximately one-tenth the oral dose (1 mg PO = 0.1 mg IV).

Example: An infant is receiving propranolol 2 mg PO every 6 hours for cardiac arrhythmias. However, the nurse observes that the infant is now not tolerating enteral feedings or oral medications and notifies the physician. The on-call house officer writes this order:

"Change propranolol to IV until tolerating feedings."
What is wrong with the order?

Answer: The IV dose should be much smaller than the oral dose because of first-pass clearance by the liver (see **PHARMACOKINETICS/PHARMACODYNAMICS** below). The order written by the house officer implies that the same dose should be given IV as PO. Serious cardiovascular toxicity could result from such an IV dose. The new order should have stated the IV dose and precautions as follows:

"Change propranolol to 0.2 mg IV every 6 hours. Infuse over 10 minutes. Monitor blood pressure and ECG."

When the infant is again tolerating oral medications, the drug should be re-ordered PO at the higher oral dose that the infant was previously receiving.

When discontinuing maintenance propranolol, taper gradually over 1–2 weeks. Hypertensive crisis may occur in patients receiving the drug for treatment of hypertension if the drug is discontinued abruptly.

Propranolol may mask the tachycardia caused by hypoglycemia or thyrotoxicosis. Use with caution in infants susceptible to hypoglycemia, especially those receiving insulin, because propranolol slows recovery of glucose concentration.[1]

Propranolol may exacerbate congestive heart failure.

Overdose—Treatment of: The following may be helpful: *atropine* for severe brady-cardia with hypotension;[3] *dopamine, dobutamine, epinephrine, norepinephrine,* or *isoproterenol* for chronotropic and inotropic support and treatment of severe hypotension (severe β-blockade may reduce or eliminate the effectiveness of these sympathomimetic agents); *isoproterenol* and/or *aminophylline* for bron-chospasm;[3] *glucagon* may be useful for bradycardia and hypotension because it has inotropic and some chronotropic effects; *transvenous pacing* may be needed for heart block;[13] *IV glucose* for hypoglycemia; *lorazepam* for seizures. *Calcium chloride* may improve cardiac and hemodynamic status.[15]

Propranolol should not be used alone to treat neonatal thyrotoxicosis, but as an adjunct to other antithyroid agents (strong iodine solution [Lugol's], pro-pylthiouracil, methimazole, sodium ipodate).[16,17] Propranolol controls the signs and symptoms of hyperthyroidism, such as tachycardia, but not thyroid function.[1,6–9]

USE

Treatment of *hypertension* (patients with high-renin hypertension are most likely to respond because the renin-angiotensin system activity is regulated, in part, by β-adrenergic-mediated stimulation of renin secretion) and of *cardiac arrhyth-mias* (supraventricular tachycardia,[2] premature ventricular contractions, tachy-cardia, digoxin-induced arrhythmias, idiopathic hypertrophic subaortic stenosis [IHSS]).[11] Used with digoxin to treat supraventricular tachycardia. Has been used alone or with digoxin to control atrial flutter or atrial fibrillation.[1] Prevents hypoxemic spells in infants with *tetralogy of Fallot.*

Used as an adjunctive agent in the treatment of *neonatal thyrotoxicosis* (neonatal Graves' disease), especially in the interval before specific antithyroid drugs become effective. It is used to treat sinus tachycardia associated with thyrotoxicosis. Abrupt withdrawal of propranolol may worsen symptoms.[6,8,9]

Used in patients with *pheochromocytoma* when there is significant persistent tachycardia or when arrhythmias recur frequently. β-blockade with propranolol should never be used in patients with pheochromocytoma without first creating α-adrenergic blockade, such as with phentolamine (Regitine).[18]

MECHANISM OF ACTION

Cardiac-Respiratory Effects: Propranolol is a nonselective (blocks both β_1 receptors in the heart and the bronchodilator/vasodilator β_2 receptors) β-adrenergic blocking agent. Drugs that are specific β_1 blockers are termed *cardioselective* because cardiac β-adrenergic innervation is β_1 in type.[19] Propranolol increases the effective refractory period of the AV node because of its β-blocking action. It is a Class II antiarrhythmic.[2] It inhibits adrenergic stimuli by competitively blocking β-adrenergic receptors within the myocardium and bronchial and vascular smooth muscle. Propranolol decreases heart rate, cardiac contractility, conduction, and cardiac output. It increases airway resistance in the lung.

Mechanism in Reducing Hypertension: Propranolol reduces cardiac output, reduces heart rate, and impairs release of norepinephrine from adrenergic nerve terminals following sympathetic nerve stimulation. It also reduces plasma renin activity by inhibiting secretion of renin by the kidney.

Metabolic Effects: Propranolol modifies carbohydrate and lipid metabolism and inhibits glycogenolysis in the heart and skeletal muscle.[1] Propranolol may impair glycogenolysis and the hyperglycemic response to endogenous epinephrine, leading to persistence of hypoglycemia and delayed recovery of blood glucose to normal levels. Propranolol decreases the release of insulin in response to hyperglycemia.[13]

ADVERSE EFFECTS

Adverse effects of propranolol are usually dose related and are extensions of the drug's β-adrenergic blocking action. Careful patient selection can help avoid two important adverse effects: heart failure and increase in airway resistance.[1] The incidence of adverse effects in children is low.[19]

Cardiovascular: Acute heart failure (especially on initiation of therapy; begin with small doses), hypotension, bradycardia,[7] heart block, asystole, depressed myocardial contractility, reduced peripheral perfusion, decreased cardiac output (rare), proarrhythmia (drug-induced worsening of arrhythmias).

CNS: Weakness, lethargy, sleep disturbances, agitation, seizures.

Endocrine: Hypoglycemia and inhibition of warning signs of hypoglycemia (tachycardia, palpitations, hunger); altered serum lipoprotein concentrations, such as elevated triglycerides and reduced high-density lipoproteins (HDL).

GI: GI upset, diarrhea, constipation, vomiting.[9]

Hematologic: Agranulocytosis (rare).

Respiratory: Increase in airway resistance, aggravation of pulmonary insufficiency in patients with chronic lung disease.[19]

PHARMACOKINETICS/PHARMACODYNAMICS

Absorption: Almost completely absorbed. The drug is equally effective when given IV as PO, but there are marked differences in dose between these two routes. Oral bioavailability may be increased (a higher serum concentration may be achieved with a given dose) in children with Down syndrome.[3] However, this may not always be true: Three infants with Down syndrome in one study had nontoxic serum concentrations of 96–132 ng/ml at a dose range of 3–4 mg/kg/day.[5]

Onset of Action:

- *IV:* 2–5 minutes.
- *PO:* 30–60 minutes.

Duration of Action: The antihypertensive effect does not correlate well with plasma concentration and exceeds the duration that would be expected based on the drug's half-life.[19]

Protein Binding: 70 percent in infants.[1]

Metabolism: Hepatic, some to active metabolites, including 4-hydroxypropranolol. Bioavailability is significantly reduced by first-pass clearance by the liver, so only about 30 percent of the dose reaches the systemic circulation. Because of the first-pass effect, plasma drug concentrations are much lower after oral dosing than after IV administration.[19] Children with Down syndrome may have a genetically linked defect in propranolol metabolism or elimination.[1]

Lipid Solubility: High. (Lipid solubility is an estimate of the drug's ability to penetrate the CNS and of its likelihood of causing adverse CNS effects.)[19]

Half-life: 2–5 hours. Half-life is prolonged in liver dysfunction.

Elimination: Urine.

NURSING IMPLICATIONS

Monitor blood pressure, blood glucose, heart rate, ECG.

Observe for worsening of respiratory status.

Watch decimal point when changing between IV and oral routes of administration.

COMMENTS

Interactions:

- Effects of propranolol may be **reduced** by: *rifampin,*[3] *aluminum hydroxide gel, barbiturates, colestipol, cholestyramine, indomethacin.*

- Effects of propranolol may be **increased** by: *cimetidine;* the antihypertensive effect is potentiated by concurrent administration of a blood pressure lowering drug *(calcium channel blocking agents, clonidine, diazoxide, hydralazine).*

- Concurrent use of *insulin* may impair glycemic control.[13] (See also **MECHANISM OF ACTION** above.)

- Concurrent administration of *halothane* may increase risk of cardiac depression and hypotension.[13]

- Concurrent use of *amiodarone, flecainide, or IV phenytoin* may potentiate cardiodepressant effects.[13]

- Concurrent use with nondepolarizing neuromuscular blocking agents *(atracurium, pancuronium, vecuronium)* may potentiate and prolong the effects of the neuromuscular block.

- Concurrent administration of *lidocaine* may reduce lidocaine elimination and increase lidocaine serum concentrations. Monitor lidocaine serum concentrations, and adjust dose as indicated to prevent toxicity.[3]

- Concurrent use of *aminophylline* or *theophylline* with propranolol may result in mutual inhibition of therapeutic effects; in addition, aminophylline or theophylline clearance may be decreased.[3]

- For sympathomimetic agents with β-adrenergic effects, propranolol may antagonize:
  - $β_1$-adrenergic cardiac effects *(dobutamine, dopamine)*
  - $β_2$-adrenergic bronchodilating effect *(albuterol, isoetharine, isoproterenol, metaproterenol, terbutaline)*
  - both *(isoproterenol)*[3]

- For sympathomimetic agents with both α- and β-adrenergic effects *(epinephrine, norepinephrine, phenylephrine),* β-blockade may result in unopposed β-adrenergic activity with risk of hypertension, excessive bradycardia, and possible heart block.[3] Propranolol does not inhibit the renal vasodilation of dopamine because this effect is mediated by dopaminergic receptors. Vasodilation by nitroglycerin and other direct-acting vasodilators is also not affected.[1]

Therapeutic Range: 20–100 ng/ml.[1,2]

REFERENCES

1. Roberts RJ. 1984. *Drug Therapy in Infants: Pharmacologic Principles and Clinical Experience.* Philadelphia: WB Saunders, 212–213, 314–315.

2. Strasburger JF. 1991. Cardiac arrhythmias in childhood: Diagnostic considerations and treatment. *Drugs* 42(6): 974–983.

3. Medical Economics Data. 2000. *Physicians' Desk Reference.* Montvale, New Jersey: Medical Economics, 3248–3250.

4. Goble MM. 1993. Hypertension in infancy. *Pediatric Clinics of North America* 40(1): 105–122.

5. Garson A Jr, Gillette PC, and McNamara DC. 1981. Propranolol: The preferred palliation for tetralogy of Fallot. *American Journal of Cardiology* 47(5): 1098–1104.

6. Gardner LI. 1980. Is propranolol alone really beneficial in neonatal thyrotoxicosis? Bradycardia and hypoglycemia evoke the doctrine of primum non nocere. *American Journal of Diseases of Children* 134(9): 819–820.

7. Newman TJ, Virnig NL, and Athinarayanan PR. 1980. Complications of propranolol use in neonatal thyrotoxicosis. *American Journal of Diseases of Children* 134(7): 707–708.

8. Smith CS, and Howard NJ. 1973. Propranolol in treatment of neonatal thyrotoxicosis. *Journal of Pediatrics* 83(6): 1046–1048.

9. Pearl KN, and Chambers TL. 1977. Propranolol treatment of thyrotoxicosis in a premature infant. *British Medical Journal* 2(6089): 738.

10. Zimmerman D. 1999. Fetal and neonatal hyperthyroidism. *Thyroid* 9(7): 727–733.

11. Gillette P, et al. 1978. Oral propranolol treatment in infants and children. *Journal of Pediatrics* 92(1): 141–144.

12. Strom JG Jr, and Miller SW. 1990. Stability of drugs with enteral nutrient formulas. *DICP: The Annals of Pharmacotherapy* 24(2): 130–134.

13. United States Pharmacopeial Convention/USP DI. 2000. *Drug Information for the Health Care Professional,* 20th ed. Rockville, Maryland: United States Pharmacopeial Convention, 605–621.

14. Bartosh SM, and Aronson AJ. 1999. Childhood hypertension. An update on etiology, diagnosis, and treatment. *Pediatric Clinics of North America* 46(2): 235–252.

15. Brimacombe JR, Scully M, and Swainston R. 1991. Propranolol overdose—A dramatic response to calcium chloride. *Medical Journal of Australia* 155(4): 267–268.

16. Fort PF, and Brown RS. 1996. Thyroid disorders in infancy. In *Pediatric Endocrinology,* 3rd ed., Lifshitz F, ed. New York: Marcel Dekker, 369–381.

17. Joshi R, and Kulin HE. 1993. Treatment of neonatal Graves' disease with sodium ipodate: A case report. *Clinical Pediatrics* 32(3): 181–184.

18. Voorhess ML. 1996. Adrenal medulla, sympathetic nervous system, and multiple endocrine neoplasia syndromes. In *Rudolph's Pediatrics,* 20th ed., Rudolph AM, Hoffman J, and Rudolph CD, eds. Stamford, Connecticut: Appleton & Lange, 1742–1750.

19. Sinaiko AR. 1993. Pharmacologic management of childhood hypertension. *Pediatric Clinics of North America* 40(1): 195–212.

PROTAMINE
(PROE-tuh-meen)

ANTIDOTE:
HEPARIN OVERDOSE

DOSE

1 mg for each 115 units of intestinal heparin or each 90 units of lung heparin. *Maximum:* 50 mg.

If time has elapsed since IV heparin injection, use a smaller dose because heparin has a short half-life (i.e., give half the usual dose if 30 minutes have elapsed since the heparin was given; give one-fourth the usual dose if more than 2 hours have elapsed). The half-life of heparin is 1–3 hours; half-life is shorter in preterm infants and in infants with thrombosis.[1,2]

Repeat doses may be needed (see **NURSING IMPLICATIONS** below).

ADMINISTRATION

IV—*Rate:* May be given slowly IV over 3 minutes, but infusion over 10 minutes is preferred. Monitor blood pressure during infusion; slow infusion if hypotension occurs.

IV—*Concentration:* May give undiluted (10 mg/ml), or may dilute further in D_5W or NS.

Compatible with: Dextrose 5 percent, sodium chloride.

Storage: Must be refrigerated.

CAUTIONS/CONTRAINDICATIONS

Severe hypotension and anaphylactoid reaction can result from rapid IV administration. Be ready to treat shock.

USE

As an antidote for heparin overdose.

MECHANISM OF ACTION

Protamine is derived from the sperm of salmon and other fish. Alone, protamine (which is strongly basic) has an *anticoagulant* effect, but when given with heparin (which is strongly acidic), a stable salt forms, resulting in loss of the anticoagulant effect of both drugs.

ADVERSE EFFECTS

Bradycardia, pulmonary hypertension, flushing, warmth, and dyspnea may also occur with too-rapid administration.

Paradoxical anticoagulation may occur with high doses of protamine because the protamine binds to platelets and various proteins such as fibrinogen.[3]

PHARMACOKINETICS/PHARMACODYNAMICS

Onset of Action: Neutralizes heparin within 5 minutes.

Duration of Action: 2 hours.

Nursing Implications

Monitor for hypotension and bradycardia.

Monitor for reversal of heparin effects using activated PTT.

Continue to monitor the infant's coagulation status for 24 hours after protamine has been given. Recurrence of bleeding has occurred 30 minutes to 18 hours after cardiac surgery despite complete neutralization of heparin with protamine.[4] Repeat dosing may be required.

References

1. McDonald MM, Jacobson LJ, and Hay WW Jr. 1981. Heparin clearance in the newborn. *Pediatric Research* 15(7): 1015–1018.

2. McDonald MM, and Hathaway WE. 1982. Anticoagulant therapy by continuous heparinization in newborn and older infants. *Journal of Pediatrics* 101(3): 451–457.

3. Roberts RJ. 1984. *Drug Therapy in Infants: Pharmacologic Principles and Clinical Experience.* Philadelphia: WB Saunders, 301.

4. Manufacturer's product literature.

PYRIDOXINE (BEESIX)
(peer-i-DOX-een)

NUTRITION:
VITAMIN SUPPLEMENT

Synonym: vitamin B_6

DOSE

Pyridoxine-Dependent Epilepsy:

- *Initial:* 100 mg/dose IV (preferred) or IM.
- *Maintenance:* 50–100 mg/dose PO given once daily. (The daily maintenance dose ranges from 2 to 200 mg PO, with an average of 50 mg.) Lifelong oral administration of pyridoxine is often required. The dose may need to be increased with age or during illnesses.[1–3]

Diagnosis of Pyridoxine-Dependent Seizures:

1. Administer pyridoxine 100 mg/dose IV slowly.

2. Observe the infant for 30 minutes or up to 1 hour if seizures have not stopped. Seizures typically stop within 10 minutes, although it can take up to 1 hour after the dose for seizures to end.

3. If severe seizures do not stop during the 30-minute test period, administer anticonvulsants.

4. If possible, monitor the EEG with the first dose. The EEG readings will normalize within minutes to several weeks after the dose.

5. If a definite response to pyridoxine occurs, continue pyridoxine 50–100 mg/dose PO once daily. The dose may need to be increased during intercurrent illnesses.

6. To confirm the diagnosis, stop the pyridoxine and monitor the EEG. Seizures usually recur within 1 week in neonates and after 2–14 days in older infants and children.[1,2,4]

Treatment of Acute Isoniazid (INH) Overdose: Give a dose of pyridoxine equal to the amount of INH ingested. Administer IM or IV in divided doses together with other anticonvulsants.

Prevention of Drug-Induced Neuritis (caused by isoniazid, hydralazine): 1–2 mg/kg/day. (See **Treatment/Prevention of Isoniazid Toxicity** under **USE** below.)

Parenteral Nutrition: 0.18 mg/kg/day.[5,6]

Recommended Daily Allowance: Birth to 3 years: 0.3–1 mg/day.[7]

ADMINISTRATION

Supplied as: Injection: 100 mg/ml. Tablet: 25 mg.

Storage: Protect from light.

IV—*Rate:* Infuse slowly over 2 minutes or more.

IV—*Concentration:* May give undiluted or diluted with saline or dextrose.

IM: May give undiluted.

PO: Give with feedings.

- No oral liquid is commercially available. The following formulation has been used to prepare an oral liquid:

Pharmacist Compounding Directions
Pyridoxine Oral Solution 1 mg/ml[8]

Add 1 ml of pyridoxine injection to 99 ml of simple syrup. Dispense in a brown glass bottle.

Stability: 30 days.

Storage: Protect from light. Refrigerate.

CAUTIONS/CONTRAINDICATIONS

Hypersensitivity to pyridoxine or any component of the product.

USE

A water-soluble vitamin used to treat and prevent vitamin B_6 deficiency.

Deficiency of Vitamin B_6: Deficiency is uncommon, even in infancy. It is usually seen in conjunction with deficiency of other B-complex vitamins. Dietary deprivation, gastric resection, or malabsorption of vitamin B_6 (with celiac disease or cystic fibrosis) results in a syndrome that includes a hypochromic, microcytic anemia; vomiting; diarrhea; failure to thrive; listlessness; hyperirritability; and seizures. Deficiency of pyridoxine may lead to xanthurenic aciduria, sideroblastic anemia, neurologic problems, seborrheic dermatitis, and cheilosis.[7]

Intake of vitamin B_6 during the last trimester of pregnancy determines the nutritional state of the infant with respect to this vitamin. Vitamin B_6 levels are greater in cord blood than in maternal blood.

High dietary protein intakes increase the need for the vitamin. Patients on hemodialysis should receive supplementation of vitamin B_6. Goat's milk is deficient in vitamin B_6.[9] Infants receiving unfortified formulas, such as evaporated milk, may need vitamin B_6 supplementation. Pyridoxine supplementation should be administered to breastfeeding infants.[10,11] Vitamin B_6 deficiency is most commonly diagnosed in the breastfed infant of the malnourished, typically adolescent, mother.[9]

Metabolic Dysfunctions: Certain congenital metabolic dysfunctions—cystathioninuria, homocystinuria, hyperoxaluria, xanthurenic aciduria—may respond to vitamin B_6 supplementation.[7]

Differential Diagnosis of Intractable Seizures: Many clinicians advocate the routine use of pyridoxine as a diagnostic approach prior to the use of anticonvulsants in infants with refractory seizures up to the age of 2 years, including those with infantile spasms.[2,4]

Treatment of Pyridoxine-Dependent Epilepsy. Pyridoxine-dependent seizures are unresponsive to the usual anticonvulsant therapy. The seizures are usually intractable until an IV injection of pyridoxine is given; then they rapidly cease. If pyridoxine is not given, the outcome can be fatal, sometimes in status epilepticus. The onset of pyridoxine-dependent seizures is typically at 4 hours of age, although onset can vary from birth to 3 months or even up to 2 years of age. The seizures are usually generalized, but they may be focal and then become generalized. Usually the EEG improves dramatically with administration of pyridoxine, but it may not return to normal for several weeks. An affected fetus can convulse during pregnancy, and the mother may recognize that rhythmic movements quite different from the usual fetal movements are occurring. If the movements are recognized as convulsions, the mother can be given pyridoxine.[3]

Treatment of Other Seizures:

- *Infantile Spasms:* Pyridoxine has not yet been shown by well-controlled trials to have therapeutic value in the management of infantile spasms, and long-term high-dose vitamin B_6 administration could cause adverse effects (see **ADVERSE EFFECTS** below). A study by Pietz and associates reported that 5 of 17 children with infantile spasms responded to high-dose vitamin B_6, 300 mg/kg/day PO. Side effects were mainly gastrointestinal, which were reversible after dose reduction. The authors commented that, considering the life-threatening side effects of treatment with adrenocorticotropic hormone (ACTH)/corticosteroids or valproate, further research using high-dose vitamin B_6 would appear justified.[12]

  Lower doses of pyridoxine (40–50 mg/kg/day) combined with low doses of ACTH (0.4 unit/kg/day) have been tried, with results similar to those achieved with high doses of ACTH.[4]

- *Recurrent Seizures:* In a randomized controlled study involving 90 infants and children with recurrent seizures, 40 were given high-dose pyridoxine (30–50 mg/kg/day) by IV infusion; 50 were control patients. Other antiepileptic therapy was similar in the two groups. Response rates in the pyridoxine and control groups were 92 versus 64 percent, respectively. No adverse effects were observed. The authors concluded that pyridoxine is a safe, effective, well-tolerated, and relatively inexpensive adjunct to routine antiepileptic drugs for treatment of recurrent seizures in children.[13]

Treatment/Prevention of Isoniazid Toxicity. Infants receiving isoniazid who are malnourished, those on milk-deficient diets, and breastfeeding infants (particularly if the mother is malnourished) may require pyridoxine supplementation to prevent peripheral neuropathy because isoniazid binds to vitamin B_6.[10,11] Pyridoxine is also used as an antidote for isoniazid overdose to terminate seizures (in conjunction with other anticonvulsants) and/or coma, prevent neuropathy, and increase excretion of the drug.[7] Isoniazid-induced seizures are thought to result from decreased γ-aminobutyric acid (GABA) within the central nervous system, possibly because isoniazid inhibits brain pyridoxal 5'-phosphate activity.

MECHANISM OF ACTION

Pyridoxine is required for the synthesis of niacin, neurotransmitters (histamine, serotonin, dopamine, norepinephrine, and GABA), heme, and prostaglandins.

Other metabolic functions include carbohydrate, protein, and fat utilization and immune development. The vitamin B_6 requirement is tied to the protein intake (20 mcg/gm of dietary protein).

Mechanism in Pyridoxine-Dependent Seizures: A pyridoxine-dependent seizure disorder is an autosomal recessive trait. It results from a defective binding of pyridoxine to its apoenzyme, glutamate decarboxylase, which catalyzes the conversion of glutamic acid to GABA. GABA acts as an inhibitory neurotransmitter in the central nervous system. Therefore, the seizure threshold is lower in infants with reduced concentrations of GABA. Administration of pyridoxine corrects the GABA deficiency.[14]

ADVERSE EFFECTS

Therapeutic doses are very well tolerated.

Occasional allergic reactions have occurred.

CNS:

- Somnolence.
- Seizures may occur with IV administration of very large doses.
- Exposure to large doses of vitamin B_6 *in utero* has been implicated in pyridoxine-dependent seizures in the neonate. (Nausea and vomiting of pregnancy are sometimes treated with pyridoxine.)[7]

Dermatologic: Local burning or stinging at injection site following IM or subcutaneous administration.

GI: Nausea.

Hematologic: Low serum folic acid concentrations.

Hepatic: Increased AST (SGOT).

Neuromuscular: Decreased sensation to touch, temperature, and vibration; paresthesia; severe hypotonia. Adverse reactions (neuropathy) to an average dose of 50 mg/day used to treat pyridoxine-dependent seizures are unlikely, but adverse effects may occur after very high doses and possibly with relatively low doses taken over a long time.[3]

Overdose of Vitamin B_6: Although pyridoxine is usually nontoxic at therapeutic doses, chronic (>2 months) administration of large doses can cause severe sensory neuropathy. Symptoms lessen over the 6-month period following discontinuation of the drug.

PHARMACOKINETICS/PHARMACODYNAMICS

Absorption: Well absorbed from the GI tract by passive diffusion in the jejunum and then transported to the liver, where it is converted to its active form, pyridoxal 5'-phosphate.[6,9]

Metabolism: The vitamin exists in three forms, which are interconverted *in vivo*: *pyridoxine, pyridoxal* (the chief metabolite), *pyridoxamine*, and the phosphorylated forms of the last two. Dephosphorylation occurs by alkaline phosphatase in the liver, predominantly to 4-pyridoxic acid, which is excreted in the urine.[6,9]

Protein Binding: Pyridoxal phosphate and pyridoxal are highly bound to plasma protein, whereas pyridoxine is not.

Half-life (biologic): 15–20 days.

Elimination: Urine, almost entirely as metabolites.[6,7,9] The excess beyond daily needs is excreted, largely unchanged, in the urine.[7] Removed by dialysis.

Nursing Implications

Monitor respiratory rate, heart rate, and blood pressure during IV administration of large doses.

Comments

Infant oral multivitamin drops (Poly-Vi-Sol) contain 0.4 mg vitamin B_6/ml.

Interactions: May decrease serum levels of phenobarbital and phenytoin.

Benzyl Alcohol Content: Pyridoxine injection contains benzyl alcohol 1.5 percent (= 15 mg/ml or 15 mg/100 mg pyridoxine). Oral, rather than IV, administration is preferred for maintenance doses to reduce risk of benzyl alcohol toxicity and other adverse effects, particularly in preterm infants. Benzyl alcohol is associated with the fatal gasping syndrome of metabolic acidosis, as well as with central nervous system, respiratory, circulatory, and renal impairment.[15] A toxic benzyl alcohol dose is approximately 100–400 mg/kg/day.

References

1. Bankier A, Turner M, and Hopkins IJ. 1983. Pyridoxine-dependent seizures—a wider clinical spectrum. *Archives of Disease in Childhood* 58(6): 415–418.

2. Roberts RJ. 1984. *Drug Therapy in Infants: Pharmacologic Principles and Clinical Experience.* Philadelphia: WB Saunders, 113.

3. Gordon N. 1997. Pyridoxine dependency: An update. *Developmental Medicine and Child Neurology* 39(1): 63–65.

4. Bourgeois BF. 1995. Antiepileptic drugs in pediatric practice. *Epilepsia* 36(supplement 2): S34–S45.

5. Greene HL, et al. 1988. Guidelines for the use of vitamins, trace elements, calcium, magnesium and phosphorus in infants and children receiving total parenteral nutrition: Report of the Subcommittee on Pediatric Parenteral Nutrient Requirements from the Committee on Clinical Practice Issues of the American Society for Clinical Nutrition. *American Journal of Clinical Nutrition* 48(5): 1324–1342.

6. Greene HL, and Smidt LJ. 1993. Water-soluble vitamins: C, B_1, B_2, B_6, niacin, pantothenic acid, and biotin. In *Nutritional Needs of the Preterm Infant: Scientific Basis and Practical Guidelines,* Tsang RC, et al., eds. Baltimore: Lippincott Williams & Wilkins, 121–133.

7. United States Pharmacopeial Convention/USP DI. 1996. *Drug Information for the Health Care Professional,* 16th ed. Rockville, Maryland: United States Pharmacopeial Convention, 2517–2520.

8. Nahata MC, and Hipple TF. 1992. *Pediatric Drug Formulations,* 2nd ed. Cincinnati: Harvey Whitney Books, 65.

9. Schanler RJ. 1988. Water-soluble vitamins: C, B_1, B_2, B_6, niacin, biotin, and pantothenic acid. In *Nutrition During Infancy,* Tsang RC, and Nichols BL, eds. Philadelphia: Hanley & Belfus, 236–252.

10. American Academy of Pediatrics, Committee on Infectious Diseases. 1992. Chemotherapy for tuberculosis in infants and children. *Pediatrics* 89(1): 161–165.

11. Heiskanen K, et al. 1996. Risk of low vitamin B_6 status in infants breast-fed exclusively beyond six months. *Journal of Pediatric Gastroenterology and Nutrition* 23(1): 38–44.

12. Pietz J, et al. 1993. Treatment of infantile spasms with high-dosage vitamin B_6. *Epilepsia* 34(4): 757–763.

13. Jiao FY, et al. 1997. Randomized controlled trial of high-dose intravenous pyridoxine in the treatment of recurrent seizures in children. *Pediatric Neurology* 17(1): 54–57.

14. Minns R. 1980. Vitamin B$_6$ deficiency and dependency. *Developmental Medicine and Child Neurology* 22(6): 795–799.

15. American Academy of Pediatrics, Committee on Drugs. 1985. "Inactive" ingredients in pharmaceutical products. *Pediatrics* 76(4): 635–643.

P

TABLE OF CONTENTS

R

RANITIDINE (ZANTAC)
(ra-NIT-ti-deen)

GASTROINTESTINAL:
HISTAMINE (H_2) ANTAGONIST

DOSE

PO: 2–4 mg/kg/day divided every 8–12 hours.[1–3]
   Maximum PO dose: 6 mg/kg/day divided every 6 hours.

IV (Preferred) or IM: 1–2 mg/kg/day divided every 6–8 hours. *Maximum IV dose:*
6 mg/kg/day divided every 6 hours.[2,4,5]

- Wiest and associates recommend 0.7 mg/kg/dose IV every 6 hours
  (= 2.8 mg/kg/day) infused over 20 minutes. They found a large degree of
  variability in pharmacokinetic parameters in their patients.[6]

Continuous IV Infusion (preferred over intermittent dosing):
   0.06–0.17 mg/kg/hour (= 1.44–4 mg/kg/day).[7–9]
   Maximum: 6 mg/kg/day.[5]

- Kelly and associates found that an IV infusion of 0.063 mg/kg/hour
  (= 1.5 mg/kg/day) was sufficient to increase and maintain gastric pH above
  4 in preterm infants receiving dexamethasone. There was no benefit from a
  higher dose of 0.125 mg/kg/hour (= 3 mg/kg/day).[9]

- Fontana and associates estimate that a continuous IV infusion of
  0.03–0.06 mg/kg/hour (= 0.7–1.44 mg/kg/day) in term newborns will achieve
  serum concentrations greater than 100–200 ng/ml.[10]

- A dose of 0.2 mg/kg/hour stopped GI hemorrhage in a 30-week-gestational-
  age newborn with anuria.[11]

Reduce dose or prolong interval in renal impairment.

Adjust to lowest dose that will maintain pH of gastric secretions above 4.

Continuous intragastric monitoring of gastric pH with a pH-sensitive electrode
   avoids problems associated with variability of gastric pH, changes in serum
   concentrations of H_2 blockers, and other problems associated with intermittent
   pH determinations.[5]

ADMINISTRATION

IV—*Rate:* May infuse IV over at least 5 minutes, but infusion over 15–30 minutes
   is preferred.

IV—*Concentration:* Dilute to at least 2.5 mg/ml.

Continuous Infusion: May infuse continuously over 24 hours. May also be given
   by continuous infusion by syringe pump or added to parenteral nutrition
   solution.

IV—*Compatibility:* May admix IV dose with parenteral nutrition solution for
   infusion over 24 hours. Be sure that intermittent IV doses of ranitidine are not
   also being given. See Appendix E: Y-Site Compatibility of Common NICU
   Drugs.

IM: May give undiluted.

PO: Oral liquid available at 15 mg/ml (7.5 percent alcohol).[12]

Use

For treatment of gastroesophageal reflux, gastric hypersecretory states, and upper GI mucosal lesions. Also used for prophylaxis of stress-induced gastric mucosal injury.[5,13,14]

Comparison with Cimetidine: Ranitidine is more potent than cimetidine and longer acting. Unlike cimetidine, ranitidine has not been associated with effects on hepatic drug metabolism, endocrine function, the immune system, or the central nervous system and therefore has fewer adverse effects and drug interactions. Ranitidine is not likely to increase theophylline levels as cimetidine does.

Mechanism of Action

Ranitidine is an H_2 blocker that is a reversible, competitive antagonist of the action of histamine on H_2 receptors. It inhibits gastric acid secretion and reduces the volume of gastric juice and its hydrogen ion concentration. Within 24 hours of birth, the preterm infant is capable of producing a gastric pH of less than 2.[9]

Adverse Effects

Usually well tolerated.[1,4]

May cause abdominal symptoms such as diarrhea or constipation, rash, and dizziness.

Uncommonly, causes a decrease in white blood cell and platelet count and increased transaminase levels.

Hypotension may occur with IV infusion over less than 5 minutes.

Tolerance to the acid-inhibiting effects of ranitidine after 2–6 weeks of continuous IV therapy has been reported in infants treated for gastric hypersecretion associated with short-bowel syndrome.[15]

Pharmacokinetics/Pharmacodynamics

Absorption: Complete and rapid, but first-pass metabolism decreases bioavailability to 50 percent; therefore, larger doses need to be given when converting from IV or IM to PO.

Volume of Distribution: 1.61 liters/kg.

Peak Effect: 1–2 hours.

Protein Binding: 15 percent.

Half-life: 3.5 hours in term newborns,[10] 2.8 hours in infants aged 6 weeks to 6 months,[15] 2 hours in older infants up to 21 months of age.[6] Half-life is prolonged with renal dysfunction.

Elimination: Mostly unchanged in the urine (70 percent).[1,2,6]

Nursing Implications

Monitor for response to therapy, including decreased irritability from reflux and prevention of stress ulcer.

Monitor hepatic and renal function.

COMMENTS

Ranitidine is usually not needed when the infant is receiving approximately 90 ml/kg/day or more of feedings, because of the buffering effect of milk.[9]

Consider converting from IV to PO ranitidine as soon as the infant is able to take oral medications, to reduce cost of therapy.

Unlike cimetidine, ranitidine is not likely to increase the half-life and serum concentrations of theophylline, caffeine, and other drugs metabolized in the liver, although idiosyncratic reactions have occurred in some patients.[16]

Interactions: Absorption of ranitidine is decreased slightly when it is given with antacids; doses should be staggered. Food does not affect ranitidine absorption.

REFERENCES

1. Blumer JL, et al. 1985. Pharmacokinetic determination of ranitidine pharmacodynamics in pediatric ulcer disease. *Journal of Pediatrics* 107(2): 301–306. (Erratum appears in *Journal of Pediatrics*, 1986, 108[4]: 630.)

2. Reed MD, Sutphen JL, and Blumer JL. 1992. Drugs used to modulate gastrointestinal function. In *Pediatric Pharmacology: Therapeutic Principles in Practice*, Yaffe SJ, and Aranda JV, eds. Philadelphia: WB Saunders, 437–465.

3. Sutphen JL, and Dillard VL. 1989. Effect of ranitidine on twenty-four-hour gastric acidity in infants. *Journal of Pediatrics* 114(3): 472–474.

4. Lopez-Herce Cid J, et al. 1988. Ranitidine prophylaxis in acute gastric mucosal damage in critically ill pediatric patients. *Critical Care Medicine* 16(6): 591–593.

5. Gedeit RG, Weigle GM, and Havens PL. 1993. Control and variability of gastric pH in critically ill children. *Critical Care Medicine* 21(12): 1850–1855.

6. Wiest DB, et al. 1989. Pharmacokinetics of ranitidine in critically ill infants. *Developmental Pharmacology and Therapeutics* 12(1): 7–12.

7. Benitz WE, and Tatro DS. 1995. *The Pediatric Drug Handbook*, 3rd ed. St. Louis: Mosby-Year Book, 371–373.

8. Eddleston JM, Booker PD, and Green JR. 1989. Use of ranitidine in children undergoing cardiopulmonary bypass. *Critical Care Medicine* 17(1): 26–29.

9. Kelly EJ, et al. 1993. The effect of intravenous ranitidine on the intragastric pH of preterm infants receiving dexamethasone. *Archives of Disease in Childhood* 69(1 spec. no.): 37–39.

10. Fontana M, et al. 1993. Ranitidine pharmacokinetics in newborn infants. *Archives of Disease in Childhood* 68(5 spec. no.): 602–603.

11. Rosenthal M, and Miller PW. 1988. Ranitidine in the newborn. *Archives of Disease in Childhood* 63(1): 88–89.

12. Manufacturer's product literature.

13. Maki M, et al. 1993. High prevalence of asymptomatic esophageal and gastric lesions in preterm infants in intensive care. *Critical Care Medicine* 21(12): 1863–1867.

14. Mallet E, et al. 1989. Use of ranitidine in young infants with gastro-esophageal reflux. *European Journal of Clinical Pharmacology* 36(6): 641–642.

15. Hyman PE, Garvey TQ III, and Abrams CE. 1987. Tolerance to intravenous ranitidine. *Journal of Pediatrics* 110(5): 794–796.

16. Kehoe WA, et al. 1996. Effect of ranitidine on theophylline metabolism in healthy Koreans living in China. *Annals of Pharmacotherapy* 30(2): 133–137.

RESPIRATORY SYNCYTIAL VIRUS IMMUNE GLOBULIN (RESPIGAM)

BIOLOGIC: IMMUNE SERUM

(res-pi-ra-TOR-e SIN-sish-al VYE-rus i-MUNE GLOB-yoo-lin)

Synonym: RSV-IGIV

DOSE

750 mg/kg/dose (= 15 ml/kg/dose) once per month during the respiratory syncytial virus (RSV) season, November through April (unless RSV activity begins earlier or ends later for the particular community).

ADMINISTRATION

Supplied as: Injection: 2,500 mg/50 ml vial (= 50 mg/ml).

IV—*Rate:* 1.5 ml/kg/hour for the first 15 minutes, *then*
3 ml/kg/hour for the next 15 minutes, *then*
6 ml/kg/hour until the end of the infusion.

    Maximum: 6 ml/kg/hour. Infusion completed over 3 hours.

Table 1-43 gives the dose, volume, and infusion rates of RespiGam to administer to infants of various weights during each time period.

IV—*Concentration:* Give undiluted.

IV—*Compatibility:* It is best to infuse RSV-IGIV into a separate line; however, if necessary, may coinfuse (Y-site administration) into a line containing dextrose in concentrations up to $D_{20}W$ with or without saline as long as the coinfusing solution does not dilute the RSV-IGIV more than 1:2. Compatibility with other solutions has not been tested.[1]

Bring to room temperature before administration.

Infusion should start within 6 hours and be completed by 12 hours after vial entry.

A filter is not required for administration. If one is used, pore size should be larger than 15 microns.

Infuse the solution only if it is colorless and not turbid.

Do not shake vial; avoid foaming.

Monitor infant's cardiopulmonary status and vital signs before beginning the infusion, before each rate change, and for 30 minutes after completion of the infusion, especially very ill infants with BPD. Slower rates of infusion may be required.[1]

Storage: Refrigerate.

CAUTIONS/CONTRAINDICATIONS

Do not use in patients who have previously had severe reactions to human immunoglobulin preparations, those with IgA deficiency, or those who are allergic to any component of the product.

TABLE 1-43 ◆ DOSE AND INFUSION RATE OF RESPIRATORY SYNCYTIAL VIRUS IMMUNE GLOBULIN INTRAVENOUS (RESPIGAM)

This chart is based on infusion rates of 1.5 ml/kg/hour for the first 15 minutes, 3 ml/kg/hour from 15–30 minutes and 6 ml/kg/hour from 30 minutes to the end of infusion. (Increase to the next rate only if the patient is tolerating the infusion.)

Weight (kg)	Dose (mg)	Total Volume (ml)	Infusion Rates		
			First 15 Minutes (ml/hour)	15–30 Minutes (ml/hour)	30 Minutes to End of Infusion (ml/hour)
2	1,500	30	3	6	12
2.5	1,875	38	3.8	6	12
3	2,250	45	4.5	9	18
3.5	2,625	53	5.3	10.5	21
4	3,000	60	6	12	24
4.5	3,375	68	6.8	13.5	27
5	3,750	75	7.5	15	30
5.5	4,125	83	8.3	16.5	33
6	4,500	90	9	18	36
6.5	4,875	98	9.8	19.5	39
7	5,250	105	10.5	21	42
7.5	5,625	113	11.3	22.5	45
8	6,000	120	12	24	48
8.5	6,375	128	12.8	25.5	51
9	6,750	135	13.5	27	54
9.5	7,125	143	14.3	28.5	57
10	7,500	150	15	30	60

From: Facts and Comparisons. 1996 (1999 looseleaf edition). *Drug Facts and Comparisons.* St. Louis: Facts and Comparisons, a Wolters Kluwer Company. Reprinted by permission.

❖ RSV-IGIV should not be given to infants with cyanotic congenital heart disease (especially those with right-to-left shunts) because these patients have shown a larger number of severe or life-threatening adverse events.[1,2]

❖ RSV-IGIV is made from human plasma and carries possible risk of blood-borne pathogens.[1]

USE

Prevention of serious lower respiratory tract infection from RSV (see also palivizumab monograph for IM RSV prophylaxis). Consider prophylactic use of RSV-IGIV in patients under 2 years old who have BPD and are receiving oxygen therapy or have received oxygen in the past 6 months and in infants with a gestational age of 32 weeks or less, even if there is no BPD.

RSV-IGIV may be substituted for IGIV during RSV season for severely immunocompromised infants who receive IGIV monthly.

❖ RSV-IGIV is not effective for *treating* RSV infections; its only use is for *prevention*.

RSV-IGIV reduces the number of RSV hospitalizations and reduces the frequency and severity of RSV infections by 40–60 percent.[2–4]

Mechanism of Action

Respiratory syncytial virus immune globulin produces passive immunization to RSV. RSV-IGIV contains immunoglobulin G selected for high titers of neutralizing antibody against RSV from pooled adult human plasma having high titers of neutralizing antibody against RSV.[1]

Adverse Effects

Many of RSV-IGIV's adverse effects relate to the rate of infusion.

Cardiovascular: Tachycardia, blood pressure changes, fluid overload in fluid-sensitive patients. If fluid overload is suspected, stop or slow the infusion. Furosemide should be available for management of fluid overload.

GI: Gastroenteritis, vomiting.

Hypersensitivity: Fever, allergic reactions, rash, anaphylaxis. If severe allergic reaction occurs, discontinue infusion and consider epinephrine and/or diphenhydramine and other supportive treatment as required.

Local: Local injection site inflammation.

Respiratory: Respiratory distress, wheezing.

Other: Aseptic meningitis syndrome may occur (rare), myalgia, arthralgia.

Pharmacokinetics/Pharmacodynamics

Half-life: Mean half-life of serum RSV neutralizing antibodies after RespiGam ranges from 22 to 28 days.

Nursing Implications

Monitor vital signs frequently during administration for increase in heart rate, respiratory rate, retractions, and rales.

Observe vital signs prior to infusion, before each rate increase, and thereafter at 1-hour intervals until 30 minutes after completion of administration.

Observe for fluid overload or allergic reaction during infusion.

Comments

Sodium content is 1–1.5 mEq/50 ml.

Interactions: Immunization with measles-containing vaccines should be delayed for 9 months after the last dose of RSV-IGIV, but no changes need be made in all other routinely given immunizations.[2]

References

1. Manufacturer's product literature.
2. American Academy of Pediatrics, Committee on Infectious Diseases and Committee on Fetus and Newborn. 1997. Respiratory syncytial virus immune globulin intravenous: Indications for use. *Pediatrics* 99(4): 645–650.

3. Groothuis JR, et al. 1993. Prophylactic administration of respiratory syncytial virus immune globulin to high-risk infants and young children. *New England Journal of Medicine* 329(21): 1524–1530.

4. PREVENT Study Group. 1997. Reduction of respiratory syncytial virus hospitalization among premature infants and infants with bronchopulmonary dysplasia using respiratory syncytial virus immune globulin prophylaxis. *Pediatrics* 99(1): 93–99.

Ribavirin (Virazole)

(rye-ba-VYE-rin)

Respiratory: Antiviral

Dose and Administration

Supplied as: 6 gm powder in 100 ml vial. When reconstituted with 300 ml sterile water, the concentration is 20 mg/ml.

Aerosol: Use a Viratek Small Particle Aerosol Generator (SPAG-2) attached to an infant oxygen hood (preferred), face mask, or oxygen tent. The SPAG-2 produces uniform particles 1.2–1.6 microns in diameter.

Administration to Patients on Mechanical Ventilation: Use with caution; the drug may precipitate in the ventilatory apparatus. Precipitation is dependent on temperature, humidity, and electrostatic forces. Deposition can lead to malfunction or obstruction of the expiratory valve, resulting in inadvertently high positive end-expiratory pressures. Use of a one-way valve in the inspiratory line, placement of a breathing circuit filter in the expiratory line, and frequent monitoring and filter replacement by trained staff have been effective in preventing these problems.[1,2]

Standard, Continuous Aerosol Delivery: Pharmacy preparation: Solubilize 6 gm ribavirin with preservative-free sterile water in the 100 ml vial supplied; then transfer to a sterilized 500 ml Erlenmeyer flask. Further dilute to 300 ml with preservative-free sterile water. Administer treatment using the SPAG-2 for 12–20 hours per day for 3–5 days (mean: 4 days; maximum: 7 days).

High-dose, Short-duration Aerosol Administration (nonventilated patients only): 2 gm over 2 hours every 8 hours. Use a concentration of 60 mg/ml (6 gm reconstituted with 100 ml preservative-free sterile water) for 3–7 days. This method maintains accessibility for patient care and limits environmental exposure of health care workers.[3] The efficacy of this method has not been proven.[1,2]

Storage: Reconstituted solution may be stored at room temperature; discard unused reconstituted ribavirin after 24 hours.

Use

An antiviral drug with a wide spectrum of activity against RNA and DNA viruses. Used primarily to treat respiratory syncytial virus (RSV), but also effective for influenza A and B and adenovirus. Indicated for certain hospitalized infants with severe lower respiratory tract infection caused by RSV (see below). (Most infants with RSV infection, even if hospitalized, do not need ribavirin and recover in 3–5 days.) Maximum benefit is derived by early treatment of high-risk patients. RSV infection is seen primarily during the winter and spring months (November through April).

The American Academy of Pediatrics recently revised its recommendations to state that practitioners should decide whether ribavirin therapy is appropriate by taking into account the particular clinical situation and their own preferences. These recommendations may be modified as new information becomes available. Consider ribavirin for the following selected infants at high risk for serious RSV disease:

- Those with congenital heart disease (including pulmonary hypertension) and BPD, cystic fibrosis, and other chronic lung disease. Previously healthy premature infants and those <6 weeks of age are at risk, but less so than those with underlying disease.
- Infants with underlying immunosuppressive diseases or therapy who have high mortality and/or prolonged RSV illness.
- Infants who are severely ill with or without mechanical ventilation. Useful guidelines for judging the degree of severity of RSV infection are blood gas measurements and the infant's response to other therapies.
- Hospitalized infants who may be at increased risk of progressing from a mild to more complicated course because they are younger than 6 weeks or have an underlying condition, such as multiple congenital anomalies or certain neurologic or metabolic diseases (e.g., myasthenia gravis).[1–4]

Use of ribavirin is controversial due to concern for potential toxicity to exposed persons, high cost, the highly variable course of illness, and questions about the efficacy of the drug in treating RSV.[5]

MECHANISM OF ACTION

Ribavirin is a synthetic nucleoside analog resembling guanosine and inosine. It interferes with the expression of messenger RNA and inhibits viral protein synthesis. RSV is an intracellular organism with an MIC of 4–10 mcg/ml.

ADVERSE EFFECTS

No appreciable toxicity has been observed in any controlled trials or other follow-up studies.[2]

Cardiovascular: Cardiac arrest, hypotension.

Dermatologic: Rash, conjunctivitis.

Hematologic: Anemia, reticulocytosis.

Respiratory: Reversible bronchospasm (0.1 percent), worsening of respiratory status, apnea, and pneumothorax.

Adverse Effects in Health Care Workers and Visitors:

- Analysis of whole blood, urine, and erythrocytes of nurses and respiratory therapists suggests that respiratory absorption of ribavirin after environmental exposure is unlikely and that exposure poses little reproductive risk to humans.[1,2,6,7] Administration of aerosolized ribavirin causes considerable environmental contamination, however, because hoods, tents, and masks exhaust ribavirin into the patient's room. The oxygen hood exhausts the highest amount of excess drug into the room air; the mask, next; and the ventilator, the least.
- The following adverse effects have occurred infrequently in health care workers: rash, breathing difficulties, headache, rhinitis, and mucous

membrane irritation. Ocular itchiness, redness, swelling, chemical conjunctivitis, photophobia, blurred vision, irritation (all reversible), and contact lens damage have been reported. Contact lenses may become cloudy from prolonged, high-concentration exposure.[8] Fetal malformations were observed in pregnant rodents administered oral ribavirin.[2] These effects were not reproduced in baboons, however, and have not been reported in humans.[1,2,7]

- The following precautions have been recommended by the American Academy of Pediatrics:[1,2,7]

  - Inform health care personnel and visitors about the potential but unknown risks of environmental exposure to ribavirin.

  - Advise pregnant women not to care directly for patients receiving ribavirin and pregnant visitors not to be in the room when ribavirin is administered.

  - Lower environmental exposure by temporarily stopping ribavirin 5 minutes prior to opening the hood and by administering the drug in a well-ventilated room (at least 6 air changes per hour).[1,2,9]

  - Contact lens wearers should wear tight-fitting protective goggles unless ribavirin is being administered in a mechanically ventilated patient. Alternatively, eyeglasses, rather than contact lenses, should be worn.[8,9]

Standard surgical masks do not block ribavirin particles (1–2 microns in size). Dermal absorption of ribavirin (even in the absence of gloves) appears to be negligible.[2]

PHARMACOKINETICS/PHARMACODYNAMICS

Absorption: About 70 percent of the aerosolized drug is deposited in the respiratory tree. The mean concentration of ribavirin in tracheal secretions after an 8-hour aerosol therapy is more than 1,000 times higher than in plasma and far exceeding the MIC required for common respiratory viruses.[10] After 8–20 hours of aerosolized ribavirin treatment, the mean plasma ribavirin concentration is 1–3 mcg/ml. The average aerosol concentration for 12 hours is 190 mcg/liter of air when using the 20 mg/ml ribavirin solution.

Onset of Action: Improvement may begin in the first 24 hours of therapy. Maximum therapeutic response occurs after 2–4 days of treatment.

Metabolism: The half-life of ribavirin in respiratory secretions is 2 hours.[3,11] Some drug is degraded in plasma and tissues to an inactive form.

Elimination: Mostly unchanged in the urine.

NURSING IMPLICATIONS

Pregnant women should not care directly for patients who are receiving ribavirin.

Warn visitors and all health care personnel about the potential risks of ribavirin.

Health care workers who are pregnant or may become pregnant should be counseled about how to reduce risk from the drug, including alternate job assignments.

Discourage employees and visitors from wearing contact lenses when exposed to ribavirin.

COMMENTS

Discontinuation of Treatment: After 3–7 days or as medical condition warrants. Use the shortest course possible. Depending on the severity of the infection and the clinical state of the patient, discontinue ribavirin if adverse effects occur.

REFERENCES

1. American Academy of Pediatrics, Committee on Infectious Diseases. 1993. Use of ribavirin in the treatment of respiratory syncytial virus infection. *Pediatrics* 92(3): 501–504.

2. American Academy of Pediatrics, Committee on Infectious Diseases. 1997. *Red Book: Report of the Committee on Infectious Diseases*, 24th ed. Elk Grove Village, Illinois: American Academy of Pediatrics, 570–574.

3. Englund JA, et al. 1990. High-dose, short-duration ribavirin aerosol therapy in children with suspected respiratory syncytial virus infection. *Journal of Pediatrics* 117(2 part 1): 313–320.

4. American Academy of Pediatrics, Committee on Infectious Diseases. 1996. Reassessment of the indications for ribavirin therapy in respiratory syncytial virus infections. *Pediatrics* 97(1): 137–140.

5. Wald ER, and Dashefsky B. 1994. Ribavirin. *Red Book* Committee recommendations questioned. *Pediatrics* 93(4): 672–673.

6. Harrison R. 1990. Reproductive risk assessment with occupational exposure to ribavirin aerosol. *Pediatric Infectious Disease Journal* 9(9 supplement): S102–S105.

7. Rodriguez WJ, et al. 1987. Environmental exposure of primary care personnel to ribavirin aerosol when supervising treatment of infants with respiratory syncytial virus infections. *Antimicrobial Agents and Chemotherapy* 31(7): 1143–1146.

8. Diamond SA, and Dupuis LL. 1989. Contact lens damage due to ribavirin exposure (letter). *Annals of Pharmacotherapy* 23(5): 428–429.

9. Munzenberger PJ, and Walker PC. 1994. Protecting hospital employees and visitors from aerosolized ribavirin. *American Journal of Hospital Pharmacy* 51(6): 823–826.

10. Connor JD. 1986. Comparative pharmacology of nucleoside analogs with antiviral activity. In *Antiviral Chemotherapy*, Mills J, and Corey L, eds. New York: Elsevier Press, 138–154.

11. Connor JD, et al. 1984. Ribavirin pharmacokinetics in children and adults during therapeutic trials. In *Clinical Application of Ribavirin*, Smith RA, Knight V, and Smith JAD, eds. New York: Academic Press, 107–123.

RIFAMPIN
(rif-AM-pin)
(RIFADIN, RIMACTANE)

Synonym: rifampicin

DOSE

Tuberculosis: 10–20 mg/kg/day as a single daily dose or divided every 12 hours.

- Alternatively, 10–20 mg/kg/dose may be given twice weekly *under direct observation* to ensure compliance (administered by an employee of the local health department or other health care professional when social or other constraints prevent reliable daily administration by a parent or guardian).[1]

Persistent Staphylococcal Infections (synergy with antistaphylococcal antibiotics and aminoglycosides): 5 mg/kg/dose given every 12 hours.[2,3]

Prophylaxis:

- *Haemophilus influenzae* type B infection:
  - <1 month of age: 10 mg/kg/dose as a single daily dose for 4 days.
  - >1 month of age: 20 mg/kg/dose as a single daily dose for 4 days.
- *Neisseria meningitidis:*
  - <1 month of age: 10 mg/kg/day divided 2 times a day for 2 days.
  - >1 month of age: 20 mg/kg/day divided 2 times a day for 2 days.

Give half the usual dose if the patient has severe hepatic dysfunction (<10 percent normal function), especially in the presence of obstructive jaundice.

ADMINISTRATION

Supplied as: Injection: 600 mg powder for injection/vial; capsule: 150 mg.

IV—*Rate:* Infuse over 30 minutes to 3 hours.

IV—*Concentration:* 1.2–6 mg/ml in D_5W (preferred) or NS. Use within 4 hours of preparation to avoid precipitation.

PO: Give 1 hour before or 2 hours after feedings to optimize absorption; however, may be given with feedings to reduce GI distress, if needed. Capsule contents can be mixed with applesauce or jelly.

Cannot be given IM or SC because of local irritation and inflammation.

Storage: Protect from light.

Although an oral liquid is not commercially available, it can be compounded by the pharmacist as follows:

Pharmacist Compounding Directions
Rifampin Oral Suspension 10 mg/ml[4-7]

Triturate contents of capsules in a mortar with a small amount of syrup; then add a quantity of simple syrup sufficient to reach the needed volume. Shake vigorously. An oral liquid can also be prepared from the injection. (Some experts discourage the use of rifampin syrup because of its instability.[1] Nahata and associates report that suspensions prepared from rifampin capsules may not provide the expected dose of rifampin. They believe that the use of plastic [instead of glass] prescription bottles in the study may have contributed to the variability of the results.)[4]

Stability: 30 days for suspension from capsules; 56 days for liquid from injection.

Storage: Store in an amber glass bottle. Refrigerate. Protect from light.

CAUTIONS/CONTRAINDICATIONS

Do not use alone, except for short-term prophylaxis for meningitis contacts, because almost all bacteria rapidly develop resistance to rifampin.

Use with caution in patients with pre-existing liver disease or those receiving other hepatotoxic agents concomitantly.

USE

Treatment of active tuberculosis in combination with other antitubercular drugs.[1,8]

Elimination of meningococci from the nasopharynx of asymptomatic *N. meningitidis* carriers.

Prophylaxis in contacts of patients with *H. influenzae* type B infection. Eradicates oropharyngeal carriage of *H. influenzae* type B.

Used with antistaphylococcal drugs and aminoglycosides to provide synergy in treatment of persistent staphylococcal infection.[1,3] Effective against coagulase-negative and coagulase-positive strains of staphylococci, but must not be used alone to treat these infections because resistance to rifampin develops rapidly. Has been used successfully in combination with vancomycin or nafcillin in the treatment of complicated CNS infections refractory to other treatments.[3] Both combinations prevent emergence of rifampin-resistant strains of staphylococci.

The spectrum of activity also includes *Mycobacterium tuberculosis, M. kansasii, M. marinum,* and some *M. avium; Haemophilus influenzae; Legionella pneumophila;* and *Flavobacterium meningosepticum.*

MECHANISM OF ACTION

Rifampin inhibits DNA-dependent RNA polymerase, thus preventing normal synthesis of RNA.

ADVERSE EFFECTS

CNS: Drowsiness, fever.

Dermatologic: Rash, allergic reactions.

GI: Vomiting, anorexia, stomatitis. The compounded oral liquid has a high osmolality and can cause diarrhea in some infants; dilute with water or feeding before administration, if possible.

GU: Elevated BUN or uric acid levels, renal failure, proteinuria, hematuria, hemoglobinuria.

Hematologic: Blood dyscrasias (leukopenia, thrombocytopenia, purpura). Acute hemolytic anemia with intermittent rifampin therapy.

Hepatic: Hepatitis, elevated liver enzymes.

Local: Irritation at injection site.

Other: Flulike reaction.

Causes urine, feces, saliva, sputum, sweat, and tears to turn reddish orange to reddish brown.

PHARMACOKINETICS/PHARMACODYNAMICS

Absorption: Well absorbed after oral administration. Food delays or reduces absorption. Give on an empty stomach, diluted with water.

Distribution: Diffuses into the CNS well when the meninges are inflamed. Distributes widely throughout almost all body tissues and fluids because of its lipophilic nature.

Mean Serum Concentration: The mean serum concentration is 6 mg/liter approximately 8 hours after a single oral dose of 10 mg/kg; after 3 days of multiple daily dosing of 10 mg/kg, the mean serum concentration is 12 mg/liter, indicating that the drug may accumulate with multiple daily dosing in neonates.[9,10]

Metabolism: Hepatic. There is significant enterohepatic circulation.

Half-life: 1.5–3 hours; prolonged with hepatic dysfunction.

Elimination: Primarily biliary; a small percentage renal.

NURSING IMPLICATIONS

Monitor CBC, liver function tests, bilirubin.

Reassure parents regarding red-orange discoloration of the infant's secretions.

Ensure that the IV dosage form is administered within 4 hours of preparation to avoid precipitation.

COMMENTS

Concomitant warfarin and rifampin administration has resulted in suboptimal anticoagulation. The warfarin dose may need to be increased by as much as 2–3 times the prerifampin requirements within about 5–7 days after rifampin is started. Monitor INR (international normalized ratio) or prothrombin time, watch for signs and symptoms of bleeding, and adjust warfarin dose as needed.

Concurrent use of other hepatotoxic drugs may increase risk of hepatotoxicity.

Interactions: Rifampin is a potent inducer of hepatic P-450 microsomal enzyme metabolism; therefore, an increased dose may be required when given concomitantly with corticosteroids, chloramphenicol, digoxin, methadone, phenytoin, propranolol, quinidine, theophylline, and antifungals such as fluconazole, itraconazole, or ketoconazole.

REFERENCES

1. American Academy of Pediatrics, Committee on Infectious Diseases. 1992. Chemotherapy for tuberculosis in infants and children. *Pediatrics* 89(1): 161–165.

2. Edwards MS. 1997. Antibacterial therapy in pregnancy and neonates. *Clinics in Perinatology* 24(1): 251–266.

3. Fan-Havard P, and Nahata MC. 1987. Treatment and prevention of infections of cerebrospinal fluid shunts. *Clinical Pharmacy* 6(11): 866–880.

4. Nahata MC, Morosco RS, and Hipple TF. 1994. Effect of preparation method and storage on rifampin concentration in suspensions. *Annals of Pharmacotherapy* 28(2): 182–185.

5. Nahata MC, and Hipple TF. 1992. *Pediatric Drug Formulations,* 2nd ed. Cincinnati: Harvey Whitney Books, 68.

6. Trissel LA. 1996. *Stability of Compounded Formulations.* Washington, DC: American Pharmaceutical Association, 233–234.

7. Allen LV. 1989. Rifampin suspension. *U.S. Pharmacist* 14: 102–103.

8. Vallejo JG, Ong LT, and Starke JR. 1994. Clinical features, diagnosis, and treatment of tuberculosis in infants. *Pediatrics* 94(1): 1–7.

9. Paap CM, and Nahata MC. 1990. Clinical pharmacokinetics of antibacterial drugs in neonates. *Clinical Pharmacokinetics* 19(4): 280–318.

10. Acocella G. 1978. Clinical pharmacokinetics of rifampicin. *Clinical Pharmacokinetics* 3(2): 108–127.

TABLE OF CONTENTS

S

S

SIMETHICONE (MYLICON)

(si-METH-i-kone)

GASTROINTESTINAL:
ANTIFLATULENT

DOSE

20 mg/0.3 ml with each feeding every 3–6 hours

ADMINISTRATION

PO: Available as simethicone drops 40 mg/0.6 ml, 30 ml dropper bottle. Shake well before using. May be mixed with infant formula or water.[1]

USE

For relief of intestinal gas and painful symptoms of gastric bloating.

Infantile Colic: Results of investigations of the efficacy of simethicone in treating infantile colic are mixed. A placebo-controlled, multicenter trial found simethicone to be no better than placebo in the treatment of infantile colic.[2] Two other studies also showed no improvement in symptoms.[3,4] However, Sethi and Sethi did find efficacy in its use, as did Becker and colleagues, who reported efficacy in 44 of 51 infants treated.[5,6]

MECHANISM OF ACTION

Simethicone is a defoaming agent that changes the surface tension of gas bubbles, causing them to coalesce. This accelerates the passage of gas through the intestine, although it does not change the actual volume of gas.

ADVERSE EFFECTS

Usually very well tolerated and nontoxic.

Does not interfere with gastric secretions or nutrient absorption.

PHARMACOKINETICS/PHARMACODYNAMICS

Absorption: None. Simethicone is a physiologically inert compound.

Elimination: Unchanged in the feces.

NURSING IMPLICATIONS

Shake well before use.

Monitor for a decrease in symptoms such as crying, fussiness, and intestinal gas.

Discontinue if there is no improvement after about 48 hours.

REFERENCES

1. Manufacturer's product literature.
2. Metcalf TJ, et al. 1994. Simethicone in the treatment of infant colic: A randomized, placebo-controlled, multicenter trial. *Pediatrics* 94(1): 29–34.
3. Dugger JA, et al. 1963. The use of silicones as an approach to the management of infantile colic. *Journal of Michigan State Medical Association* 62: 46–49.

4. Danielsson B, and Hwang CP. 1985. Treatment of infantile colic with surface active substance (sime-thicone). *Acta Paediatrica Scandinavica* 74(3): 446–450.

5. Sethi KS, and Sethi JK. 1988. Simethicone in the management of infant colic. *The Practitioner* 232(1448): 508.

6. Becker N, et al. 1988. Mylicon drops in the treatment of infant colic. *Clinical Therapeutics* 10(4): 401–405.

SODIUM BICARBONATE [NaHCO$_3$]
(SOE-dee-um bye-KAR-boe-nate)

ELECTROLYTE BALANCE: ELECTROLYTE SUPPLEMENT; ALKALINIZING AGENT

DOSE

Metabolic Acidosis: 1–2 mEq/kg/dose initially, then 0.5 mEq/kg/dose IV.
Maximum Dose: 8 mEq/kg/day IV. Alternatively, use the following formula to calculate the dose:

Weight (in kg) × 0.3 × base deficit (in mEq/liter) = dose (in mEq HCO$_3$)

- Complete correction is not recommended. Give **half** the calculated dose to minimize fluid and sodium load. Give over 8–12 hours added to the IV solution (incompatible with calcium).

Cardiac Resuscitation: Not for routine use (see **USE** below). 0.5–1 mEq/kg/dose IV. May repeat every 10 minutes or as needed as determined by arterial blood gases.

Renal Tubular Acidosis: 3–15 mEq/kg/day PO in three or four divided doses given with feedings.[1] Adjust dose according to urine pH. (Sodium and/or potassium citrate can be used instead. See monograph on potassium.)

- Individualize dose.

Clearing Occluded Central Venous Catheters: (See Appendix F: Restoring Patency to Occluded Central Venous Catheters.) Sodium bicarbonate is one alternative for clearing occluded central lines. It may dissolve occlusions caused by drugs that are soluble in an alkaline pH.

ADMINISTRATION

IV, PO, NG. May also be given intraosseous (IO).

IV—Rate: Usually over 20–30 minutes. If the infant is unstable, may infuse at 1 mEq/kg/hour or more slowly to minimize sudden changes in serum osmolality. Maximum rate of administration in emergencies: 1 mEq/kg/minute of 4.2 percent (0.5 mEq/ml).[2,3]

IV—Concentration: 4.2 percent (0.5 mEq/ml). Use the 8.4 percent (1 mEq/ml) for central line administration in fluid-restricted infants.

IV—Compatibility: Incompatible with IV solutions containing calcium (precipitation will occur). See Appendix E: Y-Site Compatibility of Common NICU Drugs.

PO: Sodium bicarbonate injection may be administered PO or NG. Dilute in feedings or with water prior to administration. For renal problems, sodium and/or potassium citrate solutions are often used. (See monograph on potassium.)

USE

For correction of persistent and severe metabolic acidosis (pH <7.15) despite maximum cardiorespiratory support.[2]

Also used for urinary alkalinization, replacement in bicarbonate deficit as in severe diarrhea,[2] and to treat hyperkalemia.

For cardiac resuscitation, use only after adequate alveolar ventilation has been established and effective cardiac compressions have been provided. Not for brief CPR, but may be beneficial during prolonged arrests that do not respond to other therapy.[4,5] There is no evidence that sodium bicarbonate is useful in the acute phase of neonatal resuscitation in the delivery room.[5]

For pulmonary hypertension, use to adjust pH >7.4 as an adjunct to other therapies to reduce pulmonary vascular resistance.

MECHANISM OF ACTION

Sodium bicarbonate buffers excess hydrogen ion, raises blood pH, and increases plasma bicarbonate.

ADVERSE EFFECTS

May cause hypernatremia, metabolic alkalosis, elevation in $PaCO_2$.

May cause nausea with oral use.

Sodium bicarbonate, particularly 8.4 percent (1 mEq/ml), is extremely hypertonic. It may cause vein erosion, which can result in IV extravasation and lead to severe tissue damage.

Rapid administration of concentrated sodium bicarbonate produces sudden increases in serum osmolality, increasing the risk of intracranial hemorrhage. The critical variables are concentration, rate, and dose. The anatomy of the immature brain includes a fragile subependymal germinal matrix, which is particularly vulnerable to bleeding when subjected to hypoxia or rapid changes in vascular pressure and osmolarity.[5] A dose of 4 mEq/kg given over 30 seconds raises the serum osmolality about 25 mOsm/kg water.[2]

Overdose from Too-Rapid or Excessive Administration: Symptoms are tetany (as a result of decreased ionized calcium), hypokalemia (as K enters the cell), and irritability.

Treatment of Overdose: Rebreathe expired air; give calcium gluconate for tetany and hyperexcitability. Treat alkalosis with chloride salts (ammonium, potassium, or sodium) as medical condition warrants.

PHARMACOKINETICS/PHARMACODYNAMICS

Absorption: Well absorbed PO.

Volume of Distribution: Approximately 0.3–0.4 liter/kg.

Metabolism: Dissociates to sodium and bicarbonate; at a proper concentration of hydrogen ion, may be converted to carbonic acid (H_2CO_3), then to CO_2 before being excreted by the lungs.

NURSING IMPLICATIONS

Use only 4.2 percent solution (0.5 mEq/ml) for peripheral administration because of hyperosmolar content. Severe tissue injury is likely with infiltration.

Monitor acid-base balance carefully and ensure that infant has established adequate ventilation to avoid CO_2 retention.

Infuse slowly.

COMMENTS

Sodium bicarbonate 8.4 percent (1 mEq/ml) is not recommended for floor stock in the NICU; stock the 4.2 percent (0.5 mEq/ml) solution.

Osmolality of 8.4 Percent Solution: 1,680 mOsm/kg water.

Composition: 1 gm of sodium bicarbonate = 12 mEq sodium and 12 mEq bicarbonate.

Interactions: Inactivates sympathomimetic amines such as epinephrine and dobutamine.

REFERENCES

1. Donckerwolcke RA. 1982. Diagnosis and treatment of renal tubular disorders in children. *Pediatric Clinics of North America* 29(4): 895–906.

2. Roberts RJ. 1984. *Drug Therapy in Infants: Pharmacologic Principles and Clinical Experience.* Philadelphia: WB Saunders, 288–291.

3. Baum JD, and Robertson NRC. 1975. Immediate effects of alkaline infusion in infants with respiratory distress syndrome. *Journal of Pediatrics* 87(2): 255–261.

4. American Heart Association, Emergency Cardiac Care Committee and Subcommittees. 1992. Guidelines for cardiopulmonary resuscitation and emergency cardiac care. Part 6: Pediatric advanced life support. *JAMA* 268(16): 2262–2275. (Comment in *JAMA*, 1992, 268[16]: 2297–2298; and *JAMA*, 1993, 269[20]: 2626.)

5. American Heart Association in collaboration with the International Committee on Resuscitation. 2000. Part 11: Neonatal resuscitation. In Guidelines 2000 for cardiopulmonary resuscitation and emergency cardiovascular care. *Circulation* 102(supplement I): I-343–I-357.

S

SODIUM CHLORIDE [NaCl]

(SOE-dee-um KLOR-ide)

ELECTROLYTE BALANCE:
ELECTROLYTE SUPPLEMENT

See citrate and citric acid solutions monograph for sodium citrate.

DOSE

Maintenance (term and preterm infants): 3–4 mEq/kg/day. Range for preterm
   infants: 2–8 mEq/kg/day.

Replacement of Deficit:[1] Use the following formula to calculate how much sodium
   to give to correct acute, serious hyponatremia:

   Weight (in kg) × 0.6 × (CD – CA) = dose (in mEq Na)

where: CD = **d**esired serum sodium **c**oncentration in mEq/liter

   CA = infant's **a**ctual, current serum sodium **c**oncentration in mEq/liter

Replace sodium gradually. Usually only half of this amount is given over
   12–24 hours.

ADMINISTRATION

IV—*Rate:* Infuse at 1 mEq/kg/hour or less to minimize sudden changes in serum
   osmolality.

IV—*Concentration:*

- ***NaCl 23.4 percent:*** Dilute in maintenance IV solution. Not for direct IV push
   or retrograde administration.

- ***NaCl 3 percent:*** May be used for retrograde or direct IV push administration.
   For emergency treatment of severe hyponatremia only.

- ***NaCl 0.9 percent "normal saline" (isotonic):*** For direct IV, retrograde, or
   maintenance fluid administration. This concentration is preferred, except in
   fluid-restricted infants.

- ***NaCl 0.45 percent ("half-normal" saline):*** For flushing IV lines. Use
   heparinized saline flush solutions only for heparin locks and to start IVs; use
   NaCl 0.45 percent without heparin for all other flushing indications.

PO: NaCl injection may be administered PO or NG. When NaCl 23.4 percent is
   used to minimize fluid volume/dose, dilute in feedings or in water prior to
   administration.

USE

Prevention and treatment of sodium and chloride deficiency.

Flushing of IV lines and as a barrier to separate incompatible medications.

Normal saline nose drops are used to facilitate suctioning of nasal secretions and to
   restore moisture. Normal saline is used to facilitate suctioning of endotracheal
   secretions.

TABLE 1-44 ◆ **SODIUM CONTENT AND OSMOLARITY OF VARIOUS SODIUM CHLORIDE CONCENTRATIONS**

Concentration	mEq/liter Na	mEq/ml Na	Osmolarity (mOsm/liter)
NaCl 0.9% (isotonic) (normal saline)	154	0.154	310
NaCl 3%	513	0.513	1,025
NaCl 23.4%	4,000	4	8,000

From: Olin BR. 1994 (bound edition). *Drug Facts and Comparisons.* St. Louis: Facts and Comparisons, a Wolters Kluwer Company, 133. Reprinted by permission.

Potassium and/or sodium citrate mixtures are used for urinary alkalinization. See Table 1-42, page 483, for comparisons of the content of some commercial citrate products. See also citrate and citric acid solutions monograph.

MECHANISM OF ACTION

Sodium chloride is the principal salt in maintenance of plasma osmolality.

ADVERSE EFFECTS

May cause hypernatremia, edema. Excessive dosage or too-rapid administration rate may cause pulmonary edema. May cause nausea with oral use.

NaCl 23.4 percent is extremely hypertonic. It may cause vein erosion, which can result in IV extravasation and lead to severe tissue damage. Table 1-44 shows sodium content and osmolarity of various NaCl concentrations.

Rapid administration of concentrated sodium chloride leads to sudden increases in serum osmolality that may result in CNS hemorrhage. Concentrated NaCl must be diluted. Inadvertent direct injection may cause sudden hypernatremia, leading to shock, CNS disorders, extensive hemolysis, cortical necrosis of the kidneys, and severe local tissue necrosis on extravasation.

Do not use bacteriostatic sodium chloride, particularly for flush solutions, in neonates because of the benzyl alcohol content. Benzyl alcohol has been associated with the fatal gasping syndrome of metabolic acidosis and CNS, respiratory, circulatory, and renal impairment. Toxic benzyl alcohol dose was approximately 100–400 mg/kg/day. Benzyl alcohol is excreted in the kidney; therefore, the risk of toxicity increases with renal dysfunction.[2]

Concentrated sodium chloride 23.4 percent is not recommended for floor stock. Doses should be prepared in the pharmacy with appropriate dilution.

PHARMACOKINETICS/PHARMACODYNAMICS

Absorption: Well absorbed PO.

NURSING IMPLICATIONS

In the low birth weight infant, consider sodium chloride flushes as a source of sodium and fluid. Monitor electrolytes carefully.

COMMENTS

Composition: 1 gm of sodium chloride = 17.1 mEq sodium and 17.1 mEq
chloride.

REFERENCES

1. Barone MA. 1996. *The Harriet Lane Handbook,* 14th ed. St. Louis: Mosby-Year Book, 219.

2. American Academy of Pediatrics, Committee on Drugs. 1985. "Inactive" ingredients in pharmaceutical products. *Pediatrics* 76(4): 635–643.

SODIUM POLYSTYRENE SULFONATE

(SOE-dee-um pol-lee-STYE-reen

SUL-fa-nate)

(KAYEXALATE)

**ANTIDOTE:
POTASSIUM
OVERDOSE**

DOSE

1 gm/kg/dose per rectum (PR) every 2–6 hours prn. Give every 6 hours PO prn. Individualize dosage.[1,2]

ADMINISTRATION

Supplied as: Sodium polystyrene sulfonate is available commercially as a liquid (also contains propylene glycol, magnesium aluminum silicate [Veegum], saccharin sodium, alcohol, sorbitol, and parabens as a preservative). However, the preservative- and flavor-free formulation in Table 1-45 is preferred for use in neonates. The commercially available liquid can be used in older infants and children.

PR preferred over PO.

PR: Administer by rectal enema. Warm to body temperature before use. May need to tape buttocks and elevate hips to retain enema in rectum for at least 30 minutes. Use caution in inserting enema, particularly in very low birth weight infants, to avoid intestinal perforation. Subsequently, irrigate colon with a non-sodium-containing solution to remove resin.[2]

PO: The PO route has been effective in children, but is used less frequently in neonates.

USE

As an adjunct to other treatment measures for hyperkalemia.

Because onset of action is delayed, other measures may be required for immediate correction of dangerously high potassium, particularly if conduction defects (widened QRS complex; tall, tented T waves; flat, wide P wave; ventricular fibrillation; and late asystole) are present.[3] These include stopping potassium intake

---

TABLE 1-45 ◆ PREPARATION OF SODIUM POLYSTYRENE SULFONATE SUSPENSION 1 GM/3 ML

Step 1: Add distilled water 24 ml to sodium polystyrene sulfonate 15 gm in a 4-ounce square wide-mouth jar. Shake vigorously.

Step 2: Add 12 ml sorbitol 70%. Shake vigorously.

Total Volume: 45 ml (with powder and liquid).

Expiration: 24 hours.

Storage: Refrigerate. To resuspend after standing, stir with tongue blade and shake vigorously.

15 gm sodium polystyrene sulfonate is approximately 4 level teaspoonfuls of powder.

Adapted from: Manufacturer's product literature.

(including medications, such as spironolactone, that elevate potassium levels), IV calcium gluconate (to antagonize the effects of hyperkalemia on the heart), sodium bicarbonate and/or glucose-insulin infusions (to shift potassium into the cell), furosemide (to enhance potassium excretion), exchange transfusion, and dialysis. Attempt to determine and eliminate the cause of the hyperkalemia.

MECHANISM OF ACTION

Sodium polystyrene sulfonate is a cation exchange resin that removes potassium from the body. Sodium ions from the resin are released into the GI tract and exchanged for potassium ions, primarily in the large intestine because of the large concentration of potassium at that site. Sodium polystyrene sulfonate exchanges approximately 1 mEq of potassium per gram of resin.

ADVERSE EFFECTS

Hypernatremia may occur because sodium is exchanged for potassium, and sodium intake may need to be restricted from other sources. Sodium content is 4.1 mEq/gm, and about one-third of this (1.4 mEq/gm) is delivered to the body because not all of the sodium is released from the resin.

Hypokalemia, hypocalcemia, hypomagnesemia.

Constipation, GI irritation, anorexia, fecal impaction, and intestinal necrosis may occur. Rarely, causes diarrhea. Adverse GI effects are dose related. Sorbitol is included in the formulation for a laxative effect to prevent constipation and fecal impaction.

PHARMACOKINETICS/PHARMACODYNAMICS

Absorption: Not absorbed.

Onset of Action: 2–12 hours after oral administration.

Elimination: In feces, primarily as potassium polystyrene sulfonate.

NURSING IMPLICATIONS

Monitor electrolytes carefully, especially serum potassium, sodium, calcium, and magnesium levels.

Continuous cardiac monitoring is required to monitor for arrhythmias and bradycardia.

Carefully administer via feeding tube and hold buttocks together for 30 minutes to ensure retention. Protect buttock skin with a barrier cream to prevent excoriation from stool and solution.

COMMENTS

Interactions: Concurrent administration of antacids or laxatives containing magnesium hydroxide or calcium carbonate may reduce the effectiveness of this drug.

REFERENCES

1. Manufacturer's product literature.

2. McEvoy GK. 1994. *AHFS Drug Information*. Bethesda, Maryland: American Society of Hospital Pharmacists, 1672–1673.

3. Gomella TL, Cunningham MD, and Eyal FG. 1994. *Neonatology: Management, Procedures, On-call Problems, Diseases and Drugs*, 3rd ed. Norwalk, Connecticut: Appleton & Lange, 211–212.

SPIRONOLACTONE (ALDACTONE)

(speer-on-oh-LAK-tone)

CARDIOVASCULAR:
DIURETIC

DOSE

1–3 mg/kg/day given as a single daily dose or in two divided doses.

Reassess and adjust dose after 3–5 days.

ADMINISTRATION

Supplied as: Tablets: 25 mg/tablet. Not available as an oral liquid; however, one can be compounded by the pharmacist. Stabilities of several formulations have been published:[1–3]

Pharmacist Compounding Directions
Spironolactone Suspension 1 mg/ml[3]

Soak 10 spironolactone 25 mg tablets in a small amount of purified water for 5 minutes. Crush tablets. Add 50 ml of carboxymethylcellulose 1.5 percent and 100 ml of simple syrup and mix. Transfer to a graduate and add a quantity of purified water USP sufficient to equal 250 ml. Shake well.

Stability: 3 months.

Storage: Refrigerate or store at room temperature.

PO: For oral administration only. May give with or after feedings.

CAUTIONS/CONTRAINDICATIONS

Do not use in patients with hyperkalemia, acute renal failure, or anuria. Use with caution in infants with hepatic or renal dysfunction, or hyponatremia.

Spironolactone is tumorigenic in chronic toxicity studies in rats at 25 to 250 times the usual human dose.[4] Breast carcinoma has occurred in men and women taking this medication, but a direct causal relationship has not yet been established.[4] Avoid unnecessary use of this drug.

USE

A potassium-sparing diuretic that may complement other diuretics in patients with diseases that increase aldosterone secretion (congestive heart failure,[5] congenital heart disease,[6] chronic lung disease [BPD],[7] or liver failure).

Also used to treat hypertension, usually in combination with other drugs.

Often used in combination with hydrochlorothiazide (see monographs on hydrochlorothiazide with spironolactone [Aldactazide] or furosemide [Lasix]) to reduce potassium loss and hypokalemia. Although fixed-combination preparations (Aldactazide) may improve compliance and simplify the drug regimen, they do not allow for individualization of dosage with each drug.

Mechanism of Action

Spironolactone is a competitive antagonist of mineralocorticoids such as aldosterone. It has a steroidlike molecular structure resembling mineralocorticoids. Spironolactone counteracts the regulatory actions of aldosterone on electrolytes in the distal segment of the nephron, resulting in increased sodium excretion and decreased potassium excretion. Spironolactone produces only a slight diuresis. Spironolactone increases excretion of calcium in the urine.[8,9] It has antiandrogenic effects.

Adverse Effects

Hyperkalemia may occur if the infant is also receiving potassium supplementation or in infants with renal dysfunction. Hyperkalemia may lead to cardiac arrhythmias and cardiac arrest. Treatment of symptomatic hyperkalemia (with ECG changes) requires prompt additional therapy. (For treatment of hyperkalemia, see monograph on potassium.)

May cause GI upset, diarrhea, drowsiness, rash, dehydration, hyponatremia (especially in combination with other diuretics), gynecomastia, transient increase in BUN, mild acidosis.

Pharmacokinetics/Pharmacodynamics

Absorption: Well absorbed after oral administration. Spironolactone shows greater absorption when ingested with meals than when given to fasting patients.

Onset of Action: 2–3 days.

Duration of Action: 2–3 days after stopping therapy. The effect is delayed because the action of aldosterone involves the synthesis of a peptide that persists for 2–3 days after drug treatment. When spironolactone is discontinued, resynthesis of adequate peptide may be delayed for an equivalent 2–3 days.[9]

Protein Binding: High (98 percent).

Metabolism: Rapidly and completely metabolized in the liver. Many of the metabolites are still active. The primary active metabolite is canrenone.

Half-life: 10–35 hours (adults).

Elimination: Urine and bile.

Nursing Implications

Monitor serum potassium, sodium, BUN and/or creatinine.

Monitor urine output and blood pressure.

Observe for dehydration.

Administer spironolactone with or after feedings to minimize stomach upset and enhance absorption.

COMMENTS

Interactions:

- Hyperkalemia may result from concurrent use with angiotensin-converting enzyme (ACE) inhibitors (captopril, enalapril, enalaprilat); concurrent potassium preparations; blood from blood bank (may contain up to 30 mEq potassium/liter plasma or up to 65 mEq potassium/liter whole blood when stored for more than 10 days).

- Spironolactone may alter the pharmacokinetics of digoxin; however, the clinical significance of this interaction is doubtful.[10] Spironolactone may falsely elevate serum digoxin levels done by radioimmunoassays (RIA); however, this is usually not a problem with the newer assays.

- Spironolactone may decrease the anticoagulant effects of heparin or warfarin. Dose adjustment of the anticoagulant may be required.[4]

REFERENCES

1. Trissel LA. 1996. *Stability of Compounded Formulations.* Washington, DC: American Pharmaceutical Association, 240–241.

2. Mathur LK, and Wickman A. 1989. Stability of extemporaneously compounded spironolactone suspensions. *American Journal of Hospital Pharmacy* 46(10): 2040–2042.

3. Nahata MC, Morosco RS, and Hipple TF. 1993. Stability of spironolactone in an extemporaneously prepared suspension at two temperatures. *Annals of Pharmacotherapy* 27(10): 1198–1199.

4. United States Pharmacopeial Convention/USP DI. 1996. *Drug Information for the Health Care Professional,* 16th ed. Rockville, Maryland: United States Pharmacopeial Convention, 1275–1280.

5. Baylen BG, et al. 1980. The occurrence of hyperaldosteronism in infants with congestive heart failure. *American Journal of Cardiology* 45(2): 305–310.

6. Hobbins SM, et al. 1981 Spironolactone therapy in infants with congestive heart failure secondary to congenital heart disease. *Archives of Disease in Childhood* 56(12): 934–938.

7. Albersheim SG, et al. 1989. Randomized, double-blind, controlled trial of long-term diuretic therapy for bronchopulmonary dysplasia. *Journal of Pediatrics* 115(4): 615–620.

8. Atkinson SA, et al. 1988. Mineral excretion in premature infants receiving various diuretic therapies. *Journal of Pediatrics* 113(3): 540–545.

9. Roberts RJ. 1984. *Drug Therapy in Infants: Pharmacologic Principles and Clinical Experience.* Philadelphia: WB Saunders, 243–244.

10. Gow RM, et al. 1993. Cardiovascular pharmacology. In *Pediatric Pharmacology and Therapeutics,* 2nd ed., Radde IC, and MacLeod SM, eds. St. Louis: Mosby-Year Book, 197–219.

SUCCINYLCHOLINE (ANECTINE)
(suk-si-nil-KO-leen)

CENTRAL NERVOUS SYSTEM: NEUROMUSCULAR BLOCKER

DOSE

IV: 1–2 mg/kg initially, then 0.3–0.6 mg/kg every 5–10 minutes as needed. Tachyphylaxis (rapid appearance of a progressive decrease in response) occurs with repeated dosing. An initial test dose of 0.1 mg/kg may determine patient's sensitivity and recovery time.

IM: Up to 3–4 mg/kg.[1–3]

ADMINISTRATION

Usually given IV, but may be given IM in infants.

IV—*Rate:* May be infused IV push over 10–30 seconds.

IV—*Concentration:* May give undiluted or dilute in D_5W or sodium chloride injection to 1–2 mg/ml. Discard diluted solution after 24 hours.

IV—*Compatibility:* Do not mix with alkaline solutions such as sodium bicarbonate or thiopental sodium. Flush line and change needle between alkaline solutions and succinylcholine to avoid inactivation and precipitation.

Storage: Refrigerate.

CAUTIONS/CONTRAINDICATIONS

Must assist ventilation.

Do not use in children with a history of malignant hyperthermia, allergy to the drug, or factors predisposing to hyperkalemia.

Do not use in patients with cholinesterase deficiency.

It is not reversed by neostigmine, as are other nondepolarizing neuromuscular blocking agents (such as atracurium and pancuronium).

USE

A short-acting neuromuscular blocking agent for skeletal muscle relaxation (paralysis) during surgical procedures and endotracheal intubation.

MECHANISM OF ACTION

Succinylcholine, a depolarizing neuromuscular blocking agent, interrupts the neuromuscular junction, thereby producing muscle relaxation or paralysis. It blocks neuromuscular transmission by first imitating the action of acetylcholine, but subsequently produces a persistent depolarization of the postjunctional membrane.[4]

ADVERSE EFFECTS

Hypoxemia resulting from inadequate ventilation.

Bradycardia is common; asystole occurs rarely. Pretreatment with atropine (0.02 mg/kg) eliminates bradycardia.[3]

Increase or decrease in blood pressure may occur. Succinylcholine has weak histamine-releasing effects.

As with other neuromuscular blockers, continuous administration over a prolonged period may result in irreversible blockade.

Myoglobinemia and myoglobinuria may occur.

Masseter muscle rigidity, defined as a transient contraction of the muscles of mastication that limits mouth opening, may indicate a susceptibility to malignant hyperthermia.[2]

Hyperkalemia.

Increases intraocular pressure.

PHARMACOKINETICS/PHARMACODYNAMICS

Absorption: Poorly absorbed from the GI tract.

Onset of Action: <1 minute.

Duration of Action: 4–6 minutes.

Metabolism: Rapidly hydrolyzed by pseudocholinesterase in the liver and plasma.

Elimination: Urine (10 percent unchanged).

NURSING IMPLICATIONS

Monitor for bradycardia.

Monitor vital signs continuously before, during, and after administration.

Drug produces only paralysis. Collaborate with physician to provide analgesia and/or sedation (e.g., fentanyl or morphine).

Refrigerate drug. When taken on transport, refrigerate immediately upon return.

COMMENTS

Mechanical ventilation must be provided during use. Does not produce analgesia or sedation, only paralysis.[4]

Neonates are relatively resistant to the relaxant effects of succinylcholine, requiring up to 4 times the adult dose.

REFERENCES

1. Roberts RJ. 1984. *Drug Therapy in Infants: Pharmacologic Principles and Clinical Experience.* Philadelphia: WB Saunders, 308–312.

2. Lerman J. 1993. Anesthesia. In *Pediatric Pharmacology and Therapeutics,* 2nd ed., Radde IC, and MacLeod SM, eds. St. Louis: Mosby-Year Book, 475–497.

3. Manufacturer's product literature.

4. Cook DR, and Fischer CG. 1978. Characteristics of succinylcholine neuromuscular blockade in neonates. *Anesthesia and Analgesia* 57(1): 63–66.

SUCRALFATE (CARAFATE)

(soo-KRAL-fate)

GASTROINTESTINAL:
ANTI-ULCER

Synonym: aluminum sucrose sulfate

DOSE

PO: 40–80 mg/kg/day divided every 6 hours.

Topical for Oral Mucositis: 1–2 ml applied topically (with swab) up to six times a day.

Topical for Perineal/Peristomal Excoriation: Apply every 4–6 hours as needed and during diaper changes or when stomal appliances are emptied. (For further information, see **USE** below.)

ADMINISTRATION

Supplied as: Suspension: 1 gm/10 ml (= 100 mg/ml). Tablet: 1 gm.

PO:

- Give 1/2 hour to 1 hour before feedings.
- Give with additional water as fluid status allows.
- Shake well.

Available commercially as an oral suspension. However, a suspension can also be compounded by the pharmacist from tablets as follows:

Pharmacist Compounding Directions
Sucralfate Oral Suspension 200 mg/ml[1–3]

Formulation #1: Crush 20 tablets of sucralfate 1 gm in a mortar. Add purified water USP while mixing. Transfer to a graduate, and add purified water USP to a volume of 100 ml. Do not use suspending agents because they may inactivate sucralfate. Shake well.

Stability and Storage: 14 days, refrigerate.

Formulation #2: Place sucralfate tablets in distilled water and allow to stand for 15–20 minutes. Equal parts of 70 percent sorbitol and cherry syrup (or any other flavoring agent) may then be added. Shake well.

Stability and Storage: 14 days at room temperature.

CAUTIONS/CONTRAINDICATIONS

- Limited experience in neonates.
- Contraindicated with hypersensitivity to sucralfate.
- Binds phosphate within the intestine. Like aluminum-containing antacids, sucralfate can cause severe hypophosphatemia. Monitor serum phosphorus.

⚬ Patients with dysphagia or GI obstruction are at increased risk for formation of bezoar (a concretion of various character sometimes found in the stomach or intestines) because of the protein-binding properties of sucralfate.

⚬ Patients with renal failure are at increased risk of aluminum toxicity from long-term use of sucralfate because of absorption of the aluminum from this drug. Monitor serum aluminum.

⚬ **Accumulation of Aluminum.** Gastrointestinal absorption of aluminum from sucralfate is low; however, absorption could be a problem in neonates because their immature renal function and limited capacity to excrete aluminum predispose them to accumulate aluminum. Infants with renal dysfunction and/or dehydration are at even greater risk of accumulating aluminum to toxic levels. Other sources add to the aluminum load, such as aluminum contamination in parenteral nutrition (PN) and aluminum-containing antacids (ACAs). Preterm infants receiving prolonged IV therapy have elevated plasma aluminum levels, as do infants receiving ACAs. When ACAs are used in conjunction with citrate, aluminum in the blood may be elevated up to fivefold. Citrate enhances intestinal absorption of aluminum.[4,5]

- Aluminum is present in PN incidental to the delivery of calcium, magnesium, phosphorus, heparin, and trace elements; calcium gluconate contributes more than 80 percent of the total aluminum contamination of PN.[6,7] The FDA intends to set an upper limit of 25 mcg/liter for aluminum in large-volume parenterals and to require manufacturers of small-volume parenterals, such as calcium and phosphate salts, to measure aluminum content and note it on the package label.[7] In preterm infants, balance studies estimate aluminum retention to be approximately 75 percent of intake.[8]

- The etiology of osteopenic bone disease in preterm infants is probably multifactorial; it has most commonly been attributed to insufficient intake of calcium and/or phosphate. However, histologic evidence shows aluminum accumulation in the bones of infants who received PN; this may be an additional factor that impairs bone mineral uptake.[8,9] Aluminum from PN, IV solutions, ACAs, and sucralfate may prevent bone uptake of calcium.

- Toxic manifestations of aluminum toxicity include hypochromic microcytic anemia, fractures, osteopenia, and osteomalacia.[10]

- Drowsiness progressing to seizures in patients with renal failure may indicate aluminum toxicity. Monitor serum aluminum concentration, if possible.[11]

USE

Prophylaxis or Short-Term Treatment of Gastric and Duodenal Ulcer Disease or Gastroesophageal Reflux[12] and Prophylaxis Against Stress-Induced Bleeding:

At least as effective as histamine H_2 receptor antagonists (ranitidine, famotidine, cimetidine).[12,13] Its advantage over these agents is that sucralfate may be associated less frequently with nosocomial pneumonia than is antacid therapy.[14,15] Although the exact reason is not clear, it may be that, at gastric pH values above 3.5 (such as those commonly seen in patients undergoing antacid therapy or those being treated with H_2 antagonists, but not in those receiving sucralfate), Gram-negative flora increase in the stomach, and their aspiration can lead to pneumonia.[12–15]

Chemotherapy-Induced Mucositis: Topical sucralfate may be tried in the prevention or treatment of chemotherapy-induced mucositis; however, there are conflicting reports, and some investigators have been unable to demonstrate any substantial effect.[16,17]

Peristomal/Perineal Excoriation: In an open-label (researchers are aware of the drug given), uncontrolled study, Hayashi and associates found that topical sucralfate was soothing, safe, and effective in 15 pediatric patients with stomal or perineal skin ulcerations. All 15 patients had failed to respond to previous therapy (a variety of steroid and/or barrier creams). With sucralfate, 13 patients had complete healing and 2 patients had partial healing. The researchers observed (1) a lag time of 2–3 days before visible healing was evident, (2) that healing occurred from the perimeter, (3) that sucralfate was soothing and reduced pain and discomfort, (4) that the drug was ineffective for fungal dermatitis, and (5) that the drug did not appear to have toxic or systemic effects. The drug was applied every 4–6 hours as needed and during diaper changes or when stomal appliances were emptied. In patients with gastrostomy tubes, sucralfate was applied every 4–6 hours as needed to maintain a visible layer. The dosage form used was either as a powder (pulverized tablets applied full strength to severely denuded and weeping areas) or as an emollient once healing was initiated (4 gm% sucralfate in a Eucerin with glycerin and water base). In one infant with severe excoriation from a badly leaking gastrostomy, sucralfate was administered via the gastrostomy so that the spillover would consist of a mixture of gastric juice and sucralfate.[18]

MECHANISM OF ACTION

Sucralfate is a basic aluminum salt of sulfated sucrose formed from sucrose octasulfate and polyaluminum hydroxide. The drug's action is local, rather than systemic. It is minimally soluble in dilute acid (e.g., gastric juice) and in alkali; and when dissolved, it breaks down into its aluminum salt and sucrose sulfate, which form a viscid gel-like substance from extensive polymerization of the drug. This gel adheres preferentially to proteinaceous exudate, such as albumin and fibrinogen, at the ulcer site. It may also act as a protective physical barrier against the action of gastric acid, pepsin, and bile acids on the damaged mucosal surfaces. Sucralfate may also increase local production of prostaglandin E_2 and gastric mucus, thus exerting a cytoprotective effect.[3,13]

Sucralfate is a protectant. It has almost no acid-neutralizing capacity.

Sucralfate may be more effective when given *before feedings* because food may buffer the acid of the stomach, increasing the pH above that which causes polymerization of the drug.

ADVERSE EFFECTS

CNS: Sleepiness.

Dermatologic: Rash.

GI: Constipation (most frequent), diarrhea, flatulence, dry mouth, gastric distress. Use of sucralfate in a nasogastric feeding tube may result in bezoar formation with other medications or enteral feedings, as a result of the protein-binding properties of the drug.

Respiratory: Laryngospasm, respiratory difficulty.

PHARMACOKINETICS/PHARMACODYNAMICS

Absorption: Up to 5 percent of the disaccharide component and less than 0.02 percent of the aluminum is absorbed from an oral dose. Free aluminum ion is released when the drug reacts with gastric acid and is absorbed systemically.

Onset of Action: 1–2 hours.

Duration of Action: Adheres to ulcerated epithelium for more than 6 hours.

Metabolism: Unbound in the GI tract to aluminum and sucrose octasulfate.

Elimination: 90 percent fecal excretion. The small amount that is absorbed is eliminated as sulfate disaccharide in the urine.

NURSING IMPLICATIONS

Monitor serum aluminum.

To avoid unnecessary aluminum accumulation, discontinue use as soon as no longer needed.

COMMENTS

Interactions:

- May cause decreased bioavailability and rate of absorption of concurrently given medications (e.g., phenytoin, ketoconazole, sodium and potassium phosphate salts, digoxin, cimetidine, ranitidine, theophylline); separate administration by 2 hours, if possible.

- Concurrent use of ciprofloxacin and other fluoroquinolones with sucralfate may decrease the absorption of these drugs. Administer these drugs 2–3 hours before sucralfate.

- Antacids and H_2 antagonists (ranitidine, famotidine, cimetidine) may reduce the effectiveness of sucralfate because its activation is dependent on the presence of gastric acid. Give antacids 30 minutes before or after sucralfate; give H_2 blockers 2 hours before sucralfate.

- Concurrent use of aluminum-containing antacids may increase total body load of aluminum because aluminum is absorbed from both medications.

- May interfere with absorption of vitamins A, D, E, and K.

REFERENCES

1. Nahata MC, and Hipple TF. 1992. *Pediatric Drug Formulations,* 2nd ed. Cincinnati, Ohio: Harvey Whitney Books, 73.

2. Schneider JS, and Ouellette SM. 1984. Sucralfate administration via nasogastric tube (letter). *New England Journal of Medicine* 310(15): 990.

3. United States Pharmacopeial Convention/USP DI. 1996. *Drug Information for the Health Care Professional*, 16th ed. Rockville, Maryland: United States Pharmacopeial Convention, 2701–2702.

4. Kirschbaum BB, and Schoolwerth AC. 1989. Acute aluminum toxicity associated with oral citrate and aluminum-containing antacids. *American Journal of the Medical Sciences* 297(1): 9–11.

5. Tsou VM, et al. 1991. Elevated plasma aluminum levels in normal infants receiving antacids containing aluminum. *Pediatrics* 87(2): 148–151.

6. Koo WWK, et al. 1986. Aluminum in parenteral nutrition solution—sources and possible alternatives. *Journal of Parenteral and Enteral Nutrition* 10(6): 591–595.

7. American Society for Clinical Nutrition (ASCN)/American Society for Parenteral and Enteral Nutrition (ASPEN), Working Group on Standards for Aluminum Content of Parenteral Nutrition Solutions. 1991. Parenteral drug products containing aluminum as an ingredient or a contaminant: Response to Food and Drug Administration notice of intent and request for information. *Journal of Parenteral and Enteral Nutrition* 15(2): 194–198.

8. Sedman AB, et al. 1985. Evidence of aluminum loading in infants receiving intravenous therapy. *New England Journal of Medicine* 312(21): 1337–1343.

9. Koo WWK, et al. 1986. Response to aluminum in parenteral nutrition during infancy. *Journal of Pediatrics* 109(5): 877–883.

10. Koo WWK, et al. 1992. Sequential serum aluminum and urine aluminum:creatinine ratio and tissue aluminum loading in infants with fractures/rickets. *Pediatrics* 89(5 part 1): 877–881.

11. Bozynski ME, et al. 1989. Serum plasma and urinary aluminum levels and tissue loading in pre-term twins. *Journal of Parenteral and Enteral Nutrition* 13(4): 428–431.

12. Arguelles-Martin F, Gonzalez-Fernandez F, and Gentles MG: 1989. Sucralfate versus cimetidine in the treatment of reflux esophagitis in children. *American Journal of Medicine* 86(supplement 6A): S73–S76.

13. Reed MD, Sutphen JL, and Blumer JL. 1992. Drugs used to modulate gastrointestinal function. In *Pediatric Pharmacology: Therapeutic Principles in Practice*, Yaffe SJ, and Aranda JV, eds. Philadelphia: WB Saunders, 437–465.

14. Driks MR, et al. 1987. Nosocomial pneumonia in intubated patients given sucralfate as compared with antacids or histamine type 2 blockers: The role of gastric colonization. *New England Journal of Medicine* 317(22): 1376–1382.

15. McCarthy DM. 1991. Sucralfate. *New England Journal of Medicine* 325(14): 1017–1025.

16. Shenep JL, et al. 1988. Efficacy of oral sucralfate suspension in prevention and treatment of chemotherapy-induced mucositis. *Journal of Pediatrics* 113(4): 758–763.

17. Solomon MA. 1986. Oral sucralfate suspension for mucositis (letter). *New England Journal of Medicine* 315(7): 459–460.

18. Hayashi AH, Lau HYC, and Gillis DA. 1991. Topical sucralfate: Effective therapy for the management of resistant peristomal and perineal excoriation. *Journal of Pediatric Surgery* 26(11): 1279–1281.

SUCROSE 24 PERCENT
ORAL SOLUTION (SWEET-EASE)

ANALGESIC:
MISCELLANEOUS

(SOOK-rose)

DOSE

The exact dose has not been established, especially in preterm infants. The International Evidence-Based Group for Neonatal Pain suggests the following doses:

- **Term:** 1–2 ml of 24 percent solution given 2 minutes prior to painful procedure, plus pacifier dipped in the sucrose solution. May repeat every 6 hours as needed after the procedure.[1]
- **Preterm:** 0.1–0.4 ml of 24 percent solution given 2 minutes prior to painful procedure, plus pacifier dipped in the sucrose solution. May repeat every 6 hours as needed after the procedure.[1]

Ramenghi and colleagues used a maximum of 1 ml of 25 percent sucrose solution in preterm infants to avoid the theoretic risk of necrotizing enterocolitis as the result of the hypertonic sucrose solution.[2]

A meta-analysis and systematic review of five studies and 271 infants showed that a dose of 0.24 gm (= 1 ml of 24 percent sucrose solution) was most effective and that a dose of 0.18 gm sucrose was ineffective. A 0.5 gm dose provided no additional benefit.[3] (Table 1-46 lists sucrose equivalents in grams and milliliters.)

ADMINISTRATION

Intraoral: Administer slowly to the anterior portion of the tongue via oral syringe and/or via pacifier.

- The total dose can be given incrementally before, during, and after the procedure. The pacifier may be dipped and administered again during the time period of the procedure.
- Discard unused portion of cup after opening.
- Do not administer with a syringe intended for parenteral use, to avoid risk of inadvertent parenteral administration. Keep a box of oral syringes and caps in the NICU for this purpose (a needle does not fit onto the hub of an oral syringe).

Supplied as: Oral solution: 24 percent, 11 ml cup with a peel-off lid suitable for dipping a pacifier or for administration with an oral syringe. Preservative free.[4]

CAUTIONS/CONTRAINDICATIONS

Avoid in preterm infants weighing <1.2 kg and/or in preterm infants receiving less than half of full enteral feedings.

Avoid in infants with feeding intolerance and/or abdominal distention.

Avoid in paralyzed or highly sedated infants at risk for aspiration.

TABLE 1-46 ◆ CONVERTING SUCROSE VOLUME (IN ML) TO SUCROSE IN GRAMS

Sucrose 24 Percent	Sucrose 12 Percent	Grams of Sucrose
0.2 ml	0.4 ml	0.05 gm
0.5 ml	1 ml	0.12 gm
0.75 ml	1.5 ml	0.18 gm
1 ml	2 ml	0.24 gm
2 ml	4 ml	0.48 gm

⟁ For treating pain of circumcision, combine with other analgesics (EMLA cream [see lidocaine/prilocaine cream monograph]), dorsal penile nerve block, acetaminophen postoperatively); do not use alone.[1]

⟁ Effective only when administered to the anterior tongue; not effective when given by gavage or via nasogastric tube. Intravenously administered sweet solutions such as $D_{10}W$ are not effective in treating pain.

⟁ Check expiration date on cup before dispensing and administering. The product becomes outdated quickly (3 months from time of manufacture) compared with other medications.

USE

Reduction of procedural pain in term and preterm neonates. Administration of sucrose solution is a noninvasive, simple, effective, inexpensive, and benign intervention to help alleviate stress and pain in the neonate.[2,3,5,6]

The International Evidence-Based Group for Neonatal Pain lists the use of a pacifier with sucrose oral solution as one suggested management approach, combined with other interventions and comfort measures, for the following procedures: heel lance, percutaneous venous or arterial catheter insertion, peripheral arterial or venous cutdown, central venous line placement, umbilical arterial or venous catheter insertion, peripherally inserted central catheter placement, lumbar puncture, subcutaneous or intramuscular injection, endotracheal suction, nasogastric or orogastric tube insertion, chest tube insertion, circumcision, and ongoing analgesia or routine NICU care and procedures.[1] Also consider using sucrose oral solution for the pain of adhesive tape removal, eye exams, dressing changes, and urinary catheterization.

Abad and colleagues showed that sucrose solution compared favorably with EMLA cream in decreasing pain responses to venipuncture in newborns.[6]

MECHANISM OF ACTION

The mechanism of sucrose solution in pain reduction is probably preabsorptive, based on sweet taste perception. This sense is well developed, even in preterm infants, at birth. The taste perception of sweetness elevates the pain threshold via the endogenous opioid system, resulting in decreased crying time and calming effects. These effects are reversed when an opioid antagonist is given.[7] The tip of the tongue is used as the administration site because about 90 percent of the taste buds are distributed within the first 2 cm from the tip of the tongue. The pacifier promotes nonnutritive sucking and calming, which may also have a synergistic effect in reducing distress from pain.[1]

Another sweet-tasting solution (Lycasin, which is hydrogenated glucose syrup 40 percent, the vehicle in the acetaminophen product Calpol [Burroughs Wellcome]) was effective in reducing crying time and pain score. Ramenghi and colleagues had subjectively observed that infants given the acetaminophen solution Calpol calmed quickly, within seconds of its administration, an effect too rapid to be attributable to the analgesic properties of acetaminophen. Their study showed that the Lycasin, the sweet-tasting solution in this product, had analgesic effects as potent as those of sucrose solutions.[7]

Sucrose is a disaccharide that when hydrolyzed is converted to dextrose and levulose.

Adverse Effects

Sucrose solution is usually well tolerated. Adverse effects have not been reported; however, the infant should be observed for these theoretical adverse effects: aspiration, hyperglycemia with repeated doses, and signs of necrotizing enterocolitis in preterm infants because of the hypertonicity of the solution. Cariogenic effects on erupted teeth have also been proposed as a potential concern.[2]

Pharmacokinetics/Pharmacodynamics

Onset of Action: Rapid. Crying almost always ceases within the first 2 minutes of sucrose administration. Two minutes are thought to be required for endogenous opioid release.[8]

Duration of Action: Calming lasts up to 5 minutes after administration.

Nursing Implications

- Consider monitoring blood glucose at bedside when repeated doses are being given.
- Monitor infant, and document effects in the medical record.
- Develop a unit protocol and order "per protocol," or obtain physician/nurse practitioner order. Document each dose.[8]

Comments

Calorie Content: Approximately 1 kcal/ml.

One pacifier dip is equivalent to approximately 0.2 ml.[4]

Osmolarity: 700 mOsm/liter.

Conversion: The studies cited in this monograph vary in terms of the percent sucrose solution and the volume of sucrose solution used. Converting the doses to common units, grams of sucrose (see Table 1-46), simplifies comparison among various research studies.

REFERENCES

1. Anand KJS, and the International Evidence-Based Group for Neonatal Pain. 2001. Consensus statement for the prevention and management of pain in the newborn. *Archives of Pediatrics and Adolescent Medicine* 155(2): 173–180.

2. Ramenghi LA, et al. 1996. Reduction of pain response in premature infants using intraoral sucrose. *Archives of Disease in Childhood. Fetal and Neonatal Edition* 74(2): F126–F128.

3. Stevens B, et al. 1997. The efficacy of sucrose for relieving procedural pain in neonates—Systemic review and meta-analysis. *Acta Paediatrica* 86(8): 837–842.

4. Manufacturer's product literature. *Sweet-Ease*. Children's Medical Ventures, 275 Longwater Drive, Norwell, MA 02061.

5. Abad F, et al. 1996. Oral sweet solution reduces pain-related behaviour in preterm infants. *Acta Paediatrica* 85(7): 854–858.

6. Abad F, et al. 2001. Oral sucrose compares favourably with lidocaine-prilocaine cream for pain relief during venepuncture in neonates. *Acta Paediatrica* 90(2): 160–165.

7. Ramenghi LA, et al. 1996. Effect of non-sucrose sweet tasting solution on neonatal heel prick responses. *Archives of Disease in Childhood. Fetal and Neonatal Edition* 74(2): F129–F131.

8. Noerr B. 2001. Sucrose for neonatal procedural pain. *Neonatal Network* 20(7): 63–67.

S

S

TABLE OF CONTENTS

T

T

TERBUTALINE (BRETHINE, BRETHAIRE)
(ter-BYOO-ta-leen)

RESPIRATORY:
BRONCHODILATOR

DOSE
Nebulization:

- *Intermittent:* 0.01–0.03 mg/kg given every 2–6 hours. Dilute to a final total volume of 3 ml with normal saline or other concurrent medications. *Minimum:* 0.1 mg. *Maximum:* 1 mg/dose.[1]
- *Continuous:* 0.4 mg/kg/hour by continuous nebulization.[2] In a study by Portnoy and Aggarwal, continuous nebulization for 1–24 hours (mean = 8 hours) was not associated with signs of toxicity such as tachycardia or arrhythmia. They considered it a safe and effective mode of treatment.[3]

MDI: Two puffs every 4–12 hours. Use with a spacer.[1,4]

ADMINISTRATION
Supplied as:

- *Injection:* 1 mg/ml amp. Use the injection (parenteral form) for nebulization.
- *Aerosol (for MDI):* 0.2 mg per actuation.

Via nebulization or MDI.

USE
A selective β_2 sympathomimetic agent for bronchodilation in reversible airway obstruction.[5]

May improve pulmonary function in infants with BPD.[6]

MECHANISM OF ACTION
Terbutaline has β_2-adrenergic effects (bronchial dilation by relaxing bronchial musculature and vasodilation) and minor β_1 effects (increased myocardial contractility and conduction). The drug stimulates adenyl cyclase, which converts ATP to cyclic AMP, which mediates cellular responses. Terbutaline also inhibits histamine release from mast cells, produces vasodilation, and increases ciliary motility.[5]

Terbutaline has greater selectivity and potency than metaproterenol.

Albuterol and terbutaline are equipotent; there is little difference between them as bronchodilator agents.

ADVERSE EFFECTS
Tachycardia, arrhythmias, tremor, increased blood pressure, and hyperglycemia.

Adverse effects are less frequent with terbutaline than with isoproterenol.

Tolerance—demonstrated by decreased intensity and duration of bronchodilator action—may develop after prolonged (several weeks) use.[7]

Fluid overload may occur with continuous nebulization.

PHARMACOKINETICS/PHARMACODYNAMICS

Onset of Action: 5–30 minutes.

Duration of Action: 3–6 hours.

Metabolism: Partially metabolized in the liver, mainly to the inactive sulfate conjugate. First-pass metabolism through the liver may occur after oral administration because a larger proportion of the dose is excreted as the sulfate conjugate after oral administration than after parenteral use.

Elimination: Primarily in the urine.

NURSING IMPLICATIONS

Monitor for tachycardia and cardiac arrhythmias.

Monitor blood pressure and respiratory status.

COMMENTS

Monitoring and Dose Titration:

- *Reduce the dose* to the next smaller dose *and/or increase the dosing interval* to the next longer interval when the heart rate exceeds 180 bpm (if baseline HR was <150 bpm) or 200 bpm (if baseline HR was >150 bpm). A moderate increase in heart rate is expected and may indicate absorption and therapeutic response. Lengthening the interval between doses should be tried when respiratory status has improved. Taper to the lowest effective dose.

- *Increase the dose* to the next larger dose *and/or decrease the dosing interval* to the next shorter interval if the infant is still in respiratory distress after a trial of 1–3 doses. Do not increase dose if infant is experiencing adverse effects from existing dose. In severe airway obstruction, frequent small doses of bronchodilator by nebulizer may be more effective than larger, less frequent doses.[8]

Discontinuation of Treatment: Monitor heart rate and blood pressure. Discontinue terbutaline if adverse effects occur or if the drug is no longer needed. If there has been no improvement in respiratory status as measured by pulmonary mechanics, blood gases, change in respiratory support, or clinical status after 3 doses, discontinue the drug.

REFERENCES

1. Galant SP. 1983. Current status of beta-adrenergic agonists in bronchial asthma. *Pediatric Clinics of North America* 30(5): 931–942.

2. Benitz WE, and Tatro DS. 1995. *The Pediatric Drug Handbook,* 3rd ed. St. Louis: Mosby-Year Book, 155–156.

3. Portnoy J, and Aggarwal J. 1988. Continuous terbutaline nebulization for the treatment of severe exacerbations of asthma in children. *Annals of Allergy* 60(4): 368–371.

4. Yuksel B, Greenough A, and Maconochie I. 1990. Effective bronchodilator treatment by a simple spacer device for wheezy premature infants. *Archives of Disease in Childhood* 65(7): 782–785.

5. Manufacturer's product literature.

6. Denjean A, et al. 1992. Dose-related bronchodilator response to aerosolized salbutamol (albuterol) in ventilator-dependent premature infants. *Journal of Pediatrics* 120(6): 974–979.

7. Isles AF, and Newth CJL. 1993. Respiratory pharmacology. In *Pediatric Pharmacology and Therapeutics,* 2nd ed., Radde IC, and MacLeod SM, eds. St. Louis: Mosby-Year Book, 243–266.

8. Robertson CF, et al. 1985. Response to frequent low doses of nebulized salbutamol in acute asthma. *Journal of Pediatrics* 106(4): 672–674.

THEOPHYLLINE
(thee-OFF-i-lin)

**RESPIRATORY:
APNEA/BRADYCARDIA;
BRONCHODILATOR**

DOSE

PO—*Loading Dose:* Theophylline 5 mg/kg

- ***Rebolus:*** In neonates, a dose of 1 mg theophylline/kg raises the serum level approximately 1.4 mcg/ml (volume of distribution in neonates is variable, with a mean of approximately 0.69 liter/kg). To raise the serum theophylline concentration by approximately 2 mcg/ml, give a dose of 1.4 mg theophylline/kg.

For example, giving a 2 kg infant a rebolus dose of theophylline 5 mg might increase serum theophylline concentration by approximately 3.5 mcg/ml:

5 mg ÷ 2 kg = 2.5 mg/kg × 1.4 mcg/ml = 3.5 mcg/ml

PO—*Maintenance Dose (begin 12 hours after loading dose):*

- ***Neonatal apnea:*** Theophylline 2 mg/kg/dose IV/PO given every 12 hours.
- ***BPD/Bronchospasm:***
  - ***6 weeks–6 months postnatal age:*** Theophylline 10 mg/kg/day PO divided every 6–8 hours.
  - ***6 months–1 year:*** Theophylline 12–18 mg/kg/day PO divided every 6–8 hours.

Adjust dose based on serum concentration.

IV: See aminophylline monograph.

ADMINISTRATION

Supplied as: Various aminophylline and theophylline products have differing theophylline content. To convert between products, use Table 1-7, page 41.

PO: An alcohol-free product (liquid, syrup, or solution) should be chosen, rather than one with alcohol (elixir) because elixirs may contain up to 20 percent alcohol. The American Academy of Pediatrics has expressed concern over the undesirable interactions, neuronal dysfunction, and hypoglycemia that can occur with ethanol-containing medications.[1] Alcohol can also alter liver function and cause gastric irritation and neurologic depression, leading to lethargy and poor feeding. Theophylline solution (5.33 mg/ml) is a readily available, easily measured, and safe concentration for most infants. Dilute in a small amount of food just prior to administration to reduce gastric irritation.

IV: See aminophylline monograph.

USE

Used to reduce the severity and frequency of neonatal apnea and as a bronchodilator in BPD. A marked reduction in the number of apneic episodes is usually seen within a few hours of initiation of therapy. May assist in weaning these infants from the ventilator. Infants not responding to theophylline or caffeine alone may respond to doxapram alone or doxapram plus caffeine or theophylline.

Caffeine is often preferred to theophylline to treat neonatal apnea because of its efficacy, greater safety, and once-daily dosing. Theophylline is preferred, however, where the added benefit of bronchodilation is desired, such as in infants with BPD.[2]

The major pharmacologic effects of two methylxanthines are listed in Table 1-8, page 42.

MECHANISM OF ACTION

Theophylline relaxes smooth muscle of the bronchi and pulmonary blood vessels, induces a small amount of diuresis, increases gastric acid secretion, and has a mild chronotropic and inotropic effect on the heart. Some of the mechanisms by which methylxanthines (theophylline and caffeine) reduce neonatal apnea include increased sensitivity of the CNS medullary respiratory centers to CO_2, stimulation of central inspiratory drive, improvement in skeletal muscle contraction, and improvement in oxygenation via increased cardiac output and decreased hypoxic episodes. (See also caffeine monograph.)

ADVERSE EFFECTS

May cause tachycardia, irritability, transient hyperglycemia, diuresis, reduced sleep, GI irritation, and jitteriness.

At serum levels >40 mcg/ml, seizures and cardiac arrhythmias may occur.

Chronic toxicity may result in poor weight gain.[3]

PHARMACOKINETICS/PHARMACODYNAMICS

Absorption: Well absorbed orally.

Metabolism: Clearance rate increases with postnatal age as liver function matures. Older infants (>1–2 months) may therefore require higher doses to achieve therapeutic levels and clinical response. Theophylline is converted to caffeine in the neonate at a serum ratio of caffeine to theophylline of 0.3 (caffeine serum concentration is about one-third as high as the concurrent theophylline serum concentration).[4]

NURSING IMPLICATIONS

Draw blood for levels after 3 or more days (steady state is reached at approximately 5 days) in preterm infants being treated for apnea. Serum levels fluctuate only about 2 mcg/ml between dosing intervals; therefore, theophylline level may be drawn at any time during dosing interval except immediately after the dose.

Monitor serum levels and for signs of toxicity such as irritability, jitteriness, feeding intolerance, and tachycardia.

Withhold the next dose and check the serum level if the heart rate increases above 180 bpm or to approximately 20 bpm above normal baseline. The dose may need to be reduced.

Discontinue oral theophylline in infants with suspected NEC to reduce gastric irritation. Use other means to control apnea.

COMMENTS

Therapeutic Range: 5–15 mcg/ml.[2]

Theophylline is methylated to caffeine in infants, with plasma theophylline to caffeine ratios sometimes reaching 0.3 to 0.4 at steady state. Thus, the overall methylxanthine effect has to account for the sum of the two drugs because both drugs are pharmacologically active.[2,5] Both caffeine and theophylline levels could be measured to determine the total methylxanthine serum concentration, although this is rarely necessary and adds to the cost of therapy.

Interactions: Cimetidine (but not usually ranitidine or famotidine) and erythromycin reduce the clearance of theophylline, resulting in higher than expected serum theophylline concentrations. Elevated theophylline levels and signs of toxicity have occurred in select patients concurrently receiving theophylline and ranitidine. This is not a general phenomenon, but rather idiosyncratic. Ranitidine does not reduce the clearance of theophylline.[6] Phenobarbital or phenytoin may decrease theophylline levels.

REFERENCES

1. American Academy of Pediatrics, Committee on Drugs. 1984. Ethanol in liquid preparations intended for children. *Pediatrics* 73(3): 405–407.

2. Aranda JV, et al. 1991. Treatment of neonatal apnea. In *Neonatal Clinical Pharmacology and Therapeutics,* Rylance G, Harvey D, and Aranda J, eds. Linacre House, Jordan Hill, Oxford: Butterworth-Heinemann, 95–115.

3. Howell J, Clozel M, and Aranda JV. 1981. Adverse effects of caffeine and theophylline in the newborn infant. *Seminars in Perinatology* 5(4): 359–369.

4. Aranda JV, et al. 1976. Pharmacokinetic aspects of theophylline in premature newborns. *New England Journal of Medicine* 295(8): 413–416.

5. Aranda JV, et al. 1979. Metabolism of theophylline to caffeine in human fetal liver. *Science* 206(4424): 1319–1321.

6. Kehoe WA, et al. 1996. Effect of ranitidine on theophylline metabolism in healthy Koreans living in China. *Annals of Pharmacotherapy* 30(2): 133–137.

TICARCILLIN (TICAR)   ANTI-INFECTIVE:
(tye-kar-SILL-in)   ANTIBIOTIC

DOSE

<1.2 kg (0–4 weeks): 75 mg/kg/dose every 12 hours[1]
1.2–2 kg:
- 0–7 days: 75 mg/kg/dose every 12 hours
- >7 days: 75 mg/kg/dose every 8 hours

>2 kg:
- 0–7 days: 75 mg/kg/dose every 8 hours
- >7 days: 75 mg/kg/dose every 6 hours[2]

Reduce dose in severe renal and/or liver dysfunction.

ADMINISTRATION

IV—*Rate:* Infuse over 30 minutes.

IV—*Concentration:* 50 mg/ml preferred, to reduce vein irritation. Maximum: 100 mg/ml.

IV—*Compatibility:* Do not admix in the same IV solution with amikacin, gentamicin, or tobramycin because ticarcillin gradually inactivates these antibiotics.[3] Inactivation also occurs *in vivo,* but only in patients with severe renal dysfunction.

IM: Reconstitute 1 gm with 2 ml sterile water or normal saline to obtain 1 gm/2.6 ml (= 385 mg/ml). Use the IM route only in extreme circumstances, when IV access is not possible, and then only for as short a time as possible.

USE

An extended-spectrum penicillin used primarily to treat Gram-negative infections, especially *Pseudomonas aeruginosa*, Proteus species, and *Escherichia coli* infections of the blood, skin and soft tissues, and respiratory tract. Often used in combination with gentamicin or tobramycin for infants with nosocomial Gram-negative enteric infections.[4–6]

Also coadministered with clavulanate potassium, which significantly enhances the antibacterial activity of ticarcillin. (A combination of ticarcillin and clavulanate potassium is marketed as Timentin. Other antibiotics are also produced in this fashion. Information on use of Timentin in newborns is limited.)[6]

Also used to treat susceptible strains of anaerobic bacteria.

Another extended-spectrum penicillin is carbenicillin.

MECHANISM OF ACTION

Ticarcillin inhibits bacterial cell wall synthesis. Its activity is dependent on its ability to enter the bacterial cell wall, avoid destruction by β-lactamases (penicillinases), and bind to penicillin-binding proteins involved in septum formation.

Combination with clavulanic acid (Timentin) protects ticarcillin from degradation by β-lactamases.

ADVERSE EFFECTS

Interferes with platelet function; bleeding may develop secondary to dose-related abnormal platelet aggregation.

Contains 4.7–5 mEq Na/gm. Maintenance sodium may need to be reduced while patient is on this drug. May cause hypernatremia and hypokalemia.

May increase urinary potassium excretion.

May produce all adverse effects associated with the penicillins, such as allergic reactions.

PHARMACOKINETICS/PHARMACODYNAMICS

Absorption: Not available in oral form.

Distribution: CSF levels are 30–50 percent of serum levels.

Metabolism: A small amount undergoes hepatic metabolism.

Half-life: Correlates with postnatal age (5–6 hours in the first few days of life, 2–3 hours by 3–4 weeks of age).

Elimination: Largely excreted unchanged in the urine.[4,5]

NURSING IMPLICATIONS

Monitor for bleeding due to possible abnormal platelet aggregation.

Monitor for decreased potassium levels.

Separate administration time by 30–60 minutes if given concurrently with aminoglycosides.

REFERENCES

1. Prober CG, Stevenson DK, and Benitz WE. 1990. The use of antibiotics in neonates weighing less than 1,200 grams. *Pediatric Infectious Disease Journal* 9(2): 111–121.

2. Nelson JD. 1996. *1996–1997 Pocketbook of Pediatric Antimicrobial Therapy,* 12th ed. Baltimore: Lippincott Williams & Wilkins, 16–17.

3. Pickering LK, and Gearhart P. 1979. Effect of time and concentration upon interaction between gentamicin, tobramycin, netilmicin, or amikacin and carbenicillin or ticarcillin. *Antimicrobial Agents and Chemotherapy* 15(4): 592–596.

4. Roberts RJ. 1984. *Drug Therapy in Infants: Pharmacologic Principles and Clinical Experience.* Philadelphia: WB Saunders, 52–53.

5. Nelson JD, et al. 1978. Clinical pharmacology and efficacy of ticarcillin in infants and children. *Pediatrics* 61(6): 858–863.

6. Sáez-Llorens X, and McCracken GH Jr. 1995. Clinical pharmacology of antibacterial agents. In *Infectious Diseases of the Fetus and Newborn Infant,* 4th ed., Remington JS, and Klein JO, eds. Philadelphia: WB Saunders, 1287–1336.

TOBRAMYCIN (NEBCIN)

(toe-bra-MYE-sin)

ANTI-INFECTIVE:
ANTIBIOTIC

DOSE

<1.2 kg (0–4 weeks): 2.5 mg/kg/dose given every 18–24 hours*
1.2–2 kg:

- 0–7 days: 2.5 mg/kg/dose given every 12–18 hours*
- >7 days: 2.5 mg/kg/dose given every 8–12 hours

>2 kg:

- 0–7 days: 2.5 mg/kg/dose given every 12 hours
- >7 days: 2.5 mg/kg/dose given every 8 hours[1,2]

Reduce dose in renal impairment.

Individualize dose based on serum concentrations.

ADMINISTRATION

Supplied as: 10 mg/ml. A 2 mg/ml solution is made by diluting 2 ml of the 10 mg/ml solution with 8 ml of sterile water.

IV preferred over IM.

IV—*Rate:* Infuse over 30 minutes. Infusing tobramycin over less than 20 minutes is not recommended because peak serum levels may exceed 12 mcg/ml.

IV—*Concentration:* No maximum concentration is stated. Volume of diluent depends on fluid status of patient.

IV—*Compatibility:* See Appendix E: Y-Site Compatibility of Common NICU Drugs.

IM: Use undiluted. May be given IM for a few doses for infants with difficult IV access. IM administration of drugs is discouraged in neonates because of their small muscle mass, poor perfusion, and trauma to the infant.

CAUTIONS/CONTRAINDICATIONS

Interactions: Aminoglycosides such as tobramycin and gentamicin have a potential curare-like effect on neuromuscular function.

Use with caution in newborns of mothers who have received magnesium sulfate. Hypermagnesemic infants are more likely to have apnea after receiving aminoglycosides.

Infants with botulism are more likely to become apneic when given aminoglycosides.

Aminoglycosides may aggravate muscle weakness in infants with myasthenia gravis.

---

* See Appendix B: Every-18-Hour Medication Worksheet.

Respiratory paralysis may occur when aminoglycosides are given soon after anesthesia or muscle relaxants.

Use

Treatment of resistant Gram-negative bacterial infections, including Enterobacter species, *Escherichia coli,* Acinetobacter species, and *Pseudomonas aeruginosa.* Should be used in combination with an antipseudomonal penicillin, such as ticarcillin, for serious systemic Pseudomonas infections.

Comparison with Gentamicin: The pharmacology and therapeutic serum levels of tobramycin and gentamicin are the same. Tobramycin has greater activity against Pseudomonas than gentamicin does.

Mechanism of Action

Tobramycin is an aminoglycoside antibiotic. Aminoglycosides act on microbial ribosomes to irreversibly inhibit protein synthesis.

Adverse Effects

May cause rash (uncommon).

Ototoxicity: Can cause both auditory (cochlear) and vestibular toxicity. Risk is greater in patients with renal impairment, with pre-existing hearing loss, with duration of therapy >10 days, with concurrent administration of furosemide, and when large amounts of drug are administered. Avoid concurrent use of other ototoxic drugs.

Renal Toxicity: Uncommon in neonates. Characterized by decreased creatinine clearance, cells or casts in the urine, decreased urine specific gravity, oliguria, proteinuria, increasing BUN and serum creatinine. Usually reversible if the drug is discontinued promptly. Avoid concurrent use of other nephrotoxic drugs.

Pharmacokinetics/Pharmacodynamics

Absorption: Poor oral absorption, but excessive levels may accumulate in neonates receiving concomitant oral and parenteral aminoglycosides.

Volume of Distribution (V_d): Gestational age and weight are inversely correlated with V_d during the first week of life. In various neonatal studies, V_d has varied from 0.51 to 1.02 liter/kg.

Peak Effect: After IM administration, 0.5–1 hour.

Metabolism: Postconceptional age is a good indicator of aminoglycoside clearance, especially after the first week of life.

Half-life: Varies from 5.6 to 11.3 hours.

Elimination: Renal.[3,4]

Nursing Implications

Infuse slowly.

Monitor urine output closely.

Monitor BUN, serum creatinine, serum tobramycin concentrations, and BAER (brainstem auditory evoked response) testing.

COMMENTS

Therapeutic Range:

- *Peak:* 4–10 mcg/ml, drawn 30 minutes after completion of a 30-minute infusion.
- *Trough:* <0.5–2 mcg/ml, drawn just before the dose.
- Draw levels at steady state (after three or four doses).
- Presence of penicillins or cephalosporins with aminoglycosides in serum samples to be assayed for tobramycin may result in falsely low tobramycin concentrations. This could lead to unnecessary upward dose adjustment, increasing the risk of toxicity. Administer the penicillin or cephalosporin after the tobramycin level is drawn to reduce the risk of this interaction.[5]

REFERENCES

1. Nelson JD. 1996. *1996–1997 Pocketbook of Pediatric Antimicrobial Therapy,* 12th ed. Baltimore: Lippincott Williams & Wilkins, 16–17.
2. Prober CG, Stevenson DK, and Benitz WE. 1990. The use of antibiotics in neonates weighing less than 1,200 grams. *Pediatric Infectious Disease Journal* 9(2): 111–121.
3. Paap CM, and Nahata MC. 1990. Clinical pharmacokinetics of antibacterial drugs in neonates. *Clinical Pharmacokinetics* 19(4): 280–318.
4. Nahata MC, et al. 1984. Effect of gestational age and birth weight on tobramycin kinetics in newborn infants. *Journal of Antimicrobial Chemotherapy* 14(1): 59–65.
5. Riff LJ, and Jackson GG. 1972. Laboratory and clinical conditions for gentamicin inactivation by carbenicillin. *Archives of Internal Medicine* 130(6): 887–891.

TOLAZOLINE (PRISCOLINE)
(toe-LAZ-oh-leen)

CARDIOVASCULAR:
VASODILATOR

DOSE

Pulmonary Hypertension:

- *Loading Dose:* 1–2 mg/kg/dose infused over 10–15 minutes into a vein that drains into the superior vena cava, such as a scalp or upper-arm vein. Taper dose gradually when arterial blood gases stabilize.

- *Maintenance Dose:* 1–2 mg/kg/hour.[1] For therapy longer than a few hours, use 0.16 mg/kg/hour for each 1 mg/kg loading dose to prevent accumulation and adverse effects.[2,3]

Vasospasm Associated with Umbilical Arterial Catheters: Heath infused tolazoline 0.25 mg/kg/hour at a concentration of 0.1 mg/ml via the umbilical artery catheter while leaving the catheters in place in two infants who required frequent arterial blood gas analyses. Catheters were positioned in the lower lumbar area to ensure perfusion to the arterial supply of the lower extremities. The regimen was also effective when given into a peripheral vein in a third infant using this dose. Venospasm improved within 10–30 minutes, but infusion should be continued to avoid recurrence. Infusion was continued for 34 hours, 72 hours, and 5 days in the three infants reported. None of the patients experienced adverse effects.[4]

Management of Aortic Thrombosis Associated with Umbilical Catheterization: 0.1–0.2 mg/kg intra-arterially.[5]

Reduce dose in patients with oliguria and/or renal dysfunction.[3]

ADMINISTRATION

IV—*Rate:* The loading dose should be infused over 10–15 minutes. The continuous infusion should be given using a neonatal syringe pump.

IV—*Concentration:* May be given undiluted or diluted based on the infant's fluid requirements.

IV—*Compatibility:* See Appendix E: Y-Site Compatibility of Common NICU Drugs.

USE

Used in some infants with elevation of pulmonary vascular resistance or pressure (persistent pulmonary hypertension of the newborn [PPHN] or persistent fetal circulation [PFC]) when oxygenation cannot be adequately maintained by the usual supportive measures, such as supplemental oxygen and/or mechanical ventilation. Improves pulmonary perfusion in some neonates, although the rate of adverse effects associated with the use of tolazoline is high. Dilates constricted pulmonary vasculature of hypoxic lambs (although effects are not specific only to the lung).[1,2]

Has also been used to treat severe vasospasm from an indwelling umbilical artery catheter.[4,6]

Newer treatment modalities such as inhaled nitric oxide show promise in treating severe PPHN.

MECHANISM OF ACTION

Tolazoline has a sympathomimetic effect, resulting in increased heart rate and cardiac output. It stimulates the GI tract, causing hyperperistalsis. It has a histamine-like effect, causing GI secretion of acid and pepsin and peripheral vasodilating action. Its α-adrenergic blocking action causes peripheral vasodilation at high doses.[1,2]

ADVERSE EFFECTS

The overall incidence of adverse effects in neonates is 30 percent. Increasing the dose to higher than that indicated, especially in patients with renal dysfunction, may increase adverse effects to 80 percent. Use of the lower continuous infusion doses suggested previously should reduce accumulation and markedly minimize adverse effects.[2]

Cardiovascular: Hypotension. Although tolazoline has been used for pulmonary hypertension, it is not a selective pulmonary vasodilator, and systemic hypotension may occur. The risk may be minimized by ensuring that the infant is in good fluid balance prior to initiation of tolazoline and using concomitant dopamine and a low-dose continuous infusion. Do not attempt to reverse hypotension with norepinephrine or epinephrine. (See **Interactions** under **COMMENTS**.) Large doses may cause tachycardia, arrhythmias.

CNS: Seizures.

GI: Increased abdominal girth, increased secretions and motility, gastric hemorrhage, perforation. Pretreatment with antacids may be beneficial.

Pulmonary: Hemorrhage.

Renal: Oliguria, hematuria, hyponatremia.

PHARMACOKINETICS/PHARMACODYNAMICS

Half-life: 3–10 hours in neonates; however, reportedly as long as 40 hours.[7] Correlates inversely with urine output.[3]

Elimination: Primarily renal.

NURSING IMPLICATIONS

Monitor ECG and blood pressure continuously.

Also monitor blood gases, urine output, fluid and electrolyte status.

Watch for signs of bleeding from GI tract or lung.

COMMENTS

If tolazoline is administered by peripheral IV, the drug may preferentially cross into the systemic circulation by means of a right-to-left shunt. This would result in peripheral vasodilation rather than pulmonary vasodilation. Reduction of systemic vascular resistance may aggravate right-to-left shunting and worsen hypoxemia.[1]

Interactions: Tolazoline may reverse the effects of epinephrine (further reduction in blood pressure, followed by exaggerated rebound). Systemic acidosis may reduce the effectiveness of tolazoline because acidosis increases pulmonary vasoconstriction.

REFERENCES

1. Roberts RJ. 1984. *Drug Therapy in Infants: Pharmacologic Principles and Clinical Experience.* Philadelphia: WB Saunders, 187–192.

2. Ward RM. 1984. Pharmacology of tolazoline. *Clinics in Perinatology* 11(3): 703–713.

3. Ward RM, Daniel CH, and Kendig JW. 1986. Oliguria and tolazoline pharmacokinetics in the newborn. *Pediatrics* 77(3): 307–315.

4. Heath RE. 1986. Vasospasm in the neonate: Response to tolazoline infusion. *Pediatrics* 77(3): 405–408.

5. Weinberg G, Brion LP, and Vega-Richf CR. 1990. Dangers of arterial catheters in critically ill neonates (letter). *Pediatrics* 85(4): 627–628.

6. Avery GB. 1983. Management of arterial spasm, thrombosis, or embolism. In *Atlas of Procedures in Neonatology,* Fletcher MA, MacDonald MG, and Avery GB, eds. Philadelphia: Lippincott Williams & Wilkins, 71.

7. United States Pharmacopeial Convention/USP DI. 1996. *Drug Information for the Health Care Professional,* 16th ed. Rockville, Maryland: United States Pharmacopeial Convention, 2893–2894.

TROMETHAMINE (THAM)
(troe-METH-uh-meen)

ELECTROLYTE BALANCE:
ALKALINIZING AGENT

DOSE

3–6 ml/kg/dose (equals approximately 1–2 mmol/kg/dose), or use the following formula:

Body weight (kg) × base deficit (mEq/liter) = dose (ml of 0.3 molar THAM)

Continuous Infusion: 2–3 ml/kg/hour. Monitor blood gases frequently.

Reduce dose in renal dysfunction, and monitor pH carefully.

Do not use in anuria.

ADMINISTRATION

Supplied as: A 0.3 molar solution, 500 ml (= 0.3 mEq/ml) (1 mEq = 1 mmol = 120 mg). Pharmacy may repackage in 10 ml sterile glass vials, using appropriate aseptic technique, to reduce drug waste.

IV: Infuse into as large a vein as possible. Not effective if given PO.

IV—*Rate:* Infuse slowly by syringe pump over 3–6 hours. Maximum rate: 1 hour.

IV—*Concentration:* May give undiluted.

Approximately 3 ml of tromethamine is equivalent to 1 ml of sodium bicarbonate (1 mEq/ml).

CAUTIONS/CONTRAINDICATIONS

Do not confuse THAM with THAM-E. THAM-E contains electrolytes and is not the product used in neonates or the product being discussed in this monograph.

Use with caution if patient is hypoglycemic because THAM may cause hypoglycemia.

USE

For correction of metabolic acidosis with adequate ventilation when sodium bicarbonate cannot be given (when maximum bicarbonate dose of 8 mEq/kg/day has already been given, in hypernatremia, or in infants with a high PCO_2). Use only if urine output is adequate.

Comparison with Sodium Bicarbonate: An advantage of tromethamine over bicarbonate is that it alkalinizes without increasing PCO_2 and sodium. Disadvantages of tromethamine include its large fluid volume per dose compared with sodium bicarbonate (1 ml of $NaHCO_3$ [at 1 mEq/ml] = 3 ml of 0.3 molar THAM).

MECHANISM OF ACTION

Tromethamine is a highly alkaline, sodium-free organic amine. Tromethamine works by combining with hydrogen ions to form bicarbonate and a cationic buffer to raise the pH and correct acidosis.

Adverse Effects

Usually well tolerated when administered as directed.

Hyperosmolality of serum with rapid infusion of large amounts.

Alkalosis and fluid overload with excessive dose; hyperkalemia (particularly in renal dysfunction), hypoglycemia, hypocalcemia may occur. Hyperkalemia and hypoglycemia were reported in animal studies, but were not confirmed in infants given tromethamine.[1,2]

Respiratory depression or apnea[1] may occur infrequently. Either is more likely in patients with chronic hypoventilation or in those treated with drugs that depress respiration. Large doses may depress ventilation because of increased blood pH and reduced CO_2 concentration. Tromethamine may decrease or cause no change in $PaCO_2$, whereas sodium bicarbonate may cause an increase in $PaCO_2$.[3]

Urine flow and electrolyte content of urine may increase because of the osmotic diuretic action of tromethamine.[4]

Check umbilical catheter placement to be sure tip is beyond the liver because direct contact with tromethamine may cause liver cell destruction. If catheter placement cannot be determined, infuse more slowly and at greater dilution. Hemorrhagic necrosis of the liver occurred in seriously ill neonates who received hypertonic (1.2 molar) preparations of tromethamine via the umbilical vein.[4]

Tissue irritation and necrosis with extravasation or from infusion into small vessel; may cause venospasm. If extravasation occurs, stop administration immediately. Treat extravasations with hyaluronidase (Wydase). Phentolamine (Regitine) by local infiltration into the vasospastic area has also been recommended.[4] (See Appendix G: Guidelines for Management of Intravenous Extravasations.) The solution's very alkaline pH of 8.6 contributes to its irritant nature.[4] The osmolality is about 350 mOsm/kg water.[3]

Tromethamine should usually not be administered for longer than 24 hours, except in life-threatening situations, because clinical experience has generally been limited to short-term use.

Pharmacokinetics/Pharmacodynamics

Absorption: Ineffective when given PO.

Metabolism: Tromethamine is a weak base that attracts and combines with hydrogen ions and their associated acid anions (i.e., lactic, pyruvic, carbonic acid); the resulting salts are excreted in the urine.

Elimination: Kidney. May accumulate in renal dysfunction.

Nursing Implications

Monitor blood gases carefully to determine response to therapy.

Monitor for hyperkalemia, hypoglycemia, respiratory depression.

Monitor IV site carefully because tissue damage occurs with extravasation.

REFERENCES

1. Roberton NRC. 1970. Apnea after THAM administration in the newborn. *Archives of Disease in Childhood* 45(240): 206–214.

2. vanVliet PK, and Gupta JM. 1973. THAM versus sodium bicarbonate in idiopathic respiratory distress syndrome. *Archives of Disease in Childhood* 48(4): 249–255.

3. Roberts RJ. 1984. *Drug Therapy in Infants: Pharmacologic Principles and Clinical Experience.* Philadelphia: WB Saunders, 291–292.

4. McEvoy GK. 1994. *AHFS Drug Information.* Bethesda, Maryland: American Society of Hospital Pharmacists, 1645–1646.

T

TABLE OF CONTENTS

UROKINASE

(yoor-oh-KYE-nase)

(ABBOKINASE)

ANTIDOTE:
OCCLUDED CENTRAL CATHETERS;
BLOOD MODIFIER:
THROMBOLYTIC AGENT

DOSE

Lysis of Large-vessel Thrombus: 4,400 units/kg IV over 10 minutes, then 4,400 units/kg/hour for 4–72 hours. Response is usually seen within 48 hours.[1,2]

- Success may be increased by pretreatment with fresh-frozen plasma.[2]
- Gal and Ransom use urokinase 100 units/kg/hour for *local infusion* to a thrombus. For *systemic therapy* of neonatal thrombosis, they begin with 100 units/kg/hour (no loading dose) and increase in increments of 400–1,000 units/kg/hour every 2–4 hours, depending on the urgency of the clinical situation (range: 1,000–10,000 units/kg/hour).[3] Hustead and Wicklund stated that the optimal dose in newborns is unknown and has varied in reports from 4,000 to 20,000 units/kg/hour for continuous infusion.[4] Therapy is guided by clinical response and serial D-dimer values. Therapy with thrombolytics is reserved for neonates who do not respond to heparin therapy.

Regional Arterial Infusion: 100 units/kg/hour.[3]

Occluded Central Venous Catheter: Use only sufficient volume to fill the lumen of the catheter, usually 0.3–0.6 ml of 5,000 units/ml, as described in Table 1-47.

ADMINISTRATION

IV: For lysis of large-vessel thrombus. Can be given intra-arterially for regional clot lysis. May also be given locally by infusing through the tip of the UAC around which a clot has developed (Table 1-47).

IV—*Rate:* Infuse loading dose over 10 minutes.

IV—*Concentration:*

- ***For systemic use:*** 1,250–1,500 units/ml; Maximum: 3,300 units/ml.
- ***For catheter patency:*** 5,000 units/ml.

IV—*Preparation:* Refrigerate powder for reconstitution. To minimize filament formation, avoid shaking the vial; instead, roll and tilt vial to enhance reconstitution. May filter with 0.45 or 0.22 micron filter.[1]

Storage: Refrigerate both the powder for reconstitution and the reconstituted solution. Reconstituted solution is stable for 24 hours at room temperature or under refrigeration.

CAUTIONS/CONTRAINDICATIONS

Manufacturing problems that had been associated with urokinase have been resolved, and the drug has been approved by the FDA. Because of the changing nature of thrombolytic use, the manufacturer focused efforts for approval solely

TABLE 1-47 ◆ **PROCEDURE FOR RESTORING PATENCY TO CENTRAL VENOUS CATHETERS USING UROKINASE**[1,7–10]

Prepare Urokinase (Abbokinase Open-Cath)

Reconstitute immediately before use to 5,000 units/ml following the manufacturer's directions. Gently roll and tilt rather than shake to minimize filament formation.

Withdraw 1 ml of the reconstituted solution into a tuberculin syringe. One vial may be used for several attempts to restore patency of the same catheter; however, the solution contains no preservative, so any unused portion should be discarded after 24 hours under refrigeration or at room temperature.

Instill Urokinase

- Aseptically disconnect the IV tubing connection at the catheter hub, and replace with a 1 ml tuberculin syringe filled with the urokinase solution.
- Carefully and slowly instill an amount of urokinase solution equal to the volume of the catheter— usually 0.3–0.6 ml.
- Fill catheter until slight resistance is felt. Avoid excessive pressure or volume to reduce risk of rupturing the catheter or forcing the clot and drug into the systemic circulation.
- Wait 5–10 minutes; then attempt to aspirate using a 5 ml syringe. Repeat every 5–10 minutes for 30 minutes (3–6 times).
- If patency is not restored in 30 minutes, cap the catheter and allow urokinase to remain in the catheter for an additional 30–60 minutes before again attempting to aspirate.
- If patency is not restored in 1–2 hours, try a second instillation of urokinase.

Follow-up

- After patency is restored and blood return is achieved, aspirate 1–2 ml of blood to remove residual clot and urokinase.
- Gently irrigate the catheter with sodium chloride 0.9 percent; then aseptically reconnect IV tubing to catheter hub.

for treatment of pulmonary embolism. (www.fda.gov/medwatch/SAFETY/2002/abbokinase.htm). See monograph on alteplase, recombinant for an alternative agent.

Do not use for systemic therapy in infants who have undergone major surgery in the preceding 10 days, who have pre-existing severe bleeding, or who have had a recent cerebrovascular accident.

USE

For lysis of neonatal thrombosis (right atrial thrombus, ventricular thrombus, aortic thrombosis secondary to umbilical artery catheterization). Use for infants who do not respond to heparin therapy. The earlier the therapy is started (best within 7 days of thrombus formation), the better the result. Some combine heparin and urokinase therapy.[5,6] See monograph on alteplase for advantages of t-PA over urokinase and streptokinase.

Alteplase is preferred over streptokinase and urokinase. (See monograph on alteplase, recombinant.)

Urokinase has been used to restore patency of central venous catheters occluded by fibrin or clotted blood. Not effective for occlusions caused by drugs or by calcium and phosphorus precipitates. (Use dilute HCl instead. See Appendix F: Restoring Patency to Occluded Central Venous Catheters and the monograph on hydrochloric acid.)[1,7,8] Alteplase is now usually used. (See monograph on alteplase, recombinant.)

MECHANISM OF ACTION

Urokinase is a fibrinolytic agent. It converts plasminogen to the enzyme plasmin, which degrades fibrin clots and fibrinogen. For urokinase to be effective, the infant must have adequate levels of plasminogen. Levels are normally 50–75 percent lower in neonates than in adults.[2,4]

ADVERSE EFFECTS

When Used for Occluded Central Line: Bleeding, if excessive amounts of urokinase are inadvertently injected into the systemic circulation. Excessive pressure or force on instillation may force the clot into the systemic circulation.

When Used for Systemic Therapy: Bleeding from puncture sites or internally, such as intracranial hemorrhage. If bleeding occurs secondary to hyperplasminemia, stop the infusion and consider replacement therapy with cryoprecipitate and fresh-frozen plasma.[2]

Rare Effects: Rash, bronchospasm, fever.

PHARMACOKINETICS/PHARMACODYNAMICS

Duration of Action: 3–4 hours.

Metabolism: Cleared rapidly by the liver.

Half-life: 20 minutes; prolonged in patients with hepatic dysfunction.

NURSING IMPLICATIONS

Recommendation is for infusion by a physician when used for occluded central venous catheters. Monitor vital signs continuously.

Reduce dose if signs of bleeding from nonpuncture sites are observed. Monitor for clinical improvement.[3]

Monitoring: Gal and Ransom measured baseline and serial D-dimer (the final breakdown product from fibrin clots) levels to guide systemic fibrinolytic therapy. The end point was a D-dimer level of >1 mcg/ml or a rising D-dimer level if the baseline was >1 mcg/ml.[3] Others have recommended serial measurements of fibrinogen, fibrin split products, and euglobulin lysis time for monitoring the status of newborns given fibrinolytic therapy.[2]

COMMENTS

Interactions: Increases risk of bleeding in infants concurrently on heparin, warfarin (Coumadin), or indomethacin.

REFERENCES

1. Manufacturer's product literature.

2. Corrigan JJ. 1988. Neonatal thrombosis and the thrombolytic system: Pathophysiology and therapy. *American Journal of Pediatric Hematology/Oncology* 10(1): 83–91.

3. Gal P, and Ransom L. 1991. Neonatal thrombosis: Treatment with heparin and thrombolytics. *Annals of Pharmacotherapy* 25(7-8): 853–856.

4. Hustead VA, and Wicklund BM. 1990. Treatment of neonatal aortic thrombosis with urokinase. *American Journal of Pediatric Hematology/Oncology* 12(3): 336–339.

5. Pongiglione G, et al. 1986. Right atrial thrombosis in two premature infants: Successful treatment with urokinase and heparin. *European Heart Journal* 7(12): 1086–1089.

6. Schmidt B, and Andrew M. 1988. Neonatal thrombotic disease: Prevention, diagnosis, and treatment. *Journal of Pediatrics* 113(2): 407–410.

7. Wachs T. 1990. Urokinase administration in pediatric patients with occluded central venous catheters. *Journal of Intravenous Nursing* 13(2): 100–102.

8. Alkalay AL, et al. 1993. Central venous line thrombosis in premature infants: A case management and literature review. *American Journal of Perinatology* 10(4): 323–326.

9. Holcombe BJ, Forloines-Lynn S, and Garmhausen LW. 1992. Restoring patency of long-term central venous access devices. *Journal of Intravenous Nursing* 15(1): 36–41.

10. Holcombe BJ, Forloines-Lynn S, and Garmhausen LW. 1993. Erratum for corrected algorithm. Restoring patency of long-term central venous access devices. *Journal of Intravenous Nursing* 16(1): 55.

URSODIOL (ACTIGALL)

(ur-so-DYE-ole)

GASTROINTESTINAL: BILE ACID

Synonyms: ursodeoxycholic acid (UDCA)

DOSE

10–18 mg/kg/day PO as a single daily dose or divided into two or three doses.[1–4] Duration of therapy is usually weeks to months. Consider discontinuing the drug when the direct bilirubin is <2.5 mg/dl.

600 mg/m^2/day has also been used.[5]

ADMINISTRATION

Supplied as: 300 mg capsules.

Oral.

Preparation: An oral liquid is not commercially available; however, a suspension can be compounded by the pharmacist. Two are described below: 25 mg/ml and 60 mg/ml.

Pharmacist Compounding Directions
Ursodiol Oral Liquid **25 mg/ml**[6]

Empty contents of ten 300 mg capsules into a glass mortar. Mix with 10 ml glycerin; then mix in 60 ml of Ora-Plus (Paddock Laboratories, Minneapolis, Minnesota), and levigate until a smooth mixture is obtained. Pour into a light-resistant prescription bottle; then add Orange Syrup, NF, to bring to a final volume of 120 ml. Shake vigorously.

Stability: 60 days.

Storage: Refrigerate or store at room temperature.

Ursodiol Oral Liquid **60 mg/ml**[7,8]

Empty contents of twelve 300 mg capsules into a glass mortar. Triturate with a small amount of glycerin to wet the powder; then add simple syrup in portions to a final volume of 60 ml. Transfer to an amber glass bottle. Shake well.

Stability: 35 days.

Storage: Refrigerate.

Alternatively, these procedures have been used:

- *Preparation of Capsules by Pharmacist:* Dosage standardization is sometimes feasible with this drug. Some centers prepare 50 and 100 mg capsules and round off doses to these increments.[7]

- *Preparation of Solution by Nurse:* Empty contents of one 300 mg capsule into a 60 ml screw-cap vial. Dilute with 10 ml water and shake well (= 30 mg/ml concentration). Withdraw appropriate volume for mg dose ordered. Date, time, and initial; then refrigerate. Discard unused portion after 24 hours. Shake well before withdrawing each dose.

CAUTIONS/CONTRAINDICATIONS

Contraindicated in patients with an allergy to bile acids.

USE

UDCA may be used in conjunction with a cholestatic treatment regimen of phenobarbital, Pregestimil infant formula, and supplemental fat-soluble (A, D, E, K) vitamins.

For cholestatic liver diseases, including parenteral nutrition cholestasis and biliary atresia, to induce hypercholeresis, stimulate bile flow, and thereby facilitate canalicular secretion of the accumulated atypical bile acids.[2,3,9] UDCA therapy improves the biochemical markers of liver function. May improve and delay end-stage liver disease, making it possible for the child to grow to a sufficient size for liver transplantation to become feasible.[1,4]

To dissolve cholesterol gallstones in selected patients with uncomplicated disease,[10] for primary biliary cirrhosis,[1,11] and to limit the progression of liver disease associated with cystic fibrosis.[12,13]

MECHANISM OF ACTION

Ursodiol is a naturally occurring bile acid found in small quantities in normal human bile and in larger quantities in the biles of certain species of bears.

Ursodiol is a hydrophilic choleretic (stimulates production of bile by the liver) bile acid that is free from hepatotoxic effects. UDCA suppresses hepatic synthesis and secretion of cholesterol and inhibits intestinal absorption of cholesterol. It changes bile composition from cholesterol precipitating to cholesterol solubilizing, thus enabling cholesterol stone dissolution.

Nittono and associates theorize that UDCA alters a constituent pattern of bile acids through the reduction of toxic chenodeoxycholic acid in the system.[3] Poupon and colleagues postulate that UDCA might displace endogenous bile acids and thus reverse their suspected cytotoxicity in primary biliary cirrhosis.[1] UDCA may also facilitate the excretion of bilirubin and bile acids into the bile through the liver and wash out bile plugs by choleretic effect, activate movements of microfilaments of bile canaliculi, and protect cell walls. UDCA reduces itching and jaundice and improves values of biochemical liver function tests.[11]

ADVERSE EFFECTS

Usually well tolerated.

Dose-related diarrhea, as well as nausea, vomiting, and abdominal pain, may occur.

May be related to UDCA use: biliary pain, cholecystitis, constipation, flatulence, stomatitis, rash, sweating, hair thinning, dry skin, headache, fatigue, arthralgia, cough, and rhinitis.

PHARMACOKINETICS/PHARMACODYNAMICS

Absorption: Absorbed in the small bowel (90 percent).

Serum Concentration: Achieves an ursodiol concentration of approximately 60 percent of the total bile acid pool. Steady state is reached after approximately 3 weeks of steady dosing.

Metabolism: Absorbed→portal vein→extracted from portal blood by liver (first pass effect)→conjugated with glycine or taurine→secreted into hepatic bile ducts→concentrated in gallbladder→expelled into duodenum in gallbladder bile in cystic and common ducts by gallbladder contraction as a response to eating.[10]

Elimination: GI tract.

NURSING IMPLICATIONS

Monitor liver function tests and bilirubin levels.

REFERENCES

1. Poupon RE, et al. 1994. Ursodiol for the long-term treatment of primary biliary cirrhosis. *New England Journal of Medicine* 330(19): 1342–1347.

2. Nittono H, et al. 1988. Ursodeoxycholic acid in biliary atresia (letter). *Lancet* 1(8584): 528.

3. Nittono H, et al. 1989. Ursodeoxycholic acid therapy in the treatment of biliary atresia. *Biomedicine and Pharmacotherapy* 43(1): 37–41.

4. Ullrich D, et al. 1987. Treatment with ursodeoxycholic acid renders children with biliary atresia suitable for liver transplantation (letter). *Lancet* 2(8571): 1324.

5. Jacquemin E, et al. 1994. A new cause of progressive intrahepatic cholestasis: 3-beta-hydroxy-C_{27}-steroid dehydrogenase/isomerase deficiency. *Journal of Pediatrics* 125(3): 379–384.

6. Mallett MS, et al. 1997. Stability of ursodiol 25 mg/ml in an extemporaneously prepared oral liquid. *American Journal of Health-System Pharmacy* 54(6): 1401–1404.

7. Zenk KE. 1991. Use of ursodiol (Actigall) in pediatrics. *Pediatric Pharmacy Network News* 1(2): 1.

8. Johnson CE, and Nesbitt J. 1995. Stability of ursodiol in an extemporaneously compounded oral liquid. *American Journal of Health-System Pharmacy* 52(16): 1798–1800.

9. Jacquemin E, et al. 1993. Ursodeoxycholic acid improves ethinyl estradiol-induced cholestasis in the rat. *European Journal of Clinical Investigation* 23(12): 794–802.

10. Manufacturer's product literature.

11. Poupon R, et al. 1987. Is ursodeoxycholic acid an effective treatment for primary biliary cirrhosis? *Lancet* 1(8537): 834–836.

12. Colombo C, et al. 1990. Effects of ursodeoxycholic acid therapy for liver disease associated with cystic fibrosis. *Journal of Pediatrics* 117(3): 482–489.

13. Ward A, et al. 1984. Ursodeoxycholic acid: A review of its pharmacological properties and therapeutic efficacy. *Drugs* 27(2): 95–131.

TABLE OF CONTENTS

VANCOMYCIN (VANCOCIN)
(van-koe-MYE-sin)

**ANTI-INFECTIVE:
ANTIBIOTIC**

DOSE

By Weight:

- **<1.2 kg (0–4 weeks):** 15 mg/kg/dose given every 24 hours
- **1.2–2 kg:**
  - 0–7 days: 15 mg/kg/dose given every 12–18 hours*
  - >7 days: 15 mg/kg/dose given every 8–12 hours
- **>2 kg:**
  - 0–7 days: 15 mg/kg/dose given every 12 hours
  - >7 days: 15 mg/kg/dose given every 8 hours[1,2]

By Postconceptional Age (PCA):

Some investigators state that PCA is a better basis than weight for establishing vancomycin doses:[3,4]

- **<30 weeks PCA:**
  - 0–7 days: 15 mg/kg/day as a single dose
  - >7 days, creatinine ≤1.2: 10 mg/kg/dose given every 12 hours
- **30–36 weeks PCA:**
  - 0–14 days: 10 mg/kg/dose given every 12 hours
  - >14 days, creatinine ≤0.6: 10 mg/kg/dose given every 8 hours
  - >14 days, creatinine 0.7–1.2: 10 mg/kg/dose given every 12 hours
- **>36 weeks PCA:**
  - 0–7 days: 10 mg/kg/dose given every 12 hours
  - >7 days, creatinine ≤0.6: 10 mg/kg/dose given every 8 hours
  - >7 days, creatinine 0.7–1.2: 10 mg/kg/dose given every 12 hours

For Older Infants (>1 Month of Age): 40 mg/kg/day divided every 6 hours. *Maximum:* 60 mg/kg/day (for CNS infections).

Oral Therapy for *Clostridium difficile* Pseudomembranous Colitis:
40–50 mg/kg/day PO divided every 6–8 hours. Continue for 7–14 days.[5,6]

Intrathecal/Intraventricular: 5 mg/day.

⊘ Reduce dose in renal impairment.

⊘ It is very important in neonates and older infants to individualize dose based on serum concentrations because there is marked interpatient variability. Empiric dosing does not reliably achieve therapeutic levels.[7,8]

---

* See Appendix B: Every-18-Hour Medication Worksheet.

ADMINISTRATION

IV, PO. Not for IM use.

IV—*Rate:* Infuse IV over 1 hour.

IV—*Concentration:* 5 mg/ml. Dilute with D_5W or $D_{10}W$ to recommended concentration (or to the greatest dilution possible considering infant's fluid balance).[9]

IV—*Compatibility:* See Appendix E: Y-Site Compatibility of Common NICU Drugs.

PO: The injectable form of the drug can also be given PO.

USE

Effective against most Gram-positive cocci and bacilli. Most Gram-negative bacteria are resistant.

Effective against methicillin (nafcillin, oxacillin)-resistant *Staphylococcus aureus* (MRSA) and *S. epidermidis* infections.

Effective against *Listeria monocytogenes.*

For pseudomembranous colitis caused by *Clostridium difficile,* vancomycin should be given orally because therapy is intraluminal. Efficacy of IV administration for this indication is uncertain. Metronidazole, rather than vancomycin, is the drug of choice for antibiotic-associated colitis because of the risk of development of vancomycin-resistant Enterococcus.[2]

MECHANISM OF ACTION

Vancomycin interferes with the phospholipid cycle of cell wall synthesis, alters plasma membrane function, and inhibits RNA synthesis.

ADVERSE EFFECTS

Usually well tolerated in infants. The ototoxicity and nephrotoxicity reported in earlier literature probably resulted from impurities in the earlier product formulation.

Hematologic: Reversible neutropenia.

Nephrotoxicity and Phlebitis: Have occurred only rarely in recent years since the use of purer vancomycin. Avoid extravasation.

Ototoxicity: Infrequent at therapeutic serum levels. Most serious adverse effect.

Red-Man ("Red-Baby") Syndrome: Erythematous rash of upper body, hypotension, and (rarely) cardiac arrest—usually from too-rapid infusion causing histamine release from cells.[10] (***Treatment:*** Stop infusion temporarily and restart at a slower rate. Treat supportively with fluids and dopamine, if needed. Consider corticosteroids.) Infusion over 60 minutes usually avoids this reaction.

Pharmacokinetics/Pharmacodynamics

Absorption: Poorly absorbed from the GI tract, but may accumulate in infants with renal dysfunction. Serum concentrations of 1 mcg/ml were reported in neonates on oral vancomycin.[11]

Distribution: CSF concentrations are 10–15 percent of concurrent serum concentrations in infants with minimal inflamed meninges, such as in ventriculoperitoneal shunt infections.

Protein Binding: 10 percent.

Metabolism: Not metabolized.

Half-life: <1 week—6–7 hours; up to 1 year—4 hours; older than 1 year—2–2.5 hours. Vancomycin clearance correlates with body weight and postnatal age.

Elimination: Excreted unchanged in the urine. Oral dose excreted in feces.[3,4,12–18]

Nursing Implications

Infuse slowly, and ensure that drug is diluted to recommended concentration.

Follow response to therapy as demonstrated by improvement in clinical condition, CBCs, and thrombocytopenia.

Monitor blood pressure and heart rate during infusion.

Monitor renal function, including urine output and BUN, creatinine.

Follow serum vancomycin levels.

Follow BAER (brainstem auditory evoked response).

Comments

Therapeutic Range:

- *Peak:* 25–40 mcg/ml. Draw blood for vancomycin peak 1 hour after completion of a 1-hour infusion (= 2 hours after start of infusion).
- *Trough:* 5–10 mcg/ml. Draw blood for trough just before dose.

Interactions: Concurrent or recent administration of indomethacin may reduce vancomycin clearance, elevating vancomycin serum concentrations. Avoid concurrent ototoxic and nephrotoxic drugs, if possible, because of potential additive adverse effects; monitor carefully.

References

1. Nelson JD. 1996. *1996–1997 Pocketbook of Pediatric Antimicrobial Therapy,* 12th ed. Baltimore: Lippincott Williams & Wilkins, 16–17.

2. Sáez-Llorens X, and McCracken GH Jr. 1995. Clinical pharmacology of antimicrobial agents. In *Infectious Diseases of the Fetus and Newborn Infant,* 4th ed., Remington JS, and Klein JO, eds. Philadelphia: WB Saunders, 1287–1336.

3. Schaible DH, et al. 1986. Vancomycin pharmacokinetics in infants: Relationships to indices of maturation. *Pediatric Infectious Disease* 5(3): 304–308.

4. Naqvi SH, et al. 1986. Vancomycin pharmacokinetics in small, seriously ill infants. *American Journal of Diseases of Children* 140(2): 107–110.

5. Manufacturer's product literature.

6. Welch DF, and Marks MI. 1982. Is *Clostridium difficile* pathogenic in infants? *Journal of Pediatrics* 100(3): 393–395.

7. Jarrett RV, et al. 1993. Individualized pharmacokinetic profiles to compute vancomycin dosage and dosing interval in preterm infants. *Pediatric Infectious Disease Journal* 12(2): 156–157.

8. Asbury WH, et al. 1993. Vancomycin pharmacokinetics in neonates and infants: A retrospective evaluation. *Annals of Pharmacotherapy* 27(4): 490–496.

9. Nahata MC, Miller MA, and Durrell DE. 1987. Stability of vancomycin in various concentrations of dextrose injection. *American Journal of Hospital Pharmacy* 44(4): 802–804.

10. Levy M, Koren G, and Dupuis L. 1990. Vancomycin-induced red man syndrome. *Pediatrics* 86(4): 572–580.

11. Schaad UB, McCracken GH Jr, and Nelson JD. 1980. Clinical pharmacology and efficacy of vancomycin in pediatric patients. *Journal of Pediatrics* 96(1): 119–126.

12. Gross JR, et al. 1985. Vancomycin pharmacokinetics in premature infants. *Pediatric Pharmacology* 5(1): 17–22.

13. Alpert G, et al. 1984. Vancomycin dosage in pediatrics reconsidered. *American Journal of Diseases of Children* 138(1): 20–22.

14. Gabriel MH, et al. 1991. Prospective evaluation of a vancomycin dosage guideline for neonates. *Clinical Pharmacy* 10(2): 129–132.

15. James A, et al. 1987. Vancomycin pharmacokinetics and dose recommendations for preterm infants. *Antimicrobial Agents and Chemotherapy* 31(1): 52–54.

16. Koren G, and James A. 1987. Vancomycin dosing in preterm infants: Prospective verification of new recommendations. *Journal of Pediatrics* 110(5): 797–798.

17. Kildoo CW, et al. 1989. Vancomycin pharmacokinetics in infants: Relationship to post conceptional age and serum creatinine. *Developmental Pharmacology and Therapeutics* 14(2): 77–83.

18. Reed MD, et al. 1987. The clinical pharmacology of vancomycin in seriously ill preterm infants. *Pediatric Research* 22(3): 360–363.

VECURONIUM (NORCURON)
(veh-kyu-ROE-nee-um)

CENTRAL NERVOUS SYSTEM: NEUROMUSCULAR BLOCKER

DOSE

0.1 mg/kg/dose. May repeat every hour, as needed.

Continuous Infusion: Begin with a loading dose of 0.1 mg/kg; then infuse at 0.05–0.1 mg/kg/hour. Individualize dose.

Dosing in Renal Impairment: Duration of action of this drug is prolonged in patients with renal impairment. Dose may need to be reduced with long-term use to prevent accumulation.

Dosing in Hepatic Dysfunction: Significant decreases in clearance and a longer elimination half-life (approximately double) may occur in severe hepatic dysfunction.

ADMINISTRATION

IV—Rate: Infuse IV push over 1–2 minutes or by continuous infusion.

IV—Concentration: Maximum: 1 mg/ml. May dilute further with saline or dextrose as desired. *Note:* Use nonbacteriostatic saline to reconstitute. Do not use the diluent provided with the product because it contains benzyl alcohol.

IV—Compatibility: See Appendix E: Y-Site Compatibility of Common NICU Drugs.

Storage: Refrigerate.

CAUTIONS/CONTRAINDICATIONS

Infants with congenital myasthenia gravis may have exaggerated pharmacologic effects (e.g., neuromuscular blockade), even with small doses. Use with extreme caution, if at all.

Use only when equipment for intubation, artificial respiration, and oxygen are available and reversal agents are present.

May mask seizures in asphyxiated infants.

Vecuronium has no analgesic or sedative effects, and the paralysis it produces may mask signs and symptoms of pain. Assess for and treat pain and agitation, if needed.

Precautions should be used to prevent corneal abrasion (tape eyelids shut, use ocular lubricant ointment).

USE

A nondepolarizing neuromuscular blocking agent (causes paralysis) for skeletal muscle relaxation during surgical procedures such as PDA ligation or during mechanical ventilation.

Potential benefits to use during mechanical ventilation are possible prevention of pneumothorax and pulmonary interstitial emphysema. May also minimize fluctuations in cerebral blood flow, an important variable associated with development of intraventricular hemorrhage.[1-3]

MECHANISM OF ACTION

Vecuronium is a nondepolarizing neuromuscular blocking agent that acts by competitive inhibition of acetylcholine for receptor sites on the postjunctional membrane. Infants less than 1 month old are especially sensitive to nondepolarizing neuromuscular blockers.

ADVERSE EFFECTS

May cause pain during injection.

Cardiovascular: Tachycardia and hypertension are less likely to occur with vecuronium than with use of other neuromuscular blockers, such as pancuronium.

From Prolonged Use: May cause fluid retention and negative effects on pulmonary mechanics (decreased pulmonary dynamic compliance and increased pulmonary resistance, resulting in the need for increased ventilatory support).[4] Muscle atrophy and weakness caused by disuse, joint contractures,[5] decubitus ulcers, and accumulation of pulmonary secretions also may occur.

Histamine Release from Mast Cells (displayed as bronchospasm, vasodilation, hypotension, cutaneous flushing): Vecuronium does not release clinically significant amounts of histamine, so cardiovascular effects are minimal. Tubocurarine releases the most histamine, followed by atracurium, then vecuronium, metocurine, and pancuronium. The latter three drugs cause the least histamine-releasing effects and are approximately equal in this respect.[3,6]

PHARMACOKINETICS/PHARMACODYNAMICS

Onset of Action: 3–5 minutes.

Duration of Action: Averages 58 minutes in infants, 18 minutes in children, and 37 minutes in adolescents. The larger the dose, the longer the duration of action.[3,7,8]

NURSING IMPLICATIONS

Have reversal agents available at bedside.

All paralyzed infants need analgesia and/or sedation in conjunction with paralyzation—consider concomitant infusion of fentanyl, morphine, or midazolam.

Provide range of motion, position changes, and eye lubrication to avoid side effects of paralyzation.

Consider need for bladder catheterization or Credé if urine output decreases.

Monitor for movement.

When drug is taken on transport, refrigerate immediately upon return.

COMMENTS

Mechanical ventilation must be provided during use. Drug does not provide analgesia or sedation, only paralysis.

Reversal of Neuromuscular Blockade:

- *Mechanism of Reversal:* Neostigmine inhibits acetylcholinesterase at the neuromuscular junction, allowing the accumulation of acetylcholine, which can successfully compete with the neuromuscular blocker at the neuromuscular junction, thus restoring muscle activity. Atropine is also given to avert the nonneuromuscular effects of neostigmine, such as increased secretions, bronchoconstriction, and bradycardia.[9]

- *Dose:* Neostigmine 0.06 mg/kg IV plus atropine 0.02 mg/kg/IV. Onset of reversal is approximately 10 minutes.

Interactions: See Table 1-13, page 77.

REFERENCES

1. Greenough A, et al. 1984. Pancuronium prevents pneumothoraces in ventilated premature babies who actively expire against positive pressure ventilation. *Lancet* 1(8367): 1–3.

2. Perlman JM, et al. 1985. Reduction in intraventricular hemorrhage by elimination of fluctuating cerebral blood-flow velocity in preterm infants with respiratory distress syndrome. *New England Journal of Medicine* 312(21): 1353–1357.

3. Buck ML, and Reed MD. 1991. Use of nondepolarizing neuromuscular blocking agents in mechanically ventilated patients. *Clinical Pharmacy* 10(1): 32–48.

4. Bhutani VK, Abbasi S, and Sivieri EM. 1988. Continuous skeletal muscle paralysis: Effect on neonatal pulmonary mechanics. *Pediatrics* 81(3): 419–422.

5. Sinha SK, and Levene MI. 1984. Pancuronium bromide induced joint contractures in the newborn. *Archives of Disease in Childhood* 59(1): 73–75.

6. Galletly DC. 1986. Comparative cutaneous histamine release by neuromuscular blocking agents. *Anaesthesia and Intensive Care* 14(4): 365–369.

7. Meretoja OA. 1989. Is vecuronium a long-acting neuromuscular blocking agent in neonates and infants? *British Journal of Anaesthesia* 62(2): 184–187.

8. Sloan M, Bissonnette B, and Lerman J. 1991. Pharmacodynamics of high dose vecuronium in children during balanced anesthesia. *Anesthesiology* 74(4): 656–659.

9. Debaene B, Meistelman C, and d'Hollander A. 1989. Recovery from vecuronium neuromuscular blockade following neostigmine administration in infants, children, and adults during halothane anesthesia. *Anesthesiology* 71(6): 840–844.

VIDARABINE (VIRA-A)

(vye-DARE-a-been)

Synonyms: adenine arabinoside, Ara-A*

DOSE

Birth to 30 Days of Age: 30 mg/kg/day infused over 18–24 hours for 10–21 days.

>30 Days of Age: 15 mg/kg/day infused over 12 hours for 10 days.[1–3]

Reduce dose in renal dysfunction.

ADMINISTRATION

IV—*Rate:* Infuse over 12–24 hours by syringe pump.

IV—*Concentration:* Dilute to 0.45 mg/ml with dextrose or saline to prevent precipitation. In fluid-restricted patients, 0.7 mg/ml may be used. Use an inline membrane filter (≤0.45 micron pore size). Do not refrigerate after dilution because precipitation may occur.

USE

A second-choice antiviral agent for neonatal herpes simplex viral (HSV) infections of the CNS, eyes, skin, and mouth and for the disseminated disease. Infants with eye involvement should also receive topical ophthalmic drug (trifluridine 1 percent, idoxuridine 1 percent, or vidarabine 3 percent).

Effective against herpes simplex virus types 1 and 2.

Early diagnosis and treatment of HSV infections are essential to reduce morbidity and mortality.

Acyclovir (see that monograph) is less toxic than vidarabine and easier to administer and therefore is the usual drug of choice for neonatal HSV infections.[4–6]

MECHANISM OF ACTION

Vidarabine is a purine nucleotide. It inhibits DNA polymerase.

ADVERSE EFFECTS

Possibility of fluid overload because of vidarabine's low solubility.

May cause thrombophlebitis.

The following have been observed in adults, but not in neonates. Monitor infants for:

- *CNS:* Tremor, myoclonus, malaise, metabolic encephalopathy.
- *Dermatologic:* Rash.
- *GI:* Mild vomiting, diarrhea.
- *Hematologic:* Decreased WBC, platelets, hemoglobin, hematocrit, and reticulocyte count.
- *Hepatic:* Elevated liver function tests and total bilirubin.

* Do not confuse with cytosine arabinoside, Ara-C, which is an antineoplastic agent.

Pharmacokinetics/Pharmacodynamics

Distribution: Distributes well into kidney, liver, spleen, skeletal muscle, brain, and body fluids.

Metabolism: Metabolized to inactive metabolite.

Half-life: 3.5–6 hours in adults.

Elimination: Excreted primarily in the urine.

Nursing Implications

Monitor blood counts, renal and hepatic function.

Observe IV site for vein irritation.

Comment

Adequate dilution and slow infusion rate are required to prevent vein irritation.

References

1. American Academy of Pediatrics, Committee on Infectious Diseases. 1994. *Red Book: Report of the Committee on Infectious Diseases,* 23rd ed. Elk Grove Village, Illinois: American Academy of Pediatrics, 569.

2. Whitley RJ, and Alford CA Jr. 1983. Towards therapy and prevention of herpetic infections. *Seminars in Perinatology* 7(1): 64–81.

3. Roberts RJ. 1984. *Drug Therapy in Infants: Pharmacologic Principles and Clinical Experience.* Philadelphia: WB Saunders, 85.

4. Whitley RJ, et al. 1980. Vidarabine therapy of neonatal herpes simplex virus infection. *Pediatrics* 66(4): 495–501.

5 Whitley RJ, et al. 1986. Vidarabine versus acyclovir therapy in herpes simplex encephalitis. *New England Journal of Medicine* 314(3): 144–149.

6. Whitley R, et al. 1991. A controlled trial comparing vidarabine with acyclovir in neonatal herpes simplex virus infection. *New England Journal of Medicine* 324(7): 444–449.

VITAMIN E (AQUASOL E)

(VYE-ta-min E)

**NUTRITION:
VITAMIN SUPPLEMENT**

Synonym: *d*-alpha-tocopherol acetate

See also the **Nutrition** section.

DOSE

Prematurity: 25 units PO daily until 36 weeks postconceptional age.

Supplementation in Cholestasis for Infants on Enteral Feedings: 50 units PO
daily in addition to oral multivitamin product (e.g., Vi-Daylin contains 4 units
vitamin E/ml and Poly-Vi-Sol contains 5 units/ml). Oral supplementation is not
needed if the infant is still on parenteral nutrition containing multivitamins. Up
to 150–300 units/day have been used in infants with persistent biliary atresia.

ADMINISTRATION

Supplied as: An oral liquid. Drops: 50 units/ml.

PO: Mix with feedings to dilute the high osmolality of this product.

USE

A fat-soluble vitamin used to prevent and treat vitamin E deficiency. Preterm
infants are at risk for vitamin E deficiency because placental transfer of the vitamin is limited. The more premature the infant, the greater the risk of deficiency.
Preterm infants also exhibit intestinal malabsorption of vitamin E because of
rapid growth and decreased bile salt production.[1]

Has been used in preterm infants to reduce the toxic effects of oxygen therapy on
the lung and the retina.

Has also been used to prevent hemolytic anemia.

Used to treat and prevent a neurologic disorder linked to vitamin E deficiency in
children with chronic cholestatic hepatobiliary disease (spinocerebellar ataxia,
loss of deep tendon reflexes, ataxia, loss of vibration and position sense, ophthal-
moplegia, muscle weakness, ptosis, dysarthria).[2]

MECHANISM OF ACTION

Vitamin E is a potent free-radical scavenger. It acts as an antioxidant, protecting
the lipid cell membranes against oxidative breakdown. It has been used in
preterm infants to reduce the incidence and severity of vitamin E deficiency
syndrome (hemolytic anemia, thrombocytosis, edema), precipitated iron
administration (an oxidant), anemia of prematurity, retinopathy of prematurity,
bronchopulmonary dysplasia, and intraventricular hemorrhage.[1,3,4]

ADVERSE EFFECTS

Osmolality of product is high (3,620 mOsm/kg H_2O).[5]

Excessive levels of vitamin E can cause creatinuria; can inhibit wound healing, fib-
rinolysis, and platelet function; and may reduce vitamin K–dependent coagulation factors.

High serum vitamin E levels following oral administration have been associated with increased incidence of sepsis and late-onset necrotizing enterocolitis.[6]

IV vitamin E has caused toxicity (thrombocytopenia, liver failure with hepatomegaly and ascites, renal failure, weight loss, and death) in preterm infants. The polysorbate emulsifiers in the now-withdrawn product E-Ferol are believed to have been the cause.[7]

PHARMACOKINETICS/PHARMACODYNAMICS

Absorption: Poor in preterm infants. Hydrolyzed in the GI tract prior to absorption. Bile salts are necessary for absorption. Vitamin E is transported via β lipoprotein in the blood to be incorporated into cellular and intracellular membranes.

NURSING IMPLICATIONS

Mix dose with feeding to dilute high osmolality.

Monitor for feeding intolerance. Space medications throughout the day to improve tolerance.

An assay for monitoring of serum vitamin E concentrations is available.[8]

COMMENTS

Begin supplementation when infant is taking full feedings, to avoid the potential detrimental effects of high osmolality on feeding tolerance.

Therapeutic Range: 1–3 mg/dl (= 10–30 mcg/ml).

Equivalency: 1 mg d-α-tocopherol acetate = 1 international unit.

Interactions: Concurrent administration of vitamin E and iron may reduce vitamin E absorption. Administer vitamin E until 36 weeks PCA; then discontinue vitamin E and begin iron supplementation.

REFERENCES

1. Olson RE. 1993. Disorders of the fat-soluble vitamins A, D, E, and K. In *Textbook of Pediatric Nutrition*, 2nd ed., Suskind RM, and Lewinter-Suskind L, eds. New York: Raven Press, 49–72.

2. Rosenblum JL, Keating JP, and Prensky AL. 1981. A progressive neurological syndrome in children with chronic liver disease. *New England Journal of Medicine* 304(9): 503–508.

3. American Academy of Pediatrics, Committee on Nutrition. 1980. Vitamin and mineral supplement needs in normal children in the United States. *Pediatrics* 66(6): 1015–1021.

4. Poland RL. 1990. Vitamin E for prevention of perinatal intracranial hemorrhage. *Pediatrics* 85(5): 865–867.

5. Ernst JA, et al. 1983. Osmolality of substances used in the intensive care nursery. *Pediatrics* 72(3): 347–352.

6. Johnson L, et al. 1985. Relationship of prolonged pharmacologic serum levels of vitamin E to incidence of sepsis and necrotizing enterocolitis in infants with birth weight 1,500 grams or less. *Pediatrics* 75(4): 619–638.

7. Arrowsmith JB, et al. 1989. Morbidity and mortality among low birth weight infants exposed to an intravenous vitamin E product, E-Ferol. *Pediatrics* 83(2): 244–249.

8. Kaufman SS, et al. 1987. Nutritional support for the infant with extrahepatic biliary atresia. *Journal of Pediatrics* 110(5): 679–686.

VITAMIN K₁ (AquaMEPHYTON)

(VYE-ta-min kay)

NUTRITION: VITAMIN SUPPLEMENT

Synonyms: phytonadione, phylloquinone

DOSE

Hemorrhagic Disease of the Newborn (HDN) and Infants of Mothers Who Received Anticonvulsants:[1-5]

- *Prophylaxis:*
  - *<1 kg:*
    IM: 0.5 mg (standard) or SC once within 1 hour after birth. Some authorities state that oral vitamin K may be used.
    PO: 1 mg PO once within 1 hour after birth. Repeat in 12–48 hours, if necessary.
  - *>1 kg:*
    IM: 1 mg (standard) or SC once within 1 hour after birth. Some authorities state that oral vitamin K may be used.
    PO: 2 mg PO once within 1 hour after birth. Repeat in 12–48 hours, if necessary.
  - *PO for infants breastfed exclusively:* 2 mg at birth; repeat 2 mg dose once at 1–2 weeks and again at 4–6 weeks of age.[5,6] IM is the preferred route of administration.
  - May repeat as soon as 6–8 hours and in 4–7 days, if necessary.
  - *Concerns about the use of PO vitamin K in place of IM vitamin K for prophylaxis of HDN:* (1) PO use has led to an increased incidence of late HDN. (2) Bioavailability of vitamin K is much lower after oral than after IM administration. (3) GI absorption of vitamin K varies greatly, with serum levels ranging from 90 ng/ml to undetectable. (4) Repeated oral doses are necessary in the first 2 months of life in exclusively breastfed infants and in at-risk infants, such as those with liver disease or chronic diarrhea.[7] This has led to compliance problems, with only 39 percent of infants receiving the recommended three doses of oral vitamin K prophylaxis by 6 weeks of age in one study.[8] See **CAUTIONS/CONTRAINDICATIONS** below.
- *Treatment:* 1 mg/day IM or SC. The prothrombin time should shorten within 2–4 hours. Give whole blood if bleeding is excessive.

To Counteract Oral Anticoagulant Overdose: 1–2 mg IM/SC every 4–6 hours.

Treatment of Vitamin K Deficiency: 1–2 mg IM/SC or 2–5 mg/day PO.

Vitamin K Supplementation in Liver Disease and Other Malabsorptive Conditions:

- For infants with diarrhea, malabsorption, cystic fibrosis, cholestasis, or atresia of the bile duct, use parenteral phytonadione (vitamin K₁).

- Monitor prothrombin time and individualize the dose. Dose frequency varies from daily to two or three times weekly. Repeated large doses are not warranted in liver disease if the response to the initial dose is unsatisfactory. This may indicate that the condition being treated is not responsive to vitamin K.[2,9]
- Infants whose feedings have a vitamin K content <100 mcg/liter should receive 1 mg of phytonadione per month IM or SC.[10]
- For breastfed infants with diarrhea of longer than several days' duration, a single 1 mg dose IM has been recommended.[10]

Recommended Daily Allowance:

- *Birth to 6 months of age:* 5 mcg/day
- *6 months to 1 year of age:* 10 mcg/day
- In the absence of sufficient data indicating otherwise, preterm infants are assumed to have the same requirements as term infants.[11,12]

ADMINISTRATION

IM, SC, PO. Because of *potential toxicity,* reserve IV use for emergency or unusual circumstances.

IM/SC—*Concentration:* 1 mg/0.5 ml (neonatal strength). The 10 mg/ml concentration may be used to minimize volume injected.

PO: Vitamin K is not available as an oral liquid. One of the following alternatives may be used to administer vitamin K orally as a liquid:

- The tablet may be crushed and mixed in a small amount of the infant's feeding to dilute and facilitate administration.
- The parenteral form may be given by mouth.[7]
- An oral liquid may be prepared by the pharmacist:

Pharmacist Compounding Directions
Phytonadione Oral Suspension 1 mg/ml[13]

Crush six phytonadione 5 mg tablets in a mortar. Mix thoroughly with 5 ml of purified water and 5 ml of 1 percent methylcellulose. Transfer to a graduate cylinder, and bring the suspension to 30 ml with 70 percent sorbitol* solution. Mix well.

Stability: 3 days refrigerated. Shake well.

Note: Formulation based on experience; chemical stability testing was not performed.

****Caution:*** This preparation could cause diarrhea because of the sorbitol diluent.

IV administration is not recommended; however, if there is no alternative, follow these guidelines:

- **IV—*Rate:*** Administer slowly over 15–30 minutes. May also be diluted in a 24-hour volume of parenteral nutrition.
  Maximum: 1 mg/minute.
- **IV—*Concentration:*** May give undiluted or diluted to a convenient volume based on the infant's fluid requirements. Dilute in the patient's maintenance IV solution, preservative-free dextrose, or saline.
- **IV—*Compatibility:*** See Appendix E: Y-Site Compatibility of Common NICU Drugs.

Storage: Protect from light.

CAUTIONS/CONTRAINDICATIONS

Oral prophylaxis seems to prevent classic HDN, but with the currently available formulations, it appears to be much less effective in preventing the late hemorrhagic disease, which occurs primarily in breastfed infants with or without hepatic disease.[7]

Deaths have occurred after IV administration. Reactions resembled hypersensitivity or anaphylaxis, including shock and cardiac or respiratory arrest. Restrict IV administration to situations in which other routes are not feasible and the risk involved is justified.[3]

USE

At birth, to prevent hemorrhagic disease of the newborn, a disorder characterized by generalized ecchymoses, GI hemorrhage, bleeding from circumcision or the umbilical stump, or sometimes intracranial hemorrhage. HDN occurs most commonly in breastfed infants who do not receive vitamin K at birth. Newborn infants of mothers who received phenobarbital, phenytoin, primidone, or warfarin are especially at risk.[10] A prompt response (shortening of the prothrombin time in 2–4 hours) is usually diagnostic.[2] Term, and especially preterm, newborns are at risk for fat-soluble vitamin deficiency disease because the placenta does not efficiently transport lipids to the fetus.[3]

Also used to treat coagulation disorders resulting from faulty formation of factors II, VII, IX, and X when the cause is vitamin K deficiency; to counteract anticoagulant-induced prothrombin deficiency; and parenterally to treat hypoprothrombinemia secondary to conditions limiting absorption or synthesis of vitamin K, such as obstructive jaundice or use of antibiotics.[2]

MECHANISM OF ACTION

Vitamin K sources are diet and synthesis by microflora in the gut. The vitamin promotes hepatic synthesis of the clotting factors II, VII, IX, and X, although the mechanism is not known.[6]

ADVERSE EFFECTS

Usually well tolerated when given at recommended doses. May occasionally cause pain and swelling at the injection site. Transient flushing with brief hypotension and rapid, weak pulse may occur. Doses >10–20 mg may cause hyperbilirubinemia and severe hemolytic anemia in neonates, particularly preterm infants (rare).

Vitamin K's onset of action is several hours; if bleeding is excessive, give whole blood or component therapy in addition to the vitamin K. Vitamin K does **not** counteract the effects of heparin (protamine is the antidote for heparin overdose).

Contains benzyl alcohol; however, the small amount in this medication should not cause toxicity when used as directed.

Reports claiming a relationship between childhood cancers and IM—but not oral—vitamin K at birth have been disproved.[6,14]

PHARMACOKINETICS/PHARMACODYNAMICS

Absorption: Vitamin K₁ is absorbed only in the presence of bile salts. Plasma phylloquinone concentrations are higher after a parenteral dose than after the same or even a greater dose PO. With 1 mg doses, the difference was 2-fold at 2 weeks, 1.5-fold at 4 weeks, and 1.2-fold at 3 months. Intramuscular administration may cause the formation of a depot at the injection site from which the vitamin is gradually released.[5]

Distribution: Probably stored in the liver. Bone may also act as a repository.

Onset of Action: Increased vitamin K levels are usually detectable within 1–2 hours; control of hemorrhage usually occurs within 3–6 hours after parenteral administration and in 6–10 hours after oral administration. Prothrombin level may normalize in 12–14 hours.[1]

NURSING IMPLICATIONS

Give within 1 hour of birth.

Monitor for adverse drug reactions.

REFERENCES

1. Tsang RC, and Nichols BL. 1988. *Nutrition During Infancy.* Philadelphia: Hanley & Belfus, 289–297.

2. Medical Economics Data. 2000. *Physicians' Desk Reference,* 54th ed. Montvale, New Jersey: Medical Economics, 1746–1747.

3. Olson RE. 1993. Disorders of the fat-soluble vitamins A, D, E, and K. In *Textbook of Pediatric Nutrition,* 2nd ed., Suskind RM, and Lewinter-Suskind L, eds. New York: Raven Press, 49–72.

4. Greer FR. 1993. Vitamin K. In *Nutritional Needs of the Preterm Infant: Scientific Basis and Practical Guidelines,* Tsang RC, et al., eds. Baltimore: Lippincott Williams & Wilkins, 111–119.

5. American Academy of Pediatrics, Committee on Fetus and Newborn. 1993. Controversies concerning vitamin K and the newborn. *Pediatrics* 91(5): 1001–1003.

6. Shearer MJ. 1995. Vitamin K. *Lancet* 345(8944): 229–234.

7. Greer FR. 1995. Vitamin K deficiency and hemorrhage in infancy. *Clinics in Perinatology* 22(3): 759–777.

8. Croucher C, and Azzopardi D. 1994. Compliance with recommendations for giving vitamin K to newborn infants. *British Medical Journal: Clinical Research Edition* 308(6933): 894–895. (Comment in *British Medical Journal: Clinical Research Edition* 1994, 308[6933]: 867–868.)

9. Kaufman SS, et al. 1987. Nutritional support for the infant with extrahepatic biliary atresia. *Journal of Pediatrics* 110(5): 679–686.

10. McEvoy GK. 2000. *AHFS Drug Information.* Bethesda, Maryland: American Society of Hospital Pharmacists, 3343–3345.

11. National Academy of Sciences. 1989. *Recommended Dietary Allowances,* 10th ed. Washington, DC: National Academy Press.

12. American Academy of Pediatrics, Committee on Nutrition. 1977. Nutritional needs of low-birth-weight infants. *Pediatrics* 60(4): 519–530.

13. Nahata MC, and Hipple TF. 1992. *Pediatric Drug Formulations,* 2nd ed. Cincinnati, Ohio: Harvey Whitney Books, 59.

14. Gellis SS. 1995. Another reminder about vitamin K. *Pediatric Notes* 19(12): 46–47.

TABLE OF CONTENTS

N

ZIDOVUDINE (RETROVIR)

(zye-DOE-vue-deen)

**ANTI-INFECTIVE:
ANTIRETROVIRAL**

Synonyms: ZDV, AZT, azidothymidine

DOSE

Prevention of Maternal-Fetal Human Immunodeficiency Virus (HIV) Transmission: Begin within 12 hours after birth and continue for 6 weeks.

- *Preterm infants—PO, IV:* 1.5 mg/kg/dose given every 12 hours from birth to 2 weeks of age; then increase to 2 mg/kg/dose given every 8 hours. (Use of the standard term infant dose, below, could result in drug accumulation and increased risk of anemia and neutropenia in preterm infants.)[1,2]

- *Term infants:*
  - *PO:* 2 mg/kg/dose given every 6 hours.
  - *IV:* 1.5 mg/kg/dose given every 6 hours.[1]

Treatment of HIV-Infected Infants:

- *Infants ≥3 months:*
  - *PO:* 160 mg/m^2/dose given every 8 hours. (Range: 90–180 mg/m^2/dose given every 6–8 hours.)[1]
  - *IV:* 120 mg/m^2/dose given every 6 hours.[1,3]
  - *Continuous IV infusion:* 20 mg/m^2/hour.[4]

- If a dose reduction is needed because of anemia and/or granulocytopenia during ZDV therapy, a minimum suggested oral dose for infants ≥4 months is 75 mg/m^2/dose given every 6 hours.[4]

- To determine the infant's body surface area in square meters for calculation of the mg/m^2 dose, refer to Table M-6, page 736.

Prophylaxis of Health Care Worker (HCW) Exposures to HIV (i.e., needlesticks)

(*Note:* These are adult doses):

- *Basic postexposure prophylaxis* (PEP): Oral zidovudine 600 mg daily in divided doses (may give as 300 mg twice daily, 200 mg three times daily, or 100 mg every 4 hours) and oral lamivudine 150 mg twice daily given for 4 weeks (28 days).[5]

- *Expanded PEP:* Oral zidovudine (600 mg daily in two or three divided doses), oral lamivudine (150 mg twice daily), and either oral indinavir (800 mg every 8 hours) or oral nelfinavir (750 mg three times daily) given for 4 weeks (28 days). Initiate therapy as soon as possible following exposure (i.e., within a few hours rather than days).[5]

The decision to recommend PEP must take into account the nature of the exposure (i.e., needlestick or potentially infectious fluid that comes in contact with a mucous membrane), the amount of blood or body fluid involved in the exposure, pregnancy in the HCW, and exposure to virus known or suspected to be

N

resistant to antiretroviral drugs. Prophylaxis may not be warranted, or the basic or the expanded PEP, above, may be indicated. The Centers for Disease Control and Prevention (CDC) states that local experts in the treatment of HIV should be consulted when using PEP.[5] The National Clinicians Post-exposure Prophylaxis Hotline at 888-448-4911 can also be consulted.

ADMINISTRATION

Supplied as: Injection: 10 mg/ml; oral syrup: 10 mg/ml.

IV—*Rate:* Infuse over 1 hour.[3,4]

IV—*Concentration:* Dilute before use. ***Maximum:*** 4 mg/ml.

PO: Administer 30 minutes before or 1 hour after feedings. Give with water. The CDC states that zidovudine can also be administered with feedings.[1] In most instances, it is not recommended that HIV-infected mothers breastfeed because of the risk of their passing HIV to their infant.

Storage: Protect from light.

🔎Do not give IM or by rapid IV infusion.

CAUTIONS/CONTRAINDICATIONS

🔎**Warning:** Ribavirin antagonizes the antiretroviral activity of ZDV by inhibiting the phosphorylation of ZDV to its active triphosphate form. ***These two drugs should not be used together.***[1,6]

🔎Do not use in patients who are hypersensitive to zidovudine or any component in the product.

🔎Use with caution in patients with anemia, bone marrow suppression, reduced renal or hepatic function (dose reduction may be required). Stop therapy if there is a rapid increase in aminotransferases.

If diagnostic testing indicates that a neonate receiving ZDV prophylaxis is HIV infected, a change to a combination antiretroviral agent regimen to treat the infection is recommended as soon as possible. Infants <12 months old are at high risk for disease progression.[4]

USE

Prevention of Maternal-Fetal HIV Transmission: ZDV reduces the risk of vertical transmission of HIV from mother to infant by two-thirds (from 26 percent to 8 percent) when given as part of a three-part regimen—antepartum, intrapartum, and newborn.[1,7] The newborn component of the ZDV regimen should be administered to the neonate even if the mother failed to receive the antepartum and/or the intrapartum component, as the following study shows:

> Wade and colleagues demonstrated that abbreviated regimens of ZDV prophylaxis reduce the rates of perinatal transmission of HIV, even if prophylaxis is begun intrapartum or in the first 48 hours of life. When treatment was begun in the prenatal period, the rate of HIV transmission was 6.1 percent; when it was begun intrapartum, the transmission rate was 10 percent;

when it was begun within the first 48 hours of life, the transmission rate was 9.3 percent. When treatment was begun on day 3 of life or later, however, the rate of HIV transmission was 18.4 percent, which does not differ significantly from the outcome when no ZDV prophylaxis is given (26.6 percent).[8]

ZDV is the best-studied antiretroviral drug in neonates. However, other agents, combinations of agents, and shorter ZDV regimens are being studied.[9] Many studies are ongoing; consult the CDC Web site (www.cdc.gov.) for current recommendations.

Treatment of HIV-infected Infants: ZDV is indicated in the treatment of infants and children >3 months of age who have HIV-related symptoms or who are asymptomatic but who have abnormal HIV-related laboratory values indicating significant HIV-related immunosuppression.

- Rohrer and colleagues reported successful treatment of a 3.5-month-old (corrected age 7 weeks; 29 weeks gestation at birth), 3.25 kg infant who was infected with HIV-1 and had encephalitis caused by cytomegalovirus (CMV). The treatment regimen included a triple-drug antiretroviral regimen using ZDV, lamivudine, and nelfinavir as well as an anti-CMV drug, ganciclovir. Therapy was well tolerated for >9 months. The infant's clinical and neurologic status improved after a few weeks, and HIV-related laboratory values improved after 9–13 months of treatment.[10]

MECHANISM OF ACTION

Zidovudine is a nucleoside reverse transcriptase inhibitor. It is a thymidine analog that is phosphorylated by cellular enzymes to the active metabolite 5'-zidovudine triphosphate, which inhibits HIV reverse transcriptase, thereby inhibiting viral DNA replication. It also terminates viral DNA chain elongation. ZDV-resistant strains of HIV emerge rapidly during long-term therapy.[3]

ADVERSE EFFECTS

Side effects are reversible and dose-related and may require either dose reduction or temporary withdrawal of the drug.[3] Sperling and colleagues reported that for the routine use of ZDV for prevention of mother-to-child HIV transmission, the only adverse effect was anemia within the first 6 weeks of life. At 18 months of age, uninfected infants did not differ in growth parameters or immune function.[11]

CNS: Lethargy, seizures, fever, insomnia, decreased reflexes.

Dermatologic: Rash; bluish or brownish pigmentation of the nails, especially in dark-skinned patients. A 4-week-old infant with ZDV-induced neutropenia developed severe paronychia of the great toes as a result of *Candida albicans* and *Escherichia coli*. The infant was successfully treated with fluconazole and topical antiseptics.[12]

GI: Nausea, vomiting; abdominal pain; anorexia; cholestatic hepatitis, hepatomegaly, elevated liver function tests.

Hematologic: Anemia (22 percent of infants) and leukopenia, mainly neutropenia (21 percent of infants), which may persist for weeks after drug discontinuation. Significant anemia usually occurs after 4–6 weeks of treatment. Patients with anemia may require blood transfusion and/or epoetin alfa (recombinant human erythropoietin; Epogen); patients with granulocytopenia may require GM-CSF (granulocyte-macrophage colony-stimulating factor; sargramostim).[1,6] Thrombocytopenia may occur.[3] Folate or vitamin B_{12} deficiency increases the myelosuppression caused by ZDV.

Metabolic: Severe transient lactic acidosis was reported in a 2.5 kg, 35-week-gestational-age infant after 9 days of prophylactic ZDV; the acidosis resolved rapidly following discontinuation of ZDV.[13]

Neuromuscular: Myalgia, myopathy, tremor, weakness.

Other: Carcinogenic in mice and rats. No childhood neoplasias were reported in a study of the safety of maternal-infant ZDV.[11]

PHARMACOKINETICS/PHARMACODYNAMICS

Absorption: Well absorbed (90 percent) in term newborns.

ZDV undergoes first-pass metabolism. The bioavailability is 65 percent in adults, compared with 89 percent in neonates ≤14 days of age and 61 percent in neonates >14 days of age.[3,6] Bioavailability decreases over the first weeks of life as hepatic glucuronidation and first-pass metabolism increase.[2] The bioavailability is greater in infants ≤14 days of age because of decreased first-pass metabolism at this age, especially in preterm infants because of immaturity in hepatic glucuronidation.[2,14]

Peak Serum Concentrations after Oral Administration: 0.5–1.5 hours.

Distribution: Distribution to CSF averages approximately 24 percent of plasma concentration in children.[6]

Protein Binding: 34–38 percent.

Metabolism: Metabolized by glucuronidation in the liver. Because ZDV is primarily cleared through hepatic metabolism, which is immature in neonates (and especially in infants 34 weeks gestation), the half-life and clearance of ZDV are prolonged in neonates compared with older infants. This is the reason for the lower doses and longer dosing intervals shown for neonates under **DOSE** above.[1]

Half-life:

- *Preterm infants 5 days of age:* 7.2 hours; *18 days of age:* 4.4 hours.
- *Term infants <14 days of age:* 3.12 hours; *>14 days of age:* 1.87 hours (compared with 1.1 hours in adults).[14]

Elimination: Eliminated in the urine.[3] Elimination is slow immediately after birth but increases rapidly in the first weeks of life in term infants (the increase is much slower in preterm infants), reaching a plateau by 4–8 weeks of age.[14]

NURSING IMPLICATIONS

Monitoring: CBC with differential to detect serious anemia or granulocytopenia; liver function tests, including ALT (SGPT), alkaline phosphatase, and AST (SGOT), as well as serum bilirubin concentration, renal function tests.[6]

Monitor blood count, liver function tests, and renal function.

Observe for signs of infection.

Advise physician of signs or symptoms of anemia or neutropenia, for possible ZDV dose reduction.

Try to administer on an empty stomach first, as recommended by the manufacturer (see **ADMINISTRATION** above). If not tolerated, may give with feedings to reduce adverse GI effects.

During discharge planning, teach the family about the signs and symptoms of anemia. Advise parents to protect infants with neutropenia from infections (such as by avoiding individuals with cold or flu symptoms and good/frequent handwashing).

COMMENTS

Interactions:

- Drugs metabolized by hepatic glucuronidation *(acetaminophen, benzodiazepines, cimetidine, indomethacin, morphine)* may compete with this pathway and increase the risk of ZDV toxicity.[3,6]

- ZDV may increase or decrease phenytoin concentrations.[1,6]

- **Bone marrow depressants *(amphotericin B, chloramphenicol, flucytosine, vidarabine, and particularly ganciclovir and interferon-alpha)* may cause additive or synergistic myelosuppression. Dose reduction or interruption of one or both drugs may be required. Monitor hematologic parameters.**[6]

- Rifampin may increase the metabolism of ZDV and decrease its serum concentrations.[6]

- Fluconazole interferes with ZDV clearance and metabolism, increasing ZDV half-life and serum concentration.[6]

- Valproic acid interferes with ZDV's first-pass metabolism, increasing ZDV plasma concentrations by increasing its bioavailability. Monitor infants receiving valproic acid and ZDV for increased ZDV adverse effects.[1,6]

- **Laboratory Interaction:** Administration of ZDV may produce erroneous results in selective screening of infants for inborn errors of metabolism because of increased urinary thymine concentrations. Sewell analyzed urine samples from three neonates for organic acids to exclude an inherited metabolic disorder. Analysis showed a large peak corresponded to thymine and suggested a possible defect in pyrimidine metabolism. Careful questioning revealed that all three neonates were born to HIV-positive mothers and had received ZDV.[15]

REFERENCES

1. Centers for Disease Control and Prevention. 1998. Guidelines for the use of antiretroviral agents in pediatric HIV infection. *MMWR* 47(RR-4): 1–43.

2. Mirochnick M, et al. 1998. Zidovudine pharmacokinetics in premature infants exposed to human immunodeficiency virus. *Antimicrobial Agents and Chemotherapy* 42(4): 808–812.

3. Patel JA, and Ogra PL. 1992. Antiviral chemotherapy. In *Pediatric Pharmacology: Therapeutic Principles in Practice,* 2nd ed., Yaffe SJ, and Aranda JV, eds. Philadelphia: WB Saunders, 365–389.

4. McEvoy GK. 2000. *AHFS Drug Information.* Bethesda, Maryland: American Society of Health-System Pharmacists, 669–683.

5. Centers for Disease Control and Prevention. 1998. Public Health Service guidelines for the management of health-care worker exposures to HIV and recommendations for postexposure prophylaxis. *MMWR* 47(RR-7): 1–33.

6. United States Pharmacopeial Convention/USP DI. 2000. *Drug Information for the Health Care Professional,* 20th ed. Rockville, Maryland: United States Pharmacopeial Convention, 3176–3181.

7. Connor EM, et al. 1994. Reduction of maternal-infant transmission of human immunodeficiency virus type I with zidovudine treatment. Pediatric AIDS Clinical Trials Group Protocol 076 Study Group. *New England Journal of Medicine* 331(18): 1173–1180.

8. Wade NA, et al. 1998. Abbreviated regimens of zidovudine prophylaxis and perinatal transmission of the human immunodeficiency virus. *New England Journal of Medicine* 339(20): 1409–1414.

9. Guay LA, et al. 1999. Intrapartum and neonatal single-dose nevirapine compared with zidovudine for prevention of mother-to-child transmission of HIV-1 in Kampala, Uganda: HIVNET 012 randomized trial. *Lancet* 354(9181): 795–802.

10. Rohrer T, et al. 1999. Combined treatment with zidovudine, lamivudine, nelfinavir and ganciclovir in an infant with human immunodeficiency virus type 1 infection and cytomegalovirus encephalitis: Case report and review of the literature. *Pediatric Infectious Disease Journal* 18(4): 382–386.

11. Sperling RS, et al. 1998. Safety of the maternal-infant zidovudine regimen utilized in the Pediatric AIDS Clinical Trial Group 076 Study. *AIDS* 12(14): 1805–1813.

12. Russo F, Collantes C, and Guerrero J. 1999. Severe paronychia due to zidovudine-induced neutropenia in a neonate. *Journal of the American Academy of Dermatology* 40(2 part 2): 322–324.

13. Scalfaro P, et al. 1998. Severe transient neonatal lactic acidosis during prophylactic zidovudine treatment. *Intensive Care Medicine* 24(3): 247–250.

14. Mirochnick M, Capparelli E, and Connor J. 1999. Pharmacokinetics of zidovudine in infants: A population analysis across studies. *Clinical Pharmacology and Therapeutics* 66(1): 16–24.

15. Sewell AC. 1998. Zidovudine and confusion in urinary metabolic screening (letter). *Lancet* 352(9135): 1227.

ZINC OXIDE, [A COMPONENT OF DESITIN OINTMENT]   TOPICAL:
(zink OX-ide)   PROTECTANT

Synonyms: ZnO, Lassar's paste

DOSE

Apply topically to affected area several times a day, as needed.

ADMINISTRATION

Supplied as:

Ointment: 20 percent ZnO in white ointment.

Paste: 25 percent ZnO in white petrolatum (Lassar's paste).

Desitin Ointment: 40 percent ZnO with cod liver oil, talc, petrolatum, lanolin, and methylparaben.

Many diaper-rash products contain ZnO. ZnO is also the major component of calamine lotion.

Pharmacist-prepared Protective Ointment: A protective ointment can be prepared by the pharmacist for severe diaper rash or perineal skin breakdown. Protective ointment stays on the skin better and protects better than zinc oxide ointment alone.

Pharmacist Compounding Directions
Protective Ointment
(Karaya Powder and Zinc Oxide Ointment)

Karaya Powder 30 ml

Zinc Oxide Ointment 30 gm

1. Pour the karaya powder into a graduated plastic medicine cup or pharmaceutical graduate cylinder to the 30 ml mark.

2. Incorporate the karaya powder into the ointment gradually. Mix to an even consistency. Package in a glass ointment jar, and store at room temperature.

Topical: Apply to skin.

CAUTIONS/CONTRAINDICATIONS

Do not use if infant is hypersensitive to any component of the product. Use of ZnO alone (rather than a ZnO product containing other components) may avoid irritation and possible allergic reactions (rare) to additives in topical products.

For topical use only; avoid contact with eyes.

Zinc oxide is a component of some baby powders. Powders can help dry the skin when vesicles or maceration is present and may play a minor role as a drying agent to reduce chafing and irritation at skin folds in obese infants. The use of baby powders should be carefully controlled because of the hazards of aspiration, accidental ingestion, allergic reaction, talc granulomas, and possible increased bacterial growth.[1–3] If powders are used, keep away from the face to avoid inhalation.

USE

Used topically to treat skin conditions such as abrasions, chafed skin, and diaper dermatitis.[1,4,5] ZnO ointment is considered the best initial choice for diaper dermatitis in terms of effectiveness, safety, and cost.[5,6] ZnO protects the skin, is a drying agent, soothes, and aids in healing of minor skin irritations. When applied after each diaper change, ZnO can serve as an occlusive barrier.[7] Its disadvantages are that it is tacky to the touch and must be removed by wiping with mineral oil.

ZnO is generally safe, but as with any medication, it should not be used unnecessarily. Prophylactic use may be considered in infants with recent diaper rash, a history of diarrhea, or a history of diarrhea while on antibiotics. Discontinue periodically to see if the ZnO is still needed.

Used as a sunscreen.

MECHANISM OF ACTION

Diaper Dermatitis: ZnO has mild astringent, antiseptic, and protective actions.

Sunscreen: ZnO provides an opaque physical barrier to sunlight. It reflects or scatters light in both the visible and the ultraviolet spectrums (290–700 nm), keeping it from penetrating the skin.

ADVERSE EFFECTS

Usually well tolerated. Possible dermatologic irritation from and allergic reactions to components in the product (rare).

When applied to denuded skin, may sting and does not stick well. See the pharmacist-prepared protective ointment (karaya powder and zinc oxide ointment) under **ADMINISTRATION** above for a possible solution to this problem.

PHARMACOKINETICS/PHARMACODYNAMICS

Absorption: Not absorbed.

NURSING IMPLICATIONS

ZnO paste can be removed easily with mineral oil. When treating diaper dermatitis, carefully remove ZNO only when needed; consider rinsing off ZnO instead of wiping to protect injured skin.

Provide parent teaching regarding hazards of baby powders.

REFERENCES

1. Liou LW, and Janniger CK. 1997. Skin care of the normal newborn. *Cutis* 59(4): 171–174.

2. Pairaudeau PW, et al. 1991. Inhalation of baby powder: An unappreciated hazard. *British Medical Journal, Clinical Research Edition* 302(6786): 1200–1201.

3. Sparrow SA, and Hallam LA. 1991. Talc granulomas. *British Medical Journal* 303(6793): 58.

4. Janniger CK, and Thomas I. 1993. Diaper dermatitis: An approach to prevention employing effective diaper care. *Cutis* 52(3): 153–155.

5. Siegfried EC. 1998. Neonatal skin and skin care. *Dermatologic Clinics* 26(3): 437–446.

6. Zenk KE. 1999. Pharmacologic aspects of good skin care of the normal newborn. *Mother Baby Journal* 4(2): 44–46.

7. Friedlander SF. 1998. Contact dermatitis. *Pediatrics in Review* 19(5): 166–171.

N

NUTRITION

Neonatal nutritional support should be initiated early and provided consistently to maintain the rate of intrauterine growth for preterm infants and of standard growth charts for term infants, increase resistance to disease, and improve response to medical and surgical therapy. Prolonged nutritional deficit can produce irreversible adverse effects on brain development. There are important links between neonatal nutritional status, brain growth, and development.[1,2]

Section II provides information on enteral and parenteral nutrition for hospitalized term and preterm infants. Enteral nutrition is always used if the infant's medical condition permits. This is because enteral nutrition is safer than parenteral nutrition, is more physiologic, stimulates development of gastrointestinal tract function, helps avoid certain adverse effects such as parenteral nutrition cholestasis, and is more cost-effective.

Enteral Nutrition

CALORIC REQUIREMENTS AND WEIGHT GAIN

The estimated enteral caloric requirement for term infants is 105–115 kcal/kg/day; for preterm infants, it is 120 kcal/kg/day (range: 105–130). Caloric requirements per kilogram decrease during the first year of life. The goal for weight gain is 15 gm/day in preterm infants and 15–30 gm/day in term infants. Weight gain, growth in length, and increase in head circumference in preterm infants should follow the intrauterine growth curve and after 40 weeks should be similar to that of term infants.[2]

Measures for optimizing weight gain include the following:

- *Maintain a neutral thermal environment.* An environmental temperature at which a newborn's oxygen consumption and metabolic rate are at their lowest while a normal body temperature is maintained—a neutral thermal environment—decreases the energy expended for thermoregulation. The temperature of a neutral thermal environment for preterm infants varies with gestational age, postnatal age, and body weight; tables are available in neonatal texts. Clothing and swaddling conserve body heat significantly. In one study, energy expenditure was 80 kcal/kg/day in unswaddled infants maintained at 28°–29°C (82.4°–84.2°F) versus 58 kcal/kg/day for swaddled infants maintained at 20°–22°C (68°–71.6°F).[3]

- *Minimize unnecessary activity.* Correct treatable causes of irritability, such as hypoxia or anemia. Keep oxygen in the higher range in the chronic-disease phase.[4] Keep the infant comfortable with good nursing care; consider sedation for the very irritable infant with bronchopulmonary dysplasia (BPD) after other causes of irritability have been ruled out. Maximum muscular activity may increase energy expenditure 70 percent above basal (resting) rate, and crying may increase metabolism by 49 percent.[5,6]

- *Optimize caloric intake.* Restrict fluid intake relative to healthy infants of similar age, but use increased-caloric-density (24–27 kcal/oz) formula or breast milk. Use supplemental energy sources such as medium-chain triglycerides (MCT oil) and/or glucose polymers (Polycose, Moducal).

Modular protein powder may also be needed to maintain the appropriate balance of nutrients. Human milk fortifier provides balanced supplementation for infants on breast milk. Establish glucose-to-lipid ratios of 3:1 or 2:1 to avoid excessive CO_2 production.[7,8]

- *Use proper feeding techniques.* About a third of the MCT may adhere to the feeding tube during gavage feeding, so administration of a higher amount than the infant requires may be necessary.[9] The syringe should be positioned vertically because human milk fat will remain in a horizontal syringe. The level of the syringe is also important: It should be below the level of the baby if possible (as when giving continuous drip feedings with a syringe pump). Because of its low density, fat will naturally rise to the upper portion of the tube and deposit there.[10] Inverting the syringe for continuous drip feedings will help to deliver fat.

PROTEIN AND FAT

Protein requirements for enteral feedings are 2.25–4 gm/kg/day, and fat requirements are 4–6 gm/kg/day. Fat should not exceed 55 percent of total calories. The distribution of calories should mirror those in human milk (6 percent of total calories from protein, 42 percent from carbohydrate, and 52 percent from fat).

INTRODUCING FEEDINGS

Feedings should be introduced incrementally in both volume and concentration to minimize the risk of adverse effects and setbacks such as feeding intolerance and necrotizing enterocolitis (NEC). Feeding advancement should be individualized based on each infant's clinical condition. For intrauterine growth restricted (IUGR) infants, base nutrition calculations on the 50th percentile of weight for age, not on the actual weight. Gastric size is proportional to age, not to weight, so IUGR infants can tolerate larger feeding volumes than premature infants can. Reflux and regurgitation are more common in preterm infants than in IUGR infants. For premature infants, begin with low volumes of breast milk or formula and gradually advance volume and caloric density. Because of their limited fluid intake, preterm infants usually require feedings containing 24–27 kcal/oz to grow and gain.

Enteral feeding deprivation causes atrophic changes in the gut and abnormal gut peptide surges such as those of the trophic hormones, gastrin, and gastric inhibitory polypeptide, which may be a key effector in the enteroinsular axis. Without enteral feedings, the gut may atrophy to the point that it becomes vulnerable to pathogenic organisms in the gut lumen or NEC. Minimal (stimulation) enteral feeding stimulates normal postnatal gut hormone surges within days, even with feeding volumes as low as 0.5 ml (that have no nutritional significance). Insulin release may be stimulated and help decrease glucose intolerance, a significant problem in very low birth weight infants on parenteral nutrition.[11,12] Stimulation feeding volumes are typically 5–15 ml/kg/day either continuously or by bolus.

TABLE 2-1 ◆ INFANT FORMULAS BY CATEGORY

Milk Protein-Based	Soy	Premature
Enfamil	Isomil	Enfamil Premature
LactoFree	ProSobee	Similac Special Care
Similac	RCF (Ross Carbohydrate Free)	
Therapeutic	**Metabolic**	**Modular**
Alimentum	Lofenalac	Casec
Nutramigen	Mono- and Disaccharide-Free Diet Powder (Product 3232A)	Enfamil Human Milk Fortifier
Portagen		MCT Oil
Pregestimil	Maple Syrup Urine Disease (MSUD) Diet Powder	Moducal
RCF (Ross Carbohydrate Free)	Phenyl-Free	Polycose
Similac PM 60/40	Protein-Free Diet Powder (Product 80056)	Similac Natural Care Human Milk Fortifier
Similac NeoSure	XP Analog	Sumacal Powder

FEEDING CHOICES

Infant enteral feeding choices comprise maternal breast milk (perhaps with a forti-fier) or a commercial infant formula. Commercial formulas may be milk-based or a therapeutic formulation.[13,14] Product categories include *standard* formulas for infants with no special requirements, *soy* formulas with a soy-protein base, *premature* formulas designed for preterm infants, *therapeutic* formulas for infants with special requirements, *metabolic* formulas for infants with inborn errors of metabolism, and *modular* formulas (Table 2-1). Modular nutrients for-tify formulas or breast milk either as fixed-nutrient supplements (e.g., Casec is added to increase protein content, MCT increases fat content, and Polycose increases carbohydrate content), or as multinutrient additives (e.g., Enfamil Human Milk Fortifier). Soy, premature, therapeutic, metabolic, and modular formulas should be used under the supervision of a dietitian and physician.

Iron-deficiency anemia can have damaging long-term consequences, especially alteration in cognitive performance. Several studies have observed lower scores on the Bayley mental-development index in iron-deficient infants.[15–19] Guidelines that have been developed by the American Academy of Pediatrics to prevent iron deficiency include (1) provide breast milk for at least 5–6 months when possible. If breastfed until older than 6 months of age, give an iron supple-ment providing 1 mg/kg/day. (2) If not breastfed, provide iron-fortified formula containing 12 mg iron/liter for the first 12 months of life. (3) Avoid whole cow's milk feeding during the first year of life because it may cause occult gastro-intestinal (GI) bleeding.[20,21] See monograph on ferrous sulfate for a discussion on iron supplementation in preterm infants.

Enterobacter sakazakii infections have been associated with the use of powdered (dry) infant formulas. Most cases of *E. sakazakii* have been in neonates with sepsis, meningitis, or necrotizing enterocolitis. Case fatality rates among infected neonates have been as high as 33 percent. Powdered infant formulas are not sterile. Formulas designed for preterm infants are available commercially only in sterile liquid form. However, "transitional" infant formulas, generally used for preterm infants after hospital discharge, are available in both powdered and liquid form. Some specialty formulas are available only in powdered form. The FDA recommends that powdered infant formulas not be used unless there is no alternative available. If the only option is to use powdered formula, risks of infection can be reduced by doing the following:

- Prepare only a small amount of reconstituted formula for each feeding to reduce the time that formula is held at room temperature.

- Minimize time formula is held, whether at room temperature or under refrigeration, before use.

- Minimize "hang time" (the amount of time the formula is at room temperature in a feeding bag or syringe on a syringe pump for enteral use and accompanying tubing). Maximum hang time is 4 hours to avoid the potential for significant microbial growth in reconstituted infant formula.

- Do not use boiling water to reconstitute powdered formula because of loss of heat-sensitive nutrients, change in physical characteristics of some formulas, inability to assure adequate destruction of *E. sakazakii,* and risk of injury to hospital staff preparing formula.[22–24]

Human Milk

Breast milk should be chosen whenever possible because of its many benefits, including immunologic benefits, better digestibility and absorption of nutrients, higher quality protein, lower renal solute load, and fostering of maternal-infant bonding. The composition of mature term human milk is:

- *Protein:* 6 percent of total calories
- *Carbohydrate:* 42 percent of total calories as lactose
- *Fat:* 52 percent of total calories
- *Iron:* 0.3 mg/liter

Because human milk contains insufficient protein, phosphorus, and calcium for preterm infants, breast milk fortifier (described later in this section) should also be given.

Commercial Milk-based Formulas

Milk-based formulas are prepared from nonfat cow's milk, vegetable oils, and carbohydrate, usually lactose. (Similac is one example.) Whey is added to some milk-based formulas to produce a ratio of 60 percent whey to 40 percent casein as in human milk. (Examples include Enfamil and a milk-based therapeutic formula, Similac PM 60/40.) These formulas are for normal term infants who do not require a special diet.[1] Of the whey-added formulas, SMA contains the least amount of sodium per liter, for infants with problems like congestive heart failure and hypertension.

Commercial Therapeutic Formulas

Therapeutic formulas are designed for infants requiring special diets. Type and sources of protein, carbohydrates, and fats are the primary differences between therapeutic and milk-based formulas.

Sources of protein for infant formulas include cow's milk, casein hydrolysate, and soybeans. The amino acid taurine is found in high concentrations (0.25–0.75 mmol/liter) in human milk. Taurine is added to all cow's milk–based formulas so that they will more closely simulate breast milk composition. Some formula manufacturers modify the type and concentration of milk protein (whey and casein) by adding cow's milk whey to skim cow's milk to achieve a ratio of 60 percent whey and 40 percent casein protein; others use unaltered cow's milk protein (18 percent whey, 82 percent casein). Whey-predominate formulas are recommended for preterm infants. The amino acid composition of the protein, in terms of essential, nonessential, and conditionally essential amino acids, differs between formulas. Essential amino acids cannot be synthesized by the body, whereas nonessential amino acids can.

The protein content of human milk adjusts to a growing term infant's needs, but is not sufficient for preterm infants because preterm infants have a higher protein requirement than is provided by human milk. The higher need is caused by a higher rate of protein utilization during the rapid-growth phase. Also, the premature infant has a greater body proportion of still rapidly growing organs. Supplementation with a commercially available human milk fortifier provides a reasonable plasma amino acid profile in the preterm infant and helps to achieve intrauterine growth rates.

Premature-infant formulas. Customized for the special needs of the preterm infant's immature GI tract, liver, and kidney, premature-infant formulas are available in higher caloric concentrations to provide adequate nutrition in smaller volumes for these fluid-restricted infants. Premature-infant formulas contain predominantly whey protein; easy-to-digest carbohydrates, including combinations of lactose, corn syrup solids, and glucose polymers; and fats that combine MCTs and long-chain triglycerides (LCTs). Preterm infants are better able to absorb MCTs than LCTs because these infants have low amounts of the bile salts required for LCT absorption. Figure 2-1 illustrates the differences between absorption of LCTs and MCTs.

Preterm formulas (Enfamil Premature, Similac Special Care) have an isotonic osmolality of approximately 300 mOsm/kg of water at a concentration of 24 kcal/oz to prevent osmotic diarrhea and reduce the risk of NEC. These formulas may contain varying amounts of extra vitamins, electrolytes, and minerals to meet the needs of the growing preterm infant.[1]

Soy-protein formulas. Soy-based formulas (Isomil, ProSobee) may be tried for infants suspected of being sensitive to milk protein. However, the American Academy of Pediatrics recommends that casein hydrolysate formulas (see below), rather than soy-protein formulas, be used for infants with a documented clinical allergy to cow's milk. This is because soy protein is probably no

FIGURE 2-1 ◆ COMPARISON OF ABSORPTION OF LONG-CHAIN (LCTs) AND MEDIUM-CHAIN (MCTs) TRIGLYCERIDES.

Long-Chain Triglycerides (LCTs)	Medium-Chain Triglycerides (MCTs)

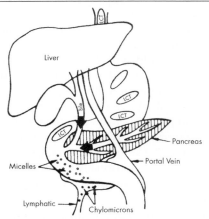
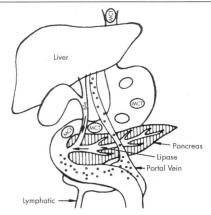

Normal digestion of fats is a relatively slow process, requiring pancreatic lipase, bile salts, and adequate intestinal surface area. Long-chain triglycerides (LCTs) are emulsified by bile salts into micelles and hydrolyzed to fatty acids and glycerol by pancreatic lipase. This emulsified fat (0.5 microns in diameter) enters the epithelial (mucosal) cells where it combines with protein to form chylomicrons, which are transferred directly into the lymphatic circulation (lacteals). The chylomicrons are transported in the form of chyle through the thoracic duct into the bloodstream and finally to the liver, where these fats are hydrolyzed and transported to the various storage areas of the body.

Medium-chain triglycerides (MCTs) contain glycerol esterified to saturated medium-chain-length fatty acids, mainly 8- and 10-carbon-atom chain lengths. The route of absorption of MCT is different from that of conventional fats. MCTs require much less pancreatic lipase and bile salts for effective digestion. MCTs are absorbed and then hydrolyzed within the mucosal cells. Furthermore, MCTs do not require micellar or chylomicron formation for digestion and absorption.

Fatty acid molecules with 10-carbon-atom chain length or less are known to be transported in unesterified form directly from the intestinal tract into the portal circulation rather than via the lymphatic system.

From: Mead Johnson Nutritionals. 1993. *Pediatric Products Handbook*. Evansville, Indiana: Mead Johnson Nutritionals, 38. Reprinted by permission.

---

less antigenic than milk protein. Soy formulas are used for infants of vegetarian parents, for infants with primary lactase deficiency (such as galactosemia), and for those with temporary lactase deficiency such as occurs in gastroenteritis.

Soy formulas contain corn syrup solids and sucrose, rather than lactose. RCF (Ross Carbohydrate Free) is a soy-protein formula that does not contain carbohydrates; the physician or nurse practitioner can select the type (glucose polymers, sucrose, dextrose) and amount of carbohydrate to be added, then titrate the dose upward as tolerated. Carnitine (see that monograph), which is necessary for optimal oxidation of fatty acids, is added because foods of plant origin have a low concentration of this substance compared with foods of animal origin.[1]

FIGURE 2-2 ◆ HYDROLYSIS OF CARBOHYDRATE.

Number of glucose units/molecule	20–2500	10–20	5–10	3–5	1–2
*Dextrose equivalents (DE)	0	10	10–20	20	50–100
Common terms	Starch	Dextrin	Maltodextrin	Corn Syrup	"Sugar"
Chemical terms			Oligosaccharides Glucose Oligomers		
			Polysaccharides		
			Glucose Polymers		

* DE reducing sugar content as percent of D-glucose

The breakdown of large starch molecules into smaller and smaller glucose polymers is achieved via hydrolysis. This process can be interrupted at any point to yield the size of glucose polymer desired. This is important in infant formula manufacture because:

1. It allows the formulation of lactose-free products with small-molecular/weight carbohydrates that can be readily utilized by infants who cannot digest lactose.

2. By varying the amounts of the various glucose polymers in the formula (i.e., starch, dextrin, corn syrup, "sugar," etc.), the osmolality of the finished product can be controlled while still providing the proper total amount of carbohydrate.

3. Starch molecules can be utilized to keep fats in a stabilized emulsion.

From: Tsang RC, and Nichols BL. 1988. *Nutrition During Infancy.* Philadelphia: Hanley & Belfus, 389. Reprinted by permission.

Lactose intolerance is uncommon in preterm infants, so using a soy-based formula just because an infant is premature is generally not recommended. The osmolality of soy formulas is lower than that of breast milk or of milk-based formulas because glucose polymers are the carbohydrate source.

Casein (protein) hydrolysate formulas. Casein hydrolysate formulas (sometimes termed *elemental* formulas) may be required in infants with a history of feeding intolerance, allergy to cow's milk, NEC, short-gut syndrome, recovery from gastroenteritis, steatorrhea, or intractable diarrhea when they are intolerant of or cannot properly absorb standard formulas. These formulas are useful for infants having difficulty transitioning from parenteral to enteral nutrition. Formulas in this category include Alimentum, Mono- and Disaccharide-Free Diet Powder (Product 3232A), Nutramigen, and Pregestimil. The protein in these formulas is casein hydrolysate—enzymatically hydrolyzed, charcoal-treated casein—rather than whole protein.

FIGURE 2-3 ◆ DIGESTION OF CARBOHYDRATES IN THE INTESTINE.

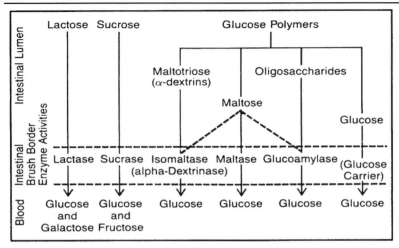

From: Mead Johnson Nutritionals. 1993. *Pediatric Products Handbook.* Evansville, Indiana: Mead Johnson Nutritionals, 11. Reprinted by permission.

The **carbohydrate** sources in elemental formulas include corn syrup solids, modified cornstarch, dextrose, sucrose, and modified tapioca starch. They do not include lactose. Figure 2-2 explains the breakdown of large starch molecules into smaller and smaller glucose polymers, notes why the breakdown process is important in infant formula manufacture, and visually defines carbohydrate terminology (glucose polymers: starch, dextrin, maltodextrin, corn syrup solids; and sugars: sucrose, lactose). Glucose polymers are a low-osmolar form of carbohydrate that help minimize the total osmolar load of the formula. They are readily digestible and are useful for infants (such as those recovering from gastroenteritis) who cannot tolerate lactose or sucrose. Figure 2-3 illustrates how carbohydrates are digested in the intestine. Note that lactose is broken down by lactase to glucose and galactose (to be avoided in galactosemia).

Elemental-infant-formula **fat** sources are MCTs and vegetable oils such as corn and safflower. Providing a portion of the fat as MCTs helps to prevent and/or relieve steatorrhea, promotes weight gain, and improves calcium absorption in preterm infants.[1]

Breast Milk Fortifiers

A breast milk (BM) fortifier (Enfamil Human Milk Fortifier, Similac Natural Care Human Milk Fortifier) may be added to breast milk when the infant is on full feedings. A fortifier increases the caloric density of breast milk to 0.8 kcal/ml and converts BM from 20 kcal/oz to 24 kcal/oz. Table 2-2 gives more information on the composition of these and other infant formulas, along with indications for their use. Table 2-3 lists the caloric content of various enteral nutrient sources.

TABLE 2-2 ◆ **INFANT FORMULAS AND ENTERAL DIET MODIFIERS: COMPOSITION AND INDICATIONS**[56–58]

Formula Name*/ Category	Composition	Indications
Alimentum[2]/ Therapeutic	*Protein:* casein hydrolysate and amino acids *Fat:* MCT (50% of fat), soy, safflower *Carbohydrate:* tapioca starch, sucrose (no lactose) *Iron:* 12.16 mg/liter	For infants who: • are sensitive to or unable to digest intact cow's milk protein • are unable to properly absorb carbohydrate or fat • are allergic to corn • show pancreatic insufficiency • have chronic diarrhea
Casec Powder[1]/ Modular	*Protein:* calcium caseinate *Fat:* none *Carbohydrate:* none *Calories:* 1.4 gm protein and 5.7 kcal/tsp	A source of extra protein. Cannot be used as the only nutritional source.
Enfamil[1]/Milk Protein-Based	*Protein:* from nonfat milk; whey-to-casein ratio 60:40 *Fat:* soy and coconut oils, soy lecithin, mono- and diglycerides *Carbohydrate:* lactose *Iron (low iron):* 4.73 mg/liter	Standard formula for infants 0–12 months who do not have special requirements. Supplemental iron needed. (See Enfamil with Iron below.)
Enfamil with Iron[1]/Milk Protein-Based	*Protein, fat, and carbohydrate:* same as Enfamil (above) *Iron:* 12.16 mg/liter	Standard formula for infants 0–12 months who do not have special requirements. Provides extra iron, as recommended by the AAP. The AAP recommends iron supplementation in the first year of life. The RDA is 6 mg/day until 6 months, then 10 mg/day between 6 months and 3 years of age.
Enfamil Premature Formula[1]/ Premature	*Protein:* from nonfat milk; whey-to-casein ratio 60:40 *Fat:* coconut and soy oils; MCT (40% of fat calories) *Carbohydrate:* corn syrup solids (glucose polymers); lactose *Iron (low iron):* 20 kcal/oz = 1.7 mg/liter 24 kcal/oz = 2 mg/liter	For rapidly growing preterm infants who have increased caloric needs but are unable to consume an adequate volume of formula. Contains easily digestible carbohydrates and fats and appropriate vitamin and mineral content for preterm infants while maintaining isotonic osmolality.
Enfamil Premature Formula with Iron[1]/ Premature	*Protein, fat, and carbohydrate:* same as Enfamil Premature Formula *Iron:* 20 kcal/oz =12.16 mg/liter 24 kcal/oz = 14.52 mg/liter	For the same infants as Enfamil Premature Formula (above), but with supplemental iron. The AAP recommends iron supplementation in preterm infants beginning at 2 months postnatal age.

continued on next page

NUTRITION

TABLE 2-2 ◆ INFANT FORMULAS AND ENTERAL DIET MODIFIERS: COMPOSITION AND INDICATIONS (CONTINUED)

Formula Name*/ Category	Composition	Indications
Enfamil Human Milk Fortifier[1]/ Modular	Protein, carbohydrates, vitamins, electrolytes (potassium, sodium, chloride), minerals (magnesium, calcium, and phosphorus), and trace elements (zinc, copper, manganese) *Calories:* 1 packet added to 50 ml raises caloric density by 2 kcal/oz; 1 packet added to 25 ml raises caloric density by 4 kcal/oz	A nutritional supplement for preterm infants to be added to mother's milk. Mother's milk collected >2 weeks postpartum may contain insufficient protein, calcium, and phosphorus—and possibly, zinc, copper, and sodium.
Isomil[2]/*Soy*	*Protein:* soy protein isolate and L-methionine *Fat:* high-oleic safflower, coconut, and soy oils. *Carbohydrate:* corn syrup, sucrose (no lactose), concentrate also contains cornstarch *Iron:* 12.16 mg/liter	For infants with cow's milk intolerance, diarrhea, or lactose-intolerance disorders caused by lactase deficiency or metabolic galactosemia. Has a low osmolality (240 mOsm/kg water) to reduce risk of osmotic diarrhea.
LactoFree[1]/*Milk Protein-Based (lactose-free)*	*Protein:* milk protein isolate *Fat:* palm olein, soy, coconut, and high oleic sunflower oils *Carbohydrate:* corn syrup solids (no lactose) *Iron:* 12.16 mg/liter	For infants up to 12 months old with lactose intolerance. Contains no lactose. Low osmolality (200 mOsm/kg water).
Lofenalac[1]/ Metabolic	*Protein:* casein hydrolysate, amino acids, *phenylalanine: approx. 0.08%* *Fat:* corn oil *Carbohydrate:* corn syrup solids, modified tapioca starch *Iron:* 12.7 mg/liter	For infants requiring restriction of phenylalanine because of hyper-phenylalaninemia, including PKU. The hydrolyzed casein in the formula is especially processed to remove most of the phenylalanine. Can be used as a formula for infants or as a basic food for older infants and children. Must be used under the supervision of a dietitian and physician. *See also* Phenyl-Free (which is more commonly used) below.
MCT Oil[1]/ Modular	*Protein, carbohydrates, and iron:* none *Fat:* medium-chain triglycerides, which contain medium-chain (C_8 to C_{10}) saturated fatty acids. Does not provide essential fatty acids *Calories:* 7.6 kcal/ml	A fat source for caloric supplementation. Easily digested and absorbed in preterm infants and others who have difficulty utilizing long-chain (C_{16} to C_{18}) triglycerides. Can be absorbed without the bile salts and pancreatic lipase needed for absorption of LCTs. Does not increase the osmolality of feedings.

continued on next page

TABLE 2-2 ◆ INFANT FORMULAS AND ENTERAL DIET MODIFIERS: COMPOSITION AND INDICATIONS (CONTINUED)

Formula Name*/ Category	Composition	Indications
Moducal[1]/ Modular	*Protein, fat, and iron:* none *Carbohydrate:* maltodextrin *Calories:* 10 kcal/tsp	A glucose polymer for caloric supplementation. Maltodextrin is a polysaccharide, a readily digestible carbohydrate that can be added to infant formulas.
Mono- and Disaccharide-Free Diet Powder (Product 3232A)[1]/ Therapeutic	*Protein:* casein hydrolysate *Fat:* MCT (28%), corn oil *Carbohydrate:* modified tapioca starch *Iron:* 12.7 mg/liter	Used in diagnosis and management of disaccharidase deficiencies (lactase, sucrase, and maltase), impaired glucose transport, and intractable diarrhea of infancy; also in the study of fructose utilization. Adequate carbohydrate must be supplied (i.e., add to the formula lactose powder in increasing amounts, as tolerated). The protein and fat in 3232A may be more easily absorbed than that in RCF (see below).
MSUD Diet Powder[1]/ Metabolic	*Protein:* individual amino acids devoid of leucine, isoleucine, and valine *Fat:* corn oil *Carbohydrate:* corn syrup solids, modified tapioca starch *Iron:* 12.7 mg/liter	For infants and children with branched-chain amino-acid disorders such as maple syrup urine disease (MSUD), methylacetoacetic aciduria, and leucine-induced hyperleucine-isoleucinemia.
Nutramigen[1]/ Therapeutic	*Protein:* hydrolyzed casein and amino acids *Fat:* palm olein, soy, coconut, and high oleic sunflower oils *Carbohydrate:* sucrose *Iron:* 12.16 mg/liter	For infants with allergy to intact protein, multiple food allergies, or persistent diarrhea or other GI disturbances due to milk-protein allergy; also for elimination diets. May be used in galactosemia.
PediaSure[2]/Milk Protein-Based	*Protein:* sodium caseinate, whey protein concentrate *Fat:* high oleic safflower oil, soy oil, MCT (20% of fat), mono- and diglycerides, soy lecithin *Carbohydrate:* maltodextrin, pureed fruits and vegetables (no lactose), gluten-free *Iron:* 13.90 mg/liter *Calories:* 1 kcal/ml	For oral or tube feeding of children 1–6 years old. Provides low osmolality (<310 mOsm/kg water) in a 1 kcal/ml formula. Preferred for the older infant and young child because nutrients are in proportion and meet RDA for this age group, especially for calcium, phosphorus, and iron. Children tolerate product better than they do adult formula products.

continued on next page

NUTRITION

TABLE 2-2 ◆ INFANT FORMULAS AND ENTERAL DIET MODIFIERS: COMPOSITION AND INDICATIONS (CONTINUED)

Formula Name*/ Category	Composition	Indications
Phenyl-Free[1]/ Metabolic	*Protein:* L-amino acids *phenylalanine:* approx. 0.08% *Carbohydrate:* sucrose, corn syrup solids, modified tapioca starch *Fat:* corn and coconut oils *Iron:* 12.2 mg/100 gm powder	A phenylalanine-free food to aid in the nutritional management of hyperphenylalaninemia, including PKU. Provides all essential amino acids (except phenylalanine), vitamins, and minerals but fewer total calories than Lofenalac (see above). Should not be used as the sole source of nutrition; regular foods such as fruits and vegetables can be used to supply the remainder of caloric needs (fat, carbohydrate), additional protein, and total phenylalanine requirement. Must be used under the supervision of a dietitian and physician to help ensure normal growth and behavioral development.
PM 60/40.	*See* Similac PM 60/40	
Polycose[2]/ Modular	*Protein:* none *Fat:* none *Carbohydrate:* glucose polymers *Calories (in liquid):* 2 kcal/ml *Calories (in powder):* 8 kcal/level tsp	Caloric supplement. Contains readily digestible carbohydrate for addition to infant formulas. The higher molecular weight of its glucose polymers helps reduce osmolality and the risk of osmotic diarrhea over other carbohydrate sources.
Portagen[1]/ Therapeutic	*Protein:* sodium caseinate *Fat:* MCT (85% of fat calories), corn oil *Carbohydrate:* corn syrup solids, sugar (sucrose) *Iron:* 12.7 mg/liter	For infants with poor ability to digest, absorb, or utilize fats, as in cystic fibrosis, intestinal resection, pancreatic insufficiency, bile-acid deficiency, lymphatic anomalies, celiac disease (gluten-induced enteropathy), steatorrhea, and disorders of long-chain fatty acid metabolism. Not for long-term use as the sole source of nutrition because it contains insufficient essential fatty acids.
Pregestimil[1]/ Therapeutic	*Protein:* casein enzymatically hydrolyzed, amino acids *Fat:* MCT oil (55% of fat calories); corn, soy, and safflower or sunflower oils *Carbohydrate:* corn syrup solids, dextrose, modified cornstarch *Iron:* 12.16 mg/liter	For infants with fat malabsorption, chronic diarrhea, intestinal resection, cystic fibrosis, or lactase or sucrase deficiency. Contains MCT as the major fat component, protein hydrolysate, and no lactose or sucrose. Used for infants with severe formula intolerance.

continued on next page

Neonatal Medications & Nutrition

TABLE 2-2 ◆ INFANT FORMULAS AND ENTERAL DIET MODIFIERS: COMPOSITION AND INDICATIONS (CONTINUED)

Formula Name*/ Category	Composition	Indications
ProSobee[1]/Soy	*Protein:* soy protein isolate, L-methionine *Fat:* Palm olein, soy, coconut, and high-oleic sunflower oils *Carbohydrate:* corn syrup solids *Iron:* 12.16 mg/liter	For infants with cow's milk intolerance. Also for management of lactose intolerance, diarrhea, sucrose intolerance, and gluten sensitivity. As a milk-free, soy-protein-based formula, it is lactose, sucrose, and galactose free (see Figure 2-3).
Protein-Free Diet Powder (Product 80056)[1]/ Metabolic	*Protein:* none *Fat:* corn oil *Carbohydrate:* corn syrup solids, modified tapioca starch *Iron:* 12.7 mg/liter	Use as an ingredient in the formulation of special diets. For patients requiring specific mixtures of amino acids, such as B_{12} independent methylmalonic aciduria, hyperlysinemia, propionic aciduria, urea cycle disorders, arginemia, and propionic and gyrate atrophy. Processed without protein or amino acids, it serves as a formula base to which protein, sodium, potassium, and chloride can be added.
RCF (Ross Carbohydrate Free)[2]/Soy/ Therapeutic	*Protein:* soy protein isolate, L-methionine *Fat:* high oleic safflower, soy, and coconut oils *Carbohydrate:* none	For infants, such as those with intractable diarrhea, who are unable to tolerate the type or amount of carbohydrate in milk or conventional infant formulas. Carbohydrate type and amount are selected by the physician, and the carbohydrate must be added before feeding. The soy protein may help infants avoid symptoms of cow's-milk-protein allergy or sensitivity.
Similac[2]/Milk Protein-Based	*Protein:* nonfat milk *Fat (in powder):* coconut and corn oils *Fat (in liquid and concentrate):* coconut and soy oils, mono- and diglycerides, soy lecithin *Carbohydrate:* lactose *Iron (low iron):* 1.49 mg/liter	Standard formula for infants 0–12 months who do not have special requirements.
Similac with Iron[2]/Milk Protein-Based	*Protein, fat, and carbohydrate:* same as Similac (above) *Iron:* 12.16 mg/liter	For infants 0–12 months who do not have special requirements except for supplemental iron. The AAP recommends iron supplementation in the first year of life. The RDA is 6 mg/day until 6 months, then 10 mg/day between 6 months and 3 years of age.

continued on next page

NUTRITION

TABLE 2-2 ◆ INFANT FORMULAS AND ENTERAL DIET MODIFIERS: COMPOSITION AND INDICATIONS (CONTINUED)

Formula Name*/ Category	Composition	Indications
Similac Natural Care Human Milk Fortifier[2]/ Modular	Protein, fat, carbohydrates, vitamins, electrolytes (potassium, sodium, chloride), minerals (magnesium, calcium, and phosphorus), and trace elements (zinc, copper, manganese) *Calories:* 24 kcal/oz (= 0.8 kcal/ml)	A nutritional supplement for low birth weight infants to be added to mother's milk or fed alternately with human milk. Not intended as a sole source of nutrients.
Similac NeoSure[2]/ Therapeutic	*Protein:* nonfat milk and whey protein concentrate *Fat:* soy, high-oleic safflower, medium-chain triglyceride, and coconut oils *Carbohydrate:* corn syrup solids and lactose *Iron:* 13.4 mg/liter	Used after hospital discharge for infants born at a gestational age of less than 32 weeks.
Similac PM 60/40[2]/ Therapeutic	*Protein:* whey protein concentrate, sodium caseinate (60:40) *Fat:* corn, coconut, and soy oils *Carbohydrate:* lactose *Iron (low iron):* 1.49 mg/liter	For infants who are predisposed to hypocalcemia and those whose renal, digestive, or cardiovascular functions would benefit from lowered mineral levels. Ca:P ratio and sodium content are similar to those in human milk. A low-sodium formula for infants with problems such as congestive heart failure and hypertension.
Similac Special Care[2]/ Premature	*Protein:* nonfat milk, whey *Fat:* MCT, soy and coconut oils *Carbohydrate:* corn syrup solids, lactose *Iron (low iron):* 2.5 mg/liter	For growing preterm infants.
Sumacal Powder[4]/ Modular	*Protein, fat, and iron:* none *Carbohydrate:* maltodextrin *Calories:* 10 kcal/level tsp	A glucose polymer for caloric supplementation. Maltodextrin is a polysaccharide, a readily digestible carbohydrate that can be added to infant formulas.
XP Analog[3]/ Metabolic	*Protein:* L-amino acids *Fat:* peanut oil, refined animal fat (pork), coconut oil *Carbohydrate:* corn syrup solids *Iron:* 10 mg/100 gm powder (2.1 mg/100 kcal)	For infants with phenylketonuria. Must be used under the supervision of a dietitian and physician. Contains no phenylalanine, but contains a balanced mixture of all other essential and nonessential amino acids, carbohydrate, fat, vitamins, minerals, and trace elements, including selenium and chromium.

* Manufacturer: [1]Mead Johnson Nutritionals, Evansville, Indiana, [2]Ross Laboratories, Columbus, Ohio, [3]Scientific Hospital Supplies, Gaithersburg, Maryland, [4]Sherwood Medical, St. Louis, Missouri.

Neonatal Medications & Nutrition

TABLE 2-3 ◆ CALORIC VALUE OF ENTERAL NUTRIENT SOURCES

Product	Caloric Content
20 kcal/oz Sources	0.67 kcal/ml
Breast milk	
Formulas:	
Alimentum	
Enfamil-20	
Enfamil Premature-20	
Isomil-20	
Nutramigen-20	
Pregestimil-20	
Similac-20	
Similac PM 60/40–20	
ProSobee-20	
22 kcal/oz Sources	0.74 kcal/ml
Similac NeoSure	
24 kcal/oz Formulas	0.8 kcal/ml
Enfamil Premature-24	
Similac Special Care-24	
Other Sources	
Breast milk fortifier (Enfamil Human Milk Fortifier)	14 kcal from 4 packets added to100 ml of breast milk Increases caloric density of breast milk by 0.14 kcal/ml; therefore, converts 20 kcal/oz breast milk to 24 kcal/oz
Casec powder	Contains 1.4 gm protein and 5.7 kcal per packed level teaspoon (tsp)
MCT oil	7.6 kcal/ml
Microlipid emulsion	4.5 kcal/ml
Moducal powder	10 kcal/tsp
Polycose liquid	2 kcal/ml
Polycose powder	8 kcal/tsp
Sumacal	10 kcal/tsp
Rice cereal	4.3 kcal/tsp
Pedialyte	0.2 kcal/ml
Ricelyte	0.13 kcal/ml

TABLE 2-4 ◆ **USUAL INFANT FLUID REQUIREMENTS (ML/KG/DAY)**[27,49,59]

	Infant Weight (gm)				
	<800	**800–1,000**	**1,000–1,500**	**1,500–2,500**	**Term Infants**
Day 1	120–140 or more	80–100	70–90	60–80	60–80
Days 2–7	120–140 or more	100–120	90–120	80–120	80–120

NUTRITIONAL SUPPLEMENTS FOR PRETERM INFANTS

Introduce nutritional supplements when the infant is tolerating full feedings. Space them throughout the day, rather than giving them all in one feeding, to avoid osmotic overload and feeding intolerance. For the same reason, do not begin several supplements all on the same day. Add a new supplement each day, as tolerated. A suggested regimen follows:

- *Multivitamins:* Begin multivitamins 0.5 ml every 12 hours when on full-strength formula; then advance to multivitamins 1 ml/day as tolerated. Some formulas designed for preterm infants (for example, Enfamil Premature, Similac Special Care) contain larger amounts of vitamins than do standard milk-based formulas. Depending on formula-intake volume, supplemental multivitamins may not be required with these formulas, or a smaller volume (such as 0.5 ml/day) may be sufficient. To calculate an infant's vitamin intake, multiply the volume of infant formula taken in by the vitamin content (see Appendix L: Composition of Feedings for Infants and Young Children in the Hospital).

- *Vitamin E/Folic acid:* Begin vitamin E 25 units PO daily and folic acid 50 mcg PO daily. Discontinue at 34–36 weeks postconceptional age (PCA).

- *Iron:* Begin ferrous sulfate drops 0.2 ml PO daily at 34–36 weeks PCA when vitamin E and folic acid are discontinued.

- *Vitamin D:* Consider vitamin D 400 units PO daily for infants weighing <1,000 gm and for those with nutritional rickets (osteopenia of prematurity).

- *Other supplements:* Add modular supplements such as fat (MCT oil for preterm infants, corn oil or microlipids for term infants), glucose polymers (Polycose, Moducal, Sumacal), and oral protein supplement (Casec powder) if needed when on full feedings.

FEEDING PROBLEMS

Problems with enteral feedings may be early signs of NEC or other serious abdominal conditions. The following signs call for assessment of the infant and potential changes in feeding orders:

- *Gastric residuals:* Residuals >30 percent of current feeding volume on two consecutive feedings

- *Bilious aspirates/emesis:* Green or yellow bilious aspirates or bilious emesis

- *Abnormalities in abdominal exam:* Increase in abdominal girth associated with visible or palpable bowel loops, decreased bowel sounds, or abdominal skin discoloration
- *Abnormalities in stooling pattern:* Occult-positive, grossly bloody, or water-loss stool
- *Emesis:* Any emesis >30 percent of feeding volume on two consecutive feedings
- *Deterioration in respiratory status:* Change from previous pattern in respiratory status and/or apnea-bradycardia spells

MONITORING INFANTS ON ENTERAL FEEDINGS

Both laboratory testing and clinical monitoring should receive attention when preterm or other infants are being fed enterally. Consider assessing blood levels of alkaline phosphatase, sodium, potassium, chloride, calcium, and phosphorus weekly to every other week for preterm infants at risk for electrolyte abnormalities and nutritional rickets. Weigh these infants daily. Plot their weight, length, and head circumference weekly.

Parenteral Nutrition

Optimal nutritional support should be provided consistently throughout hospitalization. The enteral route should be the first choice if the infant's medical condition warrants. If indicated, parenteral nutrition should be initiated on day 2 or 3 of life. Infants should not be without nutrition for more than 3 days.

FLUID REQUIREMENTS

Preterm infants are particularly susceptible to fluid losses because of their large body surface area in relation to weight, increased body water, and increased skin permeability. Insensible water loss decreases with increasing birth weight. For example, infants weighing 750–1,000 gm at birth average an insensible water loss of 64 ml/kg/day, whereas infants weighing approximately 2–3 kg lose only 20 ml/kg/day.[25] The preterm infant's total body water accounts for 75–85 percent of total body weight. Extracellular water is 45–60 percent of total body weight. These percentages decrease with growth. Intracellular water content is correlated with lean body mass and decreases as a percentage of body weight as fat content decreases. Fluid requirements consist of water for growth, plus respiratory and transepidermal losses, sweating, and urine and fecal losses.[26]

Fluid needs depend on history, gestational age, postnatal age, clinical assessment of hydration, urine specific gravity, presence or absence of patent ductus arteriosus, and increases in fluid loss associated with therapy. Urine output should be at least 1 ml/kg/hour, but it can vary widely with fluid intake, intravascular volume, osmotic status, and maturity of renal function. Healthy infants from 29 weeks gestation can tolerate a fluid intake of 100–200 ml/kg/day.[27] Infants should be weighed at least daily and the weight of attachments such as lines subtracted.[28]

TABLE 2-5 ◆ COMPARISON OF NEONATAL CAA SOLUTIONS

Amino Acid	Content (mg/100 ml)	
	Aminosyn PF 10% (Abbott)	TrophAmine 10% (McGaw)
Essential:		
Isoleucine	820	760
Leucine	1,400	1,200
Lysine	820	677
Methionine	340	180
Phenylalanine	480	427
Threonine	420	512
Tryptophan	200	180
Arginine*	1,200	1,227
Cysteine*	<16	0
Glycine*	360	385
Histidine*	480	312
Taurine*	25	70
Tyrosine*	240	40
Nonessential:		
Alanine	540	698
Proline	680	812
Serine	380	495
Glutamic acid	500	620
Aspartic acid	320	527
Osmolarity (mOsm/liter)	**875**	**829**

* These are "conditionally essential nutrients" in infants because immaturity reduces synthetic capacity below functional metabolic demands.

Adapted from: Manufacturers' product literature; and Uauy R, Greene HL, and Heird WC. 1993. Conditionally essential nutrients: Cysteine, taurine, tyrosine, arginine, glutamine, choline, inositol, and nucleotides. In *Nutritional Needs of the Preterm Infant: Scientific Basis and Practical Guidelines,* Tsang RC, et al., eds. Baltimore: Lippincott Williams & Wilkins, 267–280.

Increased fluid loss can occur from thermal stress caused by a radiant warmer or phototherapy. Overhead warmers generally call for a 50–100 percent increase in fluids. At times, insensible fluid losses may triple, requiring even greater supplementation. Phototherapy generally increases fluid requirements 30–50 percent. Fluid status may be further altered by respiratory status, ambient room temperature and humidity, cold stress, metabolic stress (such as fever, infection, or activity), and lack of effective water conservation by the immature renal system. Infants in an incubator and/or on a mechanical ventilator may have decreased fluid requirements. A plastic blanket under a radiant warmer decreases insensible water loss approximately 30–50 percent. Fluid intake must be

TABLE 2-6 ◆ CALORIC VALUE OF PARENTERAL NUTRIENT SOURCES*

Solution	Caloric Content (kcal/ml)
Dextrose†	
D_4W	0.14
D_5W	0.17
$D_{7.5}W$	0.26
$D_{10}W$	0.34
$D_{12.5}W$	0.42
$D_{15}W$	0.5
$D_{17.5}W$	0.6
$D_{20}W$	0.68
$D_{22}W$	0.75
$D_{25}W$	0.86
$D_{27}W$	0.92
$D_{30}W$	1
IV Fat Emulsion	
10%	1.1
20%	2

* Multiply the caloric content in kcal/ml on the table corresponding to the percent dextrose the baby is receiving, times the PN fluid volume to determine the total calories the infant is receiving from the solution.

† kcal/ml = % dextrose in IV solution × 0.0342.

individualized. Careful, frequent reassessments within the course of a 24-hour period are essential to properly manage infants.

Table 2-4 displays usual infant fluid requirements. The higher fluid requirements shown for very low birth weight (VLBW) infants compensate for insensible losses from the skin and help to prevent hyperkalemia, hypovolemia, and hypotension.

Several conditions call for altering the fluid balance—either restricting or liberalizing fluids:

- *Fluid restriction:* Infants with patent ductus arteriosus, bronchopulmonary dysplasia, severe respiratory distress, hypoxic-ischemic encephalopathy, and oliguric renal failure have their fluids restricted. Oliguria and hyponatremia resulting from inappropriate antidiuretic hormone (ADH) are treated by fluid restriction.

- *Fluid liberalization:* VLBW infants with excessive insensible water loss; infants under a radiant warmer; those undergoing phototherapy; those experiencing diarrhea, vomiting, or polyuria; and those undergoing frequent lumbar puncture for hydrocephalus generally require fluid augmentation.[26]

PROTEIN REQUIREMENTS

Protein is provided as CAA in PN. Begin with 0.5–1.5 gm/kg/day, and increase to 2.5–3 gm/kg/day in 1 to 5 days, as tolerated. Use a lower dose of protein (i.e., 2 gm/kg/day) in infants with an elevated BUN. Use of a neonatal-specific CAA solution is preferred.[29] CAA solutions provide balanced amino acids for infants, with the exception of cysteine, which may be added to the infusate daily (60–120 mg/kg/day). Cysteine is an essential amino acid in preterm infants because of low activity of cystathionase, the enzyme that converts methionine to cysteine in hepatic tissue.[30] Table 2-5 compares commercially available CAA solutions. Excessive protein administration can cause increased BUN, metabolic acidosis, and hyper-ammonemia (rare).

The ratio of nonprotein calories to nitrogen should be 150–200:1. To calculate grams of nitrogen being administered from grams of protein being administered, use this formula:

$$Grams\ of\ nitrogen = grams\ of\ protein \div 6.25$$

CALORIC REQUIREMENTS

Growth rates and nitrogen retention similar to *in utero* values can be sustained by IV intake of 80 kcal/kg/day when an appropriate amount of nitrogen is given. Caloric requirements are less for IV than for enteral feeding because of negligible fecal losses. However, the caloric goal for rapidly growing preterm neonates should be about 120 kcal/kg/day.[31] Caloric calculations are based on carbohydrates and fat; protein calories (4 kcal/gm) are not included in the calculations because protein should be used for anabolism, not catabolized for energy.

Carbohydrate

Dextrose, the carbohydrate used in PN, provides 3.42 kcal/gm. Begin with $D_{10}W$, which provides 6–7 mg/kg/minute of glucose, and increase every 24 hours as tolerated. Preterm infants may require lower concentrations of dextrose—such as $D_{7.5}W$, which provides approximately 5–6 mg/kg/minute of glucose—because of glucose intolerance. Daily increases of 0.5–1 mg/kg/minute are usually tolerated; VLBW infants may not tolerate as rapid an increase in dextrose concentration as term infants.[25] The steady increase in glucose infusion rate stimulates endogenous insulin secretion. An infusion rate of 11–12 mg/kg/minute is tolerated after 5–7 days of PN. If not, a continuous infusion of insulin via a separate pump may be administered to achieve an energy intake sufficient for growth.[32] Glucose load may be calculated using the following formula:[33]

$$\frac{Glucose\ load}{(mg/kg/minute)} = \frac{percent\ dextrose\ infusing \times rate\ of\ infusion\ (in\ ml/hour) \times 0.167}{baby's\ weight\ (in\ kg)}$$

The maximum concentration of dextrose that should be infused in a peripheral line is 12.5 percent because solutions of high osmolality cause local irritation and increase the risk of extravasation injury. Central PN may be gradually increased to $D_{25}W$ (rarely, to $D_{30}W$ in infants with severe fluid restrictions). Carbohydrate and fat intake should be balanced. Adverse effects of excessive

TABLE 2-7 ◆ COMPARISON OF IV FAT EMULSION PRODUCTS

	Intralipid (Clintec) 10% and 20%	Liposyn II (Abbott)	Liposyn III (Abbott)
Source of oil	Soybean	Safflower and soybean	Soybean
Osmolarity (mOsm/liter)	260	258 (20%) 276 (10%)	292 (20%) 284 (10%)
Smallest volume marketed	50 ml	200 ml (20%) 100 ml (10%)	200 ml (20%) 100 ml (10%)
Fatty acid composition (%)			
Linoleic	50	65.8	54.5
Oleic	26	17.7	22.4
Palmitic	10	8.8	10.5
Linolenic	9	4.2	8.3
Stearic	3.5	3.4	4.2

Note: All products have 1.2% egg yolk phospholipids. A larger dose of phospholipids is given with the 10% emulsion because a larger volume of product is needed for equivalent gm/kg dose of fat.

Glycerin content is 2.25% for Intralipid and 2.5% for Liposyn II and III.

Caloric content is 1.1 kcal/ml for 10% and 2 kcal/ml for 20%. The 20% emulsions contain twice as much oil, but about the same amounts of all other ingredients.

Particle size is 0.5 microns for Intralipid and 0.4 microns for Liposyn.

From: Manufacturers' product literature.

carbohydrate infusions are (1) increased CO_2 production, which increases the work load on the lungs and (2) accumulation of fat in the liver, which leads to fatty infiltration and cholestasis. These adverse effects may also occur from provision of excessive calories (overfeeding).[34] The caloric content of various dextrose-solution concentrations is shown in Table 2-6.

Fat

Administration of intravenous (IV) fat emulsion allows the clinician to provide calories adequate for growth via peripheral vein and provides essential fatty acids. Long-chain fatty acids are essential for brain development in newborns. Neonates are especially susceptible to development of essential fatty acid deficiency because their tissue deposits of linoleic acid are small and their requirements for essential fatty acids are large as a result of their rapid growth.

Concentration and caloric value. Because of its high caloric density, IV fat provides a significant portion of the infant's daily caloric needs. IV fat emulsions are available in 20 percent and 10 percent concentrations. Caloric values are as follows:

- 20 percent = 2 kcal/ml = 0.2 gm/ml
- 10 percent = 1.1 kcal/ml = 0.1 gm/ml

TABLE 2-8 ◆ AVERAGE DAILY DOSES OF ELECTROLYTES AND MINERALS

Element	Dose	Comments
Sodium	2–4 mEq/kg	
Potassium	2–3 mEq/kg	
Chloride	2–3 mEq/kg	
Acetate	1–4 mEq/kg	In infants with hyperchloremia or metabolic acidosis, the acetate salts of sodium and/or potassium may be substituted for the chloride salts.
Magnesium	0.25–0.6 mEq Mg/kg (30–80 mg MgSO₄/kg)	1 gm $MgSO_4$ = 8 mEq Mg = 100 mg elemental Mg
Calcium gluconate *Note: Calcium gluconate is preferred over calcium chloride in PN because calcium chloride dissociates more rapidly than calcium gluconate and is therefore more likely to precipitate with phosphate.*	0.2–2 mEq Ca/kg (50–500 mg calcium gluconate/kg	1 gm calcium gluconate = 4.5 mEq elemental calcium = 90 mg elemental calcium Limit concentration of calcium gluconate in peripheral lines to 3 mg/ml to reduce risk of extravasation injury. Higher concentrations can be used in central lines (percutaneous, umbilical, Broviac).
Phosphorus	0.5–2 mmol/kg (16–63 mg/kg)	1 mmol = 31 mg Maintain normal serum phosphorus (neonates: 6–8 mg/dl) to help prevent nutritional rickets.

Adapted from: Kerner JA. 1991. Parenteral nutrition. In *Pediatric Gastrointestinal Disease*, vol. 2, Walker WA, et al., eds. Philadelphia: BC Decker, 1645–1675.

The 20 percent concentration is preferred for neonates to minimize fluid volume and phospholipid intake. Phospholipid is thought to inhibit lipoprotein lipase, the main enzyme responsible for clearance of IV fat. Haumont and colleagues reported that the higher phospholipid intake in 10 percent than in 20 percent Intralipid was associated with higher plasma triglyceride concentrations and led to accumulation of cholesterol and phospholipids in low-density lipoproteins.[35] Table 2-7 provides information on the composition of available products.

Dose and administration. Begin with 0.5 gm/kg/day, and advance in increments of 0.5 gm/kg/day as tolerated. Maximum is 3 gm/kg/day and 50 percent of nonprotein calories in preterm infants or 60 percent of nonprotein calories in older infants. The maximum for extremely low birth weight infants (ELBW: birth weight <1,000 gm, less than 27–28 weeks gestation) is 2 gm/kg/day.[4] However, higher doses can be used in some ELBW infants. Careful monitoring of triglycerides, changes in blood gas tensions, and bilirubin levels determines which infants can tolerate higher doses.[4] Infuse each day's dose over 24 hours, and do not exceed a rate of 0.15 gm/kg/hour. Neonates, particularly premature and IUGR infants, have a lower tolerance for lipids than older infants and children do.[30] Only 0.5–1 gm/kg/day is needed to prevent essential fatty acid deficiency. But Gilbertson and colleagues showed no deleterious effects as a result of increasing IV lipid in sick, ventilator-dependent infants <1,500 gm from 1 to 3 gm/kg/day over days 1–4 of life compared with beginning lipids after day 8.[36]

Coinfusion of intravenous fat emulsion via Y-site injection reduces the osmolarity of the final solution and may help to maintain the vein. The osmolarity of IV fat emulsions varies from 260 to 292 mOsm/liter, depending on the product used, and is not irritating to peripheral veins.

In infants receiving PN, a solution of 70 percent ethanol in water has been used to solubilize catheter occlusions caused by IV fat. Just enough ethanol (0.3–0.6 ml) is inserted into the lumen of the catheter to fill the lumen. The catheter is locked off for one hour, then aspirated. The ethanol solubilizes the lipid/calcium/magnesium complexes (see monograph on ethyl alcohol).[37]

Monitoring and adverse effects.

- Monitor serum triglycerides (normal <150 mg/dl) daily while increasing the IV fat emulsion dose, then weekly once a stable dose is reached. Hyperlipidemia should be avoided because it may interfere with pulmonary gas diffusion.

- Potential adverse effects of IV lipids include lipid intolerance, impaired pulmonary function, increased free bilirubin concentrations, and potential interference with immune function.[38–40] Helms and colleagues found, however, that IV lipids do not adversely alter cellular immune function and may contribute to a general improvement in immune function by providing adequate calories.[41] Increased pulmonary vascular tone secondary to infusion of precursors of the vasoactive prostanoid system may occur.[42,43] Fatty acids and bilirubin competitively bind to albumin, resulting in increased unconjugated bilirubin and increased risk of kernicterus. Significant displacement occurs when the free fatty acid to serum albumin molar ratio is greater than 6; the ratio should be kept below 4, the level at which no free bilirubin is generated. Innis recommended that the use of IV fat should be carefully evaluated in infants with serum bilirubin concentrations above 12 mg/dl, in those with sepsis, or in infants whose oxygenation is severely compromised.[44] Limiting the dose to 0.5–1 gm/kg/day, sufficient to prevent essential fatty acid deficiency, should be considered in these infants.

IV fat and carnitine. Neonates have limited carnitine stores, and the enzyme systems that synthesize carnitine are immature. Carnitine facilitates transport of long-chain fatty acids through the mitochondrial membrane, which would otherwise be impermeable to them. It thus has an essential role in fatty acid oxidation for energy. Several studies have shown that carnitine 10 mg/kg/day increases fatty acid oxidation, as indicated by decreased serum plasma free fatty acid concentrations and increased ketogenesis. Higher doses may not be beneficial, however, in preterm infants given parenteral nutrition with IV fat. These higher doses may lead to increased metabolic rate, decreased fat and protein accretion, and prolonged time to regain birth weight.[45–48]

TABLE 2-9 ◆ SUGGESTED DAILY PARENTERAL INTAKE OF VITAMINS AND COMPOSITION OF A COMMERCIAL PREPARATION

Vitamin	Suggested Amount/kg/day*	Amount in 5 ml M.V.I. Pediatric
Vitamin A	280–500 mcg (933–1,667 units)	700 mcg
	• Infants with lung disease may benefit from higher doses.	
	• 0.3 mcg retinol = 1 unit vitamin A.	
	• Vitamin A is subject to photodegradation and binds to IV tubing; net loss ranges from 62% to 89%.[†]	
Vitamin E	2.8 mg	7 mcg
	• 1 unit vitamin E = 1 mg d-α-tocopherol acetate.	
Vitamin K	100 mcg	200 mcg
Vitamin D	4 mcg (160 units)	10 mcg
	• 1 mcg = 40 units	
Ascorbic acid	25 mg	80 mg
Thiamine	350 mcg	1.2 mg
Riboflavin	150 mcg	1.4 mg
Pyridoxine	180 mcg	1 mg
Niacin	6.8 mg	17 mg
Pantothenate	2 mg	5 mg as pantothenic acid
Biotin	6 mcg	20 mcg
Folate	56 mcg	140 mcg as folic acid
Vitamin B_{12}	0.3 mcg	1 mcg

* Daily dose should not exceed the amount provided by 5 ml of M.V.I. Pediatric.

[†] Shenai JP, Stahlman MT, and Chytil F. 1981. Vitamin A delivery from parenteral alimentation solution. *Journal of Pediatrics* 99(4): 661–663.

Adapted from: Heird WC, and Gomez MR. 1993. Parenteral nutrition. In *Nutritional Needs of the Preterm Infant: Scientific Basis and Practical Guidelines,* Tsang RC, et al., eds. Baltimore: Lippincott Williams & Wilkins, 225–242; and Green HL, et al. 1988. Guidelines for the use of vitamins, trace elements, calcium, magnesium, and phosphorus in infants and children receiving total parenteral nutrition: Report of the Subcommittee on Pediatric Parenteral Nutrient Requirements from the Committee on Clinical Practice Issues of the American Society for Clinical Nutrition. *American Journal of Clinical Nutrition* 48(5): 1324–1342. (Published errata in *American Journal of Clinical Nutrition*, 1989, 49[6]: 1332, and 1989, 50[3]: 560.)

ELECTROLYTE AND MINERAL REQUIREMENTS

Average daily electrolyte and mineral doses are shown in Table 2-8. Electrolyte doses should be individualized based on the infant's serum electrolytes (see Appendix M: Normal Neonatal Laboratory and Other Values), the previous day's dose, and the infant's clinical condition. Much higher doses of sodium, potassium, and/or chloride are often required for infants receiving diuretics or those with very immature kidneys. Electrolytes are not usually required on the first

TABLE 2-10 ◆ RECOMMENDED DAILY PARENTERAL INTAKE OF TRACE ELEMENTS

Trace Element	Preterm Infants mcg/kg/day	Term Infants mcg/kg/day
Zinc	400	<3 months: 250 >3 months: 100
Copper	15–20	15–20
Manganese	1	1
Chromium	0.2	0.2

Adapted from: Heird WC, and Gomez MR. 1993. Parenteral nutrition. In *Nutritional Needs of the Preterm Infant: Scientific Basis and Practical Guidelines,* Tsang RC, et al., eds. Baltimore: Lippincott Williams & Wilkins, 225–242.

day of life, but supplementation is begun on the second or third day. *Use caution to ensure adequate urine output before beginning potassium supplementation.*

VITAMIN REQUIREMENTS

Table 2-9 lists suggested daily intake for various vitamins in infants being fed parenterally. To satisfy these requirements, parenteral pediatric multivitamins (M.V.I. Pediatric from Astra Pharmaceutical Products) should be added to the daily infusate as specified in the following list. Dosage is based on weight, with smaller infants receiving a lower volume to avoid vitamin E intoxication:

- <1 kg: 1.5 ml/24 hours
- 1–3 kg: 3.25 ml/24 hours
- >3 kg: 5 ml/24 hours

Total daily dose should not exceed the amounts of the various vitamins provided by 5 ml of M.V.I. Pediatric (see Table 2-9).

TABLE 2-11 ◆ COMPARISON OF PEDIATRIC TRACE-ELEMENT PRODUCTS

Product*	Chromium (mcg)	Copper (mg)	Manganese (mg)	Zinc (mg)	Selenium (mcg)
			(concentration per ml)		
Pedtrace-4[1]	0.85	0.1	0.025	0.5	0
Multiple Trace Element Pediatric[2]	1	0.1	0.03	0.5	0
Multiple Trace Element Neonatal[2], Neotrace-4[1]	0.85	0.1	0.025	1.5	0
PedTE-PAK-4[3], P.T.E.-4[1]	1	0.1	0.025	1	0
P.T.E.-5[1]	1	0.1	0.025	1	15

* Manufacturer: [1] Lyphomed, [2] American Regent, [3] Smith & Nephew SoloPak.

Adapted from: Olin BR. 1994 (bound edition). *Drug Facts and Comparisons.* St. Louis: Facts and Comparisons, a Wolters Kluwer Company, 161. Reprinted by permission.

TABLE 2-12 ◆ MONITORING INFANTS ON PARENTERAL NUTRITION

Variable	Frequency
Weight	Daily
Weight, head circumference, and length	Plot weekly
Specific gravity, urine glucose (Double-check abnormal BG Chemstrip values with serum glucose.)	Every shift (every 12 hours) Monitor abnormal values more frequently
BG-Chemstrip (This is a safety measure to check the accuracy of the dextrose concentration in the PN solution.)	Daily, 1–2 hours after a new PN bag is hung
Sodium, potassium, chloride, BUN, creatinine, calcium, phosphorus, CO_2	Daily, then twice weekly
Triglycerides for infants on IV fat emulsion	Daily, then weekly
Hemoglobin or hematocrit	Twice weekly
Parenteral nutrition panel.* (The PN panel includes alkaline phosphatase, total and direct bilirubin, calcium, phosphorus, magnesium, total protein, albumin, alanine aminotransferase [ALT], and triglycerides. These tests alert the clinician to PN-associated cholestasis, nutritional rickets, high lipid levels, and other PN-associated imbalances.)	Weekly
Observe for clinical signs of infection, such as decreased activity, temperature instability, increased oxygen requirements, and glucose intolerance	Daily
WBC with differential, cultures to detect signs of infection	If indicated

* A customized PN panel developed by your clinical laboratory facilitates PN monitoring, uses less blood, and costs less than individual tests.

TRACE-ELEMENT REQUIREMENTS

Recommended daily parenteral intake of trace elements are outlined in Table 2-10. Pediatric trace elements are available in fixed-dose combinations of copper, zinc, manganese, and chromium. Table 2-11 compares the content of various commercial trace-element products.

Recommended dosages for term and preterm infants are as follows:

- *Term*: 0.2 ml/kg/day of PedTE-PAK-4 or P.T.E.-4
- *Preterm*: 0.2 ml/kg/day of PedTE-PAK-4 or P.T.E.-4, plus an additional 200 mcg/kg/day of zinc to provide the recommended intake (400 mcg/kg/day) of this element

Certain trace elements should be reduced or eliminated in infants with the following conditions:

- *Cholestasis:* Reduce the dose or the administration frequency of copper and manganese (e.g., give the usual daily dose at weekly intervals).
- *Renal dysfunction:* Omit chromium.

To reduce the dose of these trace elements, discontinue the use of standard fixed-dose combination trace elements, and instead use zinc and/or copper as separate individual additives in doses suggested in Table 2-10.

Selenium is not needed for short-term (<4 weeks) PN. The recommended intravenous intake of selenium is 2 mcg/kg/day.[49]

OTHER ADDITIVES

Albumin (0.5–1 gm/kg/day) and/or ranitidine (2.4–3 mg/kg/day) are compatible with parenteral nutrition and may be admixed as each infant's medical condition warrants. Note that albumin is not considered part of the protein dose. Use only the crystalline amino acids (see **PROTEIN REQUIREMENTS** above) in these calculations. For example, an infant receiving 3 gm/kg/day of protein plus 1 gm/kg/day of albumin in the PN is receiving 3 gm/kg/day of protein, not 4 gm/kg/day.

HEPARIN REQUIREMENTS

Heparin 0.5–1 unit/ml may be added to the infusate. Advantages include the following:

- Prevention of thrombosis
- Reduction in the incidence of catheter-related sepsis[49,50]
- Stimulation of the release of the enzyme lipoprotein lipase to enhance clearance of triglycerides when giving IV fat
- Possible reduction in phlebitis in peripheral lines[50]

However, the heparin dose should be minimized because of the possibility of increasing free fatty acids beyond the disposal ability of preterm infants.[49,51]

ADMINISTRATION OF PARENTERAL NUTRITION

PN should be delivered by peripheral vein, percutaneous subclavian vein catheter, or central vein by continuous infusion using a neonatal infusion pump. The solution should be filtered with a 0.22-micron filter to remove any particulate matter or bacteria. Many drugs are compatible with PN and may be administered by Y-site (see Appendix E: Y-Site Compatibility of Common NICU Drugs) or by IV push, if possible. Acyclovir, amphotericin B, metronidazole, and trimethoprim-sulfamethoxazole (Bactrim, Septra) are incompatible with PN and should be administered in a separate line or with the PN turned off.

MONITORING INFANTS ON PARENTERAL NUTRITION

The monitoring activities and laboratory tests in Table 2-12 are suggested for infants receiving parenteral nutrition. The need for laboratory tests should, however, be assessed on an individual basis.

TRANSITION FROM PARENTERAL TO ENTERAL NUTRITION

Preterm infants beginning on enteral feedings still need some parenteral nutrition. The volume of enteral feedings should be advanced slowly because these infants have a high incidence of respiratory problems, limited gastric capacity, and intestinal hypomotility. PN supplements the enteral feedings to provide adequate nutrition while avoiding stress to the immature GI tract.

PN containing high concentrations of glucose should not be discontinued abruptly; doing so may cause hypoglycemia. For example, a sudden change from central PN with $D_{25}W$ to half-strength formula could cause reactive hypoglycemia because of the marked change in dextrose concentration. (Half-strength 20 kcal/oz formula or breast milk contains approximately 3.1 gm of carbohydrate/100 ml, or dextrose 3.1 percent.) The transition to enteral feedings should be gradual, with concurrent PN tapering as enteral feedings are increased. Enteral plus parenteral nutrition should equal the infant's total daily fluid and other nutrient requirements.

Maintenance of adequate electrolyte levels during this transition should be considered as well. Transition from parenteral nutrition to half-strength formula may markedly reduce electrolyte intake and result in electrolyte imbalances. Enteral supplementation of sodium and potassium may be required.

Supplementation for Special Conditions

CHOLESTASIS

Hepatic dysfunction is one of the most common and serious complications of parenteral nutrition (PN). Inclusion of taurine in the neonatal crystalline amino acid (CAA) component of PN (Table 2-5, page 614) may lower the prevalence of cholestasis during prolonged PN. PN cholestasis is thought to be minimized by giving small enteral feedings during PN.

PN should be decreased and enteral feedings instituted or increased, if possible, to stimulate hepatic excretion of bile and gallbladder contraction. Fasting decreases gut hormones such as secretin and motilin that normally stimulate biliary secretion.[52]

If enteral feedings have been started, cycling the parenteral nutrition solution over 12- to 16-hour periods may be useful in the patient with parenteral nutrition cholestasis. Monitor closely for hypoglycemia. Weaning down the infusion rate rather than discontinuing abruptly may reduce the risk of hypoglycemia.[53]

Infants with cholestasis on enteral feedings have malabsorption of fat-soluble vitamins (A, D, E, K). This is not a problem when infants are receiving PN because vitamins in the PN infusate are delivered directly into the bloodstream and need not be absorbed in the GI tract. Supplemental fat-soluble vitamins may be discontinued once the direct bilirubin falls to less than 1 mg/dl.

Suggestions for supplementation of fat-soluble vitamins in infants on enteral feedings are:

- *Vitamin A:* Multivitamin drops 2 ml PO daily (This provides 3,000 units/day.)
- *Vitamin D:* 400 units PO daily (This, plus the multivitamin drops just mentioned, provides a total of 1,200 units daily.)
- *Vitamin E:* 50 units PO daily

- **Vitamin K$_1$:** 2.5 mg PO every other day or 1 mg given subcutaneously, weekly (The tablet may be crushed and added to a small amount of the infant's feeding. Sick, hospitalized infants on long-term antibiotics may require larger doses. Monitor PTT every 1–2 weeks until the infant is on a stable dose. Extra vitamin K may be needed if bleeding occurs.)

Infants with cholestasis should be weaned from parenteral to enteral nutrition as soon as their medical condition warrants to promote bile flow. Infant formulas with MCTs (Portagen, Pregestimil) should be used because MCTs can be absorbed without bile salts.

NUTRITIONAL OSTEOPENIA (RICKETS OF PREMATURITY)

Monitor these infants' serum calcium, phosphorus, and alkaline phosphatase as well as bone density on x-ray to observe for demineralization. A rising alkaline phosphatase (normal: <400 units/liter) in an infant on parenteral nutrition may indicate nutritional rickets is developing. Kovar and colleagues suggest screening for rickets in preterm infants with plasma alkaline phosphatase. They consider levels up to five times the upper limit of normal for adults acceptable, but levels six times adult normal should prompt an x-ray to exclude rickets.[54] Serum calcium levels will be maintained at the expense of bone (demineralization), so a normal serum calcium does not necessarily mean that adequate amounts of calcium are being delivered.[49]

Supplementation may be required to maintain serum calcium between 9 and 10 mg/dl and phosphorus between 6 and 8 units/liter for prevention and treatment of nutritional osteopenia. Optimal amounts of calcium and phosphorus should be provided to infants on PN. Infants should be weaned from parenteral to enteral nutrition as soon as their medical condition warrants. Use of specialized formulas for preterm infants (e.g., Enfamil Premature) helps to optimize intake of phosphorus, calcium, and vitamin D. Preterm infants on breast milk should also receive breast milk fortifier.

Suggestions for oral supplementation while on enteral nutrition follow:

- **Phosphorus:** 0.5–2 mmol/kg/day PO divided every 6 hours, mixed in formula. Use the injectable form of Na or K phosphate, but give PO. Higher doses may be required, based on serum phosphorus determinations. (See monograph on phosphorus.)

- **Calcium:** Calcium gluconate 200–500 mg/kg/day PO divided every 6 hours, mixed in formula. Use the injectable form of calcium gluconate (rather than calcium glubionate) PO to minimize osmolality. Calcium glubionate (Neo-Calglucon) syrup has a high osmolality and may be less well tolerated than calcium gluconate in preterm infants. Adjust the dose based on serum calcium determinations. (See monographs on calcium gluconate and calcium glubionate.)

- **Vitamin D:** 400–800 units PO daily, mixed in formula. The activated form of vitamin D, calcitriol (Rocaltrol), may also be used, in which case give calcitriol

0.01–0.05 mcg/kg/day PO as a single daily dose. Monitor serum calcium. (See monograph on calcitriol.)

Caretakers should be cautious in handling babies with nutritional rickets (e.g., during diaper changes) to avoid bone fractures.

BRONCHOPULMONARY DYSPLASIA

Infants with BPD have high caloric expenditures (120–150 kcal/kg/day or more). They often need concentrated formula for adequate growth and prevention of pulmonary edema. Unnecessary sources of fluid should be eliminated when possible. The oral medication regimen should be reviewed regularly with the goal of discontinuing unneeded drugs and administering needed drugs in as concentrated a form as available. Choose powdered nutritional supplements over liquid ones.

ASPHYXIA AND NECROTIZING ENTEROCOLITIS

Asphyxiated infants may have experienced significant insult to the gut, predisposing them to NEC. Enteral feedings are usually withheld for the first 5 days to 2 weeks after the insult, then advanced slowly. Prolonged bowel rest may arrest gut maturation, but maturation will resume when intraluminal nutrients are reintroduced.[55] Gut atrophy in the chronically parenterally fed infant may foster increased intestinal permeability of bacteria.[49]

REFERENCES

1. American Academy of Pediatrics, Committee on Nutrition. 1985. Nutritional needs of low-birth-weight infants. *Pediatrics* 75(5): 976–986.

2. Georgieff MK, et al. 1985. Effect of neonatal caloric deprivation on head growth and one-year developmental status in preterm infants. *Journal of Pediatrics* 107(4): 581–587.

3. Mestyan J, Jarai I, and Fekete M. 1968. The total energy expenditure and its components in preterm infants maintained under different nursing and environmental conditions. *Pediatric Research* 2(3): 161–171.

4. Thureen PJ, and Hay WW Jr. 1993. Conditions requiring special nutritional management. In *Nutritional Needs of the Preterm Infant: Scientific Basis and Practical Guidelines*, Tsang RC, et al., eds. Baltimore: Lippincott Williams & Wilkins, 243–265.

5. Butte NF. 1988. Energy requirements during infancy. In *Nutrition During Infancy*, Tsang RC, and Nichols BL, eds. Philadelphia: Hanley & Belfus, 86–99.

6. Murlin JR, Conklin MS, and Marsh ME. 1925. Energy metabolism of normal newborn babies: With special reference to the influence of food and of crying. *American Journal of Diseases of Children* 29: 1–28.

7. Van Aerde JE, et al. 1989. The effect of replacing glucose with lipid on the energy metabolism of newborn infants. *Clinical Science and Molecular Medicine* 76(6): 581–588.

8. Van Aerde JE. 1991. Acute respiratory failure and bronchopulmonary dysplasia. In *Neonatal Nutrition and Metabolism*, Hay WW Jr, ed. St. Louis: Mosby-Year Book, 476–506.

9. Mehta NR, et al. 1991. Adherence of medium-chain fatty acids to feeding tubes of premature infants fed formula fortified with medium-chain triglycerides. *Journal of Pediatric Gastroenterology and Nutrition* 13(3): 267–269.

10. Putet G. 1993. Energy. In *Nutritional Needs of the Preterm Infant: Scientific Basis and Practical Guidelines*, Tsang RC, et al., eds. Baltimore: Lippincott Williams & Wilkins, 15–28.

11. Dunn L, et al. 1988. Beneficial effects of early hypocaloric enteral feeding on neonatal gastrointestinal function: Preliminary report of a randomized trial. *Journal of Pediatrics* 112(4): 622–629.

12. Lucas A. 1993. Enteral nutrition. In *Nutritional Needs of the Preterm Infant: Scientific Basis and Practical Guidelines,* Tsang RC, et al., eds. Baltimore: Lippincott Williams & Wilkins, 209–223.

13. Sagraves R, Kamper C, and Doerr J. 1993. Infant formula products. In *Handbook of Nonprescription Drugs,* 10th ed., Feldman EG, ed. Washington, DC: American Pharmaceutical Association, 313–338.

14. Manufacturers' product literature.

15. Oski FA, et al. 1983. Effect of iron therapy on behavior performance in nonanemic, iron-deficient infants. *Pediatrics* 71(6): 877–888.

16. Walter T, et al. 1989. Iron deficiency anemia: Adverse effects on infant psychomotor development. *Pediatrics* 84(1): 7–17.

17. Lozoff B, et al. 1987. Iron deficiency anemia and iron therapy effects on infant developmental test performance. *Pediatrics* 79(6): 981–985.

18. Lozoff B, et al. 1991. Long-term developmental outcome of infants with iron deficiency. *New England Journal of Medicine* 325(10): 687–694.

19. Aukett MA, et al. 1986. Treatment with iron increases weight gain and psychomotor development. *Archives of Disease in Childhood* 61(9): 849–857.

20. American Academy of Pediatrics, Committee on Nutrition. 1992. The use of whole cow's milk in infancy. *Pediatrics* 89(6 part 1): 1105–1109.

21. Oski FA. 1993. Iron deficiency in infancy and childhood. *New England Journal of Medicine* 329(3): 190–193.

22. Food and Drug Administration. 2002. Health professionals letter on *Enterobacter sakazakii* infections associated with use of powdered (dry) infant formulas in neonatal intensive care units. October 10. http:vm.cfsan.fda.gov~dms/inf-ltr3.html.

23. Lai KK. 2001. *Enterobacter sakazakii* infections among neonates, infants, children, and adults. Case reports and a review of the literature. *Medicine* 80(2): 113–122.

24. van Acker J, et al. 2001. Outbreak of necrotizing enterocolitis associated with *Enterobacter sakazakii* in powdered milk formula. *Journal of Clinical Microbiology* 39(1): 293–297.

25. Barsotti MR. 1994. Fluids and electrolytes. In *Neonatology: Management, Procedures, On-call Problems, Diseases and Drugs,* 3rd ed., Gomella TL, Cunningham DM, and Eyal FG, eds. Norwalk, Connecticut: Appleton & Lange, 70–75.

26. Stephenson T, and Rutter N. 1992. Fluid requirement. In *Intravenous Feeding of the Neonate,* Yu VYH, and MacMahon RA, eds. London: Edward Arnold, 3–12.

27. Coulthard MG, and Hey EN. 1985. Effect of varying water intake on renal function in healthy preterm babies. *Archives of Disease in Childhood* 60(7): 614–620.

28. Hermansen MG, and Hermansen MC. 1999. The influence of equipment weights on neonatal daily weight measurements. *Neonatal Network* 18(1): 33–36.

29. Helms RA, et al. 1987. Comparison of a pediatric versus standard amino acid formulation in preterm neonates requiring parenteral nutrition. *Journal of Pediatrics* 110(3): 466–470.

30. American Academy of Pediatrics, Committee on Nutrition. 1993. Nutritional needs of preterm infants. In *Pediatric Nutrition Handbook,* Barness LA, ed. Elk Grove Village, Illinois: American Academy of Pediatrics, 64–89.

31. Yu VYH. 1992. Intravenous feeding in the preterm neonate. In *Intravenous Feeding of the Neonate,* Yu VYH, and MacMahon RA, eds. London: Edward Arnold, 240–249.

32. Binder ND, et al. 1989. Insulin infusion with parenteral nutrition in extremely low birth weight infants with hyperglycemia. *Journal of Pediatrics* 114(2): 273–280.

33. Zenk KE. 1984. Calculating dextrose infusion in mg/kg/minute. *PeriScope* (August): 5.

34. Mirtallo JM. 1994. Should the use of total nutrient admixtures be limited? *American Journal of Hospital Pharmacy* 51(22): 2831–2834.

35. Haumont D, et al. 1989. Plasma lipid and plasma lipoprotein concentrations in low birth weight infants given parenteral nutrition with twenty or ten percent lipid emulsion. *Journal of Pediatrics* 115(5 part 1): 787–793.

36. Gilbertson N, et al. 1991. Introduction of intravenous lipid administration on the first day of life in the very low birth weight neonate. *Journal of Pediatrics* 119(4): 615–623.

37. Pennington CR, and Pithie AD. 1987. Ethanol lock in the management of catheter occlusion. *Journal of Parenteral and Enteral Nutrition* 11(5): 507–508.

38. Puntis JW, and Rushton DI. 1991. Pulmonary intravascular lipid in neonatal necropsy specimens. *Archives of Disease in Childhood* 66(1 spec. no.): 26–28.

39. Spear ML, et al. 1985. The effect of 15-hour fat infusions of varying dosage on bilirubin binding to albumin. *Journal of Parenteral and Enteral Nutrition* 9(2): 144–147.

40. Nordenstrom J, Jarstrand C, and Wiernik A. 1979. Decreased chemotactic and random migration of leukocytes during Intralipid infusion. *American Journal of Clinical Nutrition* 32(12): 2416–2422.

41. Helms RA, et al. 1983. E-rosette formation, total T-cells, and lymphocyte transformation in infants receiving intravenous safflower oil emulsion. *Journal of Parenteral and Enteral Nutrition* 7(6): 541–545.

42. Hageman JR, et al. 1983. Intralipid alterations in pulmonary prostaglandin metabolism and gas exchange. *Critical Care Medicine* 11(4): 794–798.

43. Skeie B, et al. 1988. Intravenous fat emulsions and lung function: A review. *Critical Care Medicine* 16(2): 183–194.

44. Innis SM. 1993. Fat. In *Nutritional Needs of the Preterm Infant: Scientific Basis and Practical Guidelines,* Tsang RC, et al., eds. Baltimore: Lippincott Williams & Wilkins, 65–86.

45. Yeh Y, Cooke RJ, and Zee P. 1985. Impairment of lipid emulsion metabolism associated with carnitine insufficiency in premature infants. *Journal of Pediatric Gastroenterology and Nutrition* 4(5): 795–798.

46. Schmidt-Sommerfeld E, and Penn D. 1990. Carnitine and total parenteral nutrition of the neonate. *Biology of the Neonate* 58(supplement 1): S81–S88.

47. Helms RA, et al. 1990. Effect of intravenous L-carnitine on growth parameters and fat metabolism during parenteral nutrition in neonates. *Journal of Parenteral and Enteral Nutrition* 14(5): 448–453.

48. Tibboel D, et al. 1990. Carnitine deficiency in surgical neonates receiving total parenteral nutrition. *Journal of Pediatric Surgery* 25(4): 418–421.

49. Kerner JA. 1991. Parenteral nutrition. In *Pediatric Gastrointestinal Disease,* vol. 2, Walker WA, et al., eds. Philadelphia: BC Decker, 1645–1675.

50. Alpan G, et al. 1984. Heparinization of alimentation solutions administered through peripheral veins in premature infants: A controlled study. *Pediatrics* 74(3): 375–378.

51. Berkow SE, et al. 1987. Total parenteral nutrition with Intralipid in premature infants receiving TPN with heparin: Effect on plasma lipolytic enzymes, lipids, and glucose. *Journal of Pediatric Gastroenterology and Nutrition* 6(4):581–588.

52. Mews C, and Sinatra FR. 1994. Cholestasis in infancy. *Pediatrics in Review* 15(6): 233–240.

53. Pereira GR, and Piccoli DA. 1992. Cholestasis and other hepatic complications. In *Intravenous Feeding of the Neonate,* Yu VYH, and MacMahon RA, eds. London: Edward Arnold, 153–165.

54. Kovar I, Mayne P, and Barltrop D. 1982. Plasma alkaline phosphatase activity: A screening test for rickets in preterm neonates. *Lancet* 1(8267): 308–310.

55. Feng JJ, et al. 1987. Resumption of intestinal maturation upon reintroduction of intraluminal nutrients: Functional and biochemical correlations. *Clinical Research* 35: 228A.

56. Mead Johnson Nutritionals. 1993. *Pediatric Products Handbook.* Evansville, Indiana: Mead Johnson Nutritionals.

57. Ross Laboratories. 1990. *Product Handbook.* Columbus, Ohio: Ross Laboratories.

58. Ross Laboratories. 1991. Composition of feedings for infants and young children in the hospital. In *Product Handbook.* Columbus, Ohio: Ross Laboratories.

59. Barsotti MR. 1994. Fluids and electrolytes. In *Neonatology: Management, Procedures, On-call Problems, Diseases and Drugs,* 3rd ed., Gomella TL, Cunningham DM, and Eyal FG, eds. Norwalk, Connecticut: Appleton & Lange, 72–73.

Section III—Immunizations
Table of Contents

IMMUNIZATIONS

REFERENCES

1. American Academy of Pediatrics, Committee on Infectious Diseases. 1994. *Red Book: Report of the Committee on Infectious Diseases,* 23rd ed. Elk Grove Village, Illinois: American Academy of Pediatrics, 7–71, 510–517.

2. Manufacturer's product literature.

3. Bernbaum JC, et al. 1985. Response of preterm infants to diphtheria-tetanus-pertussis immunizations. *Journal of Pediatrics* 107(2): 184–188.

4. Centers for Disease Control and Prevention. 1999. Thimerosal in vaccines. A joint statement of the American Academy of Pediatrics and Public Health Service. *MMWR* 48(26): 563–565.

5. American Academy of Pediatrics, Committee on Infectious Diseases and Committee on Environmental Health. 1999. Thimerosal in vaccines. An interim report to clinicians. *Pediatrics* 10(3 part 1): 570–574.

6. Centers for Disease Control and Prevention. 1999. Recommendations regarding the use of vaccines that contain thimerosal as a preservative. *MMWR* 48(43): 996–998.

7. American Academy of Pediatrics, Committee on Infectious Diseases. 1993. *Haemophilus influenzae* type b conjugate vaccines: Recommendations for immunization with recently and previously licensed vaccines. *Pediatrics* 92(3): 480–487.

8. Centers for Disease Control. 1997. Recommended childhood immunization schedule—United States. *MMWR* 46(2): 35–40.

9. American Academy of Pediatrics, Committee on Infectious Diseases. 1999. Prevention of poliomyelitis: Recommendations for use of only inactivated poliovirus vaccine for routine immunization. *Pediatrics* 104(6): 1404–1406.

10. American Academy of Pediatrics, Committee on Infectious Diseases. 2003. Recommended childhood immunization schedule—United States, 2003. *Pediatrics* 111(1): 148–212.

This section gathers in one handy location the information NICU care providers need about immunizations: vaccines used, recommended schedules, and governing regulations. Table 3-1 lists and explains the meaning of the abbreviations and routes of administration for all the common vaccines (these abbreviations are used throughout the section). A standard immunization schedule is presented in Table 3-2. Figures 3-1 and 3-2 illustrate, respectively, information about regulations affecting vaccination and a suggested format physicians can use to order routine NICU immunizations. Figure 3-3 provides guidelines for the use of live-virus vaccines in patients receiving corticosteroid therapy. The section concludes with monographs for each of the common vaccines.

A permanent record of all immunizations begun in the NICU should be made by the nursing staff. Parents are provided with the original documentation, including manufacturer's name and lot number. They should be instructed regarding the importance of continued immunization of their child throughout childhood. Most agencies require signed informed consent before immunizations are given.

TABLE 3-1 ◆ VACCINES: ABBREVIATION, TYPE, AND ROUTE OF ADMINISTRATION

Abbreviation	Vaccine Name	Type
DTaP	Diphtheria and tetanus toxoids and *acellular* pertussis vaccine, adsorbed	Toxoids and inactivated bacterial components *Route:* IM
DTP-HbOC	Diphtheria and tetanus toxoids, whole-cell pertussis vaccine adsorbed (DTwP), and *Haemophilus influenzae* b conjugate vaccine	Toxoids and inactivated bacteria *Route:* IM
Hepatitis B	Hepatitis B virus vaccine inactivated (recombinant)	Inactivated viral antigen *Route:* IM
Hib conjugates	*H. influenzae* b conjugate vaccine (see Table 3-3 for specific vaccines)	Polysaccharide-protein conjugate *Route:* IM
MMR	Measles-mumps-rubella viruse vaccine, live	Live viruses *Route:* SC
Poliovirus IPV	Poliovirus vaccine, inactivated	Inactivated virus *Route:* SC
OPV	Poliovirus vaccine, live oral	Live virus *Route:* PO
Td	Tetanus and diphtheria toxoids, adsorbed	Toxoid *Route:* IM

Abbreviations: IM = intramuscular; SC = subcutaneous; PO = oral

Adapted from: American Academy of Pediatrics, Committee on Infectious Diseases. 2000. *Red Book: Report of the Committee on Infectious Diseases,* 25th ed. Elk Grove Village, Illinois: American Academy of Pediatrics, Table 1.3, pages 7–8; Table 1.4, pages 10–13.

FIGURE 3-1 ◆ VACCINE REGULATIONS.

Informing Patients and Parents

The current version of Vaccine Information Statements (VIS) must be provided to the parent or legal guardian each time a vaccine is administered. Copies of the current VISs can be obtained from state and local health departments, the Centers for Disease Control and Prevention (CDC), the American Academy of Pediatrics (AAP), and vaccine manufacturers by calling the CDC Immunization Hotline (800-232-2522 in English and 800-232-0233 in Spanish) or the Internet web sites www.cdc.gov/nip/publications/VIS/default.htm or www.immunize.org.

Documentation in the Patient's Medical Record

Vaccine manufacturer, lot number, and date of administration, name and business address of the health care professional administering the vaccine, VIS version date and date it is provided, immunizing site (such as anterior-lateral thigh), route of administration (such as intramuscular), and expiration of the vaccine. Obtaining the parent's signature to indicate that they have read and understood the material is not required; however, the AAP recommends that physicians document in the chart that the VIS has been provided and discussed with the parent or legal representative.

Patient's Personal Immunization Record

An official immunization record should be given to the parents of every newborn infant. Parents should preserve this record, present it at each visit, and physicians should record immunization data on this record at each visit. This is especially important for patients that move frequently.

Reporting Adverse Events

Before administering a subsequent dose of any vaccine, parents of patients should be questioned about adverse effects and possible reactions after previous doses. Unexpected events occurring soon after administration of any vaccine, particularly if severe enough to require medical attention, should be documented in the patient's medical record and a VAERS (Vaccine Adverse Event Reporting System) report should be made. The National Childhood Vaccine Injury Act of 1986 requires physicians and other health care professionals who administer vaccines to maintain permanent immunization records and to report occurrences of certain adverse events stipulated in the act to VAERS. Reportable events following immunizations are listed in Appendix III, p 759 of the *2000 Red Book*. Refer to the web site for the National Vaccine Injury Compensation Program at www.hrsa.dhhs.gov/bhp/vicp/ or call 800-338-2382 for further information.

Adapted from: American Academy of Pediatrics, Committee on Infectious Diseases. 2000. *Red Book: Report of the Committee on Infectious Diseases,* 25th ed. Elk Grove Village, Illinois: American Academy of Pediatrics, 4, 5, 30–34. Reprinted by permission.

IMMUNIZATIONS

TABLE 3-2 ◆ IMMUNIZATION SCHEDULE FOR HEALTHY INFANTS AND CHILDREN

Legend: ☐ range of recommended ages ▨ catch-up vaccination ■ preadolescent assessment

Vaccine ▸ / Age ▸	Birth	1 mo	2 mos	4 mos	6 mos	12 mos	15 mos	18 mos	24 mos	4-6 yrs	11-12 yrs	13-18 yrs
Hepatitis B[1]	HepB #1	only if mother HBsAg (-)	HepB #2			HepB #3					HepB series	
Diphtheria, Tetanus, Pertussis[2]			DTaP	DTaP	DTaP		DTaP	DTaP		DTaP	Td	
Haemophilus influenzae Type b[3]			Hib	Hib	Hib	Hib	Hib					
Inactivated Polio			IPV	IPV	IPV	IPV	IPV			IPV		
Measles, Mumps, Rubella[4]						MMR #1				MMR #2	MMR #2	MMR #2
Varicella[5]						Varicella	Varicella				Varicella	Varicella
Pneumococcal[6]			PCV	PCV	PCV	PCV	PCV		PCV	PPV		
Hepatitis A[7]									Hepatitis A series			
Influenza[8]								Influenza (yearly)				

Vaccines below this line are for selected populations

This schedule indicates the recommended ages for routine administration of currently licensed childhood vaccines, as of December 1, 2002, for children through age 18 years. Any dose not given at the recommended age should be given at any subsequent visit when indicated and feasible. ▨ Indicates age groups that warrant special effort to administer those vaccines not previously given. Additional vaccines may be licensed and recommended during the year. Licensed combination vaccines may be used whenever any components of the combination are indicated and the vaccine's other components are not contraindicated. Providers should consult the manufacturers' package inserts for detailed recommendations.

1. Hepatitis B vaccine (HepB). All infants should receive the first dose of hepatitis B vaccine soon after birth and before hospital discharge; the first dose may also be given by age 2 months if the infant's mother is HBsAg-negative. Only monovalent HepB can be used for the birth dose. Monovalent or combination vaccine containing HepB may be used to complete the series. Four doses of vaccine may be administered when a birth dose is given. The second dose should be given at least 4 weeks after the first dose, except for combination vaccines which cannot be administered before age 6 weeks. The third dose should be given at least 16 weeks after the first dose and at least 8 weeks after the second dose. The last dose in the vaccination series (third or fourth dose) should not be administered before age 6 months.

Infants born to HBsAg-positive mothers should receive HepB and 0.5 mL Hepatitis B Immune Globulin (HBIG) within 12 hours of birth at separate sites. The second dose is recommended at age 1-2 months. The last dose in the vaccination series should not be administered before age 6 months. These infants should be tested for HBsAg and anti-HBs at 9-15 months of age.

Infants born to mothers whose HBsAg status is unknown should receive the first dose of the HepB series within 12 hours of birth. Maternal blood should be drawn as soon as possible to determine the mother's HBsAg status; if the HBsAg test is positive, the infant should receive HBIG as soon as possible (no later than age 1 week). The second dose is recommended at age 1-2 months. The last dose in the vaccination series should not be administered before age 6 months.

2. Diphtheria and tetanus toxoids and acellular pertussis vaccine (DTaP). The fourth dose of DTaP may be administered as early as age 12 months, provided 6 months have elapsed since the third dose and the child is unlikely to return at age 15-18 months. **Tetanus and diphtheria toxoids (Td)** is recommended at age 11-12 years if at least 5 years have elapsed since the last dose of tetanus and diphtheria toxoid-containing vaccine. Subsequent routine Td boosters are recommended every 10 years.

3. Haemophilus influenzae type b (Hib) conjugate vaccine. Three Hib conjugate vaccines are licensed for infant use. If PRP-OMP (PedvaxHIB® or ComVax® [Merck]) is administered at ages 2 and 4 months, a dose at age 6 months is not required. DTaP/Hib combination products should not be used for primary immunization in infants at ages 2, 4 or 6 months, but can be used as boosters following any Hib vaccine.

4. Measles, mumps, and rubella vaccine (MMR). The second dose of MMR is recommended routinely at age 4-6 years but may be administered during any visit, provided at least 4 weeks have elapsed since the first dose and that both doses are administered beginning at or after age 12 months. Those who have not previously received the second dose should complete the schedule by the 11-12 year old visit.

5. Varicella vaccine. Varicella vaccine is recommended at any visit at or after age 12 months for susceptible children, i.e. those who lack a reliable history of chickenpox. Susceptible persons aged ≥13 years should receive two doses, given at least 4 weeks apart.

6. Pneumococcal vaccine. The heptavalent **pneumococcal conjugate vaccine (PCV)** is recommended for all children age 2-23 months. It is also recommended for certain children age 24-59 months. **Pneumococcal polysaccharide vaccine (PPV)** is recommended in addition to PCV for certain high-risk groups. See *MMWR* 2000;49(RR-9);1-38.

7. Hepatitis A vaccine. Hepatitis A vaccine is recommended for children and adolescents in selected states and regions, and for certain high-risk groups; consult your local public health authority. Children and adolescents in these states, regions, and high risk groups who have not been immunized against hepatitis A can begin the hepatitis A vaccination series during any visit. The two doses in the series should be administered at least 6 months apart. See *MMWR* 1999;48(RR-12);1-37.

8. Influenza vaccine. Influenza vaccine is recommended annually for children age ≥6 months with certain risk factors (including but not limited to asthma, cardiac disease, sickle cell disease, HIV, diabetes, and household members of persons in groups at high risk; see *MMWR* 2002;51(RR-3);1-31), and can be administered to all others wishing to obtain immunity. In addition, healthy children age 6-23 months are encouraged to receive influenza vaccine if feasible because children in this age group are at substantially increased risk for influenza-related hospitalizations. Children aged ≤12 years should receive vaccine in a dosage appropriate for their age (0.25 mL if age 6-35 months or 0.5 mL if aged ≥3 years). Children aged ≤8 years who are receiving influenza vaccine for the first time should receive two doses separated by at least 4 weeks.

For additional information about vaccines, including precautions and contraindications for immunization and vaccine shortages, please visit the National Immunization Program Website at www.cdc.gov/nip or call the National Immunization Information Hotline at 800-232-2522 (English) or 800-232-0233 (Spanish).

IMMUNIZATIONS

For Children and Adolescents Who Start Late or Who Are >1 Month Behind

Tables 1 and 2 give catch-up schedules and minimum intervals between doses for children who have delayed immunizations. There is no need to restart a vaccine series regardless of the time that has elapsed between doses. Use the chart appropriate for the child's age.

Table 1. Catch-up schedule for children age 4 months through 6 years

Dose One (Minimum Age)	Minimum Interval Between Doses			
	Dose One to Dose Two	Dose Two to Dose Three	Dose Three to Dose Four	Dose Four to Dose Five
DTaP (6 wks)	4 weeks	4 weeks	6 months	6 months[1]
IPV (6 wks)	4 weeks	4 weeks	4 weeks[2]	
HepB[3] (birth)	4 weeks	8 weeks (and 16 weeks after first dose)		
MMR (12 mos)	4 weeks[4]			
Varicella (12 mos)				
Hib[5] (6 wks)	**4 weeks:** if 1st dose given at age <12 mos / **8 weeks (as final dose):** if 1st dose given at age 12-14 mos / **No further doses needed:** if first dose given at age ≥15 mos	**4 weeks**[6]: if current age <12 mos / **8 weeks (as final dose)**[6]: if current age ≥12 mos and 2nd dose given at age <15 mos / **No further doses needed:** if previous dose given at age ≥15 mos	**8 weeks (as final dose):** this dose only necessary for children age 12 mos – 5 yrs who received 3 doses before age 12 mos	
PCV7 (6 wks)	**4 weeks:** if 1st dose given at age <12 mos and current age <24 mos / **8 weeks (as final dose):** if 1st dose given at age ≥ 12 mos or current age 24-59 mos / **No further doses needed:** for healthy children if 1st dose given at age ≥24 mos	**4 weeks:** if current age <12 mos / **8 weeks (as final dose):** if current age ≥12 mos / **No further doses needed:** for healthy children if previous dose given at age ≥24 mos	**8 weeks (as final dose):** this dose only necessary for children age 12 mos – 5 yrs who received 3 doses before age 12 mos	

Table 2. Catch-up schedule for children age 7 through 18 years

	Minimum Interval Between Doses		
	Dose One to Dose Two	Dose Two to Dose Three	Dose Three to Booster Dose
Td:	4weeks	Td: 6 months	Td[8]: **6 months:** if 1st dose given at age <12 mos and current age <11 yrs **5 years:** if 1st dose given at age ≥12 mos and 3rd dose given at age <7 yrs and current age >11 yrs **10 years:** if 3rd dose given at age ≥7 yrs
IPV[9]:	4 weeks	IPV[9]: 4 weeks	IPV[9]
HepB:	4 weeks	HepB: 8 weeks (and 16 weeks after first dose)	
MMR:	4 weeks		
Varicella[10]:	4 weeks		

1. **DTaP:** The fifth dose is not necessary if the fourth dose was given after the 4th birthday.
2. **IPV:** For children who received an all-IPV or all-OPV series, a fourth dose is not necessary if third dose was given at age ≥4 years. If both OPV and IPV were given as part of a series, a total of four doses should be given, regardless of the child's current age.
3. **HepB:** All children and adolescents who have not been immunized against hepatitis B should begin the hepatitis B vaccination series during any visit. Providers should make special efforts to immunize children who were born in, or whose parents were born in, areas of the world where hepatitis B virus infection is moderately or highly endemic.
4. **MMR:** The second dose of MMR is recommended routinely at age 4-6 years, but may be given earlier if desired.
5. **Hib:** Vaccine is not generally recommended for children age ≥5 years.
6. **Hib:** If current age <12 months and the first 2 doses were PRP-OMP (PedvaxHIB or ComVax), the third (and final) dose should be given at age 12-15 months and at least 8 weeks after the second dose.
7. **PCV:** Vaccine is not generally recommended for children age ≥5 years.
8. **Td:** For children age 7-10 years, the interval between the third and booster dose is determined by the age when the first dose was given. For adolescents age 11-18 years, the interval is determined by the age when the third dose was given.
9. **IPV:** Vaccine is not generally recommended for persons age ≥18 years.
10. **Varicella:** Give 2-dose series to all susceptible adolescents age ≥13 years.

Reporting Adverse Reactions
Report adverse reactions to vaccines through the federal Vaccine Adverse Event Reporting System. For information on reporting reactions following vaccines, please visit www.vaers.org or call the 24-hour national toll-free information line (800) 822-7967.

Disease Reporting
Report suspected cases of vaccine-preventable diseases to your state or the local health department.

For additional information about vaccines, including precautions and contraindications for immunization and vaccine shortages, please visit the National Immunization Program Website at www.cdc.gov/nip or call the National Immunization Information Hotline at 800-232-2522 (English) or 800-232-0233 (Spanish).

From: American Academy of Pediatrics, Committee on Infectious Diseases. 2003. Recommended childhood immunization schedule—United States, 2003. *Pediatrics* 111(1):212–216.

FIGURE 3-2 ◆ **SUGGESTED PHYSICIAN ORDER FORMAT FOR ROUTINE NICU IMMUNIZATIONS.**

■ Order the following vaccines when the infant is 2 months postnatal age, after informed consent has been obtained. Preterm infants should be immunized at the usual chronologic age; vaccine doses should not be reduced for preterm infants.

■ Ordering two vaccines each on 2 successive days is suggested for infants in the NICU to minimize trauma to the infant. However, if necessary, all these vaccines may be given safely and effectively on the same day.

■ Administer intramuscular (IM) injections into the anterolateral aspect of the thigh. Note that all parenteral vaccines are given IM except for IPV, which is given subcutaneously (SC).

Day 1

● Hepatitis B Vaccine*   0.5 ml IM x 1

● Diphtheria and Tetanus Toxoids and   0.5 ml IM x 1
  Pertussis Vaccine (DTP)

● Acetaminophen _____ mg† (specify
  preferred route—PO drops or PR suppository)
  30 minutes prior to DTP and every
  4 hours x 24 hours after

Day 2

● Inactivated Poliovirus Vaccine (IPV)   IPV: 0.5 ml SC x 1

● *Haemophilus influenzae* type b conjugate   0.5 ml IM x 1
  vaccine (Hib)

---

* In preterm infants who weigh <2 kg at birth and whose mothers are HBsAG-negative, vaccination with hepatitis B vaccine should be delayed until just before hospital discharge if the infant weighs ≥2 kg or until approximately 2 months of age, when other immunizations are given.

† Dose of acetaminophen (round to nearest 10 mg increment):
  2 kg: 20 mg/dose   **3 kg:** 30 mg/dose   **4 kg:** 40 mg/dose

FIGURE 3-3 ◆ LIVE-VIRUS VACCINES AND STEROID THERAPY.

Live-virus vaccines are contraindicated in immunosuppressed patients, including those on high-dose steroids, because replication of the virus may be potentiated in these patients. However, if the steroid therapy the patient is receiving is not likely to be immunosuppressive, most experts consider that live-virus vaccines (oral polio vaccine and measles, mumps, and rubella vaccine) are not contraindicated concomitantly.

The immunosuppressive effects of corticosteroid treatment vary, but many clinicians consider a prednisone dose of ≥2 mg/kg/day, (0.3 mg/kg/day of dexamethasone) to raise concern about the safety of immunization with live-virus vaccines.* (For further information, see Table 1-18, page 182.) The frequency and route of administration of corticosteroids, the underlying disease, and other concurrent therapy also are factors affecting immunosuppression. The exact interval between discontinuation of immunosuppressive therapy and re-establishment of the ability to respond to live-virus vaccines is not known, but estimates vary from 3 to 12 months.[†]

The following durations, doses, and routes of corticosteroid administration are usually *not* immunosuppressive and do not necessarily contraindicate vaccination with live-virus vaccines. However, the clinical judgment of the attending physician should prevail at all times:*

Therapeutic Doses:

- **Short-term (<2 weeks):** Low- to moderate-dose systemic corticosteroid therapy.

- **Long-term:** Alternate-day systemic corticosteroid administration with low to moderate doses of short-acting corticosteroids.

Maintenance Physiologic Doses (replacement therapy): The standard replacement dose for chronic adrenal insufficiency is 10–15 mg/m^2/day (approximately 0.3–0.5 mg/kg/day).

Routes: The following corticosteroid administration routes usually do not cause adrenal suppression:

- Topical (skin, nose, or eyes) (Note, however, that systemic immunosuppression can occur with prolonged topical corticosteroid therapy. Infants, particularly preterm infants, are very susceptible to percutaneous absorption of topically applied corticosteroids. Vaccination with live-virus vaccines should be avoided in immunosuppressed infants.)

- Aerosol

- Intra-articular, bursal, or tendon injection

Drug Duration of Action for Various Corticosteroids:

- Short-acting: hydrocortisone

- Intermediate-acting: methylprednisolone, prednisone

- Long-acting: dexamethasone

Corticosteroids differ in their duration of action. As already specified, alternate-day systemic administration with low to moderate doses of short-acting corticosteroid is usually not immunosuppressive. Alternate-day therapy provides relief of symptoms while minimizing adrenal suppression, protein catabolism, and other adverse effects. However, long-acting corticosteroids such as dexamethasone are not recommended for alternate-day therapy because they cause continuing immunosuppression even on the alternate day when they are not administered. Use of live-virus vaccines in this case is not recommended.[†]

---

* American Academy of Pediatrics, Committee on Infectious Diseases. 1994. *Red Book: Report of the Committee on Infectious Diseases*, 23rd ed. Elk Grove Village, Illinois: American Academy of Pediatrics, 55.

[†] McEvoy GK. 1994. *AHFS Drug Information*. Bethesda, Maryland: American Society of Hospital Pharmacists, 2226.

IMMUNIZATIONS

Diphtheria and Tetanus Toxoids and Pertussis Vaccine [DTP]

Biologic: Immunizing Agent

(dif-THEER-ee-a and TET-en-us TOK-soidz and per-TUSS-iss)

Synonyms:

DTwP: diphtheria and tetanus toxoids and whole-cell pertussis vaccine (DTP is the same as DTwP.)

DTaP (Tripedia, Acel-Imune): diphtheria and tetanus toxoids and acellular pertussis vaccine, now recommended by the American Academy of Pediatrics for all doses in the vaccination series[1]

Dose

0.5 ml IM. All infants receive the same dose, regardless of weight. Preterm infants receive the same dose at the normal postnatal age.[1–3]

Administer at 2, 4, and 6 months, and give a reinforcing injection 1 year after the third injection (see Table 3-2). Can use **DTaP** for all doses in the vaccination series. Extending the time interval between doses does not interfere with the final immunity achieved. Regardless of how much time has elapsed between doses, it is not necessary to start the series over.

The Advisory Committee on Immunization Practices (ACIP) and the American Academy of Pediatrics (AAP) suggest that acetaminophen be given prior to vaccination and every 4 hours for 24 hours after vaccination to infants at higher risk for seizures (those with a personal history of seizures or a family history in siblings or parents). Acetaminophen reduces the incidence of postvaccination fever.

Administration

Supplied as: 5 and 7.5 ml vials.

Normal Appearance: Markedly turbid and whitish suspension. If product contains clumps of material that cannot be resuspended with vigorous shaking, do not use.

IM: Inject the anterolateral aspect of the thigh. Do not use the same muscle site more than once during basic immunization.

Do not administer in infants with severe thrombocytopenia (platelet count <40,000/mm^3).

Storage: Refrigerate (2°–8°C [36°–46°F]). Do not freeze.

Cautions/Contraindications

Do not give if infant has had any of the following adverse reactions after previous DTP vaccine injection:

- Anaphylactic reaction to the vaccine or a constituent

- Moderate or severe illness with or without a fever
- Fever ≥40.6°C (105°F) within 48 hours after vaccination
- Collapse or shocklike state (hypotonic-hyporesponsive episode) within 48 hours
- Seizures within 3 days
- Persistent, inconsolable crying lasting ≥3 hours within 48 hours

Carefully review and consider the benefits and risks of administering DTP to infants with a family history of convulsions. Whether and when to administer DTP to infants with proven or suspected underlying neurologic disorders should be decided on an individual basis.

Do not administer in infants with severe thrombocytopenia (platelet count <40,000/mm^3).

Thimerosal in Vaccines

- There is concern about the amount of mercury from thimerosal in pediatric vaccines because the cumulative amount in all the vaccines infants receive could exceed safe limits in infants <6 months of age. Thimerosal is a mercury-containing preservative that has been used as an additive in biologics and vaccines since the 1930s because it prevents bacterial and fungal contamination, particularly in multidose containers. Infants now receive up to 12 immunizations in the first 6 months of life.

- To reduce thimerosal exposure, delay hepatitis B vaccination in healthy newborns from birth until 2 to 6 months of age (but only if the mother is negative for hepatitis B). See Table 3-5, page 647 in the hepatitis B vaccine monograph. Use thimerosal-free vaccines when possible, and use combination vaccines to reduce the number of injections. The Food and Drug Administration (FDA) is asking manufacturers to reduce or eliminate thimerosal in pediatric vaccines. Some thimerosal-free pediatric vaccines are already available, and more will be available soon.[4–6]

- The risk, if any, to infants from exposure to thimerosal is believed to be slight. The risks of not vaccinating children far outweigh the theoretical risk of exposure to thimerosal-containing vaccines during the first 6 months of life.[6]

USE

For active immunization of infants and children through 6 years of age.

DTP is used for prophylaxis only, not for treatment of the actual disease.

Children who have recovered from culture-confirmed pertussis do not need further doses of pertussis-containing vaccine.

MECHANISM OF ACTION

Contains diphtheria and tetanus toxoids and killed bacteria (pertussis) organisms. The full series confers protection against diphtheria, tetanus, and pertussis for at least 10 years.

ADVERSE EFFECTS

With DTwP (Whole-cell):

- *Local:* Erythema and induration and possible tenderness (common); pain (51 percent), swelling (41 percent), redness (37 percent). Because the product contains aluminum, a nodule may be palpable at the injection site for a few weeks. Local abscess may form.

- *Systemic:* Fever (onset within 12 hours, lasting 1–7 days), malaise, chills, irritability. Fretfulness (53 percent), drowsiness (32 percent), anorexia (21 percent), vomiting (6 percent), persistent crying (3 percent).

Rare, serious, adverse reactions may occur (see adverse reactions listed under **CAUTIONS/CONTRAINDICATIONS** above).

With DTaP (Acellular): Fever, upper respiratory tract infection, diarrhea, vomiting, rash, nodule at injection site. Rare: sterile abscess, subcutaneous atrophy at injection site.

- Adverse effects occur less frequently with DTaP than with DTwP. This is especially true of pain and tenderness, erythema, induration, swelling, and warmth at injection site. There is also less drowsiness, irritability, persistent crying, fever, and seizures.

NURSING IMPLICATIONS

Obtain consent before administering immunizations.

Provide vaccine information to parents prior to administration.

Note expiration date on vial, and assure proper storage temperature.

Document manufacturer's name, lot number, and the date, time, and site of administration.

Complete immunization card.

Monitor injection site for redness and swelling.

Monitor patient for adverse reactions, including fever and irritability.

COMMENTS

Interactions: Concurrent use of immunosuppressant drugs, including high-dose corticosteroids or radiation therapy, may result in an insufficient response to immunization. However, this is not listed as a contraindication by the AAP for giving DTP.

HAEMOPHILUS INFLUENZAE TYPE B CONJUGATE VACCINE [HIB]

BIOLOGIC: IMMUNIZING AGENT

(hem-OFF-fil-us in-flu-EN-za type BEE KON-ja-gat vak-SEEN)

DOSE

0.5 ml IM. All infants receive the same dose, regardless of weight.

See Table 3-2 for schedule.

ADMINISTRATION

Supplied as: HibTITER and ProHIBiT: 1-, 5-, and 10-dose vials. PedvaxHIB: Single-dose vials (Table 3-3).

Normal Appearance: (See Table 3-1, page 630, for identity of abbreviations):

- *HbOC (HibTITER):* Clear, colorless suspension.
- *PRP-OMP (PedvaxHIB):* Lyophilized powder, white to off-white. After reconstitution, slightly opaque white suspension.
- *PRP-T (ActHIB and OmniHIB):* Lyophilized powder, white to off-white. After reconstitution, clear, colorless suspension.

IM: Inject into the midlateral aspect of the thigh. Do not administer IV or into or near blood vessels or nerves.

- After aspiration, if blood or any suspicious discoloration appears in the syringe, do not inject. Discard contents and repeat using a new dose of vaccine at a different site.
- Do not administer IM injections in infants with severe thrombocytopenia (platelet count <40,000/mm^3).
- Hib can be given simultaneously with other routine immunizations (e.g., DTP, OPV, HBV, MMR).

Storage: Store in refrigerator at 2°–8°C (36°–46°F). Do not freeze. Improper storage can cause vaccine failure.

CAUTIONS/CONTRAINDICATIONS

- Anaphylactic reaction to the vaccine or a constituent.
- Moderate or severe illness with or without a fever.
- Hypersensitivity to any component of the vaccine, including thimerosal.
- **Thimerosal in Vaccines**
  - There is concern about the amount of mercury from thimerosal in pediatric vaccines because the cumulative amount in all the vaccines infants receive could exceed safe limits in infants <6 months of age. Thimerosal is a mercury-containing preservative that has been used as an additive in biologics and vaccines since the 1930s because it prevents bacterial and fungal contamination,

TABLE 3-3 ◆ HIB VACCINE ABBREVIATIONS

Abbreviation	Trade Name (Manufacturer)	Carrier Protein	Type
HbOC	HibTITER (Lederle)	CRM$_{197}$	**O**ligosaccharide conjugate of *Corynebacterium diphtheriae* CRM$_{197}$ mutant protein. For infants ≥2 months. DTP—HbOC (Tetramune) may be substituted for DTP and Hib, which are administered separately whenever recommended use of these 2 vaccines coincide.
HbOC-DTP	TETRAMUNE (Lederle)		HbOC in combination with DTP reduces the numbers of IM injections needed.
PRP-OMP	PedvaxHIB (Merck)	OMP	**O**uter **m**embrane **p**rotein complex of *Neisseria meningitidis.* For infants ≥2 months.
PRP-T	Pasteur Mérieux vaccines: ActHIB (Connaught) OmniHIB (Smith-Kline Beecham)	Tetanus toxoid	PRP-T may be reconstituted with DTP, manufactured by Connaught (only). For infants ≥2 months.

particularly in multidose containers. Infants now receive up to 12 immunizations in the first 6 months of life.

- To reduce thimerosal exposure, delay hepatitis B vaccination in healthy newborns from birth until 2 to 6 months of age (but only if the mother is negative for hepatitis B). See Table 3-5, page 647 in the Hepatitis B vaccine monograph. Use thimerosal-free vaccines when possible, and use combination vaccines to reduce the number of injections. The Food and Drug Administration (FDA) is asking manufacturers to reduce or eliminate thimerosal in pediatric vaccines. Some thimerosal-free pediatric vaccines are already available, and more will be available soon.[4–6]

- The risk, if any, to infants from exposure to thimerosal is believed to be slight. The risks of not vaccinating children far outweigh the theoretical risk of exposure to thimerosal-containing vaccines during the first 6 months of life.[6]

USE

For routine active immunization of infants and children 2 months to 5 years old against serious systemic bacterial diseases—such as meningitis, sepsis, septic arthritis, epiglottitis, osteomyelitis, pericarditis, and pneumonia—from capsular strains of type B *H. influenzae.*[3,7]

Hib is used for prophylaxis only, not for treatment of the actual disease.

Three Hib vaccines (HibTITER, PedvaxHIB, ActHIB/OmniHIB) are licensed for infant use. If PedvaxHIB is administered at ages 2 and 4 months, a dose at age 6 months is not required. After completing the primary series, any Hib conjugate vaccine may be used as a booster at age 12–15 months.[7]

MECHANISM OF ACTION

Promotes immunity by producing specific antibodies to *H. influenzae* type B. Hib will not protect against other types of *H. influenzae*.

ADVERSE EFFECTS

Usually mild and transient; rarely persist for longer than 24–48 hours: fever longer than 24 hours (up to 2.1 percent), erythema, induration, tenderness, diarrhea, vomiting, crying longer than 24 hours (<1.2 percent).

Reported, but causal connection not established: rash, hives, convulsions, Guillain-Barré syndrome, irritability, sleepiness, respiratory infection, otitis media, and one case of thrombocytopenia.[1]

Vaccine cannot protect from disease within the first 2 weeks following administration (the time required for the protective effects of the vaccine to develop). Infection with *H. influenzae* type B has been reported within the first 48 hours following vaccination, but this resulted from previous colonization with the organism.

NURSING IMPLICATIONS

Obtain consent before administering immunizations.

Provide vaccine information to parents prior to administration.

Note expiration date on vial, and assure proper storage temperature.

Document manufacturer's name, lot number, and the date, time, and site of administration.

Complete immunization card.

Monitor injection site for redness and swelling.

Monitor patient for adverse reactions, including fever and irritability.

COMMENTS

Interactions: Immunosuppressant drugs, including high-dose corticosteroids or radiation therapy.

Hepatitis B Immune Globulin (H-BIG)

*(hep-ah-TYE-tiss BEE
i-MUNE GLOB-yoo-lin)*

**Biologic:
Immune Serum**

Dose

0.5 ml IM administered as soon after birth as possible, preferably within 12 hours. May give at the same time as hepatitis B vaccine, but in a separate syringe at a different site.[1]

Hepatitis B vaccine 0.5 ml IM should also be given within 7 days of birth, but preferably within the first 12 hours of life.

If administration of the first dose of hepatitis B vaccine is delayed for as long as 3 months, then a 0.5 ml dose of H-BIG should be repeated at 3 months. If hepatitis B vaccine is refused, then 0.5 ml of H-BIG should be repeated at 3 and 6 months.

Administration

IM: Inject into the anterolateral thigh. Give undiluted.

- Do not administer IM injections in infants with severe thrombocytopenia (platelet count <40,000/mm^3).

- H-BIG is not for IV use because a drop in blood pressure may occur, with anaphylaxis-like symptoms.

Storage: Refrigerate. Improper storage can cause vaccine failure.

Cautions/Contraindications

Allergy to the preservative thimerosal. For concerns about use of vaccines containing this preservative, see the monograph, Hepatitis B Vaccine.

- Do not administer IM injections in infants with severe thrombocytopenia (platelet count <40,000/mm^3).

Do not give IV.

Use

Provides passive immunity to hepatitis B.

Given to infants of HBsAG-positive mothers because these infants are at risk of being infected with hepatitis B virus and becoming chronic carriers.[1]

Mechanism of Action

H-BIG is an immunoglobulin that contains a high titer of antibody to hepatitis B surface antigen (HBsAg). Infants born to HBsAg-positive mothers are at risk of being infected with the hepatitis B virus and becoming chronic carriers. About 94 percent of the infants given H-BIG plus hepatitis B vaccine immediately after birth and in the early months of life do not become carriers.

ADVERSE EFFECTS

Tenderness and pain at injection site.

Infrequent: Emesis, chills, fever, myalgia, lethargy.

Rare: Urticaria and angioedema. Isolated cases of angioneurotic edema and nephrotic syndrome have occurred.

PHARMACOKINETICS/PHARMACODYNAMICS

Onset of Action: Rapid.

Duration: short (1–3 months). Maximum serum levels of anti-HBs are seen in 2–4 days.

Half-life: About 25 days. A detectable level of circulating anti-HBs persists for about 2 months or longer.

NURSING IMPLICATIONS

Provide vaccine information to parents prior to administration.

Note expiration date on vial, and assure proper storage temperature.

Document manufacturer's name, lot number, and the date, time, and site of administration.

Complete immunization card.

Monitor injection site for redness and swelling.

Monitor patient for adverse reactions, including fever and irritability.

COMMENTS

Do not mix with other medications.

HEPATITIS B VACCINE
(hep-ah-TYE-tiss BEE vak-SEEN)
(ENGERIX-B, RECOMBIVAX HB)

BIOLOGIC:
IMMUNIZING AGENT

DOSE

Term Infants:

- *Infants with HBsAg-positive Mother.* See Table 3-4 for dose and Table 3-5 for vaccine selection. Administer IM as soon after birth as possible, preferably within 12 hours. Give at the same time as hepatitis B immune globulin (H-BIG), but in a separate syringe at a different site to ensure better vaccine absorption. Repeat dose at 1 month and 6 months of age. Test for anti-HBs and HBsAg 1–3 months after completion of immunization series.

  - An alternate four-dose schedule for Engerix-B for infants born to hepatitis B–infected mothers may be used to attain earlier immunity: 0.5 ml initially, at 1 month, 2 months, and 12 months of age.

- *Infants with HBsAg-negative Mother (Universal Hepatitis B Immunization).* See Table 3-4 for dose and Table 3-5 for vaccine selection.

  - Dose 1: At birth (preferably before hospital discharge) to 2 months of age.

  - Dose 2: 1–2 months after dose 1.

  - Dose 3: At 6–18 months of age. (*Note:* Complete the series by 6–9 months of age for high-risk populations such as Alaskan natives, Pacific islanders, and infants of immigrants from countries in which HBV is endemic.)[8]

Preterm Infants:

- *Infants with HBsAg-positive Mother.* See Table 3-4 for dose and Table 3-5 for vaccine selection. Administer IM as soon after birth as possible, preferably within 12 hours. Give at the same time as hepatitis B immune globulin (H-BIG), but in a separate syringe at a different site to ensure better vaccine

TABLE 3-4 ◆ RECOMMENDED DOSAGES OF HEPATITIS B VACCINES

	Recombivax HB (Merck)		Engerix-B* (SmithKline Beecham)	
	mcg	ml	mcg	ml
Infants of HBsAg-**negative** mothers	2.5	0.25 (peds formulation)	10	0.5
Infants of HBsAg-**positive** mothers (hepatitis B immune globulin should also be given)	5	0.5 (high-risk infant, adolescent and adult formulation) 1 (peds formulation)	10	0.5

* Engerix-B is available as a single-dose pediatric injection of 10 mcg/0.5 ml and an adult vial of 20 mcg/ml. Either one can be used for infants.

TABLE 3-5 ◆ RECOMMENDATIONS FOR HEPATITIS B VACCINATION OF NEWBORN INFANTS WITH VACCINES THAT DO NOT CONTAIN THIMEROSAL AS A PRESERVATIVE AND WITH THIMEROSAL-CONTAINING VACCINES

Mother's HBs-Ag Status at Delivery	Recommendation
Positive or Unknown	Vaccinate at birth. Use vaccine that does not contain thimerosal as a preservative; if unavailable, use thimerosal-containing vaccine.
Negative	Vaccinate at birth or by age 2 months. At birth, use vaccine that does not contain thimerosal as a preservative. At 2 months of age, use either vaccine that does not contain thimerosal as a preservative or thimerosal-containing vaccine.
Negative—high risk*	Same as "Negative" above, except thimerosal-containing vaccine can be administered at birth.

* Populations or groups that have a high risk for early childhood hepatitis B virus (HBV) transmission, including Alaskan natives, Asian-Pacific islanders, immigrant populations from countries in which HBV is of high or intermediate endemicity, and households contining persons with chronic HBV infection.

From: Centers for Disease Control and Prevention. 1999. Recommendations regarding the use of vaccines that contain thimerosal as a preservative. *MMWR* 48(43): 998.

---

absorption. Repeat dose at 1 month and 6 months of age. Test for anti-HBs and HBsAg 1–3 months after completion of immunization series.

- *Preterm Infants with HBsAg-negative Mother (Universal Hepatitis B Immunization).* See Table 3-4 for dose and Table 3-5 for vaccine selection. In infants weighing <2 kg at birth, delay vaccination with hepatitis B vaccine until *one* of the following:
  - Discharge
  - Weight is ≥2 kg
  - Other immunizations are given at about 2 months of age
- If administration of the first dose of hepatitis B vaccine is delayed for as long as 3 months, then a 0.5 ml dose of H-BIG should be repeated at 3 months. If hepatitis B vaccine is refused, then 0.5 ml of hepatitis B immune globulin should be repeated at 3 and 6 months.[1]

ADMINISTRATION

Normal Appearance: After thorough agitation, a slightly opaque, white suspension.

IM: Inject into the anterolateral thigh. Shake well.

- Hepatitis B vaccine may be given concurrently with other vaccines, including DTP, *Haemophilus influenzae* type b conjugate, MMR, and/or poliovirus vaccine. Do not inject the same muscle site more than once during the course of basic immunization.

Storage: Store in the refrigerator at 2°–8°C (36°–46°F). *Do not freeze;* freezing destroys potency. Improper storage can cause vaccine failure.

CAUTIONS/CONTRAINDICATIONS

⟋ Serious active infection, except when withholding the vaccine, entails greater risk.

⟋ Severely compromised cardiopulmonary status or when a febrile or systemic reaction could put infant at significant risk.

⟋ Do not administer IM injections in infants with severe thrombocytopenia (platelet count <40,000/mm^3).

⟋ Hypersensitivity to yeast or any component of the vaccine.

⟋ **Thimerosal in Vaccines**

- There is concern about the amount of mercury from thimerosal in pediatric vaccines because the cumulative amount in all the vaccines infants receive could exceed safe limits in infants <6 months of age. Thimerosal is a mercury-containing preservative that has been used as an additive in biologics and vaccines since the 1930s because it prevents bacterial and fungal contamination, particularly in multidose containers. Infants now receive up to 12 immunizations in the first 6 months of life.

- To reduce thimerosal exposure, delay hepatitis B vaccination in healthy newborns from birth until 2 to 6 months of age (but only if the mother is negative for hepatitis B) (Table 3-5), use thimerosal-free vaccines when possible, and use combination vaccines to reduce the number of injections. The Food and Drug Administration (FDA) is asking manufacturers to reduce or eliminate thimerosal in pediatric vaccines. Some thimerosal-free pediatric vaccines are already available, and more will be available soon.[4–6]

- The risk, if any, to infants from exposure to thimerosal is believed to be slight. The risks of not vaccinating children far outweigh the theoretical risk of exposure to thimerosal-containing vaccines during the first 6 months of life.[6]

USE

For active immunization against infection caused by the hepatitis B virus. Newborns, infants, and children respond well, with high immunogenic effects.

For both pre- and postexposure protection; provides long-term protection.

Recommended for all infants, whether the mother is HBsAg-negative or HBsAg-positive.

MECHANISM OF ACTION

Two types of hepatitis B vaccine are licensed in the U.S.: Recombivax HB and Engerix-B. Both are produced by recombinant DNA technology using common baker's yeast.

ADVERSE EFFECTS

Well tolerated in infants.

Most Frequently Reported Side Effects: Pain at injection site; fever >37.7°C (99.8°F).

CNS: Dizziness, disturbed sleep, irritability, Guillain-Barré syndrome and Bell's palsy, transverse myelitis.

Dermatologic: Rash, petechiae, purpura, herpes zoster.

GI: GI upset.

Local: 50 percent-injection site soreness; erythema, swelling.

Musculoskeletal: Arthralgia.

Respiratory: Upper respiratory infection, influenzalike symptoms.

Other: Fatigue, fever, flushing, chills, tachycardia, thrombocytopenia. Anaphylaxis is rare and has been reported only in adults.

NURSING IMPLICATIONS

Obtain consent before administering immunizations.

Provide vaccine information to parents prior to administration.

Note expiration date on vial, and assure proper storage temperature.

Document manufacturer's name, lot number, and the date, time, and site of administration.

Complete immunization card.

Monitor injection site for redness and swelling.

Monitor patient for adverse reactions, including fever and irritability.

Pneumococcal 7-Valent Conjugate Vaccine
(Diphtheria CRM$_{197}$ Protein) (Prevnar)
(NEW-moh-KOK-al 7-VAY-lent KON-ja-gat vak-SEEN)

Biologic:
Immunizing Agent

Synonym: PCV7

Dose

0.5 ml/dose as a single dose IM at 2, 4, 6, and 12–15 months of age.

The schedule usually begins at 2 months of age, but the *first* dose can be given as early as 6 weeks of age. *Two additional* doses of 0.5 ml each are given at about 2-month intervals, followed by a *fourth* dose of 0.5 ml at 12–15 months of age. Give the fourth dose 2 or more months after the third dose.

Administration

Supplied as: *Injection:* 0.5 ml dose vials.

IM: Administer into the anterolateral aspect of the thigh in infants or the deltoid muscle of the upper arm in toddlers.

- Do not administer in the gluteal area or areas where there may be a major nerve trunk or blood vessel.

Preparation of dose: This vaccine is a suspension. Shake vigorously immediately prior to administration to obtain a homogeneous white suspension. Do not use if resuspension is not possible.

Do not give IV.

Storage: Store in the refrigerator (2°–8°C [36°–46°F]).

Cautions/Contraindications

Not for treatment of active infection.

Do not give if patient is hypersensitive to any component of the vaccine, including diphtheria toxoid. Use caution in patients with possible history of latex sensitivity because the packaging contains dry natural rubber.

Postpone vaccine in cases of severe or moderate febrile illness; however, minor illnesses, such as mild upper respiratory tract infection with or without low-grade fever, are not generally contraindications.[1]

Do not give to infants with coagulation disorders or thrombocytopenia that would contraindicate IM injections, unless the benefits clearly outweigh the risks.

Infants who are immunosuppressed (from irradiation, corticosteroids, HIV infection, genetic defect, and other causes) may have reduced antibody response.

Use

Recommended for active immunization of infants and toddlers 2–23 months of age against invasive pneumococcal diseases caused by seven capsular serotypes of *Streptococcus pneumoniae.*

Two doses of PCV7 are recommended for children 24 to 59 months old at high risk of invasive pneumococcal infection—including children with functional, anatomic, or congenital asplenia; infection with human immunodeficiency virus; and primary immunodeficiency; children who are receiving immunosuppressive therapy; and children with other predisposing conditions—who have not been immunized previously with PCV7. For high-risk children 24 to 59 months old who have received no previous doses of either 23PS vaccine or PCV7, two doses of PCV7 are recommended to be given at an interval of 6 to 8 weeks, followed by a single dose of 23PS vaccine no less than 6 to 8 weeks after the last dose of PCV7. An additional dose of 23PS vaccine is recommended 3 to 5 years after the last dose.[2]

S. pneumoniae causes invasive infections such as bacteremia and meningitis, pneumonia, otitis media, and sinusitis.[1–6]

MECHANISM OF ACTION

PCV7 is a sterile solution of saccharides of the capsular antigens of *S. pneumoniae* serotypes 4, 6B, 9V, 14, 18C, 19F, and 23F, which have been individually conjugated to diphtheria CRM_{197} protein. CRM_{197} protein is a nontoxic variant of diphtheria toxin. The vaccine is aimed at the seven serotypes that cause about 80 percent of invasive pneumococcal disease in children younger than 6 years of age in the U.S., including a high percentage of resistant *S. pneumoniae* cases.[1]

ADVERSE EFFECTS

CNS: Drowsiness, irritability.

Dermatologic: Injection site reactions, such as local tenderness, redness, and edema, which are usually self-limiting and require no therapy. A nodule, caused by the aluminum component in the vaccine, may occasionally be palpable at the injection site for several weeks.

GI: Decreased appetite.

Other: Fever.

NURSING IMPLICATIONS

- Prior to administration, provide VIS (Vaccine Information Statement) to parent or other responsible adult, and discuss the importance of completing the immunization series, unless contraindicated, and the need to report any suspected adverse reaction to the infant's health care professional.[1]
- As with all vaccines, document the administration of pneumococcal vaccine on the patient's vaccine record.

COMMENTS

This vaccine does not substitute for routine diphtheria immunizations.

Immune response to PCV7 in preterm infants has not been studied.

Report suspected adverse events. The FDA Web site is http://www.fda.gov/cber/vaers/vaers.htm. The Vaccine Adverse Event Reporting System's (VAERS) toll-free number for forms and information is 800-822-7967.

Interactions:

As with other IM injections, administer with caution in infants on anticoagulants.

- Infants receiving immunosuppressive agents (large doses of corticosteroids, antimetabolites, alkylating agents, cytotoxic agents) may not respond optimally to active immunization.
- May be given simultaneously with other immunizing agents as part of the routine immunization schedule.[4]

REFERENCES

1. Medical Economics Data. 2000. *Physicians' Desk Reference, Supplement A/2000*, 54th ed. Montvale, New Jersey: Medical Economics, A105–A110.

2. American Academy of Pediatrics, Committee on Infectious Diseases. 2000. Policy statement: Prevention of pneumococcal infections, including use of pneumococcal conjugate vaccine (Prevnar), and pneumococcal polysaccharide vaccine, and antibiotic prophylaxis. *Pediatrics* 106(2 part 1): 362–366.

3. Black S, et al. 1998. Efficacy of heptavalent conjugate pneumococcal vaccine (Lederle Laboratories) in 37,000 infants and children: Results of the Northern California Kaiser Permanente Efficacy Trial. In *Programs and Abstracts of the 38th Interscience Conference on Antimicrobial Agents and Chemotherapy*, San Diego, California, September 24–27.

4. American Academy of Pediatrics, Committee on Infectious Diseases. 2001. Recommended childhood immunization schedule—United States, January–December 2001. *Pediatrics* 107(1): 202–204.

5. Overturf GD, and the American Academy of Pediatrics, Committee on Infectious Diseases. 2000. Technical report: Prevention of pneumococcal infections, including the use of pneumococcal conjugate and polysaccharide vaccines and antibiotic prophylaxis. *Pediatrics* 106(2 part 1): 367–376.

6. Centers for Disease Control and Prevention, Advisory Committee on Immunization Practices. 2000. Preventing pneumococcal disease among infants and young children: Recommendations of the Advisory Committee on Immunization Practices (ACIP). *MMWR* 49(RR-9): 1–35.

POLIOVIRUS VACCINE, INACTIVATED [IPV]

BIOLOGIC: IMMUNIZING AGENT

(POE-lee-oh VYE-rus vak-SEEN)

DOSE

0.5 ml SC. All infants receive the same dose, regardless of weight.

All children should receive four doses of IPV: at 2 months, 4 months, and 6–18 months and at 4–6 years.[9,10]

Extending the time interval between doses does not interfere with the final immunity achieved. Regardless of how much time elapses between doses, it is not necessary to start the series over.[1]

ADMINISTRATION

Supplied as: 0.5 ml single-dose syringe with integral needle or single-dose ampoule.

Normal Appearance: Clear, colorless suspension. Do not use vaccine that contains particulate matter, is turbid, or has changed color.

SC: Inject into the midlateral aspect of the thigh.

Do not administer IV or into or near blood vessels or nerves.

Do not administer IM injections in infants with severe thrombocytopenia (platelet count <40,000/mm^3).

After aspiration, if blood or any suspicious discoloration appears in the syringe, do not inject. Discard contents and repeat using a new dose of vaccine at a different site.

See Table 3-2 (page 632) for current AAP recomendations for ages of routine administration of IPV.[10]

IPV can be given simultaneously with other routine immunizations (i.e., DTP, Hib, Hep B, MMR).

Storage: Refrigerate at 2°–8°C (36°–46°F). Do not freeze. Improper storage can cause vaccine failure.

CAUTIONS/CONTRAINDICATIONS

Anaphylactic reaction to the vaccine or a constituent.

Moderate or severe illness with or without a fever.

Anaphylactic reaction to streptomycin or neomycin.

Previous clinical poliomyelitis (usually caused by only a single poliovirus type) or incomplete immunization with OPV are *not* contraindications to completing the primary series of immunizations with IPV.

IMMUNIZATIONS

Use

For routine active polio immunization of infants and children. See monograph on poliovirus vaccine, live, oral (OPV) for recommendations of when OPV, rather than IPV, should be used. For prophylaxis only, not for treatment of the actual disease.

Mechanism of Action

Promotes immunity by producing specific antibodies to poliomyelitis. IPV is a suspension of three types of poliovirus, types 1, 2, and 3. Two products are available, IPOL and Poliovax. IPOL injection is grown in monkey kidney cell cultures, and Poliovax injection is grown in human diploid cell cultures broth by a microcarrier technique.

Adverse Effects

Fever.

Significant local or systemic reactions are unlikely.

Guillain-Barré syndrome has been temporally related to administration of IPV, but a causal relationship has not been established.

Paralytic polio has not been reported in recipients of IPV.

Nursing Implications

Obtain consent before administering immunizations.

Provide vaccine information to parents prior to administration.

Note expiration date on vial, and assure proper storage temperature.

Document manufacturer's name, lot number, and the date, time, and site of administration.

Complete immunization card.

Monitor injection site for redness and swelling.

Monitor patient for adverse reactions, including fever and irritability.

Comments

Interactions: Immunosuppressant drugs, including high-dose corticosteroids or radiation therapy, may suppress normal defense mechanisms causing the patient's antibody response to any of the poliovirus vaccines to be decreased.

POLIOVIRUS VACCINE, LIVE, ORAL [OPV]

BIOLOGIC: IMMUNIZING AGENT

(POE-lee-oh-vye-rus vak-SEEN)

DOSE

0.5 ml PO. Each dose is entire volume of pipette. All infants receive the same dose, regardless of weight.[1]

Oral poliovirus vaccine (OPV) is no longer recommended as part of the Immunization Schedule for Healthy Infants and Children (Table 3-2). It may be indicated under special circumstances such as an outbreak of wild-type poliovirus infection. Please refer to the National Immunization Program website at www.cdc.gov/nip or call the National Immunization Information Hotline at 800-232-2522 for the latest information on OPV and when it should be used.[9,10]

Extending the time interval between doses does not interfere with the final immunity achieved. Regardless of how much time elapses between doses, it is not necessary to start the series over.

ADMINISTRATION

Supplied as: 0.5 ml single-dose pipette.

Normal Appearance: Clear solution; usually red or pink, but may be yellow. Color changes are unimportant provided the solution remains clear. Because of sorbitol in the vaccine, it remains fluid at temperatures above −14°C (6°F).

PO: Thaw before use. May give as is or mixed with distilled water, chlorinated tap water, simple syrup, or milk or on bread, a sugar cube, or cake.

If the infant spits up/out the dose within 5–10 minutes, repeat. If the repeat dose is not retained, neither dose should be counted, and the vaccine should be readministered at the next visit.

OPV can be given simultaneously with other routine immunizations (i.e., DTP, Hib, hepatitis B, MMR).

Storage: Store in freezer (≤0°C [≤32°F]). Thawed product can be refrozen *if* vaccine temperature never exceeds 8°C (46°F) *and* cumulative thawing time is <24 hours (maximum of 10 thaw-freeze cycles). If 24-hour time is exceeded, store vaccine in refrigerator at 2°–8°C (36°–46°F), and use within 30 days. Improper storage can cause vaccine failure.

CAUTIONS/CONTRAINDICATIONS

Anaphylactic reaction to the vaccine or a constituent of it.

Moderate or severe illness with or without a fever.

Known altered immunodeficiency (hematologic and solid tumors; congenital immunodeficiency; long-term immunosuppressive therapy) because fatal poliomyelitis has occurred after administration of live-virus vaccine. OPV should not be used to vaccinate household contacts of immunodeficient patients because those with immunodeficiency are at increased risk for vaccine-associated paralytic poliomyelitis (VAPP). Inactivated poliovirus vaccine (IPV) should be used to vaccinate these infants instead.

- Infection with HIV or immunodeficient household member (vaccine recipients should not have contact with such persons for 6–8 weeks) with HIV.

- Treatment with large amounts of systemic corticosteroids. (Exact amount/duration of steroids have not been defined. A prednisone dose ≥2 mg/kg for longer than 2 weeks is considered by many to raise concerns about immunization with live-virus vaccines.)

- IPV, rather than OPV, should be used for infants in the NICU to prevent nosocomial transmission of live poliovirus in the nursery. Other infants in the unit may be preterm infants with immature immune systems, may be on immunosuppressant drugs (high-dose corticosteroids), or be debilitated or have acute illness. Poliovirus is shed for 6–8 weeks in the stool and by the pharyngeal route. See Table 3-2 (page 632) for current AAP recommendations.

USE

For active polio immunization of infants and children. For prophylaxis only, not for treatment of the actual disease. IPV, rather than OPV, is now recommended for routine childhood immunization against poliomyelitis. See **DOSE** above for when OPV should be used.

Produces intestinal immunity, is simple to administer, is well accepted by patients, results in immunization of some contacts of vaccinated individuals, and has essentially eliminated disease associated with wild poliovirus in the U.S. However, IPV (see poliovirus vaccine, inactivated, monograph) should be used for infants in the NICU to prevent nosocomial transmission of live poliovirus in the nursery. See **CAUTIONS/CONTRAINDICATIONS** above.

MECHANISM OF ACTION

Promotes immunity by producing specific antibodies to poliomyelitis. OPV is an attenuated, live-virus vaccine that produces active immunity by simulating the infection without producing symptoms of the disease. The virus must multiply in the GI tract. OPV produces immunity to poliovirus types 1, 2, and 3.

ADVERSE EFFECTS

- Vaccine-associated paralytic paralysis (1 case/2.4 million OPV doses). Occurrence of vaccine-associated paralysis is not predictable.

NURSING IMPLICATIONS

Obtain consent before administering immunizations.

Provide vaccine information to parents prior to administration, including the risk of vaccine-associated paralytic poliomyelitis in the infant who has taken live OPV and in others who have close, personal contact with the infant (such as those who change the infant's diapers).[9]

Note expiration date on vial, and assure proper storage temperature.

Document manufacturer, lot number, and the date, time, and site of administration.

Complete immunization card.

Monitor injection site for redness and swelling.

Monitor patient for adverse reactions, including fever and irritability.

COMMENTS

Interactions: Immunosuppressant drugs, including high-dose corticosteroids or radiation therapy.

Varicella-Zoster Immune Globulin [Human] (VZIG)

(VAIR-a-sel-a ZOS-ter)

Dose

Minimum dose for infants weighing 0–10 kg: 1 vial (= 125 units of varicella-zoster virus antibody in 1.25 ml or less).

Administer entire contents of vial; do not give fractional doses, even in preterm infants.[1]

Administration

IM: Give deep IM. Do not give IV. Does not need to be diluted.

- Do not administer IM injections in infants with severe thrombocytopenia (platelet count <40,000/mm^3).
- Avoid use in patients with bleeding diatheses, if possible, as with other IM injections.[1]

Storage: Refrigerate.

Use

Provides passive immunity against chickenpox.

Can prevent or modify the course of the disease, but is not effective once the disease is established. (Consider oral or IV acyclovir in these patients.)

For maximum effect, give within 48 hours of delivery or exposure and not more than 96 hours after exposure. The American Academy of Pediatrics lists types of exposure to varicella for which VZIG is indicated:[1]

- Being in the same two- to four-bed room or in adjacent beds in a large ward
- Face-to-face (5 minutes to 1 hour or more) contact with an infected staff member or patient
- Visit by a person deemed contagious

Transmission in the nursery is extremely rare, but VZIG is recommended for some infants because of poor transfer of antibody across the placenta early in pregnancy.[1] Neonatal candidates for VZIG, provided significant exposure has occurred, are:

- Newborns whose mothers had onset of varicella-zoster (chickenpox) within 5 days before delivery or within 48 hours after delivery
- Hospitalized preterm infants (≥28 weeks gestation) whose mothers have no history of chickenpox
- Hospitalized preterm infants <28 weeks gestation or weighing ≤1 kg, regardless of maternal history
- Immunocompromised children without a history of chickenpox[1]

Mechanism of Action

Contains the globulin fraction of human plasma, primarily IgG. Provides passive immunity through IgG antibody. VZIG modifies the severity of chickenpox and reduces the frequency of death, pneumonia, and encephalitis to less than 25 percent of what would be expected without treatment.

Duration of Protection: Approximately 1 month.

Adverse Effects

No data available, but appears to be well tolerated in newborns.

Most Common: Local discomfort.

Pain, swelling, erythema, and rash may occur at injection site.

Comments

VZIG is obtained from the American Red Cross Blood Services through the hospital blood bank.

Data needed when ordering VZIG are date of exposure, weight of infant, name and patient file number, and name of physician caring for infant.

IMMUNIZATIONS

APPENDICES

APPENDIX A
SIMPLIFIED NEONATAL CALCULATIONS

Standardization simplifies drug preparation and reduces the chance of calculation errors. Standardized calculations can be performed and double-checked easily and quickly. The instructions that follow simplify some frequent calculations made in the NICU. **Use caution to ensure that the units used in the dose match the equation used. Doses of some drugs may be expressed in mcg or mg. For example, morphine may be expressed as mg/kg/hour or mcg/kg/hour, depending on decimal point placement (15–25 mcg/kg/hour = 0.015–0.025 mg/kg/hour).**

Calculations for Drugs Dosed in mcg/kg/minute

Calculations for drugs dosed in mcg/kg/minute can be time-consuming and can cause confusion among house officers, nurses, and pharmacists.[1] The standard concentrations used in older children and adults cannot be given to newborns because rates of infusion are best individualized for each infant's body weight and fluid status.

Standardizing the total volume of drug prepared at 25 ml is recommended; this volume provides a 24-hour supply of medication when infused at typical neonatal infusion rates of 0.5–1 ml/hour.

Although others recommend calculations for preparation of 100 ml, preparation of 25 ml (using Equations A-1 and A-2 below) reduces the drug cost involved in preparing a larger volume that would otherwise be wasted because of the 24-hour expiration time on IV infusions.

- The instructions that follow produce a **total volume** of 25 ml; that volume is made up of both the drug and the diluent. *The following is a common error: adding the drug to 25 ml of diluent, which produces a final volume greater than 25 ml and, thus, a lower final drug concentration and dose than ordered.*

- All continuous infusions should be administered via a neonatal syringe pump.

APPENDICES

Calculating Drug Amount Needed

Equation A-1 may be used for medications dosed in mcg/kg/minute, including continuous infusions of alprostadil, amrinone, dobutamine, dopamine, epinephrine, isoproterenol, lidocaine, midazolam, nitroprusside, and others.

To calculate milligrams of drug needed to prepare 25 ml of IV drip solution to infuse at the rate desired:

$$C = \frac{1.5\ DW}{R}$$

Equation A-1

where: C = mg of drug needed to prepare 25 ml of solution (concentration)
1.5 = constant derived from minutes/hour
D = desired dose in mcg/kg/minute
W = body weight in kg
R = desired rate of infusion in ml/hour

Example: You need to write an order for dopamine at a dose of 5 mcg/kg/minute for a 2 kg infant. You predict that the dose may need to be increased shortly and therefore want to initiate the infusion at a slow rate of 0.5 ml/hour. How many milligrams of dopamine should be ordered for a 25 ml volume of D$_5$W for a dose of 5 mcg/kg/minute for this 2 kg infant?

$$C\ (in\ mg/25\ ml) = \frac{1.5 \times D\ (5\ mcg/kg/minute) \times W\ (2\ kg)}{R\ (0.5\ ml/hour)} = \frac{1.5 \times 5 \times 2}{0.5} = 30\ mg$$

The order should read:

Dopamine 30 mg in 25 ml D$_5$W to infuse IV at 0.5 ml/hour (= 5 mcg/kg/minute)

Note: Titrating the rate and dose is simplified for nurses if the order is written so that the dose is a multiple of the rate—that is, 0.5 ml/hour for 5 mcg/kg/minute. Then for 6 mcg/kg/minute, the rate is 0.6 ml/hour, or for 10 mcg/kg/minute, it is 1 ml/hour.

Therefore, for **0.1 ml/hour = 1 mcg/kg/minute,** use the following equation:

$$C\ (mg/25\ ml) = 15 \times W\ (kg)$$

and to double-concentrate the solution so that **2 mcg/kg/minute = 0.1 ml/hour** use:

$$C\ (mg/25\ ml) = 30 \times W\ (kg)$$

CHECKING INFUSION DOSE

Equation A-1 may be changed to **Equation A-2** by solving for D (dose). It can then be used to check the dose of an existing infusion:

$$D = \frac{CR}{1.5\,W}$$

Equation A-2

or

$$Dose\ (mcg/kg/minute) = \frac{Concentration\ (mg/25\ ml) \times Rate\ of\ infusion\ (ml/hour)}{1.5 \times Weight\ (kg)}$$

where the elements are as defined for Equation A-1.

Example: As part of your change-of-shift routine you check the dose of dobutamine your infant is currently receiving for accuracy and safety. The label on the pump states the concentration infusing is 20 mg in 25 ml D_5W. The current rate on the pump is 1.2 ml/hour. Your baby weighs 1.6 kg. What is the dose of dobutamine in mcg/kg/minute?

$$D\ (mcg/kg/minute) = \frac{C\ (20\ mg/25\ ml) \times R\ (1.2\ ml/hour)}{1.5\ W\ (1.6\ kg)}$$

$$D = 10\ mcg/kg/minute$$

APPENDICES

Calculations for Drugs Dosed in mg/kg/hour

Equations A-3 and A-4 below can be used for drugs—such as doxapram, morphine, and tolazoline—that are dosed in mg/kg/hour. *The equations can also be used for fentanyl; however, fentanyl is dosed in mcg/kg/hour rather than mg/kg/hour, and the concentration is in micrograms per 25 ml rather than milligrams/25 ml.*

CALCULATING DRUG AMOUNT NEEDED

To calculate the milligrams of drug needed for 25 ml of solution to infuse at the desired rate, use:

$$C = \frac{25 \times D \times W}{R} \qquad \text{Equation A-3}$$

where: C = mg of drug needed to prepare 25 ml of solution (concentration) (for fentanyl, mcg of drug to prepare 25 ml)

25 = constant indicating 25 milliliters prepared
D = desired dose in mg/kg/hour
W = body weight in kg
R = desired rate of infusion in ml/hour.

Example: You need to order doxapram at 0.5 mg/kg/hour for a 1.5 kg infant to infuse at 0.5 ml/hour. How many milligrams should be ordered for 25 ml?

$$C = \frac{25 \times 0.5 \ mg/kg/hour \times 1.5 \ kg}{0.5 \ ml/hour} = 37.5 \ mg/25 \ ml$$

CHECKING INFUSION DOSE

To check a dose already being infused, rearrange the equation to solve for the dose:

$$D = \frac{CR}{25\,W}$$

Equation A-4

Example: Doxapram has been ordered at 22.5 mg in 25 ml D_5W to infuse at 0.6 ml/hour. You suspect that this is an overdose. How can you quickly verify the dose? The infant weighs 0.654 kg.

$$D = \frac{CR}{25\,W} = \frac{22.5 \times 0.6\ ml/hour}{25 \times 0.654\ kg} = 0.83\ mg/kg/hour$$

Calculations for Preparing a 1:10 or a 1:100 Dilution

Concentrations of medications are often manufactured for administration to adults. The concentrations are too high to permit accurate measurement of the tiny doses required by neonates. To deal with this:

- For dose volumes <0.1 ml, prepare a 1:10 dilution.
- For dose volumes <0.01 ml, prepare a 1:100 dilution.

The 0.1 ml guideline has been established because volumes less than 10 percent of a syringe's capacity cannot be measured accurately. In the 1 ml tuberculin syringe typically used to measure medications for infants, 10 percent of the volume is 0.1 ml.

1:10 DILUTION

To prepare a 1:10 dilution for administering volumes measuring <0.1 ml in a tuberculin syringe:

1. In two separate syringes, draw up
   - 0.1 ml of drug
   - 0.9 ml of diluent
2. Inject drug into diluent syringe and mix well.

Example: You need to administer digoxin 3 mcg IV. The concentration is 100 mcg/ml. The dose volume using this concentration would be 0.03 ml, which cannot be measured accurately. You need to prepare a 1:10 dilution prior to administration.

1. In two separate syringes, draw up the following:

   • 0.1 ml of digoxin (= 10 mcg)
   • 0.9 ml of diluent

Inject the digoxin into the diluent syringe and mix well. The new concentration is 10 mcg/ml. The new volume for the 3 mcg dose is 0.3 ml, which can be measured accurately in a tuberculin syringe.

1:100 DILUTION

To prepare a 1:100 dilution for administering volumes measuring <0.01 ml in a tuberculin syringe:

1. In two separate syringes, draw up

   • 0.1 ml of drug
   • 9.9 ml of diluent

2. Inject drug into diluent syringe and mix well.

Example: Hydralazine 0.07 mg is ordered for a 0.7 kg infant. Hydralazine is available as 20 mg/ml, so a 0.07 mg dose equals 0.0035 ml. A 1:100 dilution is required to measure this dose accurately.

1. In two separate syringes, draw up the following:

   • 0.1 ml of hydralazine (= 2 mg)
   • 9.9 ml of diluent

2. Inject the hydralazine into the diluent syringe and mix well. The new hydralazine concentration is 2 mg/10 ml (= 0.2 mg/ml). The volume needed for a dose of 0.07 mg—0.35 ml—can now be measured accurately.

Calculations of Dextrose Infusion Rates in mg/kg/minute

Neonates are very sensitive to minor changes in dextrose infusion rates, resulting in hyperglycemia or hypoglycemia. The mg/kg/minute rate is the most precise way to monitor and regulate dextrose infusions with the least fluctuation in serum glucose level. The concentration of dextrose alone does not really indicate how much the infant receives per unit time if rate and body weight are not considered.

Very low birth weight infants may tolerate only 3–5 mg/kg/minute. Preterm infants typically tolerate 5–8 mg/kg/minute. Infants receiving parenteral nutrition may gradually increase their tolerance to 12–16 mg/kg/minute or more. Infants of diabetic mothers with hypoglycemia at birth may require 16–18 mg/kg/minute or more. Infants usually tolerate changes of 1–2 mg/kg/minute per day well.

Equation A-5 was derived to simplify dextrose infusion rate calculations.[2] The equation takes into account percent dextrose, rate, and body weight and can be entered into a programmable calculator for routine, repeated use or calculated by hand. Dextrose from all sources should be considered, such as from the maintenance infusate plus dopamine diluted in D_5W.

Equation A-5

$$mg/kg/minute = \frac{\% \times rate \times 0.167}{kg}$$

where: % = concentration of dextrose infusing (as a *whole number*)
rate = infusion rate in ml/hour
0.167 = constant
kg = the infant's body weight in kilograms

Example: A 1.5 kg infant is receiving dextrose 10 percent at 5 ml/hour. What is the mg/kg/minute infusion rate?

$$mg/kg/minute = \frac{10\ (\%) \times 5\ (ml/hour) \times 0.167}{1.5\ (kg)} = 5.6\ mg/kg/minute$$

APPENDICES

APPENDICES

CALCULATING PERCENT DEXTROSE

Example: The same infant now requires fluid restriction, and the IV rate must be reduced to 4 ml/hour. What dextrose concentration is required to maintain the same mg/kg/minute dextrose infusion rate?

In **Equation A-6**, rearrange Equation A-5 to solve for percent dextrose:

$$\% = \frac{mg/kg/minute \times kg}{rate \times 0.167}$$

Equation A-6

$$\% = \frac{5.6 \ (mg/kg/minute) \times 1.5 \ (kg)}{4 \ (ml/hour) \times 0.167} = dextrose \ 12.5\%$$

REFERENCES

1. Zenk KE. 1980. Dosage calculations for drugs administered by infusion. *American Journal of Hospital Pharmacy* 37(10): 1304.

2. Zenk KE. 1984. Calculating dextrose infusion rates in mg/kg/minute. *PeriScope* August: 5–6.

Appendix B
Every-18-Hour Medication Worksheet

Patient Name and File Number

Medication: _____

Dose: _____

Starting Date: _____

00	01	02	03	04	05	06	07	08	09	10	11	12	13	14	15	16	17	18	19	20	21	22	23
D1	D1	D1	D1	D1	D1	D1	D1	D1	D1	D1	D1	D1	D1	D1	D1	D1	D1	D1	D1	D1	D1	D1	D1
18	19	20	21	22	23	00	01	02	03	04	05	06	07	08	09	10	11	12	13	14	15	16	17
D1	D1	D1	D1	D1	D1	D2	D2	D2	D2	D2	D2	D2	D2	D2	D2	D2	D2	D2	D2	D2	D2	D2	D2
12	13	14	15	16	17	18	19	20	21	22	23	00	01	02	03	04	05	06	07	08	09	10	11
D2	D2	D2	D2	D2	D2	D2	D2	D2	D2	D2	D2	D3	D3	D3	D3	D3	D3	D3	D3	D3	D3	D3	D3
06	07	08	09	10	11	12	13	14	15	16	17	18	19	20	21	22	23	00	01	02	03	04	05
D3	D3	D3	D3	D3	D3	D3	D3	D3	D3	D3	D3	D3	D3	D3	D3	D3	D3	D4	D4	D4	D4	D4	D4
00	01	02	03	04	05	06	07	08	09	10	11	12	13	14	15	16	17	18	19	20	21	22	23
D4	D4	D4	D4	D4	D4	D4	D4	D4	D4	D4	D4	D4	D4	D4	D4	D4	D4	D4	D4	D4	D4	D4	D4
18	19	20	21	22	23	00	01	02	03	04	05	06	07	08	09	10	11	12	13	14	15	16	17
D4	D4	D4	D4	D4	D4	D5	D5	D5	D5	D5	D5	D5	D5	D5	D5	D5	D5	D5	D5	D5	D5	D5	D5
12	13	14	15	16	17	18	19	20	21	22	23	00	01	02	03	04	05	06	07	08	09	10	11
D5	D5	D5	D5	D5	D5	D5	D5	D5	D5	D5	D5	D6	D6	D6	D6	D6	D6	D6	D6	D6	D6	D6	D6
06	07	08	09	10	11	12	13	14	15	16	17	18	19	20	21	22	23	00	01	02	03	04	05
D6	D6	D6	D6	D6	D6	D6	D6	D6	D6	D6	D6	D6	D6	D6	D6	D6	D6	D7	D7	D7	D7	D7	D7
00	01	02	03	04	05	06	07	08	09	10	11	12	13	14	15	16	17	18	19	20	21	22	23
D7	D7	D7	D7	D7	D7	D7	D7	D7	D7	D7	D7	D7	D7	D7	D7	D7	D7	D7	D7	D7	D7	D7	D7
18	19	20	21	22	23	00	01	02	03	04	05	06	07	08	09	10	11	12	13	14	15	16	17
D7	D7	D7	D7	D7	D7	D8	D8	D8	D8	D8	D8	D8	D8	D8	D8	D8	D8	D8	D8	D8	D8	D8	D8
12	13	14	15	16	17	18	19	20	21	22	23	00	01	02	03	04	05	06	07	08	09	10	11
D8	D8	D8	D8	D8	D8	D8	D8	D8	D8	D8	D8	D9	D9	D9	D9	D9	D9	D9	D9	D9	D9	D9	D9
06	07	08	09	10	11	12	13	14	15	16	17	18	19	20	21	22	23	00	01	02	03	04	05
D9	D9	D9	D9	D9	D9	D9	D9	D9	D9	D9	D9	D9	D9	D9	D9	D9	D9	D10	D10	D10	D10	D10	D10
00	01	02	03	04	05	06	07	08	09	10	11	12	13	14	15	16	17	18	19	20	21	22	23
D10	D10	D10	D10	D10	D10	D10	D10	D10	D10	D10	D10	D10	D10	D10	D10	D10	D10	D10	D10	D10	D10	D10	D10

D = Day
00 = Midnight

Instructions

1. Fill out the top of the form, including the date the form was initiated.
2. Select the time schedule corresponding to your starting time.
3. Follow the lines vertically.
4. If the administration times change, start a new sheet.
5. Start the form on the hour, not the half-hour.
6. Cross off the time as each dose is given.

Example: For gentamicin every 18 hours with a starting time of 0800, begin on day 1 (D1) at 0800, the next dose is due on day 2 (D2) at 0200, the third dose is due at 2000 on D2, and the fourth on day 3 (D3) at 1400, etc.

From: Yi K, Koeppel RM, and Zenk KE. 1993. Every 18-hour medication worksheet. *Neonatal Network* 12(8): 47. Reprinted by permission.

APPENDICES

APPENDICES

APPENDIX C
IV DRUG ADMINISTRATION METHODS

Infants, especially preterm infants, are particularly vulnerable to errors caused by faulty drug administration techniques. There has been an increasing awareness of the problems associated with accurate delivery of the small volumes of drugs and fluids these infants receive, and improved techniques are available. For example, IV pumps available for neonates today are much superior to those available a few years ago. This appendix provides some information on safe and accurate delivery of drugs via methods commonly used to administer intravenous medications and fluids to infants—syringe pump, IV push, retrograde, and burette—and discusses ways to avoid errors when making serial dilutions of concentrated medications.

SYRINGE PUMP

The syringe pump method of drug delivery is the one against which others are measured. It offers the most control over drug administration and decreases the potential for overdosing (and thus toxicity) or underdosing (and suboptimal efficacy). A syringe pump designed specifically for neonates should be used, and the pump should provide a steady, continuous flow, delivering the drug accurately in increments of 0.1 ml. The pump should have built-in safeguards against an uncontrolled flow rate and an occlusion alarm that is sensitive to low pressure. The pump should be compatible with syringe sizes from 1 to 60 ml and with low-volume tubing. It should have sturdy, heavy-duty plugs, cords, and receptacles.

To ensure accurate drug delivery, connect the syringe pump close to the patient, using low-volume tubing. The site of connection is very important in determining the speed and completeness of IV drug administration, especially in preterm infants where IV rates are very slow.[1]

Because the syringe pump method is the most accurate method of administration, it should be used for drugs given by continuous infusion (such as dopamine and nitroprusside), for drugs given in volumes >5 ml (such as intravenous fat emulsion and vancomycin), and for drugs given over a prescribed period of time (such as gentamicin). A syringe pump should also be used when incompatibility is a concern, such as when giving calcium with sodium bicarbonate or parenteral nutrition with amphotericin B.[2–4]

IV PUSH

The IV push (IVP) method of drug administration—generally defined as administration over 5 minutes or less—may be used with certain medications (e.g., ampicillin) to minimize the time the line is interrupted, thus leaving more time for infusion of nutrients or maintenance IV fluid. Of the IV administration methods, IV push requires the most skill and knowledge because of the risks involved. Injecting certain drugs too fast can cause circulatory and respiratory collapse, dysrhythmias, and even cardiac arrest. Some drugs can damage vascular walls, leading to phlebitis or IV extravasation.

FIGURE C-1 ◆ **RETROGRADE METHOD OF DRUG DELIVERY.**

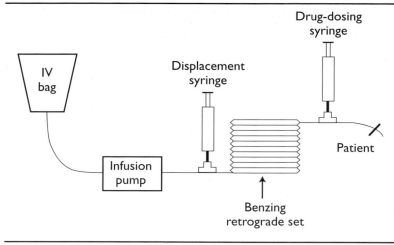

Courtesy of Medex Inc., Dublin, Ohio.

To minimize the risks of IVP administration, consult drug monograph guidelines on rate of infusion and concentration before administration. Hospitals should develop an approved list of selected medications that can be given IVP by RNs. Other IVP drugs should be administered by a physician. Most drugs should be infused over a period of at least 1 minute: the approximate amount of time it takes for blood to circulate throughout the infant's body. This ensures maximum dilution of the drug in the circulatory system. However, some drugs (e.g., adenosine) must be given very rapidly over a few seconds. Other drugs should not be given by IV push, but must be infused over 30–60 minutes.

RETROGRADE

The retrograde method of infusion reduces the number of IV access sites needed and allows administration of medications without an increase in fluid intake. In this method, a Benzing retrograde administration set (BR-10, Medex Inc., Duluth, Georgia), consisting of 2 three-way stopcocks with a segment of coiled low-volume tubing between them, is connected to the patient's main IV line. The drug-dosing syringe is attached to the stopcock closer to the patient, and that stopcock is turned off to the patient. Next, the displacement syringe is connected to the other stopcock, and that stopcock is turned off to the IV bag. The medication is introduced through the drug-dosing syringe in a retrograde direction (away from the patient and into the coil). This causes ejection of an equal volume of fluid into the displacement syringe. The infant's fluid intake ultimately remains the same (Figure C-1).[5]

To infuse the drug, turn off the stopcocks to the two syringes. The drug is usually diluted in a volume that will allow it to be delivered in 30 minutes. Thus, with a

3 ml/hour flow rate, the medication injected would be diluted to 1.5 ml; with a 10 ml/hour flow rate, the drug injected would be diluted to 5 ml. When the IV fluid and the drug are incompatible, a fluid barrier of 0.2 ml of dextrose can be used. To avoid loss of drug in the displacement syringe, do not let the dose volume exceed one-half the volume of the retrograde tubing.

Advantages of the retrograde infusion method are that it (1) saves the nursing time required to set up and disconnect a syringe pump, (2) standardizes the amount and type of diluent, (3) reduces the number of IV lines required, (4) eliminates the risk of syringe pump dysfunction, (5) simplifies fluid calculations and charting, (6) reduces the risk of fluid overload because extra fluid is not given with each dose of medication, and (7) reduces the expense of purchasing syringe pumps and administration sets.

The retrograde method should be considered for most drugs given IV over 30 minutes, such as gentamicin, amikacin, cephalosporins, aminophylline, caffeine, and bolus doses of calcium gluconate.[3,5,6]

BURETTE

In the burette method, the drug is injected into and infused with a compatible maintenance solution in the burette. This method is not usually recommended in neonates because, at their low IV infusion rates, infants may not receive the drug for several hours. For example, if the flow rate is 5 ml/hour and standard tubing (which holds, for example, 10 ml of IV fluid) is used, it would be 2 hours before the infant received the drug. In practice, it takes longer than that because drugs tend to float up the IV tubing and infuse more slowly than the IV solution.[2] (Gould and Roberts have shown that as much as 38 percent of the total drug administered may be lost in discarded IV sets.)[7] Delay in drug delivery resulting from low flow rates may lead to inaccurate estimation of the times when peak and/or trough levels occur, measurement of drug levels at inappropriate times, and inappropriate changes of drug dose. The result can be overdose toxicity or underdosing and lack of efficacy.[8]

Low-volume tubing (internal diameter of 0.06–0.14 cm) should be used to ensure optimal delivery of drugs at rates of <10 ml/hour. This type of tubing permits adequate mixing of drug and primary fluid because of higher flow velocity and increased shear forces.[9]

SERIAL DILUTION AND ACCURACY

Although pediatric dosage forms are becoming more available, many medications are manufactured with only adult dosing in mind. Serial dilutions must sometimes be made to prepare doses for infants. This provides opportunities for medication errors. If the dead space in the syringe is not appreciated, the dose delivered may be much larger than intended. The result is dilution intoxication, which has been described with digoxin. Investigators measured the amount of digoxin contained in the calibrated chamber and dead space of a TB syringe filled to the 0.05 ml level and found that it averaged 14 mcg (range 12–18 mcg), compared with the 5 mcg contained in the intended 0.05 ml dosage volume (using digoxin 100 mcg/ml). If the drug contained in the dead space were drawn into the actual delivery volume, inadvertent overdose would result.[10] An inadvertent overdose of morphine in a neonate has also been reported from inappropriate dilution technique.[11] Use a two-syringe technique to reduce errors. See Appendix A: Simplified Neonatal Calculations for further information on preparing 1:10 and 1:100 dilutions.

REFERENCES

1. Roberts RJ. 1981. Intravenous administration of medication in pediatric patients: Problems and solutions. *Pediatric Clinics of North America* 28(1): 23–34.

2. Zenk KE. 1986. Special delivery: Administering IV antibiotics to children. *Nursing 86* 16(12): 50–52.

3. Zenk KE. 1987. Intravenous drug delivery in infants with limited IV access and fluid restriction. *American Journal of Hospital Pharmacy* 44(11): 2542–2545.

4. Nahata MC, and Powell D. 1984. Effect of infusion methods on tobramycin serum concentrations in newborn infants. *Journal of Pediatrics* 104(1): 136–138.

5. Benzing G, and Loggie J. 1973. A new retrograde method for administering drugs intravenously. *Pediatrics* 52(3): 420–425.

6. Zenk KE, Cohen JL, and Craft MJ. 1985. Predictability of gentamicin infusions in infants using a new retrograde infusion device (abstract). ASHP Midyear Clinical Meeting, New Orleans.

7. Gould T, and Roberts RJ. 1979. Therapeutic problems arising from the use of the intravenous route for drug administration. *Journal of Pediatrics* 95(3): 465–471.

8. Leff RD, and Roberts RJ. 1982. Methods of intravenous drug administration in the pediatric patient. *Journal of Pediatrics* 98(4): 631–635.

9. Giacoia GP. 1987. Intravenous drug administration to low birth weight infants. *Clinical Pediatrics* 26(1): 25–29.

10. Berman W Jr, et al. 1978. Inadvertent overadministration of digoxin to low-birth-weight infants. *Journal of Pediatrics* 92(6): 1024–1025.

11. Zenk KE, and Anderson S. 1982. Improving the accuracy of mini-volume injections. *Infusion* January/February: 7–12.

APPENDIX D
UMBILICAL ARTERIAL CATHETER (UAC)
ADMINISTRATION OF DRUGS

The literature contains limited data to guide us in deciding which drugs may be infused via umbilical lines or other arterial lines (Table D-1).

- *Radial Arterial Line.* No medications should be infused via a radial arterial line because the direction of flow is toward the hand. Gangrene and loss of digits have occurred.

- *Umbilical Venous Catheter (UVC).* Use of the UVC for administration of drugs is the safest route when choosing among radial, umbilical arterial, or umbilical venous. However, there are risks even with this route. If catheter position is not correct, drugs and/or solutions can be introduced into the catheter in the liver area and may enter the liver vasculature and cause necrosis of liver tissue.

- *Umbilical Arterial Catheter (UAC).* Use of the UAC for administration of drugs is more dangerous than using the UVC because the UAC permits introduction of drugs and/or solutions *directly* into some of the major arteries (e.g., the renal artery), causing subsequent necrosis of the organ involved.

Figure D-1 shows the placement of a UAC and a UVC.

Drugs *not* recommended for UAC administration: Those that have any of these characteristics: They cause vasoconstriction, they are very irritating, or they are extremely hyperosmolar. Very irritating drugs such as phenytoin can cause vasospasm or irritation. It is risky to infuse vasopressors (i.e., dopamine, epinephrine, norepinephrine) via the UAC due to their α-adrenergic (vasoconstricting) effects on the skin and splanchnic (mesenteric) bed.

- Phentolamine (Regitine) is an α-adrenergic blocking agent (vasodilating) that may help reverse the vasoconstricting effects of these drugs.

- Tolazoline (Priscoline) has also been useful in this respect.[1,2]

Because of the potential risks, the UAC should be the last choice for infusing medications and parenteral solutions. The UVC, peripheral lines, or central venous lines are preferred.

For double-lumen umbilical catheters, infuse compatible solutions through the smaller lumen. Use the larger lumen for medication administration and for solutions incompatible with drugs infusing into the smaller lumen.

Line Flushing: Heparin 10 units is used every 8 hours for infants weighing more than 1,000 gm. Use 5 units if weight is less than 1,000 gm. Flushes should be timed with medications if possible. Dilute heparin dose with 0.5–1 ml of dextrose or saline. (See monograph on heparin sodium.)

AVOIDING PROBLEMS WITH UAC DRUG ADMINISTRATION

Physician/Nurse Practitioner/Physician Assistant: State the route of administration; don't assume that others know what you intend. Be cognizant of which

APPENDICES

TABLE D-1 ◆ UMBILICAL ARTERIAL CATHETER (UAC) ADMINISTRATION OF DRUGS

Drug	UAC Administration (Yes or No)	Comments	Reference
Albumin	Yes	Survey showed UAC administration in more than 75% of institutions.	3,8
Aminophylline	Yes	Survey showed UAC administration in more than 75% of institutions.	3,8
Ampicillin	Yes	Survey showed UAC administration in more than 75% of institutions.	3,8
Blood products	Yes		3,8
Caffeine	Yes		9
Calcium gluconate bolus	No	Very irritating.	9
Cefotaxime	Yes		9
Dextrose*	Yes	Maximum UAC dextrose $D_{15}W$ in the neonatal unit at the University of California Irvine Medical Center (UCIMC). Survey showed UAC administration in more than 75% of institutions. In the survey, 24% of units used up to $D_{25}W$ in UAC.	3,8,9
Dobutamine	No	This drug has primarily β_1 stimulating effect on the heart, but because it has a little α-adrenergic (vasoconstricting) effect, avoidance of UAC administration is preferred.	9
Dopamine	No	Adverse effects can vary from mild and reversible to severe, resulting in permanent scarring and possibly NEC. Survey showed UAC dopamine administration considered unsafe in more than 45.5% of institutions.	3,8
Epinephrine	No	It is risky to infuse vasopressors (e.g., dopamine, epinephrine, norepinephrine) via the UAC due to their α-adrenergic (vasoconstricting) effects on the skin and splanchnic (mesenteric) bed. Survey showed UAC epinephrine administration considered unsafe in more than 42.4% of institutions.	3,8
Furosemide	Yes	Survey showed UAC administration in more than 75% of institutions.	3,8
Heparin	Yes	Survey showed UAC administration in more than 75% of institutions.	3,8
Indomethacin	No	May alter blood flow velocity in the mesenteric artery.	4

* Increasing amounts of dextrose in solution increase the osmolarity of the solution.

APPENDICES

TABLE D-1 ◆ UMBILICAL ARTERIAL CATHETER (UAC) ADMINISTRATION OF DRUGS (CONTINUED)

Drug	UAC Administration (Yes or No)	Comments	Reference
Maintenance IVs with dextrose, electrolytes, and calcium	Yes	Maximum UAC dextrose $D_{15}W$ in the unit at UCIMC.	3,8,9
Norepinephrine (levarterenol)	No	It is risky to infuse vasopressors (e.g., dopamine, epinephrine, norepinephrine) via the UAC due to their α-adrenergic (vasoconstricting) effects on the skin and splanchnic (mesenteric) bed.	3
Pancuronium	Yes	Survey showed UAC administration in more than 75% of institutions.	3,8
Parenteral nutrition	Yes	Maximum UAC dextrose $D_{15}W$ in the unit at UCIMC. Survey showed UAC administration in more than 75% of institutions.	3,8,9
Phenobarbital and other barbiturates	No	May cause severe tissue damage. Possible causes: spasm of vessel, intimal damage and thrombosis, arterial blockage by acid crystals, platelet aggregation, red cell hemolysis.	5–8
Phentolamine (Regitine)	Yes	An α-adrenergic blocking agent (vasodilating) that may help reverse the vasoconstricting effects of drugs like dopamine, epinephrine, and norepinephrine. Causes vascular smooth muscle relaxation.	1–3
Phenytoin	No	Incompatible with dextrose and heparin. Line occlusion is very likely. Alkaline pH of phenytoin causes severe tissue damage in extravasation. Very irritating.	3
Sodium bicarbonate	Yes	Survey showed UAC administration in more than 75% of institutions.	3,8
Tolazoline	Yes	An α-adrenergic blocking agent (vasodilating) that may help reverse the vasoconstricting effects of drugs like dopamine, epinephrine, and norepinephrine. Causes vascular smooth muscle relaxation.	1–3

APPENDICES

FIGURE D-1 ◆ **PLACEMENT OF (A) UMBILICAL ARTERY CATHETER AND (B) UMBILICAL VEIN CATHETER. (C) CROSS-SECTION OF UMBILICAL CORD SHOWING POSITION OF UMBILICAL VESSELS.**

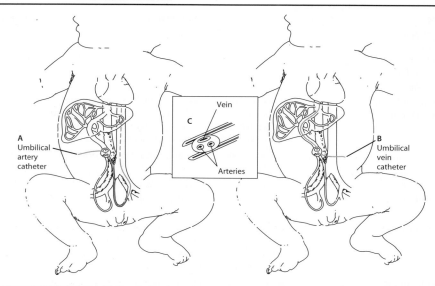

A
Umbilical
artery
catheter

B
Umbilical
vein
catheter

C

Vein

Arteries

From: Pierog SH, and Ferrera A. 1976. *Medical Care of the Sick Newborn,* 2nd ed., St. Louis: Mosby-Year Book, 317, 319. Reprinted by permission.

drugs are infusing into which lines. Avoid infusing medications into the UAC whenever possible. Avoid UAC administration of vasoconstricting, very irritating, or extremely hyperosmolar medications if possible. Examine the infant with diaper and blanket removed so that blanching in the groin area is apparent. Observe for bluish and cold extremities.

Nurse: Read orders carefully for route of administration. Be suspicious of orders for the UAC route. Verify proper line placement in a large vessel before UAC administration of drugs. Double-check which medications are infusing into which lines at change of shift or when connecting new IVs. Label all lines with infusion site at the proximal end when connecting new IVs. Label all lines close to insertion into the baby with the name of the drug or solution infusing. Develop guidelines with physicians and pharmacists on drugs that may be given via the UAC. Table D-1 provides guidelines for when the UAC should be avoided for administration of certain drugs and may be helpful in developing policies for your unit. Before giving a drug via the UAC, check nursing policies and procedures to see if the drug or solution can be infused by that route. Examine the infant in good lighting with diapers and blankets removed so that blanching in the groin area is apparent.

Pharmacist: Ask the nurse which line will be used when answering questions regarding compatibility and when reviewing drug regimens at the bedside. When reviewing medication orders, review the route of administration as well as the dose.

REFERENCES

1. Weinberg G, Brion LP, and Vega-Richf CR. 1990. Dangers of arterial catheters in critically ill neonates. *Pediatrics* 85(4): 627–628.

2. Heath RE. 1986. Vasospasm in the neonate: Response to tolazoline infusion. *Pediatrics* 77(3): 405–408.

3. Zenk KE, Noerr B, and Ward R. 1994. Severe sequelae from umbilical arterial catheter administration of dopamine. *Neonatal Network* 13(5): 89–91.

4. Coombs RC, et al. 1990. Gut blood flow velocities in the newborn: Effects of patent ductus arteriosus and parenteral indomethacin. *Archives of Disease in Childhood* 65(10 spec. no.): 1067–1071. (Comment in *Archives of Disease in Childhood,* 1991, 66[5]: 666–667.)

5. Ellertson DG, Lazarus HM, and Auerbach R. 1973. Patterns of acute vascular injury after intra-arterial barbiturate injection. *American Journal of Surgery* 126(6): 813–817.

6. Albo D Jr, et al. 1970. Effect of intra-arterial injections of barbiturates. *American Journal of Surgery* 120(5): 676–678.

7. Klatte EC, Brooks AL, and Rhamy RK. 1969. Toxicity of intra-arterial barbiturates and tranquilizing drugs. *Radiology* 92(9): 700–704.

8. Hodding JH. 1990. Medication administration via the umbilical arterial catheter: A survey of standard practices and review of the literature. *American Journal of Perinatology* 7(4): 329–332.

9. *Neonatal Services Policy and Procedure Manual.* 1998. Care of the patient with umbilical lines (UAC/UVC). University of California Irvine Medical Center.

APPENDICES

Appendix E
Y-Site Compatibility of Common NICU Drugs

Y-site administration of medications is often required for NICU infants because of limited IV access and because of numerous concurrent medications. The coinfusing drug should be injected at a site as close to the infant as possible to reduce contact time of the two medications and thereby reduce the risk of incompatibility and precipitation. The two types of incompatibilities are (1) visual (physical changes in the solution—precipitate, haze, or color change—and (2) nonvisual (chemical inactivation). Limitations and contradictions of compatibility studies are in part due to differences in buffering systems, preservatives, vehicles, temperatures, concentrations, and order of mixing. Compatibility tables usually describe the effects of mixing only two drugs, whereas three or more medications often need to be coinfused.

General rules for coinfusion include: (1) Avoid coinfusion if there is no compatibility information available; (2) when limited IV access exists, consider alternatives to administering incompatible medications such as using IV push, changing to the oral route, or even discontinuing the medication if medical condition warrants; (3) observe for signs of incompatibility while drugs coinfuse, even if positive documentation on compatibility of the drug combination is found. This appendix provides compatibility information on 70 medications commonly used in the NICU.

Please consult your pharmacist or a more detailed resource on compatibility such as Trissel's *Handbook on Injectable Drugs*[1] for current and more detailed information specific to your patient.

Y-Site Compatibility of Common NICU Drugs

Medication	Compatible with	Incompatible with
Acyclovir[1-3]	Ampicillin, cefotaxime, ceftazidime, chloramphenicol, cimetidine, clindamycin, dexamethasone, dextrose, gentamicin, lorazepam, morphine, nafcillin, potassium chloride, ranitidine, sodium bicarbonate, sodium chloride, vancomycin	Dobutamine, dopamine, parenteral nutrition*
Albumin[1-3]	Blood, dextrose, parenteral nutrition,* plasma, sodium chloride, sodium lactate	Midazolam, vancomycin *Note: Do not dilute albumin with sterile water because it may reduce the tonicity of the solution and lead to fatal hemolysis and acute renal failure.*
Alprostadil (PGE$_1$)[4]	Aminophylline, atropine, calcium chloride, cimetidine, clindamycin, dexamethasone, digoxin, dobutamine, dopamine, epinephrine, furosemide, gentamicin, glycopyrrolate, heparin, hydralazine, hydrocortisone, isoproterenol, lidocaine, metoclopramide, metronidazole, midazolam, morphine, nitroglycerin, nitroprusside, pancuronium, penicillin G potassium, phenobarbital, potassium chloride, ranitidine, sodium chloride, verapamil	No data available
Amikacin[1-3,5]	Dextrose, dexamethasone, enalaprilat, fluconazole, furosemide, heparin *(in low concentrations of 0.5 to 1 unit/ml used to maintain IV line patency)*, lorazepam, magnesium, midazolam, morphine, parenteral nutrition,* sodium chloride	Amphotericin B, ampicillin, chlorothiazide, heparin *(in high concentrations of more than 1 unit/ml used for systemic anticoagulation and in some heparin flushes)*, phenytoin
Aminophylline 1-4,6,7	Alprostadil, atracurium, calcium gluconate, ceftazidime, cimetidine, dexamethasone, dextrose, dopamine, famotidine, fluconazole, furosemide, heparin, hydrocortisone, lidocaine, methicillin, methylprednisolone, metoclopramide, morphine, nitroglycerin, pancuronium, phenobarbital, potassium chloride, ranitidine, sodium bicarbonate, sodium chloride, tolazoline, vancomycin, vecuronium	Atracurium, cefotaxime, clindamycin, dobutamine, doxapram, epinephrine, fat emulsion, hydralazine, insulin, isoproterenol, meperidine, morphine, norepinephrine, parenteral nutrition,* penicillin G, potassium

Y-Site Compatibility of Common NICU Drugs (continued)

Medication	Compatible with	Incompatible with
Amphotericin B[1–3,6,8–10]	Dextrose (5, 10, 15, and 20 percent), famotidine, fluconazole, heparin, hydrocortisone, sodium bicarbonate *Note: Amphotericin B often creates IV access problems because it must be infused alone; it also creates fluid and nutrition problems because it is irritating to peripheral veins and must be infused in dilute concentrations of 0.1 mg/ml over a prolonged period of time—usually 4–6 hours.* *Stability of amphotericin B in dextrose concentrations higher than 5 percent has recently been demonstrated. Use of such concentrations helps reduce the risk of hypoglycemia during the infusion period and improves caloric intake.* *Studies have shown that amphotericin B in 5 percent dextrose is stable at concentrations higher than 0.1 mg/ml (0.25, 0.92, 1.2, 1.4 mg/ml) for use in fluid-restricted adults through central venous catheters.[8,9] Studies are under way to assess the safety and efficacy of these higher concentrations in infants.*	Most drugs; solutions containing sodium chloride, potassium, or preservatives; calcium; fat emulsion intravenous; parenteral nutrition* *Note: Use dextrose, not sodium chloride, flushes before and after amphotericin B administration.*
Ampicillin[1–3,6,7]	Acyclovir, enalaprilat, famotidine, furosemide, heparin, hydrocortisone, insulin, magnesium, morphine, multivitamins, phytonadione, potassium chloride, theophylline, tolazoline *Note: Ampicillin is more stable in sodium chloride or in sterile water for injection than in dextrose. Do not reconstitute with dextrose solutions. When administering ampicillin with parenteral nutrition, it is probably safest to temporarily discontinue the parenteral nutrition, and administer the ampicillin by IV push over 3–5 minutes. Flush the IV line with saline before and after administration.*	Amikacin, dopamine, epinephrine, fluconazole, gentamicin, hydralazine, midazolam, parenteral nutrition,* sodium bicarbonate, sodium lactate
Atracurium[1,2]	Cimetidine, dobutamine, dopamine, epinephrine, fentanyl, gentamicin, heparin, hydrocortisone, isoproterenol, lorazepam, midazolam, morphine, nitroglycerin, nitroprusside, ranitidine, vancomycin	Aminophylline, diazepam, lactated Ringer's, sodium bicarbonate
Aztreonam[1]	Amikacin, aminophylline, ampicillin, bumetanide, cefazolin, cefotaxime, ceftazidime, ceftriaxone, clindamycin, dexamethasone, dextrose, famotidine, fluconazole, furosemide, gentamicin, heparin, insulin, metoclopramide, morphine, potassium chloride, ranitidine, sodium bicarbonate, sodium chloride	Acyclovir, amphotericin B, lorazepam, metronidazole, nafcillin

Y-Site Compatibility of Common NICU Drugs (CONTINUED)

Medication	Compatible with	Incompatible with
Bumetanide[1]	Aztreonam, D₅W, doxapram, furosemide, lorazepam, morphine, sodium chloride	Dobutamine, midazolam
Calcium chloride[1-4]	Alprostadil, dobutamine, dopamine, epinephrine, isoproterenol, lidocaine, morphine, norepinephrine, penicillin G potassium	Amphotericin B, fat emulsion intravenous, sodium bicarbonate
Calcium gluconate 1-3,7,11-16	Amikacin, aminophylline, cefazolin, dobutamine, epinephrine, erythromycin, famotidine, furosemide, heparin, heparin with hydrocortisone, labetalol, lidocaine, magnesium, meropenem, midazolam, penicillin G potassium, phenobarbital, potassium chloride, tobramycin, tolazoline, vancomycin	Amphotericin B, fluconazole, indomethacin, methylprednisolone, metoclopramide, sodium bicarbonate
	Note: Compatibility of calcium with phosphate in parenteral nutrition depends on a number of factors.	
Cefotaxime[1,2,7]	Acyclovir, aztreonam, famotidine, heparin, lorazepam, magnesium, meperidine, metronidazole, midazolam, morphine, parenteral nutrition,* tolazoline	Doxapram, fluconazole, vancomycin
Cefoxitin[1,2]	Acyclovir, aztreonam, famotidine, fluconazole, magnesium, meperidine, morphine, parenteral nutrition*	No data available
Ceftazidime[1-3,17]	Aminophylline, aztreonam, enalaprilat, famotidine, heparin, meperidine, metronidazole, morphine, ranitidine	Fluconazole, midazolam
Chlorothiazide[1-3]	Cimetidine, dextrose, lidocaine, nafcillin, ranitidine, sodium bicarbonate, sodium chloride	Amikacin, blood and blood derivatives, hydralazine, insulin, morphine, parenteral nutrition,* vancomycin *Note: Chlorothiazide should not be combined with drugs known to be unstable in alkaline media.*
Cimetidine 1,2,4,7,16	Acyclovir, alprostadil, aminophylline, atracurium, aztreonam, diazepam, enalaprilat, epinephrine, fat emulsion intravenous, fluconazole, gentamicin, heparin, inamrinone, isoproterenol, lidocaine, midazolam, morphine, pancuronium, parenteral nutrition,* sodium bicarbonate, tolazoline, vecuronium	Amphotericin B, cephalosporins, indomethacin, pentobarbital, phenobarbital
Clindamycin[1-4,6]	Alprostadil, aztreonam, enalaprilat, gentamicin, heparin, meperidine, midazolam, morphine, parenteral nutrition,* penicillin G potassium	Aminophylline, ampicillin, barbiturates, calcium gluconate bolus, fluconazole, magnesium sulfate bolus, phenytoin, tobramycin

Y-Site Compatibility of Common NICU Drugs (CONTINUED)

Medication	Compatible with	Incompatible with
Dexamethasone 1–4	Acyclovir, alprostadil, amikacin, aminophylline, aztreonam, famotidine, fluconazole, heparin, heparin with hydrocortisone, lidocaine, lorazepam, metoclopramide, morphine, nafcillin, parenteral nutrition,* potassium chloride, ranitidine, sodium bicarbonate	Doxapram, midazolam, vancomycin
Digoxin 1–4	Alprostadil, cimetidine, dextrose, famotidine, furosemide, heparin, heparin with hydrocortisone, lidocaine, midazolam, morphine, parenteral nutrition,* potassium chloride, ranitidine, sodium chloride *Note: Even when it is compatible with other drugs being used, it is best to infuse this potent and important medication alone, if possible, to ensure accurate delivery to the patient. Administer over 5 minutes.*	Dobutamine, doxapram, fluconazole
Dobutamine 1–4,7,16,18	Alprostadil, atracurium, aztreonam, bretylium, calcium chloride, calcium gluconate, dextrose (5 and 10 percent), dopamine, enalaprilat, epinephrine, famotidine, fluconazole, insulin, isoproterenol, lidocaine, lorazepam, magnesium sulfate, morphine, nitroglycerin, nitroprusside, pancuronium, parenteral nutrition,* potassium chloride, ranitidine, sodium chloride, tolazoline, vecuronium *Note: Dobutamine is compatible with dopamine, lidocaine, nitroglycerin, and nitroprusside in any combination.*	Acyclovir, aminophylline, digoxin, doxapram, furosemide, indomethacin, phenytoin, phytonadione, sodium bicarbonate
Dopamine 1,2,7,16,18	Alprostadil, aminophylline, atracurium, dextrose, dobutamine, doxapram, flumazenil, heparin, hydrocortisone, lidocaine, nitroglycerin, nitroprusside, oxacillin, pancuronium, parenteral nutrition,* potassium chloride, ranitidine, sodium chloride, tolazoline, vecuronium *Note: Dopamine is compatible with dobutamine, lidocaine, nitroglycerin, and nitroprusside in any combination.*	Acyclovir, amphotericin B, ampicillin, indomethacin, insulin, sodium bicarbonate
Doxapram 1–3	Amikacin, bumetanide, cimetidine, dopamine, epinephrine, phytonadione, pyridoxine, tobramycin *Note: Doxapram has been coinfused into a central line with fat emulsion intravenous and parenteral nutrition without precipitation or apparent loss of efficacy. The parenteral nutrition, fat emulsion intravenous, and doxapram are all hung with each day's tubing change to reduce the risk of line contamination.[19]*	Aminophylline, cefotaxime, dexamethasone, diazepam, digoxin, dobutamine, furosemide, hydrocortisone, methylprednisolone

APPENDICES

Y-Site Compatibility of Common NICU Drugs (CONTINUED)

Medication	Compatible with	Incompatible with
Epinephrine[1-4]	Alprostadil, amikacin, atracurium, calcium chloride, calcium gluconate, cimetidine, dextrose, dobutamine, dopamine, doxapram, famotidine, fentanyl, furosemide, heparin, hydrocortisone, lorazepam, midazolam, morphine, nitroglycerin, pancuronium, phytonadione, potassium chloride, ranitidine, sodium chloride	Aminophylline, ampicillin, sodium bicarbonate
Erythromycin lactobionate[1-3,6]	Acyclovir, enalaprilat, famotidine, hydrocortisone, labetalol, lidocaine, lorazepam, magnesium sulfate, meperidine, methicillin, midazolam, morphine, multivitamins, parenteral nutrition,* penicillin G potassium, potassium chloride, sodium bicarbonate	Ampicillin, fluconazole, metoclopramide
Famotidine[1-3]	Acyclovir, aminophylline, amphotericin B, ampicillin, aztreonam, calcium gluconate, cefotaxime, ceftazidime, ceftriaxone, dexamethasone, digoxin, dobutamine, dopamine, enalaprilat, epinephrine, erythromycin, fat emulsion intravenous, fluconazole, flumazenil, gentamicin, heparin, hydrocortisone, insulin, isoproterenol, lidocaine, lorazepam, magnesium sulfate, methylprednisolone, metoclopramide, midazolam, morphine, nafcillin, nitroglycerin, parenteral nutrition,* potassium chloride, sodium bicarbonate	No data available
Fat emulsion, intravenous[1-3]	Ampicillin, cefoxitin, cimetidine, clindamycin, digoxin, dopamine, erythromycin, famotidine, furosemide, gentamicin, heparin, hydrocortisone, isoproterenol, lidocaine, norepinephrine, parenteral nutrition,* penicillin G potassium, ranitidine, ticarcillin, tobramycin	Amikacin, amphotericin B, phenytoin. Undiluted 10 percent calcium gluconate used for bolus administration is incompatible with fat emulsion intravenous, but calcium gluconate that has been diluted in PN or IV solutions is usually compatible.

Note: Incompatibility can cause the fat emulsion intravenous to crack, leaving an oil and water layer, aggregation, creaming, flocculation of solution, and/or globule formation. Fat that is not emulsified must not be infused IV. Observe fat emulsion for oiling out and discontinue immediately if this occurs. If compatibility is uncertain, temporarily stop the lipid infusion. Flush the line with dextrose or sodium chloride before and after the medication.

When fat emulsion intravenous is coinfused with parenteral nutrition, the fat emulsion line should be kept higher than the parenteral nutrition line because the lower specific gravity of the fat would allow it to run up the nutrition line. If a syringe pump is used to administer the intravenous fat, position the syringe tip above the mixture point to avoid entry of parenteral nutrition into the syringe.[20]

Note: Unrecognized calcium phosphate precipitate in a 3-in-1 parenteral nutrition mixture (protein, carbohydrate, and fat emulsion together in the same bag) has resulted in patient death. Coinfusion by Y-site is preferred.

Neonatal Medications & Nutrition

Y-SITE COMPATIBILITY OF COMMON NICU DRUGS (CONTINUED)

Medication	Compatible with	Incompatible with
Fentanyl[1-3]	Atracurium, cimetidine, dobutamine, dopamine, epinephrine, furosemide, heparin, hydrocortisone, lorazepam, midazolam, morphine, nafcillin, nitroglycerin, pancuronium, potassium chloride, ranitidine, vecuronium	Pentobarbital
Fluconazole[1]	Acyclovir, amikacin, aminophylline, aztreonam, cimetidine, dexamethasone, dobutamine, dopamine, famotidine, gentamicin, heparin, immune globulin intravenous, lorazepam, metoclopramide, midazolam, morphine, nafcillin, nitroglycerin, parenteral nutrition,* ranitidine, tobramycin, vancomycin, vecuronium	Amphotericin B, ampicillin, calcium gluconate, cefotaxime, ceftazidime, ceftriaxone, clindamycin, diazepam, digoxin, erythromycin, furosemide
Furosemide 1-3,7,16	Alprostadil, amikacin, ampicillin, calcium gluconate, cimetidine, dexamethasone, digoxin, epinephrine, fat emulsion intravenous, fentanyl, heparin, hydrocortisone, indomethacin, lidocaine, lorazepam, morphine, nitroglycerin, parenteral nutrition,* penicillin G potassium, potassium chloride, sodium bicarbonate, tobramycin, tolazoline	Diazepam, dobutamine, doxapram, erythromycin, fluconazole, gentamicin, hydralazine, isoproterenol, metoclopramide, midazolam, vecuronium
Gentamicin[1,2,5,7]	Acyclovir, alprostadil, atracurium, cimetidine, clindamycin, enalaprilat, famotidine, fat emulsion intravenous, fluconazole, heparin (low concentrations of 0.5 to 1 units/ml that are used to maintain IV line patency), insulin, lorazepam, magnesium sulfate, meperidine, metronidazole, midazolam, morphine, pancuronium, parenteral nutrition,* penicillin G potassium, ranitidine, tolazoline, vecuronium Note: Ampicillin may degrade gentamicin when in the same blood sample tube, causing a falsely low serum gentamicin concentration reading. Separate ampicillin and gentamicin by 2 hours, or give ampicillin after gentamicin levels have been drawn.	Amphotericin B, ampicillin, furosemide, heparin (in high concentrations of more than 1 unit/ml used for systemic anticoagulation and in some heparin flushes), indomethacin, nafcillin, phenytoin
Heparin[1-4,6]	Acyclovir, alprostadil, aminophylline, ampicillin, atracurium, aztreonam, calcium gluconate, ceftazidime, cimetidine, clindamycin, dexamethasone, digoxin, dopamine, enalaprilat, epinephrine, erythromycin, famotidine, fat emulsion intravenous, fentanyl, fluconazole, furosemide, hydralazine, insulin, isoproterenol, lidocaine, lorazepam, magnesium sulfate, meperidine, methylprednisolone, metronidazole, midazolam, morphine, nafcillin, nitroglycerin, oxacillin, pancuronium, parenteral nutrition,* ranitidine, sodium bicarbonate, vecuronium Note: Minimize heparin use in the NICU as much as possible to reduce risk of intraventricular hemorrhage. Use plain (unheparinized) flushes whenever possible. When heparin flushes are needed, use heparin 2 units/ml in sodium chloride 0.45 percent to minimize heparin and sodium chloride dose.[2]	Amikacin, diazepam, gentamicin, phenytoin, tobramycin, vancomycin Note: Amikacin, gentamicin, and tobramycin with high heparin concentrations of more than 1 unit/ml are used for systemic anticoagulation and in some heparin flushes.

APPENDICES

Y-Site Compatibility of Common NICU Drugs (CONTINUED)

Medication	Compatible with	Incompatible with
Hydralazine[1-4]	Alprostadil, dobutamine, heparin, hydrocortisone, potassium chloride	Aminophylline, ampicillin, chlorothiazide, furosemide, phenobarbital
Hydrocortisone sodium succinate[1]	Acyclovir, aminophylline, ampicillin, atracurium, aztreonam, calcium gluconate, digoxin, dopamine, enalaprilat, epinephrine, famotidine, fentanyl, furosemide, heparin, hydralazine, insulin, isoproterenol, lidocaine, lorazepam, magnesium sulfate, morphine, pancuronium, parenteral nutrition,* penicillin G potassium, phytonadione, sodium bicarbonate, vecuronium	Diazepam, doxapram, midazolam, nafcillin, phenobarbital, phenytoin
Inamrinone[1-3]	Aminophylline, cimetidine, dobutamine, dopamine, epinephrine, famotidine, isoproterenol, lidocaine, nitroglycerin, nitroprusside, potassium chloride, sodium chloride (normal or one-half normal saline) *Note: Inamrinone may be coinfused by Y-site into a line that has dextrose infusing, but not diluted in dextrose when the drip is being prepared. Approximately 8 percent loss in potency occurs over 4 hours when diluted in 5 percent dextrose, and unacceptable losses occur over 24 hours, whereas very little loss occurs during the short time solutions are in contact during coinfusion. Dilute in normal saline or one-half normal saline.*	Sodium bicarbonate, dextrose, furosemide
Indomethacin[7,16]	Dextrose (2.5 and 5 percent), furosemide, insulin, nitroprusside, potassium chloride, sodium bicarbonate	Calcium gluconate, cimetidine, dextrose (7.5 and 10 percent), dobutamine, dopamine, gentamicin, parenteral nutrition,* tobramycin, tolazoline
Insulin [1-3,6,11,16,22]	Ampicillin, aztreonam, dextrose, digoxin, famotidine, gentamicin, heparin, indomethacin, lidocaine, meperidine, metoclopramide, morphine, nitroprusside, parenteral nutrition,* potassium chloride, sodium chloride, vancomycin *Note: Insulin adsorbs to the solution container, tubing, and in-line filter, causing decreased availability. The minimal reduction of loss in adsorption from adding albumin to parenteral nutrition does not justify its cost. To saturate the insulin binding sites in the infusion system, flush 10 ml or more of the insulin solution through and out the end of the tubing, discard, then begin the infusion. The amount of insulin adsorbed to the infusion system is unpredictable despite efforts to reduce adsorption; therefore, monitor blood glucose and the patient clinically and adjust the insulin dose accordingly.*	Aminophylline, dopamine, methylprednisolone, nafcillin, norepinephrine, phenobarbital, phenytoin

Y-Site Compatibility of Common NICU Drugs (CONTINUED)

Medication	Compatible with	Incompatible with
Isoproterenol [1–4,6,23]	Alprostadil, atracurium, cimetidine, dextrose, dobutamine, famotidine, fat emulsion intravenous, heparin, magnesium sulfate, pancuronium, parenteral nutrition,* potassium chloride, sodium chloride, vecuronium	Aminophylline, barbiturates, furosemide, lidocaine, sodium bicarbonate
Lidocaine [1–4,6]	Alprostadil, aminophylline, calcium gluconate, dexamethasone, dextrose, digoxin, dobutamine, dopamine, enalaprilat, famotidine, fat emulsion intravenous, heparin, insulin, metoclopramide, morphine, nitroglycerin, nitroprusside, parenteral nutrition,* penicillin G potassium, potassium chloride, ranitidine, sodium bicarbonate, sodium chloride *Note: Lidocaine is compatible with dobutamine, dopamine, nitroglycerin, and nitroprusside in any combination.*	Phenytoin
Lorazepam [1–3,23]	Acyclovir, albumin, amikacin, atracurium, bumetanide, cefotaxime, dexamethasone, dextrose (best diluent), dobutamine, dopamine, epinephrine, erythromycin, famotidine, fentanyl, furosemide, gentamicin, heparin, metronidazole, midazolam, morphine, nitroglycerin, pancuronium, potassium chloride, ranitidine, sodium chloride, vancomycin, vecuronium	Aztreonam
Magnesium sulfate [1–3]	Acyclovir, amikacin, ampicillin, aztreonam, cefotaxime, cefoxitin, clindamycin, dobutamine, enalaprilat, erythromycin, famotidine, gentamicin, heparin, hydrocortisone, insulin, labetalol, metronidazole, morphine, nafcillin, penicillin G potassium, potassium chloride, tobramycin, vancomycin	Amphotericin B, sodium bicarbonate
Methyl-prednisolone [1]	Acyclovir, aztreonam, cimetidine, clindamycin, dopamine, enalaprilat, famotidine, heparin, metoclopramide, metronidazole, midazolam, morphine, potassium chloride	Doxapram, nafcillin
Metoclopramide [1–4]	Acyclovir, alprostadil, aminophylline, aztreonam, clindamycin, dexamethasone, dextrose, famotidine, fluconazole, heparin, hydrocortisone, insulin, lidocaine, magnesium sulfate, meperidine, methylprednisolone, midazolam, morphine, parenteral nutrition,* potassium chloride, ranitidine, sodium chloride, verapamil	Ampicillin, calcium gluconate, erythromycin, furosemide, penicillin G potassium, sodium bicarbonate
Metronidazole [1–4]	Acyclovir, alprostadil, amikacin, aminophylline, cefotaxime, ceftazidime, enalaprilat, fluconazole, gentamicin, heparin, lorazepam, magnesium sulfate, meperidine, midazolam, morphine, tobramycin	Aztreonam, dopamine

Y-Site Compatibility of Common NICU Drugs (CONTINUED)

Medication	Compatible with	Incompatible with
Midazolam[1–4,23]	Alprostadil, amikacin, atracurium, calcium gluconate, cefotaxime, cimetidine, clindamycin, dextrose, digoxin, dopamine, epinephrine, erythromycin, famotidine, fentanyl, fluconazole, gentamicin, glycopyrrolate, heparin, insulin, lorazepam, meperidine, methylprednisolone, metoclopramide, metronidazole, morphine, nitroglycerin, nitroprusside, pancuronium, potassium chloride, sodium chloride, tobramycin, vancomycin, vecuronium	Albumin, ampicillin, bumetanide, ceftazidime, dexamethasone, furosemide, hydrocortisone, nafcillin, parenteral nutrition*
Morphine[1–4]	Alprostadil, amikacin, ampicillin, atracurium, aztreonam, bumetanide, calcium chloride, cefotaxime, cefoxitin, ceftazidime, ceftriaxone, cimetidine, clindamycin, dexamethasone, dextrose, digoxin, dobutamine, dopamine, enalaprilat, epinephrine, erythromycin, famotidine, fentanyl, fluconazole, gentamicin, glycopyrrolate, hydrocortisone, insulin, lidocaine, lorazepam, magnesium sulfate, metoclopramide, metronidazole, midazolam, nafcillin, nitroglycerin, oxacillin, pancuronium, parenteral nutrition,* penicillin G potassium, potassium chloride, ranitidine, sodium bicarbonate, sodium chloride, tobramycin, vancomycin, vecuronium	Phenobarbital, phenytoin
Nafcillin[1–3,5]	Acyclovir, cimetidine, dextrose, enalaprilat, famotidine, fentanyl, fluconazole, heparin, magnesium sulfate, morphine, parenteral nutrition,* sodium chloride	Aminoglycosides, hydrocortisone, insulin, meperidine, methylprednisolone, midazolam
Neostigmine[1–3]	Glycopyrrolate, heparin, hydrocortisone, potassium chloride	No data available
Nitroglycerin[1–4]	Alprostadil, aminophylline, atracurium, dextrose, dobutamine, dopamine, epinephrine, famotidine, fentanyl, fluconazole, furosemide, insulin, lidocaine, lorazepam, midazolam, morphine, nitroprusside, pancuronium, ranitidine, sodium chloride, vecuronium *Note: Nitroglycerin is compatible with dobutamine, dopamine, lidocaine, and nitroprusside in any combination.*	Hydralazine, phenytoin

Y-Site Compatibility of Common NICU Drugs (CONTINUED)

Medication	Compatible with	Incompatible with
Nitroprusside [1-4,16,24]	Cimetidine, dextrose (preferred diluent), dobutamine, dopamine, enalaprilat, famotidine, heparin, indomethacin, insulin, lidocaine, midazolam, morphine, nitroglycerin, pancuronium, ranitidine, vecuronium *Note: Nitroprusside is compatible with dobutamine, dopamine, lidocaine, and nitroglycerin in any combination.*	Bacteriostatic water for injection should not be used to dilute nitroprusside because preservatives increase the rate of nitroprusside decomposition.
Norepinephrine [1-3]	Amikacin, calcium gluconate, cimetidine, dextrose, dobutamine, famotidine, furosemide, heparin, hydrocortisone, lorazepam, magnesium sulfate, midazolam, morphine, nitroglycerin, parenteral nutrition,* potassium chloride, ranitidine, sodium chloride, vecuronium	Aminophylline, barbiturates, chlorothiazide, insulin, lidocaine, phenytoin, sodium bicarbonate
Pancuronium [1-4]	Alprostadil, aminophylline, cimetidine, dobutamine, dopamine, epinephrine, fentanyl, fluconazole, gentamicin, heparin, hydrocortisone, isoproterenol, lorazepam, midazolam, morphine, nitroglycerin, nitroprusside, ranitidine, vancomycin	Diazepam
Parenteral nutrition* (PN) [1-3,5,6,17,25,26]	Amikacin, azlocillin, cefotaxime, cefoxitin, ceftazidime, ceftriaxone, cimetidine, clindamycin, diazepam, digoxin, dobutamine, dopamine, epinephrine, erythromycin, famotidine, fentanyl, fluconazole, furosemide, gentamicin, heparin, insulin, isoproterenol, lidocaine, meperidine, methicillin, metoclopramide, metronidazole, morphine, nafcillin, oxacillin, penicillin G potassium, ranitidine, tobramycin, vancomycin, vecuronium *Note: Calcium and phosphate frequently cause compatibility problems in parenteral nutrition because of the large amounts of these minerals that premature infants need. The following techniques can improve calcium/phosphate solubility: (1) Use calcium gluconate, rather than chloride, (2) reduce the concentration of calcium and/or phosphate by giving some or all in other ways, (3) increase the concentration of amino acids, (4) use the correct order of mixing, (5) lower the pH of the solution, (6) avoid borderline compatibilities, (7) hang the bag as soon as possible after mixing, (8) avoid heating the bag and tubing, (9) infuse intravenous fat emulsion into a separate site, (10) increase infusion rate.*	Acyclovir, amphotericin B, ampicillin (see ampicillin above) blood, chlorothiazide, indomethacin, midazolam, phenytoin, sodium bicarbonate *Note: Unrecognized calcium phosphate precipitate in a 3-in-1 parenteral nutrition mixture (protein, carbohydrate, and fat emulsion together in the same bag) has resulted in patient death. Coinfusion by Y-site is preferred.*
Penicillin G potassium [1-6]	Acyclovir, alprostadil, calcium gluconate, clindamycin, dextrose, erythromycin, furosemide, heparin, hydrocortisone, lidocaine, magnesium sulfate, meperidine, morphine, parenteral nutrition,* potassium chloride, sodium chloride	Aminophylline, amphotericin B, dopamine, metoclopramide, sodium bicarbonate

APPENDICES

APPENDICES

Y-Site Compatibility of Common NICU Drugs (CONTINUED)

Medication	Compatible with	Incompatible with
PGE₁	See alprostadil	
Phenobarbital sodium[1-4]	Alprostadil, amikacin, aminophylline, calcium gluconate, dextrose, enalaprilat, sodium bicarbonate, sodium chloride	Hydralazine, hydrocortisone, insulin, meperidine, morphine, norepinephrine, ranitidine, vancomycin
Phenytoin[1-3]	Famotidine, fluconazole *Note:* • *If dilution of phenytoin is required, use sodium chloride 0.9 percent as the diluent, dilute immediately prior to administration, and use a 0.22-micron in-line filter. Observe admixture for precipitation.* • *Phenytoin will quickly occlude a central line, particularly in the presence of dextrose and/or heparin. (See the monograph on phenytoin for further precautions.)* • *Fosphenytoin is more soluble than phenytoin and can be diluted with dextrose or sodium chloride.*	Dextrose, dobutamine, fat emulsion intravenous, heparin, hydrocortisone, insulin, lidocaine, meperidine, morphine, nitroglycerin, norepinephrine, parenteral nutrition,* potassium chloride *Note: Phenytoin is incompatible with most medications and IV solutions.*
Phosphates[1]	Magnesium sulfate, metoclopramide, enalaprilat, famotidine, Ringer's injection, Ringer's lactate *Note: Various factors play a role in the compatibility of calcium and phosphate in parenteral nutrition: concentration of calcium, salt form of calcium, concentration of phosphate, concentration of amino acids, amino acid composition, concentration of dextrose, temperature of solution, pH of solution, presence of other additives, and order of mixing.[1]*	Dobutamine
Phytonadione [1-3,6,7]	Amikacin, ampicillin, cimetidine, dextrose, doxapram, epinephrine, heparin, parenteral nutrition,* potassium chloride, sodium bicarbonate, sodium chloride, tolazoline	

Y-Site Compatibility of Common NICU Drugs (Continued)

Medication	Compatible with	Incompatible with
Potassium chloride[1-4,16]	Acyclovir, alprostadil, aminophylline, ampicillin, aztreonam, calcium gluconate, clindamycin, dextrose, digoxin, dobutamine, dopamine, enalaprilat, epinephrine, famotidine, fentanyl, furosemide, heparin, hydralazine, hydrocortisone, indomethacin, insulin, isoproterenol, lidocaine, lorazepam, magnesium sulfate, methicillin, metoclopramide, midazolam, morphine, nafcillin, neostigmine, norepinephrine, oxacillin, parenteral nutrition,* penicillin G potassium, phytonadione, ranitidine, sodium bicarbonate, sodium chloride, vancomycin *Note: To avoid severe vein irritation and cardiac arrhythmias, coinfused bolus doses of potassium chloride must be diluted and infused very slowly (usually not greater than 40 mEq/liter = 0.04 mEq/ml and no faster than 0.5 mEq/kg/hour in a monitored infant. See standard texts for further guidelines).*	Amphotericin B, diazepam, phenytoin
Ranitidine[1-4,25]	Acyclovir, alprostadil, amikacin, aminophylline, aztreonam, bretylium, dexamethasone, dextrose, dobutamine, dopamine, enalaprilat, epinephrine, fat emulsion intravenous, fentanyl, fluconazole, furosemide, gentamicin, heparin, isoproterenol, lidocaine, lorazepam, metoclopramide, midazolam, morphine, nitroglycerin, nitroprusside, norepinephrine, pancuronium, parenteral nutrition,* potassium chloride, sodium chloride, tobramycin, vancomycin, vecuronium	Amphotericin B, atracurium, phenobarbital
Sodium bicarbonate[1-3,7,16]	Acyclovir, amikacin, aminophylline, aztreonam, clindamycin, dexamethasone, dextrose, famotidine, heparin, hydrocortisone, indomethacin, insulin, lidocaine, nafcillin, oxacillin, phenobarbital, phenytoin, potassium chloride, sodium chloride, tolazoline, verapamil *Note: Sodium bicarbonate inactivates sympathomimetic amines (dobutamine, dopamine, epinephrine, isoproterenol, and norepinephrine). This is a chemical incompatibility (nonvisual), so no precipitate will be seen.* *The combination of calcium salts such as calcium gluconate with sodium bicarbonate causes an immediate visual precipitation of calcium carbonate. Flush IV line well with saline or dextrose between these two medications to avoid line occlusion.*	Calcium chloride, calcium gluconate, cefotaxime, dobutamine, dopamine, epinephrine, glycopyrrolate, isoproterenol, magnesium sulfate, metoclopramide, midazolam, norepinephrine, penicillin G potassium
Sodium nitroprusside	See nitroprusside above	

APPENDICES

Y-SITE COMPATIBILITY OF COMMON NICU DRUGS (CONTINUED)

Medication	Compatible with	Incompatible with
Tobramycin[1-3,5-7]	Acyclovir, aztreonam, calcium gluconate, dextrose, doxapram, enalaprilat, fat emulsion intravenous, fluconazole, furosemide, magnesium sulfate, meperidine, metronidazole, midazolam, morphine, parenteral nutrition,* ranitidine, sodium chloride, tolazoline	Heparin, indomethacin *Note: Do not admix penicillins or cephalosporins in the same IV solution with tobramycin because they will gradually inactivate the tobramycin. Inactivation may also occur in vivo, but only in patients with severe renal dysfunction.*
Tolazoline (Priscoline)[1-3,18]	Aminophylline, ampicillin, calcium gluconate, cefotaxime, cimetidine, dextrose, dobutamine, dopamine, furosemide, gentamicin, phytonadione, sodium bicarbonate, sodium chloride, tobramycin, vancomycin	Indomethacin
TPN	See parenteral nutrition*	
Vancomycin[1-3,7]	Acyclovir, atracurium, calcium gluconate, dextrose, enalaprilat, fluconazole, heparin *(in low concentrations of 0.5 to 1 unit/ml used to maintain IV line patency)*, hydrocortisone, lorazepam, magnesium sulfate, meperidine, midazolam, morphine, pancuronium, parenteral nutrition,* potassium chloride, ranitidine, sodium chloride, tolazoline, vecuronium	Albumin, cefotaxime, ceftazidime, dexamethasone, heparin *(in high concentrations of more than 1 unit/ml used for systemic anticoagulation and in some heparin flushes)*, pentobarbital, phenobarbital
Vecuronium[1,2,23]	Aminophylline, cimetidine, dobutamine, dopamine, epinephrine, fentanyl, fluconazole, gentamicin, heparin, hydrocortisone, isoproterenol, lorazepam, midazolam, morphine, nitroglycerin, nitroprusside, ranitidine, vancomycin	Diazepam, furosemide
Vitamin K	See phytonadione above	

* Drugs reported as being compatible with parenteral nutrition in published studies using test solutions may not be compatible with the particular formulation your infant is receiving. Components in neonatal parenteral nutrition are individualized based on the infant's body weight, serum electrolytes, fluid, and other nutrient requirements, making most solutions unique. Observe the solution and tubing carefully for signs of precipitation during the 24-hour infusion period when drugs are coinfused. Certain drugs may be admixed into the parenteral nutrition bag. See Driscoll and associates' review of the use of parenteral nutrition as a drug vehicle.[26]

REFERENCES

1. Trissel LA. 1998. *Handbook on Injectable Drugs,* 10th ed. Bethesda, Maryland: American Society of Health-Systems Pharmacists.

2. Trissel LA. 1991. *Supplement to Handbook on Injectable Drugs,* 6th ed. Bethesda, Maryland: American Society of Hospital Pharmacists.

3. King JC. 1991. *Guide to Parenteral Admixtures.* St. Louis: Pacemarq.

4. Gannaway WL, et al. 1989. Chemical stability of alprostadil (PGE-1) in combination with common injectable medications (abstract #P-152E). *American Society of Hospital Pharmacists Midyear Clinical Meeting Abstracts* 24: 75A.

5. Kamen BA, et al. 1985. Analysis of antibiotic stability in a parenteral nutrition solution. *Pediatric Infectious Diseases* 4(4): 387–389.

6. Athanikar N, et al. 1979. Visual compatibility of 30 additives with a parenteral nutrient solution. *American Journal of Hospital Pharmacy* 36(4): 511–513.

7. Marquardt ED. 1990. Visual compatibility of tolazoline hydrochloride with various medications during simulated Y-site injection. *American Journal of Hospital Pharmacy* 47(8): 1802–1803.

8. Kintzel PE, and Kennedy PE. 1991. Stability of amphotericin B in 5% dextrose injection at concentrations used for administration through a central venous line. *American Journal of Hospital Pharmacy* 48(2): 283–285.

9. Mitrano FP, et al. 1991. Chemical and visual stability of amphotericin B in 5% dextrose injection stored at 4°C for 35 days. *American Journal of Hospital Pharmacy* 48(12): 2635–2637.

10. Wiest DB, et al. 1991. Stability of amphotericin B in four concentrations of dextrose injection. *American Journal of Hospital Pharmacy* 48(11): 2430–2433.

11. Niemiec PW Jr, and Vanderveen TW. 1984. Compatibility considerations in parenteral nutrient solutions. *American Journal of Hospital Pharmacy* 41(5): 893–911.

12. Lenz GT, and Mikrut BA. 1988. Calcium and phosphate solubility in neonatal parenteral nutrient solutions containing Aminosyn-PF or TrophAmine. *American Journal of Hospital Pharmacy* 45(11): 2367–2371.

13. Fitzgerald KA, and MacKay MW. 1986. Calcium and phosphate solubility in neonatal parenteral nutrient solutions containing TrophAmine. *American Journal of Hospital Pharmacy* 43(1): 88–93.

14. Avila E, et al. 1988. High parenteral calcium and phosphorus accretion in very low birth weight (VLBW) infants (abstract #1660). *Pediatric Research* 23: 478A.

15. Eggert LD, et al. 1982. Calcium and phosphorus compatibility in parenteral nutrition solutions for neonates. *American Journal of Hospital Pharmacy* 39(1): 49–53.

16. Ishisaka DY, Van Vleet JV, and Marquardt E. 1991. Visual compatibility of indomethacin sodium trihydrate with drugs given to neonates by continuous infusion. *American Journal of Hospital Pharmacy* 48(11): 2442–2443.

17. Wade CS, et al. 1991. Stability of ceftazidime and amino acids in parenteral nutrient solutions. *American Journal of Hospital Pharmacy* 48(7): 1515–1519.

18. Bhatt-Mehta V, and Nahata MC. 1990. Stability of dopamine hydrochloride injection in the presence of dobutamine hydrochloride, tolazoline hydrochloride, and theophylline injections. *Journal of Perinatology* 10(2): 129–133.

19. Institutional experience. University of California Irvine Medical Center, Orange, California.

20. Morgan DE, Bergdale S, and Zeigler EE. 1985. Effect of syringe-pump position on infusion of fat emulsion with a primary solution. *American Journal of Hospital Pharmacy* 42(5): 1110–1111.

21. Romanowski GL, and Zenk KE. 1991. Intravenous flush solutions for neonates (abstract #P-227E). *American Society of Hospital Pharmacists Midyear Clinical Meeting Abstracts* 26: 125A.

22. Whalen FJ, LeCain WK, and Latiolais CJ. 1979. Availability of insulin from continuous low-dose insulin infusions. *American Journal of Hospital Pharmacy* 36(3): 330–337.

23. Savitsky ME. 1990. Visual compatibility of neuromuscular blocking agents with various injectable drugs during simulated Y-site injection. *American Journal of Hospital Pharmacy* 47(4): 820–821.

APPENDICES

24. Dasta JF, et al. 1988. Comparison of visual and turbidimetric methods for determining short-term compatibility of intravenous critical-care drugs. *American Journal of Hospital Pharmacy* 45(11): 2361–2366.

25. Williams MF, Hak LJ, and Dukes G. 1990. *In vitro* evaluation of the stability of ranitidine hydrochloride in total parenteral nutrient mixtures. *American Journal of Hospital Pharmacy* 47(7): 1574–1579.

26. Driscoll DF, et al. 1991. Parenteral nutrient admixtures as drug vehicles: Theory and practice in the critical care setting. *Annals of Pharmacotherapy* 25(3): 276–283.

APPENDIX F
RESTORING PATENCY TO OCCLUDED CENTRAL VENOUS CATHETERS

SALINE OR HEPARINIZED SALINE

First, attempt to clear the occlusion and restore catheter patency by irrigating with normal saline using gentle pressure. If heparinized saline is used, do not exceed a maximum heparin dose of 40 units/kg, especially in very low birth weight infants. At this time, also attempt to reposition the catheter without dislodging it; occlusions are sometimes the result of the catheter tip sitting against the blood vessel wall or of kinking of the catheter.

ANTIDOTES

If saline irrigation is unsuccessful, choose the correct antidote from among the following: urokinase or alteplase, ethyl alcohol (ethanol), hydrochloric acid,[1–3] or sodium bicarbonate. Figure F-1 displays an algorithm for choosing the correct pharmacologic agent for clearing an occluded central line. Before using these products, please refer to the monographs for each drug and the **CAUTIONS AND CONTRAINDICATIONS** to using these agents.

- *Urokinase or Alteplase:* Use urokinase or alteplase if the occlusion is caused by blood or a fibrin clot. If the cause of the occlusion is unknown, use urokinase or alteplase first, before the other antidotes listed here.

- *Ethyl Alcohol 70 Percent:* Use ethyl alcohol if the occlusion is caused by IV fat emulsion.

- *Hydrochloric Acid 0.1N (Normal) or Sodium Bicarbonate (1 mEq/ml):*
  - If a change in pH might solubilize the precipitate, decrease the pH with hydrochloric acid 0.1N or increase the pH with sodium bicarbonate.
  - If the cause of the occlusion is strongly suspected to be calcium/phosphorus, other minerals, or a drug precipitate whose solubility can be increased by decreasing the pH, try dilute hydrochloric acid. Dilute HCl may also be tried when urokinase or alteplase has been unsuccessful at clearing the occlusions.
  - Use sodium bicarbonate for occlusions caused by basic drugs such as oxacillin, heparin,* and phenytoin.

See the monographs on alteplase, ethyl alcohol, hydrochloric acid, sodium bicarbonate, and urokinase for information on preparing and administering these agents.

Holcombe and colleagues recommend that the antidote dwell in the catheter for 1 hour (30–60 minutes for urokinase or alteplase).[4,5] If the first attempt is unsuccessful, repeat the procedure. If the second attempt is unsuccessful, allow the pharmacologic agent to dwell in the catheter overnight. For instructions on administration of alteplase, see monograph on alteplase.[6]

* Heparin causes occlusion or is incompatible with phenytoin and others (see Appendix E: Y-Site Compatibility of Common NICU Drugs).

APPENDICES

FIGURE F-1 ◆ ALGORITHM FOR ASSESSMENT AND MANAGEMENT OF OCCLUDED LONG-TERM CENTRAL VENOUS ACCESS DEVICES.

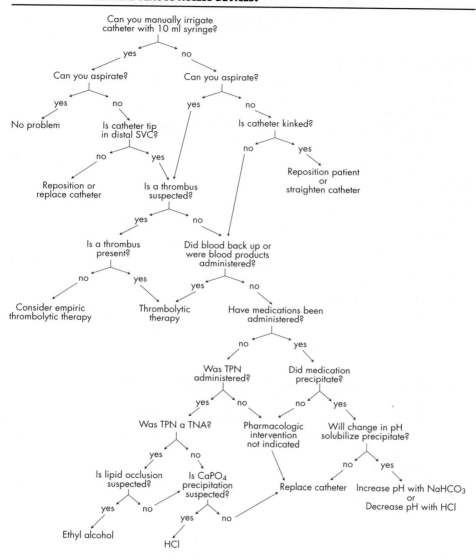

SVC = Superior vena cava

TNA = Total nutrient (3 in 1) admixture. The fat emulsion is admixed in the same bag with the amino acids, dextrose, and other components of parenteral nutrition.

From: Holcombe BJ, Forloines-Lynn S, and Garmhausen LW. 1992. Restoring patency of long-term central venous access devices. *Journal of Intravenous Nursing* 15(1): 36–41; and Holcombe BJ, Forloines-Lynn S, and Garmhausen LW. 1993. Erratum for corrected algorithm. Restoring patency of long-term central venous access devices. *Journal of Intravenous Nursing* 16(1): 55. Reprinted by permission.

APPENDICES

References

1. Duffy LF, et al. 1989. Treatment of central venous catheter occlusions with hydrochloric acid. *Journal of Pediatrics* 114(6): 1002–1004.

2. Breaux CW, et al. 1987. Calcium phosphate crystal occlusion of central venous catheters used for total parenteral nutrition in infants and children: Prevention and treatment. *Journal of Pediatric Surgery* 22(9): 829–832.

3. Shulman RJ, et al. 1988. Use of hydrochloric acid to clear obstructed central venous catheters. *Journal of Parenteral and Enteral Nutrition* 12(5): 509–510.

4. Holcombe BJ, Forloines-Lynn S, and Garmhausen LW. 1992. Restoring patency of long-term central venous access devices. *Journal of Intravenous Nursing* 15(1): 36–41.

5. Holcombe BJ, Forloines-Lynn S, and Garmhausen LW. 1993. Erratum for corrected algorithm. Restoring patency of long-term central venous access devices. *Journal of Intravenous Nursing* 16(1): 55.

6. Phelps KC, and Verzino KC. 2001. Alternatives to urokinase for the management of central venous catheter occlusion. *Hospital Pharmacy 36(3): 265–274.*

APPENDICES

APPENDIX G
GUIDELINES FOR MANAGEMENT OF
INTRAVENOUS EXTRAVASATIONS

Administration of intravenous medications in neonates can result in infiltration of the drug or solution into surrounding tissues, causing extravasation injury. Most extravasations are recognized early, remain localized, and cause no significant tissue damage. However, some infiltrations cause severe tissue necrosis, resulting in residual cosmetic defects or reduced function of the involved extremity. Extravasation injuries can prolong hospitalization and increase hospitalization costs. Prevention of these types of severe iatrogenic injuries is essential.

To prevent extravasation injury, IV sites should be checked at least hourly. During the infusion of irritating drugs, the site should be checked every few minutes so the infusion can be stopped as soon as extravasation occurs. Avoid opaque dressings over IV sites as they mask extravasations and contribute to skin breakdown—use clear tape or a transparent dressing instead, to allow for site visibility. IVs should be taped in such a way as to allow easy inspection of the area and identification of potential problems. Placing tape too tightly keeps excess fluid in the tissues from escaping, increasing pressure within a small, confined area and increasing the risk of sloughing. Infants are more prone to extravasation injury than adults because they cannot verbalize their discomfort.

NICU infants receive many medications that can cause tissue damage if allowed to infiltrate, and they have very small, fragile veins. Examples of irritating drugs are those with high osmolalities such as dextrose 10–25 percent, sodium bicarbonate 8.4 percent, and IV solutions and parenteral nutrition containing calcium and potassium salts. Sympathomimetics such as epinephrine and dopamine cause severe local vasoconstriction with ischemia of the skin when infiltration occurs; this can lead to necrosis.

Early recognition and proper treatment of IV infiltrations are important to minimize morbidity. The infusion should be stopped as soon as the infiltration is recognized. Some practitioners suggest elevation of the affected area to help reduce edema. Prompt use of hyaluronidase (Wydase) by subcutaneous injection into the site of extravasation may prevent or reduce extravasation-induced tissue injury. Hyaluronidase can be used for most drug and IV-solution extravasations in the NICU. Phentolamine (Regitine), not hyaluronidase, is used to treat extravasation injuries from dopamine and other vasoconstrictors. Complete guidelines for the use of each of these agents are found in the monograph for each drug. The discussions that follow summarize the applications for which each drug is best suited and highlight the steps in their use.

HYALURONIDASE

Use to treat extravasations of dextrose 10 percent,[1] calcium salts,[1] potassium salts, sodium bicarbonate, aminophylline,[2] radiocontrast media,[3] hypertonic saline,[3,4]

APPENDICES

nafcillin,[5] blood, parenteral nutrition,[2,6] and many other drugs such as higher concentrations of dextrose.

- *Stop infusion immediately and elevate the extremity.* Inject 0.2 ml of hyaluronidase (15 units/ml) into the needle through which the IV was running. This delivers hyaluronidase directly into the tissue plane in which the extravasation occurred. Remove the needle. (See monograph on hyaluronidase for preparation of dilution and further information on the drug.)

- *Inject* hyaluronidase locally by the subcutaneous or intradermal route using a 25 gauge needle. The dose is 15 units given in four 0.2 ml aliquots into the periphery or leading edge of the site, changing the needle after each injection, plus the 0.2 ml given into the needle, as described above, equals 1 ml total.

- *Wrap* the extremity loosely with gauze for approximately 2 hours and elevate the extremity (a skin traction stockinette dressing with a window can be used). Do not apply heat, especially moist heat, because heat can damage and macerate tissue even further.[7] Do not apply cool compresses.

- *Observe* and document the appearance of the lesion (induration, swelling, discoloration, blanching, and blister formation) every 15 minutes for approximately 2 hours.

- *Care for open wounds.* Apply silver sulfadiazine cream. Consult plastic surgery and the burn unit services, if available, early in the course of treatment. Smaller lesions will slough and heal spontaneously, whereas larger ulcers will require excision and grafting.[8]

PHENTOLAMINE

Use to treat extravasations of α-adrenergic drugs[9] such as epinephrine, phenylephrine, dopamine, and norepinephrine. (See monograph on phentolamine for preparation of dilution and further information.)

Blanching along the vein and blanching limited locally at the insertion site are not harmful and will usually reverse without treatment. It may be necessary to alternate the lines into which the α-adrenergic drug is infusing. Blanching extending more than ¼ inch (= ½-inch diameter) past the insertion site and spreading should alert the nurse to a possible extravasation. Assess the entire clinical picture: Is the area cold, hard, edematous, severely blanched, large?

- *Stop infusion and remove the needle.*

- *Cleanse* the site and surrounding area with a povidone-iodine solution.

- *Inject* phentolamine (0.5 mg/ml) locally into area of extravasation in divided increments of approximately 0.2 ml using a 25-gauge needle. Change needle between each dose increment. Phentolamine should be injected as soon as possible, but may be used up to 12 hours after the extravasation occurs.

- Phentolamine will produce noticeable local hyperemic changes within minutes of treatment.

APPENDICES

REFERENCES

1. Raszka WV Jr, Kueser TK, and Smith FR. 1990. The use of hyaluronidase in the treatment of intravenous extravasation injuries. *Journal of Perinatology* 10(2): 146–149.

2. Laurie SWS, et al. 1984. Intravenous extravasation injuries: The effectiveness of hyaluronidase in their treatment. *Annals of Plastic Surgery* 13(3): 191–194.

3. Elam EA, et al. 1991. Cutaneous ulceration due to contrast extravasation: Experimental assessment of injury and potential antidotes. *Investigative Radiology* 26(1): 13–16.

4. Zimmet SE. 1993. The prevention of cutaneous necrosis following extravasation of hypertonic saline and sodium tetradecyl sulfate. *Journal of Dermatologic Surgery and Oncology* 19(7): 641–646.

5. Zenk KE, Dungy CL, and Greene GR. 1981. Nafcillin extravasation injury: Use of hyaluronidase as an antidote. *American Journal of Diseases of Children* 135(12): 1113–1114.

6. Davies J, Gault D, and Buchdahl R. 1994. Preventing the scars of neonatal intensive care. *Archives of Disease in Childhood. Fetal and Neonatal Edition* 70(1): F50–F51.

7. Brown AS, Hoelzer DJ, and Piercy SA. 1979. Skin necrosis from extravasation of intravenous fluids in children. *Plastic and Reconstructive Surgery* 64(2): 91–96.

8. Zenk KE. 1981. Management of intravenous extravasations. *Infusion* 5(4): 77–79.

9. Siwy BK, and Sadove AM. 1987. Acute management of dopamine infiltration injury with Regitine. *Plastic and Reconstructive Surgery* 80(4): 610–612.

APPENDICES

Neonatal Medications & Nutrition

APPENDIX H
CLASSIFICATION AND SPECTRUM OF ACTIVITY OF ANTI-INFECTIVES

This appendix lists the various categories of anti-infectives (Table H-1) and some of the organisms against which they are effective. Please consult more detailed references and the infant's culture and sensitivity test results for the best choice of antimicrobial therapy to treat particular infections.

PENICILLINS AND RELATED ANTIBIOTICS

β-Lactamase (Penicillinase)-Susceptible (inactivated by penicillinase) Narrow Spectrum

- **Amoxicillin (PO):** Broader-spectrum than penicillin G or penicillin V because some Gram-negative organisms are covered. Includes coverage for Group B β-hemolytic streptococci, *Listeria monocytogenes,* and enterococci.

- **Ampicillin:** Broader-spectrum than penicillin G or penicillin V because some Gram-negative organisms are covered. Includes coverage for Group B β-hemolytic streptococci, *Listeria monocytogenes,* and enterococci.

- **Penicillin G:** Congenital syphilis *(Treponema pallidum),* tetanus neonatorum, gonococcal infection. Active against Gram-positive organisms such as Group B Streptococcus, Group A Streptococcus, and *Streptococcus pneumoniae.* Used in combination with gentamicin for neonatal Group B streptococcal disease for synergistic effect. Effective against *Listeria monocytogenes,* but IV ampicillin alone or with gentamicin is preferred. Active against certain strains of anaerobic bacteria such as Clostridium, Peptococcus, and Bacteroides *(Bacteroides fragilis* is resistant, however).

- **Penicillin V (PO):** Same spectrum as penicillin G. This is an oral drug used for mild to moderately severe infections of the upper respiratory tract, urinary tract, and skin. Used for prophylaxis of pneumococcal infections and rheumatic fever.

β-Lactamase (Penicillinase)-Susceptible (inactivated by penicillinase) Extended Spectrum (Antipseudomonal)

- **Azlocillin:** Broad range of Gram-positive and Gram-negative organisms. Active also against enterococci and many anaerobes, including *Bacteroides fragilis,* Enterobacter, and *Serratia marcescens.* Valuable for multiresistant Gram-negative enteric organisms, usually combined with an aminoglycoside.

- **Ticarcillin:** Gram-negative organisms, especially *Pseudomonas aeruginosa,* Proteus species, and *Escherichia coli.* Often used in combination with gentamicin or tobramycin for nosocomial Gram-negative enteric infections.

β-Lactamase (Penicillinase)-Resistant Antistaphylococcal

- **Cloxacillin (PO):** Penicillinase-producing staphylococci.
- **Dicloxacillin (PO):** Penicillinase-producing staphylococci.

APPENDICES

Table H-1 ◆ Classification of Anti-Infectives

Penicillins and Related Antibiotics

β-Lactamase (Penicillinase)-Susceptible

Narrow Spectrum
amoxicillin (PO)
ampicillin
penicillin G
penicillin V (PO)

Extended Spectrum (Antipseudomonal)
azlocillin
ticarcillin*

β-Lactamase (Penicillinase)-Resistant

Antistaphylococcal
cloxacillin (PO)
dicloxacillin (PO)
nafcillin
oxacillin

Carbapenems
imipenem/cilastatin*
meropenem

Others
amoxicillin/clavulanate
 (Augmentin)-(PO)*
ampicillin/sulbactam
 (Unasyn)*
ticarcillin/clavulanate
 (Timentin)*
aztreonam

Cephalosporins

First Generation
cefadroxil (PO)
cefazolin
cephalexin (PO)
cephalothin
cephapirin
cephradine (PO)

Second Generation
cefaclor (PO)
cefotetan*
cefoxitin*
cefprozil (PO)
cefuroxime
cefuroxime axetil (PO)
loracarbef (PO)

Third Generation
cefixime (PO)
cefoperazone
cefotaxime
cefpodoxime (PO)
ceftazidime
ceftizoxime
ceftriaxone

Aminoglycosides
amikacin
gentamicin
streptomycin
tobramycin

Macrolides
azithromycin
clarithromycin
erythromycin

Fluoroquinolones
ciprofloxacin

Other Antibiotics
chloramphenicol
clindamycin*
metronidazole*
mupirocin
 (Bactroban) (topical)
nitrofurantoin (PO)
rifampin
trimethoprim-
 sulfamethoxazole
 (Bactrim)
vancomycin

Antivirals
acyclovir
ganciclovir
ribavirin
vidarabine
zidovudine

Antifungals
amphotericin B
fluconazole
flucytosine
nystatin (PO) (topical)

Note: (PO) = available in oral form only.

* Spectrum of activity includes *Bacteroides fragilis.*

- *Nafcillin:* Penicillinase-producing staphylococci. Methicillin-resistant staphylococci are also resistant to nafcillin.
- *Oxacillin:* Penicillinase-producing staphylococci. Methicillin-resistant staphylococci are also resistant to oxacillin.

β-Lactamase (Penicillinase)-Resistant Carbapenems

- *Imipenem/Cilastatin:* Very broad spectrum. For most Gram-positive and Gram-negative aerobic and anaerobic bacteria, including *Bacteroides fragilis*. Effective against streptococci, *Escherichia coli*, Enterobacter, *Haemophilus influenzae*, Serratia species, *Pseudomonas aeruginosa*, *Listeria monocytogenes*, *Staphylococcus aureus*, and *Staphylococcus epidermidis*, including penicillinase-producing strains (methicillin-resistant staphylococci are resistant) and enterococci.
- *Meropenem:* Very broad spectrum. For most Gram-positive and Gram-negative aerobic and anaerobic bacteria, including *Bacteroides fragilis*. Effective against streptococci, *Escherichia coli*, Enterobacter, *Haemophilus influenzae*, Serratia species, *Pseudomonas aeruginosa*, *Listeria monocytogenes*, *Staphylococcus aureus*, and *Staphylococcus epidermidis*, including penicillinase-producing strains (methicillin-resistant staphylococci are resistant) and enterococci. Meropenem is more potent than imipenem against *Pseudomonas aeruginosa*.

β-Lactamase (Penicillinase)-Resistant Others

- *Amoxicillin/Clavulanate (Augmentin) (PO):* Broad-spectrum, includes coverage for Group B β-hemolytic streptococci, *Listeria monocytogenes*, and enterococci. Also effective for β-lactamase-producing *Branhamella catarrhalis*, *Haemophilus influenzae*, *Neisseria gonorrhoeae*, and *Staphylococcus aureus* (not MRSA).
- *Ampicillin/Sulbactam (Unasyn):* Broad-spectrum, includes coverage for Group B β-hemolytic streptococci, *Listeria monocytogenes*, and enterococci. Also effective for β-lactamase-producing strains of *Staphylococcus aureus*, *Haemophilus influenzae*, *Escherichia coli*, Klebsiella, Acinetobacter, Enterobacter, and anaerobes, including *Bacteroides fragilis*.
- *Ticarcillin/Clavulanate (Timentin):* Gram-negative organisms such as *Pseudomonas aeruginosa* and *Escherichia coli*. In addition, covers β-lactamase producing strains of *Staphylococcus aureus*, *Haemophilus influenzae*, *Branhamella catarrhalis*, *Bacteroides fragilis*, Klebsiella, and Proteus species.
- *Aztreonam:* Gram-negative aerobic bacteria, including most enteric bacilli, such as *Escherichia coli* and *Serratia marcescens*, *Pseudomonas aeruginosa*, *Klebsiella pneumoniae*, and *Haemophilus influenzae*.

CEPHALOSPORINS

In general, cephalosporins are divided into three groups (first, second, and third generation agents) by bacterial spectrum. As they progress from first generation to third, they show increased Gram-negative spectrum, reduced effectiveness against Gram-positive organisms, and more effectiveness against resistant organisms.

First Generation

- **Cefadroxil (PO):** Streptococci, staphylococci; for UTI caused by Klebsiella, *Escherichia coli,* and *Proteus mirabilis.*
- **Cefazolin:** Gram-positive aerobic cocci, including streptococci, penicillin-susceptible and penicillin-resistant staphylococci, and penicillin-susceptible pneumococci. Limited activity against Gram-negative bacteria.
- **Cephalexin (PO):** Streptococci, staphylococci, *Klebsiella pneumoniae, Escherichia coli,* and *Proteus mirabilis.* Not for enterococci.
- **Cephalothin:** Gram-positive and some Gram-negative bacteria. Ineffective against methicillin-resistant staphylococci.
- **Cephapirin:** Gram-positive and some Gram-negative bacteria. Ineffective against methicillin-resistant staphylococci.
- **Cephradine (PO):** Streptococcus, Staphylococcus; for UTI caused by Klebsiella, *Escherichia coli,* and *Proteus mirabilis.* Otitis media caused by Group A β-hemolytic streptococci, *Streptococcus pneumoniae,* or *Haemophilus influenzae.*

Second Generation

- **Cefaclor (PO):** *Staphylococcus aureus, Streptococcus pneumoniae,* and *Haemophilus influenzae.*
- **Cefotetan:** Gram-negative enteric bacilli, including *Escherichia coli,* Klebsiella, and Proteus; effective for many strains of *Neisseria gonorrhoeae.* Active against anaerobes, including *Bacteroides fragilis.*
- **Cefoxitin:** Many Gram-negative enteric organisms, as well as ampicillin-resistant *Haemophilus influenzae.* Noted for activity against anaerobic bacteria, including *Bacteroides fragilis.*
- **Cefprozil (PO):** *Streptococcus pneumoniae, Haemophilus influenzae, Branhamella catarrhalis, Staphylococcus aureus,* and *Staphylococcus pyogenes.*
- **Cefuroxime (IV and PO):** Group B streptococci, pneumococci, Gram-negative enteric bacilli (such as *Escherichia coli,* Enterobacter, and Klebsiella), as well as *Haemophilus influenzae,* meningococci, gonococci, and staphylococci.
- **Loracarbef (PO):** *Streptococcus pneumoniae, Haemophilus influenzae, Branhamella catarrhalis, Staphylococcus aureus,* and *Escherichia coli.*

Third Generation

- **Cefixime (PO):** *Streptococcus pneumoniae, Staphylococcus pyogenes, Haemophilus influenzae, Branhamella catarrhalis,* many Enterobacteriaceae, and *Neisseria gonorrhoeae.* UTI caused by *Escherichia coli* and *Proteus mirabilis.*
- **Cefoperazone:** *Haemophilus influenzae,* gonococci, meningococci, Pseudomonas, and many Gram-negative enteric bacilli.

- **Cefotaxime:** *Haemophilus influenzae*, gonococci, meningococci, and many Gram-negative enteric bacilli. *Listeria monocytogenes* and enterococci are resistant.

- **Cefpodoxime (PO):** *Streptococcus pneumoniae* or non-β-lactamase-producing *Haemophilus influenzae, Neisseria gonorrhoeae, Staphylococcus aureus* or *Staphylococcus pyogenes,* and acute otitis media caused by *Streptococcus pneumoniae, Haemophilus influenzae,* or *Branhamella catarrhalis.* UTI caused by *Escherichia coli,* Klebsiella, and Proteus.

- **Ceftazidime:** *Haemophilus influenzae*, gonococci, meningococci, Pseudomonas, and many Gram-negative enteric bacilli. *Listeria monocytogenes* and enterococci are resistant.

- **Ceftizoxime:** Gram-negative enteric bacilli such as *Escherichia coli* and Klebsiella and cocci such as Neisseria. Some variable activity against Gram-positive organisms such as Staphylococcus and Streptococcus.

- **Ceftriaxone:** Gram-negative aerobic bacteria, including *Neisseria gonorrhoeae, Neisseria meningitidis, Escherichia coli,* and *Haemophilus influenzae.* Not effective against Pseudomonas, *Listeria monocytogenes,* enterococci, methicillin-resistant staphylococci, or anaerobic organisms.

AMINOGLYCOSIDES

Amikacin: Multiple-resistant Gram-negative bacteria, including most Pseudomonas and Serratia.

Gentamicin: Gram-negative organisms—*Escherichia coli, Pseudomonas aeruginosa,* and Serratia species. Used in combination with ampicillin for Streptococcus Group D (enterococcal) infections. Also synergistic with penicillins against Streptococcus Group B, *Staphylococcus aureus, Listeria monocytogenes,* and enterococcal infections despite resistance of the microorganisms to the aminoglycosides alone.

Streptomycin: *Mycobacterium tuberculosis,* streptococcal or enterococcal endocarditis, and other nontuberculous infections such as plague, tularemia, and brucellosis.

Tobramycin: Gram-negative bacterial infections, including Enterobacter species, *Escherichia coli,* Acinetobacter species, and *Pseudomonas aeruginosa.* Used in combination with an antipseudomonal penicillin, such as ticarcillin, for serious systemic Pseudomonas infections.

MACROLIDES

Azithromycin: *Branhamella catarrhalis, Haemophilus influenzae, Staphylococcus aureus, Streptococcus pneumoniae, Mycoplasma pneumoniae, Chlamydia trachomatis,* and *Ureaplasma urealyticum.* Less active than erythromycin against most Staphylococcus and Streptococcus, but is more potent against other organisms, including some Gram-negative bacteria.

APPENDICES

Clarithromycin: *Branhamella catarrhalis, Haemophilus influenzae, Staphylococcus aureus, Streptococcus pneumoniae, Mycoplasma pneumoniae, Staphylococcus pyogenes,* and *Chlamydia trachomatis.* More potent than erythromycin.

Erythromycin: *Chlamydia trachomatis, Bordetella pertussis, Ureaplasma urealyticum,* staphylococci, streptococci, *Listeria monocytogenes,* and *Mycoplasma pneumoniae.* Not effective for Gram-negative bacterial infections.

FLUOROQUINOLONES

Ciprofloxacin: Most Gram-negative aerobic bacteria, including Enterobacteriaceae and *Pseudomonas aeruginosa.* Also for Gram-positive aerobic bacteria, including penicillinase-producing, nonpenicillinase-producing, and methicillin-resistant staphylococci. Generally less active against Gram-positive than Gram-negative bacteria. Other fluoroquinolones include enoxacin, lomefloxacin, norfloxacin, and ofloxacin.

OTHER ANTIBIOTICS

Chloramphenicol: *Haemophilus influenzae, Streptococcus pneumoniae, Neisseria meningitidis,* Group B streptococci, coliform bacteria, *Staphylococcus aureus, Listeria monocytogenes, Bacteroides fragilis,* and Salmonella. *Serratia marcescens* and *Pseudomonas aeruginosa* are resistant.

Clindamycin: Gram-positive cocci such as *Staphylococcus aureus, Streptococcus pneumoniae,* and anaerobic bacteria, especially Bacteroides species. Aerobic Gram-negative bacteria are resistant.

Metronidazole: Gram-positive and anaerobic Gram-negative bacteria (e.g., *Bacteroides fragilis)* and protozoa. Ineffective against aerobic bacteria. For *Clostridium difficile* antibiotic-associated pseudomembranous colitis (AAPC).

Mupirocin (Topical): Narrow spectrum. Mostly for Gram-positive aerobic bacteria, *Staphylococcus aureus, Staphylococcus epidermidis, Staphylococcus saprophyticus,* and Group A β-hemolytic streptococci *(Streptococcus pyogenes).* Active against penicillinase-producing, nonpenicillinase-producing, and methicillin-resistant strains.

Nitrofurantoin (PO): For UTI caused by susceptible Gram-negative and some Gram-positive organisms. Spectrum includes *Escherichia coli* and some strains of Klebsiella, Enterobacter, enterococci, Proteus, and *Staphylococcus aureus.* Pseudomonas and Serratia are usually resistant.

Rifampin: Synergistic with both antistaphylococcal antibiotics and aminoglycosides in the treatment of persistent staphylococcal infections. Treatment of active tuberculosis, elimination of meningococci from asymptomatic carriers, and prophylaxis in contacts of patients with *Haemophilus influenzae* type B infection.

Trimethoprim-Sulfamethoxazole: The common UTI organisms *Escherichia coli,* Klebsiella, and Enterobacter species, *Morganella morganii,* Proteus. Organisms from middle-ear exudate and bronchial secretions *(Haemophilus influenzae,* including ampicillin-resistant strains, *Streptococcus pneumoniae, Shigella flexneri,* and *Shigella sonnei). Pseudomonas aeruginosa* is resistant.

Vancomycin: Most Gram-positive cocci and bacilli. Most Gram-negative bacteria are resistant. Effective against methicillin- (nafcillin-, oxacillin-) resistant *Staphylococcus aureus* (MRSA) and *Staphylococcus epidermidis* infections and *Listeria monocytogenes.*

ANTIVIRALS

Acyclovir: Herpes simplex and varicella-zoster.

Ganciclovir: Cytomegalovirus (CMV).

Ribavirin: Respiratory syncytial virus (RSV).

Vidarabine: Herpes simplex virus.

Zidovudine: Human immunodeficiency virus (HIV).

ANTIFUNGALS

Amphotericin B: Wide variety of fungal infections, including candidiasis.

Fluconazole: Effective for systemic candidiasis and meningitis. Also effective against Cryptococcus, Coccidiodes, and dermatophytes.

Flucytosine: Synergistic with amphotericin B against Candida and Cryptococcus.

Nystatin: Candida.

APPENDICES

APPENDIX I
ADVERSE EFFECTS OF DIURETICS

	Type of Diuretic				
Adverse Effect	**Loop**	**Thiazide**	**Potassium Sparing**	**Osmotic**	**Carbonic Anhydrase Inhibitor**
Volume depletion	+++	++	+	+++	–
Hypokalemia	+++	++	–	++	+
Hyperkalemia	–	–	++	–	–
Hyponatremia	++	+++	–	++	–
Hypercalciuria	+++	–	–	+	–
Hypercalcemia	–	++	–	–	–
Hyperuricemia	++	++	–	–	–
Hypomagnesemia	++	++	–	–	–
Hypophosphatemia	+	+	–	+	–
Hyperglycemia	–	+	±	–	–
Hyperlipidemia	–	+	–	–	–
Alkalosis	++	++	–	–	–
Acidosis	–	–	+	+	++

Examples: Loop: furosemide; thiazide: chlorothiazide; potassium sparing: spironolactone; osmotic: mannitol; carbonic anhydrase inhibitor: acetazolamide.

Pluses and minuses indicate the degree to which the diuretic type had the adverse effect listed.

+++ = greatest effect

++ = moderate effect

+ = little effect

– = no effect

± = may or may not have the adverse effect indicated

Adapted from: Chemtob S, et al. 1989. Pharmacology of diuretics in the newborn. *Pediatric Clinics of North America* 36(5): 1231–1250.

APPENDIX J
ANTIDOTES FOR DRUGS THAT CAUSE LOSS OF RESPIRATORY EFFORT

See monographs of individual drugs for further information.

Drug Class/Examples	Antidote	Comments
Benzodiazepines 　Diazepam 　Lorazepam 　Midazolam	Flumazenil (Romazicon) 　2–10 mcg/kg IV every minute 　× 3 as needed.	Not effective for barbiturate, general anesthetic, or narcotic overdose.
Narcotics, opiates 　Codeine 　Fentanyl 　Meperidine 　Morphine 　Paregoric	Naloxone (Narcan) 　0.1 mg/kg/dose IV. May repeat every 3–5 minutes as required. • *Caution: May precipitate withdrawal; reverses analgesia.*	Not effective for barbiturate or benzodiazepine overdose.

APPENDIX K
NEONATAL WITHDRAWAL SCORE SHEET

The Neonatal Withdrawal Score Sheet in Figure K-1 is used to assess the severity of withdrawal and to assist in determining if treatment is needed for:

- Infants born to drug-dependent mothers or those with a history of drug use
- Mothers or infants with a positive urine drug screen
- Infants having withdrawal symptoms
- Infants being weaned from long-term (>2 weeks) treatment with drugs that cause physiologic dependency, such as fentanyl or midazolam

The original scoring system by Finnegan was designed for infants withdrawing from narcotics.[1] It may, however, be used as a guide for identifying infants in withdrawal from other drugs and substances such as cocaine and alcohol.

Instructions:

- Score the infant every 3–4 hours, corresponding to the frequency of feedings. Behaviors should be assessed throughout the 3- to 4-hour interval, and the form should be completed at the time of feeding. Score all that apply.

- Try nonpharmacologic measures first: Comfort the infant by swaddling, provide a pacifier, and decrease visual and auditory stimulation.

- Consider treatment of withdrawal in babies scoring 8 or above.
  - Maintain effective dose for 3–5 days before tapering begins.
  - Decrease daily dose by about 10 percent every 1–2 days, as tolerated using the withdrawal score as a guide.
  - Usually, 50 percent of babies will require 10–20 days of therapy (25 percent more, 25 percent less).
  - If a dose taper fails (score again is 8 or above), resume the previously effective dose for 3–5 days as tolerated; then begin taper again.

- Signs and symptoms of other neonatal problems—for example, sepsis, hypoglycemia, and electrolyte imbalance—may mimic some of the signs of neonatal withdrawal. These other problems need to be ruled out or corrected.[2,3]

FIGURE K-1 ◆ NEONATAL WITHDRAWAL SCORE SHEET (BASED ON FINNEGAN NEONATAL ABSTINENCE SCALE).

Signs and Symptoms	Date Time Initials								
Cry	Score								
• Excessive high-pitched (or other) crying	2								
• Continuous high-pitched (or other) crying	3								
• If intubated, continuous crying behavior	3								
Hours of Sleep after Feeding									
• Less than 1 hour	3								
• Less than 2 hours	2								
• Less than 3 hours	1								
Moro Reflex (wake the baby for this test)									
• Hyperactive	2								
• Markedly hyperactive	3								
Tremors—When Disturbed									
• Mild tremors	1								
• Marked tremors	2								
Tremors—When Undisturbed									
• Mild tremors	3								
• Marked tremors	4								
Increased Muscle Tone	2								
Generalized Seizures	5								
Gastrointestinal Symptoms									
• Frantic sucking of fists	1								
• Poor feeding	2								
• Regurgitation	2								
• Projectile vomiting	3								
Stools									
• Loose	2								
• Watery	3								
Dehydration	2								
Frequent Yawning (3–4 times/interval)	1								
Frequent Sneezing (3–4 times/interval)	1								
Nasal Stuffiness	1								
Sweating	1								
Mottling	1								

(continued on next page)

APPENDICES

FIGURE K-1 ◆ **NEONATAL WITHDRAWAL SCORE SHEET (BASED ON FINNEGAN NEONATAL ABSTINENCE SCALE) (CONTINUED).**

Signs and Symptoms	Date								
	Time								
	Initials								
Fever	Score								
• <38.3°C (37.3°C–38.3°C)	1								
• >38.3°C (38.4°C and higher)	2								
Respirations									
• More than 60/minute	1								
• More than 60/minute with retractions	2								
Excoriations of:	1								
• Nose									
• Knees									
• Toes									
4-Hour Total									

Date	Nursing Comments/Observations

Use this form to document what interventions seemed to help calm the infant and what was tried and not helpful.

Adapted from: Finnegan LP. 1985. Neonatal abstinence. In *Current Therapy in Neonatal-Perinatal Medicine*, Nelson N, ed. Philadelphia: Mosby-Year Book, 262–270. Reprinted by permission.

REFERENCES

1. Finnegan LP. 1985. Neonatal abstinence. In *Current Therapy in Neonatal-Perinatal Medicine*, Nelson N, ed. Philadelphia: Mosby-Year Book, 262–270.

2. Zaichkin J, and Houston RF. 1993. The drug-exposed mother and infant: A regional center experience. *Neonatal Network* 12(3): 41–49.

3. Levy M, and Spino M. 1993. Neonatal withdrawal syndrome: Associated drugs and pharmacologic management. *Pharmacotherapy* 13(3): 202–211.

APPENDICES

APPENDICES

APPENDIX L
COMPOSITION OF FEEDINGS FOR INFANTS AND YOUNG CHILDREN IN THE HOSPITAL

Note: Mead Johnson Nutritional products Enfamil AR, Enfamil Next Step Soy Toddler Formula, EnfaGrow products, and Kindercal are not included in this reference.

Adapted from: Mead Johnson Nutritionals. 1999. *Enfamil Family Pediatric Products Handbook*. Evansville, Indiana: Mead Johnson, 57–59; and Nestlé Carnation. 2000. *The Very Best Professional Handbook*. Glendale, California: 41–44.

APPENDICES

Nutrients per Liter

	Human Milk	Milk Protein–based Infant Formulas								
	Mature term human milk[a]	Similac® with Iron (Low-Iron)[b]	Enfamil® and Enfamil® with Iron-20 Cal[c] (Low Iron)	Similac® Lactose Free[b]	Enfamil® LactoFree®	Similac® PM 60/40[d]	Nestle® Carnation® Good Start®[e]	Nestle® Carnation® Follow-up™	Similac® with Iron 24	Enfamil® and Enfamil® with Iron-24 Cal[f] (Low Iron)
Energy, cal	699	676	680	676	680	676	670	670	806	810
Volume, ml	1,000	1,000	1,000	1,000	1,000	1,000	1,000	1,000	1,000	1,000
Protein, gm	9.09	13.99	14.5	14.46	14.3	15.00	16.1	17.4	21.85	17.4
% of total calories	5	8	9	9	9	9	10	10	11	9
Source	Mature term human milk	Nonfat milk & whey protein concentrate	Whey & nonfat milk	Milk protein isolate	Milk protein isolate	Whey protein concentrate & sodium caseinate	Reduced minerals whey protein concentrate	Nonfat milk	Nonfat milk	Whey & nonfat milk
Fat, gm	41.96	36.49	36	36.49	31	37.77	34.1	27.5	42.50	43
% of total calories	54	49	48	49	48	50	46	37	47	48
Source	Mature term human milk	High-oleic safflower, coconut, & soy oils	Palm olein, soy, coconut, & high-oleic sunflower oils	Soy & coconut oils	Palm olein, soy, coconut, & high-oleic sunflower oils	Corn, coconut, & soy oils	Palm olein, soy, coconut, & high-oleic safflower oils	Palm olein, soy, coconut, & high-oleic safflower oils	Soy & coconut oils	Palm olein, soy, coconut, & high-oleic sunflower oils
Linoleic acid, mg	3,021	6,757	5,811	8,784	5,811	8,784	5,692	4,556	10,484	6,992
Carbohydrate, gm	72.7	73.0	73	72.3	74	68.9	73.7	88.4	84.7	88
% of total calories	42	43	43	43	43	41	44	53	42	43
Source	Lactose	Lactose	Lactose	Corn syrup solids & sucrose	Corn syrup solids	Lactose	Lactose & corn maltodextrin	Corn syrup solids, lactose, & maltodextrin	Lactose	Lactose
Vitamins										
Vitamin A, IU	2,231	2,000	2,027	2,027	2,000	2,027	2,009	1,675	2,419	2,400
Vitamin D, IU	21	410	405	405	41	405	402	436	484	490
Vitamin E, IU	2.8	20.3	13.5	20.3	13.5	16.9	13.4	13	24.2	16.2
Vitamin K, mcg	2.1	54	54	54	54	54	54.9	54.3	65	65

APPENDICES

Vitamins, continued										
Thiamin (vitamin B$_1$), mcg	210	676	540	676	540	676	402	536	806	650
Riboflavin (vitamin B$_2$), mcg	350	1,014	950	1,014	950	1,014	902	643	1,210	1,140
Vitamin B$_6$, mcg	930	405	410	405	410	405	502	442	484	490
Vitamin B$_{12}$, mcg	0.28	1.69	2	1.69	2	1.69	1.5	2.1	2.02	2.4
Niacin, mcg	1,497	7,095	6,800	7,095	6,800	7,095	5,022	8,576	8,468	8,100
Folic acid (folacin), mcg	85	101	108	101	108	101	60	107	121	130
Pantothenic acid, mcg	1,797	3,041	3,400	3,041	3,400	3,041	3,013	3,216	3,629	4,100
Biotin, mcg	6.3	29.7	20	29.7	20	30.4	14.7	15	35.5	24
Vitamin C (ascorbic acid), mg	40	61	81	61	81	61	54	54	73	97
Choline, mg	92	108	81	108	81	81	80	80	129	97
Inositol, mg	149	32	41	29	115	162	121	121	38	49
Minerals										
Calcium, mg (mEq)	280 (14.0)	527 (26.3)	530 (26.5)	568 (28.3)	550 (27.5)	378 (18.9)	429 (21.5)	811 (40.4)	726 (36.2)	630 (31.5)
Phosphorus, mg	147	284	360	378	370	189	241	603	565	430
Magnesium, mg	30.1	40.5	24	40.5	54	40.5	44.9	56.3	56.5	65
Iron, mg	0.42	12.16 (1.49)	12.2 (4.7)	12.16	12.2	1.49	10	12.2	14.52	14.6 (5.7)
Zinc, mg	1.19	5.07	6.8	5.07	6.8	5.07	5	4.2	6.05	8.1
Manganese, mcg	6	34	101	34	101	34	47	47	40	122
Copper, mcg	252	608	510	608	510	608	536	509	726	610
Iodine, mcg	112	41	68	61	101	41	54	39	73	81
Selenium, mcg	20.3	14.9	18.9	14.9	18.9	12.8	13	20	20.2	23
Sodium, mg (mEq)	182 (7.9)	162 (7.1)	183 (7.9)	203 (8.8)	200 (8.6)	162 (7.1)	161 (7)	261 (11.3)	274 (11.9)	220 (9.5)
Potassium, mg (mEq)	580 (14.8)	709 (18.1)	730 (18.7)	723 (18.5)	740 (18.9)	581 (14.9)	656 (16.8)	905 (23.2)	1,065 (27.2)	880 (22.5)
Chloride, mg (mEq)	420 (11.8)	439 (12.4)	430 (12.1)	439 (12.4)	450 (12.7)	399 (11.2)	395 (11)	603 (17)	653 (18.4)	510 (14.3)
Other Characteristics										
Potential renal solute load, mosm	91.1	126.5	132	134.3	132	124.8	135.5	171.7	200.4	158
Water, gm	881	899	905	899	899	905	912	905	879	886
Osmolality, mOsm/kg water	286	300	300	230	200	280	265	326	380	360
Osmolarity, mOsm/liter	252	270	270	207	180	250	242	295	340	320

Nutrients per Liter

	Soy Protein-based Infant Formulas						Protein Hydrolysate Infant Formulas		
	Isomil®	Isomil® DFg	Enfamil® ProSobee®	Nestle® Carnation® Alsoy®	RCF®h	Nestle® Carnation® Follow-up Soy™i	Alimentum®	Enfamil® Nutramigen®	Enfamil® Pregestimil®i
Energy, cal									
Volume, ml	676	676	680	670	676	670	676	680	680
	1,000	1,000	1,000	1,000	1,000	1,000	1,000	1,000	1,000
Protein, gm	16.55	17.97	20	18.8	20.00	20.8	18.58	19	19
% of total calories	10	11	12	11	12	12	11	11	11
Source	Soy protein isolate & L-methionine	Soy protein isolate & L-methionine	Soy protein isolate & L-methionine	Soy protein isolate & L-methionine	Soy protein isolate & L-methionine	Soy protein isolate & L-methionine	Casein hydrolysate, L-methionine, L-tyrosine, L-tryptophan & L-cystine	Casein hydrolysate, L-cystine, L-tyrosine, L-tryptophan	Casein hydrolysate, L-cystine, L-tyrosine & L-tryptophan
Fat, gm	36.89	36.89	36	33.1	36.01	29.5	37.43	34	38
% of total calories	49	49	48	45	48	40	48	45	48
Source	High-oleic safflower, coconut, & soy oils	Soy & coconut oils	Palm olein, soy, coconut, & high-oleic sunflower oils	Palm olein, soy, coconut, & high-oleic safflower oils	High-oleic safflower, coconut, & soy oils	Palm olein, soy, coconut, & high-oleic safflower oils	Safflower, medium-chain triglyceride, & soy oils	Palm olein, soy, coconut, & high-oleic sunflower oils	Medium-chain triglyceride, soy, corn, & high-oleic safflower or sunflower oils
Linoleic acid, mg	6,757	8,784	5,811	6,089	6,757	5,762	12,838	5,541	7,027
Carbohydrate, gm	69.6	68.2	68	74.3	68.2	80.4	68.9	74	69
% of total calories	41	40	40	44	40	48	41	44	41
Source	Corn syrup & sucrose	Corn syrup & sucrose	Corn syrup solids	Corn maltodextrin & sucrose	Selected by physician	Corn maltodextrin & sucrose	Sucrose & modified tapioca starch	Corn syrup solids & modified cornstarch	Corn syrup solids, dextrose, & modified cornstarch
Vitamins									
Vitamin A, IU	2,027	2,027	2,000	2,064	2,027	2,077	2,027	2,000	2,600
Vitamin D, IU	405	405	410	423	405	422	304	410	510
Vitamin E, IU	20.3	20.3	13.5	20	20.3	16.1	20.3	13.5	26
Vitamin K, mcg	74.3	74	54	52.6	74	52.3	101	54	127

APPENDICES

724

Vitamins, continued									
Thiamin (vitamin B₁), mcg	405	405	540	402	405	603	405	540	530
Riboflavin (vitamin B₂), mcg	608	608	610	630	608	630	608	610	640
Vitamin B₆, mcg	405	405	410	402	405	576	405	410	430
Vitamin B₁₂, mcg	3.04	3.04	2	2.1	3.04	2.1	3.04	2	2.1
Niacin, mcg	9,122	9,122	6,800	8,669	9,122	8,040	9,122	6,800	8,500
Folic acid (folacin), mcg	101	101	108	103	101	107	101	108	106
Pantothenic acid, mcg	5,068	5,068	3,400	3,199	5,068	3,149	5,068	3,400	3,200
Biotin, mcg	30.4	30.4	20	52.6	30.4	52.3	30.4	20	53
Vitamin C (ascorbic acid), mg	61	61	81	103	61	107	61	81	79
Choline, mg	54	54	81	80	54	80	54	81	90
Inositol, mg	34	34	115	124	34	121	34	115	32
Minerals									
Calcium, mg (mEq)	709 (35.4)	709 (35.4)	710 (35.5)	702 (35.1)	709 (35.4)	905 (45.2)	709 (35.4)	640 (32)	640 (32)
Phosphorus, mg	507	507	560	413	507	603	507	43	430
Magnesium, mg	50.7	50.7	74	72	50.7	87	50.7	74	74
Iron, mg	12.16	12.16	12.2	12.4	12.16	12.1	12.16	12.2	12.7
Zinc, mg	5.07	5.07	8.1	6	5.07	8.8	5.07	6.8	6.4
Manganese, mcg	169	203	169	227	203	248	54	169	210
Copper, mcg	507	507	510	805	507	804	507	510	640
Iodine, mcg	101	101	101	54	101	54	101	101	47
Selenium, mcg	14.2	14.2	18.9	13	14.2	13	18.9	18.9	13.9
Sodium, mg (mEq)	297 (12.9)	297 (12.9)	240 (10.4)	227 (9.8)	297 (12.9)	281 (12.2)	297 (12.9)	320 (13.9)	260 (11.3)
Potassium, mg (mEq)	730 (18.7)	730 (18.7)	810 (20.7)	774 (19.7)	730 (18.7)	791 (20.2)	797 (20.4)	740 (18.9)	740 (18.9)
Chloride, mg (mEq)	419 (11.8)	419 (11.8)	540 (15.2)	475 (13.4)	419 (11.8)	529 (14.9)	541 (15.2)	580 (16.3)	580 (16.3)
Other Characteristics									
Potential renal solute load, mosm	154.1	162.2	179	164.4	173.8	186.8	170.8	172	169
Water, gm	899	899	905	905	899	905	899	905	905
Osmolality, mOsm/kg water	230	240	200	200		200	370	320	320
Osmolarity, mOsm/liter	205	220	182	181		181	332	290	290

Nutrients per Liter

	Human Milk	Human Milk Fortifier	Preterm Human Milk Plus Fortifier					Nutrient-enriched Postdischarge Formulas	
	Mature Preterm Human Milk[i]	Similac Natural Care® Human Milk Fortifier[A]	Preterm Human Milk + Similac Natural Care® 75:25 Ratio[k,l]	Preterm Human Milk + Similac Natural Care® 50:50 Ratio[k,l]	Preterm Human Milk + Similac Natural Care® 25:75 Ratio[k,l]	Preterm Human Milk + Enfamil® Human Milk Fortifier 1 pkt/50 ml[l,m]	Preterm Human Milk + Enfamil® Human Milk Fortifier 1 pkt/25 ml[l,m]	Similac NeoSure™	EnfaCare™
Energy, cal	671	806	705	739	773	730	788	746	740
Volume, ml	1,000	1,000	1,000	1,000	1,000	1,000	1,000	1,000	1,000
Protein, gm	14.09	21.85	16.00	17.95	19.92	17.31	20.48	19.40	21
% of total calories	8	11	9	10	10	9	10	10	11
Source	Mature preterm human milk	Nonfat milk & whey protein concentrate	Mature preterm human milk, nonfat milk, & whey protein concentrate	Mature preterm human milk, nonfat milk, & whey protein concentrate	Nonfat milk, whey protein concentrate, & mature preterm human milk	Mature preterm human milk, whey protein concentrate, & sodium caseinate	Mature preterm human milk, whey protein concentrate, & sodium caseinate	Nonfat milk & whey protein concentrate	Nonfat milk & whey protein concentrate
Fat, gm	38.93	43.79	40.11	41.37	42.57	38.85	38.76	41.04	39
% of total calories	52	47	51	50	50	48	44	49	46
Source	Mature preterm human milk	Medium-chain triglyceride, soy, & coconut oils	Mature preterm human milk & medium-chain triglyceride, soy, & coconut oils	Mature preterm human milk & medium-chain triglyceride, soy, & coconut oils	Medium-chain triglyceride, soy & coconut oils, & mature preterm human milk	Mature preterm human milk	Mature preterm human milk	Soy, high-oleic safflower, medium-chain triglyceride, & coconut oils	High-oleic sunflower, soy, medium-chain triglyceride, & coconut oils
Linoleic acid, mg	3,027	5,645	3,680	4,337	4,990	2,980	2,939	5,597	7,139
Carbohydrate, gm	66.4	85.5	71.2	75.9	80.7	78.8	90.8	76.9	79
% of total calories	40	42	40	41	42	43	46	41	43
Source	Lactose	Corn syrup solids & lactose	Lactose & corn syrup solids	Lactose & corn syrup solids	Lactose & corn syrup solids	Lactose & corn syrup solids	Lactose & corn syrup solids	Corn syrup solids & lactose	Maltodextrins, lactose, & citrates
Vitamins									
Vitamin A, IU	3,899	10,081	5,444	6,989	8,535	8,523	13,015	3,433	3,300
Vitamin D, IU	20	1,210	318	615	912	1,055	2,056	522	590
Vitamin E, IU	10.7	32.3	16.1	21.5	26.9	33.2	55.1	26.9	30
Vitamin K, mcg	2.0	97	26	49	73	24	45	82	59

Vitamins, continued									
Thiamin (vitamin B_1), mcg	208	2,016	660	1,112	1,564	949	1,670	1,642	1,480
Riboflavin (vitamin B_2), mcg	483	5,000	1,612	2,742	3,871	1,511	2,505	1,119	1,480
Vitamin B_6, mcg	148	2,016	615	1,082	1,549	707	1,253	746	740
Vitamin B_{12}, mcg	0.47	4.44	1.46	2.45	3.45	1.35	2.21	2.99	2.2
Niacin, mcg	1,503	40,323	11,209	20,915	30,617	16,265	30,600	14,552	14,800
Folic acid (folacin), mcg	33	298	99	166	232	156	275	187	192
Pantothenic acid, mcg	1,805	15,323	5,185	8,562	11,943	5,375	8,847	5,970	6,300
Biotin, mcg	6.0	298.4	79.1	152.2	225.3	19.3	32.1	67.2	44
Vitamin C (ascorbic acid), mg	110	298	157	204	251	166	220	112	118
Choline, mg	92	81	89	86	83	91	89	119	111
Inositol, mg	149	44	123	97	71	147	145	45	220
Minerals									
Calcium, mg (mEq)	248 (12.4)	1,694 (84.5)	610 (30.4)	971 (48.4)	1,332 (66.5)	688 (34.3)	1,116 (55.7)	784 (39.1)	890 (44.5)
Phosphorus, mg	128	935	330	531	734	348	561	463	490
Magnesium, mg	30.9	96.8	47.3	63.8	80.3	35.3	39.7	67.2	59
Iron, mg	1.21	2.98	1.65	2.10	2.54	1.17	1.17	13.43	13.3
Zinc, mg	3.42	12.10	5.59	7.76	9.93	6.87	10.24	8.96	9.2
Manganese, mcg	6	97	29	51	74	29	52	75	111
Copper, mcg	644	2,016	987	1,330	1,673	942	1,229	896	890
Iodine, mcg	107	48	93	78	63	106	104	112	111
Selenium, mcg	20.1	14.5	18.3	17.0	16.2	19.7	19.7	17.2	170
Sodium, mg (mEq)	248 (10.8)	347 (15.1)	273 (11.9)	298 (12.9)	322 (14.0)	279 (12.1)	309 (13.4)	246 (10.7)	260 (11.3)
Potassium, mg (mEq)	570 (14.6)	1,040 (26.6)	688 (17.6)	805 (20.6)	923 (23.6)	639 (16.3)	674 (17.2)	1,060 (27.1)	780 (19.9)
Chloride, mg (mEq)	550 (15.5)	653 (18.4)	576 (16.2)	602 (17.0)	627 (17.7)	630 (17.8)	706 (19.9)	560 (15.8)	580 (16.3)
Other Characteristics									
Potential renal solute load, mosm	125.4	214.9	147.6	170.0	192.5	156.1	185.5	179.1	184.1
Water, gm	879	879	879	879	879	867	855	896	902
Osmolality, mOsm/kg water	290	280	288	285	282	350	410	250	250
Osmolarity, mOsm/liter	255	250	253	251	248	303	350	224	

Nutrients per Liter

	Premature Infant Formulas		Toddler & Child Nutritional Products
	Enfamil® Premature Formula with Iron 20 (Low Iron)	Enfamil® Premature Formula with Iron 24 (Low Iron)	Enfamil® Next Step®
Energy, cal	680	810	676
Volume, ml	1,000	1,000	1,000
Protein, gm	20	24	17.57
% of total calories	12	12	10
Source	Nonfat milk & whey protein concentrate	Nonfat milk & whey protein concentrate	Nonfat milk
Fat, gm	35	41	33.78
% of total calories	46	44	45
Source	Medium-chain triglyceride, soy & coconut oils	Medium-chain triglyceride, soy & coconut oils	Palm olein, soy, coconut, & high-oleic sunflower oils
Linoleic acid, mg	7,162	8,548	5,473
Carbohydrate, gm	75.0	90	75.0
% of total calories	44	44	44
Source	Corn syrup solids & lactose	Corn syrup solids & lactose	Corn syrup solids & lactose
Vitamins			
Vitamin A, IU	8,500	10,100	2,027
Vitamin D, IU	1,830	2,200	405
Vitamin E, IU	43	51	13.5
Vitamin K, mcg	54	65	54

Vitamins, continued			
Thiamin (vitamin B$_1$), mcg	1,350	1,620	676
Riboflavin (vitamin B$_2$), mcg	2,000	2,400	1,014
Vitamin B$_6$, mcg	1,010	1,220	405
Vitamin B$_{12}$, mcg	1.7	2	1.69
Niacin, mcg	27,000	32,000	7,095
Folic acid (folacin), mcg	240	280	101
Pantothenic acid, mcg	8,100	9,700	3,041
Biotin, mcg	27	32	29.7
Vitamin C (ascorbic acid), mg	135	162	61
Choline, mg	81	97	108
Inositol, mg	115	138	32
Minerals			
Calcium, mg (mEq)	1,120 (56)	1,340 (67)	811 (40.5)
Phosphorus, mg	560	670	568
Magnesium, mg	46	55	54.1
Iron, mg	12.2 (1.7)	14.6 (2)	12.16
Zinc, mg	10.1	12.2	6.08
Manganese, mcg	43	51	47
Copper, mcg	850	1,010	608
Iodine, mcg	169	200	54
Selenium, mcg	12.2	14.6	18.9
Sodium, mg (mEq)	260 (11.3)	320 (13.9)	277 (12.1)
Potassium, mg (mEq)	700 (17.9)	840 (21.5)	878 (22.5)
Chloride, mg (mEq)	570 (16)	690 (19.4)	581 (16.4)
Other Characteristics			
Potential renal solute load, mosm	175	210	169.4
Water, gm	899	871	899
Osmolality, mOsm/kg water	260	310	270
Osmolarity, mOsm/liter	230	270	240

APPENDICES

Note: Values listed are subject to change. Refer to product label or packaging for most current information. Values are for liquid products except as noted. Values per liter are calculated from values per 100 Cal. No entry indicates value is not available.

PRSL = [Protein (gm) x 5.7] + Na (mOsm) + K (mOsm) + Cl (mOsm) + P (mOsm)

[a] Composition of human milk varies with maternal diet, stage of lactation, within feedings, diurnally, and among mothers (Refs 1,2). Total potentially available nucleotides = 72 mg/l (Ref 3). The extent of bioavailability of all sources of nucleotides has not been determined.

[b] Added free nucleotides = 72 mg/liter. With Similac Low-Iron, additional iron should be supplied from other sources.

[c] Added free nucleotides = 14 mg/liter. With Enfamil Low Iron, supplemental iron should be considered.

[d] Values are for powder at standard dilution (20 cal/fl oz). See precautions on labeling for use of Similac PM 60/40. Additional iron should be supplied from other sources.

[e] Added free nucleotides = 31.1 mg/liter.

[f] Added free nucleotides = 16.77 mg/liter. With Enfamil Low Iron 24, supplemental iron should be considered.

[g] Isomil DF contains 6 gm of added dietary fiber per liter.

[h] RCF is available as concentrated liquid. Nutrient values will vary depending on the amount of added carbohydrate and water. Values listed are for 13 fl oz of concentrated liquid with 52 gm of carbohydrate and 12 fl oz of water (20 cal/fl oz). Osmolality and osmolarity values will vary, depending on the type and amount of carbohydrate added. If carbohydrate is not added, a 1:1 dilution with water provides approximately 12 cal/fl oz (40.6 cal/100 ml).

[i] Values are for powder at standard dilution (20 cal/fl oz).

[j] Composition of preterm human milk varies with maternal diet, stage of lactation, within feedings, diurnally, and among mothers (Ref 4). Values for mature term human milk have been used for linoleic acid, biotin, choline, inositol, manganese, iodine, and selenium (Ref 1).

[k] See precautions on packaging for use of Similac Natural Care. Additional iron should be supplied from other sources.

[l] Osmolality and osmolarity are estimated.

[m] See manufacturer's cautions regarding use of Enfamil Human Milk Fortifier.

[n] Formerly Similac NeoCare®. Values are for powder at standard dilution (22 Cal/fl oz).

[o] See manufacturer's cautions regarding use of Enfamil Premature Formulas. Additional iron should be considered when using Enfamil Premature Formula Low Iron products.

REFERENCES

1. Lawrence RA. 1994. *Breastfeeding: A Guide for the Medical Profession,* 4th ed. St. Louis: Mosby-Year Book, 653–655.

2. Ogasa K, et al. 1975. The content of free and bound inositol in human and cow's milk. *Journal of Nutritional Science and Vitaminology* 21(2): 129–135.

3. Leach JL, et al. 1995. Total potentially available nucleosides of human milk by stage of lactation. *American Journal of Clinical Nutrition* 61(6): 1224–1230.

4. *Meeting the Special Nutrient Needs of Low-Birth-Weight and Premature Infants in the Hospital* (A8100). Columbus, Ohio: Ross Products Division, Abbott Laboratories, January 1998, 56.

APPENDICES

Appendix M
Normal Neonatal Laboratory and Other Values

Health care practitioners can use the information in this appendix to check the results of common laboratory tests that are monitored for abnormalities in typical neonates. The "normal range" values should be used only as guidelines. Normal values may vary depending on the laboratory doing the test and the procedures employed. Test results in the panic value range apply to all age categories and indicate a need for immediate attention and possible emergency treatment. The tables are not all-inclusive; specialized references should be consulted for normal values specific to the infant's age (gestational and postconceptional) and clinical condition.

The appendix contains tables listing the following values: blood chemistry (Table M-1), hematologic (Table M-2), cerebrospinal fluid (Table M-3), urine (Table M-4), and amniotic fluid (Table M-5). It also includes tables listing average weight and surface area by age (Table M-6), Apgar scoring criteria (Table M-7), and methemoglobin concentrations in normal infants (Table M-8).

BIBLIOGRAPHY

Adams LM, et al. 1995. Reference ranges for newer thyroid function tests in premature infants. *Journal of Pediatrics* 126(1): 122–127.

Avery GB, Fletcher MA, and MacDonald MG. 1994. *Neonatology: Pathophysiology and Management of the Newborn*, 4th ed. Philadelphia: Lippincott Williams & Wilkins, 1389–1404.

Children's Hospital of Los Angeles. 1992. *Pediatric Dosing Handbook and Formulary*. Hudson, Ohio: Lexi-Comp, 575–588.

Fanaroff AA, and Martin RJ.1992. *Neonatal-Perinatal Medicine: Diseases of the Fetus and Infant*, 5th ed. St. Louis: Mosby-Year Book, 1431–1450.

Gomella TL, Cunningham MD, and Eyal FG. 1994. *Neonatology: Management, Procedures, On-Call Problems, Diseases and Drugs,* 3rd ed. Norwalk, Connecticut: Appleton & Lange, 568.

Hathaway WE, et al. 1993. *Current Pediatric Diagnosis & Treatment,* 11th ed. Norwalk, Connecticut: Appleton & Lange, 1155–1163.

Hicks JM, and Boeckx RL. 1984. *Pediatric Clinical Chemistry.* Philadelphia: WB Saunders.

Johnson KB. 1993. *The Harriet Lane Handbook,* 13th ed. St. Louis: Mosby-Year Book, 89–96.

Lockitch G, et al. 1988. Age and sex specific pediatric reference intervals for biochemistry analytes as measured with the Ektachem-700 Analyzer. *Clinical Chemistry* 34(8): 1622–1625.

Meites S, et al. 1989. *Pediatric Clinical Chemistry: Reference (Normal) Values.* Washington, DC: American Association for Clinical Chemistry Press.

Moe PG, and Seay AR. 1997. Neurologic and muscular disorders. In *Current Pediatric Diagnosis & Treatment,* 13th ed., Hay WW Jr, et al., eds. Stamford, Connecticut: Appleton & Lange, 631–703.

Nelson JC, et al. 1993. Age-related changes in serum free thyroxine during childhood and adolescence. *Journal of Pediatrics* 123(6): 899–905.

TABLE M-1 ◆ BLOOD CHEMISTRY VALUES

Variable	Age	Normal Range	Unit	Panic Value (applies to all ages)
Albumin	<1 month	3.3–4.5	gm/dl	<2
	>1 month	3.7–5.3		
Alkaline phosphatase		150–400	units/liter	>1,000
α_1-antitrypsin	1–3 months	127–404	mg/dl	
Ammonia (arterial sample)	Newborn	Up to 150	mcg/dl	>150
	<2 weeks	Up to 130		
	>1 month	Up to 70		
Amylase		5–65	units/liter	
Bicarbonate	Preterm	18–26	mmol/liter	<14 or
	Term	20–26		>35
Bilirubin, direct		<0.5	mg/dl	>2
Bilirubin, total	≥1 month	<1.5	mg/dl	
	Cord blood	<1.8		
	Preterm			
	24 hours	<8		>15
	48 hours	<12		>20
	3–5 days	<16		
	Term			
	24 hours	<6		>15
	48 hours	<8		>20
	3–5 days	<12		>25
Blood urea nitrogen (BUN)	Preterm	3–25	mg/dl	>50
	Term	4–12		
Calcium	Preterm			
	<1 week	6–10	mg/dl	<6 or >12
	Term			
	<1 week	7–12		
	>1 week	8.6–10.8		
Calcium, ionized	<48 hours	4–4.7	mg/dl	<3.8
Carbon dioxide	Cord blood	14–22	mEq/liter	<12
	Preterm	14–27		
	Term	17–24		
Chloride		96–109	mEq/liter	<90 or >117
Creatine phospho-kinase (CPK)	Day 1	44–1,150	units/liter	>1,200
	2 days–2 weeks	Up to 440		
Creatinine	Cord blood	= mother's	mg/dl	
	Preterm			>2
	Birth	= mother's		
	10 days	1.2–1.4		
	1 month	0.6–0.7		
	Term			>2
	Birth	= mother's		
	1–4 days	0.3–1		
	>4 days	0.2–0.4		

(continued on next page)

APPENDICES

TABLE M-1 ◆ BLOOD CHEMISTRY VALUES (CONTINUED)

Variable	Age	Normal Range	Unit	Panic Value (applies to all ages)
Ferritin	<1 month	25–200	mcg/dl	
	1 month	200–600		
	2–5 months	50–200		
γ-glutamyltrans-ferase (GGT)	Preterm	56–233	units/liter	>500
	Term			>300
	0–3 weeks	0–130		
	3 weeks–3 months	4–120		
Glucose (blood)	Preterm	30–160	mg/dl	<30 or >200
	Term	40–125		<40 or >200
Lactate dehydro-genase (LDH)	Neonate	160–1,500	units/liter	>3,000
	Infant	150–360		
Lactate dehydrogenase isoenzymes:				
LD_1 (heart)		24–34	%	
LD_2 (heart, erythrocytes)		35–45		
LD_3 (muscle)		15–25		
LD_4 (liver, trace muscle)		4–10		
LD_5 (liver, muscle)		1–9		
Magnesium		1.5–2.5	mg/dl	<1.2 or >5
Osmolality (serum or plasma)		285–295	mOsm/kg	
Phenylalanine		0.7–3.5	mg/dl	
Phosphorus[1]	Preterm		mg/dl	<3 or >12
	Birth	5.6–8		
	6–10 days	6.1–11.7		
	20–25 days	6.6–9.4		
	Term			
	Birth	5–7.8		
	3 days	5.8–9		
	6–12 days	4.9–8.9		
Potassium				
Arterial/venous		3.8–6		
Capillary		4.5–7	mEq/liter	<3 or >7
Protein, total		4.5–7.3	gm/dl	
Sodium	Preterm	133–148	mEq/liter	<125
	Term	135–145		>155
T_4, free[2,3]	25–30 weeks	0.5–3.3	ng/dl	
	31–36 weeks	1.3–4.7		
	37–42 weeks	2–5.3		
Thyrotropin[2,3]	25–36 weeks	0.5–29	mU/liter	
	37–42 weeks	1–39		
Transaminases:				
AST (SGOT)		Up to 80	units/liter	>400
ALT (SGPT)		Up to 50		

(continued on next page)

APPENDICES

TABLE M-1 ◆ BLOOD CHEMISTRY VALUES (CONTINUED)

Variable	Age	Normal Range	Unit	Panic Value (applies to all ages)
Transferrin		2–3.6	gm/liter	
Triglycerides		35–150	mg/dl	>200
Uric acid		3–7.5	mg/dl	>12
Vitamin E		5–20	mcg/ml	

1. Hathaway WE, et al. 1993. *Current Pediatric Diagnosis and Treatment,* 11th ed. Norwalk, Connecticut: Appleton & Lange, 1155–1163.

2. Adams LM, et al. 1995. Reference ranges for newer thyroid function tests in premature infants. *Journal of Pediatrics* 126(1): 122–127.

3. Nelson JC, et al. 1993. Age-related change in serum free thyroxin during childhood and adolescence. *Journal of Pediatrics* 123(6): 899–905.

TABLE M-2 ◆ HEMATOLOGIC VALUES

Variable	Age or Weight	Normal Range	Unit	Panic Value
Absolute neutrophil count (ANC)		3,500–6,000	cells/mm³	<1,000
Bands	<1.5 kg 1.5–2.5 kg	7 8	%	
Bleeding time (Ivy Bleeding Time)		1.5–5.5	minutes	
Blood volume	Preterm Term	Up to 95 80	ml/kg	
Hematocrit	Birth 1–2 weeks 1–6 months	45–61 39–57 29–42	%	<20 or >70
Hemoglobin	0–3 days 1–2 weeks 1–6 months	15–20 12.5–18.5 10–13	gm/dl	
I/T (immature/total) ratio		<0.15–0.2		>0.3
Platelet count		>150,000	cells/mm³	<50,000
Reticulocytes	Newborn 1–6 months	2–6 0–2.8	%	>15
White cells (WBC)	<1.5 kg 1.5–2.5 kg	17,000 (6,000–33,000) 13,000 (7,000–15,000)	cells/mm³	<2,000 or >50,000

Absolute neutrophil count = $\dfrac{(\text{No. of segs} + \text{No. of stabs/bands}) \times \text{Total WBC}}{100}$

I/T ratio = $\dfrac{\text{No. of stabs/bands} + \text{No. of metamyelocytes} \times \text{No. of myelocytes}}{\text{Total no. of neutrophils}}$

TABLE M-3 ◆ CEREBROSPINAL FLUID VALUES

Variable	Age	Normal Range	Unit
WBC	Preterm	9 (0–29)	cells/mm^3
	Term	8.2 (0–22)	
PMN	Preterm	57	%
	Term	61	
Protein	Preterm	115 (65–150)	mg/dl
	Term	90 (20–170)	
Glucose	Preterm	50 (24–63)	mg/dl
	Term	52 (34–119)	
CSF:Blood glucose ratio	Preterm	55–105	%
	Term	44–128	

TABLE M-4 ◆ URINE VALUES

Variable	Normal Range	Unit
Sodium (spot)	10–20	mEq/liter
Osmolarity	50–600	mOsm/liter

TABLE M-5 ◆ AMNIOTIC FLUID VALUES

Variable	Age	Normal Range	Unit
L:S ratio	By 31–32 weeks	Usually 1:1	**Note: A ratio of ≥2:1 indicates mature lungs.**
			With a ratio of: 1.5–1.9:1 50% will develop RDS
	By 35 weeks	Usually 2:1	<1.5:1 73% will develop RDS
			RDS and phosphatidylglycerol (PG):
			• The presence of PG is a strong predictor that RDS will not occur, even when the L:S ratio is <2.
			• The absence of PG indicates gestational immaturity (<35 weeks) and some possibility of RDS if delivery occurs.

TABLE M-6 ◆ AVERAGE WEIGHT AND BODY SURFACE AREA (BSA) BY AGE

Age	Average Weight (kg)	Approximate BSA (m²)
Preterm (weeks gestation)		
26	0.9–1	0.1
30	1.3–1.5	0.12
32	1.6–2	0.15
38	2.9–3	0.2
Term		
40 weeks gestation	3.1–4	0.25
Postnatal		
3 months	5	0.29
6 months	7	0.38
9 months	8	0.42
1 year	10	0.49

Note: To calculate body surface area, use the following formula:

$$BSA\ (m^2) = \sqrt{\frac{Ht\ (cm)\ x\ wt\ (kg)}{3,600}}$$

To quickly approximate BSA, use this chart. For infants weighing:
  1–5 kg the BSA = (0.05 × kg) + 0.05 (m²)
  6–10 kg the BSA = (0.04 × kg) + 0.10 (m²)

TABLE M-7 ◆ APGAR SCORING

Component	Score/Criterion 0	1	2
Heart rate	Absent	<100 bpm	>100 bpm
Respiratory rate	Absent, irregular	Slow, crying	Good
Muscle tone	Limp	Some flexion of extremities	Active motion
Reflex irritability (nose suction)	No response	Grimace	Cough or sneeze
Color	Blue, pale	Extremities blue	Completely pink

Adapted from: Apgar V. 1953. A proposal for a new method of evaluation of the newborn infant. *Anesthesia and Analgesia* 32: 260. Reprinted by permission.

TABLE M-8 ◆ METHEMOGLOBIN CONCENTRATIONS IN NORMAL INFANTS

Age of Infant	Methemoglobin gm/dl Mean (Range)	Methemoglobin as Percent of Total Hemoglobin Mean (Range)
Preterm	0.38 (0.02–0.83)	2.2 (0.08–4.7)
Term newborn (1 to 10 days)	0.22 (0.00–0.58)	1.5 (0.00–2.8)
Term infant (1 month to 1 year)	0.14 (0.02–0.29)	1.2 (0.17–2.4)

Adapted from: Nathan DG, and Orkin SH. 1998. *Nathan and Oski's Hematology of Infancy and Childhood,* 5th ed., vol. 2. Philadelphia: WB Saunders, xii. Reprinted by permission.

The contributions of Linda Yang, MD, and Faez Bany-Mohammad, MD, to this appendix are appreciated.

APPENDIX N
CONVERSIONS AND EQUIVALENTS

A. METRIC VALUES

		Grams
1 kilogram (kg)	=	1,000
1 hectogram	=	100
1 decagram	=	10
1 gram (gm)	=	1
1 decigram	=	0.1
1 centigram	=	0.01
1 milligram (mg)	=	0.001
1 microgram (mcg)	=	10^{-6}
1 nanogram	=	10^{-9}
1 picogram	=	10^{-12}
1 femtogram	=	10^{-15}
1 attogram	=	10^{-18}
1,000 mg	=	1 gm
1,000 mcg	=	1 mg

- To convert milligrams to micrograms, multiply by 1,000.
- To convert micrograms to milligrams, divide by 1,000.
  Example: 30 mcg ÷ 1,000 = 0.03 mg.

B. AVOIRDUPOIS TO METRIC VALUES
Volume

1 minim	=	1/60 fluid dram	=	0.06 ml
1 teaspoon (tsp)	=			5 ml
1 dram	=	1/8 fluid ounce (fl oz)	=	3.7 ml
1 tablespoon (T)	=	1/2 fl oz	=	15 ml
2 T	=	1 fl oz	=	29.57 ml (or 30 ml)

1 cup (C)	=	8 fl oz			=	237 ml
1 pint (pt)	=	2 C	=	16 fl oz	=	473 ml
1 quart (qt)	=	2 pt	=	32 fl oz	=	946 ml
1 gallon	=	4 qt	=	128 fl oz	=	3.785 liters

1,000 milliliters (ml)	=	1 liter
1,000 microliters	=	1 ml
100 ml	=	1 deciliter (dl)

- To convert milliliters to fluid ounces, divide by 30.
- To convert fluid ounces to milliliters, multiply by 30.

Weight

1 oz	=			28.35 gm
1 grain	=			60 mg
1 pound (lb)	=	16 oz	=	453.6 gm
2.2 lb	=	1,000 gm	=	1 kg

• To convert pounds to grams, multiply by 454.

• To convert kilograms to pounds, multiply by 2.2.

Length

• To convert inches to centimeters, multiply by 2.54.

• To convert centimeters to inches, multiply by 0.3937.

C. Temperature

Centigrade (Celsius) (C)		Fahrenheit (F)
0°	Water freezes	32°
2°–8°	Refrigerator temperature for medications	36°–46°
22°	Room temperature	72°
37°	Body temperature	98.6°
100°	Water boils	212°
121°	Autoclave temperature	250°

• To convert centigrade to Fahrenheit:
  Multiply centigrade by 1.8
  Add 32

• To convert Fahrenheit to centigrade:
  Subtract 32 from Fahrenheit
  Divide by 1.8

D. Calculations Involving Milliequivalents and Millimoles

$$Milliequivalent\ weight\ (mEq) = \frac{mg}{equivalent\ weight} \tag{F-1}$$

Where:

$$Equivalent\ weight\ (eq\ wt) = \frac{gm\ molecular\ weight}{valence} \tag{F-2}$$

So:

$$mEq = \frac{gm\ molecular\ weight/valence}{1,000} \tag{F-3}$$

$$Mole = Molecular\ weight\ in\ grams\ (a\ gram\ molecular\ weight) \tag{F-4}$$

$$Millimole\ (mmol) = Molecular\ weight\ in\ milligrams \tag{F-5}$$

$$For\ single\text{-}valence\ ions \quad 1\ mmol = 1\ mEq \tag{F-6}$$

$$For\ divalent\ ions \quad 1\ mmol = 2\ mEq \tag{F-7}$$

Example: The infant formula table states the potassium content of the formula in units of milligrams, rather than in milliequivalents (the units you are used to working with). How would you convert mg of K to mEq of K?

- *Step 1.* Referring to Table N-1, you see that potassium has a molecular weight of 39.1 and a valence of 1, giving an equivalent weight of 39.1.
- *Step 2.* 1 millimole equals the molecular weight in milligrams (Equation F-5), and for single-valence ions like potassium 1 millimole equals 1 mEq (Equation F-6).

  1 mmol = molecular weight in mg = 1 mEq

Therefore, 39.1 milligrams of K equals 1 mEq of K.

- *Step 3.* The infant formula table states a potassium content of 830 mg per liter. How many mEq of potassium would this be?

  39.1 mg/1 mEq = 830 mg/X mEq

  830 mg/39 mg = X mEq = 21 mEq of potassium

Therefore, to convert potassium mg to mEq, divide the mg of potassium by the molecular weight of potassium in mg.

APPENDICES

TABLE N-1 ◆ **MOLECULAR AND EQUIVALENT WEIGHTS**

	Molecular Weight (gm)	Valence	Equivalent Weight (gm)
Calcium (Ca)	40	2	20
Chloride (Cl)	35.5	1	35.5
Magnesium (Mg)	24.3	2	12.2
Phosphate, inorganic (P)	31	2	17.2
Potassium (K)	39.1	1	39.1
Sodium (Na)	23	1	23

Adapted from: Tuckerman MM. 1994. Fundamentals of fluid and electrolyte therapy. In *Sterile Dosage Forms: Their Preparation and Clinical Application,* 4th ed., Turco S, ed. Philadelphia: Lea & Febiger, 213. Reprinted by permission.

E. OSMOLALITY

$$\text{Approximate serum osmolality} = 2 \times Na\ (mEq/liter) + \frac{glucose\ (mg/dl)}{18} + \frac{BUN\ (mg/dl)}{2.8}$$

Normal serum osmolality is 285–295 mOsm/kg.

APPENDIX O NEONATAL CARDIOPULMONARY RESUSCITATION AND POSTRESUSCITATION DRUG DOSES

Drug	Indication	Dose* (mg/kg)	Supplied	Volume of Dose (ml/kg)	Frequency	Comments
Epinephrine	• Asystole or heart rate remaining at <60 bpm after a minimum of 30 seconds of effective assisted ventilation and chest compressions • Hyperkalemia	IV, ET: 0.01–0.03 mg/kg/dose Continuous infusion: 0.05–1 mcg/kg/minute	1:10,000 Dilute to 1–2 ml with NS for ET administration.	0.1–0.3 ml/kg/dose of 1:10,000 Continuous infusion: See infusion equation[†]	Every 3–5 minutes Titrate to desired hemodynamic response.	Incompatible with sodium bicarbonate. Data on high-dose epinephrine for resuscitation of newly born infants are inadequate to support routine use. High doses may exaggerate hypertension while lowering cardiac output and increasing the risk of intracranial hemorrhage.
Normal saline or Ringer's lactate	See albumin 5% below				See albumin 5% below	See albumin 5% below
Albumin 5%	• Hypovolemia • Acute blood loss with poor response to resuscitation	IV: 0.5 gm/kg/dose Infuse over 5–10 minutes	50 ml	10 ml/kg/dose over 5–10 minutes	May be repeated if signs of hypovolemia are still present.	No longer the fluid of choice for initial volume expansion because the following have been observed: (1) limited availability of albumin 5%, (2) risk of infection, and (3) increased mortality compared with plasma protein fraction or crystalloid solution. The fluid of choice is normal saline or Ringer's lactate. May repeat after further assessment. Have on hand O negative RBCs if need is anticipated before birth.
Sodium bicarbonate	• Metabolic acidosis with adequate ventilation in prolonged arrest • Persistent metabolic acidosis • Hyperkalemia	IV: 1–2 mEq/kg/dose Infuse over at least 2 minutes Maximum: 8–10 mEq/kg/24 hours	0.5 mEq/ml (4.2%) syringe	2–4 ml/kg/dose	Every 5–10 minutes after checking pH	Incompatible with calcium and epinephrine. Flush line. Use is discouraged during brief CPR because of CO_2 generation and hyperosmolarity.

APPENDIX O   NEONATAL CARDIOPULMONARY RESUSCITATION AND POSTRESUSCITATION DRUG DOSES (CONTINUED)

Drug	Indication	Dose* (mg/kg)	Supplied	Volume of Dose (ml/kg)	Frequency	Comments
Atropine	• Bradycardia of <80 bpm in a distressed infant or one with poor perfusion or hypotension • Bradycardia with intubation attempts	*IV, ET:* 0.02 mg/kg	0.05 mg/ml syringe	0.4 ml/kg/dose	Every 5 minutes	Treat bradycardia with ventilation and oxygenation first, then atropine. Not useful in acute phase of resuscitation in delivery room.
Calcium chloride	• Hypocalcemia • Hyperkalemia • Hypermagnesemia • Calcium channel blocker overdose	*IV:* 30 mg/kg/dose Infuse slowly • Dose of calcium chloride is one-third the dose of calcium gluconate.	100 mg/ml syringe	0.3 ml/kg/dose	May be repeated once in 10 minutes. Base further doses on measured serum calcium.	Incompatible with sodium bicarbonate. Directly delivers ionized calcium. Not useful in acute phase of resuscitation in delivery room.
Calcium gluconate	• Hypocalcemia • Hyperkalemia • Hypermagnesemia • Calcium channel blocker overdose • Maintenance calcium provision	*IV:* 100 mg/kg/dose Infuse slowly *Maximum:* • *Preterm:* 500 mg/dose • *Term:* 1gm/dose	100 mg/ml vial	1 ml/kg/dose	May be repeated once in 10 minutes. Base further doses on measured serum calcium.	Incompatible with sodium bicarbonate. Metabolized in the liver to release ionized calcium. Not useful in acute phase of resuscitation in delivery room.
Dextrose	• Hypoglycemia • Hyperkalemia (with insulin)	*IV:* 0.5–1 gm/kg/dose *Hyperkalemia:* 0.4 gm/kg dextrose with 0.1 unit/kg insulin	Dextrose 10% Dextrose 25% Dilute insulin to 1 unit/ml concentration prior to measuring dose.	$D_{10}W$: 5–10 ml/kg/dose $D_{25}W$: 2–4 ml/kg/dose	May be repeated based on serum glucose. Increase maintenance dextrose.	$D_{10}W$ reduces risk of hyperosmolality, vein sclerosis, IVH. Hypoglycemia commonly occurs during first hours after resuscitation.
Flumazenil (Romazicon)	• Antidote for benzodiazepine overdose	*IV:* 2–10 mcg/kg/dose	0.1 mg/ml (100 mcg/ml)	0.02–0.1 ml/kg	Every minute up to 3 times as needed. Infuse over 30 seconds to 1 minute.	May precipitate withdrawal in chronic benzodiazepine therapy. Monitor for resedation.

APPENDICES

APPENDIX O NEONATAL CARDIOPULMONARY RESUSCITATION AND POSTRESUSCITATION DRUG DOSES (CONTINUED)

Drug	Indication	Dose* (mg/kg)	Supplied	Volume of Dose (ml/kg)	Frequency	Comments
Naloxone (Narcan)	• Antidote for narcotic overdose • Reversal of respiratory depression caused by narcotic given to mother within 4 hours of delivery	*IV, ET:* 0.1 mg/kg/dose May give SC or IM if perfusion is adequate	1 mg/ml	0.1ml/kg/dose	Every 2–5 minutes Monitor for recurrence of respiratory depression and repeat.	*Use cautiously* in infants of narcotic-addicted mothers; precipitates withdrawal. Maintain adequate ventilation.
Dopamine	• Hypotension not corrected by fluids • At low dose, increases urine output	*Continuous IV infusion:* 5–20 mcg/kg/minute *Renal dose:* 2 mcg/kg/minute	40 mg/ml	See infusion equation†	Titrate to desired hemodynamic response.	Monitor for tachycardia, decreased urine flow, dysrhythmia. Incompatible with sodium bicarbonate.
Dobutamine	• Inotropic effect to increase cardiac output • May be used with dopamine	*Continuous IV infusion:* 2–20 mcg/kg/minute	12.5 mg/ml vial	See infusion equation†	Titrate to desired hemodynamic response.	Monitor for tachycardia, dysrhythmia. Incompatible with sodium bicarbonate. Works through inotropic effects.
Isoproterenol (Isuprel)	• Adjunct in treatment of shock, low cardiac output states, congestive heart failure, bronchospasm refractory to standard therapy	*Continuous IV infusion:* 0.1–1 mcg/kg/minute	0.2 mg/ml	See infusion equation†	Titrate to desired hemodynamic response.	Monitor for tachycardia, dysrhythmia. Incompatible with sodium bicarbonate.
Amiodarone	• Pulseless ventricular fibrillation/ventricular tachycardia • Perfusing tachycardias	*IV/IO:* 5 mg/kg by rapid IV bolus—over several minutes *Loading dose:* 5 mg/kg IV/IO over 20–60 minutes	50 mg/ml	0.1 ml/kg = 5 mg/kg 0.1 ml/kg = 5 mg/kg	As needed to a maximum of 15 mg/kg/day	Hypotension most frequent adverse effect. Routine use with drugs that prolong QT interval is not recommended.

APPENDICES

APPENDIX O NEONATAL CARDIOPULMONARY RESUSCITATION AND POSTRESUSCITATION DRUG DOSES (CONTINUED)

Drug	Indication	Dose* (mg/kg)	Supplied	Volume of Dose (ml/kg)	Frequency	Comments
Lidocaine	• Ventricular fibrillation • Ventricular tachycardia • Multiple and/or multifocal premature ventricular contractions	IV, ET: 1 mg/kg/dose Maximum: 5 mg/kg total Continuous infusion: 20–50 mcg/kg/minute	10 mg/ml (1%) syringe	0.1 ml/kg/dose Continuous infusion: See infusion equation†	Every 10–15 minutes	Use lower dose of range in liver dysfunction. Overdose may cause CNS depression, seizures.
Adenosine	• Supraventricular tachycardia (SVT)	IV: 0.1–0.2 mg/kg/dose Very rapid IV push over 1–2 seconds Follow with rapid flush	3 mg/ml	0.03–0.06 ml/kg/dose	Every 2–5 minutes until SVT is resolved or until maximum dose of 0.25 mg/kg is reached	Half-life <10 seconds.

* *Intraosseous route* (IO) is not commonly used in newly born infants: The umbilical vein is more accessible, small bones are fragile, and the IO space is small in preterm infants. IO can be used as an alternative route for medication/volume expansion if umbilical or other direct venous access is not readily attainable.

† *Infusion Equation:* For drugs dosed in mcg/kg/minute, to calculate mg of drug needed to prepare 25 ml of IV drip solution to infuse at the desired rate:

$$C = \frac{1.5 \, DW}{R}$$

Where:
C = mg of drug needed to prepare 25 ml of solution
1.5 = a constant derived from minutes/hour
D = desired dose in mcg/kg/minute
W = body weight in kg
R = desired rate of infusion in ml/hour

Adapted from: Bloom RS, and Cropley C. 1990. *Textbook of Neonatal Resuscitation.* Elk Grove Village, Illinois: American Heart Association; American Heart Association, Emergency Cardiac Care Committee and Subcommittees. 1992. Guidelines for cardiopulmonary resuscitation and emergency cardiac care. Part 6: Pediatric advanced life support. *JAMA* 268(16): 2262–2275. (Comment in *JAMA*, 1992, 268[16]: 2297–2298; and *JAMA*, 1993, 269[20]: 2626.); American Heart Association, Emergency Cardiac Care Committee and Subcommittees. 1992. Guidelines for cardiopulmonary resuscitation and emergency cardiac care. Part 7: Neonatal resuscitation. *JAMA* 268(16): 2276–2281. (Comment in *JAMA*, 1992, 268[16]: 2297–2298.); Cochrane Injuries Group Albumin Reviewers. 1998. Human albumin administration in critically ill patients: Systematic review of randomised controlled trials. *BMJ* 317(7153): 235–240; American Heart Association in collaboration with the International Committee on Resuscitation. 2000. Guidelines 2000 for cardiopulmonary resuscitation and emergency cardiovascular care. Part 10: Pediatric advanced life support. *Circulation* 102(8 supplement I): I-291–I-342; and American Heart Association. 2000. Guidelines 2000 for cardiopulmonary resuscitation and emergency cardiovascular care. Part 11: Neonatal resuscitation. *Circulation* 102(supplement I): I-343–I-357.

Note: See Appendix A: Simplified Neonatal Calculations, for further information on calculation of drips.

APPENDIX P
ENDOTRACHEAL (ET) TUBE AND
SUCTION CATHETER SIZES BY INFANT WEIGHT

Weight (kg)	ET Tube Size (mm) (inside diameter)	Approximate Position at the Lips	Suction Catheter
<1	2.5	6.5 cm	#5 Fr
1–2	3.0	7.0 cm	#6 Fr
2–3	3.5	8.0 cm	#8 Fr
>3	3.5–4.0	9.0 cm	#8 Fr

APPENDICES

APPENDICES

APPENDIX Q
STANDARDIZED NICU ORAL UNIT DOSING

ADVANTAGE OF STANDARD DOSE SIZES

Certain frequently used medications can be prepared as standard sizes in advance and in bulk by the pharmacy so that they are ready for dispensing when needed. Standardized unit-dose sizes streamline the workload and reduce the risk of errors in the NICU because standardized unit doses add additional checks into the system. The unit-dose system also reduces costs: The NICU drug floor stock can be minimized because medications are dispensed from the pharmacy.

PREPARATION OF SYRINGES

The 0.5 ml oral syringe is particularly helpful to improve accuracy in measurement of small neonatal doses. Computer-generated labels for oral unit-dose syringes are efficient and neat. Labels should contain the drug name, strength, dose, volume, and expiration date so that doses can be double-checked by nursing staff before administration.

DRUGS WITH ALCOHOL AS A DILUENT

Drugs with a high alcohol content, such as phenobarbital and digoxin elixirs, should **not** be prepackaged in unit-dose syringes more than 1–2 weeks before use because of the potential for evaporation of the alcohol from the syringe.

Alcohol in medications should be avoided in infants, if possible, because of undesirable interactions, neuronal dysfunction, and hypoglycemia that could occur with ethanol-containing medications. Alcohol can also cause neurologic depression, altered liver function, and gastric irritation. Neurologic depression from alcohol in a medication could theoretically cause lethargy and poor feeding, resulting in an unnecessary workup for suspected sepsis.[1]

GUIDELINES FOR ROUNDING

To round doses per protocol to the nearest increment, follow these examples:

- If rounding to the nearest 0.5 mg increment, round 2.6 mg down to 2.5 mg; round 3.4 mg up to 3.5 mg.

- If rounding to the nearest 0.05 mg increment, round 0.26 down to 0.25 mg; round 0.78 mg up to 0.8 mg.

- If rounding to the nearest 0.1 ml increment, round 0.12 ml down to 0.1 ml; round 0.18 ml up to 0.2 ml.

- If rounding to the nearest 10 mg increment, round 13 mg to 10 mg, round 17 mg to 20 mg, and round 15 mg to 20 mg.

- If rounding to the nearest 50,000 and 100,000 unit increment, round 35,000 units to 50,000 units, round 80,000 units to 100,000 units, and round 75,000 units to 100,000 units.

APPENDICES

- If rounding to the nearest 0.5 mEq increment, round 2.6 mEq to 2.5 mEq; round 3.8 mEq to 4 mEq.
- Round to 25 units (vitamin E). Most infants receive the same dose of 25 units. If 35 units are ordered, round down to 25 units. If 45 units are ordered, round up to 50 units.
- Round to 400 units (vitamin D). Most infants receive 400 units. Round 600 units to 400 units, round 300 units to 400 units, and round 700 units to 800 units.

The prescriber may specifically request that doses not be rounded because of unusual circumstances such as extreme sensitivity to the drug.

Drugs that have a wide therapeutic range, such as acetaminophen, can be rounded in larger (10 mg) increments, as shown in Table Q-1. Drugs with a narrow therapeutic range, such as theophylline and caffeine, should be rounded in smaller increments (0.5 mg).

Doses of digoxin should not be rounded off because of its narrow therapeutic range and toxicity; give the exact dose calculated.

Rounding doses encourages use of the appropriate number of figures in calculations. Retaining too many figures in calculations wastes time, runs greater risk of careless error, and usually cannot be measured with syringes available in the NICU (e.g., the 5 in 0.125 ml).

Infants Weighing Less Than 1 Kg

Doses for infants weighing 1 kg or less should not be rounded. Rounding to the nearest standard dose may increase or decrease these very low birthweight (VLBW) infants' dose by too large a percentage. VLBW infants may not be able to handle the rounded dose because of their immature hepatic and renal functions. Exact doses based on body weight should be given to VLBW infants.

TO INSTITUTE STANDARDIZED DOSING IN YOUR UNIT

Determine the drugs and dose ranges frequently used in your unit; then list proposed standard sizes. Some suggested standard sizes are shown in Table Q-1. Discuss the concept of standard dose sizes with nursing, medicine, and pharmacy and therapeutics committees, and obtain their input and approval to dispense these standardized sizes per protocol.

REFERENCE

1. American Academy of Pediatrics, Committee on Drugs. 1984. Ethanol in liquid preparations intended for children. *Pediatrics* 73(3): 405–407.

TABLE Q-1 ◆ PHARMACIST'S SUGGESTED STANDARDIZED NICU ORAL UNIT-DOSE SYRINGES FOR USE WITH INFANTS >1 KG

Drug	Standardized Unit Dose
Acetaminophen	Round to nearest* 10, 20, 30, 40, 80 mg
Caffeine	Round to nearest 0.5 mg
Chlorothiazide	Round to nearest 0.5 mg
Ferrous sulfate (Fer-In-Sol Drops [25 mg elemental iron/ml])	Round to nearest 0.1 ml
Hydrochlorothiazide with spironolactone (Aldactazide suspension [4 mg/ml])	Round to nearest 0.1 ml
MCT oil	Round to nearest 0.5 ml
Metoclopramide	Round to nearest 0.05 mg (e.g., 0.1 mg and 0.15 mg are two frequently used sizes. The individual unit-dose syringes can be rubber-banded together for other doses such as 0.3 mg.)
Multivitamin drops	Round to 0.5 ml, 1 ml
Nystatin suspension	Round to 50,000 units and 100,000 units
Potassium chloride	Round to nearest 0.5 mEq
Potassium phosphate	Round to nearest 0.5 mmol
Ranitidine	Round to nearest 0.5 mg
Sodium chloride	Round to nearest 0.5 mEq
Sodium phosphate	Round to nearest 0.5 mmol
Theophylline	Round to nearest 0.5 mg (e.g., 1 mg and 1.5 mg are two frequently used sizes. The individual unit-dose syringes can be rubber-banded together for other doses such as 2.5 mg.)
Vitamin D	Round to 400 units
Vitamin E	Round to 25 units

* See GUIDELINES FOR ROUNDING on page 749.

APPENDICES

Section V—Indices
Table of Contents

INDICES

ABBREVIATIONS

AAPC	Antibiotic-associated pseudomembranous colitis
ACA	Aluminum-containing antacid
ACE	Angiotensin-converting enzyme
ACEI	Angiotensin converting enzyme inhibitor
ACIP	Advisory Committee on Immunization Practices
ACT	Activated clotting time
ACTH	Adrenocorticotropic hormone
ADH	Antidiuretic hormone
ADP	Adenosine 5'-diphosphate
AED	Antiepileptic drug
ALT	Alanine aminotransferase
AMP	Adenosine monophosphate
ANA	Antinuclear antibodies
ANC	Acid neutralizing capacity
aPTT	Activated partial thromboplastin time
AST	Aspartate aminotransferase
ATP	Adenosine 5'-triphosphate
ATPase	Adenosine triphosphatase
AV	Atrioventricular
BAER	Brain stem auditory evoked response
BP	Blood pressure
BPD	Bronchopulmonary dysplasia
bpm	Beats per minute
BSA	Body surface area
BUN	Blood urea nitrogen
CAA	Crystalline amino acids
c-AMP	Adenosine 3',5'-cyclic monophosphate
CBC	Complete blood count
CH	Congenital hypothyroidism
CHF	Congestive heart failure
CHO	Carbohydrate
CLD	Chronic lung disease
CMV	Cytomegalovirus
CNS	Central nervous system
COMT	Catechol-*O*-methyltransferase

CPR	Cardiopulmonary resuscitation
CPT	Carnitine palmitoyltransferase
CSF	Cerebrospinal fluid
CT	Computed tomography
CTZ	Chemoreceptor trigger zone
DIC	Disseminated intravascular coagulation
DNA	Deoxyribonucleic acid
DPPC	Dipalmitoylphosphatidylcholine
DPT	Lytic cocktail (Demerol [meperidine], Phenergan [promethazine], Thorazine [chlorpromazine])
ECG	Electrocardiogram
ECMO	Extracorporeal membrane oxygenation
EDLS	Endogenous digoxin-like substances
EDTA	Ethylenediaminetetraacetic acid
EEG	Electroencephalogram
ELBW	Extremely low birth weight
EMLA	Eutectic mixture of local anesthetics
ET	Endotracheal
ETT	Endotracheal tube
GABA	γ-aminobutyric acid
GE	Gastroesophageal
GFR	Glomerular filtration rate
GI	Gastrointestinal
GMP	Guanosine monophosphate
GU	Genitourinary
GX	Glycinexylidide
HDN	Hemorrhagic disease of the newborn
HIV	Human immunodeficiency virus
HPAA	Hypothalamic-pituitary-adrenal axis
HPLC	High-pressure liquid chromatography
HSV	Herpes simplex virus
I & O	Intake and output
ICP	Intracranial pressure
IgA	Immunoglobulin A
IgG	Immunoglobulin G
IHPS	Infantile hypertrophic pyloric stenosis
IM	Intramuscular

ABBREVIATIONS

INR	International normalized ratio
IO	Intraosseous
ITP	Idiopathic thrombocytopenia purpura
IUGR	Intrauterine growth restricted
IV	Intravenous
IVH	Intraventricular hemorrhage
IVP	Intravenous push
JRA	Juvenile rheumatoid arthritis
kcal	Kilocalorie
LCT	Long-chain triglycerides
LGA	Large for gestational age
LPL	Lipoprotein lipase
M	Molar
MAO	Monoamine oxidase
MCAD	Medium-chain acyl-CoA
mcg	Microgram
MCT	Medium-chain triglycerides
MDI	Metered dose inhaler
MEGX	Monoethylglycinexylidide
MIC	Minimum inhibitory concentration
mIU	Milli-international unit
mmol	Millimole
MRI	Magnetic resonance imaging
MRSA	Methicillin-resistant *Staphylococcus aureus*
N	Normal; defined as a solution containing 1 equivalent of replaceable hydrogen or hydroxyl per liter (e.g., 1 molar (M) HCl = 1 N)
NEC	Necrotizing enterocolitis
ng	Nanogram
NG	Nasogastric
NJ	Nasojejunal
NMS	Neuroleptic malignant syndrome
NPO	Nothing by mouth (Latin: *non per os* or *nil per os*)
NS	Normal saline
NSAID	Nonsteroidal anti-inflammatory drug
PAF	Platelet-activating factor
PCA	Postconceptional age
PDA	Patent ductus arteriosus

ABBREVIATIONS

PE	Phenytoin equivalents
PEG	Polyethylene glycol
PG	Prostaglandin (combined with specific prostaglandin, e.g., PGE_1)
PIE	Pulmonary interstitial edema
PKU	Phenylketonuria
PN	Parenteral nutrition
PO	Orally (Latin: *per os*)
PPHI	Persistent hyperinsulinemic hypoglycemia of infancy
PPHN	Persistent pulmonary hypertension of the newborn
PR	Per rectum
PR Interval	Demonstrates the time required for atrial excitation
prn	As needed; as required (Latin: *pro re nata*)
PTT	Partial thromboplastin time
PVC	Polyvinyl chloride
PVL	Periventricular leukomalacia
q	Every (Latin: *quodque*)
qid	Four times a day (Latin: *quater in die*)
qod	Every other day (Latin: *quaque altera die*)
RBC	Red blood cell
RDA	Recommended daily allowance
RDS	Respiratory distress syndrome
RIA	Radioimmunoassay
RNA	Ribonucleic acid
ROP	Retinopathy of prematurity
RSV	Respiratory syncytial virus
RTA	Renal tubular acidosis
SC	Subcutaneous
SDC	Serum digoxin concentration
SGOT	Serum glutamic-oxaloacetic transaminase (also known as AST)
SGPT	Serum glutamic-pyruvic transaminase (also known as ALT)
SIDS	Sudden infant death syndrome
SRS-A	Slow reacting substance of anaphylaxis
SVR	Systemic vascular resistance
SVT	Supraventricular tachycardia
TBG	Thyroxine-binding globulin
TBL	Total body load

ABBREVIATIONS

TBPA	Thyroxine-binding pre-albumin
TCE	Trichloroethanol
TPN	Total parenteral nutrition
TSH	Thyroid-stimulating hormone
UAC	Umbilical arterial catheter
USP	United States Pharmacopeia
UTI	Urinary tract infection
UVC	Umbilical venous catheter
VAPP	Vaccine-associated paralytic poliomyelitis
V_d	Volume of distribution
VIP	Vasoactive intestinal polypeptide
VLBW	Very low birth weight
VPA	Valproic acid
VZIG	Varicella-zoster immune globulin
WBC	White blood cell
WPW	Wolff-Parkinson-White syndrome

INDEX OF
TABLES AND FIGURES

SECTION I—DRUG MONOGRAPHS

TABLES

TABLES & FIGURES

TABLES & FIGURES

TABLES & FIGURES

TABLES & FIGURES

TABLES & FIGURES

Index

INDEX

INDEX

D

INDEX

N

INDEX

INDEX

INDEX

T

U

V

INDEX

CEU
Neonatal Medications & Nutrition
3rd Edition

Test Directions

1. Please fill out the answer form and include all requested information. We are unable to issue a certificate without complete information.

2. All questions and answers are developed from the information provided in the book. Select the *one best answer* and fill in the corresponding circle on the answer form.

3. Mail the answer form to: NICU Ink, 1410 Neotomas Ave., Suite 107, Santa Rosa, CA 95405-7533 with a check for $75.00 (processing fee) made payable to NICU Ink. This fee is non-refundable.

4. Retain the test for your records.

5. You will be notified of your test results within 6–8 weeks.

6. If you pass the test (70%) you will earn 30 contact hours (3 CEUs) for the course. Provider, Neonatal Network, approved by the California Board of Registered Nursing, Provider #FBN 3218, for 30 contact hours; Iowa Board of Nursing, Provider #189; Alabama Board of Nursing, Provider #ABNP0169; and Florida Board of Nursing, Provider #27 I 2861, content code 2505.

7. An answer key is available upon request with completion of the exam.

Objectives

After reading the text and taking the test, the participant will be able to:

1. identify special considerations for drug therapy in neonates

2. discuss common neonatal drugs as to: dose, administration, use, mechanism of action, adverse effects, nursing implications, and contraindications

3. outline the neonatal requirements for fats, proteins, and calories

4. describe recommended neonatal immunizations as to: dose, administration, cautions, mechanisms of action, adverse effects, and nursing implications

5. discuss human milk, infant formulas, and nutritional supplements as to: composition, indications for supplements, and dosage

6. describe the components and requirements of parenteral nutrition for neonates

1. In a study of 200 neonates, what percentage of babies experienced adverse drug reactions?
   a. 20   b. 25   c. 30

2. The use of sulfonamides has been implicated in the development of:
   a. abnormal dentition   b. kernicterus   c. liver failure

3. Gray baby syndrome is caused by the neonatal use of:
   a. chloramphenicol   b. hexachlorophene   c. tetracycline

4. Administration of drugs containing benzyl alcohol has been linked to a syndrome which includes:
a. jaundice   b. metabolic acidosis   c. renal failure

5. The absorption of topical steroids is enhanced with the use of:
a. alkaline soap   b. plastic diapers   c. zinc-based ointments

6. How many months after birth does it take gastric acid levels to reach adult values?
a. 12   b. 18   c. 24

7. What percentage of a neonate's body is comprised of water?
a. 68   b. 78   c. 88

8. An example of a drug that requires a higher dose in a neonate than an adult is:
a. gentamicin   b. phenobarbital   c. theophylline

9. At what age does the glomerular filtration rate reach adult values?
a. 4 months   b. 6 months   c. 8 months

10. What is the half-life of theophylline in preterm infants?
a. 10 hours   b. 20 hours   c. 30 hours

11. After what percentage change in body weight should an infant's drug dose be recalculated?
a. 5–10   b. 10–20   c. 20–30

12. The drug of choice for the treatment of herpes simplex is:
a. acyclovir   b. VZIG   c. vidarabine

13. What is the recommended initial dose of alprostadil?
a. 0.025 mcg/kg/minute   b. 0.05 mcg/kg/minute   c. 0.075 mcg/kg/minute

14. When using alteplase to clear an occluded catheter, how many hours should the drug be allowed to dwell in the catheter?
a. 1–2   b. 2–4   c. 4–6

15. Alteplase is ineffective in which of the following situations? Occlusions:
a. caused by calcium precipitate
b. found in arterial catheters
c. in catheters made of polyvinyl chloride

16. How many milligrams/kg of aminophylline is needed to raise the serum theophylline level from 6 mcg/ml to 10 mcg/ml?
a. 2.5   b. 3.0   c. 3.5

17. Following administration of a loading dose of aminophylline to a low birth weight infant, the nurse should anticipate the potential for:
a. development of a patent ductus arteriosus
b. hypertension
c. increased fluid loss

18. Amiodarone is indicated in the treatment of:
a. atrial fibrillation   c. postoperative junctional ectopic tachycardia
b. congenital heart block

19. Below what concentration does amiodarone in D_5W become unstable?
    a. 1 mg/ml   b. 0.6 mg/ml   c. 0.8 mg/ml

20. Amphotericin B is indicated for the treatment of systemic infections caused by:
    a. Candida   b. Chlamydia   c. Mycoplasma

21. Ampicillin is the drug of choice for infections caused by:
    a. *Escherichia coli*
    b. Group B β-hemolytic streptococci
    c. *Staphylococcus epidermidis*

22. What is the recommended dose of ampicillin for a 1.8 kg infant, one hour old, with suspected pneumonia?
    a. 60 mg every 8 hours   b. 90 mg every 12 hours   c. 180 mg every 12 hours

23. What is the recommended duration of Aquaphor treatment in infants <1,500 gm?
    a. 7 days   b. 14 days   c. 21 days

24. According to the skin condition grading scale, an infant with dry scales, mild erythema, and superficial fissures would be graded as a:
    a. 4   b. 5   c. 6

25. What is the maximum recommended infusion rate for arginine HCl?
    a. 1 gm/kg/hour   b. 2 gm/kg/hour   c. 3 gm/kg/hour

26. Argenine is hazardous in patients with elevated serum:
    a. chloride   b. potassium   c. sodium

27. Aztreonam is effective against:
    a. Clostridium   b. *Klebsiella pneumoniae*   c. *Staphylococcus aureus*

28. What is the recommended dose of beractant?
    a. 4 ml/kg   b. 5 ml/kg   c. 6 ml/kg

29. Nursing considerations for the administration of beractant include:
    a. diluting the supplied drug with 5 ml of normal saline
    b. shaking the medication to resuspend settled particles
    c. warming the drug to room temperature before administering

30. A drug of choice in the treatment of congestive heart failure unresponsive to diuretics would be:
    a. inamrinone   b. bretylium   c. isoproterenol

31. Compared to theophylline, the systemic side-effects of caffeine are:
    a. fewer   b. greater   c. the same

32. What is the recommended loading dose of caffeine base per kg?
    a. 2.5 mg   b. 5 mg   c. 10 mg

33. Calcitriol is an activated form of:
    a. vitamin A   b. vitamin C   c. vitamin D

34. Adverse effects of bolus infusions of calcium include:
    a. apnea   b. hypotension   c. renal vein thrombosis

35. **What is the maximum recommended concentration of calcium gluconate for infusion in a peripheral line?**
   a. 1 mg/ml   b. 3 mg/ml   c. 5 mg/ml

36. **Captopril works in the treatment of hypertension by:**
   a. blocking the conversion of angiotensin
   b. increasing the elimination of bicarbonate in the urine
   c. preventing the reabsorption of water from the renal tubules

37. **Cefazolin is effective against:**
   a. Gram-positive aerobic organisms
   b. Gram-negative organisms
   c. Gram-positive and Gram-negative anaerobic organisms

38. **Cefoperazone belongs to which generation of cephalosporins?**
   a. second   b. third   c. fourth

39. **Which of the following cephalosporins has good CSF penetration?**
   a. cefotaxime   b. cefoxitin   c. cephalothin

40. **Organisms that are resistant to cefotaxime include:**
   a. *E. coli*   b. *H. influenzae*   c. *L. monocytogenes*

41. **Which of the following drugs acts synergistically with ceftazidime against Pseudomonas?**
   a. cefoxitin   b. gentamicin   c. vancomycin

42. **Which of the cephalosporins is the drug of choice in the treatment of gonococcal infections?**
   a. ceftriaxone   b. cefuroxime   c. cephapirin

43. **To reduce the discomfort of IM injections of ceftriaxone, this drug may be diluted with:**
   a. dextrose   b. lidocaine   c. meperidine

44. **When given as a procedural sedative where deep sleep is desired, how many minutes before the procedure should chloral hydrate be given?**
   a. 10–20   b. 20–30   c. 30–45

45. **In developed countries, chloramphenicol has largely been replaced by what type of antibiotics?**
   a. aminoglycosides   b. cephalosporins   c. macrolides

46. **What is the preferred route of administration for chlorothiazide?**
   a. IM   b. IV   c. PO

47. **Cimetidine has been shown to prolong the half-life of:**
   a. phenobarbital   b. theophylline   c. vancomycin

48. **What is the recommended dose of cisapride?**
   a. 0.15–0.3 mg/kg/dose   b. 0.3–0.45 mg/kg/dose   c. 0.45–0.6 mg/kg/dose

49. **Cisapride has been associated with which of the following cardiac arrhythmias?**
   a. premature ventricular contractions
   b. prolonged QT interval
   c. supraventricular contractions

50. Citric acid is indicated in the treatment of:
    a. hypophosphatasia   b. metabolic alkalosis   c. renal tubular acidosis

51. The use of clindamycin in neonates is limited because of the risk of:
    a. allergic sensitization   c. pseudomembranous colitis
    b. intractable diarrhea

52. Adverse effects of clonidine include which of the following?
    a. diarrhea   b. hypotension   c. neutropenia

53. What is the onset of action of oral clonidine?
    a. 15–20 minutes   b. 30–60 minutes   c. 60–90 minutes

54. Following codeine administration, the maximum effect would be expected to occur in:
    a. 20–60 minutes   b. 60–120 minutes   c. 120–160 minutes

55. Cosyntropin is used in the diagnosis of adrenocortical insufficiency because, when compared to natural ACTH it is less:
    a. allergenic   c. likely to contain contaminants
    b. expensive

56. Which of the following drugs used to treat BPD is **not** a bronchodilator?
    a. albuterol   b. cromolyn   c. ipratropium

57. In addition to being a precursor to taurine, cysteine may be added to parenteral nutrition to:
    a. decrease metabolic acidosis
    b. improve glucose tolerance
    c. increase the solubility of calcium and phosphate

58. Long-term adverse effects of dexamethasone include:
    a. severe growth retardation   c. retinopathy of prematurity
    b. metabolic acidosis

59. An infant receiving dexamethasone is at increased risk for developing:
    a. diabetes mellitus   b. gastric hemorrhage   c. pulmonary hypertension

60. What is the glucose load for a 2 kg infant receiving 8 ml per hour of 10 percent dextrose?
    a. 4.7 mg/kg/minute   b. 5.7 mg/kg/minute   c. 6.7 mg/kg/minute

61. The maximum recommended concentration of glucose for infusion in a peripheral line is:
    a. 10 percent   b. 12.5 percent   c. 15 percent

62. What is the recommended dose of diazepam for the treatment of neonatal abstinence syndrome?
    a. 0.1–0.3 mg/kg/dose   b. 0.3–0.5 mg/kg/dose   c. 0.5–0.8 mg/kg/dose

63. IV doses of diazepam should be administered over:
    a. 1–2 minutes   b. 3–5 minutes   c. 5–7 minutes

64. What is the duration of action of oral diazoxide?
    a. 4 hours   b. 6 hours   c. 8 hours

65. Concurent use of diazoxide and which of the following drugs may reduce the effectiveness of both drugs?
   a. indomethacin   b. phenytoin   c. thiazide diuretics

66. The recommended dose of digoxin should be reduced in the presence of:
   a. abnormal serum magnesium levels   c. hyponatremia
   b. elevated serum potassium

67. Which of the following inotropic drugs is least likely to cause arrhythmias?
   a. dobutamine   b. dopamine   c. isoproterenol

68. Which of the following drugs should be avoided in infants receiving dopamine?
   a. aminophylline   b. furosemide   c. phenytoin

69. Which of the following drugs should be given as a local antidote for an extravasated IV containing dopamine?
   a. heparin   b. hyaluronidase   c. phentolamine

70. What is the recommended loading dose of doxapram?
   a. 2.0–2.5 mg/kg   b. 2.5–3.0 mg/kg   c. 3.0–3.5 mg/kg

71. How many mg/kg/day of elemental iron given as ferrous sulfate is recommended for neonates receiving erythropoietin?
   a. 4   b. 6   c. 8

72. The advantage of enalapril over captopril is that enalapril is:
   a. available in IV form   b. less potent   c. shorter acting

73. How many milligrams of epinephrine should be added to 25 ml of fluid to give 0.05 mcg/kg/minute to a 2 kg infant with an IV rate of 1 ml/hour?
   a. 0.075 mg   b. 0.15 mg   c. 0.3 mg

74. What is the preferred route of administration for erythropoietin?
   a. IM   b. IV   c. SC

75. Erythromycin is a member of which family of antibiotics?
   a. aminoglycoside   b. fluoroquinolone   c. macrolide

76. Which of the following prokinetic agents enhances gastric emptying by stimulating chemoreceptors in the brain?
   a. cisapride   b. erythromycin   c. metoclopramide

77. Neonates being treated with erythropoietin should also be receiving:
   a. calcium/phosphate supplements   c. vitamin A
   b. ferrous sulfate

78. The use of erythropoietin is contraindicated in patients with:
   a. cardiac failure   b. hypertension   c. sepsis

79. Ethanol may be used to restore patency in central lines blocked by:
   a. a blood clot   b. calcium precipitate   c. lipids

80. Which of the following diuretics poses the greatest risk for the development of hypercalciuria?
   a. chlorothiazide   b. furosemide   c. spironolactone

81. Which of the following H_2 antagonists binds to cytochrome P-450, altering the metabolism of other drugs?
    a. cimetidine   b. famotidine   c. ranitidine

82. How many micrograms of drug should be added to 25 ml of saline to provide an 800 gm infant with 0.5 mcg/kg/hour of fentanyl at a rate of 1 ml per hour?
    a. 10 mcg   b. 12.5 mcg   c. 15 mcg

83. How many milliliters of Fer-In-Sol would be required for a 5-week-old breastfed infant weighing 1.25 kg (desired dose = 3 mg elemental iron)?
    a. 0.15 ml   b. 0.3 ml   c. 0.5 ml

84. Compared to amphotericin B and flucytosine, fluconazole:
    a. is less bioavailable   c. results in fewer side effects
    b. has a shorter half-life

85. Fludrocortisone should be used with caution in patients with:
    a. congestive heart failure   b. hyperkalemia   c. hypoglycemia

86. Neonates on fludrocortisone who must be NPO for surgery should receive a dose of:
    a. betamethasone   b. dexamethasone   c. hydrocortisone

87. Flumazenil is used as an antidote against:
    a. chloral hydrate   b. codeine   c. lorazepam

88. Folic acid supplementation is recommended for preterm infants until the infant reaches what postconceptional age?
    a. 32 weeks   b. 36 weeks   c. 40 weeks

89. Which of the following drugs is known to be ototoxic in the presence of high serum levels?
    a. amikacin   b. clindamycin   c. imipenem

90. The risk for ototoxicity with aminoglycoside use is potentiated with the administration of:
    a. ampicillin   b. furosemide   c. phenobarbital

91. Treatment options for hypoglycemia unresponsive to dextrose infusion include:
    a. glucagon   b. metyrapone   c. propranolol

92. How many kcal per milliliter are provided by Polycose?
    a. 1   b. 2   c. 3

93. What is the average onset of action of a glycerin suppository?
    a. 30 minutes   b. 60 minutes   c. 90 minutes

94. What is the preferred concentration of heparin for line flushes?
    a. 1 unit/ml   b. 2 units/ml   c. 3 units/ml

95. What is the recommended flush solution for a 750 gm infant?
    a. D_5W b. NaCl 0.45 percent   c. NaCl 0.9 percent

96. An infiltration of which of the following substances may benefit from treatment with hyaluronidase?
    a. dobutamine   b. epinephrine   c. sodium bicarbonate

97. What is the recommended dose of IV hydralazine for hypertensive emergencies?
a. 0.05–0.01 mg/kg/dose   b. 0.1–0.4 mg/kg/dose   c. 0.4–0.75 mg/kg/dose

98. What is the role of spironolactone in Aldactazide? It:
a. inhibits sodium reabsorption
b. prevents potassium loss
c. promotes chloride excretion

99. Compared to other corticosteroids, hydrocortisone has the greatest:
a. anti-inflammatory potency   c. mineralocorticoid potency
b. biologic half-life

100. Imipenem-cilastatin is used in cases of infection caused by:
a. Bacteroides   b. Chlamydia   c. Mycoplasma

101. Immune globulin intravenous is administered to provide neonates with increased levels of:
a. IgA   b. IgG   c. IgM

102. The recommended rate of infusion for indomethacin is over:
a. 1–2 minutes   b. 30 minutes   c. 1 hour

103. The manufacturer of indomethacin recommends that the drug **not** be given to neonates with:
a. active bleeding   b. hyperbilirubinemia   c. seizures

104. In addition to hyperglycemia, insulin may be used to treat:
a. hypercalcemia   b. hyperkalemia   c. hypernatremia

105. What is the recommended dose of isoproterenol when initiating a continuous IV infusion?
a. 0.05 mcg/kg/minute   b. 0.1 mcg/kg/minute   c. 0.15 mcg/kg/minute

106. Iron dextran forms a precipitate in parenteral nutrition solutions containing a protein concentration of less than _____ percent.
a. 2   b. 3   c. 4

107. The use of iron dextran is contraindicated in patients with:
a. congestive heart failure   b. hemolytic anemia   c. hyperbilirubinemia

108. Ketamine offers which of the following advantages over barbiturate anesthesia?
a. better skeletal muscle relaxation
b. longer half-life
c. lower incidence of respiratory depression

109. Concerns regarding the use of EMLA cream in neonates have centered around the risk of the infant developing:
a. methemoglobinemia   b. pernicious anemia   c. thrombocytopenia

110. Use of lorazepam in preterm infants has been associated with:
a. chest wall rigidity   b. myoclonus   c. paroxysmal tachycardia

111. What is the daily requirement of magnesium sulfate for an infant receiving parenteral nutrition?
a. 30–60 mg/kg/day   b. 60–90 mg/kg/day   c. 90–120 mg/kg/day

112. How many calories are provided by one milliliter of MCT oil?
    a. 3.4   b. 5.8   c. 7.6

113. What is the recommended dose of the **antidote** for Demerol?
    a. 0.1 mg/kg   b. 0.2 mg/kg   c. 0.3 mg/kg

114. Meropenem is **not** recommended for infants less than _____ month(s) of age?
    a. 1   b. 3   c. 5

115. It is recommended that metaproterenol be discontinued if there is no clinical improvement following administration of how many doses?
    a. 3   b. 5   c. 7

116. What is the preferred route of administration for methadone?
    a. IM   b. PO   c. SC

117. Symptoms of methadone overdose include which of the following?
    a. bradycardia   b. hyperglycemia   c. tachypnea

118. Which of the following is a risk when steroid treatment with a drug such as methylprednisolone is withdrawn too quickly?
    a. acute adrenal insufficiency   c. rebound hyperglycemia
    b. metabolic acidosis

119. For best results, metoclopramide should be administered how far in advance of a feeding?
    a. 5–10 minutes   b. 30 minutes   c. 1 hour

120. Metronidazole is given concurrently with other antibiotics in the treatment of necrotizing enterocolitis because it is:
    a. activated by the presence of other antibiotics
    b. ineffective against aerobic bacteria
    c. synergistic with ampicillin and gentamicin

121. Mezlocillin, like other penicillins, is inactivated when it comes in contact with:
    a. aminoglycosides   c. parenteral nutrition solution
    b. latex products

122. Midazolam is a good choice for sedation prior to intubation because it:
    a. acts as a muscle relaxant
    b. drys up oral secretions
    c. may be given in the absence of an IV

123. The dose of morphine should be decreased in the presence of:
    a. a history of maternal narcotic ingestion   c. shock
    b. seizures

124. Which of the following vitamins is **not** contained in the multivitimin Tri-Vi-Sol?
    a. A   b. B   c. C

125. Nafcillin will not be effective against staphylococcal organisms which are:
    a. methicillin-resistant
    b. nosocomially-acquired
    c. penicillinase producing

126. In addition to reversing the effects of narcotics, naloxone may be indicated in the treatment of:
    a. central apnea in the first day of life
    b. hypotension caused by septic shock
    c. narcotic withdrawal

127. Neostigmine is used in the diagnosis of:
    a. myasthenia gravis
    b. systemic lupus erythematous
    c. Wolf-Parkinson-White syndrome

128. Doses of nitric oxide which exceed 20 ppm increase the risk of:
    a. circulatory collapse   b. lung injury   c. methemoglobinemia

129. Nitric oxide therapy is recommended for infants greater than how many weeks gestational age?
    a. 32   b. 34   c. 36

130. The use of PVC-containing IV administration sets can reduce the nitroglycerin concentration reaching the patient by up to what percentage?
    a. 60   b. 70   c. 80

131. Topical nitroglycerin has been used successfully in neonates to treat:
    a. diminished cardiac contractility   c. systemic hypertension
    b. dopamine extravasation injury

132. Nursing considerations in the administration of nitroprusside include which of the following?
    a. avoid using the drug if it is brown in color
    b. dilute the drug in normal saline only
    c. protect the drug from light by covering the IV bag or syringe

133. How much norepinephrine should be mixed in 25 ml of dextrose to provide 0.04 mcg/kg/minute for a 2.5 kg infant with an IV running at 1 ml per hour?
    a. 0.15 mg   b. 0.25 mg   c. 0.35 mg

134. What is the mechanism of action of octreotide? It:
    a. acts on the liver to increase glycogen conversion
    b. enhances glyconeogenesis
    c. suppresses glucagon and insulin release

135. Palivizumab is generally administered in which months?
    a. September through January   c. November through April
    b. October through March

136. Palivizumab is **not** approved for infants with:
    a. bronchopulmonary dysplasia   c. necrotizing enterocolitis
    b. congenital heart disease

137. Excessive dosing of pancuronium bromide is suggested when paralysis lasts longer than:
    a. 1–3 hours   b. 3–4 hours   c. 4–6 hours

138. Adverse effects of pancuronium include:
    a. bradycardia   b. hypertension   c. seizures

139. Paregoric is no longer recommended for treatment of neonatal narcotic withdrawal because it contains harmful ingredients, including:
    a. camphor   b. pentazocine   c. diazepam

140. What is the recommended dose of penicillin G aqueous for a 3 day old with suspected congenital syphilis?
    a. 50,000 units/kg/day   b. 100,000 units/kg/day   c. 150,000 units/kg/day

141. Unlike penicillin G aqueous, penicillin G benzathine can only be given:
    a. IM   b. IV   c. PO

142. Procaine penicillin G differs from aqueous penicillin G in that procaine penicillin G provides:
    a. high serum drug concentrations of short duration
    b. low serum drug concentrations for 1–2 days
    c. sustained serum drug concentrations for 2–3 weeks

143. What is the recommended therapeutic range of phenobarbital?
    a. 5–15 mcg/ml   b. 15–40 mcg/ml   c. 40–55 mcg/ml

144. Respiratory depression is common when phenobarbital is used with:
    a. cephalosporins   b. phenytoin   c. lorazepam

145. Phenytoin will precipitate when exposed to:
    a. dextrose   b. normal saline   c. phenobarbital

146. Which of the following routes of administration for phenytoin results in the best absorption?
    a. IM   b. IV   c. PO

147. Which of the following drugs potentiate the effects of phenytoin?
    a. aminophylline   b. cimetidine   c. furosemide

148. What is the normal serum phosphate level for a three week old infant?
    a. 4.8–6.1 mg/dl   b. 6.2–8.7 mg/dl   c. 8.8–10.2 mg/dl

149. The most important use of piperacillin is for infections caused by:
    a. Enterobacter   b. Klebsiella   c. Pseudomonas

150. What is the maximum recommended rate of infusion for an IV potassium solution?
    a. 0.5 mEq/hour   b. 1 mEq/hour   c. 1.5 mEq/hour

151. In terms of duration of effects, prednisone is classified as what type of steroid?
    a. long-acting   b. intermediate-acting   c. short-acting

152. Propranolol is indicated in the treatment of which of the following neonatal conditions?
    a. coarctation of the aorta   b. myasthenia gravis   c. thyrotoxicosis

153. Propranolol should not be used in patients with:
    a. chronic lung disease   b. renal dysfunction   c. thrombocytopenia

154. The IV dose of propranolol is much lower than the PO dose because of:
    a. first pass clearance by the liver
    b. inactivation of the drug by stomach acid
    c. poor oral absorption of the drug

155. Protamine is the **antidote** for an overdose of:
    a. heparin   b. lorazepam   c. pancuronium

156. Unlike cimetidine, ranitidine does not affect:
    a. gentamicin levels   b. hepatic drug metabolism   c. urinary output

157. Immunizations against which of the following communicable diseases should be delayed for nine months following the last dose of RSV-IGIV?
    a. diphtheria   b. hepatitis   c. measles

158. Rifampin should always be used therapeutically with another antibiotic because:
    a. bacteria rapidly develop resistance to rifampin
    b. rifampin is too nonspecific to effectively kill bacteria
    c. rifampin acts synergistically with other drugs

159. Using the formula provided, what is the calculated dose of bicarbonate for a 2.3 kg infant with a base deficit of 9 mEq/liter?
    a. 5.4 mEq   b. 5.8 mEq   c. 6.2 mEq

160. For the infant in question 159, what would be the recommended dose to be administered?
    a. 2.9 mEq   b. 3.1 mEq   c. 5.4 mEq

161. How many milliequivalents of sodium chloride are needed for an infant weighing 1.5 kg with a serum sodium of 124 mEq/liter to correct to 130 mEq/liter?
    a. 5.4   b. 6   c. 9

162. Nursing care of the infant following administration of a Kayexalate enema includes which of the following?
    a. administering an oral dose of Kayexalate if the enema was ineffective
    b. irrigating the colon with a non-sodium solution
    c. providing additional sodium intake to compensate for losses in the stool

163. Spironolactone is contraindicated in infants with:
    a. hypercalcemia   b. hyperkalemia   c. hypernatremia

164. The bradycardia which accompanies administration of succinylcholine can be avoided by pretreating the infant with:
    a. atropine   b. midazolam   c. pancuronium

165. What is the expected rise in the serum theophylline level for a 1.5 kg infant given 4.5 mg of theophylline?
    a. 3 mcg/ml   b. 4.2 mcg/ml   c. 5 mcg/ml

166. Which of the following is an advantage offered by theophylline over caffeine? Theophylline:
    a. acts as a bronchodilator
    b. has a wider therapeutic range than caffeine
    c. requires less serum drug level monitoring than caffeine

167. When mixed in the same IV solution, ticarcillin inactivates:
    a. ampicillin   b. cefotaxime   c. tobramycin

168. Aminoglycosides given to a newborn whose mother received magnesium sulfate may cause the baby to develop:
    a. apnea   b. oliguria   c. a skin rash

169. Blood to check for a peak serum level of tobramycin should be drawn how many minutes after completion of the 30 minute infusion?
    a. 15   b. 30   c. 45

170. According to Heath, what is the recommended dose of tolazoline for treatment of umbilical artery spasm?
    a. 0.25 mg/kg/hour   b. 0.6 mg/kg/hour   c. 1–2 mg/kg once

171. Tromethamine (THAM) may be indicated for the treatment of metabolic acidosis when the infant also has:
    a. hyperkalemia   b. hypernatremia   c. hypoglycemia

172. Ursodiol is administered as part of a cholestatic treatment regimen which also includes treatment with:
    a. albumin   b. parenteral nutrition   c. phenobarbital

173. The one hour recommended rate of infusion for vancomycin is designed to prevent side effects caused by:
    a. histamine release   b. local vasoconstriction   c. volume overload

174. Serum vancomycin levels may be elevated in infants who concurrently receive:
    a. aminophylline   b. dexamethasone   c. indomethacin

175. Acyclovir is preferred over vidarabine in treatment of herpes infections because compared to vidarabine, acyclovir is:
    a. cheaper   b. less toxic   c. more potent

176. Vitamin E supplements in preterm infants are recommended until what post-conceptional age?
    a. 32 weeks   b. 36 weeks   c. 40 weeks

177. IV administration of vitamin K is not recommended because of potential problems with:
    a. anaphylaxis   b. light degradation   c. precipitation in solution

178. Prophylactic zidovudine treatment should begin by how many hours after birth?
    a. 12   b. 24   c. 36

179. Caution is needed when administering zidovudine to patients with:
    a. anemia   b. hypotension   c. sepsis

180. Zinc oxide is best removed from the skin with:
    a. mild soap   b. mineral oil   c. plain water

181. What is the estimated daily caloric requirement for preterm infants?
    a. 100 kcal/kg   b. 110 kcal/kg   c. 120 kcal/kg

182. What is the iron concentration of human milk?
    a. 0.1 mg/liter   b. 0.3 mg/liter   c. 0.5 mg/liter

183. For infants with documented allergy to cow's milk protein, the American Academy of Pediatrics recommends:
    a. casein hydrolysate formula   c. soy-protein formula
    b. lactose-free formula

184. Infants with galactosemia should be fed with a formula such as:
    a. Alimentum   b. Lofenalac   c. Nutramigen

185. For a neonate weighing 1,600 gm, the maximum recommended daily intake of fat in parenteral nutrition is:

a. 2 gm   b. 3 gm   c. 4 gm

186. In addition to standard trace elements, it is recommended that preterm infants on parenteral nutrition receive additional:

a. copper   b. manganese   c. zinc

187. Drugs that are incompatible with parenteral nutrition include:

a. amphotericin B   b. dopamine   c. vancomycin

188. Immunizations which are normally given at 2 months of age include:

a. Hib   b. polio   c. MMR

189. A second dose of DTP is contraindicated in an infant who has had which of the following reactions after the first dose of DTP?

a. fever of >39°C (102.2°F) within 4 hours of vaccination
b. inconsolable crying for 4 hours on the day following vaccination
c. skin rash within 48 hours of vaccination

190. For the infant whose mother is HBsAg-positive, Hepatitis B vaccine should be given:

a. within 12 hours of birth
b. at hospital discharge
c. when the infant is 2 months old

191. The first dose of pneumococcal-7 vaccine is normally given at what age?

a. 6 weeks   b. 2 months   c. 4 months

192. To obtain the optimum protection, VZIG should be given within how many hours of exposure to chickenpox?

a. 48   b. 72   c. 96

193. An 800 gram infant is receiving 7.5 percent dextrose at a rate of 3.2 ml/hour. How many mg/kg/minute of dextrose is this infant receiving?

a. 3   b. 5   c. 7

194. Drugs which should **not** be administered through an umbilical arterial catheter include:

a. cefotaxime   b. morphine   c. phenytoin

195. Cimetidine is incompatible with:

a. cephalosporins   b. parenteral nutrition   c. sodium bicarbonate

196. Hydrochloric acid may be used to unblock a central venous catheter when the blockage is thought to result from:

a. calcium/phosphorous precipitate   c. heparin
b. fat emulsion

197. The greatest risk for hypercalciuria comes from using what type of diuretics

a. carbonic anhydrase inhibitor   c. potassium-sparing
b. loop

198. Treatment of withdrawal in neonates should be considered when the Neonatal Withdrawal Score reaches:

a. 8   b. 10   c. 12

199. How often can epinephrine be administered during a neonatal resuscitation? Every:

    a. 1–3 minutes   b. 3–5 minutes   c. 5–10 minutes

200. Naloxone should be used with caution in which of the following infants? One whose mother:

    a. has myasthenia gravis   b. is narcotic-addicted   c. was taking valium

201. Adenosine is indicated in the treatment of:

    a. complete heart block
    b. refractory hypotension
    c. supraventricular tachycardia

ANSWER FORM: Neonatal Medications & Nutrition, 3rd Edition

Please completely fill in the circle of the **one best answer** using a dark pen.

1. a. ○	2. a. ○	3. a. ○	4. a. ○	5. a. ○	6. a. ○	7. a. ○	8. a. ○	9. a. ○
b. ○	b. ○	b. ○	b. ○	b. ○	b. ○	b. ○	b. ○	b. ○
c. ○	c. ○	c. ○	c. ○	c. ○	c. ○	c. ○	c. ○	c. ○

10. a. ○	11. a. ○	12. a. ○	13. a. ○	14. a. ○	15. a. ○	16. a. ○	17. a. ○	18. a. ○
b. ○	b. ○	b. ○	b. ○	b. ○	b. ○	b. ○	b. ○	b. ○
c. ○	c. ○	c. ○	c. ○	c. ○	c. ○	c. ○	c. ○	c. ○

19. a. ○	20. a. ○	21. a. ○	22. a. ○	23. a. ○	24. a. ○	25. a. ○	26. a. ○	27. a. ○
b. ○	b. ○	b. ○	b. ○	b. ○	b. ○	b. ○	b. ○	b. ○
c. ○	c. ○	c. ○	c. ○	c. ○	c. ○	c. ○	c. ○	c. ○

28. a. ○	29. a. ○	30. a. ○	31. a. ○	32. a. ○	33. a. ○	34. a. ○	35. a. ○	36. a. ○
b. ○	b. ○	b. ○	b. ○	b. ○	b. ○	b. ○	b. ○	b. ○
c. ○	c. ○	c. ○	c. ○	c. ○	c. ○	c. ○	c. ○	c. ○

37. a. ○	38. a. ○	39. a. ○	40. a. ○	41. a. ○	42. a. ○	43. a. ○	44. a. ○	45. a. ○
b. ○	b. ○	b. ○	b. ○	b. ○	b. ○	b. ○	b. ○	b. ○
c. ○	c. ○	c. ○	c. ○	c. ○	c. ○	c. ○	c. ○	c. ○

46. a. ○	47. a. ○	48. a. ○	49. a. ○	50. a. ○	51. a. ○	52. a. ○	53. a. ○	54. a. ○
b. ○	b. ○	b. ○	b. ○	b. ○	b. ○	b. ○	b. ○	b. ○
c. ○	c. ○	c. ○	c. ○	c. ○	c. ○	c. ○	c. ○	c. ○

55. a. ○	56. a. ○	57. a. ○	58. a. ○	59. a. ○	60. a. ○	61. a. ○	62. a. ○	63. a. ○
b. ○	b. ○	b. ○	b. ○	b. ○	b. ○	b. ○	b. ○	b. ○
c. ○	c. ○	c. ○	c. ○	c. ○	c. ○	c. ○	c. ○	c. ○

64. a. ○	65. a. ○	66. a. ○	67. a. ○	68. a. ○	69. a. ○	70. a. ○	71. a. ○	72. a. ○
b. ○	b. ○	b. ○	b. ○	b. ○	b. ○	b. ○	b. ○	b. ○
c. ○	c. ○	c. ○	c. ○	c. ○	c. ○	c. ○	c. ○	c. ○

73. a. ○	74. a. ○	75. a. ○	76. a. ○	77. a. ○	78. a. ○	79. a. ○	80. a. ○	81. a. ○
b. ○	b. ○	b. ○	b. ○	b. ○	b. ○	b. ○	b. ○	b. ○
c. ○	c. ○	c. ○	c. ○	c. ○	c. ○	c. ○	c. ○	c. ○

82. a. ○	83. a. ○	84. a. ○	85. a. ○	86. a. ○	87. a. ○	88. a. ○	89. a. ○	90. a. ○
b. ○	b. ○	b. ○	b. ○	b. ○	b. ○	b. ○	b. ○	b. ○
c. ○	c. ○	c. ○	c. ○	c. ○	c. ○	c. ○	c. ○	c. ○

91. a. ○   92. a. ○   93. a. ○   94. a. ○   95. a. ○   96. a. ○   97. a. ○   98. a. ○   99. a. ○
    b. ○   b. ○   b. ○   b. ○   b. ○   b. ○   b. ○   b. ○   b. ○
    c. ○   c. ○   c. ○   c. ○   c. ○   c. ○   c. ○   c. ○   c. ○

100. a. ○   101. a. ○   102. a. ○   103. a. ○   104. a. ○   105. a. ○   106. a. ○   107. a. ○   108. a. ○
    b. ○   b. ○   b. ○   b. ○   b. ○   b. ○   b. ○   b. ○   b. ○
    c. ○   c. ○   c. ○   c. ○   c. ○   c. ○   c. ○   c. ○   c. ○

109. a. ○   110. a. ○   111. a. ○   112. a. ○   113. a. ○   114. a. ○   115. a. ○   116. a. ○   117. a. ○
    b. ○   b. ○   b. ○   b. ○   b. ○   b. ○   b. ○   b. ○   b. ○
    c. ○   c. ○   c. ○   c. ○   c. ○   c. ○   c. ○   c. ○   c. ○

118. a. ○   119. a. ○   120. a. ○   121. a. ○   122. a. ○   123. a. ○   124. a. ○   125. a. ○   126. a. ○
    b. ○   b. ○   b. ○   b. ○   b. ○   b. ○   b. ○   b. ○   b. ○
    c. ○   c. ○   c. ○   c. ○   c. ○   c. ○   c. ○   c. ○   c. ○

127. a. ○   128. a. ○   129. a. ○   130. a. ○   131. a. ○   132. a. ○   133. a. ○   134. a. ○   135. a. ○
    b. ○   b. ○   b. ○   b. ○   b. ○   b. ○   b. ○   b. ○   b. ○
    c. ○   c. ○   c. ○   c. ○   c. ○   c. ○   c. ○   c. ○   c. ○

136. a. ○   137. a. ○   138. a. ○   139. a. ○   140. a. ○   141. a. ○   142. a. ○   143. a. ○   144. a. ○
    b. ○   b. ○   b. ○   b. ○   b. ○   b. ○   b. ○   b. ○   b. ○
    c. ○   c. ○   c. ○   c. ○   c. ○   c. ○   c. ○   c. ○   c. ○

145. a. ○   146. a. ○   147. a. ○   148. a. ○   149. a. ○   150. a. ○   151. a. ○   152. a. ○   153. a. ○
    b. ○   b. ○   b. ○   b. ○   b. ○   b. ○   b. ○   b. ○   b. ○
    c. ○   c. ○   c. ○   c. ○   c. ○   c. ○   c. ○   c. ○   c. ○

154. a. ○   155. a. ○   156. a. ○   157. a. ○   158. a. ○   159. a. ○   160. a. ○   161. a. ○   162. a. ○
    b. ○   b. ○   b. ○   b. ○   b. ○   b. ○   b. ○   b. ○   b. ○
    c. ○   c. ○   c. ○   c. ○   c. ○   c. ○   c. ○   c. ○   c. ○

163. a. ○   164. a. ○   165. a. ○   166. a. ○   167. a. ○   168. a. ○   169. a. ○   170. a. ○   171. a. ○
    b. ○   b. ○   b. ○   b. ○   b. ○   b. ○   b. ○   b. ○   b. ○
    c. ○   c. ○   c. ○   c. ○   c. ○   c. ○   c. ○   c. ○   c. ○

172. a. ○   173. a. ○   174. a. ○   175. a. ○   176. a. ○   177. a. ○   178. a. ○   179. a. ○   180. a. ○
    b. ○   b. ○   b. ○   b. ○   b. ○   b. ○   b. ○   b. ○   b. ○
    c. ○   c. ○   c. ○   c. ○   c. ○   c. ○   c. ○   c. ○   c. ○

181. a. ○   182. a. ○   183. a. ○   184. a. ○   185. a. ○   186. a. ○   187. a. ○   188. a. ○   189. a. ○
    b. ○   b. ○   b. ○   b. ○   b. ○   b. ○   b. ○   b. ○   b. ○
    c. ○   c. ○   c. ○   c. ○   c. ○   c. ○   c. ○   c. ○   c. ○

190. a. ○	191. a. ○	192. a. ○	193. a. ○	194. a. ○	195. a. ○	196. a. ○	197. a. ○	198. a. ○
b. ○	b. ○	b. ○	b. ○	b. ○	b. ○	b. ○	b. ○	b. ○
c. ○	c. ○	c. ○	c. ○	c. ○	c. ○	c. ○	c. ○	c. ○

199. a. ○	200. a. ○	201. a. ○
b. ○	b. ○	b. ○
c. ○	c. ○	c. ○

Neonatal Medications & Nutrition, 3rd Edition

Print clearly

Name _____

Address _____

City _____ State _____ Zip _____

Phone (_____) _____ E-mail _____
(to receive certificate via e-mail)

Nursing License # _____ **State(s) of License** _____

Academy (ANN) Membership # _____

VISA ___ MasterCard ___ # _____ Exp. Date _____

Signature _____

Program Evaluation

		FOR OFFICE USE ONLY
Were the test directions clear?	Yes___ No___	
Were the objectives of the CEU met?	Yes___ No___	
Did the questions reflect the content of the book?	Yes___ No___	RECEIVED
Will you be able to utilize the information in your practice?	Yes___ No___	
What was the level of this course? too easy___ challenging___ too difficult___		CHECK
Do you feel the book content was comprehensive?	Yes___ No___	
How long did it take you to complete the course? ___hours		
What level unit do you practice in? I___ II___ III___		GRADE
What subjects would you like to see offered for CE courses? _____		PASSED / FAILED

Additional comments: _____

_____

CERTIFICATE ISSUED

Iowa participants may submit the evaluation directly to the Iowa Board of Nursing, 400 SW 8th St., Ste. B, Des Moines, IA 50309-4685.

Mail with a $75.00 non-refundable processing fee for 30 contact hours to NICU Ink®, 1410 Neotomas Ave., Ste. 107, Santa Rosa, CA 95405-7533.
Please make check payable to *NICU Ink*.
Enclose an additional $10.00 for rush processing.
International Participants: International Money Order drawn on U.S. bank only.

DEPOSIT DATE

REFERENCE #

Neonatal Medications & Nutrition
A Comprehensive Guide

_____ copies at $59.95/copy $ _____

$5.00 Shipping and handling for first book ordered $ _____

$2.00 Shipping and handling for each additional book $ _____

Sub Total $ _____

7.5% Sales tax (CA residents only) $ _____

Total $ _____

If ordering by mail, please allow 4–6 weeks for the order to be filled. Please print complete shipping information below:

Name: _____

Street: _____

City:_____ State:_____ Zip: _____

Country and mailing code if other than U.S. address: _____

_____ VISA   _____ MC   Expiration Date: _____

Card Number: _____

Signature: _____

You can order the book online by visiting our
website: www.neonatalnetwork.com
or
by calling our toll free number:
1-888-NICU INK (1-888-642-8465)

You can also FAX this form to 707-569-0786. If ordering by mail, please send
this form along with payment to:
NICU INK
1410 Neotomas Ave., Suite 107
Santa Rosa, CA 95405-7533

VISA and MasterCard Accepted

Cynthia
Eichelberger